Environmental Impact Assessment — Law and Practice

Stephen Tromans

Barrister

and

Karl Fuller

General Manager
Institute of Environmental
Management and Assessment

LexisNexis™ UK

Members of the LexisNexis Group worldwide

United Kingdom	LexisNexis UK, a Division of Reed Elsevier (UK) Ltd, Halsbury House, 35 Chancery Lane, LONDON, WC2A 1EL, and 4 Hill Street, EDINBURGH EH2 3JZ
Argentina	LexisNexis Argentina, BUENOS AIRES
Australia	LexisNexis Butterworths, CHATSWOOD, New South Wales
Austria	LexisNexis Verlag ARD Orac GmbH & Co KG, VIENNA
Canada	LexisNexis Butterworths, MARKHAM, Ontario
Chile	LexisNexis Chile Ltda, SANTIAGO DE CHILE
Czech Republic	Nakladatelství Orac sro, PRAGUE
France	Editions du Juris-Classeur SA, PARIS
Germany	LexisNexis Deutschland GmbH, FRANKFURT, MUNSTER
Hong Kong	LexisNexis Butterworths, HONG KONG
Hungary	HVG-Orac, BUDAPEST
India	LexisNexis Butterworths, NEW DELHI
Ireland	Butterworths (Ireland) Ltd, DUBLIN
Italy	Giuffrè Editore, MILAN
Malaysia	Malayan Law Journal Sdn Bhd, KUALA LUMPUR
New Zealand	LexisNexis Butterworths, WELLINGTON
Poland	Wydawnictwo Prawnicze LexisNexis, WARSAW
Singapore	LexisNexis Butterworths, SINGAPORE
South Africa	LexisNexis Butterworths, DURBAN
Switzerland	Stämpfli Verlag AG, BERNE
USA	LexisNexis, DAYTON, Ohio

A CIP Catalogue record for this book is available from the British Library.

ISBN 0 406 95954 4

Project Management by The Partnership Publishing Solutions Ltd, **www.the-pps.co.uk**
Printed and bound in Great Britain by Antony Rowe Ltd, Chippenham, Wilts

Visit LexisNexis UK at www.lexisnexis.co.uk

Environmental Impact Assessment — Law and Practice

7 Day

Preface

Environmental impact assessment is currently one of the fastest-expanding areas of environmental and planning law. To read the cases as they have developed is an object lesson in how environmentally-concerned private individuals can use the law to oppose powerful commercial or public interests, and in many instances win. In this respect, the UK law reflects the development of EIA jurisprudence in the US a quarter-century ago, when citizens' groups opposed to major government projects seized on the procedural requirements of EIA as a powerful weapon. The difference is that in the UK the leading cases have by and large been brought not by large citizens' groups, but by a few concerned individuals. It is furthermore remarkable to see how the courts in the UK have embraced the importance of EIA not simply as a technocratic aid to better decisions, but as a participative and democratic means of involving the public in decisions on projects.

This book seeks to provide a practical and comprehensive guide to environmental impact assessment law. It starts from the basic foundations of EC law and moves on to consider the issues of screening and procedures. It also deals with EIA outside the context of town and country planning law, and with procedures for challenging decisions on EIA grounds.

The fast-evolving nature of the case law means that by the time the book is published it will almost certainly be to some degree out of date. In general the law is stated as at 6 June 2003, the most recent decision to be covered fully being *R (PPG11 Ltd) v Dorset County Council*, though it has been possible to make some additions and changes of a more minor nature at later proof stage, including brief references to the Court of Appeal decision in R (Prokopp) v London Underground Limited (7 July 2003). However, the law has now sufficiently developed and settled to enable reasonably clear guidance to be provided on the pitfalls which may await those practising in this area. As to those pitfalls, it need hardly be said that challenges on EIA grounds present very real and serious threats to development schemes. It is hoped that this book will assist not only planning authorities and developers in recognising and avoiding such traps, but also those representing the public in ensuring that the law and its underlying purposes are respected. EIA should, it is suggested, be seen neither as an onerous set of hurdles nor as a charter for Nimbys, but as a positive set of procedures which will improve the quality of decisions, protect and enhance the environment, and also in the long run benefit developers and investors. I am therefore delighted that Karl Fuller of the Institute of Environmental Management & Assessment (IEMA) has contributed a chapter dealing with good practice in EIA, which should help lawyer readers in understanding how and why the legal requirements are of such importance. Thanks are due to his colleagues Andrew Bailey and Stefanie Simmons, who assisted him in this.

Thanks are also due to the publishers for their encouragement and assistance, and to members of the planning and environment group at my chambers, 39 Essex Street, who have collectively vast practical experience of EIA law, and whose comments and insights have undoubtedly enriched the end product.

Stephen Tromans
39 Essex Street

Contents

Appendices

Table of statutes

References in this table to *Statutes* are to Halsbury's Statutes of England (Fourth Edition) showing the volume and page at which the annotated text of the Act may be found

Paragraph numbers in **bold** type indicate where the section is set out in part or in full

Table of statutory instruments

Table of cases

*Decisions of the European Court of Justice are listed below numerically. These decisions
are also included in the preceding alphabetical list.*

CHAPTER 1

Introduction

EIA: AN INTRODUCTION

1.01   Environmental impact assessment (EIA) is one of the cornerstones of European Community law on the protection of the environment. It has proven problematic to implement correctly in most member states, as witnessed by the numerous infraction proceedings by the Commission, and by the voluminous case law in national courts. In the UK in particular, EIA has almost certainly generated more case law on the environment than any other area of EC or domestic law. It is now seen by the courts not only as a technical means of assisting expert decision making, but as an important guarantee of the democratic right of the public to be informed about the potential environmental consequences of decisions which may affect them or their surroundings, to understand the implications of those effects and how they may be avoided or mitigated, and to participate in the process by expressing their own views.

1.02   The nature of EIA has been very well explained by Christopher Wood as containing a number of strands, as follows:[1]

'... EIA refers to the evaluation of the effects likely to arise from a major project (or other action) significantly affecting the natural and man-made environment. Consultation and participation are integral to this evaluation.'

'The EIA process should supply decision-makers with an indication of the likely consequences of their actions. Properly used, EIA should lead to informed decisions about potentially significant actions, and to positive benefits to both proponents and the population at large.'

'In principle, EIA should lead to the abandonment of environmentally unacceptable actions and to the mitigation to the point of acceptability of the environmental effects of proposals which are approved. EIA is thus an anticipatory, participatory environmental management tool, of which the EIA report is only one part.'

'It should be emphasised that EIA is not a procedure for preventing actions with significant environmental impacts from being implemented. Rather the intention is that actions are authorised in the full knowledge of their environmental consequences. EIA takes place in a political context: it is therefore inevitable that economic, social or political factors will outweigh environmental factors in many instances. This is why the mitigation of environmental impacts is so central to EIA: decisions on proposals in which the environmental effects have palpably been ameliorated are much easier to make and justify than those in which mitigation has not been achieved.'

1   Wood C, *Environmental Impact Assessment: A Comparative Review* (Longman, 1995), pp 1–3.

STRATEGIC ENVIRONMENTAL ASSESSMENT AND PLAN APPRAISAL

1.03   EIA as discussed in this book is concerned with specific projects, in the form of actual development or other human physical intervention in the environment. However, attention has also turned, both in terms of domestic policy and EC law, to the desirability of assessing the effects of plans and programmes on the environment. This is now usually referred to as strategic environmental assessment (SEA).

1.04   In the UK this focus began in the early 1990s, with the recognition of the importance of embedding the principle of sustainable development within government policy making, and of ensuring that the development plan system '... takes environmental considerations comprehensively and consistently into account'.[1] Planning policy guidance on development plans and regional planning guidance[2] emphasised the need to carry through appraisal of the sustainability implications of development plans in their preparation, and this was amplified in a good practice guide.[3] More detailed good practice guidance on the environmental appraisal of development plans was published in 1993.[4] This recommended among other steps, the use of 'compatibility matrices' to appraise the relationship between specific policies and stated environmental criteria.

1   See the White Paper, *This Common Inheritance: Britain's Environmental Strategy* (Cm 1200, September 1990) para 6.24.
2   PPG 12, *Development Plans and Regional Planning Guidance* (1992).
3   Department of the Environment, *Development Plans: A Good Practice Guide* (1993).
4   Department of the Environment, *Environmental Appraisal of Development Plans: A Good Practice Guide* (1993), see Ch 5 in particular.

1.05   This focus has continued as best practice has developed and been refined, with the incorporation by local authorities of Local Agenda 21 initiatives into the planning process. PPG 12 on development plans has been revised,[1] and there is guidance on sustainability appraisal in the context of both local[2] and regional[3] planning. The issue of introducing environmental goals into planning in an integrated, accountable and transparent way was the subject of detailed consideration and criticism by the

Royal Commission on Environmental Pollution in its important 23rd Report, *Environmental Planning*.[4]

1 PPG 12, *Development Plans* (1999), see paras 4.16–4.22.
2 DETR, *Planning for Sustainable Development: Towards Better Practice* (1998).
3 PPG 11, *Regional Planning Guidance* (2000), see paras 2.30–2.37; DETR, *Good Practice Guide to Sustainability Appraisal of Regional Planning Guidance* (2000). See also the account of the Government-sponsored project on SEA in the South-West of England: E James and C Fry, *The Environmentalist*, August 2002, p 16.
4 Cm 5459, March 2002.

1.06 The EU has also been active in the area of SEA, following the publication of a draft directive on the subject in December 1996. The proposal stemmed from a report by the European Commission in 1993 on the effectiveness of the EIA Directive (Directive 85/337/EEC EIA, as now amended by Directive 97/11/EC), one of the conclusions of which was that the evaluation of some projects was taking place too late in the development planning process, thus hindering proper consideration of alternative proposals and the location of projects.[1] After a lengthy gestation period, Directive 2001/42/EC on the assessment of the effects of certain plans and programmes on the environment (the SEA Directive) was agreed in 2001.[2]

1 See S Tromans and C Roger-Machart, 'Strategic Environmental Assessment: Early Evaluation Equals Efficiency?' [1997] JPL 993.
2 OJ L197, 21.7.01, p 30.

1.07 The objective of the SEA Directive is stated at art 1 as follows:

'... to provide for a high level of protection of the environment and to contribute to the integration of environmental considerations into the preparation and adoption of plans and programmes with a view to promoting sustainable development, by ensuring that, in accordance with this Directive, an environmental assessment is carried out of certain plans and programmes which are likely to have significant effects on the environment.'

1.08 For the purposes of the SEA Directive, 'plans and programmes' is defined by art 2 to mean plans or programmes (and modifications to them):
— which are subject to preparation and/or adoption by an authority at national, regional or local level or which are prepared by an authority for adoption, through a legislative procedure by Parliament or government, and
— which are required by legislative, regulatory or administrative provisions.

1.09 An environmental assessment is required to be carried out for the plans and programmes referred to in the SEA Directive, arts 3(2)–(4) which are likely to have significant environmental effects (art 3(1)). In particular, art 3(2)(a) requires an environmental assessment for to all plans and programmes:[1]

'... which are prepared for agriculture, forestry, fisheries, energy, industry, transport, waste management, water management, telecommunications, tourism, town and country planning or land use and which set the framework for future development consent of projects listed in Annexes I and II to Directive 85/337/EEC'.

By art 3(2)(b), all plans and programmes which require assessment under the Habitats Directive[2] because of their effects on a European protected site also require environmental assessment. By art 3(3), plans and programmes which 'determine the use of small areas at local level' and 'minor modifications' to plans and programmes require environmental assessment only where the member states determine that they are likely to have significant environmental effects. By art 3(4), member states must determine, on the basis of criteria set out in Annex II, whether other plans and programmes which set the framework for future development consent for projects are likely to have significant environmental effects.

1   There is ambiguity in the relationship between the SEA Directive, arts 3(1) and 3(2), as to whether art 3(1) qualifies art 3(2) so that plans within art 3(2) only require assessment where significant effects are likely, or whether art 3(2) makes assessment mandatory in all cases. On the basis of the scheme of the Directive, and the relationship with arts 3(3) and (4), it is submitted that the second alternative is the correct interpretation.
2   Directive 92/43/EEC of 21 May 1992 on the conservation of natural habitats and of wild flora and fauna (OJ L206, 22.7.92, p 7).

1.10   By the SEA Directive, art 4(1), where environmental assessment is required, it must be carried out during the preparation of the plan or programme and before its adoption or its submission to the legislative process. The requirements for assessment follow the components of those required for EIA of projects and include the preparation of an environmental report (art 5), consultation with relevant authorities and the public (art 6), consultations with other member states where the plan or programme may have significant transboundary effects (art 7), the decision-making process (art 8) and information on the decision (art 9). The assessment of the plan or programme is without prejudice to the later requirements of EIA for any project subject to the plan (see art 11(1)).

1.11   Member states are required by the SEA Directive, art 13 to bring into force the laws, regulations and legislative provisions necessary to comply with the Directive before 21 July 2004.

1.12   The SEA Directive has obvious implications in the UK for development plans and for other types of plans or guidance, such as minerals and waste local plans, regional planning guidance, as well as local development frameworks and regional spatial strategies under the forthcoming reforms to the development planning system contained in the Planning and Compulsory Purchase Bill. The Office of the Deputy Prime Minister issued draft guidance on applying the SEA Directive to land use and spatial plans in England for consultation in October 2002.[1] The intention is to implement the Directive through legal measures, and therefore the proposed Guidance is simply to alert local planning authorities as to the requirements of SEA and help them to become familiar with the requirements and prepare for them. It explains the SEA process, how to carry out an SEA on a step-by-step basis, and discusses issues of quality assurance. In particular it explains the parallels and differences between SEA and existing procedures for sustainability appraisal of development plans and regional strategies. The draft guidance indicates clearly the complexity involved in seeking to implement the SEA Directive and to integrate the process with existing practice on sustainability appraisal of plans.[2] It has been described as '... one of the most complicated consultation papers ever issued on a planning topic. It is long, it is detailed, and it is studded with tables, figures and checklists'.[3] Quite apart from the land use planning system, there are other types of plans and programmes which will be subject to the SEA Directive. One example is local transport plans under the Transport Act 2000, Pt II.[4]

1   ODPM, Draft Guidance on the Strategic Environmental Assessment Directive (23 October 2002).
2   See paras **1.08** and **1.09** above. The Planning and Compulsory Purchase Bill (cl 38) will impose a new duty in relation to regional and local policy-making to exercise the relevant functions with a view to contributing to the achievement of sustainable development.
3   M Grant, *Encyclopedia of Planning Law and Practice*, Monthly Bulletin, November 2002, p 1.
4   See C Ferrary, 'Local Transport Plans and the Implications of the SEA Directive', *The Environmentalist*, October 2002, p 20.

COMPARISON WITH ASSESSMENT UNDER THE BIRDS AND HABITATS DIRECTIVES

1.13   It is important to note that the effect of EIA is procedural. It imposes safeguards to ensure that decisions are taken in the light of full information on the environmental effects and what can be done to avoid or mitigate them. It does not dictate the conclusion, nor offer any guarantee that environmentally damaging development will be prevented. In that respect, it is relevant to compare the procedures for the assessment of projects which may harm protected European sites under the Wild Birds Directive 79/409/EEC and the Habitats Directive 92/43/EEC. As transposed in the Conservation (Natural Habitats, & c) Regulations 1994, SI 1994/2716, Pt IV (Adaptation of Planning and Other Controls), these require the competent authority before deciding to undertake, or to consent to, a plan or project which is likely to have a significant effect on a European site to make an 'appropriate assessment' of the implications for the site.

1.14   There are obvious parallels with EIA, but the important difference is that the competent authority is constrained in its ability to agree to a plan or project which may adversely affect the integrity of the European site, having regard to the manner in which it is to be carried out and any conditions or restrictions to be imposed (see SI 1994/2716, reg 48(5) and (6)). The authority may only undertake the project or give its consent if it is satisfied that the strict criteria of reg 49 are met — namely that there are no alternative solutions and that the plan or project must be carried out for imperative reasons of overriding public interest (which are confined still more strictly where the site hosts a priority natural habitat type or a priority species).

RELATIONSHIP TO ENVIRONMENTAL INFORMATION AND PUBLIC PARTICIPATION ISSUES

1.15   As indicated above, EIA includes among its underlying purposes the informed participation of the public in the decision-making process. To that extent it forms one strand of broader and ongoing developments in the public's access to environmental information, as embodied in Directive 90/313/EEC on the freedom of access to information on the environment[1] and as implemented in the UK by the Environmental Information Regulations 1992, SI 1992/3240.

1   OJ L158, 23.6.90, p 56.

1.16   Another related area of developing law is the UNECE Convention on Access to Information, Public Participation in Decision-Making and Access to Justice in Environmental Matters (the Aarhus Convention).[1] This Convention requires Parties to ensure that public authorities make environmental information available to the public (art 4) and that systems are established to ensure there is an adequate flow of information to public authorities, and thence to the public, about existing and proposed activities which may significantly affect the environment (art 5(1)). Furthermore, by art 6(1)(a) each Party must apply the requirements of art 6 on public participation to decisions on whether to permit the activities listed in Annex I, which lists a range of activities in categories such as energy, metals, minerals, chemicals, various transport and other infrastructure projects, quarries, intensive livestock units and other types of industrial activity. Many of these are in similar, though not identical, terms to projects falling within the EIA Directive.[2] Parties must also apply art 6 to projects not listed in Annex I which may have a significant effect on the environment (art 6(1)(b)).

1   UNECE, Fourth Ministerial Conference, Aarhus, 23–25 June 1998. See M Lee and C Abbot, 'The Usual Suspects? Public Participation under the Aarhus Convention' [2003] MLR 80 for a cogent critical appraisal and R McCracken and G Jones 'The Aarhus Convention' [2003] JPL 802 for a useful summary of the underlying principles.
2   For example, the thresholds as to the number of animals in intensive livestock units is different as between the Aarhus list and the EIA Directive, the Aarhus thresholds being lower.

1.17   The process required under the Aarhus Convention, art 6 has many links and affinities with EIA, in terms of the public being notified of the proposal and supplied with specified information, including a description of the proposal, the significant effects, the mitigating measures envisaged, a non-technical summary, and an outline of the main alternatives studied (art 6(6)). A further parallel is that due account must be taken in the decision-making process of the outcome of the public participation, and the public must be informed of the decision and the reasoning on which it is based (art 6(8) and (9)). At the same time, however, it has been pointed out that in England and Wales the EIA 'regime' is at the information and nominal consultation end of the public participation spectrum, and is not securing the active public participation needed.

1   See P Stookes, *Getting to the Real EIA* [2003] JEL 141.

1.18 Implementation of the Aarhus Convention will involve changes to both EC and domestic law on environmental information. The European Commission published proposals in 2000 for a revised Directive on Access to Environmental Information,[1] not only to implement the Convention, but to address some issues identified in the working of the earlier Directive 90/313/EEC.[2] The UK government took the view that it would legislate to implement the Convention, using the specific power to make regulations contained in the Freedom of Information Act 2000, s 74, without waiting for the final version of the new Directive to be approved.[3] The government accordingly consulted on draft Environmental Information Regulations in July 2002.[4] It is fair to say that the main focus of both the European Commission and the UK government in terms of these changes has been on the general environmental information regime; there are however also possible effects for the EIA regime, given that the range of projects which the Aarhus Convention presupposes will be subject to EIA is different to, and in some respects potentially wider than, the EC regime.

1   COM/2000/0402 final.
2   COM/2000/0400 final.
3   DETR, *Proposals for the Revision of the Public Access to Environmental Information Regime* (10 October 2000).
4   DEFRA, *New Draft Environmental Information Regulations – Public Consultation* (15 July 2002).

SCHEME OF THIS BOOK

1.19 The starting point in understanding the legal requirements as to EIA is Directive 85/337/EEC.[1] The original version required compliance by member states by 3 July 1988 and was amended in a number of important respects by Directive 97/11/EC, which took effect on 14 March 1999. The Directive and the related principles of EC law are considered in chapter 2.

1   Directive 85/337/EEC of 27 June 1985 on the assessment of the effects of certain public and private projects on the environment (OJ L175, 5.7.85, p 40)

1.20 The fact that the EIA Directive was amended in 1997 means that two sets of domestic regulations have to be considered: the original Town and Country Planning (Assessment of Environmental Effects) Regulations 1988, SI 1988/1199 (TCP(AEE) Regulations 1988), and the current Town and Country Planning (Environmental Impact Assessment) Regulations 1999, SI 1999/293 (TCP(EIA) Regulations 1999). Both sets of regulations are provided as Appendices to this work. The TCP(AEE) Regulations 1988 apply to applications for planning permission made on or after 15 July 1988 and before 14 March 1999; the TCP(EIA) Regulations 1999 apply to applications made on or after 14 March 1999.

1.21 Some of the cases referred to in this work relate to TCP(AEE) Regulations 1988, others to TCP(EIA) Regulations 1999. In 2002-2003 cases were still being heard by the courts to which the 1988 Regulations applied.[1] The courts have generally pointed out that in most cases nothing will turn on the distinction, and that conclusions drawn as to the interpretation of one set of regulations will be equally valid for the other.[2] This approach has extended in some cases to instances where the local planning authority dealt with the application under the wrong set of regulations, provided that nothing turned on the differences between the 1988 and 1999 versions. So for example in *R (Goodman) v London Borough of Lewisham*,[3] the local planning authority referred erroneously to the 1988 Regulations rather than the 1999 ones. At first instance Sir Richard Tucker regarded this as 'an error of reference, not a material error of law'.[4] The Court of Appeal agreed that in the case nothing turned on the error, but 'it was not a good start'.[5]

1   See for example, *Friends Provident Life & Pensions Ltd v Secretary of State for Transport, Local Government and the Regions* [2002] JPL 958, para 20; *R (Smith) v Secretary of State for the Environment, Transport and the Regions [2003]* EWCA Civ 262; *R (Burkett) v London Borough of Hammersmith and Fulham* [2003] EWHC 1031 (Admin).
2   See for example, Richards J in *R (Jones) v Mansfield District Council* [2003] EWHC 7 (Admin), [2003] 1 P & CR 504, para 3; Waller L J in *R (Smith) v Secretary of State for the Environment, Transport and the Regions* [2003] EWCA Civ 262, para 4.
3   [2002] EWHC 1769 (Admin).
4   [2002] EWHC 1769 (Admin), para 22.
5   [2003] EWCA Civ 140, [2003] 13 LS Gaz R 28, para 11 (Buxton LJ).

1.22   The first and fundamental point to be established is whether a project is such as to fall within the ambit of the EIA Directive, the TCP(AEE) Regulations 1988 or the TCP(EIA) Regulations 1999. Here planning authorities have been prone to mistakes. The issue is addressed in chapter 3 on screening.

1.23   The heart of the EIA process is the production by the developer of an environmental statement, describing the project, its likely significant effects and the proposed mitigating measures. Again, there are traps for the unwary in the case law, which is considered in chapter 4.

1.24   Chapter 5 deals with the procedures to be followed for EIA, including the important aspects of publicity and consultation of both expert public bodies and the general public.

1.25   Chapter 6 considers the special cases which arise under the planning system in relation to non-standard planning applications and appeals — for example enforcement proceedings, permitted development rights, development by local authorities and the Crown, and the special regime for review of old mining permissions. It also addresses the problematic areas of outline planning applications and the approval of reserved matters.

1.26   Chapter 7 outlines the procedures applying to projects which are authorised outside the planning system. These include for example major power stations, overhead electricity lines, works at ports and harbours, major road schemes, oil and gas pipelines and offshore installations, forestry, land drainage, marine fish-farming, and intensive agriculture on previously uncultivated land.

1.27 Chapter 8 looks at the procedures for challenge by third parties to decisions taken in breach of domestic or EC requirements as to EIA, including the important question of time limits for bringing such proceedings.

1.28 Finally, for practitioners, the issue of the quality of the environmental assessment process, and of environmental statements, still remains an important one. Chapter 9 therefore contains a summary and discussion of good practice in relation to EIA.

Chapter 2

The European dimension and its relevance

THE IMPORTANCE OF EC LAW GENERALLY

2.01   For practitioners concerned to understand the requirements of the environmental impact assessment (EIA) process in the relevant specific statutory context, the natural starting point is the applicable domestic law. For projects within the land use planning system, this will mean the Town and Country Planning (Environmental Impact Assessment) Regulations 1999 TCP (EIA) Regulations 1999). However, the root of these requirements lies in European soil. The corpus of domestic EIA regulations implements the EC requirements contained in the EIA Directive 85/337/EEC, as now amended by Directive 97/11/EC. The development of these requirements, and their relevance in domestic law, are explained in this chapter. It is important to understand the objectives and the structure of the EC legislation, and the ECJ cases explaining it. The most spectacular successes in the courts on the part of those complaining of non-compliance with EIA procedures (and, conversely, the most spectacular defeats by government and developers) have resulted from failure properly to appreciate what EC law requires.

2.02   In a number of the leading cases, the analysis of members of the House of Lords and the Court of Appeal has been based squarely on the EIA Directive. A prime example is *R v North Yorkshire County Council, ex p Brown*,[1] the case in which the House of Lords held that the determination of the conditions to be imposed on old mineral planning permissions under the Planning and Compensation Act 1991, s 22 and Sch 2, constituted the grant of 'development consent' and as such required EIA. At that time, domestic law did not apply EIA procedures to the process of determining such conditions, and thus the issue was whether or not the Directive had been adequately transposed. Lord Hoffmann (with whose speech the other Lords agreed) established the approach by the court to the question as follows:[2]

'The appeal therefore turns on the concept of "development consent" in the Directive. This is a concept of European law, which has to be applied to the planning systems of all the member states. To ascertain its meaning, it is necessary to examine the language and in particular the purpose of the Directive. One must then examine the procedure for determining conditions as part of the United Kingdom planning system and decide whether it should be characterised as a granting of development consent within the meaning of the Directive.'

1   [2000] 1 AC 397.
2   [2000] 1 AC 397 at 401D.

2.03   From this passage, a number of salient points emerge. First, it is necessary to engage with 'concepts of European law', which have a pan-European dimension. Second, this will involve not only the language of the EIA Directive (and indeed in appropriate cases, comparison with other language versions)[1] but also the purpose of the Directive. In the context of whether a national court should seek a preliminary ruling from the ECJ under art 234 (ex art 177) of the EC Treaty, the European Court in the *CILFIT* case said this:[2]

'18. To begin with, it must be borne in mind that Community legislation is drafted in several languages and that the different language versions are all equally authentic. An interpretation of a provision of Community law thus involves a comparison of the different language versions.
19. It must also be borne in mind, even where the different language versions are entirely in accord with one another, that Community law uses terminology which is peculiar to it. Furthermore, it must be emphasised that legal concepts do not necessarily have the same meaning in Community law and in the law of the various Member States.
20. Finally, every provision of Community law must be placed in its context and interpreted in the light of the provisions of Community law as a whole, regard being had to the objectives thereof and to its state of evolution at the date on which the provision in question is to be applied.'

Judgments in the leading cases frequently make reference to the perceived purpose and objectives of the Directive, in particular as evinced by its recitals. Third, a comparison then needs to be made between the language and purpose of the Directive and the procedures applying under domestic law. The principle of autonomous construction applies, as stated by the European Court in *Luxembourg v Linster*:[3]

'The need for uniform application of Community law and the principle of equality require that the terms of a provision of Community law which makes no express reference to the law of the Member States for the purpose of determining its meaning and scope must normally be given an autonomous and uniform meaning throughout the Community; that interpretation must take into account the context of the provision and the purpose of the legislation in question.'[4]

1   For discussion of the issues arising from the plurilingual nature of EC law, see Weatherill and Beaumont, *EU Law* (3rd edn, 1999) pp 185–186.
2   Case 283/81 *Srl CILFIT and Lanificio di Gavardo SpA v Ministry of Health* [1982] ECR 3415, [1983] 1 CMLR 472, paras 18–20.
3   Case C-287/98 *Luxembourg v Linster* [2000] ECR I-6917, para 43.
4   Citing Case 327/82 *Ekvo v Produktschap voor Vee en Vees* [1984] ECR 107, para 11.

2.04   While *R v North Yorkshire County Council, ex p Brown*[1] was a case which turned on whether the EIA Directive had been properly transposed, the need to resort to the underlying EC law arises also in cases where the issue is whether the requirements of the Directive have been correctly implemented in terms of administrative processes and decisions. In *Berkeley v Secretary of State for the Environment*[2] (*'Berkeley 1'*) the House of Lords quashed a decision by the Secretary of State to grant planning permission and listed building consent to Fulham Football Club for the redevelopment of its site at Craven Cottage.[3] The issue was whether there had been compliance with the domestic regulations,[4] which it was accepted had correctly transposed the Directive.[5] The failure lay in the fact that the Secretary of State had not considered whether the project was an 'urban development project' which would be likely to have significant effects on the environment. Again giving the leading speech, Lord Hoffmann began by a description of the requirements of the Directive, starting with its recitals.[6]

1   [2000] 1 AC 397.
2   [2001] 2 AC 603.
3   The case is the leading authority on the exercise of discretion in relation to quashing decisions for non-compliance with EIA requirements, holding that the discretion not to quash is extremely limited: see para **8.44**.
4   Then the Town and Country Planning (Assessment of Environmental Effects) Regulations 1988, SI 1988/1199.
5   See [2001] 2 AC 603 at 607F (Lord Bingham of Cornhill).
6   [2001] 2 AC 603 at 609B–F.

2.05   The relevance of Lord Hoffmann's laying the ground as to the EC requirements appears later in his speech, in the section in which he considers 'Why was the planning permission ultra vires?'.[1] Again, it is instructive to consider his reasoning in some detail. Lord Hoffmann begins by a purposive approach, which requires member states to consider whether EIA is required in relation to projects falling within Annex II of the EIA Directive. As Lord Hoffmann points out, this is not expressly required by the terms of the Directive, but is necessary to give it efficacy:[2]

> 'The primary obligation under the Directive, under article 2(1), is for a member state to require an EIA before consent is given in every case in which the project is likely to have significant effects on the environment. But the decision as to whether an Annex II project is likely to have such effects is left to the member state. It depends, as article 4(2) says, on whether the member states "consider" that the characteristics of the project so require. This must mean that in Annex II cases the member states are under an obligation to consider whether or not an EIA is required. If this were not so, a member state could in practice restrict the scope of the Directive to Annex I cases simply by failing to consider whether in any other case an EIA was required or not.'

Though Lord Hoffmann does not spell it out, this approach to construing the Directive is heavily influenced by EC law. It recognises the importance of a purposive approach in the context of relatively open-textured EC drafting.[3] It stresses the importance of ensuring effectiveness of the Directive, a principle which itself finds its origins in interpretative techniques of the European Court of Justice (ECJ).[4] This is sometimes expressed in the form of a healthy mistrust of member states as willing to take advantage of any weakness or loophole in directives as a way of restricting their scope or lessening their onerous effects. It is a principle which finds clear expression in a number of the ECJ cases on EIA discussed later in this chapter.[5] At the same time, the purposive approach is not a license for indiscriminate use of the Directive to strike down permissions where there has in reality been substantial compliance; for a controversial example, see *R (Prokopp) v London Underground Limited.*[6]

1   [2002] 2 AC 603 at 614.
2   [2002] 2 AC 603 at 614B–C.
3   See Weatherill and Beaumont, *EU Law* (3rd edn, 1999) pp 186, 190–192.
4   See Tridimas, *The General Principles of EC Law* (1999) pp 276–277.
5   See paras **2.28–2.38** below.
6   CA, 7 July 2003, para **6.33** below.

2.06   A further step in Lord Hoffmann's reasoning in *Berkeley 1* was art 10 (ex art 5) of the EC Treaty, which reads as follows:

'Member States shall take all appropriate measures, whether general or particular, to ensure fulfilment of the obligations arising out of this Treaty or resulting from action taken by the institutions of the Community. They shall facilitate the achievement of the Community's tasks. They shall abstain from any measure which could jeopardise the attainment of the objectives of this Treaty.'

This article is relevant in a number of ways. It reinforces the principle of effectiveness, both in terms of interpretation and in terms of the remedies provided before domestic courts. Lord Bingham of Cornhill in *Berkeley 1* found it particularly relevant in pointing towards an order to quash the decision as being the proper response of the court.[1] Lord Hoffmann linked it to the rights of individuals to rely on the EIA Directive before national courts in relation to domestic measures which were incompatible with EC requirements,[2] and in cases where a Sch 2 project under the Planning and Compensation Act 1991 is arguably likely to have significant environmental effects, the directly enforceable right of individuals affected by the development to have the need for EIA considered before the grant of planning permission.[3]

1   [2001] 2 AC 603 at 608F.
2   [2001] 2 AC 603 at 614F. See also discussion of the ECJ case law at para **2.39** below.
3   [2001] 2 AC 603 at 615C.

2.07   On the basis of these EC principles, Lord Hoffmann considered the relevant domestic regulations.[1] The TCP (EIA) Regulations 1999, reg 4(2) prohibited the grant of planning permission without EIA in relation to Sch 1 or Sch 2 applications. Under the Regulations, the issue of whether the application fell within Sch 2 depended on the decision of the Secretary of State. Like the EIA Directive, the Regulations did not impose on the Secretary of State any general obligation to consider whether the application was a Sch 2 application or not. Lord Hoffmann found it was not difficult, in order to make reg 4(2) effective, to imply into that regulation an obligation upon the Secretary of State to consider the matter.[2] In so doing, Lord Hoffmann was applying the principle of sympathetic interpretation or indirect effect, to interpret domestic law 'as far as possible, in the light of the wording and purpose of the Directive in order to achieve the result pursued by the latter', another important aspect of EC law.[3] On that basis, unless (which was not contended) no reasonable Secretary of State could have considered the application to be within Sch 2, it was inevitable that the Secretary of State be held to have failed to comply with that implied obligation to consider the matter.[4]

1   Which at the time were the Town and Country Planning (Assessment of Environmental Effects) Regulations 1988, SI 1988/1199.
2   [2001] 2 AC 603 at 614H.
3   [2001] 2 AC 603 at 614H–615A, citing Case C-106/89 *Marleasing SA v La Comercial Internacional de Alimentacion SA* [1990] ECR I-4135 at 4159, para 8.
4   [2001] 2 AC 603 at 615B.

2.08   Thus the case illustrates many of the important themes of EC law which run through the decisions discussed later in this chapter. These are: purposive interpretation; ensuring effectiveness; sympathetic interpretation; and the recognition and vindication of the rights of individual members of the public as intended beneficiaries of the EIA process.

2.09   A final illustration of the role accorded to the EIA Directive by the courts when determining issues arising under domestic legislation is provided by the litigation involving Kingsway Business Park, Rochdale. In the first case, *R v Rochdale Metropolitan Borough Council, ex p Tew*,[1] Sullivan J quashed a bare outline planning permission for the development of a 213 ha business park. The case is discussed in detail below,[2] but the essence of the matter lay in the failure to supply adequate 'environmental information' to enable environmental assessment of the likely impacts under the applicable regulations.[3] After setting out the salient parts of the domestic regulations, Sullivan J considered the relevant recitals and provisions of the Directive.[4] Having discussed the competing submissions of the parties, including the difficult practical consequences which would flow from requiring EIA in its full rigour at bare outline stage, the judge was clearly influenced by the aims and objectives of the underlying EC legislation, as the following passage makes clear:[5]

'Notwithstanding the difficulties of describing the size, design or scale of such a project, the Members of the EC concluded that if it was likely to have significant effects on the environment, development consent should not be granted until a prior assessment of those effects had been carried out. In so far as such an assessment requires a greater degree of particularity in the description of the development that is proposed to be carried out, greater particularity must be provided. Thus, applications for such projects have been placed in a legal straightjacket *(sic)*. The reason for this is explained in Directive 97/11/EC: the environmental assessment procedure is a "fundamental instrument" of the EC's environmental policy.'[6]

1   [2000] Env LR 1, [1999] 3 PLR 74, [2001] JPL 54.
2   See paras **6.49–6.54**.
3   As in *Berkeley 1*, these were the earlier TCP(EIA) Regulations 1988.

4   [2000] Env LR 1 at 19–20.
5   [2000] Env LR 1 at 28.
6   In fact the relevant Directive was 85/337/EEC, prior to its amendment by 97/11/EC; however, Sullivan J found the recitals to the later Directive helpful in providing a 'convenient summary of the aims and importance of the earlier directive'. (See [2000] Env LR 1 at 20.)

2.10   In the second Kingsway Business Park case, *R v Rochdale Metropolitan Borough Council, ex p Milne*,[1] the deficiencies which had led to the permission in *Tew* being quashed were found to have been rectified on a subsequent application.[2] As Sullivan J pointed out, although counsel for the objectors had laid great stress on the EIA Directive, the proper starting point was the domestic Regulations.[3] This was because there was no suggestion that the TCP (EIA) Regulations 1999 did not fully and accurately transpose the Directive into domestic law.[4] Nonetheless, Sullivan J accepted that the domestic Regulations should be construed, so far as possible, to accord with the objectives of the Directive. This led to a detailed discussion in the judgment, of what the intention of the framers of the Directive might have been with regard to demand-led industrial estate development projects. The conclusion was that while EIA was an important procedural tool in helping to secure the Community's environmental policies,[5] there was no reason why the term 'description of the development' in the Directive should not recognise the reality that such projects (and possibly also 'urban development projects') are by their nature not fixed at the outset, but may be expected to evolve over a number of years depending on market demand.[6] It was for the competent domestic authority to decide whether the resulting degree of flexibility and uncertainty are such as to be unacceptable. The 'legal straitjacket' resulting from the Directive, which Sullivan J had said restrained such projects in *Tew*, was held in fact to admit of some degree of flexibility:[7]

'The directive did not envisage that the "straitjacket" would be drawn so tightly as to suffocate such projects.'

This passage is useful in emphasising that the principle of effectiveness is not a mandate for construing the Directive in the most onerous manner possible. The objectives of the Directive are to preserve and protect the quality of the environment, but not in absolute terms; the protection is procedural in nature and does not extend to all projects; the objectives involve striking a balance between the requirements of EC law and discretion allowed to member states in this respect.

1   [2001] Env LR 406, (2001) 81 P & CR 365, [2001] JPL 740.
2   See further, paras **6.55–6.59**.
3   [2001] Env LR 406 at 428 (para 82).
4   See *R v London Borough of Hammersmith and Fulham, ex p Trustees of the London Branch of the CPRE* [2000] Env LR 532; *R (Barker) v London Borough of Bromley* [2002] Env LR 631.
5   [2001] Env LR 406 at 428 (para 83); in particular referring to art 174 of the EC Treaty which includes the objective of preserving, protecting and improving the quality of the environment, but also requires account to be taken of economic and social development, and the balanced development of the Community's regions.
6   [2001] Env LR 406 at 430 (para 90).
7   [2001] Env LR 406 at 430 (para 91).

DEVELOPMENT OF THE EIA DIRECTIVE

2.11   A short account of the development of the EIA Directive may assist in understanding its objectives and structure.[1] The European Commission's Second Action Programme on the Environment in 1977[2] stated that '... effects on the environment should be taken into account at the earliest possible stage in all the technical planning and decision-making processes'. At that point the Commission announced its intention of bringing forward proposals on EIA. Behind this was the perception, expressed in the Commission's Second Report on the State of the Environment (1979) that ' ... too much economic activity has taken place in the wrong place, using environmentally unsuitable technologies'. In fact, the Commission had initiated academic research into EIA in 1975, which had in 1976 concluded that: (i) many aspects of EIA procedure already existed within member states; (ii) it should therefore be possible to introduce a harmonised European EIA system without undue disruption or US-style litigation; and (iii) the most appropriate way forward would be to introduce project-based EIA, followed at some future time by its extension to plans and projects.[3]

1   Useful accounts, on which this section is largely based, are provided in Haigh, *Manual of Environmental policy: The EU and Britain* (looseleaf) p 11.2-4 and Wood C, *Environmental Impact Assessment: A Comparative Review* (1996) pp 32–37. Also see Haigh [1987] JPL 4.
2   European Community Policy and Action Programme on the Environment 1977–1981 (OJ C139, 13.6.77).
3   This extension to plans and projects was not in fact effected until 2001, with the adoption of Directive 2001/42/EC (see para 1.06).

2.12   The political difficulties in the development of the EIA Directive have been well documented.[1] Between 1977, when the first preliminary draft was issued by the Commission, and June 1980 when a draft was formally submitted to the Council of Ministers, there were 20 internal drafts, not all of which were released. The British government then maintained consistent opposition to the proposal from September 1980 (when the first formal statement of its views on the proposal appeared) to November 1983, its main concerns including the definition of projects subject to the proposal, and the scope for delays and litigation in the planning process. The government had previously expressed interest in EIA methodology, initially in relation to onshore oil projects in Scotland during the 1970s.[2] A particular milestone was the publication in 1976 of a research report by Catlow and Thirlwall,[3] commissioned by the Department of Environment, which recommended legislative changes to embed EIA formally within the planning system. The government's response to this suggestion was at best lukewarm, with reservations being expressed as to the unacceptable calls on local government finance and manpower which it might entail. In a press release issued in 1978, the government did however go so far as to encourage the use of EIA procedures in cases of 'relatively few large and significant proposals', where it might be worthwhile.[4] This attitude did not change with the incoming Conservative government in 1979, which had a deregulatory mindset. It has been well summarised by Wood as follows:[5]

'[The government] did not actively discourage the growing acceptance of the value of EIA by local planning authorities, but it was most reluctant to introduce new procedures or statutory requirements into the existing planning system it had criticised for causing unnecessary delay.'

1   See Sheate and Macrory [1989] *Journal of Common Market Studies* 68; Wathern, *Environmental Impact Assessment: Theory and Practice* (1988).
2   See Wood C, *Environmental Impact Assessment: A Comparative Review* (1996) at pp 44–47, for a full account of early EIA interest in the UK and of attitudes to the EC proposals.
3   Catlow and Thirlwall, 'Environmental Impact Analysis' (DoE Research Report 11, 1976).
4   DoE Press Notice 488 (1978).
5   Wood C, *Environmental Impact Assessment: A Comparative Review* (1996), p 46.

2.13   This attitude explains much of the opposition to the drafts of the EIA Directive as they began to emerge from Brussels. The government's concerns were brought into focus by an important report of the House of Lords Select Committee on the European Communities, published in 1981.[1] The government, in evidence to the Committee, questioned the practicability and wisdom of the proposal.[2] Nonetheless, the Committee found that the draft directive struck an appropriate balance, in allowing existing planning controls in member states to continue without major disruption, while containing enough detail to ensure that the intention of the Directive could not be evaded. The government, however, stuck to its position. In a House of Lords debate on the Select Committee Report, the Minister Lord Bellwin said:[3]

'The Government do not believe that the present draft directive yet gets it right. As a first step in [a] new field we consider it to be over-ambitious and likely to fail in its intention.'

Nonetheless, following negotiations which limited both the scope and the requirements of the proposed directive, the UK government did eventually withdraw its opposition. This has been attributed in part to the continuing influence of the Lords' Select Committee Report[4] and to the view held within government circles that there would not be a need to extend EIA to Annex II projects.[5] Given the mass of subsequent litigation stressing the importance of proper consideration of EIA for Annex II projects, there is an obvious irony in any such reasoning.

1   Environmental Assessment of Projects (11th Report, Session 1980–81).
2   See Haigh, *Manual of Environmental policy: The EU and Britain* (looseleaf), p 11.2-5.
3   HL Official Report (5th series) vol 000, cols 1311–1347. Cited in Wood C, *Environmental Impact Assessment: A Comparative Review* (1996), p 47.
4   See Haigh, *Manual of Environmental policy: The EU and Britain* (looseleaf), p 11.2-6.
5   Wood C, *Environmental Impact Assessment: A Comparative Review* (1996), p 47.

2.14   Even following the withdrawal of the UK's objections, all was not plain sailing for the proposed directive. Denmark objected in principle to the application of EIA procedures to projects authorised by a specific Act of Parliament, on the basis that this infringed Parliamentary sovereignty. This objection was met by an amendment exempting projects the details of which were adopted by a specific act of national legislation. Directive 85/337/EEC, which had been first mooted in 1977, and formally proposed in 1980,[1] was finally published in the Official Journal in July 1985.[2] The adopted version was weaker in numerous respects than earlier drafts, to the extent that it has been suggested that the net effect of the changes has been the 'emasculation' of provisions in the earlier versions.[3] There is no doubt that it represented a political compromise. In particular, the list of projects within Annex I requiring mandatory EIA in all cases was substantially shortened, and the list of Annex II projects, for which EIA was required only if there were likely to be significant environmental effects, grew correspondingly.[4] Annex III (specifying the information to be provided in an environmental statement) was also considerably weakened in content; to some extent this may explain the rather curious format and drafting of the Directive on this issue, which has puzzled judges and commentators.[5]

1   COM/80/313 final, 11.6.80.
2   OJ L175, 5.7.85, p 40.
3   Wood C, *Environmental Impact Assessment: A Comparative Review* (1996), p 35.
4   ENDS Report 126 (July 1985) referred to a reduction of two-thirds in the original list of EIA Directive, Annex I projects, which had contained 35 types of project, the arbitrary nature of the distinction between Annex I and II projects in some cases, and that the effect of EIA practices would accordingly depend to a great extent on how member states used the greater discretion available to them.
5   See, for example, the comments of Harrison J in *R v Cornwall County Council, ex p Hardy* [2001] Env LR 25, [2001] JPL 786, para 57.

IMPLEMENTATION OF THE DIRECTIVE

2.15   Even when adopted, the EIA Directive proved troublesome in its implementation. The response of different member states was uneven, and in some cases infraction proceedings resulted. These gave rise to particular political controversy in the UK, where the then Commissioner, Carlo Ripa di Meana, suggested that work should stop on two controversial road schemes, the M3 extension at Twyford Down, Hampshire, and the East London River Crossing at Oxleas Wood.[1] The issue became tied up with general popular anti-EC sentiment and the perception of undue interference by Brussels in domestic decision making. In the event, for various reasons (including clarification of the legal position of projects which were 'in the pipeline' at the time of implementation) the Commission issued a press notice in July 1992 announcing it was terminating proceedings against the UK relating to five of the seven projects which were the subject of an art 169 infraction letter.[2] Ultimately, the Commission proceeded to a Reasoned Opinion against the UK (issued in April 1993) only in relation to the Oxleas Wood project.[3] The project was abandoned in July 1993, though the government denied that this decision was influenced by the proceedings.

1   See Haigh, *Manual of Environmental policy: The EU and Britain* (looseleaf), p 11.2-14.
2   The proceedings are chronicled by J Salter in a series of articles at [1992] JPL 14, 214 and 313.
3   The allegation was that the assessment was inadequate in relation to the data on ecological impacts on soil, fauna, mammal, reptile and amphibian populations.

2.16   The advice contained in Circular 15/88[1] when the Town and Country Planning (Assessment of Environmental Effects) Regulations 1988 (TCP(AEE) Regulations 1988) were introduced was minimalist in tone, referring to the government's aim of ensuring that 'no additional unnecessary burdens are placed on either developers or authorities'.[2] The view was that EIA would be needed for EIA Directive, Annex II projects only in three main types of case:[3]

(i) for major projects of more than local importance;

(ii) *occasionally* for projects on a smaller scale proposed for particularly sensitive or vulnerable locations; and

(iii) in a *small number of cases*, for projects with *unusually* complex and potentially adverse environmental effects, where expert and detailed analysis of those effects would be desirable.

The Secretary of State's view was that '... the number of projects falling within these categories will be a small proportion of all Schedule 2 projects; and that in most cases there should be little difficulty in deciding whether or not environmental assessment is needed'.[4]

1   Department of the Environment circular 15/88, Welsh Office circular 23/88, *Environmental Assessment* (12 July 1988).
2   Paragraph 8.
3   Paragraph 20.
4   Paragraph 21.

2.17   In view of the difficulties encountered in the UK and other countries in coming to terms with the requirements of the EIA Directive, it is perhaps not surprising that a report of the Commission in 1993 on experience in implementing the Directive[1] gave an appraisal that amounted to 'Could do better'. The Report suggested that there was evidence of some beneficial effects, but that modifications to projects as a result of EIA were mainly of a minor and non-radical nature. Changes to the Directive were proposed to increase its coverage, to improve the quality of EIA, consultation and participation, and to address the issue of transboundary effects, as required by the Espoo Convention.[2]

1   Report from the Commission of the Implementation of Directive 85/337/EEC (COM(93)28).
2   UNECE Convention on Environmental Impact Assessment in a Transboundary Context (concluded at Espoo, Finland, 25 February 1991).

DIRECTIVE 97/11/EC

2.18   The proposals of the Commission[1] for improving the EIA Directive led ultimately to the adoption in 1997 of amending Directive 97/11/EC, which applies to projects for which the request for development consent was made after 14 March 1999. To some extent, the changes made by the 1997 Directive can be seen as redressing the deficiencies caused by the political haggling over the original version. These changes can be summarised as follows:

—   Annex I (projects subject to EIA in all cases) is completely re-written, with a number of categories being added. These include road construction or modification, port or waterway developments, groundwater and water resource schemes, waste water treatment plants, gas and petroleum abstraction, pipelines, intensive pig and poultry rearing, paper and pulp production, quarrying, overhead power lines, and petroleum, petrochemical or chemical storage. Other project classes in Annex I were extended (for example a new and wider definition of 'integrated chemical installation', decommissioning of nuclear power stations and production of non-ferrous crude metals).[2]

— Annex II (projects for which EIA required if significant environmental effects are likely) is also re-written and is subjected to a large number of changes. Among the new classes added were wind farms, coastal and maritime works capable of altering the coast, groundwater abstraction and artificial recharging, permanent camp sites and caravan sites, and theme parks. Other classes were extended, for example forestry projects included deforestation, irrigation was included within water management projects for agriculture, intensive farming of any fish (not just salmon), and all waste disposal installations (not just those for industrial or domestic waste).[3] In addition, changes to Annex II projects were made subject to Annex II.

— A new art 4 and Annex III are inserted, dealing with screening (the process of determining under art 4 which Annex II projects are to be subject to EIA). This requires a formal procedure for making the determination, which must be made available to the public. Annex III specifies 'selection criteria' which are to be taken into account in setting thresholds or criteria for this purpose, or in carrying out a case-by-case examination. This change addresses concerns that some member states had exercised their discretion in relation to Annex II projects in inappropriate ways.

— A new art 5 deals with 'scoping' (the procedure by which the planning authority indicates formally what information is to be provided by the developer.

— The minimum information to be provided by the developer (art 5(3)) now includes an outline of the main alternatives studied and an indication of the main reasons for the choice.

— Article 7 now deals with procedures for collaboration between member states over potential transboundary effects.

1   COM/93/575 final, 12.5.94, p 8.
2   The full list of changes appears as Appendix IV to the DETR Consultation Paper of 28 July 1997 on implementing the revised EIA Directive.
3   The full list of changes appears as Appendix V to the DETR Consultation Paper of 28 July 1997 on implementing the revised EIA Directive.

Purpose of the Directive

2.19   Under the interpretative principles referred to above, recourse is frequently made to the recitals to the EIA Directive in order to establish its purpose. The recitals of the original Directive 85/337/EEC were relatively short.[1] They referred to the 1973, 1977 and 1983 Action Programmes as stressing that the best environmental policy consists of preventing pollution or nuisances at source, and as affirming the need to take the effects on the environment into account at the earliest possible stage in technical planning and decision-making processes. The Directive was stated to be based on art 100 of the EC Treaty as being necessary to approximate national laws on

EIA and so avoid unfavourable competitive conditions or adverse effects on the functioning of the common market. In addition, it was based on the residual powers of art 235 of the EC Treaty, in view of the lack at the time of any explicit basis in the Treaty for environmental legislation. The following recitals set out the thinking behind the structure of the original Directive as follows, in particular the distinction between Annex I and Annex II projects:

'Whereas general principles for the assessment of environmental effects should be introduced with a view to supplementing and co-ordinating development consent procedures governing public and private projects likely to have a major effect on the environment;[2]

Whereas development consent[3] for public and private projects which are likely to have significant effects on the environment should be granted only after prior assessment of the likely significant environmental effects of these projects has been carried out;[4]

Whereas this assessment must be conducted on the basis of the appropriate information supplied by the developer, which may be supplemented by the authorities and by the people who may be concerned by the project in question;[5]

Whereas the principles of the assessment of environmental effects should be harmonised, in particular with reference to the projects which should be subject to assessment, the main obligations of the developers and the content of the assessment;

Whereas projects belonging to certain types have significant effects on the environment and these projects must as a rule be subject to systematic assessment;[6]

Whereas projects of other types may not have significant effects on the environment in every case and whereas these projects should be assessed where the Member States consider that their characteristics so require;[7]

Whereas for projects which are subject to assessment, a certain minimal amount of information must be supplied, concerning the project and its effects.'

1   Reference may be made to the exact wording, which is at the APPENDIX 4.
2   In other words, the EIA Directive was seeking to augment and improve existing national procedures, and did not entail the creation of new procedures.
3   As to the meaning of 'development consent' see para **6.04**.
4   This lays the ground for the key provision on which the EIA Directive hinges, namely the prohibition of the grant of development consent, unless the environmental information required by EIA procedures has been taken into account. Hence the fact that planning permission granted in breach of the relevant requirements is unlawful.
5   Thus the prime provider of information for EIA purposes is the developer, but importantly, the role of 'people who may be concerned by the project' is also flagged up.
6   The EIA Directive, Annex I projects, for which EIA is always required.

7   EIA Directive, Annex II projects. It is probably this wording which misled the UK government into believing that EIA for such projects was effectively a matter of national discretion, and optional.

2.20   It is instructive to compare the original recitals to EIA Directive 85/337/EEC with the recitals to amending Directive 97/11/EC. The first four recitals of the latter directive in particular set out clearly the rationale for EIA under EC law, reflecting the developments which had taken place in the interim both in the importance of environmental protection as a part of EC law and policy and in the practical experience of EIA:

'(1)   Whereas Council Directive 85/337/EEC ... aims at providing the competent authorities with relevant information to enable them to take a decision on a specific project in full knowledge of the project's likely significant impact on the environment; whereas the assessment procedure is a fundamental instrument of environmental policy as defined in Article 130R of the [EC] Treaty and of the Fifth Community Programme of policy and action in relation to the environment and sustainable development;

(2)   Whereas, pursuant to Article 130R(2) of the Treaty, Community policy on the environment is based on the precautionary principle and on the principle that preventive action should be taken, that environmental damage should as a priority be rectified at source and that the polluter should pay;

(3)   Whereas the main principles of the assessment of environmental effects should be harmonized and whereas the Member States may lay down stricter rules to protect the environment;

(4)   Whereas experience acquired in environmental impact assessment, as recorded in the report on the implementation of Directive 85/337/EEC, adopted by the Commission on 2 April 1993, shows that it is necessary to introduce provisions designed to clarify, supplement and improve the rules on the assessment procedure, in order to ensure that the Directive is applied in an increasingly harmonized and efficient manner.'

2.21   Recital (5) of Directive 97/11/EC indicates that projects for which assessment is required should be subject to a requirement for development consent. By contrast, the original recitals proceeded on the assumption that there would already be development consent procedures in place for all projects subject to EIA; an assumption which proved to be unfounded. This change in perception is reflected in the requirement of art 2(1) of the amended Directive, which requires member states to adopt all measures necessary to ensure that the relevant projects are made subject to a requirement for development consent and an assessment with regard to their effects. Article 2(1) of the original Directive simply required projects to be subject to an assessment before consent was given. It is, however, right to point out that art 2(2) did envisage the possibility that new procedures might need to be established to comply with the aims of the Directive.

2.22   Recital (6) of Directive 97/11/EC records that it is appropriate to make additions to the list of projects (in Annex I) which have significant effects on the environment and which must as a rule be made subject to EIA.

2.23   Recitals (7)–(9) of Directive 97/11/EC refer to the controversial issue of Annex II projects and are worth setting out in full:

'(7)   Whereas projects of other types may not have significant effects on the environment in every case; whereas these projects should be assessed where Member States consider they are likely to have significant effects on the environment;

(8)   Whereas Member States may set thresholds or criteria for the purpose of determining which such projects should be subject to assessment on the basis of the significance of their environmental effects; whereas Member States should not be required to examine projects below those thresholds or outside those criteria on a case-by-case basis;

(9)   Whereas when setting such thresholds or criteria or examining projects on a case-by-case basis for the purpose of determining which projects should be subject to assessment on the basis of their significant environmental effects, Member States should take account of the relevant selection criteria set out in this Directive; whereas, in accordance with the subsidiarity principle, the Member States are in the best position to apply these criteria in specific instances.'

2.24   It can therefore be seen that the revised EIA Directive represents a political compromise on the thorny issue of Annex II projects, which had caused problems under the original Directive. Member state autonomy or subsidiarity is catered for by the ability of member states to set thresholds or criteria as a means of determining which Annex II projects require assessment, and as an alternative to the administrative burden of having to determine the question for each project on a case-specific basis. However, there are constraints or safeguards on this discretion. For one thing, art 4(3) of Directive 97/11/EC requires the selection criteria at Annex III to be taken into account in setting such thresholds or criteria; these relate to the characteristics and location of the project or projects in question and the characteristics of the potential impacts. Directive 97/11/EC, therefore, as it were, sets the agenda for the exercise of the discretion. In addition, as appears from the cases referred to in the following paragraphs, the ECJ has itself considered the ambit and limits of that discretion.

Implementation of the revised Directive

2.25   The government issued a consultation paper on implementation of the revised EIA Directive in July 1997.[1] This was more whole-hearted in tone than the proposals for implementing the original Directive, endorsing the use of the EIA process and suggesting that the revised Directive represented a significant improvement over the original.[2] In relation to Annex II projects, the consultation paper proposed the use of a combined system, as permitted by the Directive, of 'exclusive thresholds' for project categories, below which EIA would not be required, with case-by-case consideration of projects above those thresholds as to their likely significant effects. This would be supported by non-binding 'indicative thresholds', which would be reviewed and enhanced in the light of experience gained under the previous Regulations (TCP(AEE) Regulations 1988).[3]

1   DETR, *Implementation of EC Directive 97/11/EC on Environmental Assessment* (28 July 1997).
2   Paragraphs 18–19.
3   Paragraphs 29–33.

2.26   More detailed proposals for implementation were then put forward in the DETR consultation paper of December 1997, seeking to focus the threshold and case-by-case approaches, and introducing the use of defined 'sensitive areas' as a modification to the exclusive threshold approach.[1] The government's view was that outside these areas, the number of projects requiring EIA would be only a small proportion of EIA Directive, Annex II projects.[2] It was clear that the government saw the use of exclusive thresholds as necessary to avoid what would otherwise be a very considerable new burden on planning authorities in considering the wider range of Annex II projects on a case-by-case basis, which would require 'a dramatic increase in current levels of regulation over minor development activity'.[3] The consultation paper put it as follows:[4]

'This increase in red tape would be greatest for small businesses, farmers and statutory undertakers (affecting eg extensions/alterations to many industrial buildings; water management activities related to agriculture; and all works undertaken by statutory undertakers relating to docks, piers, harbours, roads, etc.

While the Government strongly believes that all projects with the potential to have significant effects (and in the most sensitive locations such projects could be quite small) should be properly considered on a case-by-case basis, such scrutiny is unwarranted for minor projects which could not have significant effects within the meaning of the EIA Directive.'

1   DETR, Determining the Need for Environmental Assessment (19 December 1997).
2   Paragraph 17.
3   Paragraph 20.
4   Paragraphs 20–21.

2.27   Draft Regulations were issued for consultation in July 1998, following this approach.[1] It may be noted in passing that at this stage the draft regulations followed the earlier nomenclature of 'Town and Country Planning (Assessment of Environmental Effects)'. The final terminology used in the Regulations was however Environmental Impact Assessment, reflecting the more widely-used terminology for the process,[2] and also avoiding possible confusion with the 'EA' acronym for the Environment Agency.

1   DETR, *Draft Town and Country planning (Assessment of Environmental Effects) Regulations 1998* (16 July 1998).
2   DETR, *Environmental Impact Assessment: A Guide to Procedures* (November 2000), p 6.

THE EUROPEAN CASES

Kraaijeveld

2.28   Three European cases are of particular importance in considering the purpose of the EIA Directive, and the ambit of member state discretion in relation to Annex II projects. The first is Case C-72/95 *Kraaijeveld* ('the Dutch Dykes case').[1] The case concerned the Directive in its original and unamended form. The project in question was the strengthening and replacement of dykes and embankments along the Rotterdam Waterway. This type of project fell within Annex II of the Directive, as 'canalisation and flood-relief works' or as 'dams and other installations designed to hold water or store it on a long-term basis'. As such, under art 4(3) as it then read,

> 'Projects of the classes listed in Annex II shall be made subject to an assessment ... where Member States consider that their characteristics so require.

> To this end Member States may *inter alia* specify certain types of projects as being subject to an assessment or may establish the criteria and/or thresholds necessary to determine which of the projects of the classes listed in Annex II are to be subject to an assessment ...'

1   Case C-72/95 *Aannamaersbedrijf PK Kraaijeveld v Gedeputeerde Staten van Zuid-Holland* [1996] ECR I-5403, [1997] Env LR 265.

2.29   The relevant Dutch authority adopted a plan authorising the works, which had the effect of depriving Kraaijeveld's commercial undertaking of access to the waterway. Kraaijeveld appealed to the Dutch courts, which in turn referred a number of questions to the European Court for a preliminary ruling under art 177 of the EC Treaty.

2.30   The first question was whether the expression 'canalisation or flood relief works' in the EIA Directive, Annex II was to be interpreted as covering certain types of work on a dyke running alongside the waterways. The Dutch government argued that there was a distinction between canalisation work and work on reinforcing dykes (embankments).[1] The former would change the character of the watercourse itself, so having an effect on the quality and quantity of water, and on flora and fauna, whereas the latter consisted of increasing the height of the embankment and would not affect the regulated water levels. The European Commission argued that it was necessary to take into account the purpose of the Directive, which concerned the environmental effects of projects rather than their social objective.[2] Regardless of whether the purpose was to improve navigation or to protect against flooding, the construction of dykes would affect the environment, and if those effects were significant such works should be covered by the words 'canalisation or flood relief works'. The Court's approach, in accordance with previous case law, was to compare different language versions of the Directive to see if any common meaning was yielded.[3] As there was divergence between the meaning of the various versions, the next stage was to interpret the provision by reference to the purpose and general scheme of the rules of which the provision forms part.[4] The Court agreed with the Commission that the key was the significance of the environmental effects of the works in question:[5]

> 'The wording of the directive indicates that it has a wide scope and a broad purpose. That observation alone should suffice to interpret point 10(e) of Annex II to the directive as encompassing all works for retaining water and preventing floods — and therefore dyke works — even if not all the linguistic versions are so precise.'

1   See *Kraaijeveld v Gedeputeerde Staten van Zuid-Holland* [1996] ECR I-5403, para 24.
2   See *Kraaijeveld v Gedeputeerde Staten van Zuid-Holland* [1996] ECR I-5403, para 27.
3   See Case C-283/81 *Srl CILFIT and Lanificio di Gavardo SpA v Ministry of Health* [1982] ECR 3415, [1983] 1 CMLR 472.
4   Case C-449/93 *Rockfon* [1995] ECR I-4291, para 28.
5   *Kraaijeveld v Gedeputeerde Staten van Zuid-Holland* [1996] ECR I-5403, para 31.

2.31   The second question for the ECJ in *Kraaijeveld* was whether the position under question 1 was affected by any distinction to be drawn between the construction of a new dyke, the relocation of an existing dyke, the reinforcement of an existing dyke, or the replacement in situ of an existing dyke. This turned on the interpretation of the phrase 'modifications to development projects' in Annex II of the EIA Directive. Annex II referred at that time to modifications of Annex I projects, but made no reference to modifications to Annex II projects. Rather strikingly, the governments of the UK and Italy argued that modifications to Annex II projects were caught, whereas the Dutch government and the Commission argued for a narrower construction, with such modifications not being within the scope of the Directive. The ECJ again took an approach which was both broad and purposive in holding that modifications to existing dykes were indeed caught:[1]

> '38. Since the directive provides no specific definition of "modifications to development projects" the expression must be interpreted in the light of the general scheme and purpose of the directive.
>
> 39. It has already been pointed out ... that the scope of the directive is wide and its purpose very broad. Its purpose would be undermined if "modifications to development projects" were so construed as to enable certain works to escape the requirement of an impact assessment although, by reason of their nature, size or location, such works were likely to have significant effects on the environment.
>
> 40. Furthermore, the mere fact that the directive does not expressly refer to modifications to projects included in Annex II, as opposed to modifications to projects included in Annex I, does not justify the conclusion that they are not covered by the directive. The distinction between a "project" and a "modification to a project", where projects included in Annex I are concerned, relates to the different systems to which they are subject under the directive, whereas such a distinction in the case of projects included in Annex II would relate to the general scope of the directive.'[2]

1   *Kraaijeveld v Gedeputeerde Staten van Zuid-Holland* [1996] ECR I-5403, paras 38–40.

2   The ECJ went on to refer to the case involving the Grosskrotzenburg power station (Case C-431/92 *Commission v Germany* [1995] ECR I-2189) in support of its view. See further the discussion at paras 3.40–3.42

2.32 This aspect of the decision brings home very forcefully the willingness of the ECJ to extend the scope of the EIA Directive beyond what its wording might immediately suggest, in order to safeguard or fulfil the Directive's objectives. A degree of ingenuity may be employed here, for example in the suggestion of Advocate General Elmer, adopted by the Court, that the reference to modifications to Annex I projects in Annex II is to provide that modifications to uncompleted Annex I projects are to be treated as falling within Annex II, whereas the contrary inference cannot be drawn that modifications to Annex II projects fall outside Annex II. The relevant passage from the Opinion, as well as indicating the subtlety of the approach, also demonstrates an acute awareness of the scope for avoidance of the Directive which would otherwise arise:[1]

'39. ... Thus as far as modifications to both Annex I and Annex II projects are concerned specific consideration must be given to whether the modifications may have a significant effect on the environment, so that where necessary an environmental impact assessment must be undertaken in pursuance of Articles 5 to 10 of the directive.

40. The purpose of the directive, according to which projects which may have significant effects on the environment must be subject to prior environmental impact assessment, militates decisively in favour of that interpretation. A modification of an Annex I or Annex II project which is not yet completed may very well be regarded as capable of having significant effects on the environment. Whether that is the case will however depend upon a specific appraisal. A scheme based on thresholds such as that contained in Annex I is not automatically suitable as the basis for an appraisal of the environmental impact of modifications to projects.[2] For example an increase in a projected power-station's capacity from 300 to 550 megawatts may significantly affect the environment. The increase does not however amount to 300 megawatts or more, so that it does not in itself constitute an Annex I project. Paragraph 12 of Annex II ensures in this situation that the modifications to the project and the need for a fresh environmental impact assessment are specifically considered.[3]

41. An interpretation to the effect that modifications to projects fall in general within the scope of the directive in addition prevents attempts to circumvent the directive by preparing a lesser project which does not significantly affect the environment and is therefore not subject to an environmental impact assessment and then modifying it into something which may well have significant effects on the environment.'

1   *Kraaijeveld v Gedeputeerde Staten van Zuid-Holland* [1996] ECR I-5403, Opinion, Advocate General Elmer, paras 39–41.
2   By way of explanation, the wording of the EIA Directive was such that for a number of projects in Annex I (though not all) there is a quantitative threshold: for example, for thermal power stations a heat output of 300 megawatts or more. Projects in Annex II were simply described, with no express quantitative thresholds. This remains the case with the Directive as revised.

3   Thus, perhaps counter-intuitively, the placing of modifications to EIA Directive, Annex I projects within Annex II in fact is taken to assist the objectives of the Directive.

2.33   The third question in *Kraaijeveld* is perhaps the one which has been proven to recur in other cases, namely if a member state laid down incorrect criteria or thresholds for EIA Directive, Annex II projects, whether an obligation existed to subject projects to an EIA if they were likely to have significant effects on the environment. The Dutch rules excluded EIA where the dyke was less than 5 km in length or had a cross section of less than 250 m. Effectively this would exclude all dykes in rivers (as opposed to the sea or coast). The discretion of member states under art 4(2) to specify which projects within Annex II were or were not subject to EIA, or to lay down criteria or thresholds, was held to be subject to the obligation in art 2(1) that projects must be subject to EIA where they are likely to have significant effects. A member state could not therefore lay down criteria which would have the effect of exempting all projects of a certain type, unless those projects could when viewed as a whole, be seen as not likely to have significant effects.[1] Behind the reasoning of the ECJ is the need to find limits to the discretion of member states in the use of the art 4(2) discretion, which if unconfined could lead to the exemption in advance of whole classes of project from EIA requirements.[2] Those limits are found in the obligation of art 2(1) that projects likely to have significant effects on the environment, by virtue, inter alia, of their nature, size or location, are to be subject to EIA. Whether the member state has exceeded these limits depends on '... an overall assessment of the characteristics of projects of that nature which could be envisaged in the Member State'.[3]

1   See *Kraaijeveld v Gedeputeerde Staten van Zuid-Holland* [1996] ECR I-5403, para 53.
2   *Kraaijeveld v Gedeputeerde Staten van Zuid-Holland* [1996] ECR I-5403, para 51. See also Case C-133/94 *Commission v Belgium* [1996] ECR I-2313, para 42.
3   *Kraaijeveld v Gedeputeerde Staten van Zuid-Holland* [1996] ECR I-5403, para 52.

Bozen

2.34   Similar issues arose in the second landmark ECJ case, *WWF v Bozen*,[1] a decision of the Sixth Chamber. That case concerned an attack by local residents and interest groups on a project for the restructuring of Bolzano St Jacob airfield in Italy. The airport had been used for military purposes since 1925. The project involved renovation of the runway, construction of roads, car parks and a control tower, hangars and other buildings, and the extension of the runway from 1,000 to 1,400 m. Under the relevant domestic law, the project was held not to require EIA, as it was considered to be an extension (rather than a new project) falling outside specified thresholds. Following *Kraaijeveld,* it was held that the discretion of member states to provide criteria exempting EIA Directive, Annex II projects was limited, and that the Directive covered modifications to Annex II projects, as well as such projects themselves. Further, alternative administrative procedures to those contemplated in the Directive could not be used unless it satisfied the requirements of the Directive, nor could a project approved by a legislative procedure be exempted unless the objectives of the Directive had been achieved through that procedure. The exception in art 1(4) for projects for national defence was to be construed narrowly, so as not to cover the restructuring of a military airport to allow for its commercial use.

1   Case C-435/97 *World Wildlife Fund (WWF) v Autonome Provinz Bozen* [1999] ECR I-5613, [2000] 1 CMLR 149, [2000] 2 PLR 1.

2.35   The central issue in *WWF v Bozen* was that the relevant national law provided that extensions or alterations to existing airports were subject to EIA where such projects either exceeded the thresholds for projects in EIA Directive, Annex II of the law, or where the project fell within Annex I of that law. The project did not meet these criteria, since the national law did not mention airports in Annex II, and Annex I (like the equivalent Annex in the EIA Directive) applied only to airports with a runway length of 2,100 m or more. Nevertheless, as the national court found, the project could have significant effects on the environment, by reason of its nature, size and proximity to a residential and industrial area. Not surprisingly, the Court held that member states could not use their discretion under art 4(2) to exclude in advance from EIA certain classes of Annex II projects (including modifications to such projects), unless such classes of project in their entirety could be regarded on the basis of a 'comprehensive assessment' as not being likely to have significant effects on the environment.[1] The additional feature of the decision, not present in *Kraaijeveld*, is that the principle also applies where the national discretion is used to exempt a specific project from EIA procedures.[2] Even if the legislation had referred to the specific project as exempt (which was not in fact the case), this would only be lawful if, on the date when the law was adopted, the relevant national authority was able 'to assess precisely the overall environmental impact which all the works entailed by the project were likely to have'.[3] In either case, whether in relation to a class of projects or a specific project, it was for the national court to review whether such an adequate assessment had been carried out.[4]

1   *World Wildlife Fund (WWF) v Autonome Provinz Bozen* [1999] ECR I-5613, para 49.
2   This arose because Bolzano airport was the only relevant airport in the region: see para 41.
3   *World Wildlife Fund (WWF) v Autonome Provinz Bozen* [1999] ECR I-5613, para 46.
4   *World Wildlife Fund (WWF) v Autonome Provinz Bozen* [1999] ECR I-5613, paras 48–49.

Linster

2.36   The third case in the trilogy is *Luxembourg v Linster*.[1] Here, the issue of EIA arose in the context of compulsory purchase proceedings by the Grand Duchy of Luxembourg against a number of individuals for the purpose of constructing a section of motorway link with Saarland. The main significance of the case is the clear statement by the ECJ of the general principle that national courts have an important role in reviewing whether the national authorities (including the national legislature) have kept within the limits of the discretion allowed by the EIA Directive as to its implementation. This applies equally to the discretion under art 5(1) as to the environmental information to be provided as it does to the exemption of projects under art 4(2):[2]

'35. Article 5 of the Directive requires the Member States to adopt the necessary measures to ensure that the develop supplies information, the minimum items of which are specified in Article 5(2). Under Article 6(2), they must ensure that there is public access to the request for consent to carry out the project and to the information supplied by the develop, and that members of the public have the opportunity to express an opinion before the project is initiated.

36. It is true that Article 5(1) of the Directive allows the Member States some discretion in implementing the Community provision at national level since it states that the Member States are to adopt the necessary measures to ensure that the developer supplies the required information where they consider, first, that the information is relevant to a given stage of the consent procedure and, second, that a developer may reasonably be required to compile that information.

37. However, this discretion, which a Member State may exercise when transposing that provision into national law, does not preclude judicial review of the question whether it has been exceeded by the national authorities.[3]

38. It follows that the provisions of the Directive may be taken into account by the national courts in order to review whether the national legislature has kept within the limits of the discretion set by it.

39. The answer to the first question must therefore be that a national court, called on to examine the legality of a procedure for the expropriation in the public interest, in connection with the construction of a motorway, of immovable property belonging to a private individual, may review whether the national legislature has kept within the limits of the discretion set by the Directive, in particular where prior assessment of the environmental impact of the project has not been carried out, the information gathered in accordance with Article 5 has not been made available to the public and the members of the public concerned have not had an opportunity to express an opinion before the project is initiated, contrary to the requirements of Article 6(2) of the Directive.'[4]

1   Case C-287/98 *Luxembourg v Linster* [2000] ECR I-6917.
2   *Luxembourg v Linster* [2000] ECR I-6917, paras 35–39.
3   Citing *Kraaijeveld* and also Case 51/76 *Verbond van Nederlandse Ondernemingen v Inspecteur der Invoerrechten en Accijnzen* [1977] ECR 113, paras 27–29.
4   Note again, the emphasis placed on the procedures of the EIA Directive as ensuring adequate public participation in the process.

Commission v Ireland

2.37   Another example of problems with EIA Directive, Annex II projects is provided by *Commission v Ireland*.[1] The Commission alleged that Ireland had incorrectly transposed art 4(2) of the Directive in relation to conversion of uncultivated or semi-natural land to intensive agriculture, afforestation and peat extraction projects under Annex II. Ireland had adopted size thresholds for EIA in relation to each type of project (respectively 100, 70 and 50 ha). The Commission argued that this fell foul of art 4(2) because (essentially) 'size isn't everything'. Projects which fell outside the size thresholds could still have significant effects because of their location in important nature conservation areas, or areas of geomorphological or archaeological interest. Also, such projects could, though not requiring individual EIA, have significant environmental effects when taken together with other projects. The Commission's concern was that the Irish thresholds would allow potentially damaging activities in sensitive areas such as active blanket bog, or limestone pavements in the Burren, or that a number of grant-aided projects might be developed in close proximity to one another. The Court found these concerns convincing.[2]

1 Case C-392/96 *Commission v Ireland* [1999] ECR I-5901.
2 See paras 68, 69, 79, 80.

2.38 The issue for the Court in *Commission v Ireland* was the legislative transposition of the Directive, rather than its implementation on the ground. Accordingly:[1]

'In order to prove that the transposition of a directive is insufficient or inadequate, it is not necessary to establish the actual effects of the legislation transposing it into national law: it is the wording of the legislation itself which harbours the insufficiencies or defects of transposition.'

Again, the issue was the limits of member state discretion. Article 2(1) of the EIA Directive clearly refers to EIA as being necessary for projects which are likely to have significant effects on the environment by virtue, inter alia, of their 'nature, size or location'. A member state which established thresholds by taking account only of the size of projects, without also taking their nature and location into consideration, would be exceeding the limits of its discretion under arts 2(1) and 4(2).[2] On the issue of cumulative effects, in excluding from EIA classes of projects of a particular scale, on the basis of *Kraaijeveld*, member states would have to be sure that all the projects involved, when viewed as a whole, would not be likely to have significant effects on the environment.[3] Further, it was incumbent on the member state, in setting such thresholds, to ensure that the objective of the Directive would not be circumvented by 'the splitting of projects'.[4]

1 Case C-392/96 *Commission v Ireland* [1999] ECR I-5901, para 60.
2 Paragraphs 65, 72.
3 Paragraph 75.
4 Paragraphs 76, 82.

Berkeley 2: the European cases summarised

2.39 In the case of *Berkeley v Secretary of State for the Environment, Transport and the Regions ('Berkeley 2')*[1] Schiemann LJ reviewed in detail the EC cases, and summarised 'the settled law of the Community' as follows:[2]

1   The purpose of thresholds and criteria is to render unnecessary an assessment of each individual project that comes forward — *Kraaijeveld*, para 49.
2   The criteria and thresholds set by the member state must be such that the excluded projects could when viewed as a whole be regarded as not 'likely to have significant effects on the environment' — *Kraaijeveld*, para 53.
3   The setting of the criteria or thresholds is a matter for the discretion for the member state but the discretion is circumscribed by the requirement in (2).
4   The purported exercise of that discretion can be reviewed by the ECJ on its normal principles.

1   [2002] JPL 224. The case is considered in detail in chapter 3, paras **3.65–3.68** below.
2   Paragraph 28.

EC LAW AND REMEDIES

2.40   Having considered the approach of the ECJ to the requirements of the EIA Directive, the final issue for this chapter is the implications of EC law for the purposes of remedies in the English courts. This entails consideration of the underlying principles of EC law, of indirect and direct effect. The starting point is that the rules on EIA are contained in a directive, which according to art 249 (ex art 189) of the EC Treaty:

'... shall be binding, as to the result to be achieved, upon each Member State to which it is addressed, but shall leave to the national authorities the choice of form and methods.'

The 'result to be achieved' in relation to the EIA Directive is of course the subjection to environmental assessment of the defined projects likely to have significant effects on the environment, in accordance with the procedural requirements of arts 5–10.[1]

1   See arts 2(1) and 4(1) and (2).

Effectiveness

2.41   Underlying the case law is the principle of effectiveness, which has been described as follows:[1]

'It requires the effective protection of Community rights and, more generally, the effective enforcement of Community law in national courts. Effectiveness differs from the general principles of law examined so far[2] in that it is not based directly on the laws of the Member States, but derives from the distinct characteristics of Community law, primacy and direct effect.'

In particular, the European Court has proved assertive in requiring the removal of all obstacles presented by national law or procedures which would prevent the full and effective enforcement of Community rights and requirements. Article 10 (ex art 5) of the EC Treaty[3] has provided legitimacy for this exercise:[4]

> 'Notably, Article 10 EC has proved instrumental in this development. The Court has read in it a principle of co-operation between the national and the Community judicature, from which it has derived specific obligations on national courts regarding the enforcement of Community rights.'[5]

1   Tridimas, *The General Principles of EC Law* (2000), p 277. Chapter 8 of that work contains a comprehensive discussion of the effectiveness principle and its related case law.
2   That is to say, equality, proportionality, legal certainty, legitimate expectation and fundamental rights.
3   'Member States shall take all appropriate measures, whether general or particular, to ensure fulfilment of the obligations arising out of this Treaty or resulting from action taken by the institutions of the Community. They shall fulfil the achievement of the Community's tasks. They shall abstain from any measure which could jeopardise the attainment of the objectives of the Treaty.'
4   Tridimas, *The General Principles of EC Law* (2000), p 277. See also *Berkeley 1* at para **2.04** above.
5   Key cases on the development of this approach include Case 33/76 *Rewe v Landwirtschaftskammer für das Saarland* [1976] ECR 1989 and Case 106/77 *Amministrazione delle Finanze dello Stato v Simmenthal* [1978] ECR 629.

Indirect effect and sympathetic interpretation

2.42   The principle of indirect effect is readily dealt with. It is a principle of interpretation which applies in relation to all directives, whether or not their provisions have direct effect as a matter of EC law. It can be variously referred to as 'sympathetic' or 'convergent' construction. The case of *Von Colson*[1] first established the principle that national courts must interpret national law in the light of the wording and purpose of a directive.[2] The other landmark case is *Marleasing*,[3] where the Court held that the duty of interpretation was applicable not only to national law which post-dated the relevant directive, but also to earlier national law.

1   Case 14/83 *Von Colson v Land Nordrhein-Westfalen* [1984] ECR 1891.
2   The ECJ relied on art 10 (ex art 5) of the EC Treaty in support of that proposition.
3   Case C-106/89 *Marleasing SA v La Comercial Internacional de Alimentación SA* [1990] ECR I-4135.

2.43   Thus provisions of the TCP(EIA) Regulations 1999 and other transposing EIA regulations should be interpreted sympathetically with the requirements of the EIA Directive. So, for that matter, should the general legislation in the planning and environmental field, in so far as this is relevant. An example of the approach is provided by the decision of the House of Lords in *Berkeley 1*, referred to above,[1] but this has its limits. Ensuring effectiveness by the interpretation route may require a significant departure from the wording of the national legislation.[2] However, the principle of effectiveness does not require an interpretation contra legem; nor is it the constitutional role of national judges to implement directives into national law.[3] Furthermore, to push sympathetic interpretation too far would create conflict with the important principle of legal certainty. In the case of *R v Durham County Council, ex p Huddleston*,[4] it was common ground that any attempt at sympathetic or convergent construction of the domestic legislation (on old mining permissions) by writing in words '... would set off a chain reaction likely to disrupt the whole planning regime for mineral extraction'.[5] As Sedley LJ put it, the principle stops short of 'rewriting the statute book'.[6] The Court of Appeal in the event ensured effectiveness under principles of direct effect (see below). It may be noted that if it is not possible to interpret domestic law consistently with a non-directly effective directive, then the claimant may have the alternative remedy of an action for damages against the member state.[7] Finally, it has been noted that indirect effect as a manner of interpretation is in many ways artificial and irregular, and a makeshift; it is no substitute for full, correct and certain transposition.[8]

1   See para **2.07**.
2   An example in the employment field is *Lister v Forth Dry Dock & Engineering Co Ltd* [1990] 1 AC 546.
3   See the discussion at Weatherill and Beaumont, *EU Law* (3rd edn, 1999) pp 411–412.
4   [2000] 1 WLR 1484, [2000] Env LR 488.
5   [2000] 1 WLR 1484, [2000] Env LR 488, para 10 (per Sedley LJ)
6   [2000] 1 WLR 1484, [2000] Env LR 488, para 9.
7   See para **2.67** below.
8   Jans, *European Environmental Law* (2000) p 205.

Direct effect

2.44   The principle of direct effect dates back to 1963 with the case of *Van Gend en Loos*.[1] The ECJ held that Community law, irrespective of implementation into national law, was capable of conferring rights on individuals and that those rights could be enforced in the national courts.[2] The case involved giving direct effect to a Treaty provision, which is one thing, but quite another to apply direct effect to a directive. This development occurred in the case of *Van Duyn*.[3] Some of the reasons given in the cases for attributing direct effect to a directive are more convincing than others. Among the reasons, those which are particularly apposite in considering directives such as the EIA Directive are, first, the policy argument that the effectiveness of a directive would be weakened if individuals were prevented from relying on it before national courts and, second, that a member state which is in default of its obligations under EC law to implement a directive should not be entitled to rely against an individual on its own failure to perform its obligations.[4]

1   Case 26/62 *Van Gend en Loos v Nederlandse Administratie der Belastingen* [1963] ECR 1, [1963] CMLR 105.
2   The ECJ made the well-known statements that the Treaty had created a 'new legal order', and that 'independently of the legislation of Member States, Community law ... not only imposes obligations on individuals but is also intended to confer upon them rights which become part of their legal heritage' ([1963] ECR 1 at 12).
3   Case 41/74 *Van Duyn v Home Office* [1974] ECR 1337, [1975] 1 CMLR 1.
4   This second rationale emerged in Case 148/78 *Pubblico Ministero v Ratti* [1979] ECR 1629.

2.45 The principle of direct effect has since been refined and developed in relation to directives, and the Court has laid down a number of conditions to be fulfilled for such direct effect:[1]

1 The provision in question must establish a clear, sufficiently precise and unconditional obligation on the member state.

2 The obligation must not be dependent on the taking of further implementing measures by Community institutions or member states.

3 The member states must not be left with any discretion in the implementation of the obligation.

It has been pointed out that these criteria have been relaxed over the years, and that the crucial underlying test is whether the directive is sufficiently certain to give the court enough to go on without trespassing on the role of other Community or national authorities:[2]

'The way the Court has extended the concept of direct effect in recent years justifies the assertion that the crucial criterion is whether a provision provides a court with sufficient guidance to be able to apply it without exceeding the limits of its judicial powers. Viewed thus, a provision of Community law is directly effective if a national court can apply it without encroaching on the jurisdiction of national or Community authorities.'

1 See Case C-236/92 *Comitato di Coordinamento per la Difesa della Cava v Regione Lombardia* [1994] ECR I-483.

2 See Jans, *European Environmental Law* (2000) pp 173–174.

2.46 The issue then is how these principles apply to the EIA Directive, or more precisely the various components of the Directive, since it is possible for some provisions of a measure to have direct effect, but not others. The EIA Directive comprises a bundle of obligations, within the overall requirement to ensure environmental assessment of relevant projects. These are essentially procedural in nature, in terms of the information required to be obtained and considered, the parties to be consulted, publicity to be provided, etc. The potential troublespots are relatively obvious. First, member states may adopt an unduly narrow view of what constitutes a 'development consent' under the Directive. An example is *R v North Yorkshire County Council, ex p Brown*,[1] but there is no doubt that further issues may arise on this point.[2] It is conceivable that errors could be made in defining the Annex I projects subject to mandatory EIA, but the approach now adopted of copying out the Directive's provisions verbatim makes this perhaps unlikely. What is much more likely is that the requirements as to assessment of Annex II projects are incorrectly transposed, as indeed the European cases referred to above demonstrate. Finally, it is possible that national law will not correctly or adequately transpose the procedural requirements, for example the information to be provided in the environmental statement, or the consultation procedures to be followed.

1 [2000] 1 AC 397, discussed at para **2.02** above.

2 Examples are whether the approval of reserved matters on an outline permission is a development consent (see paras **6.61–6.65**) and whether the grant of other authorisations, for

example an IPC authorisation or a PPC permit, may constitute such a consent (see paras **6.74–6.78**).

2.47   It may be argued that to some extent at least, the potentially contentious requirements of the EIA Directive allow member states some degree of discretion as to the manner of implementation. Indeed, it is precisely those measures which allow such discretion which are likely to give rise to legal disputes, rather than those which are stricter in nature. Does this mean that such provisions are not amenable to direct effect? The early cases in the national courts sent out mixed messages. In some case the national courts held that the discretion provided to member states for Annex II by the wording 'where Member States consider that their characteristics so require' in art 4(2) precluded direct effect.[1] However, in at least one early domestic case it was held that the provisions of the Directive were sufficiently clear and precise to be capable of conferring rights on individuals.[2] The answer to this conundrum lies in the fact that any discretion conferred by law will have limits, and the discretion in relation to (for example) Annex II projects is no exception. The ECJ has emphasised the importance of the inherent limits on discretion under the EIA Directive, as is clear from the cases referred to above.[3] Thus it has been correctly stated that:[4]

'The essence of direct effect is that it precludes the existence or adoption of national laws exceeding the discretion left by the directive.'

1   See *Kincardine and Deeside District Council v Forestry Comrs* [1993] Env LR 151, [1994] 2 CMLR 869, Ct of Sess; *Decision of Dutch Council of State* [1994] AB 287 (cited by Jans, *European Environmental Law* (2000) at p 178). See also *Wychavon District Council v Secretary of State for the Environment* [1993] Env LR 330; *Secretary of State for Transport v Haughian* [1997] Env LR 37; *Michael Browne v An Bord Pleanala* [1990] JEL 209, [1990] 1 CMLR 3 (Irish High Court).
2   *Twyford Parish Council v Secretary of State for the Environment and Transport* [1992] Env LR 37.
3   See paras **2.28–2.39**.
4   See Jans, *European Environmental Law* (2000) p 174.

2.48   One of the difficulties is that the European cases have perhaps not addressed the question of direct effect with the clarity that might be desirable. In *Kraaijeveld* the question of direct effect was posed squarely for the ECJ by the national court as the fourth question.[1] The transparency of the reasoning of the ECJ was not helped by the fact that it chose to amalgamate its answers to the third and fourth questions. The point was considered fully by Advocate General Elmer in his Opinion, who reasoned as follows:
1   On the basis of established case law, precise and unconditional obligations in a Directive, which have not been implemented in national law,[2]

'... may be relied on by individuals against the authorities whether in order to avert the application of contrary national rules or in order to rely on rights which may be derived therefrom.'

It is important to note that these two situations are alternatives, deriving from different strands of ECJ case law.

2   In this case the first situation did not apply, as there was no question of an authority seeking to apply a 'contrary national rule' against an individual. The issue was therefore whether the second situation applied, namely whether rights for individuals could be derived from the obligations placed on the state by the Directive.

3   Such rights could be found in the obligations under the EIA Directive, art 6(2) to make environmental information available to the public and to consult the public:[3]

> 'Where a Member State's implementation of the directive is such that projects which are likely to have a significant effect on the environment are not made the subject of an EIA, the citizen is prevented from exercising his right to be heard. The Member State's own negligent implementation of the directive thus deprives the citizen of a right under the directive.'

4   The obligation of member states under art 2 of the Directive to ensure EIA was sufficiently clear and precise to have direct effect.

1   As to the previous three questions, see paras **2.28–2.39**.
2   Case C-72/95 *Kraaijeveld v Gedeputeerde Staten van Zuid-Holland* [1996] ECR I-5403, Opinion, Advocate General Elmer, para 68.
3   Opinion, para 70.

2.49   Perhaps unfortunately the ECJ did not address the direct effect question in the same clear way as the Advocate General. Rather it focused on the question of automatic application, which it answered by saying that where under national rules a court is required to apply of its own motion binding rules of law, it must examine whether the EIA Directive has been complied with, and that where national provisions must be set aside for non-compliance, then it is for the authorities of the member state, according to their respective powers, to take all general or particular measures necessary to ensure projects are examined and where necessary are subjected to EIA. On direct effect, the ECJ made some oblique remarks that it would be incompatible with the binding effect attributed to directives by art 189 of the EC Treaty to exclude in principle the possibility of direct effect:[1]

> 'In particular, where the Community authorities have, by directive, imposed on Member States the obligation to pursue a particular course of conduct, the useful effect of such an act would be weakened if individuals were prevented from relying on it before their national courts ...'

1   Judgment, para 56.

2.50   Thus, rather than pursuing the rational analysis of Advocate General Elmer, the Court in *Kraaijeveld* simply referred to the broad brush policy of useful effect. It was left to the second decision, *WWF v Bozen* to take matters further.[1] Again the issue of direct effect arose. This time the Advocate General (Mischo A G) did not attempt full analysis, but simply referred to the ECJ's decision in *Kraaijeveld*. The Court repeated the relevant passages in *Kraaijeveld*, but went on to put the matter perhaps more explicitly as follows:[2]

'... Articles 4(2) and 2(1) of the Directive are to be interpreted as meaning that, where the discretion conferred by those provisions has been exceeded by the legislative or administrative authorities of a Member State, individuals may rely on those provisions before a court of the Member State against the national authorities and thus obtain from the latter the setting aside of the national rules or measures incompatible with those provisions.'

Again, this is clearly an extremely broad principle, which would not appear to be dependent on whether the particular provisions of the EIA Directive confer or are intended to confer rights on individuals.

1   See paras **2.34–2.35** for details of the decision.
2   Judgment, para 71.

2.51   Finally, direct effect was again considered in *Luxembourg v Linster*.[1] The issue of collateral legality of the road scheme in the absence of an EIA was raised before the national administrative court, which referred to the ECJ the question of whether it could ensure compliance with the EIA Directive by looking at whether the domestic law conformed, without having to consider the issue of direct effect and refer a question on that issue to the ECJ. Reiterating the position in *Kraaijeveld* and *Bozen*, the Court held that the role of national courts in assessing compliance with the Directive is not dependent on a finding of direct effect:[2]

'The answer to the first question must therefore be that a national court, called on to examine the legality of a procedure for the expropriation in the public interest, in connection with the construction of a motorway, of immovable property belonging to a private individual, may review whether the national legislature kept within the limits of the discretion set by the Directive, in particular where prior assessment of the environmental impact of the project has not been carried out, the information gathered in accordance with Article 5 has not been made available to the public and the members of the public concerned have not had an opportunity to express an opinion before the project is initiated, contrary to the requirements of Article 6(2) of the Directive.'

This approach represents a move away from the principles of direct effect in its classical sense of whether the Directive confers directly enforceable 'rights', and towards the review of lawfulness as a form of direct effect. It accords with principles of effectiveness and of supremacy of EC law. This is particularly significant when considering the thorny issue of horizontal direct effect, to which we now turn.

1   [2000] ECR I-6917. See para **2.36** above.
2   Judgment, para 39.

2.52   The doctrine of direct effect arose in the context of the individual wishing to assert, in the national courts, rights arising under a Directive against a member state. As indicated above,[1] one rationale for such direct effect was that the state should not be able to take advantage of its own failure to implement the EIA Directive; a principle which arguably has some resonance with private law principles. However, the ECJ soon made clear that direct effect did not extend to one individual being able to rely on a Directive which had not been transposed into national law against another individual; the so called principle of 'horizontal direct effect'.[2] While the principle that horizontal direct effect is not permissible has been attacked, the ECJ has held the line on the issue by rejecting horizontal direct effect as a concept.[3]

1   See para **2.44**.
2   Case 152/84 *Marshall v Southampton and South-West Area Health Authority* [1986] ECR 723. See also Case 80/86 *Kolpinghuis Nijmegen* [1987] ECR 3969.
3   Case C-91/91 *Faccini Dori v Recreb* [1994] ECR I-3325.

Horizontal direct effect

2.53   The cases against giving horizontal direct effect to Directives have principally concerned the situation where the Directive in question gives rights which are relevant in a contractual or employment context between two private parties. In contrast, cases arising under the EIA Directive will typically involve the eternal triangle of objector, national authority and developer. A successful claim of direct effect by the objector against the planning authority or other national authority will most likely result in the loss of planning permission, or some other substantial disadvantage, for the developer. There is effectively an indirect horizontal effect. If the general principles of no horizontal direct effect were held to apply to this situation, then in the field of EIA (and for that matter, much of the body of EC environmental law) it would be confined in practice to situations where the developer was the state, or an 'emanation of the state'.

2.54   This critical question was considered by Richards J[1] and then the Court of Appeal[2] in *R v Durham County Council, ex p Huddleston*. The case concerned the provisions of the Planning and Compensation Act 1991, s 22 and Sch 2, on old mining permissions. Under these provisions, the onus is on the holder of an old mining permission to apply for its registration, which entails the setting of conditions. The House of Lords held in *R v North Yorkshire County Council, ex p Brown*,[3] that this process is a 'development consent' and as such is subject to EIA. However, at the relevant time the national legislation made no provision for EIA — a situation which was later rectified by legislative amendment.[4] In *Huddleston*, Sherburn Stone Co Ltd held an old mining permission relating to a dormant stone quarry. The company applied for registration of the permission, and despite being requested to do so by Durham County Council as minerals planning authority, declined to provide an environmental statement. The council failed to determine the application within three months, and accordingly under Sch 2, para 2(6), the application was treated as having been granted on the conditions contained in the application. Mr Huddleston had lived in a house adjacent to the dormant quarry for 18 years, and challenged the deemed registration in judicial review proceedings.

1   [2000] Env LR 463.
2   [2000] Env LR 488.
3   See para **2.02** above.
4   See paras **6.34** et seq

2.55   Richards J dismissed the application. He rejected the argument, based on a suggested 'sympathetic interpretation'[1] that there had been no determination of the application, and that the council were still free to make their own determination. This would involve an 'unacceptable distortion' of the wording of the domestic legislation.[2] He went on to hold that to require the council to disregard the deeming provision under direct effect would involve the council, as an emanation of the state, relying on the terms of an unimplemented directive against an individual, Sherburn. Equally, Mr Huddleston could not achieve that result indirectly, by proceeding against the council and contending that the council had acted unlawfully in refusing to disapply the deeming provision; in that case Durham would have been required to give direct effect to the EIA Directive in all but name against the developer.[3]

1   See para **2.43** above.
2   *R v Durham County Council, ex p Huddleston* [2000] Env LR 463, para 28.
3   *R v Durham County Council, ex p Huddleston* [2002] Env LR 463, paras 44 and 49.

2.56   Similar issues had arisen at first instance in the case of *R v Somerset County Council, ex p Morris and Perry*.[1] There, effectively through an administrative mix-up, the application for registration of the old mining permission was not determined within the period, leading to a deemed grant. The developer sought a declaration that the conditions contained in its application were deemed to have been imposed, and an order that the council register those conditions. The authority argued that the court ought to refuse relief to the operator in order to give effect to the EIA Directive. It was held by Maurice Kay J that the court should not effectively give what was in all but name direct effect to the Directive against a private party. Richards J in *Huddleston* agreed with that reasoning, and considered it to apply with equal force to that case. While this approach may be correct on the strict legal analysis of direct effect, it could be argued that on the basis of the wide reasoning in the ECJ cases referred to above,[2] the court should simply have given effect to the Directive's requirements by setting aside the inconsistent national provisions, and in particular that, on the basis of *Linster*, considerations of direct effect were not really necessary.[3]

1   [2000] Env LR 585.
2   Paragraphs **2.28–2.39**.
3   See para **2.36**.

2.57   The Court of Appeal in *Huddleston* took a markedly different view to that of Richards J. Sedley LJ (with whom Stuart Smith LJ agreed) analysed the situation as very different from the case of a directive affecting the relationship between two private individuals (as in the employment context). Rather it concerned the rights and duties of (a) Sherburn and (b) Mr Huddleston against the state.[1] So far as Sherburn was concerned, the relevant EC obligations did not purport to limit the company's freedom of action as against other private entities, but rather concerned the conditions on which the company was entitled to obtain a benefit (planning consent) from the state.[2] Further, Sedley LJ held that the authorities showed that the enforcement of a directive against the state was not rendered inadmissible solely by its consequential effect on other parties.[3] Finally, Sedley LJ regarded the logic of Richards J as flawed, when he held that because Durham could not itself rely on the Directive against Sherburn, Mr Huddleston could not show that it had acted unlawfully or erred in law. Sedley LJ saw this as a non sequitur:[4]

'As the ECJ cases show, the failure of the state to transpose a Directive inevitably renders the state itself impotent to implement it; but for an individual with a recognised interest in proper implementation, it is precisely the state's failure which disables it from taking refuge in its own wrongdoing; and it is this which in turn entitles the citizen ... to assert rights conferred by the Directive either as a sword or as a shield against the state, though not directly against another individual. So what followed from Durham's undoubted inability to treat Sherburn as if the Directive had been implemented was not that Mr Huddleston was rendered equally powerless but, on the contrary, that he was entitled to insist that the state should act as Durham of its own motion could not act, in conformity with the Directive.'

1   [2000] Env LR 488, para 14.
2   At para 15.
3   At para 18. See Case 103/88 *Fratelli Constanzo v Commune di Milano* [1989] ECR 1839; Case C-441/93 *Pafitis v Trapeza Kentrikis Ellados AE* [1996] 2 CMLR 551; Case C-194/94 *CIA Security v Signalson* [1996] ECR I-2201.
4   [2000] Env LR 488, para 25.

2.58   Brooke LJ arrived at the same conclusion, but his judgment lays greater emphasis on the rights of Mr Huddleston. The environmental assessment process would have enabled Mr Huddleston, whose amenities both in his home and in the adjacent environment would be detrimentally affected by the proposed quarrying, to have taken a much more informed role in the consultation process, as was his right if the Directive had been properly implemented.[1] This was a 'valuable opportunity'.[2] Mr Huddleston was entitled to say to the court that the state had failed to afford him these rights, and to ask for an order which would give the Directive direct effect.[3]

1   [2000] Env LR 488, para 39.
2   At paras 40, 43.
3   At para 43.

2.59   The difference in emphasis between Sedley LJ and Brooke LJ in fact raises an important point on the question of the basis for direct effect. There are two possible approaches, not necessarily mutually exclusive. The first is that direct effect is about identifying sufficiently clear and precise rights accorded under EC law to individuals. This is how an employment lawyer, for example, would view direct effect. However, environmental law is concerned with broader issues than conferring individual rights.

2.60   Quite clearly, failure to comply with EC law may affect an individual adversely. Mr Huddleston had no right under EC law to prevent the dormant quarry being reactivated, but he did have the right or opportunity to be informed and consulted, and as Brooke LJ identified, this right was particularly important to him because of the proximity of the operations to his home. Similarly, in *Kraaijeveld*, the Kraaijeveld

family business was directly adversely affected by the relevant project; not in fact by
its environmental impacts in the normal sense, but by its effects in depriving the
business of commercial access to the waterway.[1]

1   See para **2.28** ff.

2.61   However, there is a broader public interest in the EC requirements on EIA.
Members of the public at large have an interest in the objectives of the EIA Directive
being secured, quite irrespective of harm to their direct personal interests. The public
has a general interest in being consulted. Lady Berkeley's interest, for example, in
protecting the waterfront of the River Thames from development which has not properly
been subjected to EIA is not dependent on her enjoyment of her own property being
affected. In the EIA field at least, it is suggested that the law both at European and
national level, is moving in the direction of recognising such rights and giving direct
effect, where necessary, to them. This seems to underlie the approach in *Bozen* and
Linster.

2.62   Sedley LJ recognised the point in *Huddleston*, where he drew an analogy with
the distinction between public and private law.[1] Mr Huddleston's claim was a pure
matter of public law. Public law is concerned essentially with wrongs, rather than
rights. Under domestic rules of standing, Mr Huddleston's interest did not depend on
his proximity to the quarry, though in practice that was no doubt a stimulus; his
sufficient interest lay in the legal protection of the environment. While admitting that
this was not the acid test for all horizontal direct effect issues, in Sedley LJ's view it
cast a useful light on the case, and underscored the same primary distinction as could
be seen in the case law of the ECJ.

1   [2000] Env LR 488, para 23.

2.63   The issue has also been well discussed by Jans,[1] who suggests that the
terminology sometimes used in the cases on direct effect, of the relevant provision
conferring 'rights on individuals', can be misleading. 'Rights' in this context should be
seen in a procedural rather than a substantive light; direct effect is concerned with the
precision and unconditionality of the EC provision in question, not whether it confers
some substantive individual right. Indeed Jans goes as far as to suggest that the
'right' in question is simply the procedural right to rely on the provision before the
national courts — which is the result of a finding of direct effect, rather than a
precondition for it. Jans does however acknowledge that some commentators hold
other views, that substantive rights are indeed a prerequisite for direct effect,[2] and that
some national case law seems to endorse this view.[3] While this may be a live and
extremely important issue for some types of EC environmental provisions, which require
particular environmental standards to be achieved, it is submitted that it is not a
problem that should affect the EIA Directive. That Directive, through the EIA process,
confers on each and every member of the public the right to be informed and to
participate in the process; the right is not confined to members of the public who may
be personally affected by the proposed project in some way. It is suggested that this
is a sufficiently clear and precise right to be directly effective. Naturally, the right may

be more valuable to some members of the public than others, but its value does not reside solely in whether the individual's home, property or economic interests will be affected. Its value may rest in the individual's particular or general concern for the environment that may be affected by the project.

1   Jans, *European Environmental Law* (2000), pp188–189.
2   See Hilson and Downes [1999] ELR 121.
3   Jans refers to a decision of the Dutch Council of State in *Groenendaal* [1997] M & R 92 and of the Dutch District Court *Waterpakt* [2000] MR 1.

Direct effect: a summary

2.64

Effectively therefore, the position which the UK and EC cases have arrived at in relation to EIA is that failure correctly to transpose or comply with the requirements of the EIA Directive is a ground of challenge by way of judicial review, open to anyone who meets the applicable rules for standing, and with EC law effectively trumping domestic law. Any requirement to demonstrate that the provision of the Directive relied upon meets the established criteria for direct effect has been quietly sidestepped. However, this may be inevitable in dealing with environmental measures which, by their nature, are more concerned with providing a process designed to protect the environment (of which the public forms part) than conferring specific rights on individuals (as might be the case with directives dealing with employment matters, for example). The point is that everyone has a legitimate interest in seeing that EIA procedures are followed, irrespective of the rights of information and consultation which the Directive accords them as part of the process. It is this interest or as Brooke LJ put it, 'valuable opportunity', rather than any specific 'right', which currently forms the basis of the case law.

2.65

Where no individual is involved in challenging a decision, there are two schools of thought. One (which appears from *Morris and Perry* and *Huddleston*)[1] is that the authority concerned cannot rely on failure to comply with the EIA Directive against an individual. The other (which can be drawn from the ECJ cases) is that the authority must do everything within its powers to set aside inconsistent decisions and give effect to EC law. The first view should perhaps be seen in the context of the unusual provisions on old mining permissions, which were drafted so as to create, almost inevitably, conflicts between the requirements for EIA and the effect of the legislation (and which, as mentioned above, have now been amended in any event). Such conflicts are perhaps less likely in the context of 'normal' planning permissions, where if there are defects in the EIA process, the authority would have open to it the clear, albeit costly, course of revoking the permission. In those circumstances, it would be surprising if the authority, which had failed to implement the Directive correctly, could rely on the Directive against the person entitled to the permission, so as to set it aside and thereby avoid paying compensation for revocation in cases where such revocation would be an option open to it.

1   See respectively paras **2.56** and **2.54** ff above.

2.66   The consequences of a finding of direct effect are striking. Those consequences flow from the principle of supremacy of Community law over national law, established in *Costa v ENEL*.[1] All courts, from the highest to the lowest, are obliged to disapply the offending national provision in favour of the relevant EC law. This is the effect of the important case of *Simmenthal*.[2] This does not involve the national court annulling the national provision, but simply declining to apply it. The court must act immediately to do this, and cannot wait for the provisions of national law to be set aside by legislation or by some higher court. In addition, direct effect operates at a secondary level. Not only the courts, but also other national authorities, are obliged to give priority to EC law, by declining to apply inconsistent national law if necessary: these authorities include regional and local authorities, and would include therefore a local planning authority, for example.[3] This is however subject to the principle that the authority, as an extension of the state, cannot rely on the EIA Directive as against a private individual.[4]

1   Case 6/64 [1964] ECR 585.
2   Case 106/77 *Amministrazione delle Fianze dello Stato v Simmenthal* [1978] ECR 629.
3   See Case 103/88 *Fratelli Constanzo v Milano* [1989] ECR 1839, [1990] 3 CMLR 239.
4   See Case C – 168/95 *Arcaro* [1996].ECR 4705; Case 80/86 *Officier van Justitie v Kolpinghuis Nijmegen BV* [1989] CMLR 18.

DAMAGES

2.67   Finally, the possibility may exist that failure to implement a Directive may give an individual a right in damages against the state.[1] This will only become relevant if the provision in question cannot be given direct or indirect effect by the national courts. As such it is probably unlikely to arise in the EIA context. The three basic conditions for such liability are that:

(1)   the provision must have been intended to confer rights on individuals;
(2)   the breach must have been sufficiently serious; and
(3)   there must have been a direct causal link between the breach of the obligation on the state and the damage suffered by the claimant.

The difficulty in applying these criteria to the EIA Directive lies in the fact that the rights or benefits which it confers on individuals as members of the public are procedural in nature, namely to be informed and consulted. The Directive does not guarantee any given standard of environmental quality, or any absolute protection against detrimental effects from projects.[2] If we assume that the procedures required by the Directive had not been followed in relation to a development next to the claimant's home, resulting in nuisance, detriment to amenity and loss of property value, would the claimant be able to show a sufficiently direct causal link between that procedural failure and such damage?

1   See the landmark cases of Cases C-46/93 and C-48/93 *Brasserie du Pêcheur SA v Germany* and
     R v Secretary of State for Transport, ex p Factortame Ltd [1996] ECR I-1029, [1996] 1 CMLR
     889.
2   It does however state in its recitals, that '... the effects of a project on the environment must
     be assessed in order to take account of concerns to protect human health, to contribute by
     means of a better environment to the quality of life...' (as well as ensuring maintenance of
     biodiversity and of the 'reproductive capacity of the ecosystem').

ONGOING ISSUES

2.68   It is by no means clear that problems in implementing the EIA Directive are a
thing of the past. In January 2003 the Commission reported that it was pursuing
infringement proceedings against eight member states for non-compliance with the
Directive.[1] These states were Luxembourg, the UK,[2] Austria, Italy, Spain, Finland,
Germany and Greece. A number of first or final Written Warnings were being issued in
relation to incorrect or inadequate implementation in relation to matters such as urban
development projects, the restructuring of rural landholdings, port and marina works,
waste-water treatment plant and road construction. Moreover, in relation to Ireland,
the Commission has referred to the European Court the failure to comply with the 1999
decision in *Commission v Ireland*[3] in respect of continued peat extraction, with a
proposal for daily fines of • 21,600.[4] The developing European jurisprudence is therefore
a vital part of the domestic practitioner's working knowledge on EIA.

1   Commission press release IP/03/117, 24 January 2003.
2   As to the proceedings against the UK, see further paras **6.65** and **6.72**.
3   See para **2.37** above for this case.
4   Commission press release IP/02/1950, 20 December 2002.

2.69   In June 2003 the European Commission published its latest five year report on
the implementation of the EIA Directive.[1] The report highlighted the fact that the
Directive is still not yet fully implemented in all member states; indeed some member
states have still not transposed the amendments made by Directive 97/11/EEC. Together
with the fields of nature conservation, waste and water, EIA continues to generate the
heaviest case-load of infringement proceedings, of which about 30 per cent relate to
gaps in transposition and 65 per cent to failure to apply the Directive to individual
projects. The main types of infringement are as follows:
—   inadequate screening procedures for Annex II projects
—   setting thresholds for EIA that are too high
—   failure to cover all project categories required
—   ineffective public consultation
—   failure to require EIA before the grant of development consent.

All of these issues will be familiar to UK practitioners from the domestic case-law. The
report in particular underlines shortcomings in the area of screening, with unsystematic
approaches resulting in wide variations between member states as to which Annex II
projects are subject to assessment. Failure to consider the cumulative impacts of
projects is also identified as a general problem. Another defect identified is the
inadequate incorporation of the results of the EIA process into development consent
decisions; once again, this is an issue that has taxed the UK courts. In conjunction

with publication of the report, Commissioner Margot Wallström made an important speech as part of the Commission's 'Name, Shame and Fame' seminars on EC environmental legislation. The Commissioner stressed the practical environmental benefits that may come from the EIA process,[3] the contribution made by EIA to involving citizens in the planning process, the long-term influence of the process on the quality of decisions and decision-makers, and the way in which EIA can ensure that tax-payers' money is well spent and avoid costly delays or changes to projects where unforeseen environmental issues arise. EIA is seen by the Commissioner as being particularly important in the new member states, where significant infrastructure construction will take place, often with EC funding – this explains why the Community has not granted any transition periods to accession countries in relation to the EIA Directive.

1. European Commission, 'The Application and Effectiveness of the EIA Directive: How Successful are the Member States in implementing the EIA Directive?' See Commission Press Release IP/03/876, 23 June 2003. The Report is available at http://europa.eu.int/comm/environment/eia/home.htm
2. Commission Press Release SPEECH/03/316, 23 June 2003.
3. The example given was Billund Airport, in West Denmark, where a new runway was proposed to the north, to reduce the number of homes exposed to noise. Consultation through the EIA process led to alternatives being discussed leading to the noise reductions being achieved through a change in take off procedures and routes, saving 40 million euros and avoiding the loss of 350 hectares of farmland and an old forest.

2.70   Despite these serious problems, the Commission does not presently propose any amendment to the EIA Directive. This is in part because of the very recent amendment of the Directive to reflect the requirements of the Aarhus Convention, discussed below.[1] Another reason is the forthcoming implementation of the Directive of Strategic Environmental Assessment (SEA),[2] which the Commission anticipates will form a strong link with the EIA Directive and may assist in the application of the EIA Directive; implementation of the SEA Directive may also reveal additional difficulties that will need to be taken into account in any future amendment of the EIA Directive.

1 Para 2.71. See para 1.16 for the Convention generally.
2 See para 1.06.

AMENDMENT OF THE EIA DIRECTIVE TO IMPLEMENT AARHUS CONVENTION

2.71   The implications of the Aarhus Convention on Access to Information, Public Participation in Decision-Making and Access to Justice in Environmental Matters have been noted above.[1] Directive 2003/35/EC[2] makes amendments to the EIA Directive and to Directive 96/61/EC on integrated pollution prevention and control to implement in particular art 6 of the Convention on public participation on decisions on specific activities and art 9(2) and 9(4) on access to judicial or other procedures for challenge.[3] The Directive requires transposition by Member States by 25 June 2005 at the latest.[4]

1 See para 1.18.

2.   OJ L 156, 25 June 2003. The Directive is reproduced at Appendix 11.
3.   See recitals (6)-(9) and art 1.
4.   See art 6.

2.72   In terms of EIA, art 3 of Directive 2003/35/EC makes a number of significant amendments to the EIA Directive as follows:

—   A definition is inserted into art 1(2) of 'the public' and 'the public concerned'. The latter covers not only the public affected or likely to be affected by the decision, but also those having an interest in environmental decision-making procedures; non-governmental organisations promoting environmental protection are expressly deemed to have such an interest.

—   In art 1(4) the blanket exclusion of projects serving national defence purposes is replaced by a power on the part of member states to decide on a case by case basis, if so provided by national law, not to apply the EIA Directive to projects serving national defence purposes, 'if they deem that such application would have an adverse effect on those purposes.'

—   In arts 2(3)(a) and (b), where member states decide that a specific project should be exempted from EIA under the Directive and that some other form of assessment would be appropriate, the information obtained under that other form of assessment must be made available to the public concerned, together with the information relating to the exemption decision and the reasons for it.

—   Articles 6(2) and (3), dealing with consultation of the public are replaced by long and more detailed paragraphs, setting out exactly what information is to be provided, and that this is to be provided early in the decision-making process.

—   Further arts 6(4)-(6) are added, requiring the public concerned to be given early and effective opportunities to participate in the environmental decision-making procedures and to express comments and opinions when all options are still open to the authority. The detailed arrangements for informing and consulting the public are to be determined by the member states, and reasonable time frames for the different phases are to be provided, such as to allow sufficient time for effective participation.

—   Art 7 on transboundary effects is amended.

—   Art 9(1) is amended so as to require the public to be informed not only about the main reasons for the decision, but also about the public consultation process.

—   A new art 10a is inserted, requiring that in accordance with national legal systems, members of the public concerned have access to a review procedure before a court or other independent and impartial body to challenge 'the substantive and procedural legality' of decisions, acts or omissions subject to the public participation provisions of the Directive. There is scope for member states to determine the stage at which decisions may be challenged and what constitutes a sufficient interest or impairment of right to allow standing, consistently with the objective of giving the public concerned wide access to justice; environmental protection organisations are however deemed to have sufficient interest. Such procedures must be 'fair, equitable, timely and not prohibitively expensive'.

—   Changes to or extensions of Annex I projects are brought within Annex I where the change or extension in itself meets any applicable thresholds in the Annex (such changes currently fall within Annex II).

2.73   The implications of these changes for EIA law in England and Wales are not necessarily easy to assess. In the long term authorities will have to become much more 'participation-minded'. The Ministry of Defence will have to consider and justify the exclusion of specific projects from EIA, rather than rely on a blanket exclusion. Perhaps most importantly, there will have to be an urgent re-appraisal of the procedures for EIA-based legal challenges. Whilst the current procedures of application to the High Court discussed in Chapter 8 are generally liberal in their rules on standing, and are fair and (generally) 'timely', it is difficult to argue that they are anything other than 'prohibitively expensive' in many cases where there is no eligibility for public funding. Despite the heavy expense of litigation and the real risk of paying the defendants' costs if the challenge is unsuccessful, as the cases in this book show, there have been no shortage of challenges on EIA grounds. Nonetheless, the new Directive will require a response by the government, and there can be little doubt that the volume of cases will increase if the costs and risks are reduced.

CHAPTER 3

Screening

WHAT IS SCREENING?

3.01 The term 'screening', at its broadest, refers to the process of determining whether environmental impact assessment (EIA) is required for a specific project. In that sense, it is an exercise which can be carried out by the developers, who may decide for themselves (possibly following informal discussions with the planning authority) that EIA is required, and may submit an environmental statement (ES) accordingly. More frequently, however, the term is used to denote the determination by the planning authority of whether EIA is required, which is a formal process, and one which — as we shall see — is subject to potential legal challenge.

Screening in the Directive

3.02 The EIA Directive (EIA Directive 85/337/EEC, as now amended by Directive 97/11/EC) itself does not use the term 'screening'. The concept is however inherent in the structure and requirements of the Directive, as discussed in the previous chapter. Article 2(1) requires measures to be adopted '... to ensure that, before consent is given, projects likely to have significant effects on the environment by virtue, *inter alia*, of their nature, size or location are made subject to a requirement for development consent and an assessment with regard to their effects'. These projects are defined in art 4. For Annex I projects, the fact that it is within the list is enough (see art 4(1)); the issue is therefore one of construing and applying the relevant words. For Annex II projects, by art 4(2) member states are required to determine through (a) a case-by-case examination, or (b) thresholds or criteria set by the member state, whether the project should be subject to EIA. Such projects must therefore be examined or assessed against pre-existing thresholds or criteria, to determine whether they are likely to have significant effects on the environment in art 2(1) terms.[1] By art 4(3) that process must involve taking into account the selection criteria set out at Annex III, comprising a list of factors relating to the characteristics of the project, the location of the project, and the characteristics of the potential impact. Importantly, by art 4(4), member states must ensure that the determination made by the competent authorities under art 4(2) is made available to the public.[2] Thus the Directive envisages a process which is official, structured and open in terms of its outcome.

1   As to the EC cases on how this exercise is to be conducted, see paras **2.28–2.39**.
2   It may be noted that this requirement does not expressly apply to a determination made by the competent authority as to whether or not a project falls within the EIA Directive, Annex I.

Screening in the Regulations

3.03   These requirements are addressed in the Town and Country Planning (Environmental Impact Assessment) Regulations 1999 (TCP(EIA) Regulations 1999), Pt II, under the heading 'Screening'. The structure created is one of some complexity and involves tracking through a number of provisions. The provision which gives the Regulations their 'bite' is reg 3(2) which prohibits the relevant planning authority (ie the local planning authority, the Secretary of State, or a planning inspector) granting planning permission for an 'EIA application' without having first taken the environmental information generated by the EIA process into account. An 'EIA application' means an application for 'EIA development'.[1] One then turns to the definition of 'EIA development',[2] which means development which is either:
(1)   Schedule 1 development; or
(2)   Schedule 2 development likely to have significant effects on the environment by virtue of factors such as its nature, size or location. In deciding whether Schedule 2 development is EIA development in these terms, the local planning authority or the Secretary of State is required by reg 4(5) to take into account such of the selection criteria in Sch 3 as are relevant to the development.

'Schedule 1 development' means development of a description mentioned in Sch 1.

'Schedule 2 development' means development of a description mentioned in column 1 of the table forming Sch 2 where either:
(a)   any part of the development is to be carried out in a 'sensitive area';[3] or
(b)   any applicable threshold or criterion in the corresponding part of column 2 of the Schedule is exceeded or met.

In the case of both Sch 1 and Sch 2 development, 'exempt development' (development which comprises or forms part of a project serving national defence purposes[4] or in respect of which the Secretary of State has made a direction under reg 4(4)).[5]

1   TCP(EIA) Regulations 1999, reg 2(1).
2   TCP(EIA) Regulations 1999, reg 2(1).
3   See para **3.62**.
4   See para **3.49**.
5   See para **3.49**.

3.04   It will be noted that these definitions do not use the term 'project', in the parlance of the EIA Directive.[1] Since they implement the Directive in relation only to projects subject to planning control, they use the terminology of the Town and Country

Planning Act 1990 (TCPA 1990) by referring to 'development'. This has the same meaning as under the 1990 Act by virtue of reg 2(2) which provides that expressions used both in the TCP(EIA) Regulations 1999 and in the TCPA 1990 have the same meaning for the purposes of the Regulations as they have for the purposes of the Act. Thus the Regulations only apply to projects which constitute 'development' as defined in the TCPA 1990,[2] in the sense of building, engineering, mining or other operations in, on, over or under land, or the making of any material change in the use of buildings or other land.[3]

1   As to issues arising from this, see para **3.37** below.
2   TCPA 1990, s 55(1).
3   As to changes of use as EIA development, see paras **3.43–3.44** below.

Questions to be asked on screening

3.05   Thus a planning authority, inspector or Secretary of State, faced with an application for planning permission, must ask the following questions:
1   Is the development of a description mentioned in the TCP(EIA) Regulations 1999, Sch 1? If so, is it exempt development?
2   If not within Sch 1, is the development of a description mentioned in Sch 2? Again, is it exempt development?
3   If within a description mentioned in Sch 2, is any part of it to be carried out in a 'sensitive area'?
4   If not in a sensitive area, is any criterion or threshold applicable to that description of development exceeded or met?
5   If the answer to either question (3) or (4) above is 'yes', then is the development likely to have significant effects on the environment by virtue of factors such as its nature, size, or location? In answering that question, the decision-maker must consider which of the Sch 3 selection criteria are relevant to the development and take them into account.

SCREENING PROCEDURES

Events triggering EIA

3.06   The many potential pitfalls in this exercise are considered below, but first we deal with the formal procedures provided for by the TCP(EIA) Regulations 1999 within which that decision is taken. In fact the starting point in the decision-making process lies with the developer. Under reg 4(1) and (2) there are two alternative 'events', the occurrence of which will determine that the development is EIA development. The first of these (reg 4(2)(a)) is the submission by the applicant or appellant in relation to the development of 'a statement referred to by the applicant or appellant as an environmental statement for the purposes of these Regulations'.

Decision by developer to conduct EIA

3.07   Where it is clear that EIA development is involved, the developer will prepare an environmental statement as a matter of course, as part of the planning application process. In cases where it is debatable whether EIA development is involved, the developer may well feel that his interests would be best served by preparing an environmental statement (ES), in terms of avoiding possible delay, strengthening the application, or simply following good practice. In such cases, provided the statement is expressed to be submitted as an ES under the TCP(EIA) Regulations 1999, the planning authority will then be bound to treat the application as one for EIA development under reg 4(2)(a).

3.08   It is conceivable that a developer may submit an ES under the TCP(EIA) Regulations 1999, perhaps from an abundance of caution, but the local planning authority may take the view that the application is not in fact EIA development. Circular 2/99 suggests that such cases will be 'exceptional',[1] and that a possible course is for the planning authority to request the Secretary of State for a direction.[2] A direction of the Secretary of State is determinative of the issue of whether the development is or is not EIA development.[3]

1   Department of the Environment Circular 2/99, para 53.
2   As to screening directions by the Secretary of State, see para 3.14.
3   TCP(EIA) Regulations 1999, reg 4(3).

Submission of non-statutory environmental statements

3.09   It is common for considerable amounts of environmental information to be submitted in support of planning applications. The developer may, for example, have engaged consultants to consider whether the proposed development is likely to have significant environmental effects, and reached the conclusion that it will not. The developer may wish to submit that information in support of the planning application. Circular 2/99 suggests that if environmental information is submitted, but it is not clear whether it is intended to constitute an ES under the TCP(EIA) Regulations 1999, the local planning authority should adopt a screening opinion[1] under the Regulations.[2] If the screening opinion is that the development is EIA development, then the developer may ask for the information already submitted to be treated as the formal ES, or may submit a new ES.[3] If the screening opinion is negative, then the information provided should still be taken into account in determining the planning application, so far as it is material.[4]

1   As to screening opinions, see para **3.10** et seq.
2   Department of the Environment circular 2/99, para 54.
3   Department of the Environment circular 2/99, para 54.
4   Department of the Environment circular 2/99, para 54.

Screening opinion procedures

3.10 If the developer has not triggered EIA procedures by submitting an ES, as explained above, then under the TCP(EIA) Regulations 1999, reg 4(2)(b) it is the adoption by the relevant planning authority[1] of a screening opinion to the effect that the development is EIA development which determines that the TCP(EIA) Regulations 1999 apply, subject to the powers of direction of the Secretary of State.[2]

1   'Relevant planning authority' is defined by the TCP(EIA) Regulations 1999, reg 2(1) to mean 'the body to whom it falls, fell, or would, but for a direction under section 77 [of the TCPA 1990] (reference of applications to Secretary of State), fall to determine an application for planning permission for the development in question'.
2   TCP(EIA) Regulations 1999, reg 4(1), (3) and (4).

3.11 There are two procedures in the TCP(EIA) Regulations 1999 for the giving of screening opinions. The first is the case where the developer requests such an opinion, and is dealt with under Pt II at regs 5 and 6. The second is where it appears that an application is Sch 1 or Sch 2 development, but no ES has been submitted. This is dealt with in Pt III (Procedures Concerning Applications for Planning Permission) at regs 7–9.

Prior request for screening opinion

3.12 Under the TCP(EIA) Regulations 1999, reg 5(1) a person who is minded to carry out development may request the relevant planning authority to adopt a screening opinion. A 'screening opinion' is a 'written statement of the relevant planning authority as to whether development is EIA development'.[1] No form is prescribed for such a request, but by reg 5(2) it must be accompanied by:
(a)   a plan sufficient to identify the land;
(b)   a brief description of the nature and purpose of the development and its possible effects on the environment; and
(c)   such other information or representations as the person making the request may wish to provide or make.[2]

1   TCP(EIA) Regulations 1999, reg 2(1).
2   As to the adequacy of the information to give a screening opinion, see para **3.93** et seq.

3.13 If the authority considers that insufficient information has been provided to allow them to adopt a screening opinion, they must notify the person making the request in writing of the points on which they require additional information.[1] They must adopt a screening opinion within three weeks beginning with the date of the request, or such longer period as may be agreed in writing.[2] A copy of the screening opinion must be sent forthwith to the person who made the request.[3] The important question of the formalities involved in adopting a screening opinion are considered below.[4]

1   TCP(EIA) Regulations 1999, reg 5(3).

2   TCP(EIA) Regulations 1999, reg 5(4). As to the consequences of not adopting an opinion within that period, see para **3.20**.
3   TCP(EIA) Regulations 1999, reg 5(5).
4   See para —**3.73** et seq.

Request for screening direction

3.14   A person who has requested the local planning authority to give a screening opinion can request the Secretary of State to make a 'screening direction' in two cases:[1]
(1) Where the authority fails to adopt a screening opinion within the relevant period under the TCP(EIA) Regulations 1999, reg 5(4). This applies even where the authority has requested additional information under reg 5(3), which has not yet been provided.[2]
(2) Where the authority adopts an opinion to the effect that the development is EIA development; this is effectively a form of appeal against an adverse determination. The request is made to the relevant regional government office,[3] and copied to the local planning authority.[4] With the request must be submitted:[5]
    (a) a copy of the original request under reg 5(1) and the documents that accompanied it;
    (b) a copy of any notification from the authority under reg 5(3) requesting further information, and any response to it;
    (c) a copy of any screening opinion and any accompanying statement of reasons; and
    (d) any representations the developer wishes to make.

There is a procedure for the Secretary of State to notify the developer in writing of any points on which additional information is required in order to make a direction, and to request the planning authority to provide such information as they can on those points.[6] The screening direction must be made within three weeks beginning with the date of the request, or 'such longer period as he may reasonably require';[7] unlike a local planning authority, the Secretary of State does not have to agree any extension of time with the person making the request.

1   TCP(EIA) Regulations 1999, reg 5(6). By reg 2(1) a 'screening direction' is 'a direction by the Secretary of State as to whether development is EIA development'.
2   TCP(EIA) Regulations 1999, reg 5(7).
3   Department of the Environment Circular 2/99, para 59.
4   TCP(EIA) Regulations 1999, reg 6(2).
5   TCP(EIA) Regulations 1999, reg 6(1).
6   TCP(EIA) Regulations 1999, reg 6(3).
7   TCP(EIA) Regulations 1999, reg 6(4).

Screening where application not accompanied by environmental statement

3.15   Under the TCP(EIA) Regulations 1999, Pt III, three different situations are catered for:
(1)   applications made to the local planning authority (reg 7);
(2)   applications referred to the Secretary of State for determination (reg 8); and
(3)   appeals to the Secretary of State (reg 9).

In all cases the structure is broadly similar. Where it appears to the authority or Secretary of State that (a) the relevant application falls within Sch 1 or Sch 2, (b) the development has not been subject to a screening opinion or direction and (c) the application is not accompanied by a statement referred to as an ES under the regulations, then the requirements of regs 5(3) and (4) and 6(3) and (4) respectively apply as if the receipt or referral of the application, or the appeal, were a request made pursuant to reg 5(6).[1] The effect of this is that:
(1)   the authority or Secretary of State can notify any points on which they require further information to adopt a screening opinion or make a screening direction (regs 5(3) and 6(3)); and
(2)   the authority or Secretary of State must adopt an opinion or make a direction within three weeks of the receipt of the application or the appeal, or within any applicable extension of time (regs 5(4) and 6(4)).
(3)   If the opinion or direction is that EIA is not required, then a copy must be placed on Pt I of the planning register,[2] and the application or appeal is free to be determined in the normal way. If the opinion or direction is that EIA is required, then the further procedures set out in regs 7–9 must be followed.

1   TCP(EIA) Regulations 1999, regs 7(1), 8(1), 9(1).
2   TCP(EIA) Regulations 1999, reg 20(1)(a) and (b).

Notification that EIA required

3.16   These further procedures involve the planning authority or Secretary of State notifying the applicant or appellant that the submission of an ES is required.[1] In the case of a local planning authority, it must do this within three weeks of the date of receipt of the application, or such longer period as may be agreed in writing with the applicant. In the case of the Secretary of State on a referred application, he must do this within three weeks of the date on which he received the application, or such longer period as he may reasonably require. In relation to planning appeals, the timing is more flexible, to accommodate the fact that it may not become apparent that the application is an EIA application until the planning inspector comes to deal with the matter. If at that time it appears to the inspector that it may be an EIA application, the inspector must refer the matter to the Secretary of State, and may not determine the appeal (other than by refusing permission) until a screening direction is received.[2] The Secretary of State should then give a screening direction in response to that question within three weeks or such longer period as he may reasonably require,[3] and the appellant must then be notified that an ES is required.[4] It has been held that in the context of a planning enquiry the inspector is under no duty to refer the matter to the Secretary of State for a screening direction under reg 9(2) where the Secretary of State has already made a screening direction that EIA development is not involved under regs 9(1) and 6(4).[5]

1   TCP(EIA) Regulations 1999, regs 7(2), 7(3), 8(2), 8(3), 9(2), 9(4).
2   TCP(EIA) Regulations 1999, reg 9(2).
3   TCP(EIA) Regulations 1999, reg 9(3).
4   TCP(EIA) Regulations 1999, reg 9(4).
5   See *Evans v First Secretary of State* [2003] EWHC 411 (Admin) [2003] 1 P&CR 467 where Lightman J gave summary judgement for the interested party (London Metropolitan University, who were developing new student accommodation) under CPR 24. The case is under appeal at the time of writing.

Response of applicant to notification that EIA required

3.17   Having received a notification that an ES is required, the applicant or appellant then has three weeks to write to the authority or Secretary of State with their response.[1] In the case of a planning application to the local planning authority, the applicant can either respond by accepting their view and indicating that an ES will be provided, or by stating that he is writing to the Secretary of State to request a screening direction.[2] Failure by the applicant to respond within the relevant period has draconian consequences; the application is deemed to be refused and there is no right of appeal against the deemed refusal.[3] Where the applicant responds in time to avoid such deemed refusal, the authority still may not determine the application, other than by refusing permission, until an ES has been submitted, or the Secretary of State has issued a screening direction that the development is not EIA development.[4] Circular 2/99 states that the authority should suspend consideration of the planning application, unless they are already minded to refuse permission because of other material considerations, in which case they should proceed to do so as quickly as possible.[5]

1   TCP(EIA) Regulations 1999, regs 7(4), 8(4), 9(5).
2   See TCP(EIA) Regulations 1999, reg 7(4). A request to the Secretary of State for a screening direction is made under reg 7(7), and must include the copies of documents referred to at reg 7(7)(a)–(c).
3   TCP(EIA) Regulations 1999, reg 7(5).
4   TCP(EIA) Regulations 1999, reg 7(6).
5   Department of the Environment Circular 2/99, para 70.

3.18   In the case of a planning application referred to the Secretary of State, the applicant may respond within the three-week period to say that he proposes to provide an ES.[1] If he does not respond in this way, then the Secretary of State is under no duty to deal with the application, and must notify the applicant at the end of the three-week period that no further action is being taken on it.[2] In any event, the Secretary of State may determine the application only by refusing permission if the applicant does not submit an ES and comply with the certification and publicity requirements of the the TCP(EIA) Regulations 1999, reg 14(5).[3]

1   TCP(EIA) Regulations 1999, reg 8(4).
2   TCP(EIA) Regulations 1999, reg 8(5).
3   TCP(EIA) Regulations 1999, reg 8(6). As to such requirements, see para 5.18

3.19   In the case of a planning appeal, the appellant who receives a notification that an ES is required has three weeks to write to the Secretary of State to say that he proposes to provide an ES.[1] If he does not do so, then the Secretary of State or inspector are under no duty to deal with the appeal, and at the end of the period the Secretary of State will inform the appellant that no further action is being taken on the appeal.[2] In the same way as for a referred application, the Secretary of State or planning inspector is required to determine the appeal only by refusing permission if the appellant does not submit an ES and comply with the relevant publicity requirements.[3]

1   TCP(EIA) Regulations 1999, reg 9(5).
2   TCP(EIA) Regulations 1999, reg 9(6).
3   TCP(EIA) Regulations 1999, regs 9(7) and 14(5).

Failure to issue screening opinion within relevant period

3.20   The issue may arise as to what happens where the planning authority fails to issue a screening opinion within the three-week period. The ODPM Note on EIA[1] suggests that unless a longer period is agreed with the applicant, the authority has no legal authority to issue a screening opinion outside the three-week period.[2] It goes on to suggest that if the authority considered that EIA was required outside that period, it could either seek to persuade the applicant to undertake EIA voluntarily,[3] or could request the Secretary of State to issue a screening direction that EIA is required.[4]

1   Office of the Deputy Prime Minister, *Note on EIA Directive for Local Planning Authorities* (1999 EIA Regulations), July 2002.
2   See under the heading 'Can screening opinion still be issued outside of the three-week timescale?'
3   If the developer then submits an ES expressed to be provided for the purposes of the the the TCP(EIA) Regulations 1999, the development will become EIA development: see reg 4(1)(a).
4   The Secretary of State has a general power to make a screening direction irrespective of whether he has received a request to do so: TCP(EIA) Regulations 1999, reg 4(7). Where the Secretary of State makes a screening direction after the expiry of the relevant period to the effect that the development is EIA development, the local planning authority must notify the applicant accordingly within seven days of receipt of the screening direction: reg 7(3).

3.21   However, whether these suggestions are correct is highly questionable, in the light of the obligations of the competent authorities under European law to ensure implementation of the EIA Directive.[1] The appropriate first course may well be for the local planning authority to communicate its views that EIA is required and hope the developer complies. However, if the developer does not choose to submit an ES, the local authority is under a duty to ensure compliance with the Directive's requirement that for an Annex II project there be a 'determination' in accordance with art 4(2) of the Directive, and that the determination be made available to the public under art 4(4). The local planning authority does not therefore have simply a discretion to ask the Secretary of State to issue a screening direction; this is something it must do if that is what it takes to secure compliance with the Directive. Another possible approach is to consider whether the ODPM's guidance is in fact correct in law in suggesting that the local authority has no power to issue a screening opinion outside the three-week period. The TCP(EIA) Regulations 1999 do not state this expressly, and certainly there is no provision that equates failure to respond in time with a deemed opinion that EIA is not required.[2] It could be argued on the basis of sympathetic interpretation, or indirect effect,[3] that the effect of the three-week period is simply to allow the applicant to seek a direction from the Secretary of State if no response is received,[4] not to preclude the local authority making a determination after that period.

1   See paras **2.02–2.10**.
2   Such a provision would be contrary to the EIA Directive by analogy with the cases on old mining permissions. See para **2.54** ff.
3   See para **2.42**.
4   See TCP(EIA) Regulations 1999, regs 5(6)(a) and 7(3).

3.22   Such an approach accords with that adopted by Elias J in the case of *British Telecommunications plc v Gloucester City Council*,[1] discussed further below.[2] This was a decision on the Town and Country Planning (Assessment of Environmental Effects) Regulations 1988 (TCP(AEE) Regulations 1988), rather than the TCP(EIA) Regulations 1999; nonetheless the same principles would appear to apply. In that case an outline planning application for urban redevelopment was submitted without an ES. No notice was given by the planning authority within the relevant period of three weeks under reg 9 of the 1988 Regulations,[3] requiring an ES. Elias J rejected a submission that the local planning authority had no power after that three-week period to exercise its discretion. As the following passage makes clear, his view was that the planning authority could put right an earlier failure to address the issue of EIA, whichever decision it reaches when it properly considers the matter:[4]

'It seems to me that the planning authority can put right the failure to call for an environmental statement by requiring one at any time prior to consent being granted. The Regulations themselves envisage that an applicant for planning permission can voluntarily submit a statement some time after the initial application is lodges, and I see nothing in the Regulations that would prevent an authority from requiring one. The three-week period in regulation 9 does not operate as a mandatory requirement after which no statement can lawfully be required. In my view calling for such a statement is akin to seeking an amendment to the original application. Provided the procedures relating to consultation are complied with, and the representations are before the planning authority when it makes its decision, neither logic nor common sense nor the public interest dictate that the courts should treat the exercise as invalid merely because the planning authority only realised the need for the statement late in the day. Similarly, in my view it also follows that if a decision is taken *not* to call for a statement, that is capable of being a valid decision notwithstanding that it was not taken until shortly before the permission was given. There would be no point in requiring a fresh application in which the authority would again conclude that no statement was required.'

1   [2001] EWHC Admin 1001, [2002] JPL 993.
2   See paras **3.75–3.81**.
3   SI 1988/1199, reg 9 is in similar terms to TCP(EIA) Regulations 1999, reg 7, in that it imposes
     a duty on the local planning authority to notify the applicant in writing of their view that the
     submission of an ES is required, within three weeks beginning with the date of receipt of the
     application or such longer period as may be agreed in writing.
4   [2001] EWHC Admin 1001, [2002] JPL 993 at 1007–1008, para 58.

THE SCREENING PROCESS

3.23   The remainder of this chapter considers the screening process, first in relation
to the the TCP(EIA) Regulations 1999, Sch 1 development and secondly in relation to
Sch 2 development. First however, some issues common to both Schedules are
discussed.

What is being screened?

3.24   The first issue is: what is the 'development' to be considered for the purpose of
screening? In terms of the EIA Directive, what requires assessment is the 'project',
defined to mean:[1]

> 'the execution of construction works or of other installations or schemes, [and]
> other interventions in the natural surroundings and landscape including those
> involving the extraction of mineral resources.'

The TCP(EIA) Regulations 1999, embedded as they are in the planning system, do not
refer to a 'project', but rather to 'development' as the basis for assessment. Thus
screening (in terms of the Regulations) takes place in the context of 'development'
which the applicant for a screening opinion is 'minded to carry out' (reg 5(1)), or the
development comprised in a planning application (reg 7(1) or 8(1)), or in the planning
application which forms the basis of an appeal (reg 9(1)). Under the EIA Directive
however, the concept of 'project' is distinct from the 'development consent', which is
the decision of the competent authority or authorities which entitles the developer to
proceed with the project.[2]

1   Directive 97/11/EC, art 1(2).
2   Directive 97/11/EC, art 1(2)

3.25   This in turn raises the issue of whether in order to ensure compliance with the
EIA Directive it may be necessary to apply a broader view of the 'development' than
that which may appear from the planning application, or indeed whether there could be
circumstances in which a 'project' requires EIA despite it not being development in
planning terms.[1] This second issue arose in *R (Westminster City Council) v Mayor of
London*,[2] the challenge to the confirmed Order under the Greater London Authority
Act 1999 creating the Central London Congestion Charging Scheme. One of the

unsuccessful grounds of challenge was that no EIA had been carried out before the Scheme was made. The Scheme was essentially concerned with traffic management; its only physical manifestations were cameras, signs and road markings, which either did not require planning permission at all, or were the subject of deemed permission, and in any event were not actually dealt with in the Order itself. Maurice Kay J approached the issue in two stages: first was the Scheme a 'project', and secondly, was it an 'urban development project' within Annex II? On the first issue, having considered the definition of 'project' in the Directive, and submissions for counsel for the claimant that the Scheme involved the execution of 'installations', some 'construction works' and a 'scheme', each of which entailed intervention in the townscape of London, Maurice Kay J stated that:[3]

'If Article 2(1) stood alone as the sole criterion for the application of the Directive, there might be some difficulty in holding that the Scheme is not a "project".'

However, at the second stage of the test, Maurice Kay J declined to hold that the Scheme was an 'urban development project' within Annex II:[4]

'In my judgment, it would strain the words of the Directive beyond a purposive construction to hold that "urban development project", in the precise context in which they appear, embrace this Scheme which is ... essentially a traffic management scheme. I am disposed to the view that, in general, "urban development project" connotes rather more in the nature of building and construction.'[5]

1   There are of course a number of types of project that are outside the planning system but are caught by other regimes and by separate regulations on EIA: see Chapter 7.
2   [2002] EWHC 2440 (Admin), [2002] 2 All ER (D) 494 (Jul).
3   At para 60.
4   At para 65.
5   Maurice Kay J also took comfort from the fact that the introduction of the Rome Traffic Limitation Zone was not preceded by an EIA and that no example had been forthcoming of any cognate measure which had been taken.

3.26   Thus the judgment indicates that the term 'project', like the EIA Directive in which it appears, has an expansive meaning, but that it is confined by reference to the particular types of projects referred to in the Directive. In the context of 'urban development projects', it may be noted that the term appears in Annex II under the category of 'Infrastructure projects'. Maurice Kay J's view on this issue therefore appears correct, in that a traffic management scheme is not, in itself, an 'infrastructure project'. It seems more akin to a 'plan or programme' which would fall within the SEA Directive.[1]

1   Directive 2001/42/EC. See para **1.06**.

Implications of what is the 'project'

3.27   The definition of what is the 'project' can pose other problems in terms of screening. For example, whether a project is within the EIA Directive, Annex I may depend on whether it is of a certain scale, in terms of length (for transport infrastructure) or capacity in terms of some industrial installations. The 'development' for which planning permission is sought may fall below this scale, but when combined with existing or other planned development the position may be different. Similarly the issue may arise in relation to the thresholds adopted for some Annex II projects in the TCP(EIA) Regulations 1999, Sch 2. The other issue relates to the likelihood of significant effects on the environment for Annex II projects. The more widely defined the 'project' is, the more probable it may be that the likely effects will be judged 'significant'. There are perhaps two main indications in the Directive that suggest a broad approach. First, the information required to be provided for the purposes of EIA includes a description of 'the physical characteristics of the whole project' and a description of the likely significant effects which should cover 'indirect, secondary [and] cumulative effects'.[1] Second, and perhaps more importantly, the selection criteria to be used in screening projects include the size of the project and also 'the cumulation with other projects'.[2]

1   EIA Directive, Annex IV, para 1, first indent, and para 4.
2   EIA Directive, Annex III, para 1, second indent.

Preparatory works

3.28   The scope of the 'project' may arise when considering the descriptions of the the TCP(EIA) Regulations 1999, Sch 1 and Sch 2 development. The planning application may be for preparatory works rather than the project itself. An example is the case of *R v Swale Borough Council, ex p RSPB*,[1] where planning permission was granted for land reclamation works on mud flats at Lappell Bank in the Medway estuary. It was contended by the RSPB that the works were in preparation for an extension of Sheerness Docks, and as such was development to provide a 'trading port' within Sch 1 of the TCP(AEE) Regulations 1988. Simon Brown J held that:[2]

> '... the question whether the development is of a category described in either Schedule must be answered strictly in relation to the development applied for, not any development contemplated beyond that.'

However, it is also important to note that in providing their descriptions of development, the TCP(EIA) Regulations 1999, Schs 1 and 2, in fact refer to 'the carrying out of development to provide any of the following ...'. It may be possible in some circumstances to argue that the development applied for is in fact 'to provide' later development which is within a description of Sch 1 or Sch 2.[3]

1   [1991] 1 PLR 6, [1991] JPL 39.
2   At p 16E.
3   See the discussion by Elvin and Robinson [2000] JPL 876 at 879–883.

Division of projects

3.29   As a matter of planning law there is nothing to prevent a developer from seeking planning permission for a single project by way of a number of planning applications. There may be perfectly legitimate reasons for so doing, for example commercial considerations may require a phased approach. The difficulty comes where such an approach may interfere with the proper functioning of EIA requirements. It may arise in a particularly acute form where the EIA development is defined by reference to size or capacity criteria.

3.30   At one extreme, it clearly should not be possible for a developer to circumvent the requirements of the EIA Directive by crudely subdividing a project. So, for example, if a farmer wishing to obtain permission for an installation for intensive pig-rearing with places for over 3,000 pigs (which would fall within the TCP(EIA) Regulations 1999, Sch 1) instead puts in two planning applications for adjacent installations of half that capacity, it would be legitimate for the planning authority to look carefully at whether each application is really for carrying out development to provide an installation above the relevant threshold. Equally, for transport projects, it clearly should not be possible to avoid the size criteria by dividing a road or rail project into separate sections.

3.31   Often however, the situation will not be so clear cut as this. Planning applications for different phases of a project may be separated by months or years. It may be the case that the development comprised in each separate application could well be self-sufficient and viable when viewed in isolation. The unified nature of a project may only become apparent with hindsight.

3.32   The point was touched upon by Simon Brown J in the *Swale* case, where having held that the issue of whether development fell within a particular description was to be answered in relation solely to the development as applied for, he went on to say:[1]

> 'But the further question arising in respect of a Schedule 2 development, the question of whether it "would be likely to have significant effects on the environment by virtue of factors such as its nature, size or location" should, in my judgment, be answered rather differently. The proposals should not then be considered in isolation if in reality it is properly to be regarded as an integral part of an *inevitably* more substantial development. This approach appears to me appropriate on the language of the Regulations, the existence of the smaller development of itself promoting the larger development and thereby likely to carry in its wake the environmental effects of the latter. In common-sense, moreover, developers could otherwise defeat the object of the Regulations by piecemeal development proposals.'

The use of the word 'inevitably' suggests that there must be some clear evidence to support such an approach, more than simply the potential of the earlier development to lead on to more substantial later development.[2]

1   [1991] PLR 6 at 16E, [1991] JPL 39. Emphasis added.

2   For a case applying these principles, see *BAA plc v Secretary of State for Transport, Local Government and the Regions* [2002] EWHC 1920 (Admin), para **3.35** below.

3.33   While the remarks of Simon Brown J above were clearly made in the context of screening TCP(EIA) Regulations 1999, Sch 2 projects for their likely significant effects, the guidance contained in Circular 2/99 applies them also to the applicability of any relevant thresholds:[1]

'For the purposes of determining whether EIA is required, a particular planning application should not be considered in isolation if, in reality, it is properly to be regarded as an integral part of an inevitably more substantial development. In such cases, the need for EIA (*including the applicability of any indicative thresholds*) must be considered in respect of the total development. This is not to say that all applications which form part of some wider scheme must be considered together. In this context, it will be important to establish whether each of the proposed developments could proceed independently and whether the aims of the regulations and Directive are being frustrated by the submission of multiple planning applications.'

1   Department of the Environment Circular 2/99, para 46, emphasis supplied.

3.34   In terms of whether a development is an integral part of a more substantial whole, it may be helpful in some cases to refer to the decision of the European Court of Justice in *Commission v Belgium*[1] where, in considering the definition of an 'integrated chemical installation' within the EIA Directive, Annex I, the Court held that the essence was the existence of interlinked production units forming a single unit.

1   Case C-133/94 [1996] ECR I-2323 at 2347.

3.35   A domestic example of the problems which can arise in relation to linked applications is provided by *BAA plc v Secretary of State for Transport, Local Government and the Regions*.[1] Outline planning permission had been granted before the TCP(AEE) Regulations 1988 came into force, for business development and associated access at Southampton International Airport. The Secretary of State called in two subsequent planning applications, one for the construction of a link road passing immediately to the north of the airport runway, the other for the approval of reserved matters. The Secretary of State formed the view that the first application did not require EIA because it would not have significant environmental effects, and the second did not because EIA had no application to reserved matters.[2] Turner J held that the environmental issues had been side-stepped by treating the development under the outline permission and the new road as separate schemes, whereas the correct method of approach should have been to have regard to the combined impact of both schemes.[3]

1   [2002] EWHC 1920 (Admin).
2   On this point, see para **6.47** et seq.
3   [2002] EWHC 1920 (Admin), para 69.

3.36   Referring to the passage of Simon Brown J quoted above warning of the dangers of considering proposals in isolation,[1] Turner J said that it might have been drafted with the present set of circumstances in mind:[2]

'It is clear that neither the Secretary of State nor the Inspector considered the totality of the developments for which the third defendants were seeking permissions as being capable of constituting one integral site. Had either done so as undoubtedly they ought to have done, it is inconceivable that they could have reached the conclusions which they did on this issue. If such consideration had been given to the question whether or not the two applications were part of a single development and the conclusion had been reached that they were not, it is probable that any such decision would have been vulnerable to challenge on the basis of irrationality, and this notwithstanding that the decision in question was one of fact for the Secretary of State himself to have made. Simon Brown LJ left this possibility open in his judgment in the Swale Borough Council Case ... If necessary, therefore, I would have reached such a conclusion notwithstanding the limitations of the judicial role on issues of fact.'[3]

1   Paragraph **3.32–3.33**.
2   [2002] EWHC 1920 (Admin), para 71.
3   As to the reviewability of screening decisions, see para **3.99** et seq below.

3.37   Elvin and Robinson[1] have raised the question of whether it is possible, consistently with the EIA Directive, to grant planning permission for part of a project in any circumstances. This is because it is implicit in the Directive that EIA takes place before a project is initiated, and if consent for a project is granted in parts, it is never possible to assess effectively the effects of the project as a whole. They acknowledge that in the *Bund Naturschutz* case,[2] Advocate General Gulman in the following remark suggested that there was no absolute principle against permitting projects in part:

'It must be self evident that the Directive cannot indirectly have the effect of forcing Member States to depart from the normal practice according to which long road links are executed by constructing sections over staggered periods.'

However, as Elvin and Robinson point out, this passage was not followed by the Court, which decided the case on other grounds. The Directive certainly seems to envisage a single 'development consent' which entitles the developer to proceed with the project.

1   [2000] JPL 876 at 882.
2   Case C-396/92 *Bund Naturschutz in Bayern eV v Freistaat Bayern* (the 'Bavarian roads case') [1994] ECR I-3717

3.38   Perhaps the correct view is that the EIA Directive should not be read as laying down any inflexible or absolute rule that a 'project' cannot be subdivided for 'development consent' purposes. What matters in reality is that the requirements for adequate EIA are observed and at the earliest stage possible. This certainly seems to underlie the pragmatic approach suggested by Advocate General Gulman in the Bavarian roads case:[1]

> 'The subject-matter and content of the environmental impact assessment must be established in the light of the purpose of the Directive, which is, at the earliest possible stage in all the technical planning and decision-making processes, to obtain an overview of the effects of the projects on the environment and to have projects designed in such a way that they have the least possible effect on the environment. That purpose entails that as far as practically possible account should also be taken in the environmental impact assessment of any current plans to extend the specific project in hand.
>
> For instance, the environmental impact assessment of a project concerning the construction of the first part of a power station should, accordingly, involve the plans to extend the station's capacity fourfold, when the question of whether the power station's site is appropriate is being assessed.
>
> Similarly, when sections of a planned road link are being constructed, account must be taken, in connection with the environmental impact assessment of the specific projects of the significance of those sections in the linear route to be taken by the rest of the planned road link.'

The Advocate General however declined to make 'any more specific determination' of the actual scope of the obligation in that case.

1   Case C-396/92 *Bund Naturschutz in Bayern eV v Freistaat Bayern* [1994] ECR I-3717

3.39   While no doubt presenting difficulties in application to specific circumstances, these principles do at least offer a coherent way forward for planning authorities dealing with staged or linear projects. The amount of information which it is reasonable to require concerning future stages will vary from case to case. So, for example, it will be necessary to provide more detail on the next stretch of road to be constructed, where the route will obviously be known with a reasonable degree of certainty, than on future sections which may be built many years hence, and where the alignment is much less certain.

Changes and extensions to existing development

3.40   Another issue is that of changes or extensions to existing development. It is clear from European case law that the descriptions of projects in the EIA Directive, Annexes I and II are capable of applying not only to new projects, but also to modification, extension or augmentation of existing installations.[1] Annex II of the EIA Directive, as amended in 1997, makes express mention of changes or extensions to Annex I or II projects:[2]

'Any change or extension of projects listed in Annex I or Annex II, already authorised, executed or in the process of being executed, which may have significant adverse effects upon the environment.'

1   See Case C-72/95 *Kraaijeveld* (the Dutch dykes case) [1996] ECR I-5403 (para **2.28**) above and Case C-431/92 *Commission v Germany* (the *Grosskrotzenburg* case) [1995] ECR I-2189 (construction of new block at thermal power station).
2   EIA Directive, Annex II, para (13), first indent.

3.41   Circular 2/99 makes some comments on changes or extensions to existing development which are not entirely satisfactory:[1]

'Development which comprises a change or extension requires EIA only if the change or extension is likely to have significant environmental effects.'

This does not accurately state the position under the EIA Directive or the TCP(EIA) Regulations 1999. For one thing, it ignores the possibility that a change or extension may be of such a scale as to amount to Annex I development in its own right, or may be such as to take existing development over a threshold which brings it within Annex I. In that case, if in the words of the TCP(EIA) Regulations 1999, Sch 1, it is providing an installation of the relevant description which was not there previously, there is a strong argument for saying it falls within Sch 1. Second, and perhaps more importantly, the relevant words in Annex II and Sch 2 refer not to 'significant likely environmental effects', but to 'significant *adverse* effects on the environment'. This is important, because for all other types of project listed in Sch 2 the question for screening is whether any significant effect, positive or negative, are likely.[2]

1   Department of the Environment circular 2/99, Welsh Office circular 10/99, *Environmental Impact Assessment*, para 46.
2   See para **3.74** below.

3.42   Circular 2/99 goes on to suggest that while what is to be considered are the effects from the change or extension, not the project as a whole, the context for consideration must be the whole existing development. So, for example, a relatively modest extension to an airport runway might allow larger aircraft to use the airport, thereby significantly increasing noise.[1] The effects of the existing development are also important in that they provide the baseline against which the significance of the further effects falls to be assessed. If air quality or noise levels are already affected, then an increase may result in a significant threshold being breached.[2]

1   Department of the Environment Circular 2/99, para 46.
2   See the appeal decision at [1998] (Filton aerodrome) where existing noise levels were relevant in considering the impact from extension.

CHANGES OF USE

3.43 Another situation which may give rise to difficulties is where an existing building or structure undergoes a change of use. It is possible to envisage situations where such a change of use could involve EIA development. Certainly in the terms of the EIA Directive, a change of use of a building seems capable of being described as a 'scheme', within the definition of a 'project' under art 1(2), and in any event some degree of 'construction works or other installations' might be involved, irrespective of whether this is such as to require planning permission. Since the definition of 'EIA development' under the TCP(EIA) Regulations 1999 is tied to the definition of development for planning purposes, it can include not only physical development but also a material change in the use of land.

3.44 The only express reference to changes of use in the TCP(EIA) Regulations 1999 occurs at reg 31, which provides that a change in the use of land or buildings to a purpose mentioned in Sch 1, para 9 (waste disposal installations for the incineration, chemical treatment or landfill of hazardous waste), involves a material change of use for the purposes of the definition of 'development' in the TCPA 1990, s 55. This is no doubt a reflection of the particular difficulties which can arise where the nature of waste disposed of at a particular installation changes, or indeed where waste is used as a substitute fuel, and whether such changes would constitute development.[1] Regulation 31 puts the matter beyond doubt in case where the new use is the incineration, chemical treatment or landfill of hazardous waste. However, there are many other potential situations where the same issue might arise, where the new use falls within another category of Sch 1 or Sch 2. The use of waste-derived fuels for industrial purposes, while constituting waste recovery, would not necessarily be regarded as incineration,[2] or as a change of use.[3] One possible solution would be to regard any change of use to a use falling within Sch 1 or Sch 2 as 'material' in planning terms for that very reason. However, if there is no change of use (but only, for example, a change of fuel type) there will be nothing for the concept of materiality to bite on.

1   As to the complex issues involved, see *R (Lowther) v Durham County Council* [2001] EWCA Civ 781, [2002] Env LR 349.
2   Under Directive 2000/76/EC on the incineration of waste (OJ L332, 28.12.2000, p 91) plant which uses waste as fuel, with the main purpose of generating energy or producing material products rather than disposal of waste, is termed 'co-incineration' rather than incineration (art 3(5)).
3   *R (Lowther) v Durham County Council* [2001] EWCA Civ 781, [2002] Env LR 349.

Schedule I projects

3.45 There ought not in principle, other than in the areas of controversy described above, to be too much doubt in deciding whether development falls within the TCP(EIA) Regulations 1999, Sch 1. It is a matter of applying the words used, and any size or other criteria, to the development. In most cases the descriptions of development are reasonably clear and self-explanatory, and what is required is attention to the detail of

the wording. Reference should be made to the Schedule itself, which is set out at
Appendix 1.

Schedule 2 projects

3.46   It is in relation to Sch 2 projects that most difficulties arise in practice. This is
partly a reflection of the fact that some of the categories of development within Sch 2
are very broad in scope, partly because of the approach adopted in the TCP(EIA)
Regulations 1999 of applying thresholds and criteria to the various categories, and
partly because of the judgment which is required to be made of whether development
falling within Sch 2 is likely to have significant effects on the environment. Each of
these aspects is discussed below.

Deciding whether development falls within a Schedule

3.47   As considered below,[1] in reviewing screening decisions by planning authorities,
the courts generally apply a test of irrationality or *Wednesbury* unreasonableness.
This is an appropriate standard where the question is one of judgment as to the
significance of likely effects; however the approach requires modification where the
issue is whether a particular development falls within one of the scheduled descriptions.
In *R v Swale Metropolitan Borough Council, ex p RSPB*,[2] Simon Brown J held that
questions of classification were matters of fact and degree, not law, and were subject
only to *Wednesbury* challenge. This line was followed by Sir Richard Tucker in *R
(Goodman) v London Borough of Lewisham and Big Yellow Property Co Ltd*,[3] where
the issue was whether a development of self-storage units was within the category of
'infrastructure' projects.[4] However, in that case the Court of Appeal disagreed
decisively, holding that the meaning of expressions used in the Schedule was a matter
of law.[5] Buxton LJ (with whom Brooke LJ and Morland J agreed) recognised that the
terms 'infrastructure' and 'urban development projects' are very wide and to some
extent obscure expressions, where there may be legitimate disagreement about their
application to the facts of a given case, but then went on:[6]

> 'However fact-sensitive such a determination may be, it is not simply a finding
> of fact, nor of discretionary judgment. Rather, it involves the application of the
> authority's understanding of the meaning in law of the expression used in the
> Regulation. If the authority reaches an understanding of those expressions that
> is wrong as a matter of law, then the court must correct that error: and in
> determining the meaning of the statutory expressions the concept of reasonable
> judgement as embodied in *Wednesbury* simply has no part to play.'

1   See para **3.99**.
2   [1991] 1 PLR 6, 16C; cited by Sullivan J in *R (Malster) v Ipswich Borough Council* [2001]
    EWHC 711 (Admin), [2002] PLCR 251, para 62.
3   [2002] EWHC 1769 (Admin), paras 25–26.
4   See below, para **3.56**.
5   [2003] EWCA Civ 140, [2003] 13 LS Gaz R 28.
6   [2003] EWCA Civ 140, [2003] 13 LS Gaz R 28, para 8.

3.48　However, Buxton LJ went on to make clear that this was not the end of the matter. The meaning of an expression used in the TCP(EIA) Regulations 1999 might be so imprecise that in applying it to the facts (as opposed to determining its meaning) a range of different conclusions may be legitimately acceptable.[1] In such cases, the approach, following the test stated by Lord Mustill in *R v Monopolies and Mergers Commission, ex p South Yorkshire Transport Ltd*,[2] was that the court should substitute its own opinion for that of the decision-maker where 'the decision is so aberrant that it cannot be classed as rational'.[3]

1　[2003] EWCA Civ 140, [2003] 13 LS Gaz R 28, para 8.
2　[1993] 1 WLR 23.
3　[1993] 1 WLR 23 at para 32G.

Exempt development

3.49　Both Sch 1 and Sch 2 of the TCP(EIA) Regulations 1999 exclude 'exempt development', defined as:[1]

'... development which comprises or forms part of a project serving national defence purposes or in respect of which the Secretary of State has made a direction under regulation 4(4)'.

As to the first limb of this definition, art 1(4) of the EIA Directive provides that 'projects serving national defence purposes are not covered by this Directive'. In *WWF v Bozen*[1] the ECJ (Sixth Chamber) gave a restrictive interpretation to this exclusion, so that:[2]

'... only projects which mainly serve national defence purposes may therefore be excluded from the assessment obligation.'

It followed from this that the project for restructuring an airport to simultaneously serve both civil and military purposes, but whose main use was commercial, was held to be within the scope of the EIA Directive.

1　Case C-435/97 *World Wildlife Fund v Autonome Provinz Bozen* [1999] ECR I-5613; [2000] 1 CMLR 149; [2000] PLR 1. See para **2.34** above.
2　At para 65.

3.50　As to the second limb of 'exempt development', the TCP(EIA) Regulations 1999, reg 4(4) allows the Secretary of State to direct that particular proposed development is exempted from the application of the Regulations in accordance with art 2(3) of the EIA Directive (but without prejudice to art 7). A copy of the direction must be sent to the relevant planning authority, which must make the direction available for public inspection for a period of at least two years,[1] and must place a copy on Pt I of the planning register in relation to any relevant planning application.[2]

1　TCP(EIA) Regulations 1999, reg 20(2).
2　TCP(EIA) Regulations 1999, reg 20(1).

3.51 Article 2(3) of the EIA Directive allows a member state, 'in exceptional cases', to exempt a specific project in whole or in part from the provisions laid down in the Directive. In this event, the member state must:

(a) consider whether another form of assessment would be appropriate and whether the information collected should be made available to the public;

(b) make available to the public concerned the information relating to the exemption and the reasons for granting it; and

(c) inform the Commission, prior to granting consent, of the reasons justifying the exemption granted, and provide it with the information made available to its own nationals. The Commission shall immediately forward the documents received to the other member states, and must report annually to the Council on the application of the provision.

3.52 It is not clear from the EIA Directive what is contemplated by the 'exceptional cases' referred to in art 2(3); the recitals simply say that ' ... it may be appropriate in exceptional cases to exempt a specific project' from the assessment procedures laid down by the Directive. What is clear is that such exemption must be project specific, and cannot be applied to a class or category of projects. While the EIA Directive suggests that partial exemption is possible ('may ... exempt a specific project in whole or in part'), the power of direction under reg 4(4) of the TCP(EIA) Regulations 1999 appears to be on an 'all or nothing' basis. In any event, the power to exempt is without prejudice to the requirements of art 7 of the EIA Directive, dealing with projects likely to have significant effects on the environment in another member state.[1] Thus the power of exemption cannot be used so as to avoid the entitlement of the potentially affected member state and its citizens to participate in the EIA process for the project concerned.

1   See further, paras 5.37–5.39.

Descriptions of Sch 2 development

3.53 As for TCP(EIA) Regulations 1999, Sch 1 projects, reference should be made to the detailed wording of Sch 2, column 1, for the types of development covered. Most of these descriptions are self-explanatory, and there should be little doubt as to whether the project falls within the description or not; many involve particular industrial or manufacturing processes. There are however some categories which merit particular attention.

CATEGORY 10: INFRASTRUCTURE

3.54 This category (TCP(EIA) Regulations 1999, Sch 2, para 10) contains some extremely broad descriptions of development, for example '(a) Industrial estate development projects', '(b) Urban development projects, including the construction of shopping centres and car parks, sports stadiums, leisure centres and multiplex cinemas' and '(f) construction of roads'. The term 'urban development project', which has not as yet been defined or subject to much judicial scrutiny, is particularly wide in its potential scope.[1] It may cover sports stadia schemes,[2] housing development,[3] retail and storage units.[4]

1   See J Pugh-Smith [2002] JPL 1316 at 1317.
2   *Berkeley v Secretary of State for the Environment, Transport and the Regions (Berkeley 1)* [2001] 2 AC 603.
3   *Berkeley v Secretary of State for the Environment, Transport and the Regions and London Borough of Richmond upon Thames (Berkeley 2)* [2002] JPL 224 (block of flats); *R (Francis) v London Borough of Brent* CO/1939/2001 (local planning authority undertook not to act on resolution to grant permission for residential development on 3.5 ha at the former Hirst Research Centre, Wembley, which it had considered not to be an urban development project); *R (Prophet) v York City Council* [2002] EWHC 588 (Admin) (24 flats on 0.51 ha site; permission granted for judicial review).
4   *R (Roplas) v Kingston upon Hull City Council (Roplas 1)* CO/2897/2001 (local planning authority submitted to judgment for failure to screen 1,000 m2 retail and 3,000 m2 first floor healthcare scheme on just over 0.5 ha site); *R (Goodman) v Lewisham London Borough Council and Big Yellow Warehouse Co* [2003] EWCA Civ 140, [2003] 13 LS Gaz R 28 (16 externally accessed B8 storage units with 2,780 m2 of floorspace; discussed below).

3.55   The main authority on the category is *R (Goodman) v London Borough of Lewisham and Big Yellow Property Co Ltd*.[1] Planning permission was given for the construction of a warehouse and self-storage blocks on the site of a former dairy of marginally over 0.5 ha. At first instance, Sir Richard Tucker applied a test of irrationality to whether the local planning authority was correct to conclude that this was not an 'urban development project',[2] an approach which the Court of Appeal held was erroneous.[3] Sir Richard Tucker agreed that Sch 2 of the TCP(EIA) Regulations 1999 was concerned with major development and that it was not intended that all industrial and commercial development should be included. Having regard to the scale and intensity of the development, he held that it could not be said to be irrational or perverse to conclude it was not an 'urban development project'.[4] The Court of Appeal focused on the view of a planning officer, expressed in correspondence, that a 'storage and distribution use' did not fall within the Sch 2 categories. It seemed plain to the Court that the officer was deciding and reporting that storage and distribution as a category of project did not fall within Category 10(b), and that this view was outside the range of reasonable responses open to the authority.[5]

1   [2003] EWCA Civ 140, [2003] 13 LS Gaz R 28.
2   [2002] EWHC 1769 (Admin).
3   See para **3.47** above.
4   [2002] EWHC 1769 (Admin) para 31.
5   [2003] EWCA Civ 140, [2003] 13 LS Gaz R 28, paras 13–14.

3.56   Buxton LJ in *Goodman* commented that 'infrastructure project' and 'urban development project' are 'terms of wide ambit, perhaps more easily understood by those versed in planning policy than by mere lawyers'.[1] However, the examples of urban development projects used in the TCP(EIA) Regulations 1999, Sch 2, para 10(b) showed that the term 'infrastructure' went far wider than the normal understanding of the term as installation such as roads, power stations, sewers and housing, which could be said to form the 'economic foundations' of the country.[2] Buxton LJ could not accept that a storage and distribution facility, especially when providing services to business and the community at large, could never be said to be part of 'infrastructure' as understood in the Regulations.[3] Morland J in agreeing stated:[4]

> 'Storage and distribution of goods and materials are very much the lifeblood of commerce and trade. The words 'including the construction of shopping centres and car parks, sports stadiums, leisure centres and multiplex cinemas' are not words of limitation but of description which emphasises the wide ambit encompassed by 'urban development projects'.

1   [2003] EWCA Civ 140, [2003] 13 LS Gaz R 28, para 13.
2   [2003] EWCA Civ 140, [2003] 13 LS Gaz R 28, para 13, the words used citing the Shorter Oxford English Dictionary definition.
3   [2003] EWCA Civ 140, [2003] 13 LS Gaz R 28, para 13.
4   [2003] EWCA Civ 140, [2003] 13 LS Gaz R 28, paras 23–24.

3.57   Thus it is clear that the examples given in the TCP(EIA) Regulations 1999, Sch 2, para 10(b) of types of urban development project are at most indicative rather than exclusive, and that the fact that a particular type of use is not expressly named does not mean it cannot be caught by para 10(b). At the same time, it would be for the planning authority to determine whether such a use was or was not on its facts within para 10(b), whereas for those types of use expressly included (such as sports stadiums and leisure centres) there will be no doubt.

CATEGORY 11: OTHER PROJECTS

3.58   While many of the descriptions within this category (TCP(EIA) Regulations 1999, Sch 2, para 11) are of a somewhat esoteric nature, for example knackers' yards and test benches for engines or turbines, there are two broad and important descriptions: '(b) Installations for the disposal of waste' and '(c) Waste-water treatment plants'.

CATEGORY 12: TOURISM AND LEISURE

3.59   This category (TCP(EIA) Regulations 1999, Sch 2, para 12) includes '(c) Holiday villages and hotel complexes outside urban areas', '(e) Permanent camp sites and caravan sites' and '(f) Golf courses and associated developments'.

CATEGORY 13: CHANGES OR EXTENSIONS

3.60   The potentially thorny issue of changes or extensions to existing development has already been considered.[1] Schedule 2 of the TCP(EIA) Regulations 1999 deals with this by including '(a) Any change to or extension of development of a description listed in Schedule 1 or [Schedule 2], where that development is already authorised, executed or in the process of being constructed, and the change or extension may have significant adverse effects on the environment'.[2] The relevant thresholds and criteria for Sch 2 projects (see column 2 (i)) and Sch 1 projects (see column 2 (ii))[3] are to be applied to the change or extension, and not to the development as changed or extended.

1   See para **3.40**.
2   For the implications of this wording, see para **3.41**.
3   For the TCP(EIA) Regulations 1999, Sch 1 projects, the thresholds or criteria from corresponding Sch 2 projects are applied across.

Thresholds and criteria

3.61   Having concluded that a development falls within one of the TCP(EIA) Regulations 1999, Sch 2 descriptions, and is not exempt development, it is then necessary to consider whether it is Sch 2 development as defined under reg 2(1), namely where either:
(a)   any part of the development is to be carried out in a sensitive area; or
(b)   any applicable threshold or criterion in the corresponding part of column 2 in Sch 2 is respectively exceeded or met in relation to that development.

Sensitive areas

3.62   It will be appreciated from the definition in the preceding paragraph that thresholds or criteria are not relevant where any part of the development falls within a sensitive area. This means any of the following:
(a)   land notified as a site of special scientific interest under the Wildlife and Countryside Act 1981, s 28;
(b)   land to which a nature conservation order under the Wildlife and Countryside Act 1981, s 29(3) applies;
(c)   an area to which the General Development Procedure Order 1995, art 10 (u)(ii) (consultation areas around SSSIs (Sites of Special Scientific Interest)) applies;
(d)   a national park;
(e)   the Broads (see the Norfolk and Suffolk Broads Act 1988);
(f)   a property appearing on the World Heritage List kept under the UNESCO Convention for the Protection of the World Cultural and Natural Heritage, art 11(2);
(g)   a Scheduled monument under the Ancient Monuments and Archaeological Areas Act 1979;
(h)   an area of outstanding natural beauty designated under the National Parks and Access to the Countryside Act 1949; and
(i)   a European site of nature conservation interest as defined by the Conservation (Natural Habitats, etc) Regulations 1994, reg 10.[1]

It will be appreciated that some of these areas could be very extensive and may, for example, in the case of a World Heritage Site encompass large urban areas (for example the historic centre of Bath). This means that in such areas, particular care will have to be taken in considering whether development may constitute an 'urban development project', given the absence of any size thresholds.

1   A European site includes special areas of conservation under the Habitats Directive 92/43/EEC and classified special protection areas under the Wild Birds Directive 79/409/EEC, and is defined to include sites over which consultation at European level is still continuing; reference should be made to the detailed wording of reg 10(1) on this issue.

Applying the thresholds and criteria

3.63   Reference should be made to the precise wording of the relevant threshold or criterion in each case. In most instances the threshold is based on size, but the area involved is variously phrased, so that in some cases the reference is to the area of 'the development', in others 'the works' and in others the 'floorspace'. Other thresholds relate to production or storage capacity (for example intensive fish farming, hydroelectric installations or chemical storage facilities).[1] In other instances, criteria may apply; for example whether the development is to be sited within 100 m of controlled waters (for example, the surface storage of fossil fuels, installations for the disposal of waste, sludge deposition or the storage of scrap metal).[2] Height is mentioned as a threshold in only two cases: a 15 m hub height for wind farm turbines or other structures, and a 15 m height for any building or other structure for ski-runs, ski-lifts or cable-cars.[3] There are a few cases where there is no threshold, so that all development within the description is Sch 2 development — these are the reclamation of land from the sea, extraction of minerals by fluvial dredging, coast protection and sea defence works.[4] All installations for the disposal of waste by incineration are Sch 2 development, such disposal being a criterion in its own right.[5]

1   TCP(EIA) Regulations 1999, Sch 2, Table, paras 1(d), 3(h), 6(c).
2   TCP(EIA) Regulations 1999, Sch 2, Table, paras 3(e), 11(b), (d) and (e).
3   TCP(EIA) Regulations 1999, Sch 2, Table, paras 3(i), 12(a).
4   TCP(EIA) Regulations 1999, Sch 2, Table, paras 1(e), 2(c), 10(m).
5   TCP(EIA) Regulations 1999, Sch 2, Table, para 11(b)(i).

Mechanistic application of the thresholds

3.64   For projects within Annex II, the EIA Directive allows member states to determine whether EIA is required through either 'a case-by-case examination', or 'thresholds or criteria set by the Member States'.[1] As discussed above, this does not confer an unlimited discretion; the approach adopted must be consistent with the overarching objectives of the Directive.[2] The TCP(EIA) Regulations 1999 adopt both approaches — use of thresholds and criteria as an initial sieve,[3] followed by case-by-case assessment of the likely effects for those developments caught by the sieve. It is however possible to conceive of cases where a development of the relevant description might fall outside the size or other criteria, but have possible significant effects. One example might be a tall building with a small footprint; another might be an urban development project below the size threshold, but involving the clean-up of highly-contaminated land in proximity to residential property which might be affected. Could it be argued that the mechanistic application of the threshold in such cases is contrary to EC law?

1   EIA Directive as amended, art 4(2).
2   See paras **2.28–2.38**.
3   Subject of course to projects in sensitive areas, where the thresholds do not apply.

3.65   In *Berkeley 2*[1] a planning inspector granted permission on appeal for a development of a building with 30 one or two bedroom flats at Mortlake. No EIA was required, as the 0.5 ha threshold for an urban development project had not been crossed, and the development was not in a 'sensitive area' as defined. Lady Berkeley challenged the decision on the basis that there was no power to grant permission. In the Court of Appeal, counsel for Lady Berkeley made two main submissions: first that the inspector had erred in not referring the decision on whether the development was EIA development to the Secretary of State, and secondly that if there was no obligation on the inspector to do so, then the EIA Directive had not been transposed correctly. Schiemann L J analysed the Directive and the European cases in terms of the tension between the purpose of thresholds and criteria being to render unnecessary an assessment of each individual project that comes forward, and the limitations on the discretion of member states in setting those thresholds and criteria.[2] Under reg 4(8) of the TCP(EIA) Regulations 1999 it is possible for the Secretary of State to direct that development of a description within Sch 2 is EIA development despite the fact that the relevant threshold or criterion is not met. Schiemann L J held however that the Secretary of State is never obliged to make such a direction.[3]

1   *Berkeley v Secretary of State for the Environment, Transport and the Regions and the London Borough of Richmond upon Thames and Berkeley Homes (West London) Ltd* [2002] JPL 224.
2   [2002] JPL 224 at 236, para 28. See also para **2.39** above.
3   [2002] JPL 224 at 239, para 39(5). From the context of the passage it seems clear, though unstated expressly, that Schiemann L J was at this point referring to the Secretary of State's obligation purely in terms of the domestic regulations.

3.66   On the fundamental issue of whether the transposition of the EIA Directive in relation to urban development projects was compliant with EC law, Schiemann LJ's judgment set out six points which the Court regarded as clear:[1]

1   The amended EIA Directive is not intended to prevent all development which is likely to have a significant effect on the environment. It is intended to improve the quality of the decision-making process in a group of cases. If the proposed development falls within that group, then EIA procedures are to be followed before permission is granted.

2   In respect of development falling within Annex I the Community has decided that the nature of the development itself is such that EIA procedures must always be followed.

3   In relation to development falling within Annex II the Community has recognised that in some cases it will be desirable to insist that the EIA procedures be gone through, but that this will not be desirable in all cases.

4   In relation to Annex II development the Community has, 'in accordance with the subsidiarity principle' (Recitals to EIA Directive) in principle left it to member states to identify the parameters of the group of development for which permission cannot be granted without EIA.

5   However, the Community has in Annex III set out selection criteria to be applied by member states in identifying those parameters. If a member state fails to apply those criteria then its resulting regulations will not be Community Law compliant.

6   The Secretaries of State in making the TCP(EIA) Regulations 1999 have expressly purported to have taken into account the Annex III selection criteria: the recital to the Regulations states that the Secretaries of State make the Regulations, 'having taken into account the selection criteria in Annex II to Council Directive 97/11/ EC'.

From this base, Schiemann LJ went on to hold that the Annex III criteria referred to a broader range of matters than just the size of the development. However, it did not follow logically from this that the thresholds set by member states had to refer to each or all of these matters.[2] Schiemann LJ accepted that in setting thresholds, member states are under a duty under art 2 of the EIA Directive to consider whether the criteria they have established will '... ensure that, before consent is given, projects *likely* to have *significant* effects on the environment'[3] will be subject to an EIA. In doing so the member states must take into account possible cumulative effects and the Annex III criteria. However, there was no reason to suppose that the Secretaries of State had failed to do this; nor was the end result either irrational or surprising.[4] The Court declined to refer the point to the ECJ.

1   [2002] JPL 224 at 240–241, para 47.
2   [2002] JPL 224 at 241, para 48.
3   Schiemann LJ's emphasis.
4   [2002] JPL 224 at 241, para 50. Schiemann LJ contrasted the position in Case C-392/96 *Commission v Ireland*, where the non-compliance with Community law was manifest: see para **2.37**.

3.67   Thus the *Berkeley 2* decision provides endorsement at Court of Appeal level, for the view that the size thresholds set for urban development projects are compliant with Community law.[1] The problem is that such thresholds can only be a blunt instrument; as Schiemann LJ himself pointed out, it is always possible to conceive of circumstances where there are special circumstances which could result in significant environmental effects.[2] This could arise from cumulative effects, or from particular circumstances relating to the location of the development, or from unusual complications such as contaminated land. If the domestic approach is examined, it is clear that some of the selection criteria in the EIA Directive, Annex II are reflected, for example in the concept of 'sensitive areas'. Others are not, most obviously cumulation with other projects,[3] but also for example whether the area likely to be affected is 'densely populated'.[4] A category such as 'urban development projects' could obviously encompass a huge range of possible circumstances and permutations, so that to press to its logical conclusion the approach that the member state must be satisfied in advance that application of the threshold would never lead to development with significant environmental effects, thus avoiding the requirements of EIA, would mean in reality that each case would have to be assessed on an individual case-by-case basis. This would negate the discretion expressly given by art 4(2) to make the determination through thresholds or criteria. The difficulty lies perhaps in the structure of the EIA Directive, in that the selection criteria in Annex III are in fact the same for both case-by-case examination and the setting of thresholds. Some of the criteria are simply not capable of being translated into thresholds, and it is arguable that what have to be considered are the '*relevant* selection criteria'.[5] Similarly, what has to be considered under art 2(1) in setting such criteria is whether significant effects are *likely*, not whether they are impossible. On this basis, it is understandable that the Court of Appeal declined to find that the 0.5 ha threshold was in breach of EC law. However, there remains the fact that in some case the environmental impact of an urban development project may arise from its height, rather than its footprint.[6] It would have been possible for some form of height threshold to be incorporated into Sch 2 for such projects, in the same way as for wind turbines and ski-lifts.[7] It may well be that this issue will arise in future cases.

1 The Court expressly confined its decision to such projects: see [2002] JPL 224 at 241, para 52.
2 [2002] JPL 224 at 241, para 49.
3 EIA Directive, Annex III (1), indent 2.
4 EIA Directive, Annex III (2), indent 3 (g).
5 EIA Directive, art 4(3).
6 An example given by counsel for Lady Berkeley was the London Eye.
7 See para **3.63** above.

3.68 What is perhaps the more problematic issue arising from *Berkeley 2*, assuming the size threshold to be lawful, is whether in any circumstances there is an obligation on the decision-maker to 'go behind' the relevant threshold in view of possible effects arising from special circumstances. Neither a local planning authority nor a planning inspector has power to require EIA for development which falls outside the the the TCP(EIA) Regulations 1999, Sch 2 thresholds; the Secretary of State however does have that residual power under reg 4(8). That power must have been inserted for some good reason; presumably because it was recognised that there might be cases where development falling outside the relevant Sch 2 threshold would still require EIA in order to comply with the Directive's requirements. The issue then arises as to in what circumstances a local planning authority or inspector should refer the issue to the Secretary of State to consider making a reg 4(8) direction. In *Berkeley 2* the suggestion was made in written submissions that such an examination should be carried out by the Secretary of State in every case; this was rejected as 'manifestly unsustainable' and was not pursued in oral submissions. However, the alternative (and much more attractive) submission was made that in cases where a plausible argument was made to the planning inspector that the Secretary of State might make a reg 4(8) direction, then the inspector should under reg 9(2) refer the question to the Secretary of State.[1] The Court of Appeal rejected this submission but, with respect, its reasons for doing so are unclear. The judgment focuses on the issue of compliance with EC law in setting the thresholds,[2] but this is logically a separate point to whether the thresholds allow the decision-taker to ignore possible significant effects which might justify making an exception in the interests of securing effective EIA. It might be asked how the Secretary of State is to exercise his power of direction under reg 4(8) unless the decision-taker refers the matter to him. What underlies the Court of Appeal decision in *Berkeley 2* is the assumption that there was no reason to suppose that the quality of the decision-making process would have been significantly improved by the carrying out of an EIA.[3] This however is contrary to the approach taken in deciding whether a decision should be quashed for non-compliance with EIA requirements, where it is certainly no answer to say that the EIA process would have made no difference, or would not have improved the decision-making process.

1   Compare *Evans v First Secretary of State* [2003] EWHC 411 (Admin) [2003] 1 P&CR 467 (para 3.16 above) where the Secretary of State had previously made a direction.
2   See paras 2.28–2.38 above.
3   [2002] JPL 224 at 241, para 51.

Contaminated sites

3.69   A case which illustrates the potential difficulties of the approach of the Court of Appeal in *Berkeley 2* is *Gillespie v First Secretary of State and Bellway Urban Renewal Southern,*[1] discussed more fully below.[2] In that case a successful challenge was made to a decision to grant planning permission for predominantly residential development of a 3.5 ha former gasworks site in Stepney. Objectors to the proposal had argued that no proper EIA had been undertaken on the issue of decontamination of the site, and possible effects of decontamination measures on adjoining residential areas. The inspector and Secretary of State both concluded that EIA was not required. Since the development was over the 0.5 ha threshold for urban development projects, the question was whether it was likely to have significant effects, an issue discussed below. At first instance Richards J held that the decision not to require EIA was flawed, and that the suitability and effectiveness of proposed decontamination measures should have been discussed and assessed in the context of EIA procedures. Responding to a submission from counsel for the first Secretary of State that such a conclusion would mean that an EIA was required in the case of any development on contaminated land, Richards J indicated that this would not be a conclusion that caused him any alarm:[3]

> 'There are legitimate public concerns about the risks of development on contaminated land and, although that is not in itself a reason for requiring an EIA, the EIA procedure should ensure that the public is fully informed of, and given a full opportunity to comment on, the extent of those risks and the measures proposed to meet them.'

While the case did not involve consideration of the threshold issue, the risks and effects referred to by Richards J could apply equally whether the site was above or below the 0.5 ha threshold. It is suggested therefore that where a planning authority has reason to believe that development of a contaminated site of less than 0.5 ha is likely to give rise to significant environmental effects, it should invite the developer to submit an ES dealing with those issues on a voluntary basis, or if the developer refuses, refer the matter to the Secretary of State to consider making a direction under the TCP(EIA) Regulations 1999, reg 4(8).

1   [2003] EWHC 8 (Admin), [2003] 1 P & CR 745; upheld by the Court of Appeal [2003] EWCA Civ 400, [2003] 14 LS Gaz R 30.
2   At para **3.81** et seq.
3   [2003] EWHC 8 (Admin), [2003] 1 P & CR 745, para 80.

Likely significant effects

3.70   The ultimate stage in the screening process for TCP(EIA) Regulations 1999, Sch 2 development is to consider whether it is 'likely to have significant effects on the environment by virtue of factors such as its nature, size or location'.[1] It is this which results in Sch 2 development becoming 'EIA development' and as such, subject to the EIA process. In making the decision, the authority must take into account such of the selection criteria set out in Sch 3 as are relevant to the development.[2] It is this exercise which has proven to be particularly fraught with difficulty and potential legal pitfalls for planning authorities and developers alike, as the cases referred to in the following paragraphs make clear.

1   TCP(EIA) Regulations 1999, reg 2(1).
2   TCP(EIA) Regulations 1999, reg 4(5).

3.71   An initial and very important point is that the exercise of judgment on likely significant effects is a formal process, and must be treated as such. This bears on the procedures for delegation, and on the actual process and its documentation.

Delegation

3.72   As to delegation, it will most often be the case that screening decisions are taken by planning officers. Such decisions are important, and if they are to be taken by officers, then the proper delegation procedures must be followed. In *R v St Edmundsbury Borough Council, ex p Walton*[1] a planning application was submitted by the brewers Greene King for the construction of a new access road to their brewery. It was accompanied by traffic, ecological and landscape reports, but no ES was prepared. The decision that the development was not likely to have significant environmental effects, and thus that EIA was not required, was taken by a council planning officer. However, there was no formal delegation for this purpose. Hooper J held that if a planning authority wishes to delegate such an important decision to an officer, it must do so by formal procedures. The decision could not be regarded as a purely 'procedural' matter. Accordingly the officer's decision and the planning permission were both quashed. This decision may be compared with that in *R v Powys County Council, ex p Andrews*,[2] where the defect resulted from failure by the Director of Architecture and Planning to consult with certain members of the Planning Committee before taking the screening decision. Although this meant that the decision not to require EIA was taken without the necessary power, Jowitt J exercised his discretion not to quash the planning permission; in so doing he asked himself in reality,[3]

'... whether the applicants have lost a real, as opposed to a fanciful, chance of obtaining a decision from the planning authority that an environmental assessment should be obtained.'

Looking at all the evidence before him, Jowitt J concluded that no real chance had been lost by the failure of the Director to consult members. He appears to have been particularly influenced by a letter from the Secretary of State in response to a request by local residents that he direct EIA be required. The Secretary of State had concluded that the development (an extension of a quarry) did not require EIA because it was not likely to have significant effects on the environment. In these circumstances, even if the local planning authority had required an ES to be prepared, the developer faced with that requirement would have been entitled to seek a direction form the Secretary of State. Thus while judicial discretion may in some cases provide a way to avoid the drastic consequences of defective delegation, it should not be assumed that it will assist, particularly in the light of the courts' more recent hard line on the use of discretion in EIA cases.[4] The need for circumspection in the exercise of delegated powers, and the limitations of judicial discretion in relation to such defects, have been emphasised by the Court of Appeal in *R (Carlton-Conway) v London Borough of Harrow*.[5]

1   [1999] Env LR 879, [1999] 3 PLR 51.
2   [1997] Env LR 170.
3   [1997] Env LR 170 at 187.
4   See para **8.44**.
5   [2002] EWCA Civ 927, [2002] JPL 1216.

Formality

3.73   Decisions on screening should be taken in a formal and principled way, and the reasoning should preferably be documented if future problems are to be avoided. As discussed below, there is no obligation in the TCP(EIA) Regulations 1999 to give reasons for a screening opinion that EIA is *not* required. However, as the ODPM's guidance points out:[1]

'... it would be prudent for the authority to make and retain for its own use a clear record of the issues considered and the reasons for its decision. This would be very useful in the vent of any challenge to the planning decision based on EIA grounds.'

The importance of rigour and discipline in the process is well illustrated by the case of *R (Lebus) v South Cambridgeshire District Council*.[2] In considering an application for a large egg production unit, senior planning officers held an informal meeting, at which no notes were kept, where it was decided that EIA was not required. In response to a letter from solicitors acting for local residents, various reasons were given as to why EIA was not required. Subsequently the council prepared a checklist table of environmental impacts which was put on the planning file, and the views of officers that EIA was not required were recorded in various committee reports. Sullivan J held that none of this constituted the adoption of a screening opinion. There was no document constituting such an opinion, and it was not permissible to engage in a paperchase to try and assemble such an opinion from the various materials before the court.[3]

1   *Note on EIA Directive for Local Planning Authorities* (June 2002).
2   [2002] EWHC 2009 (Admin), [2003] 2 P & CR 71.
3   [2002] EWHC 2009 (Admin)), [2003] 2 P & CR 71 at paras 37, 38. Compare however the approach of Elias J in *British Telecommunications plc v Gloucester City Council* (para **3.76** below).

All significant effects are relevant

3.74   One mistake which has been made by local planning authorities is to proceed on the basis that only significant *negative* effects are relevant to the screening exercise. This is not what the TCP(EIA) Regulations 1999 in fact say. The definition of EIA development refers to 'significant effects', not 'significant adverse' or 'negative' effects. (This can be compared with the definition of changes and extensions as Sch 2 development, where there is express reference to 'significant adverse effects'.)[1] The reason not to confine the screening process to adverse effects is clear. If confined, it would be open to the planning authority carrying out the screening process to conclude that individual effects would not be adverse or that the overall impact would be neutral or even beneficial, thereby avoiding the scrutiny and public dialogue as to the nature of effects and the appropriate mitigating measures which the EIA process is designed to facilitate.

1   See para **3.41** above.

3.75   This appears most clearly from the decision in *British Telecommunications plc v Gloucester City Council*.[1] In that case outline planning permission was granted for the first phase of redevelopment of the Blackfriars area of Gloucester, a scheme which had been mooted since 1987. The initial development included a multiplex cinema, cafes, bars, restaurants and a multi-storey car park. The Blackfriars area was of Roman and Medieval archaeological interest, and included some notable listed buildings. However, despite this, the area had 'extremely poor' visual and townscape qualities, and a significant proportion of vacant or unused buildings and surface-level parking.[2] The challenge to the permission, and to related listed building and conservation area consents, was made by British Telecommunications and another landowner, who were affected by compulsory purchase orders consequent upon the grant of planning permission. One of the heads of challenge was on EIA grounds. The application for outline permission did not include an ES; no screening opinion was sought, and the local planning authority did not require an ES under the TCP(ΛEE) Regulations 1988, reg 9, which were then applicable. There was some correspondence between solicitors acting for the developer and the planning officer with day-to-day responsibility for the application; the officer was of the view that an ES should be prepared, but the solicitors put forward various reasons, relying in particular on Circular 15/88, why it need not. The matter was then considered by a more senior planning officer, Mr Scott, who agreed with the view of the solicitors for the developer. No formal note of the decision was made, nor was the view in fact communicated to the solicitors.

1   [2001] EWHC Admin 1001, [2002] JPL 993.
2   [2001] EWHC Admin 1001, [2002] JPL 993 at 997, para 4 (Elias J).

3.76   Elias J held that a decision had in fact been taken by Mr Scott, despite the lack of formality, though it was 'certainly most unfortunate that no formal note of the decision was made'.[1] However, he went on to find the decision to be flawed in a number of important respects. For present purposes, the most important finding was that the planning authority had approached screening by asking the wrong question — namely whether the development was likely to have significant adverse effects on the environment. As Elias J pointed out, the TCP(EIA) Regulations 1999 draw a distinction between significant effects and significant adverse effects, and there was no justification for treating the term 'significant effects' in the definition of Sch 2 projects as qualified by the word 'adverse'.[2] This conclusion was buttressed by the purpose of the EIA Directive in requiring an

'... inclusive and democratic procedure ... in which the public, however misguided or wrong headed its views may be, is given the opportunity to express its opinion on the environmental issues.'[3]

It was implicit in this process that individuals can 'form their own judgment on the significance of the environmental issues raised by the project'.[4] As Elias J put it:[5]

'This involves a recognition that it is not always clear whether an impact is beneficial or not. In particular, where the development of sites of historic or architectural interest are concerned, there will generally be a range of views held about the artistic and aesthetic features of the scheme and whether they best preserve the true character of the area which is the subject of the development. It would frustrate the process of debate about the merits of such a development if the planning authority could determine that the impact was beneficial and as a consequence rule that no environmental statement was needed. In this context benefit, like beauty, is in the eye of the beholder.'

Accordingly, it is not open to a planning authority to conclude that EIA is not required because in its view a particular significant effect is beneficial rather than adverse; nor (perhaps more pertinently) to reach such a conclusion on the basis that the positive aspects of the proposal outweigh the adverse effects.[6]

1   [2002] JPL 993 at 1007, para 57. Compare however the approach of Sullivan J in *R (Lebus) v South Cambridgeshire District Council* (para **3.73** above).
2   [2002] JPL 993 at 1009, paras 64–67.
3   [2002] JPL 993 at 1009–1010, para 68.

4   Elias J was here quoting from the HMSO Publication, *Environmental Assessment: A Guide to the Procedures* (1989) p 4.
5   [2002] JPL 993 at 1010, para 69.
6   [2002] JPL 993 at 1011, para 71. The same conclusion was stated obiter by Brooke LJ in *R (Barker) v Bromley London Borough Council* [2001] EWCA Civ 1766; [2002] Env LR 631, para 65 (decided the working day before judgment was handed down in *British Telecommunications plc v Gloucester*) and was shared by Deputy Judge George Bartlett QC in *R (Prophet) v York City Council* [2002] EWHC 588 (Admin), para 14.

Can mitigating measures render effects insignificant for screening purposes?

3.77   A planning authority faced with a proposal for development will be aware that should permission be granted, planning conditions will be imposed for the purpose of minimising potential adverse effects such as noise. Equally, there may be other forms of statutory control, such as an IPPC (Integrated Pollution Prevention and Control) Permit or a waste management licence, which will have that effect. To what extent is it open to the authority to take those controls into account at the screening stage to reach the conclusion that the development will not have significant environmental effects? The same issue may arise in the different context of whether adequate information has been provided as part of the environmental statement (ES).[1]

1   See paras 4.45–4.47

3.78   The issue arose in *British Telecommunications plc v Gloucester City Council*, discussed above.[1] The planning officer in that case took the view that it was likely that adequate steps could be taken to ensure that the development would have only a minimal impact on the archaeology of the site. There had been difficulties in evaluating part of the site in archaeological terms, because the owners would not allow access. Elias J held that it was not open to the planning authority to conclude that there would be significant effects, but for the scheme of mitigating measures to be put in place. The purpose of the EIA process was to enable public discussion to take place on the effectiveness of such measures, or indeed whether more effective measures might be put in place:[2]

'In my opinion ... the question whether or not there are likely to be significant environmental effects should be approached by asking whether these would be likely to result, absent some specific measures being taken to ameliorate or reduce them. If they would, the environmental statement is required and the mitigating measures must be identified in it.'

1   [2001] EWHC Admin 1001, [2002] JPL 993; see para **3.75** above.
2   [2001] EWHC Admin 1001, [2002] JPL 993 at 1011, para 73.

3.79   The same principle applies to controls under other legislation, whether it be on listed buildings, ancient monuments, pollution control, highways, nature conservation, or whatever. The existence of such controls of itself cannot justify a planning authority concluding that EIA is not required.[1] Again the *British Telecommunications plc v Gloucester City Council* case deals with this issue. Elias J regarded as rightly made a concession by counsel for the planning authority that it would be wrong to take account of separate listed building and conservation area controls in deciding whether EIA was required.[2] The ES should provide a single and accessible compilation of the relevant information; this would be frustrated if EIA was dealt with under related legislation.

1   As to the relationship between EIA and pollution control regimes, see also para **6.74** et seq.
2   [2001] EWHC Admin 1001, [2002] JPL 993 at 1012, para 75. Circular 15/88 had suggested (Annex A, para 17) that in relation to urban development schemes in sensitive locations such as historic town centres, listed building controls ensure that the effects on the built heritage are considered. The passage is not repeated in the corresponding guidance (paras A18–A19) in Circular 2/99.

3.80   The approach in *British Telecommunications plc v Gloucester City Council* was followed in other first instance cases. It was another basis for quashing the permission in *R (Lebus) v South Cambridgeshire District Council*.[1] The officers in that case (so far as their reasoning could be discerned) were held to have erred by approaching the matter on the basis that the significant adverse impacts could be rendered insignificant if suitable conditions were imposed. Sullivan J cited the relevant passages from *British Telecommunications v Gloucester* and said that the proper approach '... was to say that potentially this is a development which has significant adverse environmental implications: what are the measures that should be included in order to reduce or offset those adverse effects?'.[2] Sullivan J did however accept that each case will no doubt turn on its own facts, and stated that it may well be perfectly reasonable 'to envisage the operation of standard conditions and a reasonably managed development'.[3]

1   [2002] EWHC 2009 (Admin), [2003] 2 P & CR 71. See para **3.73** above.
2   [2002] EWHC 2009 (Admin), [2003] 2 P & CR 71, para 51.
3   [2002] EWHC 2009 (Admin), [2003] 2 P & CR 71, para 45.

3.81   The reference by Sullivan J to 'standard conditions' highlights a potential difficulty in pressing the *British Telecommunications v Gloucester* approach to its ultimate conclusion. Almost any development could give rise to significant environmental effects, in the course of construction if nothing else, if undertaken with complete disregard for local amenity in terms of noise, dust, waste disposal, hours of working, and so on. This issue was considered by the Court of Appeal in *Gillespie v First Secretary of State and Bellway Urban Renewal Southern*.[1] *Gillespie* concerned development of a former gasworks site, which was contaminated. It had been partially investigated, but a full picture of the contamination could not be obtained until large structures on the site had been removed. At first instance Richards J, while endorsing the *British Telecommunications v Gloucester* approach, discussed those problems.[2] He held that the Secretary of State's view that significant environmental effects were not likely must have been based in part on an assessment that the proposed remediation measures would be effective to prevent the significant environmental effects that would otherwise arise. Thus he fell into the *British Telecommunications v Gloucester* trap. Richards J put the point clearly as follows:[3]

> '... where an EIA is required, the regulatory scheme requires separate information to be provided on (i) likely significant environmental effects and (ii) measures to avoid, reduce or remedy the adverse effects, so as to enable the public to make representations on the suitability and effectiveness of the proposed remediation or mitigation measures. That suggests that, in deciding whether an EIA is required, the focus should be on likely significant environmental effects rather than on remediation or mitigation measures; and if a decision runs the two issues together and rest on the view that remediation measures will be effective to prevent otherwise significant effects, it deprives the public of the opportunity to make informed representations in accordance with the EIA procedures about the adequacy of such measures.'

1   [2003] EWCA Civ 400, [2003] 14 LS Gaz R 30.
2   [2003] EWHC 8 (Admin), [2003] 1 P & CR 475. This was a case based on the TCP(EIA) Regulations 1999, rather than the TCP(EAA) Regulations 1988 as in *British Telecommunications v Gloucester*.
3   [2003] EWHC 8 (Admin), [2003] 1 P & CR 475, para 73.

3.82   At the same time, Richards J acknowledged that the approach was not free from difficulties. It could not be right, he felt, that standard controls over matters such as noise and dust during construction were to be ignored when determining whether a development is likely to have significant effects.[1] Accepting there was a tension between the general reasoning in *British Telecommunications v Gloucester* and *Lebus*, and exceptions of this type, the matter was one of fact and degree, and the general approach was sound. In *Gillespie* the mitigating measures in question, involving the clean-up of potentially serious contamination, were clearly not just standard conditions, but were 'special and elaborate remediation measures'.[2]

1   [2003] EWHC 8 (Admin), [2003] 1 P & CR 475, at para 75. Richards J also referred (at para 75) to the similar approach adopted in relation to the adequacy of environmental statements by Sullivan J in *R v Rochdale Metropolitan Borough Council, ex p Milne* (2001) 81 P & CR 365, [2001] Env LR 406, [2001] JPL 470. See further para **6.55**.
2   [2003] EWHC 8 (Admin), [2003] 1 P & CR 475, para 79.

3.83   The Court of Appeal recognised the same tension in the cases. It rejected any test based on whether the mitigating condition in question could or could not be described as 'standard'.[1] The Court however, did not hold that mitigating measures were to be ignored in every case as a matter of law; rather it suggested a flexible and fact-sensitive approach. Pill L J held that the Secretary of State was not obliged to shut his eyes to the remedial measures submitted as part of the planning application, or to 'put into separate compartments the development proposal and the proposed remedial measures and consider only the first when making his screening decision'.[2] In so far as the judges in the first instance cases referred to above suggested otherwise, these views must be regarded as overruled, though Pill L J did not in any event read the decisions of Richards J and Sullivan J in that way.[3]

1   [2003] EWCA Civ 400, para 26 (Pill L J, Laws and Arden L J J agreeing).
2   [2003] EWCA Civ 400, para 36.
3   [2003] EWCA Civ 400, para 36. No reference was made in this context by Pill L J to the
     statement of Elias J in *British Telecommunications v Gloucester* (see para **3.78** above), which
     in the light of *Gillespie* appears to be stated too broadly.

3.84   Where the Secretary of State was held to have gone wrong was in assuming
that the existence of a condition requiring remediation necessarily provided a complete
answer to whether significant effects were likely. Fuller scrutiny was required.[1] This
involved looking at the extent of investigations, the impact of the development, the
nature of the proposed remedial measures, the extent to which they were particularised,
their complexity, and the prospects of their successful implementation.[2] The Secretary
of State should have considered the contingencies inherent in the proposed condition,
and the uncertainties of successful implementation. Instead, he had simply assumed a
successful outcome. Thus he had applied the wrong test; the Court was not saying
that had he applied the correct test he could not have rationally have concluded that
the project was unlikely to have significant effects.[3]

1   [2003] EWCA Civ 400, paras 39–40.
2   [2003] EWCA Civ 400, para 39.
3   [2003] EWCA Civ 400, paras 40–41.

3.85   While the basic principle from the case is clear, the three Court of Appeal
judges in *Gillespie* all stated their reasons in slightly different ways, which may lead to
the need for clarification in future. As indicated above, Pill LJ confined himself to
saying that the Secretary of State had applied an incorrect test. Laws LJ stated the
reasons in his own terms as follows:[1]

> 'Where the Secretary of State is contemplating an application for planning
> permission for development which, but for remedial measures, may or will have
> significant environmental effects, I do not say that he must inevitably cause an
> EIA to be conducted. Prospective remedial measures may have been put before
> him whose nature, availability and effectiveness are already plainly established
> and plainly uncontroversial; though I should have thought there is little likelihood
> of such a state of affairs in relation to a development of any complexity. But if
> prospective remedial measures are not plainly established and not plainly
> uncontroversial, then as it seems to me the case calls for an EIA. If then the
> Secretary of State were to decline to conduct an EIA, as it seems to me he would
> pre-empt the very form of enquiry contemplated by the Directive and Regulations;
> and to that extent he would frustrate the purpose of the legislation.'

1   [2003] EWCA Civ 400, para 46.

3.86   Arden LJ agreed with both Pill and Laws LJJ, but added her own view that
whether proposed remedial measures could properly be taken into account turns not
on the complexity or controversiality of the development, but on the nature of the
proposed remedial measures:[1]

'Such measures can be taken into account if, fairly considered, they are of themselves unlikely to have significant effects on the environment because, for example, they are of limited impact or well-established to be easily achievable within the process of the development.'

1   [2003] EWCA Civ 400, para 49.

3.87   To put the matter in context it is worth recalling that the remediation scheme in *Gillespie* was to tackle serious soil contamination, on a site in close proximity to dense residential development and a school, where the success or failure of the clean-up measures (and the way in which they were carried out) could have very serious implications for the environment and human health.[1] Effectively the condition involved having a 'temporary contaminated waste treatment and disposal facility' in that area.[2] It can easily be appreciated how the assumption in that case that 'all will be well' would deprive local residents of the protective benefits of the EIA process. It can be anticipated that difficult borderline case may arise where the issue is what level of certainty that planning authority must have as to the effectiveness of the proposed measures and the absence of adverse effects arising from them. The passage from Laws LJ's judgment, cited above, suggests that a high degree of assurance will be required and that if there is any doubt, then EIA should follow.

1   See the first instance decision, [2003] EWHC 8 (Admin), paras 21 and 34.
2   See the letter from the Greater London Authority, summarised by Richards J at [2003] EWHC 8 (Admin), para 34.

3.88   It is foreseeable that local residents may well not be satisfied by a simple assurance by a planning officer that he considers that proposed mitigation will prevent, and will itself not give rise to, significant effects. The mitigation measures are themselves, as pointed out by Elias J in *British Telecommunications v Gloucester*, an important part of the EIA exercise.[1] It might be said that in such cases the decision of the planning authority will require careful scrutiny if the objectives of the Directive are not to be compromised. Whether in such cases the courts will be content to judge the decision simply on an irrationality test remains to be seen. However, the practical answer is that planning authorities should tread very carefully when taking proposed mitigating measures into account and that the safest course may well be to require EIA in anything but the most straightforward of cases.

1   See para **3.22**.

Conditions to minimise non-significant effects

3.89   Another case decided by Richards J, *R (Jones) v Mansfield District Council*,[1] addressed somewhat similar issues. This was a case under the TCP(AEE) Regulations 1988 and involved the grant of permission for the development of a 28 ha site as an industrial estate. A variety of factors led the planning officer to conclude that EIA was not required, and these were referred to in an initial report to committee. A second report referred in detail to various ecological surveys carried out, and concluded that there would not be likely significant adverse effects (in particular to over-wintering golden plover populations). Various conditions were imposed on the permission to minimise adverse ecological effects, including further surveys before development was commenced. The case predominantly deals with the separate issue of the amount of information and the degree of certainty necessary to reach a conclusion that significant effects are not likely, considered below.[2] However, it is also helpful in indicating that it may be appropriate, consistently with the approach in *British Telecommunications v Gloucester* and *Lebus*, having determined that such effects are not likely, to impose conditions designed to reduce the possible effects still further. As Richards J found in that case, the planning authority had sufficient information that it was able properly to conclude that the development was unlikely to have significant effects in relation to bats. The permission was subject to conditions and an undertaking which included additional survey work and protective measures in relation to bats. Richards J said:[3]

'Having regard to the information already available, it was reasonable to conclude that the development was unlikely to have significant effects in relation to bats; but it was still appropriate to adopt further measures to ensure that, if there were any bats on the site, account was taken of them in the timing of the work carried out and by way of other mitigation.'

1   [2003] EWHC 7 (Admin), [2003] P & CR 504.
2   See para **3.94**.
3   [2003] EWHC 7 (Admin), [2003] P & CR 504, at para 59.

What is a significant effect?

3.90   As has been stressed previously, in taking screening decisions under the TCP(EIA) Regulations 1999, the planning authority must take into account such of the selection criteria under Sch 3 as are relevant to the development.[1] These criteria do not in themselves provide detailed guidance, but are simply a checklist of characteristics relating to the development, its location and its potential impact. Circular 2/99 contains more detailed guidance, both in general terms and in relation to particular descriptions of development. Generally, it advises that there are three main types of case in which EIA for Sch 2 projects is likely to be required:[2]
(a)   major development that is of more than local importance;
(b)   development proposed for particularly environmentally sensitive or vulnerable locations; and
(c)   development with unusually complex and potentially hazardous environmental effects.

More specifically, Annex A to the Circular gives indicative criteria or thresholds for each class of Sch 2 development which indicate 'the types of case in which, in the Secretary of State's view, EIA is more likely to be required'.[3] Thus for example in relation to wind farms, para A15 states that EIA is more likely to be required for commercial development of five or more turbines, or more than 5 MW of new generating capacity. For urban development projects, para A18 states that EIA is unlikely to be required for the redevelopment of land unless the new development is on a significantly greater scale than the previous use (or the types of impact are of a markedly different nature or there is a high level of contamination) and para A19 suggests that for sites which have not been previously intensively developed, the scheme is more likely to require EIA if the site is over 5 ha in size, or it would provide over 10,000 m² of new commercial floorspace, or would have 'significant urbanising effects in a previously non-urbanised area' (eg over 1,000 new dwellings).

1   TCP(EIA) Regulations 1999, reg 4(5).
2   Department of the Environment Circular 2/99, Welsh Office Circular 10/99, *Environmental Impact Assessment*, para 33.
3   Department of the Environment Circular 2/99, para 44.

3.91   It should go without saying that these guidelines are not intended to be applied rigidly, as indeed Circular 2/99 makes clear.[1] It should not be assumed either that development outside them cannot have significant effects; or conversely that development within them must have such effects. The acid test is whether the proposed development, in its proposed location, may have significant effects. The guidance in the Circular is simply that — guidance, not a substitute for the local planning authority's own judgment. As such there is no objection to the planning authority having regard to it, together with other relevant considerations.[2]

1   Department of the Environment Circular 2/99, para 44.
2   See *R v Powys County Council, ex p Andrews* [1997] Env LR 170 at 175.

Effects on an individual's amenity

3.92   EIA is based on the likelihood of significant effects on the environment. This is not necessarily the same thing as effects on the amenity of a limited number of neighbours of the proposed development, material as that may be in planning terms. These points are illustrated by the decision of Sullivan J in *R (Malster) v Ipswich Borough Council and Ipswich Town Football Club*.[1] Mrs Malster was concerned at the development of a new North Stand at Ipswich Town FC. There would be a significant shadowing effect from the development on a few properties adjacent to the stand, but only two properties (not including hers) would as a result fail to meet the authority's standards on shadowing. Sullivan J put it this way:[2]

'The 1999 Regulations are concerned to protect the environment in the public interest. Whilst this may have the effect of avoiding harm to residential amenity, the purpose of the 1999 Regulations is not to protect the amenity of individual dwelling-houses. There may be a "significant" impact upon a particular dwelling or dwellings without there being any likely "significant effect on the environment" for the purposes of the Regulations.'

It would therefore seem to be an issue of fact and degree as to the point at which effects on the amenity of a sufficient number of people may be capable of being regarded as an effect on the environment.

1   [2001] EWHC 711 (Admin), [2002] PLCR 251.
2   [2001] EWHC 711 (Admin), [2002] PLCR 251 at para 73.

ADEQUACY OF INFORMATION FOR SCREENING

3.93   Screening decisions may arise in various contexts. If a local planning authority is faced with a request for a screening opinion under the TCP(EIA) Regulations 1999, reg 5, then it will have the minimum information provided for by reg 5(2).[1] If it considers that it has not been provided with sufficient detail to adopt an opinion, it may notify in writing the points on which it requires further information.[2] If the screening decision arises in the context of a planning application submitted without an ES, and the local planning authority considers it requires further information to reach a screening decision, again it can notify the applicant of the further points on which it requires information.[3] These provisions raise the issue of how much information a planning authority needs for the purpose of deciding whether significant environmental effects are likely.

1   See para **3.12** above.
2   TCP(EIA) Regulations 1999, reg 5(3).
3   TCP(EIA) Regulations 1999, reg 5(3) as applied by reg 7(1).

3.94   The issue was addressed by Richards J in the case of *R (Jones) v Mansfield District Council*, referred to above.[1] While the question of likely significant effects calls for an exercise of judgment on the part of the planning authority, there is a 'logically prior question' for the authority, namely whether it has sufficient information to enable it to form a sensible judgment.[2] Richards J regarded a number of factors as being relevant to that issue. In particular, the TCP(EIA) Regulations 1999 contemplate that less information will be available at the screening stage than at the later stage of substantive EIA; reg 5 for example contemplates a speedy screening decision based on relatively limited information.[3] Indeed, were it otherwise there would be the strange situation where EIA was necessary in order to determine whether or not EIA was necessary. Whether sufficient information is available for the purpose of screening is a matter for the authority, subject to review on *Wednesbury* principles.[4] Richards J summarised the overall position as follows:[5]

> 'The authority must make an informed judgment, on the basis of the information available to it and having regard to any uncertainties that may exist, as to the likelihood of significant environmental effects. The gaps and uncertainties may or may not make it impossible reasonably to conclude that there is no likelihood of significant environmental effects. Everything depends on the circumstances of the individual case.'

1   [2003] EWHC 7 (Admin), [2003] 1 P & CR 504. See para **3.89**.

2   [2003] EWHC 7 (Admin), [2003] 1 P & CR 504, para 48.
3   [2003] EWHC 7 (Admin), [2003] 1 P & CR 504, para 49(ii).
4   [2003] EWHC 7 (Admin), [2003] 1 P & CR 504, para 49(iv).
5   [2003] EWHC 7 (Admin), [2003] 1 P & CR 504, para 52.

3.95   The alleged 'gaps and uncertainties' in *Jones* related to the presence of species such as bats and golden plover. In both cases it was held that there was sufficient information before the committee to enable it to conclude that it was unlikely there would be significant effects.[1] Although it was intended there would be further surveys, there was information to enable the committee to be satisfied that significant environmental effects were likely to be disclosed by those further surveys.[2]

1   [2003] EWHC 7 (Admin) paras 57, 58, 65.
2   [2003] EWHC 7 (Admin) paras 62, 65.

3.96   An alternative way of dealing with uncertainties (though the information available in *Jones* made this unnecessary) would be to consider the issue on 'worst case' assumptions, ie that birds or bats would be present, and on that basis to consider whether the effects on such birds or bats would be significant.[1]

1   [2003] EWHC 7 (Admin), [2003] 1 P & CR 504, para 65.

3.97   Similarly in *R (Gillespie) v First Secretary of State*[1] Richards J at first instance held that the Secretary of State's decision that sufficient information was held to determine that significant effects were not likely was subject to review only on *Wednesbury* grounds. Considered in that way, the First Secretary of State had enough information concerning site conditions and proposed remediation to be reasonably entitled to conclude that this was sufficient for screening purposes, despite the fact that parts of the site could not be fully investigated until development commenced and structures were dismantled.[2] The error of the First Secretary of State instead lay in how he had dealt with the proposed remediation measures in determining whether the effects were likely to be significant.[3]

1   [2003] EWHC 8 (Admin), [2003] 1 P & CR 475, para 83(i). See para **3.81** above.
2   [2003] EWHC 8 (Admin), [2003] 1 P & CR 475, paras 83(ii) and (iii).
3   See para **3.84**.

3.98   The issue of whether there is sufficient information for screening purposes can arise in a particularly problematic form where outline planning applications are concerned. The point is somewhat akin to that which arises with outline applications in relation to the adequacy of the ES in cases such as *R v Rochdale Metropolitan Borough Council, ex p Tew*[1] and troubled Elias J in the *British Telecommunications v Gloucester City Council* case.[2] The application in that case was for outline permission and matters of design, external appearance and landscaping were reserved. Matters of appearance were important because of the architectural sensitivity of the setting. Having stated that the authority's view on whether it had sufficient information could only be upset on *Wednesbury* grounds,[3] Elias J was not satisfied that the relevant officer had ever properly turned his mind to the question of whether sufficient information was available and was strongly inclined to the view that in the circumstances the officer could not have properly concluded there was sufficient information:[4]

'In a situation where the development relates to a conservation area which is a sensitive site of high archaeological, historical and architectural interest, I find it difficult to see how the likely potential effects can be confidently determined without information about the style and design and, although to a lesser extent, the external appearance of the buildings and landscaping. The proposed development would plainly be capable of affecting the cultural heritage. It seems to me unlikely that information about siting and design alone give sufficient details to enable these effects to be determined. It is true that there was an illustrative design, but that cannot as a matter of law be relied upon when determining the potential effects since the ultimate design may depart significantly from it.'

However, having said that, Elias J was not willing, in the absence of expert or other evidence, to find that the lack of information on design must *inevitably* mean that in a conservation area no proper assessment could be made.[5] The decision could therefore not be overturned on *Wednesbury* grounds.

1   [2001] JPL 54, [2000] Env LR 1. See para **6.49** above.
2   [2001] EWHC Admin 1001, [2002] JPL 993. See para **3.75** above.
3   [2001] EWHC Admin 1001, [2002] JPL 993 at 1012, para 78.
4   [2001] EWHC Admin 1001, [2002] JPL 993 at 1013, para 80.
5   [2001] EWHC Admin 1001, [2002] JPL 993 at 1014, para 86.

CHALLENGING SUBSTANTIVE DECISIONS ON SCREENING

3.99   The general consensus from the cases is that a decision by the planning authority that a development is or is not likely to have significant environmental effects is subject to review on *Wednesbury* grounds.[1] In *R v Swale Borough Council, ex p RSPB*, Simon Brown J had stated that questions of classification of development as falling within the EIA regime are essentially questions of fact and degree, not law:[2]

'The decision whether any particular development is or is not within the Scheduled descriptions is exclusively for the planning authority in question, subject only to *Wednesbury* challenge.'

The fullest judicial discussion of the issue occurs in the judgment of Sullivan J in *R (Malster) v Ipswich Borough Council*,[3] where it had been argued that the question of whether a development was likely to have significant environmental effects was one of 'jurisdictional fact' on which the court could submit its own view for that of the planning authority. Sullivan J rejected that submission. He held that the TCP(EIA) Regulations 1999 entrust the screening decision to the planning authority:[4]

'A detailed knowledge of the locality and expertise in assessing the environmental effects of different kinds of development are both essential in answering that question, which is pre-eminently a matter of judgment and degree rather than a question of fact. Unlike the planning authority, the court does not possess such knowledge and expertise.'[5]

1   See *R (Gillespie) v First Secretary of State* [2003] EWHC 8 (Admin), [2003] 1 P & CR 475, para 10; *R (Jones) v Mansfield District Council* [2003] EWHC 7 (Admin), [2003] 1 P & CR 504, para 7; *R (Goodman) v London Borough of Lewisham* [2003] EWCA Civ 140, [2003] 13 LS Gaz R 28, para 9.
2   [1991] PLR 6 – Compare however the Court of Appeal in *R (Goodman) v London Borough of Lewisham* [2003] EWCA Civ 140 para 3.47 above.
3   [2001] EWHC 711 (Admin), [2002] PLCR 251. See para **3.92** above.
4   [2001] EWHC 711 (Admin), [2002] PLCR 251, para 61.
5   The lack of such specialist expertise in Sullivan J's view rendered the situation quite different to that in New South Wales, where the Specialist Land and Environment Court could properly adopt such an interventionist approach: see *Timbarra Protection Coalition v Ross Mining* [1999] NSWCA 8 (New South Wales Court of Appeal).

3.100   A similar unwillingness to interfere with an authority's decision appears from *R (Kathro) v. Rhonnda Cynon Taff County Borough Council*,[1] a decision of Richards J dealing also with human rights issues. The project was a community learning centre covering 11.5 ha of an undeveloped valley. The authority issued a screening opinion saying EIA was not required on the basis that no significant effects on traffic, biodiversity, ecology or pollution were likely, and that visual effects would not extend beyond the immediate locality of the site. Extensive evidence was before the court from the case officer and a planning consultant acting for the claimants. It was held to be clear on the evidence that the authority had given careful consideration to the matter, and the conclusion that it was not EIA development was reasonably open to it.

1   [2001] EWHC Admin 527, [2002] JPL 304

3.101   It should be noted that the straight *Wednesbury* test will not necessarily apply to every aspect of screening. It does not apply, as pointed out above, to decisions as to the meaning of descriptions of Scheduled development,[1] and there are doubts as to how it would apply to decisions on screening which involve taking mitigating measures into account.[2] The irrationality test was applied by Turner J in *BAA plc v Secretary of State for Transport, Local Government and the Regions* to the issue of whether developments should be considered together for screening purposes.[3]

1   See para **3.47**.
2   See para **3.88**.
3   [2002] EWHC 1920 (Admin), para 71; see para **3.35** above.

Reasoning

3.102   Where a local planning authority adopts a screening opinion, or the Secretary of State makes a screening direction, to the effect that development is EIA development, the opinion or direction must be accompanied by 'a written statement giving clearly and precisely the full reasons for that conclusion'.[1] There is no statutory obligation to give reasons for an opinion or direction that EIA is *not* required. In *R v Secretary of State for the Environment, Transport and the Regions and Parcelforce, ex p Marson*[2] the Court of Appeal on an application for permission for judicial review, in considering the TCP(AEE) Regulations 1988, refused to import any general duty to give express reasons for a negative opinion, and found that reasons had in fact been given, albeit in summary form.[3] Pill LJ set out the Court's reasoning in 11 points.[4] Of particular interest is the suggestion by Pill LJ that it would be difficult to identify a more elaborate form of wording 'which could sensibly prove the negative averment that an environmental assessment is not required'. Moreover, further 'gratuitous comment' by the Secretary of State to support the view that EIA was not required could possibly 'prejudice the local authority decision-maker against the environmental interest which it is the object of [Mr Marson] to protect'.[5]

1   TCP(EIA) Regulations 1999, reg 4(6).
2   [1998] Env LR 761, [1998] 3 PLR 90.
3   If so, such reasons were extremely summary, since the opinion merely stated that in the Secretary of State's opinion the development (a 17 ha parcels handling facility near Coventry airport) was unlikely to have significant effects by virtue of factors such as its nature, size or location.
4   [1998] Env LR 761 at 769–770.
5   [1998] Env LR 761 at 770, points (9) and (10).

3.103   It was argued in *Marson*[1] that an obligation to give reasons applied as a result of Community law, on the basis that individuals had rights to ensure that EIA was undertaken in appropriate cases, and that such rights could not be protected effectively unless reasons were given; in the absence of reasons, no proper decision could be taken as to whether to seek judicial review, and there would be no effective recourse to the courts.[2] These submissions were rejected by the Court on the basis that what was involved was a preliminary procedure involving an exercise of judgment and discretion by the decision-maker. There was no bar to a judicial review of the decision, in relation to which considerable information was available, nor was there anything to prevent the third party from raising environmental issues as material considerations in the normal way prior to the grant of planning permission. Accordingly the 'fundamental right' relied on by Mr Marson was 'far removed' from the fundamental rights of free access to employment considered by the ECJ in the cases relied on by Mr Marson.[4]

1   [1998] Env LR 761 at 767.
2   Relying on Case C-70/95 *Sodemare SA v Regione Lombardia* [1997] ECR I-3395, para 19, and Case 222/86 *UNECTEF v Heylens* [1987] ECR 4097, para 14.
3   [1998] Env LR 761 at 769–70, points (3)–(7).
4   The issue in *Heylens* related to the refusal to recognise a diploma qualification of the national of another member state.

3.104 It might be thought that the reasoning in *Marson* could require reappraisal in the light of the decision of the House of Lords in *Berkeley 1*, stressing the importance of the individual's right to participate in the formal EIA process.[1] Indeed, such reappraisal formed part of the judgment of Richards J in *Gillespie*.[2] Richards J, like the Court of Appeal in *Marson*, regarded the line of cases in the ECJ on 'fundamental rights' as distinguishable. Perhaps more importantly, Richards J did not regard the lack of reasons as seriously prejudicing the ability to obtain judicial review, and *Marson* was still regarded as good law, despite the partial inconsistency of its approach with *Berkeley 1*:[3]

> 93. ... importantly, effective judicial review is possible in this case without any further statement of reasons. The material upon which the Secretary of State's judgment was based is fully known to the parties and the lawfulness and rationality of that judgment can be challenged. Indeed, the claimant's success on ground 1 is a prime illustration of the availability of effective judicial review.
>
> 94. Although the judgment of the Court of Appeal in *Marson* was on a permission application, it was a detailed judgment and is of strong persuasive authority. I accept that the decision of the House of Lords in *Berkeley* has undermined part of the reasoning, namely reliance on the fact that the applicant had the opportunity to make representations on the environmental considerations and the authority was supplied with information on those considerations. But that does not affect the balance of the reasoning, the broad thrust of which seems to still to hold good.'

1   [2001] 2 AC 603.
2   [2003] EWHC 8 (Admin), [2003] 1 P & CR 475.
3   [2003] EWHC 8 (Admin), [2003] 1 P & CR 475, paras 93–94. It may be noted however that in *R (Prophet) v York City Council* [2002] EWHC 588 (Admin) Deputy Judge George Bartlett QC referred to *Berkeley* as support for his view that in the particular circumstances of that case (see para **3.107** below) reasons for any view that EIA was not required should be given.

3.105 It is still perhaps a moot point whether arguments could arise at this stage under the European Convention on Human Rights, art 6(1), on the basis that the civil rights of a third party to participate in the EIA process are being determined, and that fairness requires that reasons be given in order that a view can be taken on whether there are grounds for judicial review of the decision. Article 6(1) was raised in *Marson*,[1] but the Court's decision centred on the question of whether fundamental rights under Community law were involved rather than on the human rights issue. Given sufficiently strong facts, it is possible that the human rights issue may arise in future cases, but the facts would probably need to be very striking to give a realistic prospect of success. Implementation of the UNECE Aarhus Convention on public participation and information[2] may well require reconsideration of this issue.

1   [1998] Env LR 761 at 768.
2   See para **1.16** above.

3.106 In summary, therefore, there is currently no legal obligation to give reasons for a screening opinion that EIA is not required. However, it may well be sensible as part of the process of good administration to provide such reasons, but in the knowledge that where they are given they will be subject to scrutiny by the court.[1] Certainly the courts are more likely to be impressed by reasons given contemporaneously than those which are only put forward later in response to proceedings.

1   For example as in *R (Lebus) v South Cambridgeshire District Council* [2002] EWHC 2009 (Admin), [2003] 2 P & CR 71, para 39. See para **3.63** above.

'RETROSPECTIVE' SCREENING

3.107   In cases where a challenge is made to a resolution to grant permission on EIA grounds, the planning authority may subsequently seek to adopt a screening opinion to the effect that EIA is not required. In *R (Prophet) v York City Council,*[1] a decision on permission for judicial review, Deputy Judge George Bartlett QC held that despite the fact that no screening opinion had been issued within the time period contemplated by the TCP(EIA) Regulations 1999[2] it was open, under the Regulations, for the planning authority and developer to agree an extension of time for a screening opinion to be given. The Deputy Judge gave permission for judicial review, but stayed the proceedings for three months to allow the council the opportunity to rectify defects in the screening process.[3] He also expressed the view that in those circumstances, it would be appropriate for the planning authority, if deciding that the development did not require EIA, to give reasons for that view.[4]

1   [2002] EWHC 588 (Admin).
2   See para **3.20** above.
3   [2002] EWHC 588 (Admin), para 21.
4   [2002] EWHC 588 (Admin), para 22.

REVISITING THE ISSUES WHERE THERE IS NEW INFORMATION

3.108   The decision in *Fernback v Harrow London Borough Council*[1] addresses the question of whether a planning authority which has given a screening opinion that EIA is not required can or should revisit the issue before granting permission, in the light of new information. In that case a screening opinion that EIA was not required was given in relation to residential and associated development at RAF Stanmore. Objectors argued that additional material on likely traffic impacts had later become available, and the matter should have been reconsidered. Richards J was of the view that the fundamental provision was the prohibition in the TCP(EIA) Regulations 1999, reg 3, on granting permission for EIA development without taking the environmental information into account. By TCP(EIA) Regulations 1999, reg 4(2)(b), a positive screening opinion by the local planning authority is expressed to be determinative that the development was EIA development, but a negative opinion has no such express statutory effect. By contrast, under reg 4(3) a direction of the Secretary of State is stated to be determinative either way.[2] Thus Richards J held that the Regulations deliberately left open the possibility for the authority which had given a negative screening opinion to change its mind and hold that EIA was required.[3] Since the Regulations make no provision for a new screening opinion to be adopted in the absence of a request from the developer, this might entail the authority having to ask the Secretary of State to make a screening direction.[4] The ability of the Secretary of State to make such a direction, in Richards J's view, told against there being any power for the local planning authority to adopt a new screening opinion in the absence of a request for one from the developer.

1   [2001] EWHC Admin 278, [2002] Env LR 10.
2   The term used in the TCP(EIA) Regulstions 1999, reg 4(3) is simply 'direction', not 'screening direction'. This may reflect the fact that the Regulations provide for more than one type of direction by the Secretary of State: see regs 4(4), 4(7) and 4(8).
3   [2001] EWHC Admin 278, [2002] Env LR 10, para 50(ii).
4   [2001] EWHC Admin 278, [2002] Env LR 10, para 50(iii).

3.109   Richards J also recognised the alternative possibility of a local planning authority which had given a negative screening opinion, but whose view had subsequently changed, notifying the developer under the TCP(EIA) Regulations 1999, reg 7(2) of its view that an ES was now required. This followed from the fact that a negative screening opinion was not decisive of the status of development as in EIA terms, as set out in the previous paragraph:[1]

'A change of mind would be at risk of challenge on ordinary public law grounds in the absence of good reasons for it ... But in an appropriate case a change of mind might be justified by a change in circumstances since the date of the screening opinion.'

However, any such notification would, by reg 7(3), in Richards J's view have to be given within three weeks of the application.[2]

1   [2001] EWHC Admin 278, [2002] Env LR 10, para 50(v), endorsing the advice given in Department of the Environment Circular 2/99, para 66.
2   [2001] EWHC Admin 278, [2002] Env LR 10, para 50(vi). See also the discussion at para **3.20** above.

3.110   Having held that there were such residual powers to revise a negative screening opinion, Richards J went on to hold that there was no express or implied *duty* for the authority to reconsider the adopted opinion. The issue of traffic had been considered in the original opinion, and the additional detail which had become available was not such as to make failure to reconsider *Wednesbury* unreasonable. That there was likely to be some traffic impact was undeniable, but it could not be said that the only reasonable conclusion was to require EIA.[1] In this respect the decision should perhaps be seen as turning on its own facts. No party had requested that the matter of screening be reconsidered, or that the new information was such as to make the development EIA development.[2] It is possible to envisage a case where the changes in knowledge or in circumstances after the original screening opinion might well be such as to require reconsideration, though as explained above, the decision as to significance of effects remains at all times one for the planning authority.[3]

1   [2001] EWHC Admin 278, [2002] Env LR 10, para 50(x).
2   [2001] EWHC Admin 278, [2002] Env LR 10, para 50(ix).
3   See para **3.99** et seq.

CHAPTER 4

Environmental statements

EC REQUIREMENTS

4.01 Production of an environmental statement (ES) is a fundamental part of the environmental impact assessment (EIA) process. In terms of EC law, the starting point is the EIA Directive (85/337/EEC, as amended by Directive 97/11/EC), art 5. In the case of projects which are subject to EIA, member states must, under art 5(1):

> '... adopt the necessary measures to ensure that the developer supplies in an appropriate form the information specified in Annex IV inasmuch as:
> (a) the Member States consider that the information is relevant to a given stage of the consent procedure and to the specific characteristics of a particular project or type of project and of the environmental features likely to be affected;
> (b) the Member States consider that a developer may reasonably be required to compile this information having regard *inter alia* to current knowledge and methods of assessment.'

4.02 The EIA Directive, Annex IV sets out the information referred to in art 5(1). Reference should be made to the precise wording of the Annex (see APPENDIX 2 to this work), but the categories of information may be broadly summarised as follows:

1 A description of the project, including its physical and land use characteristics, the production processes (if relevant) and estimated residues and emissions resulting from its operation.

2 An outline of the main alternatives studied by the developer and an indication of the main reasons for his choice.

3 A description of the aspects of the environment likely to be significantly affected by the project (followed by a non-exhaustive list of such aspects).

4 A description of the likely significant effects of the proposed project on the environment resulting from its existence, use of natural resources, emission of pollutants and creation of nuisances. There must also be under this heading a description of the forecasting methods used to assess environmental effects.

5   A description of measures envisaged to prevent, reduce and where possible offset any significant adverse effects on the environment.
6   A non-technical summary of the above information.
7   An indication of any difficulties encountered in compiling the required information (technical difficulties or lack of know-how).

4.03   The EIA Directive, art 5(3) sets out a list of minimum information, in the sense that the information provided by the developer must include at least the following:
—   a description of the project comprising information on the site, design and size of the project,
—   a description of the measures envisaged in order to avoid, reduce and, if possible, remedy significant adverse effects,
—   the data required to identify and assess the main effects which the project is likely to have on the environment,
—   an outline of the main alternatives studied by the developer and an indication of the main reasons for his choice, taking into account the environmental effects,
—   a non-technical summary of the information mentioned in the previous indents.

4.04   Thus it can be seen that the EC requirements form a somewhat complex scheme which places qualified obligations on member states in relation to the information in the EIA Directive, Annex IV, but is subject to certain irreducible requirements in art 5(3). This is no doubt a product of the political controversy surrounding the Directive and of the uneasy tension between allowing member states a certain degree of flexibility and ensuring that the fundamentals of the EIA process are not thereby undermined or circumvented. To summarise, what the Directive requires is as follows:
1   Member states must adopt measures to ensure that the developer supplies at least the information contained in the five indents of art 5(3).
2   Beyond this, member states must adopt measures to ensure that the information specified in Annex IV is supplied.
3   However, the obligation to ensure the Annex IV information is supplied is subject to the potentially important caveats of art 5(1)(a) and (b), which only require the information to be supplied so far as the member state considers that:
    —   it is relevant to a given stage of the consent procedure (art 5(1)(a)),
    —   it is relevant to the specific characteristics of the project or type of project and to the environmental features likely to be affected (art 5(1)(a)),
    —   a developer may reasonably be required to compile the information having regard inter alia to current knowledge and methods of assessment (art 5(1)(b)).

4.05   The EIA Directive's scheme merits further consideration. Part of the difficulty is that the types of information set out in Annex IV, while worded more fully in some cases, are essentially no different to the minimum requirements set out in art 5(3). The most obvious difference is that Annex IV includes at point 7 an indication of difficulties encountered in compiling the information; this does not feature in art 5(3). In other cases there are minor and inexplicable differences of wording. For example, art 5(3), second indent, refers to the measures envisaged to '*avoid*, reduce and, if possible, *remedy* significant adverse effects'; whereas point 5 of Annex IV refers to measures envisaged to '*prevent*, reduce and where possible *offset* any significant adverse effects on the environment'. It is not clear why the different wording should be used.

4.06 So far as the EIA Directive, Annex IV information is concerned, the three qualifications mentioned at para 4.4(3) above are also somewhat curious. The first implies that EIA may be a staged process, with different information being relevant at different stages. In relation to the planning system, the UK has however implemented the Directive in a 'once for all' manner, the grant of planning permission (whether outline or full) equating to the 'development consent' referred to in the Directive.[1] The second qualification, that the information be relevant to the specific characteristics of the project and to the environmental features likely to be affected, one would imagine is a general requirement which applies equally to the information listed in art 5(3) as it does to that in Annex IV. Presumably, even in relation to the minimum information under art 5(3), the Community did not intend that member states would be required to elicit *irrelevant* information.

1   See further para **6.05** below.

4.07 The third qualification, the extent to which a developer can reasonably be expected to compile the information, is perhaps more logical on its face, but still presents some difficulties. Article 5(1)(b) of the EIA Directive refers specifically to current knowledge and methods of assessment as limiting factors on the amount of information it may be reasonable to ask a developer to provide. More to the point is the cost of providing that information, which is not specifically mentioned. This could be particularly relevant in relation to the forecasting of likely effects, which may involve expensive modelling work, and which may in any event produce a result which is still uncertain, in that it may only provide confidence between broad parameters, or may be dependent upon controversial assumptions. Depending on how far the developer is required to go in providing 'an outline' of the main alternatives studied,[1] this may be a very onerous exercise. It is submitted that a common sense view is required here. Some effects may be more crucial than others, and it may well be reasonable to expect a developer to devote more technical and financial resources to the assessment of those effects. So for example, in the case of a planning application for a hazardous waste incinerator, one would expect considerable attention to be paid to air modelling in relation to potential emissions of concern. The same level of cutting-edge technical assessment would perhaps not be required in relation to, say, possible odour nuisance from a livestock unit. Similarly, the level of sophistication required in simulating and assessing the visual effects of, say, a standard industrial unit in a mixed use area will be different to that expected in relation to a new tall building of striking design in an area of historic and architectural interest.[2]

1   As to alternatives, see para **4.50**.
2   See the discussion below, para **4.29**, as to the guidance in Department of the Environment Circular 2/99.

ENVIRONMENTAL STATEMENTS IN DOMESTIC LAW

Prohibition on granting planning permission without considering environmental information

4.08   The starting point of the Town and Country Planning (Environmental Impact Assessment) Regulations 1999 (TCP(EIA) Regulations 1999) is the prohibition in reg 3(2), that the planning authority (whether the local authority, Secretary of State or an inspector) shall not grant planning permission pursuant to an application for EIA development 'unless they have first taken the environmental information into consideration'.[1] The environmental information is defined to include:[2]
— the environmental statement,
— any further information,[3]
— any representations made by a body required under the Regulations to be invited to make representations,[4]
— any representations duly made by any other person about the environmental effects of the development.

Thus unless there is an ES, there cannot be environmental information adequate to satisfy the requirements of reg 3(2). However, it is also important to bear in mind that the EIA process includes all elements of the environmental information, listed above. As Newman J put it in *R (Burkett) v London Borough of Hammersmith and Fulham*,[5] it is ' ... a dynamic process, which starts with the statement from the developer but it does not end with the statement'.

1   TCP(EIA) Regulations 1999, reg 3(2) also contains an obligation that they shall state in their decision that they have done so.
2   TCP(EIA) Regulations 1999, reg 2(1).
3   'Further information' means any further information which the developer may be required to provide under TCP(EIA) Regulations 1999, reg 19(1). See further, para **4.24** below.
4   See para **4.22**.
5   [2003] EWHC 1031 (Admin), [2003] All ER (D) 203 (May), para 8(vi).

Definition of the ES

4.09   By the TCP(EIA) Regulations 1999, reg 2(1), the ES is defined to mean a statement:
  '(a) that includes such of the information referred to in Part I of Schedule 4 as is reasonably required to assess the environmental effects of the development and which the applicant can, having regard in particular to current knowledge and methods of assessment, reasonably be required to compile, but
  (b) that includes at least the information referred to in Part II of Schedule 4.'

It will be appreciated that this definition follows the approach of the EIA Directive. Schedule 4, Pt I, and para (a) of the TCP(EIA) Regulations 1999 correspond to the qualified obligation as to the contents on an ES in art 5(1) and Annex IV of the Directive; para (b) and Sch 4, Pt II correspond to the irreducible minimum information referred to in art 5(3). The required elements of the ES are transposed substantially word for word from the Directive, subject to substitution of the terms 'development' and 'applicant' for the terms 'project' and 'developer' as used in the Directive. The domestic Regulations thus share some of the curious features of the drafting of the Directive, discussed above.

Importance of the ES

4.10   The importance of the ES lies not just in the information which it contains, but in its presentation of that information in comprehensive and accessible form to members of the public, including a non-technical summary. Thus the requirements of the TCP(EIA) Regulations and the EIA Directive will not be met by the provision of the same information in some other form. This is clear from the House of Lords' decision in *Berkeley 1*.[1] There it was argued for the Secretary of State that although there had been no formal ES, its equivalent was to be found in the statements of case prepared for the planning inquiry, cross-referenced with the comprehensive officer's report to the planning committee, and in turn the background papers or letters from consulted specialist bodies, together with proofs of evidence put in at the inquiry. It was said that members of the public had access to all these documents. Perhaps not surprisingly, the House of Lords rejected that submission. In the words of Lord Hoffmann:[2]

> 'My Lords, I do not accept that this paper chase can be treated as the equivalent of an environmental statement. In the first place, I do not think it complies with the terms of the Directive. The point about the environmental statement contemplated by the Directive is that it constitutes a single and accessible compilation, produced by the applicant at the very start of the application process, of the relevant environmental information and the summary in non-technical language. It is true that Article 6.3 gives member states a discretion as to the places where the information can be consulted, the way in which the public may be informed and the manner in which the public is to be consulted. But I do not think it allows member states to treat a disparate collection of documents produced by parties other than the developer and traceable only by a person with a good deal of energy and persistence as satisfying the requirement to make available to the public the Annex III information[3] which should have been provided by the developer.'

1   [2001] 2 AC 603. Further, see paras **2.04–2.05** above. See also *R (Burkett) v London Borough of Hammersmith and Fulham* [2003] EWHC 1031 (Admin), [2003] All ER (D) 203 (May), para 8(vii) where Newman J stressed that the information made available must be sufficient to enable a member of the public to exercise their democratic right to respond to the significant effects identified in the ES *and* to examine the project to see whether it is likely to give rise to any effects *not* identified in the ES.
2   [2001] 2 AC 603 at 617D–F.
3   Lord Hoffmann was referring to the original version of the EIA Directive 85/337/EEC.

4.11   Apart from the requirements of the EIA Directive, Lord Hoffmann went on to point out that the relevant Regulations (the Town and Country Planning (Assessment of Environmental Effects) Regulations 1988 (TCP(AEE) Regulations 1988)) represented the way in which the UK had chosen to implement the Directive. It was no answer to non-compliance with those Regulations to say that a different and less strict form of transposition might possibly have been adopted,[1] a point which applies with equal force to the TCP(EIA) Regulations 1999. Similarly in *R (Lebus) v South Cambridgeshire District Council* [2] one of the reasons advanced by the local planning authority for not requiring an ES was that the relevant information on environmental impacts was that which it should rightfully expect to receive in sufficient detail in any event as part of the planning application process. Sullivan J held that this was an error of law in that it proceeded 'from the impermissible premise that it is unnecessary to obtain a formal environmental statement if the information will be received in sufficient detail as part and parcel of the material one might expect with an application'.[3]

1   [2001] 2 AC 603 at 617G–H.
2   [2002] EWHC 2009 (Admin), [2003] JPL 466.
3   [2002] EWHC 2009 (Admin), [2003] JPL 466, para 39.

Compilation of the ES

4.12   It is the developer's responsibility to prepare the ES,[1] and there is no shortage of guidance as to good practice in that regard.[2] Circular 2/99 points out that there is no obligation to consult anyone in preparing the ES,[3] and the developer may, if he so chooses, plough a solitary furrow in that regard. However, there are good reasons why the preparation of the ES should be preceded by informal discussions with the planning authority, other statutory bodies, non-governmental organisations, and indeed the public at large. All may have useful information which may assist in the preparation of the ES and in consideration of possible effects and mitigating measures. Such consultation is at the discretion of the developer as to its timing and the terms on which it takes place.[4] As explained in the following paragraphs, there are some statutory procedures which may assist, but non-statutory procedures may well be equally, if not more, effective. For example, while it may be possible to engage with English Nature as a statutory consultee under the formal procedures laid down in the TCP(EIA) Regulations 1999, non-statutory bodies such as local wildlife trusts or societies engaged with particular species may have equally valuable local information.

1   Department of the Environment Circular 2/99, para 86.
2   For example, the Department of the Environment Planning Research Programme: *Preparation of Environmental Statements — A Good Practice Guide* (HMSO, 1995). See chapter 9 of this work for detailed discussion of these issues.
3   Department of the Environment Circular 2/99, para 87.
4   Department of the Environment Circular 2/99, para 88.

Statutory procedures relating to the preparation of an ES

4.13   The TCP(EIA) Regulations 1999, Pt IV (Preparation of Environmental Statements), contain procedures designed to facilitate the process of preparing an ES.

These are essentially the process which is known as 'scoping' (regs 10 and 11) and a procedure to elicit relevant information from public bodies (reg 12). Scoping involves a procedure for obtaining from the planning authority a statement as to its opinion on what information should be included in the ES. It is referred to in art 5(2) of the EIA Directive as follows:

'(2) Member States shall take the necessary measures to ensure that, if the developer so requests before submitting an application for development consent, the competent authority shall give an opinion on the information to be supplied by the developer in accordance with [art 5(1)] ... The competent authority shall consult the developer and authorities referred to in Article 6(1) before it gives its opinion. The fact that the authority has given an opinion under this paragraph shall not preclude it from subsequently requiring the developer to submit further information.

Member States may require the competent authorities to give such an opinion, irrespective of whether the developer so requests.'

Scoping opinions from the local planning authority

4.14   By the TCP(EIA) Regulations 1999, reg 10(1), a person who is minded to make an EIA application may ask the relevant planning authority to state in writing their opinion as to the information to be provided in the ES (a 'scoping opinion'). The purpose of the procedure is summarised by Circular 2/99 as follows:[1]

'This provision allows the developer to be clear about what the local planning authority considers the main effects of the development are likely to be and, therefore, the topics on which the ES should focus.'

1   Department of the Environment Circular 2/99, para 89.

4.15   A request for a scoping opinion must include:[1]
(a)   a plan sufficient to identify the land;
(b)   a brief description of the nature and purpose of the development and its possible effects on the environment; and
(c)   such other information or representations as the person making the request may wish to provide or make.

Circular 2/99 suggests that the developer may wish to consider submitting a draft outline of the ES, to provide a focus for the local planning authority's considerations.[2] An authority which feels that it has not been provided with sufficient information to adopt a scoping opinion may notify the person making the request of the points on which it requires further information.[3]

1   TCP(EIA) Regulations 1999, reg 10(2).
2   Department of the Environment Circular 2/99, para 90.
3   TCP(EIA) Regulations 1999, reg 10(3).

4.16   Before adopting a scoping opinion the planning authority must consult with the person making the request and with the 'consultation bodies'.[1] It must also take into account the following:[2]

(a) the specific characteristics of the particular development;

(b) the specific characteristics of development of the type concerned; and

(c) the environmental features likely to be affected by the development.

As regards (a), the authority will be largely dependent upon the information supplied by the developer. In relation to (c), the views of the consultation bodies may be particularly important. Circular 2/99 advises that authorities should study the statutory definition of an ES and the guidance at paras 81–85 and Annex A of the Circular;[3] in addition it refers local planning authorities to the European Commission's 'Guidance on Scoping' which was sent to all local planning authorities late in 1996.[4]

1   See TCP(EIA) Regulations 1999, reg 10(4). The term 'consultation bodies' is defined in reg 2(1). See further, para **5.12**.
2   TCP(EIA) Regulations 1999, reg 10(6).
3   Department of the Environment circular 2/99, para 91.
4   *Environmental Impact Assessment — Guidance on Scoping* (DG XI, May 1996).

Time limits for scoping

4.17   It will be appreciated that scoping, if undertaken thoroughly, is an exacting process. Notwithstanding this, the local planning authority is obliged to adopt a scoping opinion and send a copy to the person making the request within five weeks beginning with the date of receipt of the request, or such longer period as may be agreed in writing.[1] Should the authority not comply with this time limit, then the person who requested the opinion may under the TCP(EIA) Regulations 1999, reg 11(1) ask the Secretary of State to make a scoping direction as to the information to be provided in the ES.[2] Such a request can be made even though the local planning authority has notified points on which it requires further information and such additional information has not yet been supplied.[3] Given that the whole rationale for scoping is a co-operative process between the developer and the planning authority, it seems unlikely in most cases that a developer would wish to refer the matter to the Secretary of State while withholding requested information from the local planning authority. Whereas there is some debate as to whether a local planning authority has power to issue a screening opinion outside the statutory time period, a scoping opinion has no binding effect in terms of limiting information that may later be required by the planning authority.[4] Accordingly, there seems no reason why, provided the matter has not been made the subject of a request to the Secretary of State under reg 11, the local planning authority should not provide a scoping opinion after the expiry of the five-week period.

1   TCP(EIA) Regulations 1999, reg 10(4).
2   TCP(EIA) Regulations 1999, reg 10(7).
3   TCP(EIA) Regulations 1999, reg 10(8).
4   TCP(EIA) Regulations 1999, reg 10(10). See para **4.21** below.

Scoping and screening combined

4.18 A request for a scoping opinion may be combined with a request for a screening opinion under the TCP(EIA) Regulations 1999, reg 5. In such cases the authority will first determine the screening issue. If it issues a screening opinion to the effect that EIA is required, it should then go on to issue the scoping opinion within a period of five weeks beginning with the date on which the screening opinion was adopted, or such longer period as may be agreed in writing.[1]

1   TCP(EIA) Regulations 1999, reg 10(5).

Scoping directions by the Secretary of State

4.19 A request to the Secretary of State for a scoping direction may be made where the local planning authority fails to issue a scoping opinion within the relevant period of five weeks or any longer agreed period.[1] The procedure is set out in the TCP(EIA) Regulations 1999, reg 11, which deals with the documentation to be submitted and copied to the local planning authority,[2] the ability of the Secretary of State to request further information,[3] the obligation to consult the person making the request and the consultation bodies,[4] and to take into account the matters referred to in reg 10(6).[5] The Secretary of State should make the scoping direction within five weeks beginning with the date of the receipt of the request, or 'such longer period as he may reasonably require'.[6] There is no mechanism to resolve a dispute between the developer and local planning authority over the content of a scoping opinion: however Circular 2/99 points out that in the event of a call-in or appeal the Secretary of State will need to form his own view on the matter.

1   TCP(EIA) Regulations 1999, reg 10(7).
2   TCP(EIA) Regulations 1999, reg 11(1) and (2).
3   TCP(EIA) Regulations 1999, reg 11(3).
4   TCP(EIA) Regulations 1999, reg 11(4).
5   TCP(EIA) Regulations 1999, reg 11(5). See para **4.16**.
6   TCP(EIA) Regulations 1999, reg 11(4).

Publication of scoping opinions/directions

4.20 The local planning authority is required to take steps to secure that a copy of any scoping opinion or direction made or received is available for public inspection with the planning register for at least two years.[1] Where a planning application in relation to the development is subsequently made, the opinion or direction must be placed on Pt I of the register.[2]

1   TCP(EIA) Regulations 1999, reg 20(2).
2   TCP(EIA) Regulations 1999, reg 20(1)(c) and (d).

Non-binding nature of scoping opinions/directions

4.21   As indicated above, the EIA Directive expressly states that the fact that a
scoping opinion has been given must not prevent the competent authority requesting
further information at a later stage.[1] This is reflected in regs 10(9) and 11(6) of the
TCP(EIA) Regulations 1999. Regulation 10(9) states that the authority which has
adopted a scoping opinion is not precluded from requiring additional information[2] in
connection with any ES that may later be submitted in connection with an application
for planning permission for the same development. Regulation 11(6) provides that
where the Secretary of State has made a scoping direction, neither he nor the local
planning authority is precluded from requiring additional information in connection
with any later ES. Conversely, as Circular 2/99 points out, failure to comply with a
scoping opinion or direction does not render an ES invalid; however, since these
documents represent the considered view of the local planning authority or Secretary
of State, an ES which does not cover the relevant ground will probably be subject to
requests for further information under reg 19.

1   See para **4.13**.
2   See para **4.24** as to such requests.
3   Department of the Environment circular 2/99, para 95.

Provision of information by consultation bodies

4.22   It may well be the case that bodies such as the Environment Agency, English
Nature or the relevant Countryside Agencies have information which may be useful in
preparing an ES — an example might be data on water quality or on the nature
conservation interest of land. Much of this information may well already be accessible
to the developer through the electronic or paper publications of the body concerned,
or on request. The developer, like any other member of the public, will also have rights
to request that such bodies make available 'environmental information' under the
Environmental Information Regulations 1992.[1] In addition, the TCP(EIA) Regulations
1999, reg 12 provide a separate procedure to facilitate the production of relevant
information. This fulfils the obligation under art 5(4) of the EIA Directive that member
states 'shall, if necessary, ensure that any authorities holding relevant information ...
shall make this information available to the developer'. The procedure is that any
person intending to submit an ES may give notice to the local planning authority or
Secretary of State, as the case may be, which must include the information necessary
to identify the land and the nature and purpose of the development, and must indicate
the main environmental consequences to which it is proposed to refer in the ES.[2] The
local planning authority or Secretary of State must then notify the consultation bodies
under reg 12(3), and inform the developer of the names and addresses of the consultation
bodies so notified. The effect of such notification is that the consultation bodies and
the relevant planning authority must, if requested by the developer, enter into
consultation to determine whether the body has in its possession any information
which they or the developer consider relevant to the preparation of the ES.[3] If they
have such information, it must be made available.

1   SI 1992/3240, as amended.
2   TCP(EIA) Regulations 1999, reg 12(1) and (2).
3   TCP(EIA) Regulations 1999, reg 12(4).

4.23   Thus the process goes further than the Environmental Information Regulations 1992, where the onus is on the person making the request to identify the information they require; under reg 12 the relevant bodies must co-operate with and assist the developer in identifying what information may be useful. Regulation 12 does not however require the disclosure of information which is required to be treated as confidential, or is capable of being so treated, under the Environmental Information Regulations 1992, reg 4.[1] The consultation body, or local planning authority, may make a reasonable charge reflecting the cost of making the relevant information available.[2] It may be noted that these procedures also apply where an applicant for planning permission who has not submitted an ES is then notified by the planning authority or Secretary of State that one is required, and responds indicating that they intend to provide an ES.[3]

1   TCP(EIA) Regulations 1999, reg 12(5). For example: matters that are at issue in any legal proceedings or inquiry; or would involve the supply of documents in the course of completion, or of any internal communication; or would affect commercial confidentiality; or the disclosure of which would contravene any statutory provision; or where the information was supplied voluntarily to the consultation body by a third party who has not consented to its disclosure.
2   TCP(EIA) Regulations 1999, reg 12(6).
3   TCP(EIA) Regulations 1999, regs 12(3), 7(4)(a), 8(4), 9(5). On these procedures, see para **3.17** above.

Further information

4.24   As is discussed below, the adequacy or otherwise of a submitted ES is predominantly a matter for the planning authority to whom it is submitted.[1] The TCP(EIA) Regulations 1999, reg 19(1) states that where a local planning authority, the Secretary of State or a planning inspector is dealing with an application or appeal in relation to which an ES has been submitted, and is of the opinion 'that the statement should contain additional information in order to be an environmental statement', they shall notify the applicant or appellant in writing accordingly, and the applicant or appellant shall provide such 'further information'. The duty to notify under reg 19 only applies where the deficiencies in the information provided are such as to mean that the statement provided cannot be regarded as an ES as the term is defined in the TCP(EIA) Regulations 1999. The consequences of this are serious, because, if the defect is not rectified, then under reg 3(2) the only course is to refuse the application or appeal. Circular 2/99 stresses that reg 19 should not be used simply 'to obtain clarification or non-substantial information', and that additional delay and costs imposed by the use of reg 19 should be kept to the minimum consistent with securing compliance with the Regulations.[2] Regulation 19 contains detailed procedural provisions on how 'further information' is to be handled and publicised, which are discussed elsewhere.[3] It is clear that the need for further information may well arise in the context of an inquiry when the Secretary of State or inspector looks at the ES with fresh eyes. The issue may be dealt with before the inquiry opens, if the problem is spotted soon enough; otherwise it may be necessary to adjourn the inquiry in order for the necessary information to be provided.

1   See para **4.30**.
2   Department of the Environment Circular 2/99, para 111.
3   See para **5.23**.

Verification

4.25   There is a separate power under reg 19(10) of the TCP(EIA) Regulations for the planning authority, Secretary of State or inspector to require in writing an applicant or appellant to produce such evidence as they may reasonably call for to verify any information in the ES. This may involve the provision of background data or methodology, and perhaps the disclosure of any unused data. In the context of an inquiry this is likely to be dealt with by way of evidence to the inquiry.

Additions to the ES by the developer

4.26   There is a potentially important gap in the TCP(EIA) Regulations, in that they do not address later amendments or additions to the ES submitted voluntarily by the developer. Such additional material does not fall naturally within the concept of 'further information' requested under reg 19. The problem is essentially one of publicity and consultation, and is addressed in the chapter dealing with procedures.[1]

1   See para **5.19**.

Adequacy of ES

4.27   In the interests of good administration, and to avoid later delays, the planning authority in receipt of an ES should obviously take steps to satisfy itself as early as possible that the ES meets the requirements of the Regulations and to consider whether the authority is obliged to request further information under the TCP(EIA) Regulations 1999, reg 19.[1] It is possible that there may be grey areas, particularly in the difficult distinction between information which is mandatory, and that which is qualified in terms of what is 'reasonably required' to assess the environmental effects of the development, and in terms of what the developer can 'reasonably be required to compile'.[2] When discussing the issue above,[3] a pragmatic approach was advocated, and this is supported by the advice in Circular 2/99,[4] which states that 'Whilst each ES must comply with the requirements of the Regulations, it is important they should be prepared on a realistic basis and without unnecessary elaboration.'

1   See Department of the Environment Circular 2/99, para 109. As to guidance, see DoE, Planning Research Programme, *Evaluation of Environmental Information for Planning Projects — A good Practice Guide* (HMSO, 1994).
2   See para **4.7** above.

3   Para **4.7**.
4   Department of the Environment Circular 2/99, para 82.

4.28   Consideration of the wording of the TCP(EIA) Regulations, Sch 4 (which in turn mirrors the wording of the EIA Directive), indicates that an exercise of judgment is required by the planning authority when considering the contents of an ES. Even in relation to the mandatory minimum requirements of Sch 4, Pt II, it is not every possible effect that has to be considered. Pt II, para 3 refers to the data required to identify and assess the *main* effects which the development is likely to have on the environment; para 2 requires a description of the measures envisaged in order to avoid, reduce and, if possible, remedy *significant* adverse effects. Equally, in Sch 4, Pt I, even before considering whether it is reasonable to expect the information to be provided, a judgment is required as to what aspects of the environment are likely to be *significantly* affected (para 3), what are the likely *significant* effects that need to be described (para 4) and what are the *significant* adverse effects in relation to which measures to prevent, reduce or offset need to be described.

4.29   In this respect, Circular 2/99 urges a selective approach:[1]

'Whilst every ES should provide a full factual description of the development, the emphasis of Schedule 4 is on the "main" or "significant" environmental effects to which a development is likely to give rise. In many cases, only a few of the effects will be significant and will need to be discussed in the ES in any great depth. Other impacts will be of little or no significance for the particular development in question and will need only very brief treatment to indicate that their possible relevance has been considered.'

1   Department of the Environment Circular 2/99, para 82.

ADEQUACY IS NOT A QUESTION OF PRIMARY FACT FOR THE COURTS

4.30   As with the decision on whether the likely effects of development are significant so that EIA is required, the question arises as to whether the adequacy of the environmental information provided by the developer is fundamentally a matter for the planning authority or for the courts. Sullivan J answered this question in *R v Rochdale Metropolitan Borough Council, ex p Milne*[1] by holding emphatically that the question was not one of primary fact on which the courts could differ from the view of the planning authority. The case raises important issues as to the approach to EIA in cases of outline planning applications, and is discussed at length below in that context.[2] Sullivan J in the salient passage held as follows:[3]

'Whether the information provided about the site, design, size or scale of the development proposed is sufficient for these purposes is for the local planning authority, or on appeal or call in, the Secretary of State, to decide. I reject [counsel for Mr Milne's] submission that the issue is one for the court to decide, as a question of primary fact ... The local planning authority's or the Secretary of State's decision is subject to review on *Wednesbury* grounds.'

Further, Sullivan J went on to state the limited nature of the court's jurisdiction, and the reasons for it:[4]

'The question whether such information does provide a sufficient "description of the development proposed" for the purposes of the assessment regulations is, in any event, not a question of primary fact, which the court would be well equipped to answer. It is pre-eminently a question of planning judgment, highly dependent on a detailed knowledge of the locality, of local planning policies and the essential characteristics of the various kinds of development project that have to be assessed.'

1   [2001] Env LR 406.
2   See paras 6.55–6.59.
3   [2001] Env LR 406 at para 106.
4   [2001] Env LR 406 at paras 108–110.

4.31   Similarly, in the case of *R v Rochdale Metropolitan Borough Council, ex p Tew*,[1] the precursor to *Milne*, Sullivan J had stated that the underlying objective of EIA, that decisions be taken 'in full knowledge' of a project's likely significant effects still left scope for the planning authority to exercise its discretion and judgment:[2]

'That is not to suggest that full knowledge requires an environmental statement to contain every conceivable scrap of environmental information about a particular project. The directive and the Assessment Regulations[3] require likely significant effects to be assessed. It will be for the local planning authority to decide whether a particular effect is significant ...'

1   [2000] Env LR 1, discussed below at paras 6.49–6.53.
2   [2000] Env LR 1, at 29.
3   In that case the TCP(AEE) Regulations 1988.

4.32   The respective roles of the courts and planning authorities in relation to the adequacy of an ES was also considered by Ouseley J in *R (Bedford and Clare) v London Borough of Islington and Arsenal Football Club plc*.[1] In that case there was no doubt that the development (a new football stadium with associated enabling or financially supporting development) required EIA. An ES was produced, following a formal scoping opinion, but it was alleged that the ES was so deficient that it could not be regarded as an ES for the purposes of the TCP(EIA) Regulations. Ouseley J, having analysed the relevant provisions of the Regulations, stated as follows:[2]

'The Environmental Statement, therefore, is not just a document to which the developer refers as an Environmental Statement; it is that document plus the other information which the local planning authority thinks that it should have in order for the document to be an Environmental Statement. Accordingly, it is the local planning authority which judges whether the documents together provide what Schedule 4 requires by way of a description or analysis of the likely significant effects.'[3]

1   [2002] EWHC 2044 (Admin), [2002] All ER (D) 538 (Jul).
2   [2002] EWHC 2044 (Admin), [2002] All ER (D) 538 (Jul), para 199.
3   Ouseley J also cited in support of that proposition the judgment of Sullivan J in *Milne* (see above), and the approving comments made on that judgment by the Court of Appeal in *R (Barker) v Bromley London Borough Council* [2002] Env LR 638, paras 32, 33 and 65.

4.33   While acknowledging that it was important not to be over-impressed simply by the volume or weight of documents comprising an ES, and that even very lengthy documents can omit significant matters, Ouseley J was sceptical whether the alleged deficiencies in the ES could be such as to mean that the local planning authority could not reasonably regard the material as constituting an ES:[1]

'It is inevitable that those who are opposed to the development will disagree with, and criticise, the appraisal, and find topics which matter to them or which can be said to matter, which have been omitted or to some minds inadequately dealt with. Some or all of the criticism may have force on the planning merits. But that does not come close to showing that there is an error of law on the local planning authority's part in treating the document as an Environmental Statement or that there was a breach of duty in regulation 3(2) on the local planning authority's part in granting planning permission on the basis of that Environmental Statement.'

In fact, on examining the alleged deficiencies individually and in detail on the evidence before him, Ouseley J concluded that there was no such error on the part of the planning authority.[2]

1   [2002] EWHC 2044 (Admin), [2002] All ER (D) 538 (Jul), para 203.
2   [2002] EWHC 2044 (Admin), [2002] All ER (D) 538 (Jul), paras 204–232. These included alleged deficiencies in relation to transport modal splits, loss of waste-handling facilities through the redevelopment of existing waste transfer sites for the new stadium, noise, contaminated land and dust. The passage is worth reading for an example of the careful judicial approach to the evidence on such alleged shortcomings.

4.34   A further example of an unsuccessful attack on the adequacy of an ES is provided by *R (Burkett) v London Borough of Hammersmith and Fulham*.[1] That case concerned a 32-acre development site at Imperial Wharf, Fulham, formerly used for operational purposes by British Gas, and proposed for mixed use development including over 1,800 residential units, a hotel, retail, office, leisure and community uses.[2] The ES included nine technical reports, dealing with planning, design, transport, air quality, archaeology, ecology, trees, contamination and landscape/visual appraisal. The ES was reviewed by the Institute of Environmental Assessment, which identified some omissions and inadequacies in the assessment of 'residuals' associated with site run-off, dust, spoil and noise. The officers in their report to committee advised that these identified weaknesses had been satisfactorily overcome through subsequent meetings, and did not warrant refusal.

1   [2003] EWHC 1031 (Admin), [2003] All ER (D) 203 (May).
2   For this case in the context of time-limits for challenge, see paras **8.08–8.16**.

4.35   The first ground of challenge was that since details of design, external appearance and landscaping had been reserved, the potential effects in relation to these matters could not have been assessed. Newman J, while accepting that there might be cases where this would be so, rejected this argument on the basis that the local planning authority were entitled to conclude that they had sufficient information about these matters to enable likely *significant* effects to be assessed.[1] As counsel for the local planning authority pointed out, the EIA Directive and the TCP(EIA) Regulations 1999 require that the description of the development should include information on design, but not that every detail of the design must be described, including the particular design of individual components.[2] A further aspect of this head of challenge was that one issue of siting had also been reserved, namely the siting for Phase 3 of the development. The reason for this was that local amenity groups had in consultation asked for a historic dock to be excavated and reinstated, which meant that some adjustment might be needed to the siting of Phase 3. Thus, as the judge pointed out, the reserved siting was itself a product of the consideration given to environmental maters and was in any event properly regarded by the authority as not significant in the context of the development as a whole.[3]

1   [2003] EWHC 1031 (Admin), [2003] All ER (D) 203 (May), para 33.
2   [2003] EWHC 1031 (Admin), [2003] All ER (D) 203 (May), para 19.
3   [2003] EWHC 1031 (Admin), [2003] All ER (D) 203 (May), para 34.

4.36   The second ground of attack in *Burkett* was in respect of the assessment of traffic impact. A planning condition had been imposed preventing the commencement of future stages of the development until either a new station and passenger train service had been provided to serve the development, or a Transport Impact Assessment had been submitted which demonstrated to the council's reasonable satisfaction that the development could proceed without causing adverse traffic conditions on the highway network. The officers' report to committee indicated that the transport study submitted by the developers was believed to be flawed, and in fact the authority carried out its own assessment with the assistance of an independent expert. Newman J regarded it as 'manifest' that the authority had assessed the impact of traffic within the parameters of the known size of the development, national and UDP planning policies, its own assessment, and its own policies on car use.[1] The authority was clearly entitled to conclude that the likely significant effects had been assessed and provided for. While not referred to in the judgment, the point could also be made that the effect of the condition in question was that development consent was not in fact granted for the later stages unless the traffic issues could either be resolved or be demonstrated not to give rise to significant effects.

1   [2003] EWHC 1031 (Admin), [2003] All ER (D) 203 (May), para 35.

4.37   Another ground of challenge related to the approach taken to contamination. The site was contaminated as a result of its former use by British Gas. However, before planning permission had been granted, British Gas had in fact completed statutory remediation works, by excavating and removing contaminated soils ands structures. Thus the issue was confined to the risk of contamination to local residents during construction. Newman J found there was no factual basis to suggest that the assessment was inadequate in relation to such effects: it did not follow that because site workers might need to wear protective equipment that this also applied to local residents, any there was or basis for asserting that the works would give rise to a need for residents to tape up their windows.[1]

1   [2003] EWHC 1031 (Admin), [2003] All ER (D) 203 (May), para 36.

4.38   The judgment of Newman J in *Burkett* provides a useful reminder that it is inadequate simply to focus on alleged deficiencies in an environmental statement without having regard to the totality of the 'dynamic process' of assessment, and that it is necessary to keep in mind that the objective of EIA is not to frustrate development but improve the quality of judgment in the planning process.[1] At the same time, an obvious and glaring error is an ES which is not noticed by the authority may give rise to an arguable case that the decision was flawed.[2]

1   [2003] EWHC 1031 (Admin), [2003] All ER (D) 203 (May), paras 33, 37.
2   See Crichton v Wellingborough Borough Council [2002] EWHC 2988 (Admin) where the ES contained an obvious arithmetical error on the likely percentage increase in aircraft movements, this being one of the most controversial aspects of the application (paras 18 – 28).

Errors of law as to adequacy of ES

4.39   The approach of considering decisions as to adequacy of information on a *Wednesbury* basis does not mean that local authorities will always be immune from attack. There are examples of successful challenges where the authority has been found to have erred in law or to have acted irrationally.

4.40   One such example is *R v Rochdale Metropolitan Borough Council, ex p Tew*,[1] where the issue was the adequacy of the description of the development and on mitigating measures. The case concerned the problems of applying EIA to bare outline applications, and together with its sequel, *R v Rochdale Metropolitan Borough Council, ex p Milne*, is considered more fully in that context below.[2] For present purposes, the main point of *Tew* is that the application was for bare outline permission for a major business park, which would be developed over a number of years. The project and its effects were therefore not fully described at the outset, and (unlike the later case of *Milne*) there was nothing to confine the ultimate form of the development so as to conform with the illustrative details on which the ES had been based. Sullivan J held that the local planning authority could determine what effects were significant;[3] what it could not do consistently with the requirements of the TCP(EIA) Regulations

1999 and the underlying purpose of the EIA Directive was to defer a description of the development and any measures to avoid, reduce or remedy it, to a later stage.[4]

1   [2000] Env LR 1.
2   See para **6.49** below.
3   See *R (Burkett) v London Borough of Hammersmith and Fulham* [2003] EWHC 1031 (Admin), [2003] All ER (D) 203 (May), para **4.34** above.
4   [1999] Env LR 1 at 29.

Possible error in a 'wait and see' approach

4.41   Another example of how a planning authority can fall into error is *R v Cornwall County Council, ex p Hardy*. A planning application was made to extend an existing landfill site. The ES raised a number of issues relating to badgers, liverwort and lesser horseshoe bats. In particular, the excavation of new areas for waste deposits would involve the loss of most habitats within the area of the proposed extension. This included a number of old mineshafts within that area. The site was however regarded by the ES as being of limited nature conservation interest. Nature conservation bodies which were consulted, including English Nature and the Cornwall Wildlife Trust, did not object to the proposal, but advised that bat and badger surveys be carried out. The Trust suggested that because of the need to fell woodland to obtain access, the surveys of the mineshafts for bats would best be carried out after permission was granted; in addition, surveys needed to be carried out immediately prior to development to provide an up-to-date picture of the exact location of habitats. The authority resolved to grant planning permission, subject to a condition that no development should take place until additional surveys had been undertaken and mitigation measures in relation to the relevant species submitted for approval.

1   [2001] Env LR 473.

4.42   Having concurred with Sullivan J in *Milne* that it was for the relevant planning authority to judge the adequacy of the environmental information, subject to review on normal *Wednesbury* principles, Harrison J in *Hardy* went on to refer to TCP(EIA) Regulations 1999, Sch 4 as follows:[1]

'Paragraphs 1 to 3 of Part II of Schedule 4 are not, it seems to me, in a logically correct sequence. Firstly, the environmental statement must contain a description of the development (paragraph 1). Secondly, it must contain the data required to identify and assess the main effects of the development is likely to have on the environment (paragraph 3). Thirdly, it must contain a description of the measures envisaged to avoid, reduce and, if possible, remedy significant adverse effects (paragraph 2). The requirement to provide the paragraph 2 information relating to the measures to be taken does not arise if, in the planning authority's view, there are no "significant adverse effects" Similarly the requirement to provide the paragraph 3 information relating to the data does not arise if, in the planning authority's view, it is not required to identify and assess the "main effects" of the development.'

1   [2001] Env LR 473 at para 57.

4.43   The issue was accordingly whether the local planning authority could rationally conclude that the relevant nature conservation aspects did not amount to 'significant effects' or 'main effects'.[1] The problem was that the planning authority had accepted two inconsistent positions; first that of the ES that the development would not affect protected species and, second, that of the advice of English Nature and the Cornwall Wildlife Trust that further surveys should be carried out to ensure that protected species of bats would not be adversely affected. The advice that surveys be carried out must have entailed the conclusion that bats might be present in the shafts, and given their European protected status, it was in the view of Harrison J an 'inescapable conclusion' that adverse effects on them would be a 'significant effect' or 'main effect'.[2] The facts of the case were therefore very striking: having accepted that surveys should be carried out, the planning authority were simply not in a position to conclude there were no significant adverse effects, or to know whether they had the full information required by the Regulations in relation to such effects.[3] Notwithstanding the practical difficulties, the correct course was to await the results of surveys before determining the application.

1   [2001] Env LR 473, at para 58.
2   [2001] Env LR 473 at para 61.
3   [2001] Env LR 473 at paras 62 and 64.

4.44   It is submitted that *Hardy* is not authority for the proposition that where there is uncertainty as to the presence of species a planning authority can never rationally conclude in the absence of a survey that significant effects are not likely, or that planning permission can never be subject to conditions requiring further surveys. It may be possible on the basis of what is known to conclude that even on a *worst case* basis where the species is present, the effects would not be significant. It would probably have been difficult to conclude this in *Hardy*, since the development would inevitably lead to the destruction of the shafts in which the bats might have been present. If such a conclusion can properly be reached, then there should in principle be no objection to granting planning permission coupled with conditions on surveys and other mitigating measures designed to minimise such effects as there may be.[1] Such an approach would seem to be consistent with the tentative conclusions reached by Harrison J in *Hardy* as to effects on badgers and liverworts, where he indicated that in relation to the badgers there was no evidence of significant adverse effects, and that it was open to the planning authority to conclude as a matter of judgment that the liverworts need not be significantly affected by proposed ditches or pipelines.[2]

1   See para **3.89** above, on the same issue in the context of screening.
2   [2001] Env LR 473 at para 65.

Further survey work permissible

4.45   The validity of an approach which involves further survey work after the grant of planning permission is demonstrated by *R (PPG 11 Ltd) v Dorset County Council*, another landfill case.[1] This decision involved a resolution to grant planning permission for the extension of a clay quarry and its restoration by landfill, including the construction of a 1.2 km access road. This road was routed so as to avoid areas of possible ecological sensitivity in the heathland adjoining the site. There had been an ecological desk study and some survey work. The County Ecologist advised the waste planning authority that although he considered that a full fauna survey for reptiles and birds would have been helpful, this did not prevent him concluding that the measures proposed would not have significant adverse effects on habitats or species.[2] The resolution included conditions requiring further surveys as to habitats and protected species. In attacking the resolution, the claimant relied heavily on *Hardy*.

1   [2003] All ER (D) 68 (Jun).
2   For a similar conclusion, where the information in the ES was properly regarding as adequate despite the survey not having been carried out at the best time of the year see *Crichton v Wellingborough Borough* [2002] EWHC 2988 (Admin) (Gibbs J; permission application), para 37

4.46   Mackay J in *PPG 11* regarded as interesting the distinction between *Hardy* and the case of *R (Jones) v Mansfield District Council*.[1] In *Jones* (a case on screening)[2] the fact that the authority thought it would be beneficial for further bird surveys to be carried out to gain a better understanding of *any* adverse effects was not inconsistent with their reaching a conclusion, on the information available, that the development would not have *significant* effects. Mackay J put the point of distinction as follows:[3]

'*Hardy* does not mean that a defendant cannot form the decision that it does not need a survey to reach a conclusion about the absence of significant effect; and where such a defendant in fact goes on to obtain or make provision for a survey that is no more than a prudent approach, such as was in play in *Jones*, to establish whether any changes had taken place on the ground between the last survey and the starting of work, events which could well be up to 5 years or more apart in time.'

1   [2003] EWHC 7 (Admin), [2003] 1 P & CR 504.
2   The case is fully discussed in this context at para **3.89**.
3   [2003] EWHC 1311 (Admin), [2003] 1 P & CR 504, para 46.

4.47   It was held that the authority had not fallen into the trap suggested by counsel for the claimant of having reached a contingent conclusion on significance of effects which was dependent on further information. The cases (dealing with screening)[1] where such a trap had been sprung were all cases where there were clear deficiencies on the information before the authority, which could not be rectified by information gained later under post-grant survey conditions.[2] Considering the matter overall, the officer's and ecologist's reports in this case indicated that neither believed there was likely to be a significant adverse effect on the relevant ecology and that there was material on which each was entitled to form this view independently of the putative effects of mitigation; second, both thought that whatever adverse, non-significant effects there might be, these would be met by the post-grant conditions proposed. This, it was held, was not an unlawful approach.[3] It is an approach which accords with the practicalities of dealing with protected species which are mobile, and where further survey work will be advisable or necessary, immediately prior to undertaking the relevant works, to ensure that any individual members of the species which may be affected are identified and appropriately preserved. The desirability of such surveys does not dictate a conclusion that there has been inadequate prior assessment of likely significant effects.

1   These cases being *Tew, British Telecommunications v Gloucester, Lebus, Gillespie* and *Hardy.* With the exception of *Hardy,* all are discussed in   chapter 3 above.
2   [2003] EWHC 1311 (Admin), [2003] 1 P & CR 504, paras 49–50.
3   [2003] EWHC 7 (Admin), [2003] 1 P & CR 504, para 53.

Interrelationship of heads of information

4.48   A further point on which provides helpful guidance is the approach to the matters itemised for inclusion in an ES *R (PPGII Limited) v Dorset County Council,*[1] when considering whether the ES is adequate. In particular these include in Sch 4, PE II:
1   A description of the development comprising information on the site, design and size of the development.
2   A description of the measures envisaged in order to avoid, reduce and, if possible, remedy significant adverse effects.
3   The data required to identify and assess the main effects which the development is likely to have on the environment.

The TCP(EIA) Regulations 1999, Sch 4, Pt I, 1(a)–(c) includes:
   '(a) a description of the physical characteristics of the whole development and the land-use requirements during the construction and operational phases;
   (b) a description of the main characteristics of the production processes, for instance, nature and quantity of the materials used;
   (c) an estimate, by type and quantity, of expected residues and emissions (water, air and soil pollution, noise, vibration, light, heat, radiation, etc) resulting from the operation of the proposed development.'

The claimant in *PPG 11* argued that each of these matters had to be the subject of discrete consideration by the local planning authority — in other words that the authority could not simply conclude that because mitigating measures under point 2 of Sch 4, PE II could be assured there was no need to identify and assess main effects under point 3. On the basis of authorities dealing with scoping,[2] Mackay J however concluded that in whatever sequence these requirements were considered, the authority was not required to consider each item in that 'rather mechanistic, sequential and discrete way', ignoring all material advanced in relation to the other items.[3] While accepting that the requirements of Sch 3, Pt II were to be construed purposively, Mackay J regarded it as significant that the second item embraces both information as to mitigation measures and significant adverse effects, 'under the same roof, so to speak, and in that order.'[4]

1   [2003] EWHC 1311 (Admin).
2   In particular, *Milne* (para 114) and *Gillespie* (first instance) para 76 and *Gillespie* (Court of Appeal) para 36.
3   [2003] EWHC 1311 (Admin) paras 47(4), 48, 52(3) and 54.
4   [2003] EWHC 1311 (Admin) para 48.

4.49   It would seem to follow logically from this approach that in considering whether all significant potential effects have been identified, the planning authority can properly have regard to the proposed mitigating measures in assessing the significance of such effects, provided that it considers the likely effectiveness of such measures in doing so. In this respect, it would also have to consider any representations made by the statutory consultation bodies and by members of the public which might cast doubt on the effectiveness of such measures. In that way the democratic and participative objectives of the EIA Directive and TCP(EIA) Regulations 1999 are secured. It needs to be borne in mind that in *PPG 11* the mitigation measures in relation to the reptiles potentially affected (sand lizards and slow worms, which are both European protected species) could be very readily ensured by well-understood techniques of survey and translocation.[1] Moreover, from the information available the areas of potential habitats, and hence the potential numbers of animals affected, were known to be small, with plenty of suitable habitat for any translocation. There was no attack on the rationality of this conclusion as such, nor did consultation with English Nature or the Herpetological Conservation Trust cast any doubts on the practicability or effectiveness of such measures. In other cases it may not be so straightforward for the planning authority to conclude that the possible effects will not be significant.

1   [2003] EWHC 1311 Admin, para 54.

ALTERNATIVES

4.50   One of the difficulties which frequently taxes those drafting an ES is how to deal with the issue of alternatives. The TCP(EIA) Regulations 1999 require at least 'an outline of the main alternatives studied by the developer or appellant and an indication of the main reasons for his choice, taking into account the environmental effects'.[1] In *R v Secretary of State for the Environment, Transport and the Regions, ex p Challenger*,[2] Harrison J did not interpret this requirement over-onerously. The case concerned a Transport and Works Order for the Thameslink 2000 project, affecting the important conservation area of London Bridge and Borough Market. The objectors were promoting an alternative route. They argued that the discussion of alternatives in the ES was perfunctory and out of date. The inquiry inspector ruled on the matter to the effect that the ES met the relevant statutory requirements.[3] It was held that the ES did in fact give the necessary information in outline and the main reasons. While the objectors would have liked more detailed information, this was not required by the Rules.

1 TCP(EIA) Regulations 1999, Sch 4, Pt II, para 4. The wording in Sch 4, Pt I, is in fact in the same terms.
2 [2001] Env LR 209.
3 The Transport and Works (Applications and Objections Procedure) Rules 1992, SI 1992/ 2902, Sch 1, para 2(d).

4.51   The issue of alternatives also arose in *R (Bedford and Clare) v London Borough of Islington* (the Arsenal FC case) referred to above.[1] In commenting on a submission which had been abandoned, that the ES should have considered alternative sites outside the M25, Ouseley J commented that the Regulations were 'quite clear' on the point:[2]

'What needs to be covered in the Environmental Statement are the alternatives which the developer has considered. This the Environmental Statement did. The Regulations do not require alternatives which have not been considered by the developer to be covered, even though the local planning authority might consider that they ought to have been considered.'

1 [2002] EWHC 2044 (Admin), [2002] All ER (D) 538 (Jul); see para **4.32** above.
2 [2002] EWHC 2044 (Admin), [2002] All ER (D) 538 (Jul), para 224.

4.52   Thus the logical starting point will be the extent to which the developer feels that the existence of alternatives will be a material consideration for the planning authority, or on appeal. If the developer feels that the consideration of alternatives will assist the application, then the ES will have to deal with those alternatives which have been considered. Furthermore, as Circular 2/99 points out, the consideration of alternatives (whether sites, choice of processes or the phasing of construction) is widely seen as good practice, and resulting in a more robust planning application:[1]

'Ideally, EIA should start at the stage of site and process selection, so that the environmental merits of practicable alternatives can be properly considered. Where this is undertaken, the main alternatives considered must be outlined in the ES.'

1 Department of the Environment Circular 2/99, para 83. See also the discussion in Chapter 9.

SOCIO-ECONOMIC CONSIDERATIONS

4.53   Many developments will have social or economic effects which may be either positive or negative: local housing may be lost, communities dislocated and jobs may be created or may be lost. Whether such factors should be included in an ES is a potentially important question. The information required by the EIA Directive includes 'population' within the 'aspects of the environment', which are to be described, and on which the significance of the project's effects are to be assessed.[1] So, for example, a large urban mixed-use development, including commercial, residential, leisure, hotel and retail elements, might have both positive and negative potential effects of a socio-economic nature. On the positive side might be permanent and temporary employment creation, secondary benefits for the local economy, the provision of housing and services, and the creation of leisure and amenity opportunities. On the negative side might be increased demand on limited local school and healthcare resources, the creation of retail competition and the displacement of local business, and housing provision which is inappropriate in terms of affordability. These are of course all matters of planning policy, but this in itself does not mean that they do not need to be the subject of EIA procedures. They may in some cases figure in the ES under other headings, for example health effects may be considered in relation to air quality assessment, or the effects of community severance may figure in the transport assessment.

1   Annex IV, points 3 and 4.

4.54   The point did in fact arise in *R (on the application of Portland Port Ltd and Portland Harbour Ltd) v Weymouth and Portland Borough Council* though no conclusive answer emerged.[1] Harrison J was faced with a challenge by Portland Port Limited (the harbour authority for Portland Harbour) to the proposed grant of planning permission by Weymouth and Portland Borough Council for the development by the South West Regional Development Agency of an area called Osprey Quay for a mixed use of residential, leisure, retail and commercial development. The area adjoined Mere Tank Farm, which was part of the operational land of the harbour and was used for storing hazardous substances.

1   [2001] EWHC Admin 1171, [2002] JPL 1099.

4.55   Numerous points were made by the Port in the course of its unsuccessful challenge to the decision. Among them was the suggestion that the data presented in the ES was incomplete in various respects, in that it did not include the detail required by the TCP(EIA) Regulations 1999, Sch 4, Pt II. One of the alleged deficiencies related to possible socio-economic effects. It was said that while the ES did in fact have a section on socio-economic effects, including the number of jobs to be created by the proposed development, there was no mention of the possible adverse effect on harbour-related jobs or on the operation of the Port if the use of Mere Tank farm for storage of hazardous substances were sterilised. Leading counsel for the Port ultimately did not press the submission that an ES was required to contain an assessment of socio-economic effects as a matter of law. Rather, his point was that the picture presented was one-sided. The court, however, held that the Port had been allowed to address the planning sub-committee and thus had ample opportunity to rectify the balance and tell the sub-committee what they thought the adverse effects might be.

4.56   Reading the TCP(EIA) Regulations 1999, Sch 4, there are somewhat mixed messages as to whether socio-economic effects fall within the 'Information for Inclusion in Environmental Statements' referred to in that Schedule. The 'description of the development' certainly appears to refer to its physical characteristics and its physical effects (such as emissions). The statement will also refer to the likely significant effects on the environment, which by TCP(EIA) Regulations 1999, Sch 4, Pt I, para 4, should cover indirect as well as direct effects, secondary and cumulative effects resulting not only from the 'emission of pollutants' and the 'creation of nuisances', but also effects resulting from 'the existence of the development'.

4.57 It is of course possible to argue that the intention is to assess environmental effects in their traditional sense, on flora, fauna, soil, water, air, etc. However, by TCP(EIA) Regulations 1999, Sch 4, Pt I, para 3, the 'aspects of the environment' to be described, if they are likely to be significantly affected, include 'population', which of course can be affected in many ways going beyond simply pollution, loss of amenity, and so forth. Having said that, the thrust of the Sch 3 'Selection Criteria for Screening Schedule 2 Development' is very much in the direction of the physical characteristics and effects of the development. Comparison of the coverage of EIA systems in other jurisdictions suggests that this is generally something of a grey area.

1   See Wood C, *Environmental Impact Assessment: A Comparative Review* (1995) Longman, ch 7.

4.58 The problem is that, as in the *Portland Port* case, such uncertainty can leave it open to the developer to pray in aid socio-economic factors (urban regeneration or job creation) by referring to them in the environmental statement, without necessarily having to confront by rigorous analysis the other possible side of the coin. It may be that case law, either at domestic or EC level, will clarify the issue, and clearer guidance on assessment methodologies and techniques would assist.

Procedure

INTRODUCTION

5.01 This chapter considers the procedures required for determining planning applications or appeals to which the Town and Country Planning (Assessment of Environmental Effects) Regulations 1988 (Town and Country Planning (Environmental Impact Assessment) Regulations 1999 (TCP(EIA) Regulations 1999) apply). Specific problems relating to particular aspects of procedure (for example, outline applications and enforcement appeals) are dealt within in chapter 5. It is important to note at the outset that these procedures are not mere 'formalities', capable of being modified or waived by the authority and developer. Rather they should be seen as important safeguards to ensure that decisions are taken in full knowledge of the likely environmental effects, that potential harmful consequences are avoided or minimised, and that the rights of members of the public to participate in the process are secured.

EC REQUIREMENTS

5.02 In terms of the EIA Directive 85/337/EEC, as amended by Directive 97/11/EC), the essential procedural requirements are to be found in arts 6–9. However, it is also relevant to bear in mind the overarching requirement of art 3:

'The environmental impact assessment shall identify, describe and assess in an appropriate manner, in the light of each individual case and in accordance with the Articles 4 to 11, the direct and indirect effects of a project on the following factors:
— human beings, fauna and flora,
— soil, water, air, climate and the landscape,
— material assets and the cultural heritage;
— the interaction between the factors mentioned in the first, second and third indents.'

The process therefore involves identification of effects, description of effects and assessment of effects. As is clear from the procedures in arts 6–9, this is a collaborative process involving not only the decision-taker and developer, but also other relevant bodies and the general public. In cases of transboundary effects, it also involves competent authorities and the public in other member states.

Consultation of relevant authorities

5.03 The EIA Directive, art 6(1) requires member states to take the measures necessary to ensure that 'the authorities likely to be concerned by the project by reason of their specific environmental responsibilities' are given an opportunity to express their opinion on the environmental statement (ES) and on the application for development consent. Member states must designate the authorities to be consulted, either in general terms or on a case-by-case basis. The ES and any other information gathered pursuant to art 5 shall be forwarded to those authorities, and detailed arrangements for consultation shall be laid down by the member state.

Consultation of the public

5.04 By the EIA Directive, art 6(2), member states shall ensure that any request for development consent and any information gathered pursuant to art 5 '... are made available to the public within a reasonable time in order to give the public concerned the opportunity to express an opinion before the development consent is granted'. Article 6(3) requires the detailed arrangements for such information and consultation to be determined by the member state. Five indents indicate those areas in particular which are to be the subject of such arrangements, depending on 'the particular characteristics of the projects or sites concerned':
— the public concerned,
— the places where information can be consulted,
— the way in which the public may be informed, eg bill-posting, newspaper publication, organised exhibitions,
— the manner of consulting the public, eg by written submissions or public inquiry, and
— time limits for the various stages of the process, in order to ensure that a decision is taken within a reasonable period.

Transboundary effects

5.05 The EIA Directive, art 7 outlines the procedures to be followed where a project in one member state (MS A) is likely to have significant effects on the environment in another member state (MS B). Essentially:
— MS A must send to MS B as soon as possible (and no later than when informing its own public) a description of the project, any available information on its possible

transboundary impact, and information on the nature of the decision that may be taken (art 7(1)). This may include the ES.

— MS B must be given a reasonable time in which to indicate whether it wishes to participate in the EIA process (art 7(1)).

— If MS B indicates that it does intend to participate in the process, MS A (if it has not already done so) must send to MS B the ES and other relevant information, and the request for development consent (art 7(2)).

— The information must be made available, within a reasonable time, to the relevant authorities and to the public concerned in MS B (art 7(3)(a)).

— Those authorities and the public concerned must be given an opportunity, before development consent is granted, to forward their opinion within a reasonable time to the competent authority in MS A (art 7(3)(b)).

— The MSs must enter into consultations within a reasonable time frame to be agreed regarding the potential transboundary effects and the measures envisaged to reduce or eliminate such effects (art 7(4)).

— The detailed arrangements for implementing the Article may be determined by the MSs concerned (art 7(5)).

— When the decision has been taken, MS A must forward to MS B the relevant information (art 7(2)).

Taking account of information and consultation responses

5.06   By the EIA Directive, art 8, the results of consultations and the information gathered pursuant to arts 5–7 must be taken into consideration in the development consent procedure.

Information on decisions

5.07   By the EIA Directive, art 9, when the decision to grant or refuse development consent has been taken, the relevant competent authority or authorities must inform the public of the decision and make the following information available:

— the content of the decision and any conditions attached thereto,

— the main reasons and considerations on which the decision is based, and

— a description, where necessary, of the main measures to avoid, reduce and, if possible, offset the major adverse effects (the Directive refers here to *major* effects, rather than *significant* or *main* effects, as used elsewhere).

STRUCTURE OF THE DOMESTIC REGULATIONS

5.08   Turning to the TCP(EIA) Regulations 1999, Pt V deals with 'Publicity and Procedures on Submission of Environmental Statements'. This Part covers the following issues:

— The procedure where an ES is submitted to a local planning authority with a planning application (reg 13).

— The procedure where the ES is submitted after the application for planning permission (reg 14).
— The provision of an ES to the Secretary of State on a called in application, or on appeal (reg 15).
— The procedure where an ES is submitted to the Secretary of State (reg 16).
— The availability of copies of the ES and charges for copies of the ES (regs 17–18).
— Procedures relating to the provision of 'further information' where this is called for (reg 19).

These requirements have the appearance of being somewhat fragmentary in nature. The explanation for this is that they are not an entirely self-contained code and require to be read in conjunction with the more general procedural requirements contained in the Town and Country Planning (General Development Procedure) Order 1995 (TCP(GDP) Order 1995).[1] In addition, Pt VI of the TCP(EIA) Regulations deals with publicity of material and of decisions (reg 20) and the duties as to information where an environmental impact assessment (EIA) application is determined.

1　The relevant parts of the Town and Country Planning (General Development Procedure) Order 1995, SI 1995/419 , are reproduced at APPENDIX **8**.

Previous Regulations

5.09　The procedures in relation to EIA for planning applications lodged on or after 15 July 1988 and before 14 March 1999 are governed by the Town and Country Planning (Assessment of Environmental Effects) Regulations 1988 (TCP(AEE) Regulations 1988),[1] which are explained in Circular 15/88, *Environmental Assessment*[2] and in *Environmental Assessment: A Guide to the Procedures*.[3] The structure of these Regulations is as follows:
— Procedure on applications made to a planning authority without an ES (reg 9).
— Procedure on applications referred to the Secretary of State without an ES (reg 10).
— Procedure on appeals to the Secretary of State without an ES (reg 11).
— Publicity where a planning application is accompanied by an ES (reg 12).
— Publicity where an ES is submitted in the course of planning procedures (reg 13).
— Procedure where an ES is submitted to the planning authority (reg 14).
— Procedure where an ES is submitted to the Secretary of State (reg 15).
— Availability of copies of the ES and charges (regs 18 and 20).
— Further information and evidence where this is called for (reg 21).

1　SI 1988/1199, as amended by SIs 1990/367, 1992/1494 and 1994/677.
2　Department of the Environment Circular 15/88, Welsh Office Circular 23/88, *Environmental Assessment* (12 July 1988).
3　Department of the Environment/Welsh Office, 1989.

Scotland

5.10   The current regulations governing EIA on planning applications and appeals in Scotland are the EIA (Scotland) Regulations 1999,[1] Ch 5 of which deals with publicity and procedures on the submission of environmental statements. The procedures are similar, as might be expected given the need to transpose the Directive, but are not identical. Thus, for example, the Scottish procedures differ in terms of publicity requirements (reg 13) and in the detail of the procedures for consultation with consultation bodies (reg 14). In the case of reg 14, for instance, a period of four weeks is allowed for responses, as opposed to 14 days under the English and Welsh Regulations;[2] moreover, under the Scottish Regulations, there is an express procedure whereby the consultation body may inform the planning authority that it does not consider consultation to be required for any case or class of case, or in relation to any specified area.[3]

1   SSI 1999/1.
2   TCP(EIA) Regulations 1999, reg 14(3).
3   TCP(EIA) Regulations 1999, reg 14(4).

Northern Ireland

5.11   The relevant regulations for Northern Ireland are the Planning (EIA) Regulations (Northern Ireland) 1999.[1] Part IV deals with procedures on receipt of applications and Pt V deals with publicity. Again the procedures are comparable to those in England and Wales, but reflect the fact that planning applications are made to the Department of the Environment and that appeals are dealt with by the Planning Appeals Commission. The drafting is in fact simpler and more straightforward than the corresponding regulations in Great Britain.

1   SR 1999/73.

CONSULTATION BODIES

5.12   The TCP(EIA) Regulations 1999 define the bodies which must be consulted as part of the EIA process (the consultation bodies) as follows (reg 2(1)):
(a)   any body which the relevant planning authority[1] is required to consult (or would be required if an application for planning permission for the development concerned had been made) the TCP (General Development Procedure) Order 1995, art 10,[2] or by virtue of any direction made under art 10; and
(b)   the following bodies (if not within (a)):
   (i)   any principal council[3] for the area where the land is situated, if not the relevant planning authority;
   (ii)   where the land[4] is situated in England, the Countryside Commission and English Nature;
   (iii) where the land is situated in Wales, the Countryside Council for Wales; and

(iv) the Environment Agency.

1   The 'relevant planning authority' is defined as the body to whom it falls, or would fall, to determine a planning application for the development in question.
2   Town and Country Planning (General Development Procedure) Order 1995, SI 1995/419; art 10 is reproduced at **APPENDIX 8**.
3   'Principal council' has the meaning given by the Local Government Act 1972, s 270(1).
4   'The land' means the land on which the development (or presumably any part of the development) would be carried out, or has already been carried out.

RESPONSIBILITIES OF THE APPLICANT WHEN SUBMITTING AN ES

5.13   The applicant for planning permission for EIA development, when submitting an ES which is referred to as an ES for the purposes of the TCP(EIA) Regulations 1999, must provide the relevant planning authority with three additional copies for transmission to the Secretary of State (reg 13(1)). In terms of copies for the consultation bodies, the applicant has a choice; he may serve a copy of the ES on such bodies, and if so by reg 13(1) must at the same time:
(a) serve with the ES a copy of the application and any plan submitted with it (unless these have already been served on the body in question);
(b) inform the body that representations may be made to the relevant planning authority; and
(c) inform the authority of the name of everybody whom he has so served, and of the date of service.

Alternatively, if the applicant does not serve the consultation bodies with a copy of the ES, the relevant planning authority is required to do so by reg 13(2)(c), and the applicant must send to the planning authority the copies required for this purpose. Thus there are potential advantages in terms of time saving for the applicant to take the initiative in terms of serving the ES on the consultation bodies.

RESPONSIBILITIES OF THE PLANNING AUTHORITY WHEN ES SUBMITTED

5.14   The planning authority which receives an ES which is described as such, must under the TCP(EIA) Regulations 1999, reg 13(2):
(a) send three copies of the ES and one copy of the application and supporting documents to the Secretary of State within 14 days of receipt of the ES;
(b) inform the applicant of the number of copies of the ES required for forwarding to any consultation body which has not already received a copy direct from the applicant; and
(c) forward copies of the ES when received to such consultation bodies and inform them that they may make representations.

The planning authority must then allow 14 days to expire from the last date on which a copy of the ES was served on the Secretary of State or on a consultation body, before determining the application (reg 13(4)).

PUBLICITY FOR EIA APPLICATIONS

5.15   Where an EIA application is accompanied by an ES, the TCP(GDP) Order 1995 (art 8(2)(a)) requires that the application be publicised in the manner specified in art 8(3), that is to say, by display of a site notice in accordance with the definition of 'site display' in art 1(2) for not less than 21 days, and by advertisement in a local newspaper. There is a special form of notice under TCP(GDP) Order 1995, art 8 and Sch 3, to be used in cases of EIA applications, which gives details of where and at what hours members of the public can inspect copies of the application, plans and ES, and from where and at what charge copies of the ES may be obtained. It also must state that anyone wishing to make representations about he application may write to the planning authority (giving the address) by a date which must give at least 21 days from the date of initial display of the site notice, or 14 days from publication in a local newspaper, as the case may be.

Material to be placed on the planning register

5.16   Where the particulars of an EIA application are placed on Pt I of the planning register in accordance with the TCP(GDP) Order 1995, art 25(3), there must also be placed on that Part the materials specified at paras (a)–(h) of the TCP(EIA) Regulations 1999, reg 20(1). As well as the various opinions, directions or notifications which may have been given in connection with the screening or scoping processes, these include the ES and any 'further information' which has been provided.

Availability of the ES

5.17   Under the TCP(EIA) Regulations 1999, reg 17, the applicant must ensure that a reasonable number of copies of the ES are made available at the address stated in the notices publicising the application. By reg 18 a reasonable charge may be made to a member of the public for a copy of the statement, reflecting printing and distribution costs. Such costs may be significant, given the scale and sophistication of the ES in many cases. However, it will often be more useful, for the average member of the public, to make available the non-technical summary, or as is often the case a more simplified leaflet or brochure.[1] Circular 2/99 states that applicants and local planning authorities may wish to consider whether the ES should be made available through the council offices, in which case the authority's staff may have to deal with the collection of charges for copies.[2]

1   Department of the Environment Circular 2/99, para 105, urges applicants to make copies of the non-technical summary available free of charge as a separate document.
2   Department of the Environment Circular 2/99, para 101.

Publicity for an ES submitted late

5.18 In cases where no ES was submitted with the planning application, but is submitted later (perhaps in consequence of notification under the EIA Directive, art 7(2)),[1] the applicant must follow the procedures in TCP(EIA) Regulations 1999, reg 14. This entails the applicant who proposes to submit an ES publishing a notice in a local newspaper, giving the details required by reg 14(2)(a)–(j) as to the application, the availability of the ES and other documents, and the ability to make representations about the application. It must state that the documents will be available for inspection for a period not less than 21 days after the date of publication of the notice (reg 14(2)(e)). The applicant must also post a notice on the land where the development is to be carried out, giving equivalent information (reg 14(3) and (4)). It will be appreciated that these requirements reflect those which would have applied under the TCP(GDP) Order 1995, art 8, if the ES had been submitted with the application. Compliance with these requirements must be certified by the applicant when the ES is submitted.[2] Where the applicant has indicated that he proposes to provide an ES in these circumstances, consideration of the application (other than by considering refusal) must be suspended by the planning authority until the ES and relevant certificates have been received, and then a further period of 21 days (beginning with the date of receipt) must be allowed before the application can be determined.[3]

1   See para **3.16** above.
2   TCP(EIA) Regulations, reg 14(5). False or misleading certification made knowingly or recklessly is an offence by reg 14(7).
3   TCP(EIA) Regulations, reg 14(6).

SUPPLY OF THE ES TO SECRETARY OF STATE ON CALL-IN OR APPEAL

5.19 The TCP(EIA) Regulations 1999, reg 15, deals with the position where an ES or further information has been submitted to the local planning authority and then either:
(1)   the application is called in for determination by the Secretary of State under the Town and Country Planning Act 1990 (TCPA 1990), s 77, or
(2)   there is an appeal under s 78 against actual or deemed refusal of the application.

In such cases the applicant must supply the Secretary of State with three copies of the ES and any further information. This obligation does not apply in the case of a called-in application where the local planning authority has already supplied three copies when referring the application to him.

Procedure where the ES is submitted to the Secretary of State on call-in or appeal

5.20 The TCP(EIA) Regulations 1999, reg 16, governs the position where an EIA application is before the Secretary of State or an inspector for determination, or is the subject of an appeal, and the applicant or appellant at that stage submits an ES. This may occur where the relevant Regional Office or an inspector identifies the need for an ES. The applicant or appellant must submit four copies of the ES to the Secretary of State, who must then send one copy to the relevant planning authority (reg 16(2)). The procedures then follow those of reg 13, where an ES is submitted to the local planning authority, in terms of ensuring that the consultation bodies are sent a copy of the ES (either by the applicant/appellant or the Secretary of State) and in allowing a period of at least 14 days for those bodies to comment before the application or appeal is determined.[1] The requirements of regs 17 and 18 as to making copies of the ES available to the public also apply, as do the requirements for notification and certification under reg 14.[2]

1   See para **5.13**.
2   See para **5.17** The TCP(EIA) Regulations 1999, reg 14 applies to all applications including those referred to the Secretary of State (see reg 14(2)(j)) and to appeals (see reg 14(8)).

PROCEDURES FOR 'FURTHER INFORMATION'

5.21   Reference has already been made to the duty of the planning authority, Secretary of State or inspector to call for 'further information' in cases where the ES is deficient to the point that it is not an ES for the purpose of the Regulations.[1] The TCP(EIA) Regulations 1999, reg 19(3)–(9) provides procedures for dealing with such 'further information'. Essentially this repeats the requirements which apply to an ES in terms of publication of a notice in a local paper (reg 19(3)), the forwarding of copies to the consultation authorities and Secretary of State (reg 19(4)–(6)), the availability of copies at a reasonable charge (reg 19(8) and (9)), and the suspension of determination of the application or appeal for a period to allow for consultation responses and representations by the public (reg 19(7)). 'Further information' must also be placed on Part I of the planning register (reg 20(1)(g)).

1   See para **4.24**.

'Further information' required for public inquiries

5.22   The provisions of TCP(EIA) Regulations 1999, reg 19(3)–(9) described above do not apply to 'further information' which was provided for the purpose of a planning inquiry pursuant to a request which stated it was to be provided for such purposes.[1] Such information will be regulated instead by the rules relating to the submission of evidence to local planning inquiries.[2] In particular, the further material will in practice form part of the statement of case, or statement of common ground, or proofs of evidence. In each case, the relevant rules provide for members of the public to have the opportunity to inspect and, where practicable, take copies of these documents.[3]

1   TCP(EIA) Regulations 1999, reg 19(2).
2   See Department of the Environment Circular 2/99, para 113.

3   See the TCP (Inquiries Procedure) (England and Wales) Rules 2000, SI 2000/1624, rr 6(13), 13(7) and 14(2); the TCP Appeals (Determination by Inspectors) (Inquiries Procedure) (England) Rules 2000, SI 2000/1625, rr 6(13), 14(7) and 15(2).

ADDITIONS OR MODIFICATIONS TO THE ES

5.23   It will sometimes be the case that the developer wishes to modify or add to an ES which has been submitted — for example because further information has come to light, or because of some change in the detail of the proposal. This is not a situation where the previous ES is being withdrawn and a new one submitted, nor where the planning authority is requiring further information under reg 19. The TCP(EIA) Regulations 1999 do not make provision for this situation, which is a potentially serious gap, because if the new information is not properly consulted on and publicised there will not have been compliance with the procedural requirements of the EIA Directive. The best course will be to follow the advice in the ODPM Guidance, as follows:[1]

'The safest approach is to treat any addition or amendment as an ES submitted during the course of a planning application and to advise the applicant to advertise the whole of the ES, with the amendment/addition, in compliance with regulation 14. This will ensure compliance with the general intent of the EIA Directive to notify and inform people of the possible environmental effects of a proposed development.'

Of course, the developer may decline to follow such advice, but it would be rash to do so and risk losing the permission on a later legal challenge. The developer would also be well advised to consider how best to present such changes to avoid the charge that the public has to engage in a 'paper chase' to assimilate the ES and its modifications. It may be preferable to re-issue the relevant parts or chapters of the ES in their entirety if the changes are substantial.

1   ODPM, *Note on EIA Directive for Local Planning Authorities* (2002), reproduced at **APPENDIX** 7.

USE OF POWERS ON FURTHER INFORMATION

5.24   In *R (on the application of Smith) v Secretary of State for the Environment, Transport and the Regions*,[1] Silber J considered the use of the power to call for further information contained in the TCP(AEE) Regulations 1988, reg 21 (now TCP(EIA) Regulations 1999, reg 19). Two successive planning applications for the extension of a quarry to facilitate its use for landfill were refused by the local planning authority. Each was accompanied by an ES. It was alleged by the claimant that the first ES was defective, the defects being remedied by the second ES. Only the first planning application refusal was appealed. On the appeal, the inspector took both ESs into account, the environmental information in relation to the second application being described in the inspector's decision letter as 'subsumed into the evidence before me'. It was argued for the claimant that the inspector should not have followed this course, but should have used his reg 21 powers to call for further information in relation to the (allegedly) defective first ES. This was rejected by Silber J for three reasons. First, the inspector, having in his possession both the first and the second ES, did not need 'further information';[2] second, he had no reason to believe there was further information available which was not then before him;[3] and third, there was nothing in the Regulations to say that reg 21 was the sole and exclusive way in which further information could be obtained.[4] The claimant's submission would involve '... re-writing regulation 21 so as to contain words to the effect that no environmental evidence could be relied on by the inspector other than that contained in the actual planning application or in the ES actually submitted with it unless the inspector invokes regulation 21'.[5]

1   [2001] EWHC 1170 Admin. The decision was appealed, unsuccessfully, on other grounds: see
     [2003] EWCA Civ 262, [2003] All ER (D) 36 (Mar), (para 5.46).
2   [2001] EWHC Admin 1170, para 34.
3   [2001] EWHC Admin 1170, para 35.
4   [2001] EWHC Admin 1170, para 36.
5   [2001] EWHC Admin 1170, para 36.
6   [2001] EWHC Admin 1170, para 36.

5.25   In considering the first instance decision in *Smith*, it has to be borne in mind that the wording of the current provisions is somewhat different. As Silber J pointed out in *Smith*, TCP(AEE) Regulations 1988, reg 21 was partly facultative and partly mandatory.[1] TCP(EIA) Regulations 1999, reg 19(1) is entirely mandatory rather than facultative. It would be rash to assume that a planning authority, faced with an inadequate ES, would be entitled simply to ignore reg 19 and 'subsume' into the environmental information material from other sources. This would be contrary to the principle that the public should have access to a single ES, and not be required to engage in a 'paperchase'.[2] However, as indicated above,[3] under the TCP(EIA) Regulations 1999, the provisions on publicity in reg 19(3) (which had been inserted into reg 21 of the previous Regulations (the TCP(AEE) Regulations 1988) by amendment in 1990)[4] do not apply in relation to further information provided for the purpose of an inquiry. In *Smith*, it seems clear that the second ES had been published and had been available for comment by the public at the inquiry.[5] It is not therefore apparent that the public had been disadvantaged by failure to follow the reg 21 procedure.

1   [2001] EWHC Admin 1170, para 33.
2   See para **4.10**.
3   At para **5.22**.
4   SI 1994/677, reg 2 and Schedule, para 12.
5   [2001] EWHC Admin 1170, para 19.

TIME LIMITS FOR DETERMINING EIA APPLICATIONS

5.26   By the TCP (EIA) Regulations 1999, reg 32(2)(a),[1] the normal period of eight weeks for determination of a planning application is extended to 16 weeks in the case of EIA applications, beginning with the date on which the application was received.

That period will not begin to run until the ES has been submitted, together with the other documents which should accompany it.[2] In determining whether the period after which an appeal in respect of deemed refusal can be made, in case where the authority has notified the applicant under reg 7(2) that an ES is required and the Secretary of State has given a screening direction, no account is to be taken of any period before the issue of the direction.[3]

1   Modifying the TCP(GDP) Order 1995, art 20(2).
2   TCP(EIA) Regulations 1999, reg 32(2)(b), inserting art 20(3)(ba) into the TCP(GDP) Order 1995.
3   TCP(EIA) Regulations 1999, reg 32(1).

MAKING THE DETERMINATION

5.27   Before determining the application, the relevant planning authority, the Secretary of State or the inspector must first take the environmental information into consideration.[1] The environmental information means:[2]

— the ES,
— any 'further information',
— any representations made by a consultation body, and
— any representations duly made by any other person about the environmental effects of the development.

This fulfils the obligation under the EIA Directive, art 8 that the results of consultations and the relevant information must be taken into consideration.[3]

1   TCP(EIA) Regulations 1999, reg 3(2).
2   TCP(EIA) Regulations 1999, reg 2(1).
3   See para **5.06** above

DECISIONS AND PUBLICITY

5.28   EIA is essentially a procedural process; it does not dictate any given conclusion or restrict the grant of development consent. It is perfectly possible to grant planning permission for a development which has serious adverse effect if other material considerations outweigh those effects. EIA ensures that those effects are properly assessed and weighed, and that consideration is given to how they may be avoided or mitigated. The requirements of EIA relating to the decision are therefore essentially procedural in nature.

5.29   TCP(EIA) Regulations 1999, reg 3(2) requires the planning authority, Secretary of State or inspector not only to take the environmental information into account, but also to state in their decision that they have done so. This is not of course an obligation to give reasons for the decision, but such an obligation flows from reg 21. TCP(EIA) Regulations 1999, reg 21(1) imposes various duties to inform the Secretary of State and the public when a local planning authority determines an EIA application. The authority must:

(a)   inform the Secretary of State in writing of the decision;

(b)   inform the public by publishing a notice in a local paper; and

(c)   make available for public inspection at the location where the planning register is kept a statement containing the following:

  (i)   the content of the decision and any conditions attached to the permission;

  (ii)   the main reasons and considerations on which the decision is based; and

  (iii)   a description, where necessary, of the main measures to avoid, reduce and if possible offset the major adverse effects of the development.

This fulfils the obligations under the EIA Directive, art 9(1).[1] Where the decision is taken by the Secretary of State or an inspector, the Secretary of State must notify the local planning authority of the decision and provide the authority with a statement giving the relevant particulars.[2] The local planning authority must then inform the public of the decision and make the statement available for inspection.[3]

1   See para **5.07**.
2   TCP(EIA) Regulations 1999, reg 21(2).
3   TCP(EIA) Regulations 1999, reg 21(3).

Approach to procedural breaches on post-decision publicity requirements

5.30   In *R v Cornwall County Council, ex p Hardy*[1] Harrison J considered alleged procedural breaches of the TCP(EIA) Regulations 1999, regs 3 and 21 on an obiter basis, having already decided that the planning decision was unlawful on other grounds.[2] It was accepted that there had been a breach of reg 3(2), in that the planning authority had not stated in its decision that it had taken the environmental information into account. Counsel for the planning authority submitted that the breach could be properly dealt with by accepting an undertaking that such a statement would be made, or by the court ordering the authority to make such a statement. Harrison J was inclined to agree that the breach of reg 3 could have been appropriately dealt with by the court by way of a mandatory order, rather then by quashing the grant of permission.[3]

1   [2001] Env LR 473.
2   See paras **4.41–4.43** above.
3   [2001] Env LR 473, para 67.

5.31   There was also an alleged breach of TCP(EIA) Regulations 1999, reg 21, in that the statement which the authority had made available, purportedly under reg 21(1), simply attached the report of the Planning Director, the s 106 agreement (under TCPA 1990) entered into by the applicants, the decision notice and the approved plans. Harrison J held that while this would have satisfied reg 21(1)(c)(i) relating to the decision and the conditions attached to it, it did not contain the main reasons and considerations on which the decision was based, as required by reg 21(1)(c)(ii).[1] In view of this finding, the statement in Circular 2/99 that the reg 21(1)(c)(ii) requirement may in practice be met by the relevant planning officer's report to committee,[2] should perhaps be treated with caution. The question of what relief should be granted in respect of this breach, Harrison J found, was not so straightforward, but as the permission was being quashed in any event he did not regard it as necessary or desirable to express an opinion as to whether the breach could have been dealt with by a mandatory order, or whether it would necessitate the quashing of the permission.[3] It is submitted that despite the importance rightly attached by the courts to compliance with the procedural safeguards in the EIA procedures,[4] there are cogent arguments why a breach of this type could properly be dealt with by a mandatory order rather than by quashing the permission. The requirement in the EIA Directive and in the transposing Regulations to provide a public statement of the main reasons and considerations on which the decision is based is one which applies after the decision has been taken, and is there purely to inform the public (and no doubt to assist in ascertaining whether there might be grounds for further legal challenge of the decision). Provided the Directive and Regulations have been fully complied with at the stages prior to the decision to grant permission, the public's interest in participating in the decision-making process will have been protected. The further interest in being informed as to the considerations underlying the decision can be adequately protected by an order requiring that information to be provided, without the potentially serious consequences in terms of delay and resources that would follow from quashing the decision.[5] The counter-argument is perhaps that requiring the authority to re-take the decision in the knowledge that it will have to provide a statement of reasons may affect the outcome of the decision.

1   [2001] Env LR 473, para 68.
2   Department of the Environment Circular 2/99, para 127.
3   [2001] Env LR 473, para 69.
4   See para **8.44**.
5   A similar approach was taken in *Brayhead (Ascot) v Berkshire County Council* [1964] 2 QB 303, [1964] JPL 185 to the statutory obligation to give reasons for planning conditions.

5.32   Two further cases provide authority for this suggested flexible and pragmatic approach to the procedural requirements of regs 3 and 21. In *R (Burkett) v London Borough of Hammersmith and Fulham*[1] one of the grounds of challenge was non-compliance with reg 4(2) of the TCP(AEE) Regulations 1988, which required the planning authority to state in its decision that the environmental information had been taken into consideration. Newman J had no doubt that a failure to comply with this requirement went to the validity of the decision. However, it did not follow that the decision would be invalidated, in cases where it was plain that the substantive statutory purpose of the provision (that the environmental information should be taken into account) had been met.[2] The court in such cases should be cautious about the degree of indulgence extended to the failure to comply, and should considered carefully the material disclosing that the statutory purpose had been met, and any prejudice to interested parties by failure to meet the strict procedural requirements.[3] In this case, Newman J was satisfied that there was no compelling evidence that the failure to make the statement required by reg 4(2) was an error and was not to be interpreted as an indication that the environmental information was not taken into account; in fact, the material before the court suggested the contrary.[4] Also, there was no prejudice to the claimant or any other interested party resulting from the failure. Newman J was clearly influenced in this approach by the fact that the procedural point had been taken only at the last moment, when skeleton arguments were being prepared for the hearing, and that the litigation (which had involved a hearing in the House of Lords on the issue of time limits for challenge) had previously not been conducted on that basis.[5] He held that, if he was wrong in concluding that the court could find that there had been substantial compliance, he would have refused relief on discretionary grounds, because of the late stage at which the point was taken, the lack of any demonstrated prejudice to the claimant, and the unconscionable prejudice that would be sustained by the developer and the local planning authority if the permission were quashed.[6]

1   [2003] EWHC 1031 (Admin).
2   [2003] EWHC 1031 (Admin) para 41.
3   [2003] EWHC 1031 (Admin) para 41.
4   [2003] EWHC 1031 (Admin) para 44 (i)-(iii).
5   [2003] EWHC 1031 (Admin) para 43.
6   [2003] EWHC 1031 (Admin) para 45.

5.33   The second decision is that of Richards J in *R (Richardson) v North Yorkshire County Council*.[1] Planning permission had been granted for the extension of a sand and gravel quarry. Among the grounds of challenge were failure to comply with regs 3(2) and 21(1) of the TCP(EIA) Regulations 1999. A 'notice of decision' had been issued by the mineral planning authority, which contained a 'Note' stating that the accompanying environmental information had been taken into account. This referred to Article 22(2) of the TCP(GDP) Order 1995, but not to the TCP(EIA) Regulations 1999. The actual minute of the resolution to grant permission contained no such statement. Richards J held that for the purposes of reg 3(2) the 'decision' was not the resolution (which in itself had no immediate legal effect) but rather the notice of decision.[2] It was further held that the 'Note' to the notice of decision was sufficient to comply with reg 3(2), since Article 22(2) of the TCP(GDP) Order 1995 was clearly intended to achieve the same result and, fairly construed, the Note was referring to the environmental information encompassed within reg 3(2).[3]

1   [2003] EWHC 764 (Admin).
2   [2003] EWHC 764 (Admin) para 31. In so holding, Richards J refered to the decision of the House of Lords in *Burkett* that time for challenge runs from the grant of permission, rather than the preceding resolution (see para 8.13).
3   [2003] EWHC 764 (Admin) para 32. In terms of the drafting history, the requirement to state that the environmental information had been taken into account was introduced in 1994, by para 3 of the Schedule to the TCP(AEE) (Amendment) Regulations 1994, and given the integration of EIA procedures into the general planning regime, Richards J regarded Art 22(2) of the 1995 Order as consonant with that requirement: [2003] EWHC 764 (Admin) para 32(iv).

5.34   Richards J went on to hold that if, contrary to that view, there had been a failure to comply with the relevant requirement in reg 3(2), he would not regard that as a sufficient reason to quash the grant of planning permission. He distinguished between the fundamental requirement of reg 3(2) (to take the environmental information into account) and the important, but essentially procedural and secondary requirement, to state that this had been done.[1] Thus the alleged procedural failure in this case was not such as to render the decision ultra vires. Nor, in Richards J's view, would it be contrary to European law to exercise the judicial discretion not to quash the permission in a case where the primary obligation to take the environmental information into account had been complied with, and the only error lay in the wording of the statement made.[2]

1   [2003] EWHC 764 (Admin) para 33(ii)-(iv). This distinction was reinforced by the wording of reg 3(2) which prohibits the grant of permission unless the environmental information has been taken into account, and imposes a separate requirement to state that it has been; this contrast with the wording of the 1988 Regulations as originally amended, in which the requirement to make the statement was also governed by the word 'unless'.
2   [2003] EWHC 764 (Admin) para 33(vi). On the issue of discretion, see para **8.44**.

5.35   A further ground of challenge in *Richardson* was the failure to comply with reg 21(1)(c)(ii) to make available for public inspection a statement containing the main reasons on which the decision was based. Richards J held that for the purposes of this requirement (as for reg 3(2)) the 'decision' was the grant of permission, and that whilst there was no time stated in the regulation, it must be implied that the statement be made available to the public either as soon as reasonably practicable or within a reasonable time of the decision.[1] In this case the notice of decision placed on the public register contained no statement of reasons, and accordingly there was a continuing breach of the requirement.[2]

1   [2003] EWHC 764 (Admin) para 46((i)-(iii).
2   [2003] EWHC 764 (Admin) para 46(v)-(vi).

5.36   However, as demonstrated by the range of the cases cited, from various statutory and administrative contexts, the consequences of a failure to comply with a requirement to give reasons will depend very much on the context and circumstances of the particular case.[1] In analysing the requirements of reg 21(1), Richards J regarded it as important that the requirement to make reasons available is concerned not with the decision-making process itself or matters prior to the decision, but with the position after the decision has been made.[2] This led Richards J to the view that such non-compliance ought not to lead necessarily to the quashing of the decision, but should be capable of being remedied by a mandatory order requiring the appropriate statement to be made available to the public.[3]

1   [2003] EWHC 764 (Admin) para 47.
2   [2003] EWHC 764 (Admin) para 49.
3   [2003] EWHC 764 (Admin) para 50.

5.37   In considering the appropriate judicial response to the non-compliance in this case, the problem faced by Richards J was that the statutory requirement to provide a statement of reasons had simply never been drawn to the committee's attention. This was clearly, in the words of Richards J,[1]

'… a most unfortunate oversight. It meant that members did not have imposed upon them the same disciplined and structured approach as might have been thought appropriate had they been aware of the duty to make a statement of main reasons available. It also meant that they missed the opportunity to agree in terms on a specific set of reasons.'

Despite this unsatisfactory resulting situation, Richards J was ultimately able to conclude that it was not justified to quash the grant of planning permission. He was influenced by the fact that there was evidence from members of the committee who had been asked to cast their minds back and state the reasons for their decision; all of this evidence, read with 'a limited degree of beneficence' indicated that members accepted the reasoning and conclusions in the officer's report to the committee.[2] On that basis the appropriate order was held to be simply a mandatory order requiring the statement of reasons to be placed on the public register.[3]

1   [2003] EWHC 764 (Admin) para 52.
2   [2003] EWHC 764 (Admin) para 53(i)-(iii). Compare the strict approach against ex post facto rationalisation of decisions discussed at para 8.41.
3   [2003] EWHC 764 (Admin) para 53(v).

5.38   Thus the requirements of stating that environmental information has been taken into account, and providing public reasons for decisions, should certainly not be regarded as optional extras. They serve the important purposes of informing the public, providing assurance as to compliance with the substantive requirements of EIA, and imposing discipline on the decision-making process. At the same time, pending any decisions of the appellate courts or the European Court, they do not stand on the same level as failure to comply with the fundamental substantive requirements of the Regulations and Directive, in that non-compliance will not necessarily be fatal to the permission. On the other hand, there may be cases where the defect is fatal on the facts, and the onus will be on the planning authority to make good its case that the fundamental objectives of the EIA legislation were met and that the decision was taken on a principled basis; at the very least, failure to comply will entail a real and substantial risk that the planning permission may be invalidated.

CONDITIONS AND MITIGATION

5.39   TCP(EIA) Regulations 1999, reg 21(1)(c)(iii) requires a description of the main measures to avoid, reduce and, if possible, offset the major adverse effects of the development. This raises the question of how such mitigating measures are to be secured. In terms of planning permission, the most obvious ways are by conditions or a s 106 obligation (under TCPA 1990). However, many potential effects, particularly in terms of the ongoing operation of industrial processes, will in practice be controlled by conditions imposed on other consent, for example integrated pollution prevention and control, waste management licensing, radioactive substances, etc.

5.40   The basic point to keep in mind is perhaps that the planning authority faces two related but separate issues; first what are the relevant mitigating measures emerging from the ES, consultation responses and other environmental information and, second, how in practice those measures are going to be secured. It is the first question which is of primary relevance when stating those measures under TCP(EIA) Regulations 1999, reg 21(1)(c)(iii). Thus the statement is primarily concerned with the *content* of those measures, not the legal regime under which they are to be secured. As to the second question, there is nothing in the TCP(EIA) Regulations 1999 or the EIA Directive which requires a local planning authority to seek to secure all those mitigating measures under the planning permission (or in the Directive's terms, the 'development consent') if there are more appropriate mechanisms by which they can be imposed.[1] What seems important is that, by one means or another, the key aspects of mitigation stated in the ES are translated into clear and enforceable requirements. Otherwise, the developer will be under no obligation to implement the measures put forward in the ES.

1   See also Department of the Environment Circular 2/99, para 122.

Incorporation of mitigation measures into conditions

5.41   Where a planning authority may run into difficulties is by seeking to incorporate mitigation measures stated in the ES wholesale into planning conditions. Circular 2/99 cautions against this approach:[1]

'Conditions attached to a planning permission may include mitigation measures. However, a condition requiring the development to be "in accordance with the Environmental Statement" is unlikely to be valid unless the ES was exceptional in the precision with which it specified the mitigation measures to be undertaken. Even then, the condition would need to refer to the specific part of the ES, rather than the whole document.'

The problem is whether such a condition can meet the general test of being enforceable and precise. In addition to these traditional tests, there is a strong argument that members of the public ought to be able to understand the terms on which permission is given and the mitigating measures emerging from the EIA process, without having to trawl through or cross-refer to other lengthy and highly technical material. Unfortunately, the first Secretary of State did not appear to heed his own advice in relation to the grant of planning permission to Minosus Ltd for the use of rock salt caverns at Winsford Rock Salt Mine, Middlewich, as a waste disposal facility.[2] The permission included a condition that the development should only be carried out in accordance with a list of documents, including the ES. On a challenge to the permission[3] the first Secretary of State submitted to the quashing of the permission on the basis that it was incorrect to include the ES in its entirety by reference as a planning condition. It appears that in so agreeing, the first Secretary of State was influenced by the undesirability of the public having to refer to separate and substantial documents to try and make sense of the planning permission.[4]

1   Department of the Environment Circular 2/99, para 121.
2   Ref APP/z0645/v/01/000273, Decision letter dated 26 July 2002.
3   CO/4140/2002.
4   Personal communication with Minosus Ltd.

5.42   Another area of potential difficulty in relation to translating mitigating measures into conditions is where conditions leave over matters which may impact on the environment for future determination, for example by approval of a detailed scheme. This issue is exemplified by the case of *Smith v Secretary of State for the Environment, Transport and the Regions*,[1] and is discussed below.[2]

1   [2003] EWCA Civ 262, [2003] All ER (D) 36 (Mar).
2   See para **5.44**.

Procedural fairness and conditions

5.43   It should also be borne in mind that the process of considering conditions at a public inquiry or hearing is subject to normal rules of procedural fairness, and that failure to involve third-party objectors in the process may be a ground for quashing a decision. This was the case in *Jory v Secretary of State for Transport, Local Government and the Regions*,[1] where, having heard representations from all sides as to noise conditions on a proposed auditorium development, the inspector later sought the view of the appellant and the council on an alternative form of wording. While the objector's forte might not have been drafting planning conditions, Sullivan J held that elementary fairness demanded that he be given the opportunity to comment.[2]

1   [2002] EWHC 2724 (Admin), [2003] 03 LS Gaz R 33.
2   [2002] EWHC 2742 (Admin), [2003] 03 LS Gaz R 33, paras 38–40.

THE RISKS OF LEAVING MATTERS OVER

5.44   The grant of planning permission will not necessarily dot every 'i' and cross every 't'. In outline planning permission, reserved matters will be approved at a later stage, and the potential difficulties which this can present in EIA terms are discussed below.[1] But even where full planning permission is concerned, there may well be conditions which require matters of detail to be subject to later approval, often by the preparation of a scheme to be submitted to the planning authority for its later approval. In practical terms, this may well be a sensible administrative approach by leaving discrete issues of detail to be worked out after the principle of granting permission has been settled. However, as a process it can sit uneasily with the EIA process, for various reasons. Members so the public may well feel that they have been denied the opportunity to subject these matters to the EIA process, leaving them to be worked out in private between the developer and the planning authority.

1   See para **6.61**.

5.45   One potential problem is that if the matters left over involve the mitigation of potential environmental effects, whether such mitigation can be properly taken into account in considering whether or not significant effects are likely. Examples could be schemes to ensure the control of noise, or the remediation of contaminated land. The issue here will essentially be whether the mitigation measures provide the authority with sufficient confidence for this purpose.[1] If the detail of the measures will only become apparent when put forward and approved, it will be all the more difficult to satisfy this test.

1 See paras **3.81–3.88**.

5.46 Another problem is the extent to which leaving matters over means that either the development, or the likely significant effects, or the mitigating measures, cannot be described sufficiently to comply with Schedule 4 of the TCP(EIA) Regulations. If not, then the planning authority will have fallen foul of the reg 3(2) prohibition on granting permission without having first taken the environmental information into account. The problem is encapsulated in the Court of Appeal decision in *Smith v Secretary of State for the Environment, Transport and the Regions*.[1] Mrs Smith challenged under s 288 of the TCP Act 1990 the grant of permission by a planning inspector to extend a stone quarry and to allow its use for landfill over a ten year period. The focus was on various conditions imposed on the grant of permission. These required: (1) that development should be carried out in accordance with various specified plans unless otherwise agreed in writing by the local planning authority; (2) that development should not take place until a detailed scheme for the landscaping of the site had been submitted to and approved in writing by the local planning authority; and (3) that no development should take place until a scheme to suppress dust had been submitted to and approved in writing by the local planning authority. Thus the first condition permitted departure from the approved plans, whereas the second and third were of a 'Grampian' nature, preventing the commencement of development until the relevant details had been approved.

1 [2003] EWCA Civ 262.

5.47 Giving the main judgment,[1] Waller L J deduced two particular propositions from the case law. The first was that the inspector or the local planning authority would fail to comply with the relevant requirement[2] if they attempted to leave over questions which related to the significance of the impact on the environment and the effectiveness of any mitigation; essentially because the public would not have been allowed to debate the relevant environmental issues.[3] The second, and Waller L J felt the most difficult area, was that it is possible to leave final details of, for example, a landscaping scheme to be clarified in the context of a reserved matter or a condition on full permission.[4]

1 Black J agreed; Sedley L J produced a judgment which agreed, whilst expressing important doubts.
2 The case concerned the TCP(AEE) Regulations 1988, the equivalent provision of which was reg 4(2).
3 [2003] EWCA Civ 262, para 27.
4 [2003] EWCA Civ 262, para 28.

5.48   This led to a detailed debate as to the proper meaning of the words used in the relevant conditions, and whether the operation of those conditions could lead to a situation where there could be possible impacts on the environment that had not been properly considered. In relation to the first condition dealing with approved variations from the plans, as Waller L J put it:[1]

> 'Do the conditions allow the LPA to approve a deviation from the plans which might have a significant adverse impact on the environment, or are the LPA constrained when considering the landscaping scheme to dealing with details within the parameters identified by the plans?'

Waller L J solved this question by reading the conditions in the context of the inspector's decision letter, and concluding that read in this way, it was not contemplated that the local planning authority could go outside the constraints placed by the plans and '... in effect reconsider the impact on the environment and vary the conditions imposed by the plans.'[2] Similarly, in relation to the conditions requiring approval of a landscape scheme and dust suppression measures, the inspector was held to have been entitled, having set the parameters of the planning permission on matters such as contours and tree planting, to form the view that the local planning authority could be left to deal with the details in such a way as to mitigate adverse effects.[3]

1   [2003] EWCA Civ 262, para 37.
2   [2003] EWCA Civ 262, para 45.
3   [2003] EWCA Civ 262, para 49.

5.49   Sedley L J delivered a robust judgment in which he stated that anybody reading the conditions could be forgiven for concluding that instead of fulfilling his duty to set conditions to mitigate adverse effects, the inspector had 'simply passed the buck' to the local planning authority.[1] If this were indeed the case, Sedley L J would have had little hesitation in holding the decision to constitute 'an abdication of the inspector's functions.'[2] Sedley L J was prepared to agree with the other members of the court that the conditions could be read in such a way as to avoid that consequence, but expressed serious doubts as to whether this was putting a gloss on the conditions, and whether condition with such elastic wording was appropriate for decisions on which the developer and public alike were entitled to expect legal certainty.[3] In particular, Sedley L J called into question the common practice of planning inspectors using model conditions in Circular 11/95 so as to remit matters such as landscape management plans to the local planning authority. Sedley L J suggested that it might seem more appropriate that the Secretary of State should reserve them for himself so as to keep the public in the picture:[4]

> 'It would be odd if such a carefully structured regime could be circumvented in this way by the surrender of public judgment to private negotiation'.

1   [2003] EWCA Civ 262, para 54.
2   [2003] EWCA Civ 262, para 55.
3   [2003] EWCA Civ 262, para 56.
4   [2003] EWCA Civ 262, para 58.

5.50   The decision in *Smith* offers much food for thought. Clearly it may be preferable where possible for both local planning authorities and inspectors to avoid such conditions. Where they are used, this should only be in cases where it is clear that they will not sanction a departure from the development and mitigating measures which was subject to EIA, so as to allow changes which are significant in environmental terms. Their wording will also require close scrutiny in this respect, to avoid undue elasticity or ambiguity. So far as planning inquiries are concerned, the use of such conditions may often be driven by the constraints of the inquiry timetable, leaving insufficient time for these matters of detail to be worked out and resolved. Developers and local planning authorities could potentially assist in this by putting forward more detail before the inquiry, and seeking to reach common ground where possible as to the content of such schemes, which would then be open for members of the public to consider and comment on as part of the inquiry process. As it is, these matters are too often in practice left until too late in the day, at a session at the end of the inquiry dealing with conditions. Obviously there may in some cases be good reasons why a detailed scheme of landscaping cannot be put forward sooner, but it is suggested that developers and their consultants should address the question of whether it is practicable to make such material available sooner, and indeed possibly include it within the environmental statement.

TRANSBOUNDARY EFFECTS

5.51   One final aspect relates to the requirement of the EIA Directive for special procedures in the case of EIA development which may have significant environmental effects in another member state.[1] This is addressed by the TCP(EIA) Regulations 1999, regs 27 and 28, as amended by the TCP(EIA) (England and Wales) (Amendment) Regulations 2000.[2]

1   See para **5.05**.
2   SI 2000/2867, reg 2(1) and (4).

Development likely to have effects in another EEA state

5.52   TCP(EIA) Regulations 1999, reg 27 applies in circumstances where it comes to the attention of the Secretary of State that development proposed to be carried out in England or Wales is the subject of an EIA application and is likely to have significant effects on the environment in another EEA state, or where another EEA state likely to be significantly affected so requests. It should be noted that the provision applies to any EEA state, defined as a party to the Agreement on the European Economic Area, not just EU member states. The Secretary of State is concerned not only with the EC EIA Directive in this regard, but also with the UNECE Convention on EIA in a Transboundary Context (the Espoo Convention).[1] In such cases, relevant particulars of the development must be published in the *London Gazette* and sent to the EEA state concerned (reg 27(1) and (2)). Where the EEA state indicates within the reasonable time allowed to it, that it wishes to participate in the EIA procedure, then the Secretary of State must:

— Send to the EEA state a copy of the ES and other relevant information (reg 27(3)).
— Arrange, 'insofar as he is concerned', for particulars to be made available to the consultation authorities and the public concerned in the EEA state and to ensure they are given an opportunity to forward their opinion, within a reasonable time, before permission is granted (reg 27(4)). The words 'insofar as he is concerned' no doubt reflect the fact that the responsibility for these aspects under art 7(3) of the EIA Directive is shared between both states concerned.
— Enter into consultations with the EEA state in accordance with art 7(4) of the Directive (reg 27(5)).
— Inform the EEA state of the ultimate decision and forward to it a statement of the content of the decision, the main reasons on which it is based and a description of the main mitigating measures (reg 27(6)).

1   Cm 1645.

5.53   Circular 2/99 suggests that developments that are likely to have significant effects on the environment of other countries will be rare in England.[1] If such developments are identified, then the Secretary of State is likely to make a direction under the TCP(GDP) Order 1995, art 14, that planning permission may not be granted until the end of such time as is necessary for the international procedures to be concluded.[2] Further, such development is likely to be a candidate for exercise of TCPA 1990, s 77 call-in powers.[3]

1   Department of the Environment Circular 2/99, para 116.
2   Department of the Environment Circular 2/99, para 116.
3   Department of the Environment Circular 2/99, para 117.

Development likely to have transboundary effects in England and Wales

5.54   TCP(EIA) Regulations 1999, reg 28 caters for the converse situation where the Secretary of State receives information from another EEA state of proposed development there, which may have significant effects in England and Wales. The Secretary of State must:
— Enter into consultations with the other EEA state in accordance with art 7(4) of the Directive (reg 28(1)(a)).
— Determine in agreement with the other EEA state a reasonable period within which members of the public may submit to the competent authority in the other EEA state their representations before development consent is given (reg 28(1)(b)).
— 'Insofar as he is concerned', arrange for the information received from the other EEA state to be made available to the authorities in England and Wales which he considers are likely to be concerned by the project by reason of the specific environmental responsibilities, and to the public concerned (reg 28(2)(a)).
— Again, 'insofar as he is concerned', ensure that those authorities and the public concerned are given an opportunity, before development consent is given, to forward to the competent authority within the relevant EEA state their opinion on the information supplied (reg 28(2)(b)).

CHAPTER 6

Special cases

INTRODUCTION

6.01   There are a number of procedures under the domestic planning system which require special consideration in terms of the application of environmental impact assessment (EIA) procedures. Some of these are expressly dealt with in the Town and Country Planning (Environmental Impact Assessment) Regulations 1999 (TCP(EIA) Regulations 1999), Pt VII ('Special Cases'). These are:
— Development by a local planning authority (reg 22).
— Permission granted by simplified planning zone (SPZ) and enterprise zone (EZ) schemes (regs 23 and 24).
— Unauthorised development and enforcement procedures (regs 25 and 26).
— Review of old mineral planning permissions (ROMP) applications (reg 26A).

6.02   As well as these provisions in the TCP(EIA) Regulations 1999, there are specific provisions in the Town and Country Planning (General Development Procedure) Order 1995, SI 1995/419 (TCP(GPD) Order 1995) as to the relationship between EIA development and permitted development rights.

6.03   In addition to these specific provisions, issues arise as to other aspects of the planning system, for example procedures relating to outline planning applications and the approval of reserved matters; applications under the Town and Country Planning Act 1990 (TCPA 1990), ss 73 and 73A; and whether EIA requirements should extend to other types of consent where these are necessary in addition to planning permission (in particular, pollution prevention and control (PPC) permits).

'DEVELOPMENT CONSENT'

6.04   The general point which it is important to keep in mind throughout is that the EIA Directive bites on 'development consent' being given for a project within the Directive. 'Development consent' is defined by art 1(2) to mean:

'the decision of the competent authority or authorities which entitles the developer to proceed with the project',
the 'project' being defined as both:
— the execution of construction works or of other installations or schemes, and
— other interventions in the natural surroundings and landscape including those involving the extraction of mineral resources.

6.05   Under the EIA Directive (85/337/EEC, as amended by Directive 97/11/EC), art 2 the EIA may be integrated into the existing procedures for consent to projects, or into procedures established for that purpose. So far as the planning system is concerned, the UK has engrafted the EIA requirements onto the existing procedures for the grant of planning permission, the grant of permission being the 'development consent'. A project may however require a number of consents in addition to the planning permission which authorises its construction. As will be seen, there can be differing views as to whether a particular requirement of consent which governs some aspect of the operation of the project is to be regarded as a 'development consent' for the purposes of the Directive.

6.06   In *R v North Yorkshire County Council, ex p Brown*,[1] in considering this issue, Lord Hoffmann referred to those cases involving the application of the Directive to 'pipeline' cases where the procedure for obtaining consent, or the principal consent, was already under way before the relevant commencement date. In particular he referred to *R v Secretary of State for the Environment, ex p Greenpeace Ltd*,[2] in which it was argued that EIA requirements applied to the grant of authorisation under the Radioactive Substances Act 1993 for the discharge of radioactive waste from a nuclear reprocessing facility at Sellafield, for which planning permission had been granted in outline in 1978, and full permission in 1983. There Potts J held that the grant of authorisation under the Radioactive Substances Act 1993 was not the 'development consent' which entitled the applicant to proceed with the 'project' of disposing of nuclear waste (though obviously the plant could not lawfully have operated without such authorisation). The waste disposal aspects were all part of one project, starting with the construction of the plant, for which consent had been given before the Directive came into force. From this case and others, Lord Hoffmann discerned a clear principle:[3]

'... the Directive does not apply to decisions which involve merely the detailed regulation of activities for which the principal consent, raising the substantial environmental issues has already been given.'

It is suggested that this distinction needs to be borne in mind in considering the specific situations discussed in this chapter.[4]

1   [2000] 1 AC 397.
2   [1994] 4 All ER 352.
3   [2000] 1 AC 397 at 405C.
4   See for example the approach of the Court of Appeal in *R (Prokopp) v London Underground Limited* (CA, 7 July 2003) to whether subsequent regulation of a project as it progresses (for example under planning conditions) is a 'development consent' (para **6.33** below).

DEVELOPMENT BY A LOCAL PLANNING AUTHORITY

6.07   The EIA Directive draws no distinction in its requirements between public and private projects. This is made clear by art 1(1) which expressly refers to 'public and private projects' and by the definition of 'developer' at art 1(2), which includes '... the public authority which initiates a project'.

6.08   The Town and Country Planning (Assessment of Environmental Effects) Regulations 1988 (TCP(AEE) Regulations 1988) originally contained reg 17 on obtaining planning permission by local authorities under the Town and Country Planning General Regulations 1976, SI 1976/1419. This system was repealed and replaced in turn by the Town and Country Planning General Regulations, SI 1992/1492. In consequence, reg 17 was repealed by SI 1992/1494 and replaced with a new reg 25A, dealing with local authority planning applications. These provisions were carried forward into reg 22 of the TCP(EIA) Regulations 1999, reg 22.

6.09   TCP(EIA) Regulations 1999, reg 22 addresses the situation where the relevant planning authority for the purposes of the Regulations is also the applicant or proposed applicant (whether alone or jointly with some other party). Effectively the TCP(EIA) Regulations 1999 apply to such applications, subject to certain modifications. Thus the authority will have to prepare an environmental statement (ES), and publish and consult on it in the normal way.

6.10   TCP(EIA) Regulations 1999, regs 5 and 6 on screening opinions do not apply (reg 22(1)(a)). Instead there is a specific power for a planning authority which is minded to make a planning application to adopt a screening opinion or request the Secretary of State in writing to make a screening direction (reg 22(2)). The Secretary of State may request the authority to provide additional information for this purpose (reg 6(3)) and the authority is under a duty to send such information as may be requested (reg 22(5)).

6.11   It is to be hoped that in cases of development falling within TCP(EIA) Regulations 1999, Sch 1 or 2, the planning authority would address the issue of screening before submitting a planning application, and submit an ES with the application if this is required. However, if an application is made for Sch 1 or 2 development without an ES, and there has been no screening opinion, then the authority will be required to adopt a screening opinion within three weeks (reg 5(3) as applied by reg 22(1)(b)).

6.12   The procedures for scoping in TCP(EIA) Regulations 1999, regs 10 and 11 obviously do not apply (reg 22(1)(c)), since these would involve the authority in formally giving an opinion on the scope of its own ES. However, the procedures in reg 12(4) for consultation with relevant authorities as to information which they may hold will apply (reg 22(1)(d)) and may be useful.[1]

1   See para **4.22** on these procedures.

6.13   TCP(EIA) Regulations 1999, reg 13 apply, with modifications, so that the authority when lodging an ES must serve a copy on each consultation body, inform the bodies that representation may be made to the planning authority, and send three copies of the ES plus the application and supporting documents to the Secretary of State (reg 22(1)(e)). Regulation 13(4) will apply so that the authority may not determine the application for a 14-day period from the last date on which a copy of the ES was served in accordance with these requirements. Where the ES is submitted after the planning application, reg 14 on the publicity procedures to be followed will apply in its entirety.[1]

1   See para **5.18** above.

6.14   If the authority's planning application for TCP(EIA) Regulations 1999, Sch 1 or 2 development is called in by the Secretary of State, and no ES has been submitted or screening opinion adopted, then reg 8 will apply as with any other application, so that the Secretary of State may notify the authority that the submission of an ES is required. If an ES is then submitted, the consultation procedures of reg 13 will apply (see reg 22(1)(f)). The procedures under reg 19 for the Secretary of State or inspector to call for 'further information' if the ES is deficient will also apply.

6.15   The requirements of TCP(EIA) Regulations 1999, regs 17 and 18 on making the ES available to the public will also apply, as will the publicity requirements of reg 20 and the requirement for a notice and statement informing the public of the decision under reg 21.

CROWN DEVELOPMENT

6.16   The issue of development by the Crown is dealt with at para 157 of Circular 2/99, which states as follows:[1]

'Like the Town and Country Planning Act, the [EIA] Regulations do not bind the Crown. Developments by Crown bodies which would require planning permission if they were proposed by any other person and which require EIA under the terms of the Regulations are likely to be uncommon in England. When any such development is proposed, the Crown body concerned will submit an Environmental Statement to the local planning authority when consulting them under the arrangements set out in Part IV of the Memorandum to Circular 18/84. In addition, the Ministry of Defence will, in appropriate circumstances and subject to considerations affecting national security, provide Environmental Statements in respect of major defence projects.'

1   Department of the Environment Circular 2/99, para 157.

6.17   It may be noted that the EIA Directive expressly does not apply to 'projects serving national defence purposes'.[1] Leaving such projects aside, the Directive will apply to all other types of Crown development falling within Annexes I and II, except those which are the subject of specific exemption in accordance with art 2(3), or the details of which are adopted by a specific act of national legislation.[2] The vast majority of the types of project mentioned in the Directive will be carried out by private entities, and the Circular is therefore correct in drawing attention to the rarity of the need to apply EIA procedures to Crown development in this country. Nonetheless, where such requirements do apply, it may be noted that the Directive not only requires that such projects are subject to EIA, but also that they are subject to 'a requirement for development consent'. Under the law as it presently stands, this will not be the case for Crown development, unless the decision of the Crown body to proceed with the project is regarded as the 'development consent'. The difficulty with this is that the Directive clearly appears to contemplate that the development consent is a decision taken by a competent authority, which entitles the developer (which can include a public authority) to proceed.[3]

1   EIA Directive, art 1(4). See further para **3.49** above.
2   EIA Directive, art 1(5).
3   EIA Directive, art 1(2).

SIMPLIFIED PLANNING ZONES AND ENTERPRISE ZONES

Old schemes and orders

6.18   By the TCP(EIA) Regulations 1999, reg 23(1), any SPZ scheme[1] or EZ order[2] which had effect immediately before the commencement of the Regulations (on 14 March 1999) ceased to have effect on that date:

(i)   to grant planning permission for Sch 1 development, and

(ii)   to grant planning permission for Sch 2 development unless a screening opinion has been adopted or a screening direction made, to the effect that the particular proposed development is not EIA development.

1   A simplified planning zone (SPZ) scheme has the effect of granting planning permission within the zone for development, or any class of development, specified in the scheme: see TCPA 1990, s 82(2).
2   An enterprise zone (EZ) order (made originally under the Local Government, Planning and Land Act 1980, Sch 32) has effect to grant planning permission for development, or any class of development, specified in the scheme: see TCPA 1990, s 88(1).

6.19   By TCP(EIA) Regulations 1999, reg 23(2) this does not however affect the completion of any development begun before the commencement date of 14 March 1999. For this purpose, in accordance with reg 2(2), the expression 'begun' will be subject to the TCPA 1990, s 56 ('Time when development begun'), which specifies the circumstances in which development of land is taken to be 'initiated'. The arrangements which applied to SPZs and EZs prior to the 1999 Regulations are explained in Circular 24/88.[1]

1   Department of the Environment Circular 24/88, Welsh Office Circular 48/88, Environmental Assessment (12 July 1988). See also Environmental Assessment: A Guide to Procedures (Department of the Environment/ Welsh Office, 1989).

New schemes and orders

6.20 By the TCP(EIA) Regulations 1999, reg 24, the same restrictions apply to SPZ schemes adopted or approved, EZ orders made, or modified EZ schemes approved after the commencement date of 14 March 1999. Such schemes or orders do not grant permission for Sch 1 development, or for Sch 2 development, unless a negative screening opinion or direction has been obtained.

UNAUTHORISED DEVELOPMENT

6.21 Planning permission can of course be granted in the context of an enforcement notice appeal under the TCPA 1990, s 177(1)(a), which provides that on determination of an appeal under s 174 (Appeal against enforcement notice) the Secretary of State may:

> 'grant planning permission in respect of the matters stated in the enforcement notice as constituting a breach of planning control, whether in relation to the whole or any part of those matters or in relation to the whole or any part of the land to which the notice relates.'

Thus EIA is required to be incorporated into these procedures in order to secure compliance with EC law. This was not immediately appreciated by the government when EIA was introduced in 1988, and the necessary procedures were introduced by the TCP (Environmental Assessment and Unauthorised Development) Regulations 1995 which came into force on 2 October 1995.[1]

1   SI 1995/2258, explained in Department of the Environment Circular 13/95 (Welsh Office Circular 39/95).

6.22 TCP(EIA) Regulations 1999, reg 25(1) now provides an overarching requirement that the Secretary of State shall not grant planning permission under the TCPA 1990, s 177(1)(a) in respect of EIA development which is the subject of an enforcement notice (termed 'unauthorised EIA development') unless he has first taken the environmental information into account, and he must state in his decision that he has done so. The remainder of reg 25 then lays down the associated procedures.

Procedures on service of enforcement notice

6.23 Where a local planning authority intends to serve an enforcement notice in respect of matters which appear to comprise or include TCP(EIA) Regulations 1999, Sch 1 or Sch 2 development, the authority must, before the notice is issued, adopt a screening opinion (reg 25(2)). Where in the light of this opinion it appears that these matters comprise or include EIA development, they must serve with the enforcement notice a notice (termed 'a regulation 25 notice') which includes the screening opinion and the reg 4(6) statement giving reasons for this opinion, and which requires any appeal against the enforcement notice to the Secretary of State to be accompanied by four copies of an ES relating to the EIA development (reg 25(3)). The authority must also send a copy of the reg 25 notice to the Secretary of State and the consultation bodies (reg 25(4)), and the Secretary of State must be provided with a list of the other persons to whom a copy of the notice is sent (reg 25(5)). The recipient of a reg 25 notice who disagrees with the view that the development is EIA development may apply to the Secretary of State for a screening direction in accordance with the procedures of reg 25(6).

Preparation of ES

6.24   Where a TCP(EIA) Regulations 1999, reg 25 notice is served, similar procedures apply for the facilitation of the preparation of the ES as will apply in normal cases.[1] The planning authority and the consultation authorities are required enter into consultation if requested, to determine whether the consultee has relevant information (reg 25(7)).

1   See para **4.22**.

Appeals where there is no screening opinion or direction

6.25   TCP(EIA) Regulations 1999, regs 25(9)–(11) cover the situation where on consideration of an enforcement appeal it appears to the Secretary of State that the matters alleged to constitute the breach of planning control comprise or include Sch 1 or Sch 2 development, but there has been no screening opinion or direction. The Secretary of State must first make a screening direction (reg 25(9)) and may call for such additional information as he requires from the appellant for that purpose (reg 25(10)). Failure to provide such information within the reasonable period specified in the Secretary of State's notice will result in the deemed application for permission and any appeal under ground (a) (that planning permission ought to be granted) lapsing (reg 25(11)).

Appeals without an ES

6.26   Where the Secretary of State is dealing with an enforcement appeal and the matters alleged to constitute the breach of planning control comprise or include EIA development, but the documents submitted do not include an ES referred to as such, the procedures of TCPA(EIA) Regulations, 1999, reg 25(12) will apply. In this situation there will have been a prior screening opinion by the local planning authority under reg 25(2), or a screening direction under reg 25(6) or (9). The Secretary of State must within three weeks of receipt of the appeal, or such longer period as he may reasonably require, notify the appellant of the requirement to submit four copies of an ES within a specified period or such longer period as the Secretary of State may allow (reg 25(12)(a) and (c)). Failure by the appellant to comply with such a requirement will result in the deemed application and ground (a) appeal lapsing (reg 25(12)(e)). The Secretary of

State need not however call for a separate ES for the purpose of the enforcement appeal in cases where the appellant has submitted an ES for the purposes of a TCPA 1990, s 78 appeal against refusal of planning permission which relates to the same development and is to be determined at the same time as the enforcement appeal; in that case the ES (and any further information and representations made in relation to it) are to be treated as the ES for the purpose of the enforcement appeal (reg 25(12)(b)).

Procedure and publicity where ES submitted on appeal

6.27   Where the Secretary of State receives in connection with an enforcement appeal an ES which the appellant refers to as an ES for the purposes of the TCP(EIA) Regulations 1999, then various procedures are to be followed. This applies irrespective of whether the ES is submitted at the outset, or in response to later notice from the Secretary of State. First the Secretary of State must send a copy to the local planning authority and inform them that they may make representations; the consultation bodies to whom a copy of any reg 25 notice was sent must also be notified and sent a copy of the ES (or part of it) if they so request within the seven-day period allowed (reg 25(13)(a)–(c)). Second, the procedures of reg 19 whereby the Secretary of State may request further information[1] apply with minor modifications; the sanction for failure to provide such information is that the deemed application and ground (a) appeal will lapse (reg 25(14)). Further, the local planning authority must publicise the ES by notice in a local newspaper (reg 25(16)–(18)) and make the ES and associated documents available for public inspection (reg 25(19)).

1   See paras .**4.24** and **5.21**.

Procedures where planning permission granted on enforcement appeal

6.28   Where the Secretary of State grants planning permission for EIA development on an enforcement appeal, the relevant particular must be placed on the planning register (TCP(EIA) Regulations 1999, reg 25(20)) and the same requirements as to placing a statement on the planning register as apply to normal grants of planning permission[1] will apply (reg 25(21)).

1   See para **5.29**.

Unauthorised development with significant transboundary effects

6.29   In those cases (presumably extremely rare) where unauthorised development is likely to have significant effects in another EEA state, the requirements of TCP(EIA) Regulations 1999, reg 27[1] will apply with appropriate minor modifications (reg 26).

1   See para **5.52**.

EIA requirements and enforcement discretion

6.30   An important issue is the extent to which the need to ensure effectiveness of the EIA Directive's requirements may have an effect on the discretion of local planning authorities as to whether in the words of the TCPA 1990, s 172(1)(b), it is 'expedient' to issue an enforcement notice where there has been a breach of planning control which involves, or may involve EIA development. Failure to enforce would mean that the development is allowed to continue or to remain, without EIA.

6.31   In *R (Prokopp) v London Underground Ltd*,[1] the scheme was the highly contentious development of the Bishopsgate Goods Yard for the East London Line Extension. Planning permission for the relevant works had lapsed. The local planning authorities concerned, Hackney and Tower Hamlets, requested that London Underground submit a fresh planning application and environmental statement. However, the authorities then resolved that they would not enforce against the scheme if London Underground entered into a planning obligation to give effect to the conditions on the original planning permission, in varied form. The case for Mr Prokopp was that the development fell within the EIA Directive, Annex II, para 10(h) and the TCP(EIA) Regulations 1999, Sch 2, para 10(i) ('elevated and underground railways ... used exclusively for passenger transport') and that failure to enforce was in effect a decision entitling the developer to proceed, and thus a 'development consent'.[2]

1   [2003] EWHC 940 Admin (Collins J); reversed by CA 7 July 2003 (see para **6.33** below). For a further case on the same project, see *R (Hammerton) v London Underground Limited* [2002] EWHC 2307 Admin.
2   Relying on *R v North Yorkshire County Council, ex p Brown* [2000] 1 AC 397.

6.32   Following an interim injunction granted by Ouseley J to restrain the works, the matter came before Collins J, who held that the injunction was correctly granted. Collins J held that the decision not to enforce was a grant of development consent for the purposes of the EIA Directive, and so in principle EIA was required, unless on the facts there had been substantial compliance with the requirements by what had gone before when the whole history of the matter was taken into account.[1] As Collins J put it:[2]

> 'The use of a decision not to take enforcement action coupled with conditions to be imposed in a s 106 agreement as a means of permitting a development to proceed is not unlawful. But it cannot avoid the requirement to provide an EIA if the development falls within the Directive and an EIA is required.'

Tower Hamlets LBC had not considered whether the Directive required them to enforce,[3] and neither authority had adequately addressed the issue of whether adequate conditions were in place to ensure adequate protection for the listed structures involved. Nonetheless, there had been an EIA in 1993 when the planning permission was originally granted, and in the view of Collins J, there it would be open to the local planning authorities to conclude there had been substantial compliance with EIA requirements; developments since 1993 were not such as to justify re-opening the decision. Moreover,

Collins J expressed the view that not only had there been substantial compliance, but that the decision now only involved the detailed regulation of an activity for which the principal consent had been given.[4]

1   [2003] EWHC 960 (Admin), [2003] 19 EG 119 (CS), para 25.
2   [2003] EWHC 960 (Admin), [2003] 19 EG 119 (CS), para 26.
3   This was because they had been advised, wrongly so Collins J held, that to take enforcement action would involve giving direct effect to the Directive in an unlawful way: see [2003] EWHC 960 (Admin), [2003] 19 EG 119 (CS), para 36.
4   [2003] EWHC 960 (Admin), [2003] 19 EG 119 (CS), para 38.

6.33   The decision of Collins J would have had significant implications for planning authorities. It was, however, reversed by the Court of Appeal on 7 July 2003. The Court held that there was no breach of the Directive in the circumstances of the case where EIA had been undertaken initially, and the permission had lapsed because of breach of conditions imposed by the national authority, which were not required by the EIA Directive.[1] The entitlement of the developer to proceed was held in the circumstances to stem from the planning permission granted in 1997 and not from the later negotiations of the local planning authority.[2] Buxton L J was satisfied that EC law did not require the surprising conclusion that in the circumstances of the case, the EIA process would have to be re-commenced. The fact that a further consent might be required in the course of the project by virtue of domestic law did not mean that such consent has a 'development consent' engaging the Directive.[3] The planning authority's 'failure to interrupt' the project was not such a development consent in the case.[4] At first sight the decision may seem a set back to the use of EIA by opponents to decisions.[5] It should however be seen in context. The breach of condition which had led to the permission lapsing was not in itself a matter for EIA or something which had significant environmental effects. The case does not affect the position where failure to enforce against development where there has never been an adequate EIA, in which case it is suggested EC law may require enforcement.[6] The case is thus very much one on its own special facts.

1   See Schiemann L J at para 42. Kennedy L J agreeing.
2   See Schiemann L J at para 46–47. Kennedy L J agreeing.
3   See paras 59–61.
4   See paras 61.
5   A petition for leave to appeal was dismissed by the House of Lords.
6   See Schiemann L J at para 38.

ROMP APPLICATIONS

6.34   The somewhat esoteric procedures for the review of old mining and mineral permissions (ROMP) have given rise to particular difficulties in the EIA context. The Planning and Compensation Act 1991, s 22 and Sch 2, introduced a scheme for the review of 'old mining permissions' for mineral working and the deposit of mineral waste, which were authorised under wartime Interim Development Orders (IDOs) and for which planning permission was retrospectively deemed to be granted under the

Town and Country Planning Act 1947, s 77. This involves the making of an application to determine the conditions to which the permission is to be subject and the registration of the permission, failing which the permission ceases to have effect. The objective is of course to ensure that such operations, if they are to continue, are subject to modern standards of environmental protection, rather than the rudimentary or non-existent controls when they were originally imposed. The Environment Act 1995, s 96 and Schs 13 and 14, extended this approach to require the review of old mineral permissions granted between 1948 and 1982 (Sch 13) and the ongoing periodic review of all mineral permissions (Sch 14). There is a useful description of the working of the statutory scheme by Lightman J in *R v North Lincolnshire County Council, ex p Horticultural and Garden Products Sales (Humberside) Ltd.*[1]

1   (1997) 76 P & CR 363.

6.35   The importance of the decision of the House of Lords in *R v North Yorkshire County Council, ex p Brown*[1] is that it made clear that the process of setting such conditions (and thereby allowing the mining activity to continue) constitutes 'development consent' and as such must be subject to EIA procedures. In 1999 the DETR issued a consultation paper, *Review of Old Mineral Permissions and Environmental Impact Assessment*, which led ultimately to reform of the legislation.

1   [2000] 1 AC 397.

6.36   The changes to the legislation to deal with EIA for ROMP applications were effected by the TCP(EIA) (England and Wales) (Amendment) Regulations 2000,[1] which inserted reg 26A into the TCP(EIA) Regulations 1999.[2] Unfortunately, the amendments are made in a perhaps unnecessarily complex way. It is necessary to read in amendments made by regs 26A(2)–(15) and to superimpose a number of additional provisions in reg 26A(16)–(30). The new provisions apply to ROMP applications and ROMP development. A ROMP application is an application to the relevant mineral planning authority to determine the conditions to which a planning permission is to be subject under the Planning and Compensation Act 1991, Sch 2, or under the Environment Act 1995, Schs 13 or 14.[3] ROMP development is development *which has yet to be carried out* (hence the provisions are not retrospective) and which is authorised by a mineral permission in respect of which a ROMP application is made. In general terms the TCP(EIA) Regulations 1999 apply to ROMP applications and ROMP development as they apply to the grant of any other planning permission, subject to various modifications and additions.[4]

1   SI 2000/2867.
2   Commencement date 15 November 2000.
3   TCP(EIA) Regulations 1999, reg 2(1).
4   TCP(EIA) Regulations 1999, reg 26A(1).

6.37   The TCP(EIA) Regulations 1999, reg 3 prohibition on granting permission without having taken the environmental information into account, and the requirement to state it has been taken into account, apply to ROMP applications received on or after 15 November 2000.¹ The provisions on screening apply, as do the procedures whereby the applicant may be required to submit an ES, save that the period within which the applicant can indicate that they intend to provide an ES is extended from three to six weeks.² The requirements as to publicity in Pt V of the Regulations apply where an ES is submitted with a ROMP application as for a normal planning application with consequential modifications, and the requirements of the Town and Country Planning (General Development Procedure) Order 1995, SI 1995/419 (TCP(GDP) Order 1995), art 8 and Sch 3 (publicity for applications for planning permission) are applied to such cases.³

1   TCP(EIA) Regulations 1999, reg 26A(2).
2   TCP(EIA) Regulations 1999, reg 26A(3)(a) and (5)(a).
3   TCP(EIA) Regulations 1999, reg 26A(9).

6.38   As well as the modifications to the normal provisions of the TCP(EIA) Regulations 1999 to apply to ROMP applications, reg 26A of the Regulations also contains some freestanding additions to the regime, in particular:
— as to the suspension of the planning permission to which the ROMP application relates, so that it will not authorise any minerals development¹ if the applicant does not respond to a request for an ES or for further information within the relevant period (reg 26A(17) and (18)) until the relevant information is provided;
— the deeming provisions in all three ROMP regimes,² whereby failure by the planning authority to determine the application within the prescribed period or any agreed extension results in the authority being deemed to have imposed those conditions put forward in the application, do not have effect unless a screening opinion or direction has determined that the ROMP development is not EIA development (reg 26A(22)(a));³
— the provisions as to the register of applications under the TCPA 1990, s 69 and the TCP(GDP) Order 1995 (art 25) apply to ROMP applications (reg 26A(22)(b));
— the usual requirement under the Planning and Compensation Act 1991, Sch 2, para 4(4), to give written notice of its decision as soon as reasonably practicable does not apply (reg 26A(23));
— the authority has a period of 16 weeks to give notice of its decision beginning with the date of receipt of the application, for which purpose the ROMP application is not received until the authority has received a copy of the ES, any documents required to accompany it and any additional information which the authority has notified the applicant that the ES should contain (reg 26A(24) and (25)) and failure to give notice of determination within that period gives a right of appeal to the Secretary of State (reg 26A(26));
— the requirements of the TCP(EIA) Regulations 1999 apply to ROMP applications made by a mineral planning authority, subject to consequential modifications (reg 26A(28)–(30)).

1   This means development consisting of the winning and working of minerals or involving the deposit of mineral waste (TCP(EIA) Regulations 1999, reg 26A(21)). Such suspension does not however affect minerals development carried out before the date of suspension (reg 26A(20)).
2   See the Planning and Compensation Act 1991, Sch 2, para 2(6)(b) and the Environment Act 1995, Sch 13, para 9(9) and Sch 14, para 6(8).

3   These were the provisions which gave rise to difficulties in *R v Somerset County Council, ex p Morris and Perry (Gurney Slade Quarry) Ltd* [2000] Env LR 585, [2000] PLCR 117 and *R v Durham County Council, ex p Huddleston* [2000] Env LR 488.

6.39   The Court of Appeal considered the approval of conditions for 'old minerals permissions' under the Environment Act 1995, Sch 13, and the relationship between these provisions and EIA, in *Payne v Caerphilly County Borough Council.*[1] The developer had had submitted an application under Sch 13 in relation to permissions granted in 1955 and 1961. The 1955 permission had been granted for proposed development described as 'disposal of colliery rubbish', while the 1961 permission had been granted for 'removal of the tip' and was subject to a condition which stated that the permission expired on 31 December 1971. The Council returned the Sch 13 application, stating in a letter that no application could be made in respect of the 1961 permission because as a time-limited permission it was not included on the First List, and had ceased to have effect. However, the 1955 permission for colliery waste tipping on the site was not subject to any such time limit on duration and was, therefore, included on the First List as a dormant site. An application could made to determine new conditions for that permission under Sch 13, para 9, prior to any commencement of works on site. However the authority went on to say that the permission and new conditions would not authorise removal of spoil, but only renewed tipping of colliery waste.

1   [2003] EWCA Civ 71, [2003] All ER (D) 75 (Jan).

6.40   The developer sought a declaration that the authority should be treated as having determined that the conditions to which the two permissions were subject should be those proposed in the application. At first instance, Sullivan J found that there was such a deemed determination in relation to the 1955 permission.[1] On appeal the authority submitted that Sullivan J had been wrong to grant the declaration in relation to the 1955 permission for two main reasons: first, the application had not been a valid application at all so that the application was a nullity; and second, if the application was valid, the TCP(EIA) Regulations 1999 applied, on the basis that the development fell within the description of 'underground mining' or 'installation for the disposal of waste' under Sch 2, so that, by reason of reg 26A(22)(a), the 'deeming' provisions of Sch 13 to the Environment Act 1995 did not apply.

1   [2002] EWHC 866 (Admin), [2002] PLCR 496.

6.41   The Court of Appeal upheld Sullivan J's conclusions as to the Council's first argument, holding that the application had not been a nullity. In relation to the EIA submissions, the Court held that disposal of colliery rubbish did not fall within either of the two descriptions relied upon by the authority: the tipping of colliery rubbish on a site could not properly be described as the carrying out of works to provide 'underground mining', and the disposal of colliery rubbish could not be said to be the provision of an installation 'for the disposal of waste' within the meaning of the TCP(EIA) Regulations 1999, Sch 2.

PERMISSION GRANTED BY GENERAL DEVELOPMENT ORDER

6.42   Under the TCP(GPD) Order 1995, art 3(1) planning permission is granted for the classes of development described as 'permitted development' under Sch 2 of the Order. However, by art 3(10)[1] Sch 1 or Sch 2 development under the TCP(EIA) Regulations 1999 is not permitted unless:
(a)   the local planning authority has adopted a screening opinion that the development is not EIA development; or
(b)   the Secretary of State has made a screening direction to such effect; or
(c)   the Secretary of State has given a direction that the development is exempted under the TCP(EIA) Regulations 1999, reg 4(4).

A screening opinion to the effect that the development is EIA development, which has not been reversed by a screening direction of the Secretary of State, means that the development is treated as development which is not permitted by the TCP(GPD) Order 1995 (art 3(11)).

1   Substituted by the TCP(EIA) Regulations 1999, reg 35(3).

6.43   By art 3(12) of the TCP(GDP) Order 1995[1], art 3(10) does not apply to certain types of permitted development, so that art 3(1) can operate in the normal way. The provision has been amended, and the current types[2] of permitted development within art 3(12) are as follows:
—   development consisting of the carrying out of works by a drainage body within the meaning of the EIA (Land Drainage Improvement Works) Regulations 1999;[3]
—   development within Part 7 (Forestry buildings and operations);
—   development within Part 8, Class D (Deposit of waste from an industrial process on land comprised in site used for that purpose on 1 July 1948);
—   development within Part 11 (Development under local or private acts or orders);
—   development within Part 12, Class B (Deposit by a local authority of waste on land comprised in a site used for that purpose on 1 July 1948);
—   development within Part 17, Class F(a) (Development by a public gas transporter required for the purposes of its undertaking consisting of the laying underground of mains, pipes or other apparatus);
—   development within Part 20, Classes A and B (Coal mining development in mines started before 1 July 1948);
—   development within Part 21, Class B (Deposit on land comprised in a site used for the deposit of waste materials or refuse on 1 July 1948 of waste resulting from coal mining operations);
—   development within Part 20, Class C or D (Development required for the purposes of a mine carried out at an authorised site);
—   Part 21, Class A (Deposit of mineral waste on premises used as mine or on ancillary mining land);
—   Part 22, Class B (Development comprising boreholes, seismic surveys or other excavations for mineral exploration) — provided in each case that the development is carried out on the same land as that on which the same type of permitted development was carried out before 14 March 1999; and

— the completion of any development begun before 14 March 1999.

1   Amended by the TCP(EIA) Regulations 1999, regs 34 and 35 and Sch 5.
2   Two of the original categories (projects serving national defence purposes and electricity supply lines) were revoked by the TCP(EIA) Regulations 1999, save in relation to applications, appeal or enforcement proceedings pre-dating 14 March 1999. National defence projects have their own exemption from EIA (see para **3.49**). As to electricity projects, see para **7.34**.
3   SI 1999/1783; see further para **7.29**.

6.44   These provisions as set out above are summarised only in broad terms, and reference should be made to the detailed wording of the TCP(GPD) Order 1995 in each case.[1] It will be seen that one common thread running through art 3(12) is the safeguarding of the continuation of activities such as mining and waste disposal on land which was subject to that use prior to the requirements of the EIA Directive, as otherwise there could be an argument that new deposits or extraction could be development subject to EIA and as such outside the scope of permitted development rights. In other cases, the intention is to exclude projects which are not within the Directive; in particular development under local or private acts or orders. In line with the approach of construing exemptions narrowly, this should only exempt development which is specifically designated in the relevant act or order.[2]

1   See also the summary in Department of the Environment Circular 2/99, paras 151–154.
2   See Department of the Environment Circular 2/99, para 152.

Screening permitted development

6.45   Circular 2/99 advises that any request for a screening opinion in relation to permitted development (PD) should be made in accordance with the normal procedures under the TCP(EIA) Regulations 1999, reg 5.[1] Where the relevant category of PD rights requires pre-notification of the local planning authority it may be convenient to make a sreeening opinion request at the same time.[2] The Circular also emphasises the importance of a prompt response by planning authorities in such cases:[3]

'Local planning authorities are reminded that in exercising their functions under the [EIA] Regulations they are to determine the significance or otherwise of the likely environmental effects of the proposed development, rather than judge its planning merits. They should, therefore, make every effort to minimise disruption and delay, particularly where urgent development is required, for example for safety or security purposes or for essential improvements to public water and sewage treatment systems, or in other case where improvements to public utilities are proposed.'

1   Department of the Environment Circular 2/99, para 64.
2   Department of the Environment Circular 2/99, para 64.
3   Department of the Environment Circular 2/99, para 65.

OUTLINE PLANNING APPLICATIONS

6.46 Outline planning permission, and the concomitant procedure for approval of reserved matters, are not addressed expressly by the TCP(EIA) Regulations 1999. Outline permission is in principle treated no differently to full permission, so far as EIA is concerned. However, as can be seen from the case law, these procedures sit somewhat uneasily with the requirements of the EIA Directive.

Outline procedures

6.47 TCPA 1990, s 92 defines 'outline planning permission' to mean permission granted with the reservation for subsequent approval by the local planning authority or Secretary of State of matters not particularised in the application ('reserved matters'). By the Town and Country Planning (Applications) Regulations 1988, reg 2,[1] 'outline planning permission' is defined to mean planning permission for the erection of a building, subject to a condition requiring the subsequent approval of the local planning authority with regard to one or more reserved matters, that is to say:
(a) siting,
(b) design,
(c) external appearance,
(d) means of access, and
(e) the landscaping of the site.

1   SI 1988/1812. See also the TCP(GDP) Order 1995, art 1(2).

6.48 It will be readily apparent that any of these matters could potentially have a bearing on the likely environmental effects of a development; for example the siting of a building within the red line of the permission, or the routing and width of an access way. By the TCP(GDP) Order 1995, art 3(1), where an application is made for outline planning permission, the local planning authority may grant permission subject to a condition specifying reserved matters for the authority's subsequent approval. By art 3(2) it is open to the authority, if they are of the opinion that in the circumstances the application ought not to be considered separately from any of the reserved matters, to notify the applicant within one month of the receipt of the application that they are unable to determine it unless further details (which the authority must specify) are submitted.

Tew: the problem identified

6.49 The potential difficulty in complying with the requirements of the EIA Directive when making an outline planning application is one of lack of information at the stage when the outline permission (the 'development consent' for the purposes of the Directive) is granted. The grant of outline permission will settle the principle of the development but, depending on what matters are reserved, some of the information needed to describe the development and all its likely effects will be lacking. This problem arose squarely in *R v Rochdale Metropolitan Borough Council, ex p Tew.*[1]

1   [2000] Env LR 1, [1999] 3 PLR 74, [2001] JPL 54.

6.50   The case concerned a bare outline permission for the development of some 170 ha of largely open land at junction 21 of the M62 motorway. The permission referred to a 'proposed business park consisting of general and light industry, offices distribution and storage, research and development with associated and complementary retail, leisure, hotel and housing land'. An associated full permission was granted for the construction of a spine road within the site. The local planning authority had a long-standing policy in favour of the development — known as Kingsway Business Park. One of the grounds of challenge was that there was failure to give the information required by the TCP(AEE) Regulations 1988.

6.51   An ES had been prepared by consultants for the developers, based on the proposed master plan for site layout and indicative figures as to floor space. However, the planning permission expressly stated that the illustrative master plan was not approved, and that a further 'framework document' showing overall design and layout was to be submitted and approved. On that basis it was argued that there was no sufficient description of the development to comply with the TCP(AEE) Regulations 1988 and that the decision had not been taken in full knowledge of the project's likely effects on the environment.

6.52   Sullivan J approached the requirements as to the content of the ES (at that time TCP(AEE) Regulations 1988, Sch 3) on a purposive basis. Without a description of the development proposed, the likely impact 'could not begin to be assessed' and the underlying purpose of providing information in the ES would be frustrated. An ES based on a bare outline application, Sullivan J suggested, ' ... could not begin to comply' with the requirements for an ES. The matter was seen as one of degree, depending on how many matters were reserved, and ultimately whether an ES complying with the TCP(AEE) Regulations 1988 could be produced. Sullivan J acknowledged the difficulties this would create for demand-led commercial developments where the final form would only emerge over the course of time; however in applying EIA to 'urban development projects', the EC had placed applications for such projects in 'a legal straitjacket'. Deferring the description of a likely significant effect and the measures to mitigate it would not be in accordance with the terms of the Regulations, would conflict with the public's right to make an input into the environmental information and would, therefore, conflict with the underlying purpose of the EIA Directive.

6.53   In making these comments, Sullivan J suggested a possible way out of the 'legal straitjacket': the fundamental difficulty was that the ES described the effects of the development by reference to an illustrative master plan, but the ultimate form of the development was not tied in any way to that plan. Sullivan J did not wish to rule out the master plan approach, provided it was tied, for example by the imposition of a condition, to the description of the development permitted. Similarly, if illustrative figures for floor space were given, it could be possible for the ES to assess the effects of development within those ranges, and for conditions to be imposed to ensure that any permitted development remains within those ranges.

6.54   The approach in *Tew* was followed by Richards J, in the context of permission granted by the Secretary of State following a public inquiry, in *Elmbridge Borough Council v Secretary of State for Environment, Transport and the Regions*,[1] where eight public inquiries had been held into proposed motorway service areas on the M25. Rival developers obtained the quashing of the outline permission granted to the successful applicant, on the basis (among others) that the information contained in the outline application was not adequate, as a matter of fact and degree, to satisfy EIA requirements. As in *Tew*, there was nothing to tie the development to any particular form, the conditions leaving almost everything open to reserved matters approval. On that basis, Richards J found the case indistinguishable from *Tew*,[2] and the lack of an adequate description to form the basis of the ES meant that the outline permission was unlawful under the TCP(AEE) Regulations 1988, regs 4(2) and 25. However, like Sullivan J, Richards J emphasised that the issue was one of fact and degree, and he was not saying that outline permission could never be lawfully granted for EIA development. Richards J also accepted, without deciding, the possibility that the breach of the Regulations could be cured by an appropriate condition tying the grant of permission to the illustrative material on which the inspector's conclusions, as accepted by the Secretary of State, were based.[3]

1   [2000] Env LR 1.
2   [2000] Env LR 1, para 205.
3   [2000] Env LR 1, para 210.

Milne: *the solution approved*

6.55   The sequel to *Tew* was *R v Rochdale Metropolitan Borough Council, ex p Milne*.[1] Following their defeat in *Tew*, the developers made extensive revisions to the outline application, minor revisions to the spine road application and added a new application for full permission to construct the estate roads leading off the spine road. Sullivan J found that the application was no longer a 'bare outline';[2] it incorporated into the application an attachment describing the development, a Schedule of Development, a Development Framework and a Masterplan. This operated by dividing the site into 20 plots, in relation to each of which the hectarage, floorspace, Use Class, height and car parking numbers were summarised. Based on these documents, an ES was prepared, which Sullivan J described as 'a model of its kind'.[3] The planning permission then contained conditions requiring the development to be carried out in substantial accordance with the layout in the Development Framework, including matters such a phasing and the height of buildings.

1   [2001] Env LR 406, 81 P & CR 365.
2   [2001] Env LR 406, para 19.
3   [2001] Env LR 406, para 26.

6.56 Sullivan J held that this process complied with the relevant requirements (by this time the TCP(EIA) Regulations 1999). The reality of the matter was that for a large-scale and market-led scheme such as the Kingsway Business Park, the project would not be fixed at the outset, but would evolve in accordance with the demands of the market over a period of years. In including industrial estate developments within the category of EIA projects, there was no reason to suppose that the framers of the EIA Directive intended to be unduly prescriptive as to what would amount to an adequate description of the project; the amount of information which it was possible to provide would vary depending on the nature of the project within the various categories of development mentioned.[1] The Directive did not require the 'legal straitjacket' referred to be Sullivan J in *Tew* to be 'drawn so tightly as to suffocate such projects'.[2]

1   [2001] Env LR 406, paras 89–90, 94.
2   [2001] Env LR 406, para 91.

6.57 Sullivan J identified the essential underlying requirements as to the description of the project as twofold: first, enough information must be provided to enable the 'main' or 'likely significant' effects to be assessed, and the mitigation measures to be described; and, second, the development which is described and assessed must be the development which is proposed to be carried out.[1] The first of these issues was a matter for the judgment of the planning authority,[2] and the second was a question of whether there were adequate conditions tying the final form of the development to that which had been assessed.

1   [2001] Env LR 406, paras 104–105.
2   See further, para **4.30**.

6.58 Sullivan J also emphasised the importance of considering what matters were actually reserved in the outline permission. The ES was not required to consider every possible environmental effect, however minor. So, for example, landscaping as a reserved matter was not likely to have significant effects on the environment, despite the fact that neighbouring householders might regard it as significant from their point of view.[1] It had been submitted for the claimant that the environmental impact of a project could be significantly affected by the detailed design at reserved matters stage, for example by the use of materials such as reflective glass, or by some striking 'landmark building'. Sullivan J dealt with this submission by injecting an element of realism:[2]

'It is true that at the reserved matters stage the council might theoretically approve a building in a particularly shocking colour, or with a particularly visually intrusive roof design, but that is not the test, since it can be satisfied that it is not likely to do so, hence the effect, for example, of a rainbow coloured building, or a bizarre "landmark" building is not a "likely effect", let alone a "likely significant effect" on the environment.'

In the same way that the authority undertaking EIA was entitled to assume that the authorities dealing with emissions to air, water and land would fulfil their duties with a reasonable degree of competence, Sullivan J held that the same assumption could properly be made in relation to the local planning authority's own function in approving reserved matters:[3]

> 'Mistakes may occur in any system of development control, but one is identifying and mitigating the "likely significant effects", not every conceivable effect, however minor or unlikely, of a major project.'

1   [2001] Env LR 406, para 113.
2   [2001] Env LR 406, para 127.
3   [2001] Env LR 406, para 128.

6.59   Milne therefore provides a guide to the practical solution of the legal problems facing the developer of a major project of the type for which outline permission procedures was designed. It does not give a licence for developers to avoid providing information which they could reasonably be expected to provide. For many kinds of infrastructure project (for example a water engineering works) a high level of detail may be expected to be available at the outset and incorporated in the project description; thus there may be types of development for which outline planning permission and EIA procedures will remain seriously incompatible.

Use of s 106 obligations with outline permission

6.60   In *Milne* the essential step of tying the development permitted to the details submitted with the application was by way of planning conditions. In *R (Portland Port Ltd) v Weymouth and Portland Borough Council*[1] the linkage was provided by an agreement under the TCPA 1990, s 106. The decision had been made to grant outline permission for mixed use development incorporating leisure, employment, retail and residential uses. The application was accompanied by an illustrative master plan, a design statement and a draft s 106 agreement. The s 106 agreement included a covenant by the developer that any application submitted for the approval of details of the development 'shall include only development of the quantity and disposition around the site described in the Master Plan and the Environmental Statement'. Harrison J rejected a submission that a condition tying these matters together was required; the same result could be achieved by a s 106 agreement, and looking at the relevant documents, Harrison J was satisfied that the proposed development would be kept within the parameters on the environmental assessment on which consultation took place.[2]

1   [2001] EWHC Admin 1171, [2002] JPL 1099. The case was a judicial review permission hearing, where Harrison J, having heard detailed argument, considered the issue of permission on a threshold of whether the claim had a reasonably good chance of success (see *R v Cotswold District Council, ex p Barrington Parish Council* (1998) 75 P & CR 515).
2   [2001] EWHC Admin 1171, [2002] JPL 1099, paras 19 and 26.

APPROVAL OF RESERVED MATTERS

6.61 By the TCP(GDP) Order 1995, art 4, an application for approval of reserved matters must:

(a) be made in writing giving sufficient information to enable the authority to identify the outline permission in respect of which it is made;

(b) include such particulars, and be accompanied by such plans and drawings, as are necessary to deal with the matters reserved in the outline permission; and

(c) be accompanied by three copies of the application, plans and drawings.

The underlying principle adopted by the courts to the approval process is that the principle of the development has been settled at outline stage. This has two main consequences. First, the planning authority cannot seek to deny the principle of development by refusing approval if they now consider permission should not have been granted; equally they can only impose conditions in relation to those matters which have been reserved, for example by seeking to restrict the amount of floorspace.[1] The other side of the same coin is that an applicant cannot, in submitting an application for approval of reserved matters, seek to change the nature or scope of the development approved at outline stage.[2]

1   See, for example, *Camden London Borough Council v Secretary of State for the Environment* [1993] JPL 466; *R v Newbury District Council, ex p Chieveley Parish Council* [1999] PLCR 51.

2   See, for example, *Shemara v Luton Corpn* (1967) 18 P & CR 520; *Calcaria Construction Co (York) v Secretary of State for the Environment* (1974) 27 P & CR 435.

6.62 An important issue of principle is whether EIA procedures can apply to the approval of reserved matters. In general, application for approval of any reserved matter must be made within a period of three years, beginning with the date of the grant of outline permission.[1] Leaving aside therefore what should now be rare 'pipeline' cases where outline permission was granted before EIA became a legal requirement and there has been a long delay sanctioned by the planning authority in seeking approval of reserved matters, there should not be cases where approval of reserved matters involves considering issues that should not have been the subject of EIA at outline stage. The situation is therefore not really akin to that contemplated by the House of Lords in *R v North Yorkshire County Council, ex p Brown*,[2] where the approval of conditions on old mining permissions, which had been granted without any serious consideration of the environment in modern terms, could be regarded as 'a new and freestanding examination of the issues'[3] and accordingly as a development consent for EIA purposes. However, there could undoubtedly be instances where it is alleged that there has been some defect in the original EIA process at outline stage (either a deficient assessment, or no assessment at all due to an screening error) and that this should be rectified at the stage of reserved matters. This might be regarded as giving third-party objectors 'a second bite at the cherry' in terms of a challenge or, equally, giving the planning authority a second opportunity to put matters right and comply with domestic and EC law.

1   TCPA 1990, s 92(2)(a) and (3).

2   [2000] 1 AC 397. See para **6.06** above.
3   [2000] 1 AC 397 at 405E–F (Lord Hoffmann).

6.63   These considerations may usefully be kept in mind in considering the decision of the Court of Appeal in *R (Barker) v London Borough of Bromley*.[1] The case concerned the controversial development of Crystal Palace Park for leisure and recreational facilities, including 52,000 m² of new buildings and 1,200 car parking spaces. Outline permission was granted in March 1998, on the basis that EIA was not required because it was unlikely to have significant environmental effects. There was then an unsuccessful challenge to the outline permission based on architectural and parking matters. Reserved matters were then approved at a public meeting, at which the council was advised that although an informal ES could be obtained, this could not justify the council in refusing to deal with the application for approval of reserved matters. The claimant was held at first instance[2] to be out of time to challenge the grant of outline permission on EIA grounds, and permission to appeal on that basis was not forthcoming. The contention of the claimant in the Court of Appeal was that the planning process was a staged process involving both the grant of outline permission and the approval of reserved matters, and that the EIA Directive requires consideration of the need for EIA at both stages.

1   [2001] EWCA Civ 1766, [2002] Env LR 631.
2   [2001] Env LR 1, [2000] PLCR 399 (Jackson J).

6.64   Latham LJ rejected this argument. In so doing he referred to the 'consensus' which had emerged from previous cases that the grant of outline permission (and not any subsequent approval of reserved matters) was the 'development consent' for EIA purposes, in the way in which these requirements had been transposed by the domestic regulations (the TCP(EIA) Regulations 1999).[1] He also rejected any analogy with the approach of the House of Lords in *Brown*, essentially for the reasons stated above.[2] In addressing the argument that the planning authority should protect the public and 'remedy the mischief' of not having required EIA at the outline stage by requiring it now, Latham LJ accepted that mistakes could be made or indeed that circumstances could change after the grant of outline permission; neither of these was however a reason for requiring EIA as part of approving reserved matters.[3] He indicated that the planning authority was not powerless in these circumstances, in that it could if necessary revoke the outline permission (subject to the payment of compensation). He concluded that there was no lacuna in the domestic regulations and that a reference to the ECJ was neither necessary nor appropriate.[4] Brooke LJ and Burton J delivered judgments agreeing with Latham LJ.

1   [2001] EWCA Civ 1766, [2002] Env LR 631, paras 31–39. Latham LJ referred in this context not only to *Tew* and *Milne* (see paras **6.49–6.59**) above, but also to the decisions at permission stage of Richards J and of the Court of Appeal in *R v London Borough of Hammersmith and Fulham, ex p CPRE* [2000] Env LR 532 at 541 and (2001) 81 P & CR 73, para 42.
2   [2001] EWCA Civ 1766, [2002] Env LR 631, para 42.
3   [2001] EWCA Civ 1766, [2002] Env LR 631, para 45.
4   [2001] EWCA Civ 1766, [2002] Env LR 631, para 47.

6.65   Logical though the approach of the Court of Appeal undoubtedly is, it will clearly not remain the last word on the subject. The House of Lords gave permission to appeal on 9 October 2002 and on 30 June 2003 the Appellate Committee referred the matter to the European Court for a preliminary ruling under Art 234 of the EC Treaty on three related issues:

1.   Whether identification of the decisions of the competent authority which entitles the developer to proceed with the project under Art 2 of the Directive is exclusively a matter for the national court applying national law.
2.   Whether the Directive requires EIA approval of reserved matters stage where no EIA was carried out at outline permission stage.
3.   Whether national law can, consistently with the Directive, preclude a competent authority from requiring EIA be carried out at a later stage of the planning process, where it provides for EIA at an initial stage.

In addition, the European Commission has referred the UK to the ECJ in relation to the project, for failure to carry out environmental assessment at the outline stage, and also in relation to the general question of how whether the UK procedures effectively exclude reserved matters from EIA procedures.[1]

1   Commission Press Release IP/03/117, 24 January 2003.

APPLICATIONS UNDER TCPA 1990, S 73

6.66   TCPA 1990, s 73, provides a procedure by which application can be made for planning permission for the development of land without complying with conditions subject to which a previous planning permission was granted. This procedure is useful where the developer wishes to modify previous conditions. Though the application is for planning permission, by s 73(2) the planning authority is to consider only the question of the conditions, and whether permission should be granted subject to the original conditions or whether it should be granted subject to different conditions, or no conditions at all. In *R v Coventry City Council, ex p Arrowcroft Group plc*[1] Sullivan J, while emphasising that the outcome of a successful application under s 73 is a fresh planning permission,[2] held that the council's ability to impose conditions is limited to such conditions as could lawfully have been imposed on the original permission.

1   [2001] PLCR 113.
2   [2001] PLCR 113, para 33.

6.67   How EIA procedures may apply to such applications is an interesting question. At one level, it could be argued that the application is for planning permission and as such, if the development is within Sch 1 or 2, the requirements of the TCP(EIA) Regulations 1999 will apply.[1] However, the underlying purpose of the provision is clearly not to revisit the principle of the development, but to consider the conditions on which it should be granted. It could therefore be said that the process is concerned with the detailed regulation of activities for which the principal consent has already been given, as envisaged by Lord Hoffmann in *Brown*.[2]

1   It certainly appears to have been accepted by Schiemann L J in R (Prokopp) v London
    Underground Limited (CA 7 July 2003, para 43) that this was the case.
2   See para **6.06** above.

6.68   Neither of these extreme positions is perhaps entirely correct. In some cases
the effect of modifying a condition may be neutral in terms of its environmental effects;
an example might be the relaxation of a personal occupancy condition. However, in
other instances significant effects might flow from the modification; for example a
change in permitted hours of working, or in permitted noise levels, or in the type of
waste permitted to be received at a site, or in extending or removing a time-limiting
condition. It is suggested that if the development covered by the planning permission
falls within the TCP(EIA) Regulations 1999, Sch 1 or 2, the planning authority should
consider whether the proposed modification could have significant environmental
effects. If so, then EIA procedures should be followed in terms of requiring an ES and
consultation and publicity in relation to the application for planning permission under
s 73.

6.69   A potentially problematic issue is the scope of such assessment; can the
authority confine itself to the effects consequent upon the change to the condition, or
should the development as a whole as authorised by the TCPA 1990, s 73 permission
be assessed? It should be remembered here that it is quite possible that a s 73 application
may be made in relation to an old permission which was not subject to EIA procedures
when granted. Section 73 allows the authority to revisit all the conditions subject to
which it was granted, not just those which are the subject-matter of the application. It
could be argued, taking a purposive approach, that the authority ought to consider
whether any additional or stricter conditions could properly be imposed to mitigate
against significant environmental effects, and that EIA is a necessary component of
that exercise. So, for example, if one assumes that a planning permission was granted
in 1980 for the use of land as a scrap yard, subject to a personal occupancy condition,
an application under s 73 for removal of the personal occupancy condition would
result in the reopening of the environmental effects of the use. In *R (Prokopp) v
London Underground Limited* [1] Collins J accepted, obiter, that EIA would be required
for a s 73 application, albeit that consideration of the matter would be limited to
conditions.

1   [2003] EWHC 960 (Admin), [2003] 19 EG 119 (CS), para 25.

APPLICATIONS UNDER TCPA 1990, S 73A

6.70   TCPA 1990, s 73A allows planning permission to be granted for development
carried out before the date of the application, whether without planning permission at
all, or under a time-limited permission, or in breach of some condition. Since the effect
of such permission will be either to authorise the development retrospectively, or to
allow it to be carried on after it would otherwise have expired (see s 73A(3)(a) and (b)),
it is submitted that if the application is for Sch 1 or Sch 2 development then the

requirements of the TCP(EIA) Regulations 1999 will apply, and the procedures should be followed as for any other application for planning permission.

CERTIFICATES OF LAWFULNESS OF EXISTING USE OR DEVELOPMENT

6.71   TCPA 1990, s 191 allows applications to be made to ascertain whether existing uses of land, or prior operations, or failure to comply with planning conditions or limitations is, in each case, lawful. Such matters are defined by s 191(2) to be lawful if no enforcement action may be taken against them (whether because the time for enforcement action has expired, or because they did not constitute development requiring planning permission). Such certificates are a means by which the lawfulness of the use or operations can be established conclusively: s 191(6) states that the lawfulness of any use, operations or other matters for which a certificate is in force 'shall be conclusively presumed'. It might be thought therefore that the grant of the certificate is not 'development consent' within the EIA Directive's meaning of the decision of the competent authority which entitles the developer to proceed, since such entitlement does not arise from the certificate but from the underlying facts. All that the certificate does is to provide a means of conclusively proving those facts and their effect.

6.72   It seems however that the European Commission takes a different view. Commission Press Release IP/03/117 (24 January 2003) states that the UK is to be sent a 'final written warning' in relation to its system of 'allocating certificates of lawful development to projects like scrap-yards' which may be covered by the EIA Directive. This is apparently viewed as protecting the operator from prosecution and thus effectively exempting such projects from the requirement of planning permission and, hence, EIA. The Commission considers that such certificates should be granted 'only if the rules with regard to EIAs are respected'. It may be that this matter can be resolved by the Commission being provided with a better understanding of how the certification system works, but if there is a problem, then presumably it does not lie in the certification process, but rather in the underlying rules which mean that planning permission is not required.

CERTIFICATES OF LAWFULNESS OF PROPOSED USE OR DEVELOPMENT

6.73   Under TCPA 1990, s 192, an application may be made for a certificate to ascertain whether any proposed use of land or proposed operations are lawful. If this involves considering whether proposed operational development fall within permitted development rights, then the implications of the TCP(GPD) Order 1995, art 3(10), as discussed above,[1] need to be considered. An example of this is the Ministerial appeal decision of 27 September 2001, against the refusal of Lancashire County Council to grant a lawful development certificate for the proposed use of land and buildings at Burscough Industrial Estate, for the incineration of meat and bonemeal (MBM).[2] There were two issues in the appeal: one relating to whether the proposed use was an 'industrial process' within the Town and Country Planning (Use Classes) Order 1987 and the other as to whether proposed operational development for a 15 metre-high chimney stack was permitted development. On the inspector's recommendation, the Secretary of State asked the appellant for further information as to the level of dispersion of pollutants provided by the stack. The appellant stated that this could not be provided without undue expense. The Secretary of State held that it was crucial to determine whether the development, involving TCP(EIA) Regulations 1999, Sch 2 development (an installation for the disposal of waste), was EIA development, since if it was the permitted development rights would not apply. This could only be determined by considering whether significant environmental effects were likely. The onus of proof as to lawfulness of the proposed development lay on the appellant,[3] and the failure to provide the requested information meant that this onus had not been discharged. The appeal was accordingly dismissed.

1   See para **6.41–6.42** above.
2   [2002] JPL 118.
3   See TCPA 1990, s 191(4) and Department of the Environment Circular 10/97, para 8.12.

IPPC AND OTHER REGIMES

6.74   Planning permission is in many cases not the only form of consent required to undertake a project falling with the EIA regime. A multitude of other regulatory consents may be relevant. These include PPC permits under the Pollution Prevention and Control (England and Wales) Regulations 2000 (PPC Regulations 2000)[1] and waste management licences under the Environmental Protection Act 1990, Pt II.

1   SI 2000/1973.

6.75   In most cases the EIA process can legitimately be confined to the planning permission stage. The basis for this is two-fold. First, subsequent regulatory controls over the operation of the site or process can be regarded as matters of detailed regulation, which do not go to the principle of development consent.[1] Second, both the developer when preparing the ES, and the planning authority when considering it, should be entitled when undertaking EIA at the stage of planning permission to rely on the operation of such controls with a reasonable degree of competence by the authority concerned.[2]

1   See *R v North Yorkshire County Council, ex p Brown* [2000] 1 AC 397 and the discussion of *R v Secretary of State for the Environment, ex p Greenpeace Ltd* [1994] 4 All ER 352 at para **6.06** above.
2   See *R v Rochdale Metropolitan Borough Council, ex p Milne* [2001] Env LR 406, para 128 (para **6.55** above).

6.76   However, further consideration needs to be given to the relationship between EIA and pollution prevention control (PPC). Directive 96/61/EC concerning Integrated Pollution Prevention and Control[1] (IPPC) requires measures to ensure that no new installation falling within the scope of the Directive is operated without a permit issued in accordance with the Directive (art 4). The categories of industrial activities covered by the IPPC Directive are not the same as the categories of projects subject to EIA, but there is a significant degree of overlap. In particular, art 6(1) of the IPPC Directive requires that an application for an IPPC permit contains a description of various matters (and indeed a non-technical summary) many of which will be equally relevant to an ES. Also, as with EIA, the IPPC Directive requires coordination between the various relevant authorities involved (art 7) and the ability of the public to participate in the process (art 15). Article 6(2) states that where the requirements of art 6(1) for information are fulfilled by information supplied in accordance with EIA requirements, such information may be included in or attached to the IPPC application. Under the PPC Regulations 2000 'any relevant information obtained or conclusion arrived at in relation to the installation' pursuant to EIA must be included within the application for a permit for a Part A installation.[2]

1   OJ L 257, 10.10.96, p 26.
2   Pollution Prevention and Control (England and Wales) Regulations 2000, SI 2000/1973, Sch 4, para 1(1)(m). Part A installations are those defined as such in the PPC Regulations 2000, Sch 1 and as such are subject to the full PPC regime.

6.77   In the light of this, can it be argued that a PPC permit can constitute a development consent within the terms of the EIA Directive? Clearly the permit is one which entitles the applicant to operate the installation. The issue has arisen, and has been referred to the ECJ, in the case of *R (Horner) v Environment Agency and Castle Cement Ltd.*[1] Essentially the Environment Agency had granted a variation under the Environmental Protection Act 1990, s 11, to an integrated pollution control (IPC) authorisation[2] held by Castle Cement. The effect was to allow Castle to burn 'Cemfuel', a form of substitute liquid fuel (SLF) derived from wastes, in one of its cement kilns. The Environment Agency regarded Cemfuel as itself being a hazardous waste. It was argued in the claim for judicial review that this fell within the terms of the EIA Directive, either because it was a change to an Annex I or II project and as such within Annex II, para 13 (the project being either within Annex I as a waste disposal installation for the incineration of hazardous waste[3] or within Annex II as an installation for the manufacture of cement).[4] The problem arose in this form because a change in the type of fuel so as to burn waste will not necessarily constitute a material change of use requiring planning permission.[5] The Environment Agency's response was that the variation decision was not a development consent and the use of Cemfuel not a 'project'. The Agency also raised issues of substantial compliance and direct effect.[6] The Secretary of State also opposed the application on the basis that the variation was not concerned with a 'project' in the sense of physical development, and that operational changes, such as a change of fuel, fall squarely within the sphere of pollution control under the IPPC Directive.

1   CO/961/2001. Permission to proceed with judicial review was given by Sullivan J on 11 May 2001, and the reference to the ECJ was made by Ouseley J on 6 February 2002 [2002] EWHC 513 (Admin).
2   IPC being the system introduced by Part I of the EPA 1990, and the precursor to PPC.
3   EIA Directive, Annex I, paras 9 and 10.
4   EIA Directive, Annex II, para 5(a).

5   See *R v Durham County Council, ex p Lowther* [2001] Env LR 332, 81 P & CR 27, especially
    at para 82 where Gibbs J held that it was neither necessary nor indeed reasonable for the
    planning authority to commission a full EIA in deciding whether there had been such a change
    of use. See also the Court of Appeal decision at [2002] Env LR 349. See also para **3.44** above.
6   See para **2.44** above.

6.78   It may well be that the ECJ will take a broader view of the scope of the EIA
Directive than the UK government. The EIA Directive defines 'project' not only by
reference to the 'execution of construction works or of other installations or schemes',
but also 'other interventions in the natural surroundings or landscape' (art 1(2)).
Without unduly stretching the language, a change of fuel in a major industrial
installation on a basis which gives rise to new significant effects might be said to be an
intervention in the natural surroundings (though at the same time, it may be noted that
the provision refers specifically to interventions involving the extraction of mineral
resources, from which it might be argued that the term 'intervention' is designed to
cover physical interventions which do not amount to construction works or to a built
installation). In relation to complaints made by local residents on a similar issue at a
site in Durham, the Commission has indicated that it has questioned with the UK
government in a letter of formal notice (a) whether it is correct to rely on the test of
material change of use as an additional hurdle in deciding whether projects are required
to undergo EIA, and (b) whether, by focusing only on the land use planning process,
the requirements of art 3 of the Directive were being complied with.[1]

1   Letter of European Commission to Weardale Action Group (30 April 2001) on Complaints
    97/4549 and 98/4016.

IMPLICATIONS OF THE PLANNING AND COMPULSORY PURCHASE BILL

6.79   The Planning and Compulsory Purchase Bill (introduced in 2002 and in June
2003 carried over into the next Parliamentary session) will make significant changes to
the system of development control in a number of significant respects, which will have
EIA implications. At the time of writing, in the absence of the regulations to be made
under the proposed new Act, it is impossible to do more than outline those implications,
as they appear from the Bill as introduced into Parliament.

Local development orders

6.80   It is proposed to insert into the TCPA 1990 a new s 61A, making provision for
local development orders. Such orders may be made by local planning authorities to
implement policies in the development plan documents, and may grant planning
permission for development specified in the order, or for development of any class
specified in the order. Under the proposed s 61C, such planning permission may be
granted unconditionally, or subject to such conditions as are specified in the order.

6.81 Proposed Sch 4A to the TCPA 1990 deals with the procedure for local development orders. Essentially the procedure will be prescribed in Regulations. In order to comply with the EIA Directive, presumably there will need to be provision as for EZs and SPZs, that planning permission is not granted for EIA development unless there has first been a negative screening opinion.

6.82 Such orders are equivalent to the planning permission granted by simplified planning zone schemes or enterprise zone orders in that they will constitute development consent for EIA purposes.[1]

1   See para **6.18** above.

Statement of development principles

6.83 The proposed new s 61D of the TCPA 1990 will allow a local planning authority to issue a statement of development principles in relation to a proposed development in their area, if they are requested to do so by any person. The statement must indicate whether the local planning authority agrees or disagrees with the principle of the proposed development, and the statement will be a material consideration for the purposes of determining any planning application for planning permission in respect of a similar development made within the period of three years, or such other period as the authority may direct. Where a statement of development principles has been issued, outline planning permission must not be granted for a similar development within that period.

6.84 Thus it can be seen that the procedure for statements of development principles is an alternative to outline planning permission. It could indeed be used to supplant outline planning permission entirely, and provision is made in Schs 3 and 6 of the Planning and Compulsory Purchase Bill for the repeal of s 92 of the TCPA 1990 dealing with outline planning permission. The government's intention, as indicated in Committee stage in the Commons, is that the outline planning permission procedure will be repealed if and when it appears that statements of development principles are working successfully.[1] It is also the case that if at some stage outline planning permission procedures were held to be incompatible with the EIA Directive's requirements,[2] then the statement of development principles procedure could allow a developer to obtain at least an indication of the acceptability of a development proposal, without the grant of a development consent which would trigger the EIA process.

1   See [2003] JPL B11 (Current Topics).
2   See paras **6.46–6.59**.

Major infrastructure projects

6.85 By the proposed new s 76A of the TCPA 1990, the Secretary of State may, in relation to applications for planning permission to which the new section relates, direct that the application be referred to him instead of being dealt with by the local planning authority. The section applies to those applications which the Secretary of State thinks relate to development which is of national or regional importance. Having made a direction, the Secretary of State must appoint an inspector to consider the application, and the procedure will be governed by regulations. Clearly provision will have to be made as to how EIA requirements will be incorporated into this procedure, and these will presumably be similar to those applying in other cases where planning applications are called in for determination by the Secretary of State.

CHAPTER 7

Non-planning development and EIA

INTRODUCTION

7.01 The EIA Directive 85/337/EEC, as amended by Directive 97/11/EC applies to a number of projects which for various reasons are not subject to planning control. This may be because they are not within the concept of 'development' (eg agricultural activity) or because they fall within other regulatory regimes. Therefore specific regulations or arrangements have been made to implement the Directive. This chapter briefly describes those arrangements, but without going into the detail of the previous chapters on the Town and Country Planning (Environmental Impact Assessment) Regulations (TCP(EIA) Regulations 1999.

ORIGINAL ARRANGEMENTS

7.02 When the EIA Directive was first transposed in 1988, a number of regulations were made in relation to projects not subject to planning control. These were described in Pt III of the Government's Guide to EIA procedures published in 1989,[1] and were as set out in paras 7.03–7.09 below.

1   Department of the Environment/Welsh Office, *Environmental Assessment: A Guide to the Procedures* (1989) pp 16–22.

7.03 The Highways (Assessment of Environmental Effects) Regulations 1988 (SI 1988/1241) (Highways (AEE) Regulations 1988) — applying to all new trunk roads and motorways over 10 km in length, or over 1 km where passing through or within 100 m of a sensitive area, and to other trunk road improvements likely to have a significant effect on the environment. Such schemes are subject to approval under procedures in the Highways Act 1980.[1]

1   Department of the Environment/Welsh Office, *Environmental Assessment: A Guide to the Procedures* (1989) paras 47–50.

7.04   The Electricity and Pipe-Line Works (Assessment of Environmental Effects) Regulations 1989 (SI 1989/167) — applying to applications made to the Secretary of State for Energy for:

(i)   the construction or extension of a nuclear power station;
(ii)   the construction or extension of a non-nuclear power station with a heat output of 300 MW or more;
(iii)   the construction or extension of a non-nuclear power station of less that 300 MW output where likely to have significant effects on the environment; and
(iv)   the placement of an overhead line or construction or diversion of a pipeline of 10 miles or more in length, where likely to have significant environmental effects.

At the time, oil and gas pipelines of more than 10 miles in length were authorised under the Pipelines Act 1962, s 1. Power stations and overhead lines were at that time proposed by the Central Electricity Generating Board and Area Electricity Boards, and were approved under arrangements with the Secretary of State for Energy, whereas non-nuclear power stations proposed by private developers were subject to normal planning procedures, as were oil and gas pipelines of less than 10 miles long. However, the Electricity Act 1989 would shortly introduce new procedures whereby the Secretary of State's consent would be required to construct or extend a power station with a capacity of 50 MW or more.[1] Following these changes, the Electricity and Pipe-Line Works (Assessment of Environmental Effects) Regulations 1990 (SI 1990/442)[2] were made to apply environmental impact assessment (EIA) to the consent procedures under the Electricity Act.

1   Department of the Environment/Welsh Office, *Environmental Assessment: A Guide to the Procedures* (1989) paras 51–58.
2   In turn amended by SI 1996/422.

7.05   The Environmental Assessment (Afforestation) Regulations 1988 (SI 1988/1207) — requiring EIA of any afforestation project before grant could be given, in any case where, in the opinion of the Forestry Commission, the project would be likely to have significant environmental effects.[1] The procedures adopted by the Forestry Commission were further explained in a guide, *Environmental Assessment of Afforestation Projects* (August 1988).

1   Department of the Environment/Welsh Office, *Environmental Assessment: A Guide to the Procedures* (1989), paras 56–59.

7.06   The Land Drainage Improvement Works (Assessment of Environmental Effects) Regulations 1988 (SI 1988/1217) — these Regulations were intended to cover improvements to existing land drainage works undertaken by drainage bodies and the National Rivers Authority (then the relevant authority before the creation of the Environment Agency) under permitted development rights (TCP General Development Order 1988, Sch 2, Pts 14 and 15). New land drainage works, including flood defence and coastal protection works, were within the normal planning system.[1]

1   Department of the Environment/Welsh Office, *Environmental Assessment: A Guide to the Procedures* (1989), paras 60–61.

7.07   The Harbour Works (Assessment of Environmental Effects) Regulations 1988 (SI 1988/1336) — these Regulations amended the Harbours Act 1964 in respect of harbour revision orders and harbour empowerment orders made to the Minister of Agriculture, Fisheries and Food or the Secretary of State for Transport, for harbour works. Other harbour works not falling within these procedures and not requiring planning permission were covered by the Harbour Works (Assessment of Environmental Effects) (No 2) Regulations 1989 (SI 1989/424).[1]

1   Department of the Environment/Welsh Office, *Environmental Assessment: A Guide to the Procedures* (1989) paras 62–63. Scottish procedures were later brought into line by the Harbour Works (Assessment of Environmental Effects) Regulations 1992, SSI 1992/1421.

7.08   The Environmental Assessment (Salmon Farming in Marine Waters) Regulations 1988 (SI 1988/1218) — these Regulations required EIA before the grant of a lease by the Crown Estate Commissioners for offshore facilities for salmon farming. Development for onshore salmon farming was within the normal planning system.[1] The Crown Estate published Guidelines on siting and design of marine fish farms in 1987, covering both fish and shellfish farming.[2]

1   Department of the Environment/Welsh Office, *Environmental Assessment: A Guide to the Procedures* (1989), para 64.
2   The Crown Estate, *Fish Farming: Guidelines on Siting and Design of Marine Fish Farming in Scotland* (December 1987).

7.09   Marine dredging for minerals — dredging for minerals offshore did not require planning permission but required a dredging licence form the Crown Estate Commissioners. No regulations were made, but the Crown Estate put in place procedures to require an environmental statement and to consult interested bodies and obtain a 'Government view' from the relevant government department.[1]

1   Department of the Environment/Welsh Office, *Environmental Assessment: A Guide to the Procedures* (1989), para 65.

PRESENT ARRANGEMENTS

7.10   The regulations mentioned above were replaced when it became necessary to transpose the amended EIA Directive. In addition, there have been further areas identified as requiring regulations in order to comply with the Directive. A number of the arrangements are described in Section 3 of the current Guide on EIA procedures,[1] to which reference may be made in Appendix 6 to this work.

1   DETR/National Assembly for Wales, *Environmental Impact Assessment; A Guide to Procedures* (November 2000), pp 25–35.

7.11   The current regulations, more fully outlined below, are set out in the following table. For ease of reference, details of the equivalent Scottish, Welsh and Northern

Irish Regulations (where relevant) are also given, though the commentary which follows refers to the English Regulations.

Regulations	Type of project
The Highways (Assessment of Environmental Effects) Regulations 1999, SI 1999/369 Scotland SSI 1999/1, Pt III NI 1999 /89	Highways
The Pipe-line Works (Environmental Impact Assessment) Regulations 2000, SI 2000/1928	Onshore pipe-lines
The Public Gas Transporter Pipe-line (Environmental Impact Assessment) Regulations 1999, SI 1999/1672	Pipe-line works by public gas transporters
The Offshore Petroleum and Pipelines (Assessment of Environmental Effects) Regulations 1999, SI 1999/360	Offshore petroleum exploration and development and construction of pipelines
EIA (Fish Farming in Marine Waters) Regulations 1999, SI 1999/367 NI 1999/415	Marine fish farming
EIA (Land Drainage Improvement Works) Regulations 1999, SI 1999/1783 Scotland 1999/1, Part IV NI 2001/394	Land drainage
EIA (Forestry) (England and Wales) Regulations 1999, SI 1999/2228 Scotland, SSI 1999/43 NI 2000/84, amended by SI 2002/249	Forestry
Electricity Works (Assessment of Environmental Effects) (England and Wales) Regulations 2000, SI 2000/1927 Scotland, SSI 2000/320	Power stations (including nuclear power stations) and overhead power lines
Nuclear Reactors (EIA for Decommissioning) Regulations 1999, SI 1999/2892	Decommissioning nuclear reactors
Harbour Works (EIA) Regulations 1999, SI 1999/3445, amended by SI 2000/2391 NI 2003/136	Harbour works
EIA (Uncultivated Land and Semi-Natural Areas) (England) Regulations 2001, SI 2001/3966. Wales 2002/2127 (W 214) Scotland, SSI 2002/6 NI 2001/435	Use of previously uncultivated or semi-natural land for intensive agricultural purposes
Water Resources (EIA) (England and Wales) Regulations 2003, SI 2001/164	Water abstraction, impounding and other water management projects
EIA (Extraction of Minerals by Marine Dredging) Regulations (forthcoming)	Marine minerals dredging

Trunk roads

7.12 The EIA Directive covers:
(i) construction of motorways and express roads[1] (Annex I, para 7(b)).
(ii) construction of new roads of four or more lanes, or realignment and/or widening of an existing road of two lanes or less so as to provide four or more lanes, where such new road, or realigned and/or widened section of road would be 10 km or more in a continuous length (Annex I, para 7(c)).
(iii) construction of roads not within Annex I (Annex II, para 10(e)).
(iv) changes or extensions of roads within Annex I or II (Annex II, para 13, first indent).

1   For the purposes of the EIA Directive, an 'express road' is stated to mean a road which complies with the definition in the European Agreement on Main International Traffic Arteries of 15 November 1975 (UNECE, Consolidated Text 5 April 2002). Annex II defines an express road as 'a road reserved for motor traffic accessible only from interchanges or controlled junctions and on which, in particular, stopping and parking are prohibited on the running carriageway(s)'.

7.13 Road construction and improvements can fall within one of three categories:
(i) Trunk road network construction or improvement, for which the Secretary of State or the National Assembly for Wales is the highway authority. Such projects are approved under the Highways Act 1980.[1] The Highways (AEE) Regulations 1999[2] apply to these projects.
(ii) Roads constructed or improved as part of the local authority highways network. These are subject to normal planning control and EIA procedures.
(iii) Roads constructed or improved by private developers. These are again subject to normal planning control and EIA procedures.

1   Motorways ('special roads', for which special classes of permitted traffic are prescribed) are authorised by schemes approved by the Secretary of State under the Highways Act 1980, s 16, other trunk roads under s 10, and side roads (roads that cross or adjoin trunk roads or classified roads) under s 14.
2   SI 1999/369.

7.14 The Highways (AEE) Regulations 1999 amend the Highways Act 1980 by inserting a new Part VA (Environmental Impact Assessments) comprising ss 105A–105C. Where the Secretary of State is considering a project for constructing or improving a highway for which he is the highway authority he must, before details of the project are published, determine whether or not it falls within Annex I or II of the EIA Directive (s 105A(2)). If he considers it falls within Annex I then an environmental statement (ES) must be published not later than the date when details of the project are published (s 105A(3)(a)). If he considers it to fall within Annex II, then he must consider whether it is a 'relevant project' and if so, whether it should be made subject to EIA, having regard to the selection criteria in Annex III of the Directive, in which case an ES must be published (s 105A(3)(b)). For this purpose, a 'relevant project' means one where the area of the completed works together with any area occupied during construction by plant, equipment, spoil heaps or other facilities exceeds 1 ha, or where any such area is situated in whole or in part in a 'sensitive area'.[1] Where the project is for construction or improvement of a special road and falls within Annex II, then it must be treated as having characteristics requiring it to be subject to EIA (s 105B(2)). The ES must contain the information referred to in Annex IV of the Directive, to the extent that the Secretary of State considers that the information is relevant to the specific characteristics of the project and the affected environmental features, and that the information may be reasonably gathered (s 105A(4)).

1   Highways Act 1980, s 105A(1). This is a threshold in EIA Directive terms. 'Sensitive area' is defined by s 105A(6) in similar terms to the TCP(EIA) Regulations 1999.

7.15   The Highways Act 1980, s 105B, deals with the procedures for EIA in such cases. Essentially there must be consultation with defined consultation bodies and the opportunity for the public to express their views, and there must be publicity of the ES and of the ultimate decision, the reasons and the mitigating measures. The Highways Act decision-making procedure involves the confirmation of statutory orders, and in most cases there will be a public inquiry before an inspector.[1] Section 105C contains procedures applying where there may be significant transboundary effects.

1   The procedural requirements are in Sch 1 to the Highways Act 1980, and involve the publication of a draft scheme. See also the Special Road Schemes and Highways Orders (Procedure) Regulations 1993 (SI 1993/169) and the Highways (Inquiries Procedure) Rules 1994 (SI 1994/ 3263).

7.16   Given the long time-scales involved in major highways projects, the issue of the date at which these requirements bite, and on what they bite, is important. The Highways (AEE) Regulations 1999 came into force on 13 March 1999. Projects begun before that date are governed by the Highways (AEE) Regulations 1988. Specific provision for the transition is made by reg 3 of the 1999 Regulations, which states that the 1999 Regulations do not apply:
(a) to a project for which the Secretary of State has published an ES before the commencement date, but for which no draft order or scheme had been published;
(b) to a project in relation to which a draft order or scheme had been published prior to the commencement date;
(c) to a project for which a draft order or scheme was not required and for which the works contract had been let before the commencement date.

Onshore pipelines

7.17   Pipelines for the transport of gas, oil or chemicals with a diameter of more than 800 mm and a length of more than 40 km are within Annex I of the EIA Directive (para 16). Oil and gas pipelines which are below either of these thresholds are within Annex II (para 10(i)).

7.18   Onshore pipelines other than those of public gas transporters (see below) and which are more than 10 miles long require a pipe-line construction authorisation from the Secretary of State for Trade and Industry under the Pipe-lines Act 1962. These are covered by the Pipe-Line Works (EIA) Regulations 2000, which came into force on 1 September 2000[1] and apply to England, Scotland and Wales. Shorter pipelines are approved under normal planning permission. The Regulations apply to authorisations under s 1(1) of the Pipe-lines Act 1962 for the construction of a cross-country pipeline, the purpose of which is the conveyance of oil, gas or chemicals. Any pipeline for oil and gas is covered, and any pipe-line for chemicals exceeding 40 km in length and 800 mm in diameter.[2] There are procedures for directions on whether an ES is required (reg 4), scoping (reg 5), publicity (reg 7) and transboundary effects (reg 10)

1   SI 2000/1928. The Electricity and Pipe-line Works (Assessment of Environmental Effects) Regulations 1990 are continued in force by the Electricity and Pipe-line Works (Assessment of Environmental Effects) Regulations 2000, reg 1(3) in relation to applications for oil or gas pipe-lines received by the Secretary of State before 1 September 2000.
2   See the definition of 'relevant pipe-line' at reg 2.

7.19   A separate regime applies to companies licensed as public gas transporters under the Gas Act 1995, who do not require consent under the Pipe-lines Act 1962. Moreover, such works benefit from permitted development rights under the Town and Country Planning (General Development Procedure) Order 1995 (TCP(GPD) Order 1995), Sch 2, Pt 17, Class F(a). The Public Gas Transporter Pipe-line (EIA) Regulations 1999[1] apply to such projects. They do not apply to works which were commenced by the public gas transporter before the commencement date of 15 July 1999, or in respect of which the public gas transporter invited tenders before that date (reg 1(3)(a)). Nor do they apply to works in respect of which a direction under the Town and Country Planning (General Development Procedure) Order 1995, SI 1995/419 (TCP(GPD) Order 1995), art 4, has been given, where permitted development rights have been withdrawn and planning permission is required (Public Gas Transporter Pipe-line (EIA) Regulations 1999, regs 1(3)(b) and 4). The Regulations apply to the completion of works which have already been started, where a direction made by the Secretary of State determines that EIA is required (reg 2(2)).

1   SI 1999/1672.

7.20   The Public Gas Transporter Pipe-line (EIA) Regulations 1999 constitute a detailed and self-contained EIA code for such projects. For projects falling within Sch 3, Pt 1, that is pipe-line works in respect of a pipeline with a diameter of more than 800 mm and a length of more than 40 km, the developer must give the Secretary of State notice of preparation of an ES before commencing works (reg 3(1)). For those within Sch 3, Pt 2 either the developer must give such a notice or request an 'environmental determination' — the equivalent of a screening direction (reg 3(2)). These are works where either (a) the whole or any part of the pipeline or of its 'working width'[1] will be within a sensitive area,[2] or (b) where the pipeline will have a design operating pressure exceeding 7-bar gauge. Where the developer gives notice of preparation of an ES, or the Secretary of State determines that one is required, the public gas transporter may not commence or continue pipeline works without first applying for and obtaining the consent of the Secretary of State under reg 14 (see reg 3(5)).

1   'Working width' means the area occupied by apparatus, equipment, machinery, plant, spoil heaps or other facilities or stores required for the construction or installation works (reg 2(1)).
2   'Sensitive area' is defined by reg 2(1) in similar terms to the definition under the TCP(EIA) Regulations 1999.

7.21   There are procedures for screening (Public Gas Transporter Pipe-line (EIA) Regulations 1999, reg 6), scoping opinions (reg 7), co-operation with consultation bodies (reg 9), publicity (reg 10), further information (reg 11), transboundary effects (reg 13), the giving of consents and consequent publicity (reg 14), applications to the High Court by persons aggrieved by the grant of consent or conditions attached (regs 15 and 16), applications to court by the Secretary of State to restrain works being carried out without consent or requiring the removal of unconsented works (reg 17) and offences (reg 18). One interesting point to note is that reg 18, as well as making it an offence to carry out works without consent, or in breach of the terms of a consent, also makes it an offence intentionally or recklessly to submit an ES or any other information which is false or misleading in a material particular. Schedule 1 prescribes the information to be included in the ES and Sch 2 lists the matters to be taken into account in making an environmental determination as to whether EIA is required.

Offshore petroleum and pipelines

7.22   The extraction of petroleum and natural gas for commercial purposes, where the amount extracted exceeds 500 tonnes per day for petroleum and 5,000 m^3 per day for gas, falls within Annex I, para 14 of the EIA Directive. Other 'deep drillings' are within Annex II, para 2(d). The grant of offshore oil and gas exploration and production licences was the subject of litigation in *R v Secretary of State for Trade and Industry, ex p Greenpeace Ltd*,[1] though in relation to the requirements of the Habitats Directive 92/43/EC rather than EIA. The licences challenged related to areas of the North-East Atlantic outside UK Territorial Waters but within the UK Continental Shelf. Maurice Kay J held that the Habitats Directive, in using the phrase 'in the European territory of the member states', applied to projects outside territorial waters. The Habitats Directive is now implemented in relation to such projects by the Offshore Petroleum Activities (Conservation of Habitats) Regulations 2001.[2]

1   [2000] Env LR 221. An application by Greenpeace in relation to an earlier Round of licensing had failed on grounds of delay: see *R v Secretary of State for Trade and Industry, ex p Greenpeace* [1998] Env LR 415 (see para **8.14**).
2   SI 2001/1754. These regulations came into force on 31 May 2001.

7.23   In any event, the government had, prior to that case, introduced the Offshore Petroleum and Pipelines (Assessment of Environmental Effects) Regulations 1999[1] which came into force on 14 March 1999, replacing the Offshore Petroleum and Pipe-lines (Assessment of Environmental Effects) Regulations 1998.[2] The Regulations, which are of considerable complexity in their drafting, apply to licences granted by the Secretary of State for Trade and Industry under the Petroleum Act 1998, s 3 (licences to search and bore for and get petroleum). By reg 4(1) the Secretary of State may not grant a licence which does not require the licensee to obtain the prior consent of the Secretary of State for the following specified operations wholly or partly in the 'relevant area':[3]

(a) commencing or re-commencing the drilling of any well;[4]

(b) extracting petroleum[5] where the amount exceeds the 500 tonnes/500,000 m[3] thresholds for oil and gas; or

(c) erecting any structure[6] in connection with a 'development', that is any project which has as its main objective the getting of petroleum as opposed to establishing its presence, quantity or quality.[7]

1   SI 1999/360
2   SI 1998/968
3   The 'relevant area' is defined to cover (a) tidal waters and parts of the sea between the low water mark and the seaward limits of territorial waters, (b) waters in areas designated as Continental Shelf, and (c) the seabed and subsoil under the waters referred to at (a) and (b) (see Offshore Petroleum and Pipelines (Assessment of Environmental Effects) Regulations 1999, reg 3(1)).
4   A 'well' is any well or borehole drilled for, or in connection with, the getting of petroleum or exploring or testing for it, but does not include wells drilled to a depth of 350 m or less below the seabed for the main purpose of testing stability (Offshore Petroleum and Pipelines (Assessment of Environmental Effects) Regulations 1999, reg 3(1)).
5   'Petroleum' includes both mineral oils and natural gas (Offshore Petroleum and Pipelines (Assessment of Environmental Effects) Regulations 1999, reg 3(1)).
6   A 'structure' is any structure used for the getting of petroleum, storing it or conveying it to land, which is intended to be permanent, and is not designed to be moved without major dismantling nor to be used only for searching for petroleum (Offshore Petroleum and Pipelines (Assessment of Environmental Effects) Regulations 1999, reg 3(1)).
7   SI 1999/360, reg 3(1).

7.24   In addition, by Offshore Petroleum and Pipelines (Assessment of Environmental Effects) Regulations 1999, reg 4(4), notwithstanding any provision in a licence, the prior written consent of the Secretary of State is required to use: (1) a floating installation in connection with a 'relevant project' comprising a development, or (2) any mobile installation for the extraction of petroleum where the principal purpose is the testing of any well. A 'relevant project' is defined[1] to mean a project comprising:

(a) the drilling of an exploration well;[2]

(b) a development;

(c) the construction of a pipe-line for the conveyance of petroleum, other than one which is to form an integral part of any development;

(d) the use of a mobile installation for the extraction of petroleum where the principal purpose is the testing of any well.

1   SI 1999/360, reg 3(1).
2   An 'exploration well' is any well other than one drilled for the purposes of, or in connection with, a 'development'.

7.25   The Offshore Petroleum and Pipelines (Assessment of Environmental Effects) Regulations 1999, reg 5 then constrains the Secretary of State in the granting of 'consents'. These are essentially consents required under Petroleum Act licences, consents to use floating installations, and authorisations for construction and use of pipelines under the Petroleum Act 1998, s 14.[1] Subject to certain exceptions in reg 5(2),[2] consent may not be granted in respect of a 'relevant project'[3] unless either the application for consent is accompanied by an ES or is the subject of a direction given under reg 6 that no ES need be prepared.

1   See Offshore Petroleum and Pipelines (Assessment of Environmental Effects) Regulations 1999, reg 3(1).
2   These essentially relate to cases where (a) a consent for getting petroleum is being renewed or extended and where the increase in the rate of production would not exceed stated thresholds, or (b) the consent is for construction or extension of a pipe-line which would not extend more than 500 m from a well or fixed installation, and where in either case the Secretary of State has decided that the operation would not be likely to have a significant effect on the environment.
3   For the meaning of 'relevant project', see para **7.23** above.

7.26   The Offshore Petroleum and Pipelines (Assessment of Environmental Effects) Regulations 1999 contain provision as to the matters to be expected; applications for directions that EIA is not required (reg 6), consultation and publicity (regs 9 and 10), projects affecting other member states (reg 12).

Marine fish farming

7.27   'Intensive fish farming' is an Annex II project under the EIA Directive (para 1(f)). Development in connection with onshore fish farming, for example excavation to create ponds,[1] will fall within the normal planning system, including development on the foreshore between the high and low water marks. Consideration will, however, need to be given in such cases as to whether permitted development rights for agricultural buildings and operations may apply, since rights under the TCP(GPD) Order 1995, Sch 2, Pt 6, extend to 'fish farming', defined to mean the 'breeding, rearing or keeping of fish or shellfish', including cetaceans and molluscs.[2] The detail of the terms and limitations of such permitted development rights, and their relationship to the system of EIA, will need to be considered.[3]

1   See *West Bowers Farm Products Ltd v Essex County Council* (1985) 50 P & CR 368, [1985] JPL 857; *Fayrewood Fish Farms Ltd v Secretary of State for the Environment* [1984] JPL 267.
2   See TCP(GPD) Order 1995, Sch 2, Pt 6, para D.1. 'Livestock' includes farmed fish or shellfish.
3   See in particular TCP(GPD) Order 1995, Sch 2, Pt 6, A.1(i), A.2(2)(d) and B.1(e), as well as the general provisions in art 3(10) removing permitted development rights in relation to EIA development (as to which see para **6.42**).

7.28   Offshore fish farming facilities are not within the planning system, but require a lease from the Crown Estate Commissioners (or in appropriate cases, the Shetland Islands Council[1] or Orkney Islands Council[2]). The EIA (Fish Farming in Marine Waters) Regulations 1999[3] came into force on 14 March 1999 and apply to Scotland as well as England and Wales. They apply where any person is minded to make an application after the commencement date to the Crown Estate or to the appropriate Council for fish farming, defined by reg 2(1) as 'keeping live fish, excluding shellfish, (whether or not for profit) with a view to their sale or their transfer to other marine waters'. The expression used in the EIA Directive is *intensive* fish farming, which obviously gives some scope for subjective judgment as to what is 'intensive'. The Regulations deal with this by confining their scope (reg 1(3)) to fish farming where:

(a) any part of the proposed development is to be carried out in a 'sensitive area'; or

(b) the proposed development is designed to hold a 'biomass' of 10 tonnes or greater; or

(c) the proposed development will extend to 0.1 ha or more of the surface area of the marine waters, including any proposed structures or excavations.

1   Under the Zetland County Council Act 1974, s 11, where within the coastal area defined in that Act.

2   Under the Orkney County Council Act 1974, s 11, where within a harbour area defined in that Act.

3   SI 1999/367.

7.29   Again, the EIA (Fish Farming in Marine Waters) Regulations 1999 form a self-contained code for EIA of such projects, closely following the scheme for the planning system. The provisions include: prohibition on the grant of a licence or consent without considering the environmental information (reg 3), screening opinions (reg 4), scoping opinions (reg 6), publicity and consultation (regs 8 and 9), intimation of decisions (reg 11), transboundary effects (reg 15), selection criteria (Sch 1), matters for inclusion in the ES (Sch 2), and bodies to be consulted (Sch 3). The Crown Estate Commissioners, in consultation with the Scottish Executive Rural Affairs Department (SERAD), have issued a Guidance Manual for marine salmon farmers on EIA, and SERAD has published guidance on the practical implications of the Regulations.[1]

1   SERAD, *Guide to the EIA (Fish Farming in Marine Waters) Regulations 1999* (March 1999).

Land drainage

7.30   The EIA Directive includes within Annex II 'water management projects for agriculture, including irrigation and land drainage projects' (para 1(c)). It also includes under the general category of agricultural projects 'reclamation of land from the sea' (Annex II, para 1(g)), and under infrastructure projects both 'canalization and flood-relief works (para 10(f)) and 'coastal work to combat erosion and maritime works capable of altering the coast through the construction, for example, of dykes, moles, jetties and other sea defence works, excluding the maintenance and reconstruction of such works' (para 10(k)). The government's guide to EIA procedures suggests that new land drainage works, including flood defence works and defences against the sea, require planning permission.[1] On the other hand, the TCP(GPD) Order 1995, Sch 2, Pts 14 and 15 provide permitted development rights for development by drainage bodies and the Environment Agency 'in, on or under any watercourse or land drainage works and required in connection with the improvement, maintenance or repair of that watercourse or works'.[2] The EIA (Land Drainage Improvement Works) Regulations 1999 are intended to apply to drainage improvement works which would otherwise not require planning permission.[3]

1   DETR/National Assembly for Wales, *EIA: A Guide to Procedures* (November 2000) para 80.

2   See TCP(GPD) Order 1995, Sch 2, Pt 14 and Pt 15, Class A(b). Under Pt 14 a 'drainage body' is defined by reference to the Land Drainage Act 1991, s 72(1), but excluding the Environment Agency, ie an internal drainage board or any other body having power to make or maintain works for the drainage of land.

3   SI 1999/1783. Permitted development rights are not removed in respect of development falling within the EIA (Land Drainage Improvement Works) Regulations 1999: see TCP(GPD) Order 1995, art 3(12(b)).

7.31   The EIA (Land Drainage Improvement Works) Regulations 1999 apply to 'improvement works' carried out by a 'drainage body' (the Environment Agency, an internal drainage board, or a local authority). 'Improvement works' means works which are permitted development under the TCP(GPD) Order 1995, Sch 2, Pts 14 and 15, and which are 'the subject of a project to deepen, widen, straighten or otherwise improve any existing watercourse[1] or remove or alter mill dams, weirs or other obstructions to watercourses, or raise, widen or otherwise improve any existing drainage[2] work'.

1   'Watercourse' is very broadly defined to include any river and stream, and any ditch, drain, cut, culvert, dike, sluice, sewer (other than a public sewer) and any passage through which water flows (EIA (Land Drainage Improvement Works) Regulations 1999, reg 2(1)).

2   'Drainage' includes defence against water, including sea water (EIA (Land Drainage Improvement Works) Regulations 1999, reg 2(1)).

7.32   By the EIA (Land Drainage Improvement Works) Regulations 1999, reg 3(1) a drainage body shall not carry out any improvement works unless they have complied with the requirements of the Regulations. In relation to all improvement works the drainage body must, taking into account the selection criteria in Sch 2, determine whether the proposed improvement works are likely to have significant effects on the environment (reg 4). If the drainage body consider that they are not likely to have significant effects, this must be announced and particulars published in local newspapers and made available to the consultation bodies including English Nature and the Countryside Council for Wales (reg 5(1) and (2)). If representations are made to the effect that the works are likely to have significant environmental effects, and the drainage body maintains its position that this is not likely, then the drainage body must apply to the Secretary of State for Environment, Food or Regional Affairs, or to the Welsh Assembly, for a determination on the issue (reg 5(5)). Where it is determined that significant effects are likely, an ES containing the information specified in Sch 1 must be prepared (reg 7) and published (reg 10). In determining whether the works should proceed, the drainage body must assess the direct and indirect effects of the proposed works in the light of the ES and any representations made on it (reg 12(1)). If objections as to likely effects are made and are not withdrawn, then the drainage body must refer the proposal to the Secretary of State or Welsh Assembly for determination (reg 12(4)). Powers of enforcement are provided for the Secretary of State and Welsh Assembly by reg 14 in cases where a drainage body carries out improvement works without complying with the Regulations; an application may be made to the county court or High Court for an order restraining works and requiring removal and reinstatement of works carried out, and in default the authority may carry out works itself and recover the cost as a debt from the drainage body.

Forestry

7.33   Annex II of the EIA Directive catches 'initial afforestation and deforestation for the purposes of conversion to another type of land use' (para 1(d)). The EIA (Forestry) (England and Wales) Regulations 1999[1] came into force on 6 September 1999 and apply to four types of project (reg 3(2)):

(a)   afforestation;[2]
(b)   deforestation;
(c)   forest road works;[3] and
(d)   forest quarry works.[4]

By reg 4(1)(c) such projects will only be a 'relevant project' for the purposes of the Regulations if they fall outside any class of Sch 2 projects in the TCP(EIA) Regulations 1999, or do not involve development within the planning system, or involve development for which there are permitted development rights under of the TCP(GPD) Order 1995, Sch 2, Pt 7 (Forestry Buildings and Operations). Thus the Regulations in a sense constitute a 'safety net' to catch afforestation or deforestation projects which would not be caught by EIA under the planning system. Also, in order to be a relevant project, the project must be likely to have significant effects on the environment (reg 3(1)(b)).

1   SI 1999/2228.
2   'Afforestation' and 'deforestation' have the same meaning as in the EIA Directive (EIA (Forestry) (England and Wales) Regulations 1999, reg 2(1)).
3   Defined by EIA (Forestry) (England and Wales) Regulations 1999, reg 2(1) to mean the formation, alteration or maintenance of private ways on land used or to be used for the purposes of forestry.
4   Defined to mean operations on forestry land, or land held or occupied with such land, to obtain the materials for forest road works.

7.34   By the EIA (Forestry) (England and Wales) Regulations 1999, reg 4, no person may carry out on any land works or operations relating to a relevant project unless consent has been granted by the Forestry Commissioners, or by the Secretary of State or the National Assembly for Wales, and the project is carried out in accordance with the consent. Regulations 5 and 6 contain a screening procedure whereby the proposer of a project may apply in writing to the Commissioners for their opinion whether the project is a relevant project. There is also a procedure for directions on the issue to be given by the Secretary of State or Welsh Assembly (reg 9). As might be expected, provision is made for scoping opinions (reg 9), further information (reg 11), publicity (reg 13), transboundary effects (reg 14), determination of applications for consent (reg 15), notification of decisions (reg 16) and applications to the court by persons aggrieved (reg 19). Because the Regulations are creating an entire new consent procedure they also deal with the mechanics of that procedure, in particular applications (reg 10), imposition of conditions (reg 18), appeals against refusal or consent or against conditions imposed (reg 17), enforcement in respect of unconsented works (regs 20–23) and public registers (reg 24).

Power stations and electricity works

7.35   A range of energy-related projects fall within Annexes I and II of the EIA Directive:

Annex I
— thermal power stations and other combustion installations with a heat output of 300 MW or more (para 2, first indent)
— nuclear power stations and other nuclear reactors (para 2, second indent)
— construction of overhead electrical power lines with a voltage of 222 KV or more and a length of more than 15 km

Annex II
— other industrial installations for the production of electricity, steam and hot water (para 3(a))
— industrial installations for transmission of electrical energy by overhead cables (para 3(b))
— installations for hydroelectric energy production (para 3(h))
— wind farms (para 3(i))
— changes or extensions to Annex I or II projects (para 13).

7.36   The construction or extension of power stations exceeding 50 MW capacity and the installation of overhead power lines both require consent from the Secretary of State for Trade and Industry under ss 36 and 37 of the Electricity Act 1989. The EIA Directive is implemented in relation to such consents through the Electricity Works (Assessment of Environmental Effects) Regulations 2000,[1] which came into force on 20 July 2000. They apply to applications under the Electricity Act 1989, s 36, for consent to construct, extend or operate a generating station, and to applications under s 37 for consent to install or keep installed an electric line above ground (reg 1(2)). EIA is required for all projects within Annex I (all nuclear stations and non-nuclear stations with a heat output of 300 MW or more).[2] Screening is required for all generating stations not within Annex I, for the extension of generating stations where a s 36 consent is required, for all overhead lines of 132 KV or more, and for other above ground electric lines installed in 'sensitive areas'.[3] Overhead power lines below the 132 KV threshold are not normally expected to have significant environmental effects and do not need to be considered for EIA unless local circumstances demand it.[4] There are procedures for seeking a screening opinion (reg 5), for screening determinations where an application is made without an ES (reg 6), scoping (reg 7), publicity and procedures (Pt IV) and transboundary effects (reg 12).

1   SI 2000/1927.
2   SI 2000/1927, Sch 1.
3   SI 2000/1927, Sch 2.
4   DETR/National Assembly for Wales, *EIA: A Guide to Procedures* (November 2000) para 73

Nuclear power station decommissioning

7.37   Annex I, para 2 of the EIA Directive includes the dismantling or decommissioning of nuclear power stations and other nuclear reactors. An EIA regime for this activity is provided by the Nuclear Reactors (EIA for Decommissioning) Regulations 1999,[1] which came into force on 19 November 1999 and apply to Scotland as well as England and Wales. The Regulations do not apply to any dismantling or decommissioning work commenced prior to their coming into force,[2] nor to any project serving national defence purposes.[3] Decommissioning will in practice be the subject of conditions under the nuclear site licence.[4] The holder of the nuclear site licence may not commence a decommissioning 'project'[5] unless he has applied to the Health and Safety Executive (HSE) for a consent and a consent has been granted (reg 4).

1   SI 1999/2892.
2   SI 1999/2892, reg 3(2).
3   SI 1999/2892, reg 3(3).
4   See Tromans and Fitzgerald, *The Law of Nuclear Installations and Radioactive Substances* (1997) para 2-43.
5   'Project' means the carrying out of any dismantling or decommissioning work, but excludes removal of elements or waste in accordance with normal or routine operations (Nuclear Reactors (EIA for Decommissioning) Regulations 1999, reg 2(1)). Dismantling or decommissioning is not treated as having commenced unless plant or equipment is disabled or removed for the purpose of permanently preventing the continued operation of the station or reactor.

7.38   There are no procedures for screening, since the project will require EIA in every case. There are procedures for seeking a pre-application opinion from the HSE as to the content of the ES (Nuclear Reactors (EIA for Decommissioning) Regulations 1999, reg 6), for the procedure to be followed by the HSE in dealing with applications for consent (reg 8), publicity (reg 9), further information (reg 10), information as to decisions (reg 11), transboundary effects (reg 12), and for considering whether changes or extensions to consented projects, or to those commenced before the regulations came into force, are such as to require further EIA (reg 13). Enforcement is dealt with by incorporating the relevant provisions on offences and enforcement in the Health and Safety at Work, etc Act 1974, ss 18–26 and 33–42 (reg 16).

Port and harbour works

7.39   Annex I of the EIA Directive includes 'trading ports, piers for loading and unloading connected to land and outside ports (excluding ferry piers) which can take vessels of over 1,350 tonnes' (para 8(b)). Annex II includes 'construction of harbours and port installations, including fishing harbours' (para 10(e)) as well as changes or extensions to port projects within Annex I (para 13).

7.40   Port and harbour developments above the low water mark will be development requiring planning permission.[1] Permitted development rights for statutory undertakers under the TCP(GPD) Order 1995, Sch 2, Pt 17, Class B (operational land of dock, pier, harbour and water transport undertakings) will not apply in relation to EIA development.[2]

7.41   However, harbour works may also be authorised by harbour revision and empowerment orders under the Harbours Act 1964, ss 14 and 16, for securing harbour efficiency and for improving or constructing harbours. For this purpose, a 'harbour' includes natural or artificial harbours or ports, estuaries, tidal and other rivers or inland waterways, which are navigable by sea-going ships, and also docks and wharfs.[1] Development which is authorised by such orders, designating specifically the nature of the development and the land on which it may be carried out, is permitted development under the TCP(GPD) Order 1995, Sch 2, Pt 11, Class A(b).

1   Harbours Act 1964, s 57(1).

7.42   For such works as do not require planning permission, the EIA Directive is implemented for England, Scotland and Wales by the Harbour Works (EIA) Regulations 1999, which came into force on 1 February 2002.[1] These Regulations fall into two parts: Pt II provides a procedure for harbour works below the low water mark, while Pt III amends the procedures applying to orders under the Harbours Act 1964.

1   SI 1999/3445 as amended by SI 2000/2391, which simply corrects a typographical error and three incorrect cross-references in the 1999 Regulations.

7.43   Part II of the Harbour Works (EIA) Regulations 1999 applies to all harbour works (defined by reg 2(1) as works involved in the construction of a harbour or in the making of modifications to an existing harbour) below the low water mark, but excluding:[1]
(a)   works subject to planning control;
(b)   works authorised by a harbour revision or empowerment order under the Harbours Act 1964;
(c)   works authorised in any enactment conferring power to carry out works at a harbour;
(d)   works authorised under the Transport and Works Act 1992;[2]
(e)   works consented by the Crown Estate Commissioners under the EIA Regulations dealing with fish farming.[3]

Harbour works constituting a project within Annex II of the EIA Directive are to be treated as not falling within the Annex unless either:[4]
(a)   the area of the works exceeds 1 ha, or
(b)   any part of the works is to be carried out in a sensitive area,[5] or
(c)   the appropriate authority[6] determines that the works should be treated as falling within the Annex.

1   SI 1999/3445, reg 3.
2   See para 7.54.
3   See paras 7.26.
4   SI 1999/3445, reg 2(3).
5   Defined in the usual terms at reg 2(1).

6   The authority is (a) the Secretary of State for the Environment, Food and Regional Affairs for fishery harbours in England, (b) the National Assembly for Wales for fishery harbours in Wales, (c) the Secretary of State for Transport, Local Government and the Regions for other harbours in England and Wales, and (d) the Scottish Ministers for any harbour in Scotland. See the Transfer of Functions (Fishery Harbours) Order 2001, SI 2001/3503.

7.44   The procedures under the Harbour Works (Environment Impact Assessment) Regulations 1999, Pt II apply where an application or notice is given under any of the procedures listed in reg 5(1) in relation to harbour works covered by Pt II. These include applications under the Coast Protection Act 1949, notices given under regulations made under the Merchant Shipping Act 1988 in relation to navigation, and applications for any approvals required under local acts or harbour revision or empowerment orders.[1] There is a procedure under reg 4 whereby the person minded to make such an application can obtain the opinion of the appropriate authority as to whether EIA is required and, if so, what information should be supplied in the ES. Where the appropriate authority determines that EIA is required, then it directs the developer to supply it with an ES in such form as it may specify and containing such of the information referred to in Sch 1 as the authority considers is relevant and that the developer may reasonably be expected to compile (see reg 5 dealing with applications where a prior opinion under reg 4 has been given, and reg 6 dealing with applications where no such prior opinion has been given).

1   The making of such orders themselves is dealt with in Pt III of the Harbour Works (Environment Impact Assessment) Regulations 1999.

7.45   Further provisions then deal with publicity for the ES (Harbour Works (Environment Impact Assessment) Regulations 1999, reg 7), cases with potential transboundary effects (reg 8), consultation with other bodies (reg 9(1)–(3)), the holding of public inquiries into the proposal where the relevant authority thinks fit (reg 9(4)), decisions by the appropriate authority on applications for consent (reg 10), applications for variations in relation to changes or extensions to works (reg 12), and procedures for enforcement and penalties in the case of works carried out without consent (regs 11, 13 and 14).

7.46   Part III of the Harbour Works (Environment Impact Assessment) Regulations 1999 amends the Harbours Act 1964 by substituting a new Sch 3, dealing with the procedure for making harbour revision or empowerment orders. Essentially these procedures require the person applying for a harbour revision order which directly or indirectly authorises a 'project'[1] to give notice to the Secretary of State of his intention to make the application (Harbours Act 1964, Sch 3, para 3). The Secretary of State then decides whether the project falls within Annex I or II of the EIA Directive, and if within Annex II, whether it is a 'relevant project'[2] (Sch 3, paras 4–6). If the decision is that EIA is required, then the application for the order must comply with Sch 3, para 8, and be accompanied by an ES. There are procedures for publicity (para 10), consultation (para 15), cases of potential transboundary effects (para 16), for the holding of inquiries into objections (para 18), and the making and notification of decisions (paras 19 and 20).

1   'Project' is defined in the same terms as in the EIA Directive to include the execution of construction works or other installations or schemes and other interventions in the natural surroundings (Harbours Act 1964, Sch 3, para 1).
2   A 'relevant project' is one which is likely to have significant effects on the environment by virtue of factors such as its nature, size or location (Harbours Act 1964, Sch 3, para 1).

7.47   By the Harbours Act 1964, Sch 3, Pt III, para 32, the same procedures apply to applications for harbour empowerment orders. The Government's guidance suggests that in general, works under harbour empowerment orders are likely to fall within Annex I of the Directive, whereas works under harbour revision orders are likely to fall within Annex II.[1] The distinction is that harbour revision orders are made for achieving defined objectives set out in the Harbours Act 1964, Sch 2, in relation to harbours managed by a harbour authority in the exercise and performance of its statutory powers and duties, whereas any person wishing to construct a dock or harbour, or to improve a harbour, port, or waterway navigable by sea-going ships may apply for a harbour empowerment order.

1   DETR/National Assembly for Wales, *EIA: A Guide to Procedures* (November 2000), para 86.

Extraction of marine minerals by dredging

7.48   The extraction of minerals by marine or fluvial dredging is within Annex II of the EIA Directive (para 2(c)). These operations, if below the low water mark, will not require planning permission. The intention is to introduce a new statutory system to apply to marine dredging, requiring dredging permissions. In 2002, the government introduced MMG 1, providing guidance on sea-bed minerals dredging.[1] This Guidance is intended to cover both current practice whereby dredging licences are issued by the Crown Estate, subject to a 'government view' (GV) on the acceptability of the environmental effects,[2] and the new statutory system of dredging permissions, when it is introduced. The guidance indicates that it is government policy that all applications for dredging permissions in previously undredged areas will require EIA,[3] that applications to vary conditions attached to old GV licences will be considered on a case by case basis as to the need for EIA,[4] and that in most cases prospecting and sampling operations are unlikely to require EIA if they remove no more than 5,000 tonnes of material,[5] unless operations may impact on a European conservation site or other sensitive area.[6] Annex A of MMG 1 contains detailed guidance on EIA in relation to such applications, since obviously the potential impacts are of a rather different nature than those from terrestrial projects.

1   Marine Minerals Guidance Note 1 (MMG 1): Guidance on the Extraction by Dredging of Sand, Gravel and Other Minerals from the English Seabed (ODPM, 2002).
2   MMG 1, paras 4, 6.
3   MMG 1, para 16.
4   MMG 1, para 17.
5   MMG 1, para 18.
6   For example, designated shell fisheries or marine archaeological sites.

Use of uncultivated and semi-natural land

7.49   Projects for the use of uncultivated land or semi-natural areas for intensive agricultural purposes are within Annex II of the EIA Directive (para 1(b)). EIA was only introduced as a formal requirement for such projects by the EIA (Uncultivated Land and Semi-Natural Areas) (England) Regulations 2001,[1] which came into force on 1 February 2002. These Regulations only apply in relation to this type of project if it is not caught by one of the other regimes for planning, forestry or land drainage, as described above (reg 3(2)). By reg 4, no person may begin or carry out a project without first obtaining a screening decision, and reg 5 lays down a screening procedure. One point to note is that by reg 5(10) a screening decision is time limited, in that it ceases to have effect after three years if the project has not been commenced within that time. By reg 6 no person may begin or carry out a 'relevant project' (one determined as likely to have significant effects) without first obtaining consent from the Secretary of State.

1   SI 2001/3966.

7.50   The EIA (Uncultivated Land and Semi-Natural Areas) (England) Regulations 2001 then make provision for scoping (reg 7), consent applications (including the ES, consultation and publicity) (reg 9), additional information (reg 10), possible transboundary effects (reg 11), procedures for consultation where part of the land concerned is in Scotland or Wales (reg 12), the consent decision (reg 13), the review of decisions where a site subsequently becomes a European nature conservation site (reg 14 and Sch 3), appeals against decisions (regs 15–17), applications to the court by persons aggrieved (reg 18), and offences and enforcement (regs 19–25). The strict nature of the regime is emphasised by the fact that consents are to be subject to conditions that they will lapse if the project is not commenced by the carrying out of a material act within one year, and that the consent will expire (in the sense of not authorising further operations or continued use) if the project is not completed within three years (reg 13(11)).

Water resources

7.51   An area likely to be a growing concern in environmental terms is that of water resources. There are a number of types of project falling within Annexes I and II of the EIA Directive relating to water which may not necessarily fall within the planning system's concept of development. These are:

Annex I
— groundwater abstraction or artificial recharge schemes (para 11)
— works for the transfer of water resources between river basins (para 12).

Annex II
— water management projects for agriculture, including irrigation (para 1(c))
— deep drillings, in particular drilling for water supplies (para 2(d))

— groundwater abstraction and artificial groundwater recharge schemes not within Annex I (para 10(l))
— works for the transfer of water resources between river basins not included in Annex I (para 10(m)).

7.52   It may be that in many cases such projects will involve engineering operations such as to constitute development requiring planning permission. Statutory undertakers for the supply of water benefit from permitted development rights for various projects under the TCP(GPD) Order 1995, Sch 2, Pt 17, Class D. However, such rights are withdrawn in the case of EIA development by art 3(10) of the Order. It is possible to contemplate cases where abstraction or irrigation might be carried out without the need for planning permission, and might have significant environmental effects, for example in relation to large scale and intensive crop irrigation systems.

7.53   Water abstraction is subject to the requirement of a licence from the Environment Agency under the Water Resources Act 1991, Pt II, Ch II (Abstraction and Impounding). The regulations governing the procedure for such licences date back to 1965,[1] long before EIA. This gap in transposition has now been addressed by the Water Resources (EIA) (England and Wales) Regulations 2003,[2] which came into force on 1 April 2003. These require (reg 3(1)) that EIA shall be carried out in relation to a 'relevant project'. By reg 3(2) a project is a 'relevant project if:
(a)   it is a water management project for agriculture, including an irrigation project;
(b)   in the case of water abstraction, it involves the abstraction of more than 20 cubic metres in any 24 hour period; and
(c)   it would be likely to have significant effects on the environment.

A project will not be covered if it involves development requiring planning permission, or if it constitutes drainage improvement works within the EIA (Land Drainage Improvement Works) Regulations 1999 (reg 3(3)).

1   The Water Resources (Licences) Regulations 1965, SI 1965/534 (having continued effect by virtue of the Water Consolidation (Consequential Provisions) Act 1991, s 2(2) and Sch 2, Pt I, para 1(1), (2)).
2   SI 2003/164.

7.54   The EIA (Land Drainage Improvement Works) Regulations 1999 bite on applications for an abstraction or impounding licence under the Water Resources Act 1991, Pt II, Ch II. However, there may be cases where such a licence is not required, and in such cases a new consenting procedure is introduced by Pt III of the Regulations. There are procedures for obtaining a prior determination as to whether a project is a relevant project (reg 4), the provision and content of an ES (regs 5 and 6), publicity (reg 7), determination of applications (reg 8) and registers (reg 16).

The Transport and Works Act 1992

7.55   The Transport and Works Act 1992 (TWA 1992) allows orders to be made by the Secretary of State authorising the construction or operation of railways, tramways, trolley vehicle systems, other guided transport systems, and inland waterways. Such orders may be coupled with a direction that planning permission is deemed to be granted: see TCPA 1990, s 90(2A), inserted by TWA 1992, s 16(1). Effectively, the TWA 1992 provides an extra-Parliamentary process for projects that would previously have been the subject of the Private Bill procedures; s 9 does however require Parliamentary involvement in proposals which are of national significance. The TWA is amended by the Transport and Works (Assessment of Environmental Effects) Regulations 1998 (TWA(AEE) Regulations 1998),[1] to insert provisions to give effect to requirements of the EIA Directive.

1   SIs 1998/2226 and 2000/3199.

7.56   The following heads under Annexes I and II of the EIA Directive may be relevant to projects authorised by TWA orders:

Annex I
— construction of lines for long-distance railway traffic (para 7(a))
— inland waterways which permit the passage of vessels of over 1,350 tonnes (para 8(a)).

Annex II
— construction of railways and intermodal transshipment facilities (para 10(c))
— inland waterway construction (para 10(f))
— tramways, elevated and underground railways, suspended lines or similar lines of a particular type, used exclusively or mainly for passenger transport (para 10(h))
— changes or extensions to Annex I or II projects (para 13).

7.57   The procedures for making such orders under the TWA 1992, Pt I, are found in the Transport and Works (Applications and Objections Procedure) (England and Wales) Rules 2000,[1] made under TWA 1992, s 6, and which came into force on 16 October 2000. These contain provisions to implement the EIA Directive, and replace the previous Rules (SI 1992/2902). The relevant requirements are as follows:
1   Where the order for which application is to be made would authorise any works or other matters comprising a project for the purposes of Annex I or II of the EIA Directive, notice is required to be given not less than 28 days before making the application to specified bodies (see art 5(2) and Form 1, Sch 3).
2   There is a procedure for the promoter to request relevant information from public bodies (art 6(1)).
3   The applicant is required to submit an ES (termed an 'applicant's statement of environmental information') in relation to Annex I projects, and for Annex II projects unless notified that EIA is not required (art 7(1) and (2)). The content of the ES is dealt with by art 11 and Sch 1.

4   There is a procedure to seek a screening decision from the Secretary of State (art 7(3)–(14)).
5   There is a procedure for obtaining a scoping opinion (art 8).
6   The publicity procedures are set out at art 14.
7   There is a procedure for projects with likely significant effects on the environment in Scotland, Northern Ireland, the Isle of Man, the Channel Isles, and other member states of the European Economic Area (art 16, the reference to the EEA being inserted by SI 2000/3199, reg 3).[2]
8   Further information can be required to be provided by the promoter under art 17.
9   The determination of the application must state that the ES and other environmental information has been considered, and the notice of determination must contain a description of the main measures to avoid, reduce and if possible remedy the major adverse environmental effects (TWA 1992, s 14(3A) and (3AA), inserted by the TWA(AEE) Regulations 1995, SI 1995/1541 and the TWA(AEE) Regulations 1998, SI 1998/2226).

1   SI 2000/2190.
2   The power to make such provision is contained in TWA 1992, s 6A (as inserted by SI 1998/2226 and amended by SI 2000/3199).

CONCLUSION

7.58   As will have been clear from the account in this chapter, transposing the EIA Directive has not been an entirely straightforward process. This is because of the non-comprehensive nature of the planning system when compared with the Directive's list of projects, and the existence or non-existence of alternative statutory procedures which covered some types of project. In some cases there has been a ready-made system onto which EIA procedures could be engrafted; in others there has been the need to create a new consent procedure. This illustrates the force of the requirement in arts 2(1) and (2) of the EIA Directive, which may require new procedures to be established in order to ensure that relevant projects are made subject to a requirement for development consent as well as EIA. As Art 2(2) puts it:

'The environmental impact assessment may be integrated into the existing procedures for consent to projects in the Member States, or, failing this, into other procedures or into procedures to be established to comply with the aims of this Directive.'

7.59   As the history of implementation shows, the government has not always fully realised the implications of the EIA Directive in this regard, and regulations have had to be made, in some cases belatedly, to fill gaps in transposition. It is therefore relevant to conclude this chapter by considering whether there may be other gaps remaining to be filled.

7.60   One main area of continued uncertainty relates to one of the EIA Directive's more obscure classes of project: 'projects for the restructuring of rural land holdings'

(Annex II, para 1(a)). The scope of this wording is by no means certain, but clearly the consolidation of holdings into the large-scale enterprises in many parts of England (East Anglia in particular) has had very significant environmental effects. The European Commission has referred Austria to the ECJ following the failure of a number of *Länder* to adopt rules to ensure that projects involving the restructuring of rural landholdings are subject to an EIA.[1]

1   See Commission Press Release IP/03/117, 24 January 2003.

7.61   Probably because of the lack of clarity as to what is covered, and the lack of any regulatory controls over such restructuring, the government has steered clear of transposing the Directive in this regard. In order to qualify as a 'project', the restructuring of a holding would have to entail the execution of construction works or schemes, or other interventions in the natural surroundings and landscape. It is therefore the physical manifestations of consolidation or restructuring which are caught. A starting point at least would be to implement the Directive through the tougher measures now applying to operations likely to damage the special interest of sites of special scientific interest under the Wildlife and Countryside Act 1981, Pt II, as introduced by the Countryside and Rights of Way Act 2000, s 75(1) and Sch 9. EIA could in principle be introduced as part of the procedure for English Nature or the Countryside Council for Wales considering applications for consent. However, in order to implement the Directive fully, wider application than simply to SSSIs would be required.

CHAPTER 8

Challenges

INTRODUCTION

8.01 This chapter deals with the issue of challenges made to decisions on EIA grounds. As will have been clear from previous chapters, such challenges have increased dramatically in frequency in recent years, and have had a relatively high success rate. In terms of procedures, EIA-based challenges are no different to other types of challenge and indeed EIA is often coupled with other grounds of challenge, for example procedural fairness, non-compliance with procedural requirements, lack of formal delegation, or human rights contraventions. There are, however, two issues which have run as recurrent themes through the cases, and which are explored in this chapter. These are the timing of challenges and the exercise of discretion in terms of remedies where a breach of EIA requirements has been found.

DISTINCTION BETWEEN JUDICIAL REVIEW AND STATUTORY APPEAL

8.02 An initial and important point arises from the Town and Country Planning (Environmental Impact Assessment) Regulations 1999 (TCP(EIA) Regulations 1999), reg 30, which provides that for the purposes of the Town and Country Planning Act 1990 (TCPA 1990), Pt XII (validity of certain decisions), the reference in s 288 to action of the Secretary of State which is not within the powers of the Act, is to be taken to extend to a grant of planning permission by the Secretary of State in contravention of regs 3 or 25. By way of reminder, reg 3 prohibits the Secretary of State (or any planning authority or inspector) from granting planning permission pursuant to an EIA application unless he has first taken the environmental information into account. TCP(EIA) Regulations 1999, reg 25 imposes the same prohibition on the Secretary of State in relation to the grant of planning permission under TCPA 1990, s 177 in the context of an enforcement notice appeal. Thus the grant of permission by the Secretary of State, whether on a called-in application, s 78 appeal or enforcement notice appeal, if it is to be challenged on the basis that EIA was non-existent or deficient, will fall within the ambit of s 288. It may be noted that the same also applies to the determination of ROMP applications[1] by the Secretary of State by virtue of the TCP(EIA) Regulations

1999, reg 26A(14) as amended. The same provision also appears in the original Town and Country Planning (Assessment of Environmental Effects) Regulations 1988 (TCP(AEE) Regulations 1988).[2]

1   As to such applications, see para **6.34**.
2   SI 1988/1199, reg 25.

8.03   The effect of this provision, in the words of TCPA 1990, s 288(1), is that in relation to claims that the Secretary of State has granted permission in breach of EIA requirements:

'If any person— ...
(b)   is aggrieved by any action of the part of the Secretary of State ... and wishes to question the validity of that action on the grounds—
    (i)   that the act is not within the powers of this Act [including breach of regs 3 and 25], or
    (ii)   that any of the relevant requirements have not been complied with in relation to that action,
he may make application to the High Court under this section.'

8.04   Thus limb (b)(i) deals with the situation where the granting of planning permission is in breach of the TCP(EIA) Regulations 1999, regs 3 or 25(1) and is hence unlawful, because the environmental information was not taken into account. It should be noted that under limb (b)(ii), s 288 also applies to persons wishing to question actions on the basis of non-compliance with procedural requirements. Such 'relevant requirements' are defined by TCPA 1990, s 288(9) to include any requirements of the TCPA 1990 or of any orders, regulations or rules made under that Act which are applicable. It would thus cover procedural breaches of the requirements of the TCP(EIA) Regulations 1999 by the Secretary of State, even where such breaches did not result in a breach of regs 3 or 25(1).

8.05   The practical consequences of TCPA 1990, s 288 applying are as follows. First, by TCPA 1990, s 284(1)(f), the validity of the Secretary of State's decision may not be questioned in any legal proceeding other than under s 288. Thus challenge by judicial review is not permitted. Second, by TCPA 1990, s 288(3) there is a strict time limit in that any application must be made within six weeks from the date of the Secretary of State's decision. Third, as to remedies, by s 288(5) the High Court may: (a) suspend the operation of the decision on an interim basis, until final determination; and (b) if satisfied that the action is not within the powers of the Act (by TCP(EIA) Regulations 1999, reg 30 (this will include non-compliance with regs 3 and 25(1)) or that the interests of the applicant have been substantially prejudiced by failure to comply with a relevant requirement, quash the decision.

8.06   Thus there are effectively two regimes for challenge: TCPA 1990, s 288 applying to decisions of the Secretary of State, and judicial review in relation to decisions of a local planning authority

Time limits: TCPA 1990, s 288

8.07   If a decision of the Secretary of State is to be challenged under TCPA 1990, s 288, observance of the six-week statutory time limit is crucial. This contrasts with the flexible approach, based on the concept of promptitude, which applies in relation to judicial review. The right of challenge under s 288 is extinguished after six weeks, even where the allegation is that the decision was unlawful or ultra vires.[1] Moreover, the six-week period runs from the date the Secretary of State's decision is signed and dated,[2] not the date on which notice of it was received, which may result in a portion of the six-week period being effectively lost. It has been held that the strict six-week period is not incompatible with the ECHR, art 6 (on determination of civil rights), nor in conflict with the Human Rights Act 1998, s 7.[3]

1   See *Smith v East Elloe RDC* [1956] AC 736, followed in *R v Secretary of State for the Environment, ex p Ostler* [1977] QB 122, CA (distinguishing *Anisminic Ltd v Foreign Compensation Commission* [1969] 2 AC 147).
2   *Griffiths v Secretary of State for the Environment* [1983] 2 AC 51. As to calculation of the period, see *Okolo v Secretary of State for the Environment* [1997] 2 All ER 911, [1997] JPL 1005.
3   *Matthews v Secretary of State for the Environment, Transport and the Regions* [2001] EWHC Admin 815, [2002] JPL 716 (Sullivan J).

Time limits: judicial review

8.08   In bringing an EIA challenge by way of judicial review, the normal requirements will apply: the claimants must make their application by filing the claim form (a) promptly and (b) in any event not later than three months after the grounds to make the claim first arose.[1] A significant body of case law was built up on this requirement, with two particular conundrums prominent — first, the date from which time ran, in particular where the formal grant of planning permission had been preceded by a resolution to grant permission, and second, whether promptitude involved applying by analogy the requirement to bring a statutory challenge within six weeks. Both of these issues were addressed by the House of Lords in *R (Burkett)v London Borough of Hammersmith and Fulham*,[2] which is now the starting point on the issues of delay and what is the correct target for judicial review.

1   CPR 54.5(1).
2   [2002] UKHL 23, [2002] 1 WLR 1593. For the substantive decision in the case, see para 4.34.

8.09   *Burkett* concerned a challenge by judicial review to a decision of the planning committee of Hammersmith and Fulham to grant outline planning permission for a large-scale development at Imperial Wharf, Fulham; indeed the scheme was at the time one of the largest in London. The 32-acre site had formerly been used by British Gas, and the proposed development was for 1,800 residential units (including 500 affordable dwellings), a hotel, retail, restaurant leisure and community uses, Class B1 offices, public open space, car parking and a riverside walk. Mrs Burkett lived in a maisonette immediately adjacent to the site and was concerned about the possible effects on her and her family. In particular her concerns were as to dust from the development and soil contamination. The timing of the challenge was as follows:

15 September 1999 — resolution to grant planning permission[1]
6 April 2000 — application for permission for judicial review
12 May 2000 — planning permission granted.[2]

At that time the relevant provision on time limits for judicial review was RSC Ord 53, r 4(1), which was to the same effect as CPR 54.5(1) though couched in slightly different language. It required the application to be made 'promptly and in any event within three months from the date when grounds for the application first arose'. Thus if time ran from the date of the resolution the application was clearly out of time in terms of the three-month longstop period. Richards J and the Court of Appeal refused permission on that basis.

1   Subject to completion of a satisfactory TCPA 1990, s 106 agreement and to the Secretary of State not imposing an EIA Directive, art 14 direction preventing the grant of permission.
2   The delay was attributable to the fact that the Secretary of State imposed a holding EIA Directive, art 14 direction which was lifted on 24 February 2000 and to the negotiation of a TCPA 1990, s 106 agreement, which was executed on 12 May 2000.

8.10   The main speech in the Lords was given by Lord Steyn, and adopted by Lord Slynn of Hadley, Lord Hope of Craighead, Lord Millett and Lord Phillips of Worth Matravers. The House of Lords first of all rejected a procedural submission on the basis of *In re Poh*[1] that they had no jurisdiction to hear an appeal against the decision of the Court of Appeal on the permission point.[2]

1   [1983] 1 WLR 2.
2   See [2002] UKHL 23, [2002] 1 WLR 1593 at 1596F, para 7 (Lord Slynn), 1597–1598, paras 10–14 (Lord Steyn), 1611–1612C, paras 56–58 (Lord Hope).

8.11   Having referred to the EIA Directive, Lord Steyn noted that it created rights for individuals enforceable in the courts and that there was an obligation on national courts to ensure that individual rights are fully and effectively protected:[1]

'The Directive seeks to redress to some extent the imbalance in resources between promoters of major developments and those concerned, on behalf of individual or community interests, about the environmental effects of such projects.'

1   [2002] UKHL 23, [2002] 1 WLR 1593 at 1599D, para 15.

8.12   Lord Steyn then referred to the provisions of CPR 54.5 and RSC Ord 53, r 4. He also noted what he described as a useful reserve power in some cases, for the court to refuse to grant permission or any relief sought under the Supreme Court Act 1981, s 31(6), where it considers there has been 'undue delay' and that the granting of the relief sought would be 'likely to cause substantial hardship to, or substantially prejudice the rights of, any person or would be detrimental to good administration'.

Date from which time runs

8.13   The competing contentions were, for the local authority and the developer, that time ran from the date of the resolution and, for the claimant, that time ran from the date of the grant of permission or alternatively the date that the Secretary of State decided not to call in the application. Lord Steyn regarded the real choice as between the date of the resolution and the date of the grant. The fact that the application for judicial review referred to the resolution was held to be not fatal, as the emphasis should be on substance not form, and if the correct target was the grant, the application could be amended accordingly.[1] Lord Steyn regarded it as significant that the resolution to grant permission was 'inchoate' in that it gave rise to rights and obligations only when the conditions precedent to it (including the uncertain successful negotiation of a complex TCPA 1990, s 106 agreement) were satisfied.[2] Further, as a matter of law the planning authority could revoke a resolution to grant permission.[3]

1   [2002] UKHL 23, [2002] 1 WLR 1593 at 1604D, para 31.
2   [2002] UKHL 23, [2002] 1 WLR 1593 at 1604E–1605B, paras 32–34.
3   [2002] UKHL 23, [2002] 1 WLR 1593 at 1606E, para 39.

8.14   As a matter of construction of the domestic procedural rules, the issue turned on the words 'from the date when the grounds for the application first arose'. Lord Steyn did not regard the RSC and CPR versions as materially different in this regard. Applying the general words to the specific case of planning applications, Lord Steyn held that it was certainly *possible* to challenge a resolution to grant permission if such grant would be unlawful;[1] the issue was however whether the challenge *had* to be made at that stage. Lord Steyn's analysis of the resolution as 'inchoate' suggested that the date of the resolution was not decisive in this respect. The counter view, forcefully expressed by Laws J in *R v Secretary of State for Trade and Industry, ex p Greenpeace Ltd*[2] and adopted by the Court of Appeal in *Burkett*, was that the claimant should move at the earliest possible opportunity against the substantive act or decision which was the real basis of his complaint. Lord Steyn however rejected any argument that the alleged defects in EIA underlay the resolution as well as the grant and that therefore time must be measured from the resolution:[3]

> 'For my part the substantive position is straightforward. The court has jurisdiction to entertain an application by a citizen for judicial review in respect of a resolution before or after its adoption. But it is a jump in legal logic to say that he *must* apply for such relief in respect of the resolution on pain of losing his right to judicial review of the actual grant of planning permission which does affect his rights. Such a view would also be in tension with the established principle that judicial review is a remedy of last resort.'

1   [2002] UKHL 23, [2002] 1 WLR 1593 at 1606B–C, para 39.
2   [1998] Env LR 415.

8.15   Drawing examples from other areas of judicial review, Lord Steyn showed that the contrary approach could be wasteful of time and money, if it requires the citizen to challenge a provisional decision. Lord Steyn also made reference to three important points of principle favouring the date of the formal grant of permission as the decisive date:

1   The deprivation by time limits of the citizen's right to challenge an abuse of power could involve not only individual rights but also community interests.[1] This weighs in favour of 'a clear and straightforward interpretation which will yield a readily ascertainable starting date'.

2   'Legal policy favours simplicity and certainty rather than complexity and uncertainty'.[2] The citizen, local authority and developer should know where they stand. The approach in *Greenpeace* did not give rise to such certainty.

3   The preparation of a judicial review application, particularly in a planning case, is a burdensome task, requiring full and frank disclosure by the applicant, a full statement of grounds, and extensive documentation. A private applicant is at risk of having to pay substantial costs, or alternatively there is a heavy cost to the Legal Services Commission. On that basis it is unreasonable to require an applicant to move against a decision which may never take effect, or to subject an applicant to the uncertainty of a retrospective assessment of a judge as to the date of triggering the time limits.[3]

1   [2002] UKHL 23, [2002] 1 WLR 1593 at 1608F–G, para 45. By 'community', Lord Steyn in this context meant the community of the relevant members of the public, not the European Community.
2   [2002] UKHL 23, [2002] 1 WLR 1593 at 1608H–1609B, paras 46–47.
3   [2002] UKHL 23, [2002] 1 WLR 1593 at 1610C–E, para 50.

8.16   Having resolved this issue on a construction of the domestic rules, Lord Steyn did not see the need to consider arguments which had been made on European law, nor to refer a question to the ECJ.[1]

1   [2002] UKHL 23, [2002] 1 WLR 1593 at 1610G, para 52. See also 1596E, para 6 (Lord Slynn).

Promptitude

8.17   A second issue arose for consideration in *Burkett*, though the case did not turn upon it. This was the issue of when an applicant may be said to have acted 'promptly'. Lord Steyn dealt with this point briefly. Following the decision of Laws J in *R v Ceredigion County Council, ex p McKeown*,[1] a body of case law had arisen to suggest that the six-week period allowed for statutory challenges in planning cases was to be used as a yardstick for promptness in judicial review or, in an extreme formulation, had supplanted the three-month limit. Lord Steyn rejected the extreme formulation as a 'misconception': 'The legislative three months' limit cannot be contracted by a judicial policy decision.'[2] Lord Steyn went on to query whether indeed the requirement to apply 'promptly' was sufficiently certain to comply with both European law and the European Convention on Human Rights.[3] As Lord Steyn suggested, it might be preferable to deal with delay by the refusal of relief in appropriate cases under the Supreme Court Act 1981, s 31(6). Lord Hope of Craighead expressly shared these concerns: under the principle of legality, any rule restricting Convention rights must be formulated with sufficient certainty to enable the citizen to regulate his conduct and to foresee to a reasonable degree the consequences of given actions.[4] The problem is that the word 'promptly' is inherently imprecise, and the relevant rules provide no criteria by reference to which the test is to be judged. Lord Hope contrasted the position in Scotland, where there is no statutory provision on delay, and where the issue is governed by the common law concepts of delay, acquiescence and personal bar, rather than simply the passage of time.[5] Lord Hope felt that these concepts could provide the certainty required by European law, and provide a 'sufficiently clear and workable rule'.[6]

1   [1998] 2 PLR 1.
2   [2002] UKHL 23, [2002] 1 WLR 1593 at 1610H–1611A, para 53.
3   [2002] UKHL 23, [2002] 1 WLR 1593 at 1611A–B, para 53.
4   [2002] UKHL 23, [2002] 1 WLR 1593 at 1612E–F, para 60, referring to *Sunday Times v United Kingdom* (1979) 2 EHRR 245, 270–271, paras 47, 49.
5   [2002] UKHL 23, [2002] 1 WLR 1593 at 1613D–F, para 63.
6   [2002] UKHL 23, [2002] 1 WLR 1593 at 1614D, para 66.

8.18   The observations of Lords Steyn and Hope on the possible incompatibility between the requirement of promptness and the European Convention on Human Rights were obiter. In the subsequent case of *R (Young) v Oxford City Council*[1] the Court of Appeal held that unless and until the issue is resolved adversely to the promptness requirement, it remains a feature of English law:[2]

'Those who seek to challenge the lawfulness of planning permission should not assume, whether as a delaying tactic or for other reasons, that they can defer filing their claim form until near the end of the three-month period in the expectation that the word "promptly" in the rule is a dead letter.'

1   [2002] EWCA Civ 990, [2002] All ER (D) 226 (Jun).
2   [2002] EWCA Civ 990, [2002] All ER (D) 226 (Jun), para 38 (Pill LJ).

Approach to time requirements post-*Burkett*

8.19   Where then does *Burkett* leave applicants, planning authorities and developers as regards challenges in EIA cases? The obvious point is that the challenger faced with a resolution to grant permission will have the choice whether to challenge the resolution or wait until permission is granted before issuing proceedings. This has a number of practical consequences. One is that the challenger, rather than being forced to take immediate action to avoid prejudicing their position, may have a greater incentive to enter into discussion with the authority as to his or her concerns, thereby providing an opportunity for defects to be rectified before permission is formally granted. The converse position is of course that a challenger may choose to simply bide their time until permission is granted, thereby causing maximum disruption. The appropriate way for the court to deal with this problem would probably lie in the exercise of its discretion under TCPA 1990, s 31(6) in relation to undue delay.

8.20   Another practical consequence, pointed out by Lord Steyn in *Burkett*, was that there will probably now be greater incentive for planning authorities and developers to reduce the time between the resolution and the grant of permission, and thereby minimise the uncertainty. Lord Steyn quoted from a recent article to this effect:[1]

> 'There would be a greater incentive for both the planning authority and the developer to move to ensure that the formal grant of planning permission is issued more speedily. This could be of advantage to developers wishing to progress the development of the site. From a public policy point of view it is important that speedy progress is made to issue the formal planning permission for appropriate development.'

There may of course be good reasons why there is delay, which may in some cases lie outside the control of the parties, for example a direction of the Secretary of State preventing the grant of permission, or the necessity to conclude a TCPA 1990, s 106 agreement (as in *Burkett* itself).

1   [2002] UKHL 23, [2002] 1 WLR 1593 at 1608D (para 44) citing *Jones and Phillpot* [2000] JPL 564 at 588.

8.21   It might be asked what the position would be where there is some action prior to any resolution to grant permission which is capable of challenge. The obvious example is a screening opinion by the authority that the development is not EIA development. Such a decision is (or should be) a formal and public decision. In the case of a screening opinion it does not however have conclusive effect that the development is not EIA development (unlike a positive opinion, which does have the effect of making the development EIA development by TCP(EIA) Regulations 1999, reg 4(2)(b)). In *R (Malster) v Ipswich Borough Council*[1] Sullivan J expressed the strong view that if a challenge is to be made to a screening opinion, it is not appropriate to wait until planning permission has been granted:[2]

> 'It is not appropriate to wait until after the planning permission has been granted, when it is too late to remedy the omission, and then complain that the screening opinion, which has been on the public register for some months, was erroneous. Each case will of course depend on its own particular facts but, as a general rule, where there is a discrete challenge to a screening opinion, it should, in my judgment, be made promptly so that any error, if there is one, can be remedied before the planning application is considered by the local planning authority.'

1   [2001] EWHC Admin 711 [2002] PLCR 251.
2   [2001] EWHC Admin 711 [2002] PLCR 251 at para 99. Sullivan J referred to the comment by Richards J in *R (Kathro) v Rhondda Cynon Taff County Borough Council* [2001] EWHC Admin 527, [2002] Env LR 402 at para 40, that it would not generally be appropriate to make a challenge following the issue of a screening opinion but before the grant of planning permission, where in that case there was no direct challenge to the screening opinion itself.

8.22   In practical terms, Sullivan J's comments have some force. However the position after *Burkett* would seem to be that while clearly it would be possible to challenge a screening opinion on the basis of error of law, equally it would be open to challenge the later grant of planning permission for unlawfulness under TCP(EIA) Regulations 1999, reg 3(2). Indeed Lord Steyn in *Burkett* specifically referred to the possibility that under the reasoning which he had rejected, time might start to run when a planning authority accepted a deficient ES and placed it on the public register.[1] Thus on his reasoning, the time for challenge would not start to run until the grant of permission. In the case of *R (Lebus) v South Cambridgeshire District Council* [2] an attempt was made to rely on the earlier comments in *Malster* to argue that relief should be refused in that there had been no separate challenge to the defective screening process. It will be recalled that in this case there had been no formal screening opinion.[3] Sullivan J regarded the facts as being far removed from *Malster*. The solicitors for Lebus had made it clear throughout to the council that EIA was required and that any planning permission granted without EIA would be unlawful:[4]

> 'In truth, the claimants have been saying for a very long time that the Council's approach under the Regulations was in error: the lack of a proper screening opinion is but one aspect of that complaint.'

1   [2002] UKHL 23, [2002] 1 WLR 1593 at 1609G, para 49.
2   [2002] EWHC 2009 (Admin), [2003] 2 P & CR 71.
3   See para 3.73.
4   [2002] EWHC 2009 (Admin), [2003] 2 P & CR 71 para 55. Sullivan J also regarded it as important that *Malster* was an application for permission to apply for judicial review, so that delay was a live issue, whereas in *Lebus* permission had already been given.

8.23   However, there may be a potential trap for challengers so far as screening directions by the Secretary of State are concerned. This is not so much to do with time limits as with the effect of such a direction. By TCP(EIA) Regulations 1999, reg 4(3) a direction determines for the purposes of the Regulations whether *or not* development is an EIA development. Thus if a negative screening direction goes unchallenged, a later challenge to the grant of permission could be met with the argument that since the direction has determined that the development is not EIA development, there has been no breach of reg 3(2), which only applies to an application for EIA development. The challenger might therefore be well advised to avoid that potential problem by challenging the direction, rather than waiting.

Promptitude

8.24   *Burkett* is clearly helpful in laying to rest the idea that six weeks is some sort of norm or surrogate statutory time limit in terms of promptness. However, that will still leave the question of whether within the three-month time limit the claimant acted promptly, or if the three-month limit is exceeded, whether it may be extended under CPR 3.1(2)(a).

8.25   In this respect it is probably true to say that the courts have gradually shown greater sympathy for the difficulties faced by the individual claimant, and the comments by Lord Steyn in *Burkett*, referred to above,[1] provide powerful support in this respect. In particular it may be relevant that the claimant was unaware of the decision but acted expeditiously once he became aware,[2] or that there was a delay in obtaining community legal funding.[3] The approach may also be extended to extensions of time; in *Crichton v Wellingborough Borough Council*[4] Gibbs J gave an extension of time where the claimants were a day out of time on the basis that they should not be shut out from raising an arguable point for such delay.

1   [2002] UKHL 23, [2002] 1 WLR 1593 at 1610C–E (para 50). See para **8.15** above.
2   *R v Secretary of State for Home Department, ex p Ruddock* [1987] 1 WLR 1482; *R v Secretary of State for Foreign and Commonwealth Affairs, ex p World Development Movement Ltd* [1995] 1 WLR 386.
3   See *R v Stratford-upon-Avon District Council, ex p Jackson* [1985] 1 WLR 1319
4   [2002] EWHC 2988 (Admin).

8.26   In *R v Waveney District Council, ex p Bell*[1] Sullivan J provided some useful comments on the rationale for the requirement of promptitude and its practical application to the facts of the case. A challenge was made on EIA grounds to a resolution made on 25 January to grant planning permission for a new printing works. The application for judicial review was made on 3 March, a little over five weeks from the date of the resolution. Planning permission was granted on 23 March. The authority conceded that there had been a breach of the TCP(EIA) Regulations 1999, but argued that the planning permission should not be quashed, on the basis that there had been undue delay in making the challenge. Sullivan J stated the general principles as to delay in the following terms:[2]

> 'Whilst it is perfectly true that there are numerous authorities which emphasise the need for the utmost promptitude in challenging a grant of planning permission, that requirement should not be considered as an abstract ideal divorced from the facts of the particular case. The purpose of requiring the utmost promptitude in planning cases is so that there is not prejudice to third parties who might for example be entering into contractual arrangements. There is prejudice to good administration if members of the public rely upon public decisions and perhaps take actions or abstain from taking actions to their detriment.'

In that case there was no evidence of any *specific* prejudice to the developer, beyond the normal type of prejudice to be expected in any case where a permission is quashed; nor was there any evidence of prejudice to good administration, other than the delay which would naturally follow any quashing.[3] Sullivan J held there was no obligation on the claimant to provide evidence as to the reasons for the short delay in issuing proceedings; the grounds were substantial and a significant number of documents had to be collated. There was nothing to suggest that the claimants simply sat on their hands and waited for a while before deciding to apply for judicial review.[4] Sullivan J also realistically recognised that in terms of financial resources and familiarity with the legal system, individual claimants would not be in the same position as a commercial organisation bringing a challenge to the planning permission of a rival developer;

accordingly no direct parallels could be drawn with cases which had considered promptitude in relation to such challenges.[5]

1   [2001] Env LR 465.
2   [2001] Env LR 465, para 9.
3   The courts will in any event be wary of arguments based on prejudice to good administration, since administration beyond the law is not by definition 'good administration' See *R v Hammersmith and Fulham London Borough Council ex p Burkett* [2001] Env LR 684, part 29 I *R v Restormel Borough Council, exp Corbett* [2001] 1 PLR 108, para 32.
4   [2001] Env LR 465, para 13.
5   [2001] Env LR 465, para 14.

8.27   In line with the emphasis on viewing time issues as a practical matter in the context of the facts, rather than as some abstract ideal, it is possible that there may be circumstances relating to the development which require particular promptness. In *R (Malster) v Ipswich Borough Council*[1] a challenge to a resolution passed on 25 April was made on 1 June — a period of shortly over one month. Sullivan J held that, all other things being equal, this would be sufficiently prompt. But as Sullivan J put it, 'all other things are not equal'.[2] Ipswich Football Club had made clear the urgent need to proceed with the development of a new stand during the closed season, and demolition of the old stand began immediately and had been completed by the time the judicial review application was made. It was not a case where the development had come out of the blue to the local residents, who indeed could see the demolition proceeding. On that basis, Sullivan J held that the challenge had not been made promptly and that the lack of promptness had resulted in substantial prejudice to the Club.[3] It should be noted, however, that the decision does not provide authority to encourage a developer who is aware of a possible pending challenge to press on and incur expenditure in an attempt to defeat a challenge on promptness grounds; Sullivan J made it clear that the evidence presented by the Club showed that if it had appreciated that there was any doubt as to the lawfulness of the permission, it would not have proceeded to demolish the existing accommodation.

1   [2001] EWHC 711 (Admin), [2002] PLCR 251.
2   [2001] EWHC 711 (Admin), [2002] PLCR 251, para 100.
3   [2001] EWHC 711 (Admin), [2002] PLCR 251, para 101.

8.28   The history of dealings between the challenger and the authority will also be relevant in this context, as is shown by the decision of the Court of Appeal in *R (Young) v Oxford City Council*.[1] In that case a challenge was made within three months of the date of planning permission, but more than three months from the prior resolution. The Court of Appeal applied *Burkett* so that time ran from the date of the grant of permission. There was however a further argument as to whether, even on that basis, the claimant had acted promptly. Both Pill LJ and Potter LJ (with whose judgments Judge LJ agreed) stressed the importance of the claimant having time to seek information from the council to establish whether he had an arguable case. The claimant was held to have acted reasonably in seeking by some five letters over a period of three weeks to obtain such information. The council was criticised for not responding, not even stating that there were no surviving notes to explain the procedures followed.

It was only having threatened judicial review that the claimant had received more co-operation, and a letter some two months later which purported to be a 'complete explanation' was in fact nothing of the kind. The result, in the words of Potter LJ, is that the claimant was 'kept in the dark as to the process or reasoning applied by the council'.[2] Accordingly there had been no lack of promptness. Potter LJ stated the underlying rationale as follows:[3]

> '... such a requirement [promptitude] should not, in my view, oust the countervailing consideration that it is undesirable for a litigant to proceed blindly towards challenge of a decision in relation to which he suspects a fault or omission susceptible of review in a case where, for the purposes of clarification, he reasonably requires further information from the decision-making body so that he can consider in an informed manner whether proceedings are justified or worthwhile. Not only is he entitled to consider the wisdom of embarking on the trouble and expense of litigation from his own point of view, it is also undesirable that the machinery of litigation and the engagement of the court process be set in motion before there has been an effort to resolve the matter in pre-trial correspondence.'

1   [2002] EWCA Civ 990, [2002] All ER (D) 226 (Jun).
2   [2002] EWCA Civ 990, [2002] All ER (D) 226 (Jun), para 44.
3   [2002] EWCA Civ 990, [2002] All ER (D) 226 (Jun), para 43.

8.29   In summary therefore, the emphasis is on the reasonableness of the conduct of the parties, and on open-handedness in accordance with the spirit of modern litigation. Pending any further consideration of the compatibility of the promptness requirement with European human rights law, applicants will still have to move promptly following the grant of permission, and cannot simply stay silent until the last possible moment. If there are doubts as to the validity of the action proposed or taken, these should be voiced as early as possible, and any further information needed should be requested. Planning authorities should be responsive to such concerns or requests, and should consider, if planning permission has not yet been granted, whether any additional steps need to be taken in the light of the concerns expressed. Applicants should also be alert to possible prejudice which a developer may suffer from relying on the decision, and clear warning should be given. In terms of litigation, a developer who claims to have suffered prejudice will need to put their cards on the table by providing the specific evidence to back up those assertions.

PROCEDURES: STATUTORY CHALLENGE TO SECRETARY OF STATE DECISIONS

8.30   Where a challenge is made under the TCP Act 1990, s 288 (as applied by the TCP(EIA) Regulations 1999, reg 30) to a decision by the Secretary of State which is in breach of reg 3 or 25 of the TCP(EIA) Regulations 1999, then under CPR Sch 1, RSC Ord 94 the procedure is as follows:

1   The jurisdiction is exercisable by a single judge of the Queen's Bench Division (RSC Ord 94, r 1(1)).
2   The application must be made by claim form, which must state the grounds of application (RSC Ord 94, r 1(2)).
3   No permission is needed to make the claim.
4   The claim form must be filed at the Administrative Court office, and served, within the six-week time limit (RSC Ord 94, r 2(1)).
5   The claim form must be served on the Secretary of State and on the planning authority directly concerned with the decision (RSC Ord 94, r 2(2)(a) and (d)). Service should be on the Treasury Solicitor, who is the solicitor authorised for service in relation to the Secretary of State.[1]
6   Evidence is by way of witness statement or affidavit (Ord 94, r 3(1)).
7   Any witness statement in support of the application must be filed within 14 days after service of the claim form, and a copy must be served on the respondent (Ord 94, r 3(2)).
8   Any witness statement in opposition must be filed by the respondent within 21 days after service of the applicant's witness statement on him, and at the same time a copy must be served on the applicant (Ord 94, r 3(4)).
9   When filing a witness statement at the Administrative Court office, a copy of the statement and a copy of any exhibits must be left for the use of the court (Ord 94, r 3(4)).

1   See CPR Sch 1, RSC Ord 77, r 4(2)(a) and (b); Crown Proceedings Act 1947, s 18; also the Cabinet Office Note, *Crown Proceedings Act 1947* set out as the Annex to CPR PD 19 (19PD-007 to 010). The address is: The Treasury Solicitor, Queen Anne's Chambers, 28 Broadway, London SW1H 9JS. The address for service in the case of the National Assembly for Wales is: the Counsel General to the National Assembly for Wales, Cathays Park, Cardiff, CF10 3NQ.

Position of developer under statutory challenge

8.31   RSC Ord 94 makes no express provision as to the position of a developer where planning permission is challenged under this procedure. Reference should be made to CPR Pt 19 as to the addition of parties.

Procedures: challenge by judicial review

8.32   Under CPR 53 the following procedures apply:
1   The court's permission is required to proceed with the claim (CPR 54.4).
2 ᵻ The claim form must be filed (a) promptly and (b) in any event not later than three months[1] after the grounds to make the claim first arose (CPR 54.5(1)).
3   The claim form is Form N461.
4   The claim form must contain the matters referred to in CPR 8.2 and 54.6(1).
5   The claim form must be accompanied by the documents required by the relevant practice direction (CPR 54.6(2)).
6   The claim form must be served within seven days after the date of issue on (a) the defendant and (b) any person the claimant considers to be an interested party

(CPR 54.7).

7   Any person served with the claim form who wishes to take part in the proceedings must file an acknowledgment of service in Form N462 no more than 21 days after service of the claim form, and must serve copies on the claimant and on any other person named in the claim form, as soon as practicable and in any event not later than seven days after it is filed (CPR 54.8(1)–(3)).

8   The acknowledgment of service must set out a summary of the grounds for contesting the claim, where it is intended to do so (CPR 54.8(4).

9   Failure to serve an acknowledgment of service within the relevant time limits means that the relevant party may not take part in any permission hearing unless the court allows this; however, provided the later requirements of detailed grounds for contesting the claim are met, failure to acknowledge service will not prevent the party taking part in the full hearing (CPR 54.9(1)).

10   In most cases the court will deal with the permission application on the papers. The court may decide to hold a hearing in some cases, for example if there are arguments as to delay.[2]

11   On giving permission to proceed the court may also make directions (CPR 54.10).

12   Having given permission, the court will serve the order on the claimant, the defendant, and on any other party which filed an acknowledgment of service (CPR 54.11).

13   Where permission is refused without a hearing, or is given only on some of the grounds, the court will give its reasons (CPR 54.12(1)).

14   The claimant may file a request within seven days of being given the reasons for the refusal of permission, that the decision be reconsidered at a hearing (CPR 54.12(3) and (4)).

15   When permission to proceed is given, neither the defendant nor any other party may apply to set the order aside (CPR 54.13).

16   A defendant and any other person wishing to contest the claim must file and serve (a) detailed grounds for contesting the claim and (b) any written evidence, within 35 days after service of the order giving permission.

17   The court's permission is required if the claimant seeks to rely on grounds other than those for which he has been given permission to proceed (CPR 54.15).

1   In *Crichton v Wellingborough Borough Council* [2002] EWHC 2988 (Admin) Gibbs J was inclined to the view that the day on which the notice of decision was given should be included in the 3-month calculation, though the contrary was arguable (para 56(a))

2   See *Crichton v Wellingborough Borough Council* [2002] EWHC 2988 (where a full day permission hearing was held, contested by both defendant and interested party).

8.33   In particular, care is required in preparing the claim form and accompanying documents, which will include copies of the relevant decision under challenge, any written evidence in support of the claim, copies of the relevant statutory provisions and any case law, and a list of essential reading, with relevant passages sidelined. This material must be placed in a paginated and indexed bundle, two copies of which must be lodged.[1] The time and effort required to assemble and draft this material should not be underestimated. The process is 'front-loaded' and is akin to preparing for a trial. It should also be remembered that the claimant is under a duty to make full and frank disclosure of all material facts. The key purposes of the proper presentation of the material are to provide sufficient information to enable the defendant and any interested party to provide an acknowledgment of service, and to enable the judge considering the application on the papers to identify the issues and to establish whether there is an arguable case.

1   See CPR PD 54. PD-005.
2   CPR 54.6(3).

Standing: statutory challenge to Secretary of State decisions

8.34   By TCPA 1990, s 288(1) the right of challenge applies to any 'person aggrieved' by the relevant action on the part of the Secretary of State. The approach taken by the courts to these words has been fairly liberal in including local amenity groups opposing a decision or any other person who in the ordinary sense of the word is 'aggrieved', and the requirement does not seem to be a serious bar to local residents or groups making EIA-based challenges.[1] For example, in the leading case of *Berkeley v Secretary of State for the Environment*,[2] there was no objection in terms of standing to Lady Berkeley, who lived in a house near the site, had taken a course in ecology and was concerned about the effects of the development on the diversity of species in the Thames, had written to the Secretary of State urging the application be called in, and had appeared in person at the planning inquiry.[3] The tendency has been to move the concept towards the liberal approach to standing in judicial review,[4] though there are limits to this approach.[5] The question is whether the challenger has a genuine grievance because their interests may be prejudicially affected.[6] Those interests are not necessarily financial.

1   See *Turner v Secretary of State for the Environment* (1973) 28 P & CR 123; *Bizony v Secretary of State for the Environment* [1976] JPL 306; *Times Investments Ltd v Secretary of State for the Environment* (1990) 61 P & CR 98, [1991] JPL 67. As to public authorities as 'persons aggrieved', see *Cook v Southend Borough Council* [1990] 2 QB 1; *Strathclyde Regional Council v Secretary of State for Scotland* [1990] 2 PLR 8.
2   [2001] 2 AC 603.
3   [2001] 2 AC 603 at 612F–H.
4   *Cook v Southend Borough Council* [1990] 2 QB 1, at 7, per Woolf LJ.
5   See para 8.35.
6   See *R v Liverpool Corporation, ex p Liverpool Taxi Fleet Operators' Association* [1972] 2 QB 299, at 308 – 309 per Lord Denning MR.

8.35   The issue of 'person aggrieved' arose recently in *Trevett v Secretary of State for Transport, Local Government and the Regions*.[1] The case shows that there are limits to the concept of 'person aggrieved', and that it is not necessarily as wide a concept as standing in judicial review. Planning permission had been granted on appeal for three telecommunications masts belonging to three different operators at three separate locations in the Stroud area, but up to 15 km apart. Mrs Trevett challenged the decisions under TCPA 1990, s 288. Sullivan J referred to the broad approach taken by the previous authorities, but noted that the grounds in support of the application merely stated that '[she] lives near to one of the sites and was involved with the community prior to the inquiry concerning the police station site'. She lived in close proximity to that site and had concerns about her children attending the local school; however, her solicitors argued that the principle under challenge applied equally to all three sites. Sullivan J held that there was 'no conceivable basis' on which the claimant could claim to be a person aggrieved in relation to the other two sites.[2] A single inquiry had been held into the three masts. The claimant had been unable to attend because of a trip to America, but had shared her concerns with those who were attending. Sullivan J was prepared to assume that the claimant was a person aggrieved in relation to the site close to her home, but even if she could establish that a common legal flaw underlay all three decisions, the court had no jurisdiction to quash the other decisions on her application, in respect of which she was not a person aggrieved.[3] In that regard, the concept was held to be narrower and less flexible than that of standing in judicial review proceedings.[4]

1   [2002] EWHC 2696 (Admin), [2002] All ER (D) 361 (Nov).
2   [2002] EWHC 2696 (Admin), [2002] All ER (D) 361 (Nov), para 6.
3   [2002] EWHC 2696 (Admin), [2002] All ER (D) 361 (Nov), paras 8–9.
4   See para **8.36** below.

Standing: challenge by judicial review

8.36   The requirement for judicial review is that the claimant have 'sufficient interest' in the matter to which the claim relates: Supreme Court Act 1981, s 31(3). The tendency has been towards an increasingly liberal approach to standing, and in fact it is rare for permission to be refused in EIA cases on standing grounds. This is because, as emphasised by Sedley J in his comprehensive judgment in *R v Somerset County Council, ex p Dixon*,[1] public law is fundamentally about the review of wrongs, rather than the existence of rights. Thus, if an arguable case of misuse of power can be made out on an application for leave, '... the court's only concern is to ensure that it is not being done for an ill motive'.[2] This is true for concerned individuals, for responsible interest groups with a serious interest in the subject matter,[3] and indeed those such as rival developers who have a commercial motivation for the challenge.[4]

1   [1997] Env LR 111, [1997] JPL 1030. See also *R v Secretary of State for Foreign and Commonwealth Affairs, ex p World Development Movement Ltd* [1995] 1 WLR 386.
2   [1997] Env LR 111, 121.
3   *R v HM Inspectorate of Pollution ex p Greenpeace Ltd* [1994] 4 All ER 329, at 350 c-j
4   See for example *R v Plymouth City Council, ex p Plymouth & South Devon Co-operative Society Ltd* [1993] 2 PLR 75; *R v Thurrock Borough Council, ex p Tesco Stores Ltd* [1993] PLR 114; *R v Monopolies & Mergers Commission, ex p Argyll Group plc* [1986] 1 WLR 763, 774B.

8.37   In *R (Kides) v South Cambridgeshire District Council*[1] the Court of Appeal drew an important distinction between an interest in obtaining the *relief* sought, and an interest in the *grounds* on which that relief was based. Thus an individual with a genuine interest in challenging a decision or quashing a permission should not be debarred from relying on grounds in which he had no personal interest. As Jonathan Parker L J put it:[2]

> 'It seems to me that a litigant who has a real and genuine interest in challenging an administrative decision must be entitled to present his challenge on all available grounds.'

1   [2002] EWCA Civ 1370, [2003] 1 P & CR 298.
2   [2002] EWCA Civ 1370, [2003] 1 P & CR 298, para 134, Aldous and Laws L J J agreeing.

8.38   This approach was followed by Ouseley J in *R (Hammerton) v London Underground Ltd*.[1] There the claimant was arguing that planning permission for a rail extension had lapsed. The claimant's concern was to avoid the demolition, as part of the project, of the Victorian Bishopsgate Goods Yard, a structure of considerable architectural and historical importance. The ground on which it was argued that the permission had lapsed was the failure to comply with a planning condition as to the provision of exchange land. On the issue of standing, Ouseley J rejected an argument that the claimant had to show that there was no one else who could bring such proceedings: the fact that local authorities or English Heritage might have done so, but chose not to, did not preclude Mr Hammerton having standing.[2] Ouseley J expressed initial reservations about whether Mr Hammerton had standing to argue that permission had lapsed on the basis of conditions as to exchange land which were of no personal interest to him. However, on considering the decision of the Court of Appeal in *Kides*, he could see no sensible distinction to be drawn between the cases, and his initial reservations were accordingly dispelled.[3]

1   [2002] EWHC 2307 (Admin), [2002] 47 EG 148 (CS).
2   [2002] EWHC 2307 (Admin), [2002] 47 EG 148 (CS), para 201.
3   [2002] EWHC 2307 (Admin), [2002] 47 EG 148 (CS), para 209.

EVIDENCE

8.39   As indicated above, both for challenges under the TCPA, s 288 and by way of judicial review, evidence will be given by way of witness statement, though it is possible in exceptional cases for the court to require oral evidence and cross-examination. It increasingly common for voluminous evidence to be submitted for the claimant, the defendant and often an interested party. The courts have however, on various occasions, criticised parties for producing large volumes of documents, often disorganised and duplicated, which are not in the event used or referred to in court.[1] This was recently the subject of strong criticism by the Court of Appeal in *R (Prokopp) v London Underground* where the production of the amount of material was described as a 'grotesque' waste of resources, public money and judicial time and energy.[2]

1   *Bruce v Worthing Borough Council* [1994] 26 HLR 223, av 224.
2   CA, 7 July 2003, paras 52, 90, 91.

8.40 For the claimant, written evidence presents the opportunity to trace the claimant's interest and involvement in the matter, to exhibit relevant documents and correspondence, and where relevant to explain why any delay has occurred. In some cases claimants may submit detailed technical evidence as to the alleged shortcomings of the EIA process, though careful thought needs to be given as to whether such evidence will be helpful or relevant. The court will be concerned with whether the decision of the authority fell within the bounds of reasonableness, not with which of the two competing expert views is correct.

Late reasons

8.41 For the defendant authority, evidence may well seek to flesh out the decision-making process and to explain the steps taken by way of consultation and consideration.[1] The risk is that such evidence may stray into the realm of retrospective rationalisation of the decision in order to meet the grounds of challenge.[2] It will be far preferable for the reasons for the decision to be made clear and recorded in the minutes or other relevant documents. The Court of Appeal sounded a clear warning against retrospective reasoning in *R (Young) v Oxford City Council*.[3] In something of a twist in that case the applicant sought to rely on written statements from a number of councillors as to what had transpired at the relevant meeting. The Court allowed this, despite the fact that the councillors had not been approached prior to the original substantive hearing. The Court recognised that it would be undesirable and very difficult effectively to place the onus on the applicant to approach councillors at any earlier stage; this would almost certainly be met with a hostile response and might give rise to allegations of improper pressure.[4]

1 See M Fordham, 'Fresh Evidence in Judicial Review' [2000] JR 18.
2 For cases advocating caution in relation to late reasons, see *R v Westminister City Counci, ex p Ermakovl* [1996] 2 All ER 302; *R (Nash) v Chelsea Royal College of Art* [2001] EWHC Admin 538, [2001] All ER (D) 133 (Jul) (Stanley Burnton J) and *Leung v Imperial College of Science, Technology and Medicine* [2002] EWHC 1358 (Admin), [2002] All ER (D) 103 (Jul) (Silber J).
3 [2002] EWCA Civ 990, [2002] All ER (D) 226 (Jun), para 20 (Pill L J).
4 [2002] EWCA Civ 990, [2002] All ER (D) 226 (Jun), para 23 (Pill L J) and 47–49 (Judge L J).

8.42 Equally, the court will be wary of a planning authority which carries out a non-statutory reconsideration exercise in the light of the challenge, and then argues that the decision would have been the same in any event.[1] The court will be mindful of the risk that the matter is not being approached completely open-mindedly and impartially.[2]

1 See *R (Carlton-Conway) v London Borough of Harrow* [2002] EWCA Civ 927, [2002] JPL 1216.
2 See *R v Legal Aid Board, ex p Donn & Co* [1996] 3 All ER 1 (Ognall J).

8.43 From the point of view of the developer, as an interested party, it can be a difficult question as to how much evidence to put in. Obviously any factual inaccuracies in the claim should be corrected, and it may be helpful to give information, so far as this is relevant, on the process and procedures relating to the ES and to consultation. Also, if it is alleged that delay by the claimant has resulted in prejudice, then as full and specific evidence as possible should be provided to back this up.[1] In *Crichton v Wellingborough Borough Council* [2] at the permission hearing it was made clear that prejudice from delay could be recanvassed at the substantive hearing and that any evidence should be filed at least 21 days before the hearing.

1   See para **8.27** above.
2   [2002] EWHC 2988 (Admin) paras 59–60.

DISCRETION AND REMEDIES: GENERALLY

8.44   The general principle that remedies in public law are matters for the discretion of the court[1] has to be modified in relation to EIA matters in the light of the decision of the House of Lords in *Berkeley v Secretary of State for the Environment*.[2] This was a challenge to a decision of the Secretary of State and accordingly was made under TCPA 1990, s 288. It therefore concerned the discretion of the court under s 288(5)(b) to quash the decision. Lord Bingham of Cornhill held that even in the purely domestic context, where the action of granting planning permission is outside the powers of the Secretary of State, any discretion to do anything other than quash is very narrow, and that in the Community law context it becomes narrower still, being confined to violations 'so negligible as to be truly de minimis'.[3] Lord Hoffmann doubted whether the discretion conferred on the court by the word 'may' in s 288(5)(b) could be exercised consistently with the court's obligations under European law to uphold a planning permission which had been granted contrary to the requirements of the EIA Directive.[4] As is often the case, the fundamental principle established in *Berkeley* has been modified in subsequent cases where the circumstances are less clear-cut. In *R v Derbyshire County Council, ex p Murray*[5] Maurice Kay J considered *Berkeley* and held it was never intended to apply to a case where a document had been produced as an ES and been treated by all parties as such up to and beyond a planning permission, and where that 'at the very least, substantially complied with the requirements of the Regulations'.[6] In cases dealing with purely procedural requirements on post-decision publicity, discretion has been exercised not to quash the permission.[7]

1   As to the normal principle, see *Bolton Metropolitan Borough Council v Secretary of State for the Environment* (1990) 61 P & CR 343, [1990] JPL 241.
2   [2001] 2 AC 603. See also para **2.04**.
3   [2001] 2 AC 603 at 608D–E.
4   [2001] 2 AC 603 at 616E.
5   [2001] Env LR 494.
6   [2001] Env LR 494 at 505.
7   See paras **5.32–5.38** above. See also *R (Prokopp) v London Underground Limited* (CA 7 July 2003) para 87 (Buxton L J)

Remedies and discretion: s 288 challenges

8.45   Under TCPA, s 288(5) the court may quash the action of the Secretary of State, if satisfied that the action was not within the powers of the Act, or that the interests of the applicant have been substantially prejudiced by a failure to comply with any of the relevant procedural requirements. In most EIA cases the argument will be that the action of granting planning permission was outside the relevant powers, being in breach of reg 3(2) of the TCP(EIA) Regulations 1999. However, it is possible to envisage cases where there has been compliance with reg 3(2) but procedural requirements (for example as to publicity) have not been complied with.[1] Certainly where there has been a failure to comply with reg 3(2), on the basis of the general principles set out above, the decision is likely to be quashed.

1   See paras 5.32–5.38 above.

Remedies and discretion: judicial review

8.46   The options open to the court are the normal quashing orders, mandatory orders, declarations and injunctions. In cases where breach of EIA requirements is made out, the normal course will be a quashing order. By CPR 54.19 where the court makes a quashing order it may remit the matter to the decision maker and direct it to reconsider the matter and reach a decision in accordance with the judgment of the court.

CHAPTER 9

Good practice in EIA

INTRODUCTION

9.01   The law, in terms of directives, regulations and court judgments, sets the context within which environmental impact assessment (EIA) is required to operate. They establish the minimum requirements or the essential issues that a project proponent and his team must take account of if they are to avoid potential legal challenge and serious delays to the project. However, the actual work of undertaking an EIA is less of a legal exercise and more a product of a range of other skills and disciplines: communication and presentation, project management, environmental and social sciences, engineering and art. This chapter is concerned with the deployment of these skills and disciplines in a way that can result in an effective EIA. It outlines common approaches and gives guidance on those that, from experience, appear to work well.

9.02   Good practice in EIA is dealt with here in two ways. The first considers the EIA process, takes each of the stages and examines its purpose, common approaches, the pitfalls and aspects that exemplify good practice. The second addresses the assessment of impacts that are common to many types of development in the UK. A generic framework for the assessment of impacts is provided and then the different types of impact are addressed in more detail. While it is not possible in this chapter to provide comprehensive guidance on good practice, it will provide an outline of:
— common sources of impacts
— issues to consider when determining the scope of the study into a particular impact
— methods for gathering baseline environmental information, predicting impacts and assessing significance.

DEFINING GOOD PRACTICE

9.03   Before considering the detail it is worth attempting to define what is meant by good practice. The interpretation of good practice may be different to different types of stakeholder. For example, the developer may consider a good practice EIA to be one that has cost as little as possible and yet has resulted in the proposed development receiving consent. Alternatively, the representative of the non-governmental organisation or the academic may consider a good-practice EIA to be one that consists of a range of comprehensive studies that have been undertaken in an objective manner, have advanced the state of the art of environmental science and have resulted in the development being stopped or redesigned to meet sustainability criteria. There are likely to be other views falling between these extremes.

9.04 To develop a more objective interpretation of good practice it is informative to consider the objectives of EIA Directive 85/337/EEC, as amended by Directive 97/11/EC. The preamble to the amended Directive states that: 'European Community policy is based on the principle that preventative action should be taken, that environmental damage should as a priority be rectified at a source and that the polluter should pay'.[1]

1   DETR (2000), *Environmental Impact Assessment: A Guide to the Procedures*, Thomas Telford Publishing: Appendix 1, Consolidation of Directive 85/337/EEC on the assessment of the effects of certain public and private projects on the environment.

9.05 Other elements within this part of the EIA Directive refer to: 'the need to achieve objectives in protection of the environment and the quality of life', ensuring that consent for certain projects is only given following an assessment of the likely significant impacts and that this should be based on appropriate information. The Directive also emphasises, in a recital, the role of EIA in protecting human health, protecting the environment and improving the quality of life:

'The effects of a project on the environment must be assessed in order to take account of concerns to protect human health, to contribute by means of a better environment to the quality of life, to ensure maintenance of the diversity of species and to maintain the reproductive capacity of the ecosystem as a basic resource for life.'

9.06 These highlighted elements of the EIA Directive emphasise two key roles for EIA; namely contributing to the protection of the environment and influencing decision making. The World Bank also emphasises the role of EIA in affecting decision making, particularly those early decisions taken with regard to the nature and design of a project:[1]

'2. The purpose of EA is to improve decision making and to ensure that the project options under consideration are environmentally sound and sustainable. All environmental consequences should be recognized early in the project selection, siting planning, and design. EAs identify ways of improving projects environmentally, by preventing, minimizing, mitigating, or compensating for adverse impacts. These steps help avoid costly remedial measures after the fact. By calling attention to environmental issues early, EAs:
(a) allow project designers, implementing agencies, and borrower and Bank staff to address environmental issues in a timely and cost-effective fashion;

(b) reduce the need for project conditionality because appropriate steps can be taken in advance or incorporated into project design, or alternatives to the proposed project can be considered; and

(c) help avoid costs and delays in implementation due to unanticipated environmental problems. EAs also provide a formal mechanism for interagency coordination on environmental issues and for addressing the concerns of affected groups and local non-governmental organizations (NGOs). In addition, the EA process plays an important role in building environmental management capability in the country.

1   World Bank (1991), Operational Directive 4.01 *Environmental Assessment*, World Bank Washington, DC.

9.07   The dual role of protecting the environment and affecting decision making can be used as two benchmarks against which the success of EIA can be judged, or good practice in EIA can be defined. The first of these roles is influenced by professional practice, in terms of ensuring that there is a sufficient understanding of the existing environment and its functional systems, and the likely effects of a proposal on it. The latter is more influenced by procedural efficiency and the integrity of decision makers. The roles are, nevertheless, inextricably linked; for example, excellence in the understanding of the environment and the effects of a project upon it can be completely undermined by a decision-making process that does not take adequate account of this information and use it to form a judgment as to the nature of a proposal or whether the proposal should proceed or not. These measures of success of EIA can best be summarised in a simple question: 'Does it make a difference?'.[1] Have environmental effects been avoided or reduced as a result of an EIA? Has the environment been protected and/or enhanced as a result of an EIA?

1   Sippe R (1993), personal communication.

9.08   The above discussion provides a clear purpose for EIA and an objective for the development of good practice, but does little to define the nature of good practice for anyone undertaking an EIA, or trying to evaluate an environmental statement (ES). Focusing exclusively on the protection of the environment and the effect on decision making could suggest that there should be no other constraints under which EIA should operate. This is clearly not the case. EIA has to be undertaken within the context of legal and institutional requirements, social and business expectations and time and resource constraints. For example, EIA should be undertaken in a timely fashion so to work with the planning and development process, and there must also be limitations on the resources that are devoted to EIA. Guidance is required at three levels to bring the notion of good practice to an operational level. Setting good practice principles that underpin the whole of the EIA process provides a set of standards to guide the conduct of an EIA. Establishing the components of a good practice process provides a road map for the conduct of an EIA. Methodological guidance enables the practitioner to undertake an EIA in accordance with both of these elements, or the reader of an ES to determine whether the process has been consistent with a good-practice approach.

9.09   In 1999 the Institute of Environmental Assessment worked with the International Association for Impact Assessment to establish principles of good practice in EIA. The result was a document that addressed the first two guidance levels referred to above. The Basic Principles set the standards which should underpin the conduct of the EIA process and the Operating Principles established the components of a good practice EIA process. Both are reproduced in full below as a reference point for good practice. The Operating Principles provide the template for the analysis of good practice in the EIA process.

9.10   The Basic Principles include components designed to meet the requirements of stakeholders in the EIA process, as well as achieving the objective of environmental protection. This can create a tension between some of the objectives and accordingly the need to have a balanced approach to their application is emphasised. For example, adopting a participative approach could appear to be at odds with the need for the EIA to be efficient, and with minimising costs in terms of time and resources.

Box 1: Principles of Environmental Impact Assessment Best Practice[1]
Basic principles

Environmental Impact Assessment should be:

Purposive — the process should inform decision making and result in appropriate levels of environmental protection and community well-being.

Rigorous — the process should apply 'best practicable' science, employing methodologies and techniques appropriate to address the problems being investigated.

Practical — the process should result in information and outputs which assist with problem solving and are acceptable to and able to be implemented by proponents.

Relevant — the process should provide sufficient, reliable and usable information for development planning and decision making.

Cost-effective — the process should achieve the objectives of EIA within the limits of available information, time, resources and methodology.

Efficient — the process should impose the minimum cost burdens in terms of time and finance on proponents and participants consistent with meeting accepted requirements and objectives of EIA.

Focused — the process should concentrate on significant environmental effects and key issues; ie, the matters that need to be taken into account in making decisions.

Adaptive — the process should be adjusted to the realities, issues and circumstances of the proposals under review without compromising the integrity of the process, and be iterative, incorporating lessons learned throughout the proposal's life cycle.

Participative — the process should provide appropriate opportunities to inform and involve the interested and affected publics, and their inputs and concerns should be addressed explicitly in the documentation and decision making.

Interdisciplinary — the process should ensure that the appropriate techniques and experts in the relevant bio-physical and socio-economic disciplines are employed, including use of traditional knowledge as relevant.

Credible — the process should be carried out with professionalism, rigor, fairness, objectivity, impartiality and balance, and be subject to independent checks and verification.

Integrated — the process should address the interrelationships of social, economic and biophysical aspects.

Transparent — the process should have clear, easily understood requirements for EIA content; ensure public access to information; identify the factors that are to be taken into account in decision making; and acknowledge limitations and difficulties.

Systematic — the process should result in full consideration of all relevant information on the affected environment, of proposed alternatives and their impacts, and of the measures necessary to monitor and investigate residual effects.

Box 1: Operating Principles

The EIA process should be applied:

— As early as possible in decision making and throughout the life cycle of the proposed activity;
— To all development proposals that may cause potentially significant effects;
— To biophysical impacts and relevant socio-economic factors, including health, culture, gender, lifestyle, age, and cumulative effects consistent with the concept and principles of sustainable development;
— To provide for the involvement and input of communities and industries affected by a proposal, as well as the interested public;
— In accordance with internationally agreed measures and activities.

Specifically the EIA process should provide for:

Screening — to determine whether or not a proposal should be subject to EIA and, if so, at what level of detail.

Scoping — to identify the issues and impacts that are likely to be important and to establish terms of reference for EIA.

Examination of alternatives — to establish the preferred or most environmentally sound and benign option for achieving proposal objectives.

Impact analysis — to identify and predict the likely environmental, social and other related effects of the proposal.

Mitigation and impact management — to establish the measures that are necessary to avoid, minimize or offset predicted adverse impacts and, where appropriate, to incorporate these into an environmental management plan or system.

Evaluation of significance — to determine the relative importance and acceptability of residual impacts (ie, impacts that cannot be mitigated).

Preparation of environmental impact statement (EIS) or report — to document clearly and impartially impacts of the proposal, the proposed measures for mitigation, the significance of effects, and the concerns of the interested public and the communities affected by the proposal.

Review of the EIS — to determine whether the report meets its terms of reference, provides a satisfactory assessment of the proposal(s) and contains the information required for decision making.

Decision making — to approve or reject the proposal and to establish the terms and conditions for its implementation.

Follow up — to ensure that the terms and condition of approval are met; to monitor the impacts of development and the effectiveness of mitigation measures; to strengthen future EIA applications and mitigation measures; and, where required, to undertake environmental audit and process evaluation to optimize environmental management.

1   International Association for Impact Assessment (IAIA) and Institute of Environmental Assessment (1999), *Principles of Environmental Impact Assessment Best Practice*, IAIA, Fargo, ND, USA.

GOOD PRACTICE AND THE EIA PROCESS

9.11   In Box 2 below and in most of the writing on EIA, a discussion on the EIA process commences with an examination of 'screening', being the process of determining whether a proposed project requires an EIA. However, in reality there are many decision-making points which precede the screening phase that can have a significant influence on the environmental effects of an activity. The decision of a developer to invest in a new facility, or of a government or local authority to enhance public infrastructure, will usually incorporate a consideration of alternative courses of action. It is therefore appropriate that a discussion on good practice in the EIA process considers how the environment can be incorporated into these early decisions in the development process.

Considering alternatives

9.12   A brief survey of the projects listed in the EIA Directive, Annexes 1 and 2[1] will indicate that any one of them is likely to be considered a major investment. Even for agricultural or forestry projects, which would rate as requiring a lower capital investment compared to other projects, the size of the investment is still likely to be considered to be significant by those providing the funds. Given the magnitude of the decision on whether to proceed with the investment or not, it is almost unthinkable that a developer would not consider the options available and attempt to determine the best course of action. In the case of a significant investment in upgrading the infrastructure for a town or region the decision may be made on the basis of years of feasibility studies, economic assessments and strategy studies. At this early decision point in the development planning process, the issues at stake may range from an evaluation of strategic alternatives to meet stated objectives, to decisions on the best location for a project or the nature of the technology to be adopted. The results of these decisions are likely to have a profound effect on the nature of the environmental effects of a proposal and these decision points represent the best opportunity to avoid the most significant environmental effects. Including environmental factors in the consideration of these alternatives is therefore critical to the success of EIA in protecting the environment.

1   *Consolidation of Directive 85/337/EEC on the assessment of the effects of certain public and private projects on the environment as amended by Directive 97/11/EC.* DETR, *Environmental Impact Assessment: A Guide to the Procedures,* Thomas Telford.

9.13   Early consideration of environmental factors is not just good practice in environmental terms. The environment is becoming a more important factor in consent decisions, the test of sustainability is increasingly being applied to decisions and environmental factors are consistently being used as a lever for objectors to proposals to delay or in some cases stop development. In this context, early consideration of environmental factors is increasingly associated with *good* decision making, not just *environmental* decision making. It provides a means of reducing the risks of a proposal being rejected or seriously delayed.

9.14   An important challenge is therefore to ensure that environmental issues have an equal seat at the table when the key strategic decisions are being taken. The best model for this type of integrated decision making is to be found in those industries that have learnt that an inadequate consideration of the environment at an early strategic stage can prove to be costly. The oil industry, in particular, has increasingly included the environment as a major factor in their early decision making.

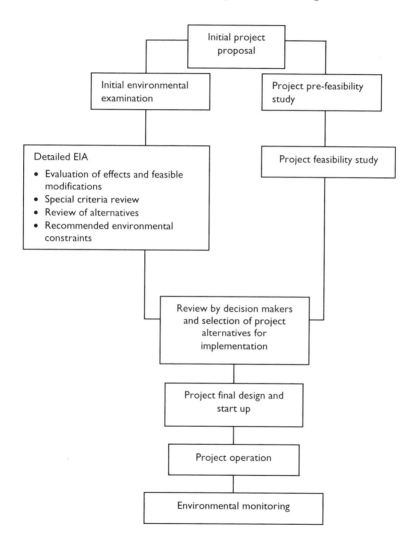

Figure 1: Project Planning and Environmental Assessment
Source: Based on Jones, M (c.1999)

9.15   Figure 1 illustrates how environmental issues are to be considered alongside the feasibility studies for an oil project. This approach, used by Shell, helps to ensure that any major environmental constraints are identified at an early stage and taken into account in the design of the project. An alternative, if the environmental constraints appeared to be insurmountable, is that the company could choose not to pursue the project. The early environmental work will have enabled this decision to be taken before there has been significant investment in the planning and design of the project. The oil industry is now developing this approach to undertake strategic assessments when seeking to begin activities in a new country or region, or before making a significant addition to existing operations. The purpose of the strategic assessment is to gain a clear understanding of business risks and benefits that could be encountered. It is undertaken prior to a major investment programme, rather than for the benefit of a single project.

9.16   Figure 2 is taken from a United Nations Environment Programme (UNEP) publication and advocates a similar approach to the early consideration of environmental issues in EIA. In this case UNEP promote the development of a project planning cycle that enables the lessons learned from one development to inform the development of the next project. While this approach may be applicable for companies that undertake EIA on a regular basis, the reality for many UK developers is that they may only undertake an EIA on a few occasions during the history of the company. Nevertheless, major property developers, utility companies, minerals companies and oil companies would do well to adopt such an approach.

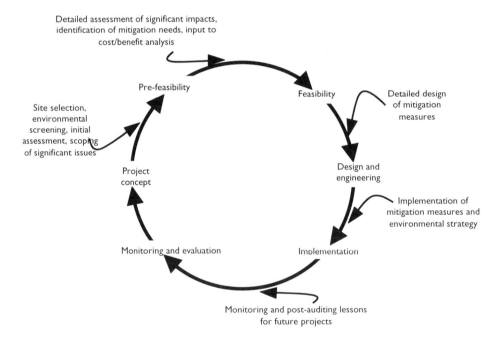

Figure 2: EIA and the Project Planning Cycle
Source: EIA Basic Procedures for Developing Countries, UNEP (1988)

Types of alternatives

9.17 In the UK there has been a general reluctance to make the consideration of alternatives a requirement. There are a number of reasons for this, including the following:
— The development planning system provides a basis for considering alternative sites and therefore it is inappropriate for the EIA to do so.
— The inability of those who already own a site to consider in practical terms sites that they do not own and may have no realistic prospect of owning.
— The impracticability of considering alternative sites when decision makers have little practical authority to direct a developer to an environmentally preferred site.
— The treatment of alternatives can become an academic exercise where a developer owns a site and only has limited options for developing it.
— The consideration of alternative sites based on environmental factors frequently conflicts with commercial interests.

9.18 In marked contrast to the UK reluctance to consider alternatives, there is the Federal EIA system in the USA. The consideration of alternatives has been described as being at the heart of their EIA system. Similarly, there are many other EIA systems around the world that have a regulatory requirement for alternatives to be considered. In Europe, the Netherlands is an example of a system that emphasises the need to examine alternatives. Specifically, they require the 'no action' and the most environmentally-friendly alternatives to be considered.

9.19 The regulatory requirement for alternatives to be addressed in many EIA systems indicates that it is not considered by all governments (and possibly other stakeholders) to be entirely incompatible with commercial interests. Part of the resistance in the UK may be an assumption that the term 'alternatives' is synonymous with the consideration of alternative sites. While an analysis of alternative locations is an approach that can be important in avoiding significant environmental impacts, there may well be a range of other alternatives that are available to all developers, including those that own a site and have no realistic prospect of developing another plot of land. Alternatives should be interpreted as 'a different way of doing things' rather than limiting the options to a decision on location.

9.20 The range of options open to a developer will be increased the earlier that they are considered within the project planning process. This also offers the best opportunity to avoid significant environmental effects and thereby enhance the probability of receiving development consent for a proposal. In addition, it is not always true that the best environmental option will not be the best commercial option. Taking the environmental perspective can result in significant cost savings. For example, reducing the footprint of a project to reduce the impact on ecosystems could be a saving when compared with a purely engineering-led approach. A creative approach to energy management to reduce CO_2 emissions could also result in significant cost savings.

9.21 A hierarchy of alternatives are available to the developer. These range from strategic decisions on the type and form of development to the details of the layout of a site or the technology to be employed for a particular part of a process. The World Bank encourages a 'step-by-step' approach to the consideration of alternatives:[1]

— **Define objectives**: This will help to set the boundaries of the alternatives considered. For example, if the purpose of the project is to generate income for the landowner, alternative sites are likely to be irrelevant, but alternative types of development could be a possibility. If the objective is to provide a particular service or produce a particular type of product then the technological options may be limited, but the locational decision could offer a means of reducing the environmental impact.

— **Identify alternative technologies or strategies to meet objectives**: It may be easy to dismiss some of the options for environmental, economic or other reasons. The technologies or strategies that remain will help to define the requirements for the site.

— **Identify alternative sites**: Based on the requirements of the technology or the strategy.

1   World Bank (1996), *Environmental Assessment Sourcebook Update, Analysis of Alternatives in Environmental Assessment*, World Bank, Washington DC.

9.22   Following the identification of a specific site and an increased understanding of the associated environmental effects, other alternatives can be considered:

— **Operational alternatives**: detailed technological options may still be available.

— **Site layout or configuration**: it may be possible to avoid more sensitive locations within the site boundary.

— **Mitigation alternatives**: while this may only contribute to reducing the impact rather than avoiding it, some mitigation measures may be demonstrably better than others. This can also be regarded as an opportunity to enhance the benefits of the proposal.

Methods for considering alternatives

9.23   Much of the EIA literature includes complex quantitative approaches to the consideration of alternatives. In reality these are rarely used within the UK. More extensive approaches have been used to assess strategic alternatives. However, in most cases the comparison of alternatives can be a relatively simple exercise. For example, for a site selection process, the following approach is frequently used:

— Identify the criteria that the selected option must meet. This may or may not include factors that are non-environmental. If they are excluded it would be expected that a separate economic and engineering feasibility appraisal would be undertaken.

— Use the criteria to draft a matrix that can be used for rating the options.

— Using the matrix, identify how well the options perform against each of the criteria.

9.24   A scoring system can be used in conjunction with the matrix, although it is usually preferable to avoid this approach, as there is a temptation to add the scores for each issue to give a total impact score. If integrating non-environmental factors into the appraisal this can imply that poor environmental performance can be traded against good economic or engineering performance. Even if the non-environmental factors are omitted, the approach still indicates that a poor performance against one environmental factor can be traded against a positive performance against another environmental factor. Symbols or shading are commonly used to indicate the performance of the options against each of the criteria. An example is illustrated by Figure 3.

SITE	Land availability	Compatibility with planning policy	Proximity to areas of major waste arisings	Proximity to approved Lorry Route Network	Compatibility with surrounding land uses	Landscape/townscape sensitivity	Potential impact on areas of ecological interest	Potential impact on areas of archaeological interest	Potential impact on areas of high quality agricultural land	Potential for CHP
① Land at Millennium Chemicals										
② Immingham Landfill										
③ Pyewipe Depot and Materials Recycling Facility (MRF)										
④ North Moss Lane, Stallingborough										
⑤ Europa Way, Stallingborough										
⑥ M180 Interchange, Grimsby										
⑦ A180 Moody Lane, Grimsby										
⑧ Gilbey Road, Grimsby										
⑨ Hewitts Avenue Business Park, Humberston										
⑩ South Marsh Road, Stallingborough (1)										
⑪ South Marsh Road, Stallingborough (2)										
⑫ Hobson Way, Stallingborough										
⑬ Europarc, English Partnerships site										
⑭ Land at Hydro Agri										
⑮ Land at Kiln Lane/A1173 roundabout										
⑯ Land at Novartis										
⑰ Land North of Synthomer, Stallingborough										

○ meets criterion   ◐ partially meets criterion   ● does not meet criterion

Figure 4.2 Alternative sites: assessment matrix

Figure 3: Alternative sites assessment matrix
Source: Terence O'Rourke (2000), Proposed Integrated Waste Management Facility Stallingborough, North East Lincolnshire, Environmental Statement, NEWLINCS Development Ltd.

9.25 This is a subjective judgment and it is valuable to test the conclusions against the views of the stakeholders in the EIA process (if possible), or someone with a different expertise. An alternative approach is to simply list the advantages and disadvantages of the options. Again, this may or may not include environmental factors. In most cases, these simple approaches are sufficient to identify the option that performs best in environmental terms. Presentation of the analysis in the environmental statement (ES) demonstrates a transparent approach. In the event that the best environmental option is not the one selected as the preferred option, it will be important to ensure that the ES includes a full justification for the alternative selected.

9.26 It is not anticipated that the above approach would be used for all of the alternatives available throughout the planning of a project. For example, a consideration of alternative mitigation measures would usually result in the self-selection of the best environmental option. The level of analysis required should be consistent with the stage of the project planning process and the environmental implications of the decision. A more exhaustive, more systematic approach is better suited to the strategic decisions that are likely to have a fundamental effect on the nature of the environmental impact of the project.

SCREENING

9.27   Screening is the process of determining whether a proposal requires an EIA before a consent decision is taken. At the simplest level, it is a case of determining whether the type of project is included in the list of those that are stated to require EIA. In most cases it will require a weighing of the issues to determine whether the impacts of a project are likely to be significant to the extent that they require a detailed assessment.

9.28   A screening decision is the responsibility of the determining authority, and is often taken following a request for a decision from the developer. In order to aid the decision, the developer is required to provide basic information about the proposal including a plan of the site identifying the proposed development, a description of the nature and purpose of the proposal and its likely environmental effects.[1] In the event that a developer considers that an EIA may be required for the proposal and would like to seek the view of the determining authority, the minimal disruption to the project planning process will be achieved if this is undertaken early, well before the submission of the planning application. If an EIA is decided upon, a minimum of three to four months will be required to undertake the most straightforward of EIAs, and considerably longer if the development or its environmental effects are particularly complex.

1   DETR (2000), *Environmental Impact Assessment: A Guide to the Procedures*, Thomas Telford Publishing.

9.29   A developer can elect to take a decision to provide an ES without seeking a formal opinion as to whether the determining authority would require an EIA. Many developers consider that if there is any question of an EIA being required for a project then they will undertake one anyway because:

— Environmental issues that make the screening decision a borderline one are likely to have to be addressed in any case.
— It demonstrates a willingness to be transparent about the development and its environmental effects, whereas a reluctance to undertake EIA could be interpreted as the developer having 'something to hide'.
— It may make the decision-making process easier and quicker.
— If any environmental problems can be designed out of the project or at least minimised, then there is a greater likelihood of the project receiving consent.
— It avoids the risk of a negative screening decision being challenged in court.

9.30   Undertaking an EIA when one may not be formally required may be regarded as a high-cost strategy. However, the costs of an EIA are usually a tiny proportion of the capital cost of a project (usually less than 0.5%[1]) and can pale into insignificance when compared with the cost of significant delays to the project and particularly the cost of a public inquiry.

1   Land Use Consultants (1996), *Environmental Impact Assessment — A Study on Costs and Benefits* (Final Report, Vol 1: Main Report), European Commission, Brussels.

Criteria for screening decisions

9.31   EIA is to be applied to projects in the EIA Directive, Annex 2 if they are likely to have significant effects on the environment. This decision has to be taken at a time when there is precious little information on the project and the receiving environment on which to base a decision. A judgment is therefore taken based on generic information on the likely impacts resulting from a particular type of project, and the sensitivity of the receiving environment. In order to promote some consistency in screening decisions, criteria have been provided both within the EIA Directive and in guidance relating to both the Directive and the Town and Country Planning (Environmental Impact Assessment) Regulations 1999 (TCP(EIA) Regulations 1999) in England and Wales.

9.32   Box 2 regarding selection criteria referred to in EIA Directive, art 4(3) demonstrates how the criteria at the European level attempt to steer those taking screening decisions towards considering the range of factors associated with a project when coming to a decision. While this is likely to promote a systematic consideration of the issues, it is unlikely to result in a consistency in screening decisions.

Box 2: Selection criteria

Annex III
Selection criteria referred to in Article 4(3)

1   CHARACTERISTICS OF PROJECTS

The characteristics of projects must be considered having regard, in particular, to:
— the size of the project
— the cumulation with other projects
— the use of natural resources
— the production of waste
— pollution and nuisances
— the risk of accidents, having regard in particular to substances or technologies used.

2   LOCATION OF PROJECTS

The environmental sensitivity of geographical areas likely to be affected by projects must be considered, having regard, in particular, to:
— the existing land use
— the relative abundance, quality and regenerative capacity of natural resources in the area
— the absorption capacity of the natural environment, paying particular attention to the following areas:
  (a) wetlands;
  (b) coastal zones;
  (c) mountain and forest areas;
  (d) nature reserves and parks;
  (e) areas classified or protected under Member States' legislation; Special Protection Areas designated by Member States pursuant to Directive 79/409/EEC and 92/43/EEC;
  (f) areas in which the environmental quality standards laid down in Community legislation have already been exceeded;
  (g) densely populated areas;
  (h) landscapes of historical, cultural or archaeological significance.

3   CHARACTERISTICS OF THE POTENTIAL IMPACT

The potential significant effects of projects must be considered in relation to criteria set out under 1 and 2 above, and having regard, in particular, to:
— the extent of the impact (geographical area and size of the affected population)
— the transfrontier nature of the impact
— the magnitude and complexity of the impact
— the probability of the impact
— the duration, frequency and reversibility of the impact.

9.33 A more systematic checklist has been published by the European Commission.[1] This checklist is designed to be used by the determining authority. It asks specific questions about the development and its likely environmental effects in an attempt to lead the user to a logical decision as to whether an EIA is required. An extract from the checklist is provided in Box 3. There is no formula to indicate that a particular number of answers that indicate a potentially significant effect will trigger an EIA. Nevertheless, systematic use of this checklist or any similar screening tool should help the decision maker to develop a clear picture of the potential environmental effects of a proposal and the need for an EIA.

Box 3: Extract from sample screening checklist

Questions to be considered	*Yes/No? Briefly describe*	*Is this likely to result in a significant effect? Yes/No? Why?*
Brief description of the project:		
1. Will construction, operation or decommissioning of the Project involve actions which will cause physical changes in the locality (topography, land use, changes in waterbodies, etc)?	Yes. The Project will involve development of a large site currently in agricultural use and crossed by a small river.	Yes. Loss of agricultural land and diversion of river.
3. Will the Project involve use, storage, transport, handling or production of substances or materials which could be harmful to human health or the environment or raise concerns about actual or perceived risks to human health?	No, except in the small amounts typically used by householders.	No.
4. Will the Project produce solid wastes during construction or operation or decommissioning?	Yes. Construction will require excavation of a small hill and transport and disposal or re-use of a large quantity of spoil.	Yes. Transport could have significant impact on neighbouring village.
9. Will the Project result in social changes, for example, in demography, traditional lifestyles, employment?	No. The existing village was mainly built in the 1950s.	No.

Source: ERM (2001)

---

1   Environmental Resources Management (2001), *Guidance on Environmental Impact Assessment: Screening*, European Commission, Brussels.

9.34   The UK approach to screening seeks to promote a greater consistency in screening decisions from one determining body to another by:
— defining the term 'sensitive area'
— providing a list of thresholds for the size of projects below which an EIA will not be required
— providing a list of thresholds for the size of projects above which an EIA will normally be required.

While the latter list provides an indication of the likelihood for the requirement of an EIA, it does not preclude the determining authority from requiring an EIA for a project that falls below the indicative threshold. Figure 4 illustrates the role of indicative thresholds in guiding determining authorities and others on the need for an EIA for project proposals.

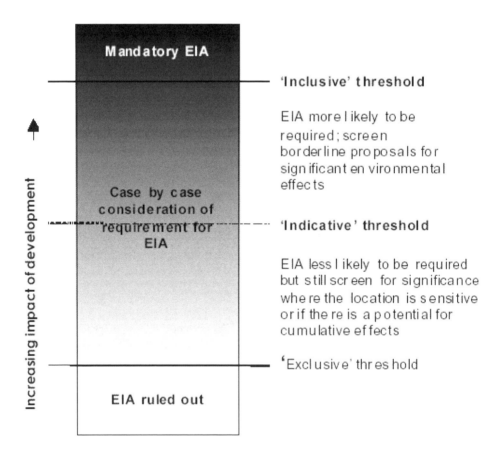

Figure 4: Indicative thresholds
Source: Consultation paper on the DETR (1998), Implementation of Directive 97/11/EC

9.35 Screening criteria are not the only assistance available for making screening decisions. The following can also assist in the determination of whether impacts are likely to be significant or not:
— assistance from colleagues and statutory consultees
— examples of previous environmental statements
— public interest and concerns relating to the project.

9.36 Public opposition to a project is not, in isolation, considered to be sufficient grounds for requiring an EIA. However, it is often worth examining the reasons underpinning any such concerns or opposition. The significance of an impact is often a subjective issue and public interest in a project may be an indicator that they consider that significant environmental effects are likely to result.

Approaches for determining authorities

9.37 Good practice in screening is measured by ensuring that all projects (within the scope of the TCP(EIA) Regulations 1999) that are likely to result in significant environmental effects are subjected to an EIA. Checklists and guidance are tools that aid screening. Equally important is a systematic process that captures the projects. Figure 5 is taken from the European Commission guidance on screening, and illustrates a systematic approach to screening projects. A determining authority that adopts this type of approach and applies it to all projects for which consent is applied for (within reason) should have a defensible, transparent and replicable approach to screening projects.

9.38 Notable in the EC guidance is the identification of two different routes to requiring an EIA. The first is under the terms of the EIA Directive, and the second is under the terms of the Habitats Directive.[1] An assessment under the Habitats Directive is known as an 'appropriate assessment'. It is not triggered by the type of project, but by a proposal potentially affecting a Natura 2000 site. Even small-scale projects could trigger the requirement for an assessment. If a project is in either Annex 1 or 2 of the EIA Directive and may affect a Natura 2000 site, then an EIA is likely to be required as the project could affect a sensitive area. An appropriate assessment would also be required, but could be incorporated into the EIA with the agreement of the relevant authorities.

1 Directive 92/43/EEC on conservation of natural habitats and of wild fauna and flora. See para **1.13** above.

9.39 In the event that a project requires an assessment under the Habitats Directive, but not the EIA Directive, it is important to recognise that the scope, objectives and responsibility for undertaking the assessment will be different from an EIA.

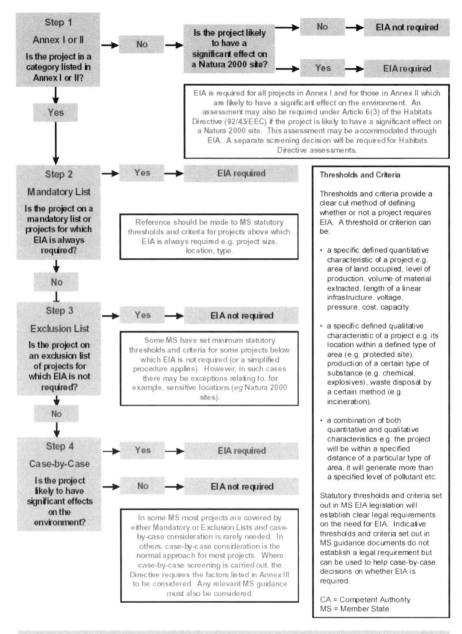

Figure 5: Illustration of a systematic approach to screening projects
Source: *ERM, 2001.*

SCOPING

9.40 Scoping is undertaken to focus the EIA on significant environmental effects. It ensures that the resources dedicated to the EIA are focused on the important issues. Scoping is one of the most important stages in the EIA process. If successful, it can set the terms of reference for the conduct of the EIA and ensure that it addresses the interests of the various stakeholders in the process as well as the easily identifiable impacts. An inadequate scoping phase can result in an EIA that is unfocused, omits key issues, does not address the concerns of key stakeholders and could hinder rather than aid the decision-making process. A study into the costs and benefits of EIA examined the reasons for delays to projects that involved EIA.[1] A key reason was the lack of a proper scoping exercise to determine the direction and focus of the EIA. In such cases additional work is required to provide sufficient information for a decision to be made.

1   Land Use Consultants (1996), *Environmental Impact Assessment — A Study on Costs and Benefits* (Final Report, Vol 1: Main Report), European Commission, Brussels.

9.41 Scoping is also important for the cost effectiveness of an EIA. Sufficient time and effort spent on focusing the EIA on the important issues will reduce the time and resources devoted to investigating impacts that are unlikely to be significant. Conversely, the inclusion of these issues may give the appearance of completeness, but can result in a document that is voluminous and obscures the key issues on which the decision is likely to be based.

9.42 While scoping is widely acknowledged to be one of the most important elements of the EIA process, current practice in the UK rarely matches up to the standards of international best practice. The lack of a regulatory requirement has meant that little emphasis has been placed on developing the methods and approaches that are considered to be good practice. Inadequacies usually relate to:

—   A failure to include a sufficiently wide range of stakeholders, especially the public.
—   A failure to eliminate issues that, in the context of the project and the location, are not significant.
—   Inadequate terms of reference for the conduct of the EIA, providing little assurance for the quality of the work that follows.
—   Treatment of scoping as a one-off activity, rather than a process that continues throughout the EIA to the preparation of the ES.

Objectives of scoping

9.43 Scoping should result in terms of reference that identify the key issues, define the boundaries of the EIA and sets out the methods that will be used to investigate impacts and assess their significance. This approach enables scoping to be a significant influence on the quality of the remainder of the process. The correct information can be gathered, using the appropriate techniques and the resulting ES should be focused on the key issues and aid the decision-making process.

9.44   In order to ensure that it addresses the key issues of interest to a range of stakeholders, scoping should be an open, participative process that includes the affected communities as well as statutory and non-statutory consultees. The increasing emphasis by the courts on the role of the public in EIA and the influence of compliance with the Aarhus Convention is likely to result in a greater role for public participation at the scoping phase of an EIA in the future.[1]

1   See para **1.16** above.

Guiding principles

9.45   Guiding principles for carrying out the scoping process include the following:
—   recognise scoping is a process rather than a discrete activity or event
—   design the scoping process for each proposal, taking into account the environment and people affected
—   begin scoping as soon as there is sufficient information available
—   specify the role and contribution of the stakeholders and the public
—   take a systematic approach but implement flexibly
—   document the results to guide the preparation of an EIA
—   respond to new information and further issues raised by stakeholders
—   analyse the results of scoping so as to focus on the key issues.

9.46   Scoping is undertaken following screening, a stage when there is likely to be only a relatively modest amount of information available on the project and the receiving environment. At this stage, the issues identified during scoping are a 'best guess' based on the available information and the professional judgment of the stakeholders involved. It is inevitable that as the EIA process continues and more information becomes available, this is likely to affect the scope of the EIA. For example, additional information on the project may result in the identification of other environmental effects or the downgrading of those that were initially considered to be a problem. Similarly, additional information on the receiving environment is likely to change the importance of some of the effects initially identified. An EIA that does not adapt to new information and changes to the project risks being only partially relevant to the consent decision that has to be taken. Scoping should therefore be revisited throughout the process and those responsible for the EIA should be willing to alter its focus in response to new information.

9.47   While there is a range of statutory and other consultees that are likely to be contacted for most EIAs, it is important that each scoping process is designed for each particular project. For example, a standard shopping-list approach to the identification of consultees is likely to result in local community groups being ignored, as these will be specific to each location. The approaches used to canvass the opinions of stakeholders are also likely to alter in relation to:
—   the stakeholder's familiarity with EIA
—   the time and budgets available for consultation
—   the social status and education of the affected communities

— public opposition or concern in relation to the proposal
— the relationship between the likely significance of impacts and the various specialisms of the consultees.

9.48 A clear definition of the role and expectations of the various stakeholders should help to focus the inputs of the stakeholders to meet the requirements of the scoping process. For example, if the objective of consultation with the public is identified as the identification of their environmental concerns and the incorporation of them into the scope of the EIA, the consultation process can be designed to elicit this type of response and discourage the voicing of a range of objections to the project that then have to be 'unpicked' to make a contribution to the EIA. Similarly, if a local planning authority is made aware that they are expected to comment on the methods of assessment as well as the issues to be addressed then they are more likely to ask the appropriate questions during their discussions with statutory consultees.

9.49 The scoping process should be documented throughout. This enables the developer to demonstrate a transparent approach to the identification of the issues by indicating how issues that have not formed part of the final scope of the EIA have been dealt with. For example, the traffic impact of a project may be initially raised during scoping, but dismissed due to the low vehicle numbers generated by the development. If the issue simply does not appear in the final scoping document then it could appear that it has been ignored. If the process has been documented then it will be easy to demonstrate that the issue was considered, but dismissed, following discussion with a wider range of stakeholders, as it is not regarded as one of the significant effects of the development.

Stakeholder involvement in scoping

9.50 Scoping is a process of communication. It requires seeking the views of other parties on the likely environmental effects of the proposed project. As a minimum, the determining authority should be asked for their opinion. It is critical that an EIA is directed toward their concerns. In practice, the determining authority consults with other statutory consultees and incorporates their views into any response. There are likely to be other stakeholders whose views should be considered at the outset, but it will be the responsibility of the developer to seek these. This is important as these groups may submit comments and concerns when the application for consent is submitted. For example, a failure to consult the Royal Society for the Protection of Birds is likely to be seen as a critical failing of the EIA if a significant effect on birds is identified at a later stage, and particularly if it is the RSPB that identify the issue. Box 4 provides a generic list of groups that should be considered for consultation at the scoping stage.

Box 4: Groups to be considered for consultation

Checklist of Consultees for Scoping

1   ENVIRONMENTAL AUTHORITIES:

— regional and local authorities
— authorities responsible for pollution control including water, waste, soil, noise and air pollution
— authorities responsible for protection of nature, cultural heritage and the landscape
— health and safety authorities
— land-use control, spatial planning and zoning authorities
— authorities in neighbouring countries where transfrontier impacts may be an issue.

2   OTHER INTERESTED PARTIES:

— local, national and international environmental and social interest groups
— sectoral government departments responsible for agriculture, energy, forestry, fisheries, etc whose interests may be affected
— international and transfrontier agencies whose interests may be affected eg cross-border river basin commissions
— local employers' and business associations such as Chambers of Commerce, trade associations, etc
— employees' organisations such as trades unions
— groups representing users of the environment, eg farmers, fishermen, walkers, anglers, tourists, local wildlife groups
— research institutes, universities and other centres of expertise
— the general public.

3   THE GENERAL PUBLIC:

— landowners and residents
— general members of the local and wider public
— elected representatives and community figures such as religious leaders or teachers
— local community groups, residents groups, etc.

Source: ERM (2001), Guidance on EIA: Scoping, European Commission.

9.51   In contrast to most other EIA systems, there is no requirement in the UK or in the EIA Directive for the public to be involved in the scoping phase of an EIA. Even the Aarhus Convention,[1] which requires early and effective public participation does not define the timing of this. As a result, current practice in the UK is to ignore the public during scoping in all but the most controversial of projects, or where the developer is committed to complying with best practice. However, several trends indicate that this position will not be sustainable in the long term:

— Increasing public awareness of the requirements of the EIA Directive and challenging compliance in order to delay or block development.
— The likely interpretation of the Aarhus Convention to include an expectation of participation during the scoping stage of an EIA.
— Trends in other fields (eg planning, community design, etc) are moving towards increased public participation, underpinned by the principles of sustainable development, including citizen participation.

1   UN/ECE (1998) Convention on Access to Information Public Participation in Decision-Making and Access to Justice in Environmental Matters. Fourth Ministerial Conference, Aarhus, Denmark, 23–25 June 1998. See para **1.16** above.

9.52   The involvement of the public at an early stage ensures that there is a clear understanding of their concerns at the outset and provides the opportunity for the EIA to address them directly. Where there is likely to be significant opposition to a project, early involvement of the affected communities is increasingly regarded as the only means of overcoming this. Early identification of the community's concerns may allow many of them to be taken into account as part of the design of the project. Box 5 provides a case study of a water storage project located close to a community that had a significant track record of successfully opposing proposed developments. A formal EIA was not required, but was regarded as a means for addressing the environmental issues and incorporating the concerns of the local community. A policy of early and meaningful participation of the local community was adopted and resulted in the project receiving consent with no formal objections to the proposal.

Box 5: Severn Trent Water — Witches Oak Waters

CONTEXT

Severn Trent Water (STW) sought planning permission for a project at Witches Oak Waters, to the south of Derby, that involved construction associated with bankside storage. An EIA was not required by the local authority, but was carried out as an aid to decision making and as a way to consider all of the wider environmental issues.

It was considered that securing the approval and trust of local residents was key to gaining planning permission. Local residents were well organised and environmentally aware, having previously contested landfill, quarrying and bypass proposals. An application to use the pits for recreational purposes instead of returning them to agricultural use had also antagonised local residents and reactivated local pressure groups. Therefore, it was considered that traditional decide–announce–defend approaches might not be successful. An approach was required that would establish a trusting relationship between STW and local residents. Potentially this could also influence the long-term success of the company in terms of securing future water supplies.

MECHANISM FOR PARTICIPATION

STW decided that local communities would be involved from the earliest stages of the project in a partnership approach and invited to participate in decision making. Local people were invited to participate in developing proposals for the final restoration of the site.

Invitations to participate in a series of workshops were sent to every household in each of the three villages directly affected. An interest in attending the sessions was expressed by over 100 individuals and it was decided that a maximum of 50 people should be invited. The workshops involved STW's trained facilitators and an independent environmental expert. They were held from 7.00 pm to 9.00 pm, one at the village hall and one at a school. Bus transport was provided.

The first workshop set out STW's objective in terms of the use of the River Trent in 'plain English'. Questions from participants were answered to ensure that there were not any misunderstandings. Working in small groups, assisted by the facilitators and the independent environmental expert, participants explored the issues involved. The local community came to their own conclusions about the use and restoration of the mineral workings and the long-term involvement of the local communities.

The independent environmental expert used the results from the workshops to prepare a draft report. This was presented to a further workshop prior to being adopted by STW.

After the workshops a questionnaire was used to determine whether, for example, the participants felt that they had had the opportunity to express their views and opinions and whether they believed that STW was serious about working with participants to achieve the best possible mutual outcome.

An awareness campaign was also undertaken involving local newsletters, direct mail drops and exhibitions.

OUTCOME

— Local communities started to identify themselves with the scheme, feeling involved with it.
— The results of a questionnaire survey indicated that STW had gained trust from the local communities.
— Planning permission was achieved without any objections from the local communities within the required timescale.
— The process was considered to have contributed to restoring the trust and goodwill of present and future customers and added to the company's ability to secure supplies.
— Local people are expected to maintain an active role in the development of the site by their involvement on a site conservation management board.
— Although the process of participation may have been perceived at first as causing unnecessary delay, the speed with which this ambitious scheme reached completion demonstrates the cost effectiveness and efficiency of this approach.

Source: Institute of Environmental Management and Assessment (2002), Perspectives — Guidelines on participation in environmental decision making, IEMA, Lincoln.

Terms of reference from scoping

9.53 Scoping is a significant opportunity to affect the quality of the remainder of the EIA, but this can only be achieved if scoping is used as an opportunity to develop a full terms of reference for the EIA. This should expand on what is going to be assessed by describing how it is going to be assessed. Typically terms of reference include:
— The regulatory context of the project consent.
— Reference to other regulatory regimes that may be relevant to the project (eg Habitats Directive or IPPC Directive[1]).
— Details of the alternatives to be assessed.
— Details on the key environmental effects to be addressed by the EIA, including any time and space boundaries.
— Information on the methods to be used to gather baseline data.
— Information on the methods to be used to predict impacts.
— Details of the significance criteria to be used for specific impacts. This could include details of legislative limits or standards to be used.
— The types of mitigation that will be under consideration.

— Details of consultation and participation programmes that are to be undertaken during the EIA.

1   Directive 96/61/EC of 24 September 1996 concerning integrated pollution prevention and control, OJ L257, 10.10.96, p 26.

9.54   One of the key benefits of preparing terms of reference and subjecting them to consultation with a range of other stakeholders is that it separates any disagreement on the *approach* to the EIA from disagreements on the *results* of the EIA, particularly the interpretation of the data and the judgments on the significance of effects.

9.55   The requirements of the EIA Directive can overlap with the requirements of other regulatory regimes, with the IPPC Directive being the most often quoted example. In some cases this has caused some disagreement on the approach to the EIA, typically when little information is provided on the impacts that are likely to be covered by the requirements of the IPPC Directive. It is good practice to ensure that the relevant information is provided to both consent regimes. If the applications for consent are developed in parallel, the EIA can be used as a tool for communicating information on the environmental effects to both consent regimes. Regardless of the approach adopted, consultation on this issue at the scoping stage will help to identify whether the approach is acceptable to the relevant authorities and if not, clarify the approach they would like to see.

9.56   Prior to reaching the scoping stage it is likely that a range of alternatives have already been considered and dismissed when compared with the preferred option. Nevertheless, it is important to address the issue of alternatives during scoping for the following reasons:
— If scoping is undertaken at an early stage in the project planning process, it is likely that a range of options are still available, particularly relating to the detail of the project.
— An early identification of the alternatives that other stakeholders consider it appropriate to address, and may consider to be acceptable, will help to reduce later arguments on this issue at a stage when it is likely to be much more costly to abort or adapt plans that would then have been developed to a considerable level of detail.
— Other stakeholders may identify alternatives that may not have been considered by the developer, but are nevertheless technically and economically acceptable. If there are indications that these alternatives are likely to be more acceptable, then their consideration could enhance the chances of receiving consent for the project.

9.57   The key purpose of scoping is to identify the environmental issues that are to be addressed by the EIA. It is important that this is undertaken in sufficient detail for other stakeholders to understand the approach being taken. For example, if the noise impact of a proposal is to be assessed, the sources of noise that will form part of the assessment should be identified (eg plant noise, traffic and construction). Most of this detail can be provided by explaining the approaches and methods being used to gather the baseline information and to predict the environmental effects of the proposal.

This should include an indication of the time and space boundaries relating to the proposal and the identification of any sensitive locations. For example, the details of a noise impact assessment could include a broad indication of the types of locations and communities from which noise will be monitored and for which predictions will be made. Box 6 provides an example of the type of information that could be provided for the assessment of impact of a proposal on the ecology of an area.

Box 6: An example of Terms of Reference for the component of an EIA addressing the impact of the proposal on the ecology of the area.

— Identification of any known sensitivities at the proposed project location (eg designated sites, presence of protected species).

— Identification of the ecological groups on which the project is expected to have an effect including the sources of the effect.

— Description of the methods to be used to gather baseline information to include:

— Organisations to be contacted for information.

— Existing publications and data sources to be used.

— Survey methods and identification of the ecological groups to be surveyed, including time and space boundaries and the timing of the surveys in relation to any seasonality considerations.

— Methods and criteria to be used to evaluate the importance and sensitivity of the site (e g designations, protected species lists, biodiversity action plans, criteria for selection of Sites of Special Scientific Interest,[1] etc).

— Methods to be used to predict the impacts of the proposal (e g quantification of habitat loss, reference to studies on the response of species to particular types of effect, application of professional judgment).

— Methods and criteria to be used to assess the significance of effects.

— Mitigation measures at this stage will be under consideration to avoid or reduce the environmental effect, recognising that others will be developed as the nature of the effects is clarified.

Source: K Fuller.

---

1   JNCC (Joint Nature Conservation Committee) (1995). *Guidelines for the Selection of Biological SSSIs.* Joint Nature Conservation Committee, Peterborough, UK.

9.58   The early identification of the criteria to be used to assess the significance of effects can eliminate later arguments and avoid subsequent delays to the decision-making process. When the significance criteria published in an ES all appear to be mysteriously slightly in excess of the predicted environmental effects, there is an understandable suspicion that the criteria have been selected or manipulated to demonstrate that the impacts of the proposal are not significant, thus undermining the credibility of the document. Identification of significance criteria during scoping means that they are being selected without a clear understanding of what the predicted effects are likely to be. The approach to the EIA therefore appears to be objective, credible and can achieve the trust of other stakeholders.

9.59   At the scoping stage little may be known about the detail of mitigation measures to be applied to reduce the impact of the proposal. Nevertheless, if there are any obvious impacts that will have to be mitigated for the project to receive consent, it is likely to be helpful to address the issue at this early stage. It indicates that early consideration has been given to the environmental effects. For example, in the event that an ecologically-sensitive area is likely to be affected, the relevant authorities and other wildlife groups are likely to find it helpful to know that mitigation measures such as habitat creation or species translocation are under active consideration. A lack of reference to these types of issues could undermine the environmental credibility of the proposal even at this early stage of the process.

9.60   Seeking the advice, opinions and concerns of a range of stakeholders is critical at the scoping stage, and it should be the start, rather than the end, of the participation programme. The terms of reference should provide an indication of the how stakeholders will be involved throughout the remainder of the process. This may range from simple informal consultations with the appropriate authorities to clarify issues and approaches as more information becomes available, to a comprehensive public participation programme involving newsletters, workshops and 'drop-in' centres. This information will indicate to the stakeholders whether they are likely to be able to continue to influence the process, or whether they should prepare themselves to respond to the publication of the ES.

Methods and approaches to scoping

9.61   Approaches to scoping in the UK have primarily focused on the application of professional judgment of those undertaking the EIA and consultation, primarily with the determining authorities and statutory consultees. It is good practice to spread the net wider than this and there is an expectation, if not a requirement, in most EIA systems that the public should be involved in the process.

9.62   More formal methods for scoping do exist, but are used rarely in UK practice. These are covered in some detail elsewhere in the EIA literature.[1] Matrices are often identified as being one of the main scoping tools, but while they may not be used frequently to identify the environmental effects of a proposal in practice, they are often used as a presentational tool in the ES to demonstrate the interactions of the proposal with the environment.

1   For example see Wathern P, *EIA Theory and Practice* (1990) Routledge; or Canter L, *Environmental Impact Assessment* (1996) McGraw Hill.

9.63 Checklists for scoping the environmental effects of a proposal are also available. The most prominent are those produced by the European Commission[1] and the Environment Agency.[2] Those issued by the Environment Agency are presented on a project-specific basis and present information on the possible sources of impact as well as an indication of the environmental factors which could be affected by the project. Guidance manuals, such as the *Design Manual for Roads and Bridges*, Vol 11,[3] also provide clear guidance on the scope of the EIA for particular projects. While these give a clear direction for the EIA, it is important not to use them as a replacement for the application of professional judgment and consultation with stakeholders. A particular project, in a particular location, could result in environmental effects that were not anticipated during the drafting of such a manual.

1   ERM (2001), *Guidance on EIA: Scoping*, European Commission.
2   Environment Agency (2002), *Environmental Impact Assessment: A handbook for scoping projects*, Environment Agency.
3   Highways Agency et al (1993), *The Design Manual for Roads and Bridges, Vol 11, Environmental Assessment*, Highways Agency.

9.64 There is no evidence that use of formal methods improves the effectiveness of the scoping phase, and it is much more important that a sufficient range of stakeholders are given the opportunity to influence the conduct of the EIA at this stage. Some practitioners do, nevertheless, find such methods useful to act as a check on the results of consultation and to help confirm that no key issues have been overlooked.

Focusing on key issues

9.65 Good practice in scoping is widely regarded as including a wider range of stakeholders. One of the inevitable results is that a long list of possible effects is identified. In the event that each of these is addressed by the EIA, the resulting ES is likely to be voluminous and unfocused. There is some evidence that this represents the current situation in the UK. The size of ESs has increased and both consultants and determining authorities are often drawing up a wide-ranging scope for an EIA in order to 'cover their backs'. Consultation with a range of stakeholders is being used to replace rather than supplement a technical analysis of the issues.

9.66 The results of stakeholder involvement should be subject to technical analysis to filter out those issues that, while undoubtedly being environmental effects of the project, in the context of the whole range of effects could not be considered to be significant. The resulting list should be shorter and more focused, but it is important that the issues that are not to be addressed in detail are not ignored. Ideally, the scoping process should include a period of negotiation where further discussion is held with the stakeholders with the objective on gaining agreement on the final list of significant effects to be addressed by the EIA. This will require a clear rationale for dismissing some of the effects originally raised during stakeholder involvement. This will be more time consuming than the standard approaches to scoping, but it is likely that time spent at this stage can be justified by avoiding time spent later on issues that the various stakeholders can agree, after some negotiation, are not significant effects of the development.

Conclusions on scoping

9.67   Scoping is one of the key stages of the EIA process and will have a fundamental effect on the conduct of the remainder of the EIA and the results that appear in the ES. An approach to scoping with the purpose of simply establishing a list of issues enhances the risk of an EIA which lacks focus and a resulting ES which confuses rather than aids the decision-making process. Resources could also be wasted, as there is no clear direction on which issues really matter and no understanding of the depth to which the environmental effects need to be investigated. In contrast, an approach that is designed to establish a terms of reference for the EIA, to focus on the significant environmental effects and gain the agreement of stakeholders on both of these issues, is more likely to result in cost efficient and effective EIA.

ASSESSING ENVIRONMENTAL EFFECTS

9.68   The main purpose of EIA is to assess the environmental effects of a proposal. This section addresses generic issues. EIA has been described as falling between an art and a science.[1] The mixture of the use of scientific facts with interpretation, judgment and opinion and the problems of communication with other stakeholders means that a successful EIA relies on more than just the scientific rigour of the analysis. EIAs are undertaken in the context of resource and time constraints and are the responsibility of the developer of the project, who is generally not regarded as having a neutral standpoint, despite the fact that an EIA should be an objective analysis. There is therefore a range of factors that will influence whether the impact analysis component of an EIA is successful. Fundamental to this is whether the analysis can be considered to be credible and, given that the EIA is being undertaken by the developer, a transparent approach to the EIA will make a significant contribution to this credibility. A consideration of the following factors is important to achieving this:

Fact, interpretation, judgment and opinion
— It is important that an EIA identifies the difference between facts, interpretation of facts and judgment or opinions based on facts. In the event that any of these are confused then the credibility of the EIA will be undermined.

Constraints
— All EIAs are undertaken in the face of a range of constraints. These can vary from the time and resources devoted to the EIA, to the state of the art of environmental science that enable accurate predictions to be made. It is important that the constraints are identified and communicated to the other stakeholders together with the implications for the impact analysis. For example, if the timing of the EIA

results in an ecological survey being undertaken at a less than ideal time of year then this should be identified and the potential effect of incomplete data discussed.

Communication of information
— EIAs should be based on a scientifically-rigorous approach. However, the documents that result from the process will primarily be read by people who are not specialists in the various disciplines that have contributed to the analysis. It is one of the roles of contributors to EIAs to ensure that their information is understandable to the non-specialist. Any attempt to express the information in scientific or engineering jargon could be interpreted as an attempt to 'blind the reader with science'. The requirement for a non-technical summary of the ES does not imply that the main document can be entirely technical.

1   Wathern P (ed), *Environmental Impact Assessment: Theory and Practice* (1988) Unwin Hyman.

Dimensions of impacts

9.69   The characteristics of environmental impacts vary. Typical parameters to be taken into account in impact prediction and decision making include:
— nature (positive, negative, direct, indirect, cumulative);
— magnitude (severe, moderate, low);
— extent/location (area/volume covered, distribution);
— timing (during construction, operation, decommissioning, immediate, delayed, rate of change);
— duration (short-term, long-term, intermittent, continuous);
— reversibility/irreversibility;
— likelihood (probability, uncertainty or confidence in the prediction); and
— significance (local, regional, global).

9.70   The characteristics of the impact should be identified as far as is possible at the scoping stage as this will affect the nature of the methods adopted to investigate the impact. For example, more resources and greater in depth study are likely to be required for an impact that is adverse, certain to happen, permanent and significant at an international level than for one that is positive and significant at only a local scale.

Nature

9.71   The most obvious impacts are those that are directly related to the proposal, and can be connected (in space and time) to the action that caused them. Examples of direct impacts are: loss of habitat caused by 'footprint' of the project; or an increased levels of particulates in the air as a result of an increase in traffic.

9.72   Indirect or secondary impacts are changes that are usually less obvious, occurring later in time or further away from the impact source. Examples of these types of impacts include: the changes in the ecology of a water course as a result of changes in water quality; a reduction in trade at a tourist attraction as a result of the visual impact of a new cement works.

9.73   Cumulative effects, typically, result from the incremental impact of an action when combined with impacts from projects and actions that have been undertaken recently or will be carried out in the near or foreseeable future. These impacts may be individually minor but collectively significant because of their spatial concentration or frequency in time.

Magnitude

9.74   Estimating the magnitude of the impact is of primary importance. Typically, it is expressed in terms of relative size of the impact and is quantified where possible; for example, changes in the levels of biological oxygen demand in a receiving watercourse. For some issues quantification is not feasible and classification systems are often used that categorise the impacts under terms such as 'major', 'moderate' or 'low'. In these cases it is important that these terms are defined in the context of the impact being addressed.

Extent/location

9.75   The spatial extent or zone of impact influence can be predicted for site-specific versus regional occurrences. Depending on the type of impact, the variation in magnitude will need to be estimated; for example, alterations to the range or pattern of species, or dispersion of air and water pollution plumes. This is much easier for direct impacts, but can be attempted for other types of impacts.

Timing

9.76   Impacts arising from all of the stages of the project should be considered (i e during construction, operation and, where relevant, decommissioning). Some impacts will occur immediately, while others may be delayed, sometimes by many years.

Duration

9.77   Some impacts may be short-term, such as the noise arising from the operation of equipment during construction. Others may be long-term, such as the changes to habitat as a result of reclamation of salt marsh area. Certain impacts, such as blasting, may be intermittent, whereas others, such as emissions from a plant that operates on 24-hour basis, may be continuous.

Significance

9.78   Significance is arguably the most important characteristic. The other characteristics describe the make-up of the impact, whereas the evaluation of significance indicates whether the impact matters in terms of its importance to decision making and in terms of maintaining the integrity of the existing environmental conditions. Significance is discussed in more detail later.

Assessment

9.79   There are three key activities associated with the assessment of impacts. The first is to develop a clear understanding of the baseline environmental conditions. This is usually the same as the existing conditions, but it will be seen that there are occasions on which it is necessary to predict the baseline conditions. When a full understanding of the existing conditions has been developed, the changes to the environment as a result of the project can be predicted. This is expressed in terms of the size or the magnitude of the impact. Finally, the impact is evaluated to determine its significance.

9.80   Interaction between the members of the EIA team is critical during the impact analysis stage. They will need to keep each other informed of their findings and discuss how this might affect the approaches to the assessment of their particular impact. For example, noise impacts are routinely assessed only in terms of their effects on humans, but if the ecologist in an EIA team discovers the presence of a bird species that may be sensitive to noise disturbance, then it may be necessary for the noise assessor to measure baseline levels at a new location, make predictions of the new noise levels for the same location and undertake research on the relevant thresholds that should not be exceeded to avoid disturbing the birds.

9.81   The assessment of impacts will also lead to the development of mitigation measures that are designed to avoid, reduce or offset the impacts of the proposal. Interaction between the various specialists will again be important as mitigation measures can have their own environmental impacts. For example, barriers that are established to reduce the noise impact of a proposal could have a significant landscape and visual impact. This impact may have to be assessed, or an alternative approach to reducing noise levels adopted.

THE BASELINE CONDITIONS

9.82   The baseline conditions describe the environment that exists before the changes that are brought about by the proposed project. It provides a benchmark against which the impact of the project can be compared. In most case this will be consistent with the existing conditions, but it is still necessary to account for changes in environmental conditions that are likely to occur in the absence of the project. It is rare that any environmental conditions are a constant and do not change over time. Air quality is likely to change as a result of traffic growth, changes in vehicle technology and other influences; noise levels will be similarly influenced by other developments; habitats are subject to species succession that will alter them over time; and the landscape can be changed significantly as a result of changes in agricultural practices or policies. Some of these changes may be predictable by extrapolating from existing trends, or the application of scientific knowledge about environmental change. Consented projects or land use plans may also indicate the likely changes to environmental conditions. Other matters, such as significant policy changes, will not be predictable and the status quo may have to be assumed. The requirement to predict the baseline conditions is likely to increase where a project has a long lead in time and may not commence or be completed for some years.

9.83   Where there is a significant predictive element to the baseline, judgments will have to be made about what it is reasonable to assume. To resolve these, and in order to avoid later arguments it is prudent to consult with the determining authority and other relevant experts. For example, if assumptions are to be made about ecological change it would be appropriate to discuss the approach with English Nature (EN), Scottish Natural Heritage (SNH) or the Countryside Council for Wales (CCW), as appropriate. These discussions will form part of the discussions on the scope of the EIA.

9.84   Having established the approach to be taken to establishing the baseline conditions, the necessary information will need to be gathered. This is usually undertaken by a combination of researching existing published data, consulting with other organisations (statutory consultees are obliged to provide relevant data) and undertaking surveys specific to the site and the area likely to be impacted on by the proposal. Where data from other sources is used, it is important to recognise the reasons for the collection of the original data and evaluate how relevant the data is likely to be to the EIA. For example, bird counts for a large Ramsar site[1] may be of only limited usefulness for describing the importance of an extreme corner of the site. Similarly, water quality data may not include levels for pollutants that are relevant to the proposed development.

1   Convention on Wetlands signed in Ramsar, Iran, 1971.

9.85   Having gathered the baseline data, the information must be evaluated to determine the importance of the existing environmental resources and their sensitivity to change. This will be an important component when assessing the significance of the environmental effects. The basis for the evaluation needs to be clearly stated, along with any assumptions.

9.86   Baseline studies can be considered to be the relatively easy part of the technical work undertaken as part of an EIA. As a result there can be a temptation for baseline surveys to demand resources at the cost of work undertaken on predicting impacts and evaluating the significance of impacts. An additional pressure, often quoted, is the desire of statutory agencies to use EIAs as a means of gathering data on issues that, while interesting, are not necessary for predicting the impacts of the proposal. It is important that the time and resources devoted to baseline studies is balanced against the needs for predicting impacts and assessing their significance.

Impact prediction

9.87   The prediction of impacts is usually undertaken on the basis of empirical measurements (eg footprint of buildings), professional judgments, modelling, previous case studies and occasionally experiments or physical models. Regardless of the methods used to make the predictions it is important that the following information is recorded and included in the ES:
—   a description of the methods used to predict the impacts;
—   a statement of the assumptions on which predictions have been based and their underlying rationale;
—   the reliability of any predictions and any confidence limits associated with the predictions;
—   a description of the characteristics of the impacts; and
—   a statement of any uncertainty associated with the predictions.

9.88   As with baseline information, there is a preference for impacts to be predicted in quantitative terms, while accepting that some issues will not be appropriate for this type of approach. The predictions should, as a minimum, take into account the effect of mitigation measures. Ideally predictions are provided without the mitigation measures taken into account and then revised to incorporate the effectiveness of the measures. This helps to demonstrate the effectiveness of any mitigation measures and also indicates the magnitude of the impact in the event that the mitigation measure is not implemented or is unsuccessful.

Dealing with uncertainty

9.89   Predicting impacts is essentially an attempt to predict the future, and inevitably uncertainty is inherent. This uncertainty may be enhanced due to a number of factors:
—   **Scientific uncertainty** — associated with the limitations of the environmental or social science that forms the basis for predictions.
—   **Data uncertainty** — associated with the limitations of information relating to the proposal or insufficient data on the baseline conditions.
—   **Policy uncertainty** — associated with unclear objectives or standards for managing environmental effects.

9.90   Poor environmental statements are often characterised by the way they deal with such uncertainty. However, the following are good-practice approaches that attempt to deal with the uncertainty:
Worst case scenarios — in the face of scientific or data uncertainty, an assessment that tends toward the worst case (within reason) will help to ensure that impacts are not underestimated. An EIA will retain its credibility if impacts are overestimated, but risks losing it if they are underestimated.

Use of impact ranges — these can also be used to address scientific uncertainty and avoid an impression being given of spurious scientific certainty where there may be considerable uncertainty. For example, climatic conditions can have a significant effect on noise levels and it may be more appropriate to provide the impacts in terms of ranges rather than provide a single figure.

Sensitivity analysis — these will help to demonstrate how small changes in factors that will affect the impact will change the magnitude of the impact.

Risk assessment — to indicate the risk of a significant effect occurring where it is difficult to predict the circumstances under which the impacts will occur.

9.91   An additional type of uncertainty is the subjective response to environmental effects. For issues such as landscape and visual impacts, such subjectivity cannot be avoided and approaches for dealing with this are well established. It is important for all stakeholders to appreciate that many types of impact have a subjective element that should not be ignored. For example, responses to noise are subjective and the provision of a single figure for a noise impact could prove to be misleading in some circumstances. Where the subjective element of impacts could be important, a good EIA deals with rather than ignores the subjectivity. Methods for addressing this include:

— Demonstrating rather than describing the impacts (e g using photomontages to illustrate the visual impact of a proposal).
— Clearly describing the reasons underlying the judgment on the magnitude of the impact. In the event that other stakeholders disagree with the judgment, this can have the benefit of separating the facts from the opinion and thus more accurately identifying the issues over which the parties disagree.
— Subjecting the judgments to consultation with other stakeholders prior to the finalisation of the ES.
— Acknowledging the existence of contrary opinions in the ES alongside the judgments offered by those undertaking the EIA.

Significance

9.92   Significance is a thread that runs throughout the EIA process. With each stage the degree of detail with which significance is assessed is greater. At the screening stage the likelihood of significant environmental effects is the trigger for undertaking an EIA, particularly for those projects for which screening decision is required (those within Annex 2 of the EIA Directive). At this stage the assessment of significance is based on the judgment of a small number of people. At the scoping stage the issues to be addressed by the EIA are identified according to those that are considered to be significant. While a detailed analysis is not undertaken, the judgment of what is considered to be significant is opened up to a wider number of stakeholders and their views are taken into account. When the impacts of a project are being assessed the significance of the impacts is subjected to a detailed analysis, requiring thorough supporting arguments and comparison with relevant regulations and accepted standards.

9.93   When assessing the significance of an impact it should be recognised that significance is a subjective issue. The affected community is likely to take a different view on the significance of an impact that directly affects them than, for example, the developer. The determining authority may take a different position from both parties, but there is no objective means of determining who is right. Criteria can be used to bring as much objectivity as possible into the analysis, but an impact that falls below any thresholds may still not be considered to be insignificant by the affected party. It is the task of the determining authority to weigh these different opinions and make their own judgment as to the significance of the impact and the acceptability of the proposal (note that significance and acceptability are not interchangeable terms).

9.94   The use of standards and criteria can assist in making the analysis more objective, but the selection of those criteria may not be an objective exercise. It is for this reason that it is considered to be good practice to select any standards or criteria to be used to assess significance at the scoping stage, when little is known about the magnitude of the impact. If selected after the impact has been quantified those undertaking the EIA could be accused of selecting the criteria in order to demonstrate that the impact is not significant.

9.95   The significance of an impact is usually described as a function of the magnitude of the impact and the importance of the receptor. The evaluation of the significance of impacts without mitigation taken into account will help to set priorities for those impacts for which mitigation will need to be developed in order for the impact to be considered acceptable. The assessment of the significance of the mitigated impacts will help to determine whether mitigation is sufficient to avoid any clearly unacceptable effects.

9.96   In order to assist the assessment of significance, criteria are usually applied. These may be based on regulation, policy, standards, or opinion (usually of those undertaking the EIA) and will be based on emissions or the environmental quality of the receptor.

9.97   Emissions based criteria are typically used for issues such as emissions to air and water. They may be enshrined in regulation, established as a policy, or based on a published standard. In some cases the emissions based criteria may be established on a case-by-case basis, such as limits contained in a discharge consent for emissions to water. In rare cases they may be poorly defined, but based on the level of public concern. For example, a proposal for a nuclear facility may meet all regulatory discharge and safety requirements, but public concern regarding radioactive emissions may still be considered to be a significant concern of sufficient importance to prevent the proposal from proceeding.

9.98   Environmental quality criteria are more frequently used for issues such as landscape and ecology. They often be based on legislation (e g Special Protection Areas or Sites of Special Scientific Interest), policy (e g Areas of Outstanding Natural Beauty) or may be related to the opinions and status of other stakeholders, for example, species of birds that are on the RSPB list of bird species of conservation concern, or National Trust land.

9.99   Regardless of the criteria that are used to assess significance, the credibility of an ES will be enhanced if the criteria are explained and their use is justified. This is essential where criteria have been developed by those undertaking the EIA (typically for landscape and visual impacts).

9.100   The following approach to the use of criteria should help to deliver a robust assessment of significance:
— Where possible, use of criteria that are derived from regulation or policies is preferable as these will have official standing and be relevant to the decision to be made.
— In the absence of regulatory or policy guidance, official standards can be used (eg ISO or British Standards).
— International standards and guidance can be consulted in the absence of any national regulations or guidance. It may also be appropriate to 'borrow' standards from other countries.
— In some circumstances, it may be useful to examine the differences between the international and national standards and the reasons for them. The EIA may be considered to be more robust if the more precautionary approach is selected.
— Where criteria are developed by those undertaking the EIA, a full explanation and justification of the criteria is required.

9.101   Most of the regulations, policies and standards from which significance criteria are derived were not developed for the purpose of use in the EIA. While they provide a useful benchmark, there can be circumstances under which the simplistic application of these criteria can be misleading. For example, environmental quality criteria based on the designation of sites or species can give the impression that any resources not included in the relevant lists are not important.

9.102   Emissions-based criteria usually operate on the basis of a simple threshold that environmental conditions should not exceed (eg National Air Quality Objectives). Typically these are compared with the predicted environmental concentrations of pollutants and if the thresholds are not exceeded then it is concluded that the impact is not considered to be significant. This approach does not account for the contribution to the level of pollutants that result from the proposed project. Therefore a large increase in the levels of particulates in the air could still be considered to be insignificant so long as the resultant levels are below the relevant thresholds. In this circumstance it might be appropriate also to apply criteria that take account of the change in the levels of pollutants. These would need to be developed by those undertaking the EIA.

9.103   The discussion above on the prediction of impacts addressed the issue of uncertainty. It is important that the assessment of the significance of impacts also takes account of this. For example, the assessment could be based on the worst-case scenario prediction rather than a 'best guess'.

MITIGATION AND MANAGEMENT

9.104 The purpose of mitigation is to find a way of achieving the objectives of the proposal with a reduced environmental effect. Mitigation is closely associated with the consideration of alternatives, as one of the key ways in which impacts can be avoided is to consider the alternatives available.

9.105 Mitigation is typically shown in the EIA process as following the assessment of impacts. This presupposes that methods to reduce impacts are only developed when the significant impacts have been identified and quantified. The reality is that, for most projects, many of the likely significant effects are known at the outset and work to reduce them would be integrated with the planning and design of the project. Mitigation that is developed following the assessment of impacts is more likely to be in the form of 'end-of-pipe' solutions and landscape design of the site. More fundamental mitigation may involve a redesign of the project.

Mitigation hierarchy

9.106 A widely-accepted good practice approach to mitigation is to follow a hierarchy:
— Avoid adverse impacts.
— Minimise or reduce adverse impacts to as low as practicable.
— Remedy or compensate for adverse impacts that are unavoidable.

A fourth element of the approach to mitigation is to seek opportunities to enhance the beneficial effects of the proposal. Examples of different types of mitigation measures can be found in Box 7.

9.107 Identifying mitigation in accordance with the above hierarchy requires the measures to be considered at the very early stages of project planning. As the project is developed in increasing detail, the options for avoiding impacts will often be limited and the remaining options for mitigation will be aimed at impact reduction or compensation.

9.108 The avoidance of impacts may include measures such as a different site design, using alternative technologies, identifying specific measures so as to avoid specific impacts (e g an airport not undertaking night flying in order to avoid a sleep disturbance problem).

9.109 The reduction of impacts can be achieved by changing the scale of development, applying alternative technology or adding additional elements to the proposal.

9.110   Compensation for impacts can be in financial terms, but it is generally accepted as good practice for this to be the last resort. Where possible, compensation should be related to the impact of the proposal. For example, the reduction in a wetland area could be compensated by the creation of another wetland area in another location.

Box 7: Examples of different types of mitigation measures

AVOIDANCE OR MINIMISATION AT SOURCE:

—Siting the project to avoid a valuable habitat or historic monument
—Selecting cleaner production technology
—Selecting lorry routes to avoid communities
—Moving noisy plant to the side of the site furthest away from sensitive receptors.

ABATEMENT ON THE SITE:

— Installing air pollution control of effluent treatment plant
— Enclosing plant to contain noise or odours
— Constructing a noise barrier or visual screen at the site boundary
— Installation of balancing ponds to regulate site run off.

ABATEMENT AT THE RECEPTOR:

— Planting trees to hide the site at the nearest residential properties
— Installing noise insulation at the receptor property
— Advance warning of blasting given to residents
— Relocating rare species
— Setting up an archaeological watching brief and allowing time for rescue work if required during excavation.

REPAIRING OR REMEDYING THE IMPACT:

— Installing clean-up equipment for spills and training staff in its use
— Dismantling and relocating historic buildings and structures
— Replacing rights of way.

COMPENSATION:

— Replacing home and other property
— Creating new habitats to replace those changed by the proposal
— Carrying out landscape restoration and improvement works
— Providing community facilities to compensate for unwanted development.

Source: Based on ERM (1997).

Mitigation in the environmental statement

9.111 The description of mitigation measures within the ES is important. These are the measures that are designed to prevent or minimise the significant environmental effects. The determining authority and other stakeholders will require confidence that the measures will be implemented and will be effective in achieving their task. A detailed description of the mitigation measures will give the reader of the ES a clear understanding of what is to be implemented and how. A useful test of whether a description is adequate is to question whether sufficient information has been provided for the reader of an ES to verify clearly whether a mitigation measure has been implemented or not during construction or after completion of the project.

9.112 The effectiveness of mitigation measures can be described in terms of the extent to which the environmental impact will be reduced. Any timing issues associated with the effectiveness will also need to be discussed. For example, any planting of trees that are designed to screen a development will take some years to become effective.

9.113 Not all mitigation is certain of being successful in reducing the environmental effects. For example, the success of translocation can be variable depending on species type, the similarity of the soil conditions between the host and the receptor site and other factors. Where there is uncertainty this should be clearly stated.[1] For example, the predicted probability of success of the measure can be given in the ES. If there is a high degree of uncertainty regarding the success of the measure an indication of the action to be taken in the event of failure can be described. It may also be appropriate to predict the impact of the proposal as that without the mitigation measure taken into account.

1   As to the legal issues arising from such uncertainty, see para **3.81**.

9.114 A common failure of many ESs is the lack of clarity of the mitigation measures that are to be implemented as opposed to those that are under consideration and those that will be implemented if the developer is forced to do so by the regulator. Only the mitigation measures that the developer is committed to implementing are certain to reduce the impact of the proposal. It is therefore appropriate that only these are taken into account when making predictions. Often, the commitment of the developer to the implementation of mitigation measures can be indicated by the extent to which they have been incorporated into the design of the project. Those measures that are to be treated as options, or which the developer is deliberately being ambiguous about, often appear to be 'add-ons' or 'end-of-pipe' solutions.

9.115 The treatment of mitigation in the ES is important to the determining authority, as this will form the basis for many of the conditions should the project receive consent. A developer is not obliged to implement mitigation measures that are described in an ES unless these have been specifically imposed as conditions by the determining authority.[1] Research undertaken for the Department of the Environment (published in 1997[2]) indicated that there were sufficient powers within the planning system to deliver mitigation measures, but it was important that local planning authorities set out planning conditions or legal agreements to cover the measures that they considered to be essential to the implementation of the project. Clarity of mitigation measures is also important because the determining authority is required to publish the main mitigation measures.[3] Failure to do this adequately could provide another avenue for legal challenge.

1   As to the legal issues arising, see para **5.32.**
2   Environmental Resources Management (1997), *Mitigation Measures in Environmental Statements*, Department of the Environment, London.
3   See para **5.29.**

9.116   To make the process of conditioning the mitigation measures less painful for the determining authority and the developer, the Department of the Environment research referred to above suggested that it is helpful for the ES to include a schedule of environmental commitments. Thus the ES would set out all of those mitigation and management measures that the developer is committed to implementing. This then becomes a working document that is modified as negotiations over the proposal take place and the project is modified to take account of the determining authority's views and those of other stakeholders. The final version, following the grant of consent, can then be used as a checklist to ensure that the environmental commitments are delivered on site.

Follow-up and environmental management

9.117   EIAs have generally had a poor record in relation to implementing follow-up activities. These can be defined as those environmental activities that are undertaken as part of the implementation of the project. Their purpose is to ensure that the work undertaken to identify and reduce the significant environmental effects of the development has results on the ground in terms of improved environmental protection. The lack of results of some EIAs 'on the ground' is one of the factors that have resulted in the value of EIA being questioned. Follow-up measures can include:

— Environmental management measures that are designed to respond to environmental effects as they occur: for example, the use of water bowsers to mitigate a dust impact during construction.
— Monitoring to ensure that environmental effects are compliant with required targets or thresholds: for example, noise monitoring of construction to ensure that limits imposed as conditions are not exceeded.
— Processes designed to address the environmental effect of changes to the design of the project or methods of working: for example, a change control process that ensures that any changes are environmentally screened.

9.118   Follow-up measures will be implemented as part of the implementation of the project, but it is during the assessment of impacts and the development of the mitigation measures that the scope for follow-up needs to be thought through and planned. The increased awareness of the need to ensure that the environmental effects are reduced in practice, as well as on paper, has led to the increased use of environmental management plans (EMPs). These incorporate the key mitigation and management measures to be implemented. Ideally, a first draft of the plan can be incorporated into the ES and might replace the mitigation schedule referred to above. As the project nears implementation, the EMP can be developed to identify the personnel responsible for delivery of the measures. Where necessary, the EMP can then be used as a basis for auditing the implementation of the mitigation measures.

9.119   Follow-up may be required in the following cases or to meet the following conditions:
— A need for the developer to demonstrate compliance with conditions or other environmental regulations. In some cases monitoring of environmental effects may be a requirement of other environmental regulation.
— Uncertainty relating to the magnitude or significance of an impact or the success of mitigation measures may be a further reason for implementing follow up. In the case of uncertain impacts, monitoring may be undertaken to identify whether a more significant impact occurs that requires additional mitigation measures. Similarly, in relation to mitigation measures for which success is uncertain, monitoring progress will help to identify whether any additional interventions are required.
— A risk of a significant environmental effect in the event that predictions prove to be inaccurate or mitigation measures fail. Monitoring can provide early warning to identify the need for additional interventions or for avoiding action to be taken.

9.120   Typically, EMPs are applied to the construction phase of a development. Where the operational phase of a development is in the control of the developer a commitment may be made to include the environmental commitments within a formal environmental management system. The continued commitment to environmental management for developments that are sold on by the developer is more problematical.

THE ENVIRONMENTAL STATEMENT

9.121   The Environmental Statement (ES) is one of the main products of the EIA process. It is the document that is the main communication tool for providing information on the nature of the development, the existing environment, the environmental effects of the proposal and the measures that are to be put in place to reduce these. The ES is also the document upon which people will focus in order to seek opportunities to challenge decisions and delay or block the progress of the application for consent. The ES is of immense importance in the EIA process, but it should not be regarded as the end of the process. When setting out to undertake an EIA, the objective should not be to produce an ES, but to develop a proposal that is consistent with protecting the environment. The ES is a vehicle for communicating the information that has been gathered to achieve this main objective. The content and presentation of the ES is also one of the main indicators of the commitment of the developer to protection of the environment in the course of developing the project.

9.122   Previous sections have given some indication of the information that should be included in an ES with regard to baseline conditions, etc. This will not be repeated here, but attention will be given to key principles of successful presentation of an ES.

Principles of presentation

9.123   The ES is the document of the developer. This association means that in perception, if not in reality, the ES will be viewed as being biased in favour of the developer and the proposal. There is some anecdotal evidence to confirm that this is the case. For example, there are few, if any, ESs which indicate that the impact of the project is so significant that it is questionable whether it should proceed or not. Even those that clearly state that significant impacts are likely to occur generally attempt to 'soften the blow' by arguing that the impact is not as bad as it may first appear, or that the mitigation and compensation is sufficient to render the impact as being acceptable.

9.124   The ES can influence the relationship and attitude of the decision-making body and the public to the developer, his advisors and the project. Given the propensity for stakeholders to perceive the ES as a biased document, it is important those responsible for producing the ES work hard to retain the credibility of the document and the findings of the EIA. The following principles will help to guide this effort:
— objectivity
— transparency
— communication
— retaining scientific rigour
— integrating the information.

Objectivity

9.125   Stakeholders will be very alert and sensitive to the objectivity of the document and it is important that those undertaking the EIA take an independent stance in the presentation of the information. Minimising the significance of environmental effects, emphasising benefits or positive impacts of the proposal or placing 'spin' on the presentation of significant environmental effects are all indicators that the document is not objective. Given the relationship between the developer and those responsible for undertaking the EIA, it is probably inevitable that some bias will creep into the ES, but a conscious effort to minimise this should limit any damage to the credibility of the document. Examples of approaches that enhance the objectivity of an ES are:
— Clearly and unambiguously stating when a significant impact is to occur.
— Recognising and describing the limitations on any of the EIA work and giving the underlying reasons for this, e g ecological surveys undertaken at a sub-optimal time of year.
— Being clear about any uncertainty relating to the prediction of impacts or the success of mitigation measures.

— Describing the decision-making processes relating to any details that may be determined after the main project decision and indicating if, and how, the public and other stakeholders can influence those processes.

Transparency

9.126 A transparent approach to the presentation of the information will also help to enhance the objectivity of the ES. Transparency relies on the description of processes, underlying arguments and the acknowledgment of the opinions of others. Compliance with the approaches listed under 'Objectivity' is also consistent with a transparent approach. Other factors will also be important:
— Demonstrating the reasons for decisions.
— Separating fact from opinion.
— Demonstrating how the ES meets the requirements of other stakeholders, e g by including their responses to the original scoping document or terms of reference.
— Acknowledging opinions and interpretations that are not consistent with those presented in the ES.
— Involving stakeholders in the assessment of significance where subjective judgments are required.

Communication

9.127 Communication, in the context of an ES, has two components: the presentation of the information in the ES, and the access to the document. ESs are often written in the style of scientific reports. However, their key role is as a communication device to the determining authority and other stakeholders. The ESs that are widely regarded as working best in terms of their presentation and communication of information are those that are written with this main readership in mind, rather than those that follow the conventions of technical or scientific reports. The following typify the approach of such ESs:
— use language that is understandable to the non-specialist;
— use maps and diagrams where these can illustrate issues more successfully than descriptions in text;
— avoid burying information in a large document;
— the reader will have to assimilate all of the information in a limited amount of time so the size of the document should be kept to a minimum consistent with ensuring that it is credible and robust;
— focus on the key issues; and
— organise the material for the convenience of the reader, not those assembling the information.

Retaining scientific rigour

9.128   The presentation of an ES is about achieving a balance between a range of objectives. Consistent with implementing principles of good communication, it is important that the ES retains a scientific rigour that supports the credibility of the document. Over-simplification of arguments, in order to satisfy the criteria of writing for the non-specialist, is likely to be criticised. Full and complete information should be provided, but the language used should not be aimed at the scientific community. Where technical terms are unavoidable they should be explained in the text or in a glossary.

Integrating the information

9.129   Poorly presented ESs are often characterised by a series of separate technical reports that are bound together. An introduction describing the development may be included and some general conclusions may be found toward the end of the ES. The separate technical reports may be technically sound, but will be written in a range of styles, will potentially repeat information and will demonstrate that there has been little integration of the different disciplines while the EIA was being undertaken. In some cases there will be inconsistent data between the different reports.

9.130   The ES should appear as a coherent document, written in a single style and with the information integrated to the extent that it is consistent and concise, as well as sufficiently extensive. The separate technical documents should be the source material that is used to draw up the coherent ES. If they have been heavily summarised they could be included as appendices to the ES to enable those wishing to look at the full detail to do so. Another advantage is that it demonstrates that the ES is a fair reflection of the original technical report. The disadvantage is that the inclusion of the reports will create a large document.

Review and decision making

9.131   There is no requirement in the UK for formal review of an ES by determining authorities. This contrasts with most other EIA systems around the world. Review is a well-established and widely-accepted component of good practice in EIA. It is undertaken in order to analyse the adequacy and relevance of the environmental information that will be used as part of the basis for decision making. In the event that the ES is found to be inadequate then additional information can be requested to fill any data gaps. Determining authorities have a similar responsibility to identify any additional information required before a decision is made. They are also responsible for ensuring that the ES complies with the requirements of the legislation, but are not required to conduct a formal review to fulfil either of these obligations. Nevertheless, a formal review is a systematic approach that will provide the information to fulfil their responsibilities and provide a more complete picture of the adequacy of the ES. Consistent with other EIA systems, EIA Regulations in the UK do require that the public be given an opportunity to review the ES and submit their comments to the determining authority. EIA review therefore has two components: the technical review that formally analyses the adequacy of the ES; and the public review that provides for the opinions of other stakeholders to be considered in the decision-making process.

9.132 The purpose of review is to determine the adequacy of the ES. Key issues can be identified that help to explain what is meant by the term 'adequate'. Sadler has described the process of review as submitting the ES to the triple 'A' test:[1]
— Appropriateness (coverage of the key issues)
— Adequacy (of impact analysis)
— Actionability (does the report provide the basis for informed decision making?).

These terms can be further broken down to set out the key expectations of an ES in the form of review criteria. These are discussed in more detail below.

1   Sadler B, *International Study of the Effectiveness of Environmental Assessment: Environmental Assessment in a Changing World — Evaluating Practice to Improve Performance* (1996) International Association for Impact Assessment and Canadian Environmental Assessment Agency, Ottawa.

Methods of review

9.133 Most EIAs are undoubtedly reviewed in some form, but the methods used to do this are usually not clear, particularly where the review is undertaken internally. There are few local planning authorities that employ individuals specifically for their EIA expertise. Other determining authorities may receive ESs on a more frequent basis and have a greater level of expertise, for example, in the oil and gas sector. Nevertheless, the methods adopted for the review are usually not clear in either case.

9.134 As a minimum, all authorities are required to consult with the statutory consultees and seek their opinion as to the adequacy of the information in the ES, in relation to their specialist area. In most cases, these authorities will also be indicating whether they have any fundamental objections to the project being given consent and will outline the main mitigation measures they would require in the event that the project does proceed. Technical comments can also be expected from many of the non-governmental organisations that may participate in the public review.

9.135 Where a more formal review of the whole of the EIA is undertaken, one of three methods is usually adopted:[1]
— The ad hoc review — based on the experience and knowledge of those undertaking the review.
— The review based on the scope or terms of reference.
— Review using published review criteria.

1   Fuller K, *Quality and Quality Control in Environmental Impact Assessment* in J Petts (ed), *Handbook of Environmental Impact Assessment,* Vol 2 (1999) Blackwell Science, Oxford.

9.136   The ad hoc review is the least systematic of the three options. It relies on the reviewers having an appropriate level of expertise in EIA and some knowledge of environmental and social science disciplines relevant to the project. The flexibility of the approach may enable the reviewer to identify issues that would not have been identified by more formal approaches. Conversely, there is a risk that relatively straightforward issues will be overlooked as there is no guide to the review process.

9.137   The review based on the scope or the terms of reference of the EIA is formalised within some EIA systems (e g The Netherlands). In order for this to be a thorough review, detailed terms of reference will be required at the outset. The review simply examines the ES to determine whether it has covered all the issues that were identified as part of the scoping phase and to the depth that was agreed with the various stakeholders. In cases where this is applied the reviewers usually retain the right to address issues that were not necessarily identified in the original terms of reference. For example, if additional information obtained during the EIA should have resulted in an adjustment to the terms of reference, then it would be legitimate for the review to question why the additional issues were not addressed.

9.138   The use of review criteria is becoming increasingly prominent. Many examples of review criteria have been published, but all reflect similar approaches. They essentially provide a checklist of issues that should be included in an ES that is consistent with compliance with regulations and good practice. The requirements are set down as principles of assessment that should be present in an ES rather than as requirements on specific technical issues. There are few differences in content between the various review criteria, so a review conducted using one should come up with similar findings to a review using alternative criteria. A short extract of review criteria published by the European Commission is given in Box 8.[1] This small section deals with the information provided in the ES on the scoping of the EIA. In total the European Commission Criteria has 144 questions with space for reviewers to add their own questions that may have particular relevancy to their own EIA system or the particular project with which they are dealing.

Box 8: Review criteria

Section 4: Description of the likely significant effects of the project

No. Review question	Relevant?	Adequately addressed?	What further information is needed?
Scoping of effects			
4.1 Is the process by which the scope of the environmental studies was defined described?			
4.2 Is it evident that a systematic approach to scoping was adopted?			
4.3 Is it evident that full consultation was carried out during scoping?			
4.4 Are the comments and views of the consultees presented?			

1 Environmental Resources Management, *Guidance on EIA: EIS Review*, European Commission, Brussels (2001).

9.139   Review criteria provide a systematic basis for undertaking a review and give considerable support to the non-specialist to evaluate the environmental information. A more thorough review is likely to result if undertaken by an individual familiar with EIA and with some knowledge of environmental and social sciences. When using the review criteria, the reviewer is required to answer each question systematically, first of all determining whether it is relevant to the particular project (for example, storage of hazardous substances is not likely to be relevant for an EIA of a windfarm) and then deciding whether the issue has been adequately addressed. In the event that the information is considered to be inadequate, the reviewer sets out the additional information required. An alternative approach offered is to grade the quality of the ES on a scale of A–E, where A is considered to be excellent and E very poor. Similar grading systems are associated with many other published review criteria. The attribution of these grades is a subjective judgment, but experience indicates that two people undertaking a review will generally judge the grades to be the same or within a grade of each other. If those two people then discuss their findings and the reasons for awarding a particular grade there is usually little difficulty in reaching agreement on the grade to be awarded.

9.140   The use of review criteria encourages a systematic approach to review that should aid consistency from one review to another and from one project to the next. They also add transparency to the process as those undertaking the EIA can be aware of the standard against which their ES will be judged.

9.141   The limitations of using review criteria are similar to those criticisms levelled at using any type of checklist approach in EIA. By using a set framework there is a danger that the reviewers will restrict their analysis to those issues contained in the criteria. Issues that may be specific to a proposal, but otherwise rarely occur in EIA (and are therefore not included in the criteria), may not be identified by the reviewers. The transparency of the review criteria approach can also lead to ESs being written to address the criteria rather than address the real issues related to the EIA. In most cases the difference between these approaches would be subtle and probably immaterial, but in some cases it could lead to important issues not being addressed.

Who should undertake a review?

9.142   Review is primarily the responsibility of the determining authority. This activity may be undertaken 'in-house', but many authorities do not possess the appropriate expertise. In many cases they will contract a third party to undertake the review; this may be a university department, a consultant, or the Institute of Environmental Management and Assessment. This organisation provides a review service, but does not involve itself in undertaking EIAs. It is a membership organisation that includes organisational members from consultancies, businesses, the education and public sectors. The approach is therefore to be independent of any particular stakeholder interest in the EIA process.

9.143   The absence of a formal review system in the UK means that the results of a review have no special status other than being additional environmental information. Some authorities choose to address all of the outstanding issues that the review identifies; others evaluate their relevance to the decision and only ask for additional information on those issues that they consider to be most important.

9.144   Review is essentially a quality control process and can have a role to play in the internal quality control within consultancies. For example, it might be appropriate for a consultancy to conduct an internal review using people not associated with project or the EIA. In some cases it may be helpful to contract a third party to undertake an independent review. These can be undertaken prior to the project and the ES being submitted into the decision-making process. The results of the review will provide the developer and his advisors with the opportunity to address any problems before they are identified within the decision-making process.

Public review

9.145 The only requirements for public review is that a copy of the ES is made available at an appropriate location for the public to view and that it is made available for the public to purchase. The implementation of these requirements has often been a barrier to effective public involvement. ESs are made available for viewing often at council offices, or other locations that require the members of the affected public to be available during working hours. Clearly, a significant proportion would be working and would be unable to attend the venue where the ES could be viewed. Even if they could, most ESs are of such a size that it is clearly unrealistic for a member of the public to stay at a particular location for the time it would take to read and analyse the ES.

9.146 For ESs that are made available for purchase the developer is allowed to charge a fee that covers the reproduction costs of the ES. Many of the charges levied have operated as a barrier to public access to information. Many examples exist of over £500 being charged for an ES, but there have been no legal challenges to charges of this level.

9.147 The growth of the Internet provides a potential solution to both of the problems described above. The creation of an electronic version of the ES can be produced relatively cheaply given that the document is likely to have been produced in this format anyway. There are now several examples of websites being created specifically for the purpose of informing people about a development, including its environmental effects. An electronic version of the ES can be included on this for people to download. Where the size of the document is large it may be appropriate to provide the different chapters of the ES as separate files.

9.148 More proactive approaches to public involvement are possible, but require the commitment and initiative of either the developer or the determining authority. Many other EIA systems have a requirement for public meetings or hearings to be held. Other techniques discussed in the public participation section may be more effective. The benefits of holding an event to seek public views as part of the review are:
— Expanding the range of opportunities and means by which the public can make their views known.
— Demonstrating a transparent approach to the decision-making process.
— Ensuring the public remain informed about the development and its environmental effects if they have been unable to access a copy of the ES.

Decision making

9.149 There has often been a question of the influence and use of the ES in decision making. The five-year review of the implementation of the original EIA Directive raised concerns about the incompleteness of information that was being used in decision-making processes and the limited use of the environmental information. These concerns influenced some of the changes to the EIA Directive that were included in the amending

Directive of 1997. Most notable is the requirement for determining authorities to publish their decision along with the main reasons for it and, if the project has received consent, a description of the main mitigation measures. There have been few studies undertaken to determine whether these changes have had an influence on the role of the ES in decision making. On the face of it, there is a greater challenge to those making decisions to think about how they could justify them in environmental terms. In the UK the means of publication could be more transparent and give the public easier access to the information, as currently the decision and related information is simply published in the planning register (for planning projects in England and Wales).

CROSS CUTTING ISSUES

9.150   The previous sections of this Chapter discuss EIA practice in the context of the EIA process, in approximately the order that events would happen in when undertaking an EIA. There are some issues, that are linked to each other and cut across the whole of the EIA process, and which warrant specific attention, rather than simply examining their role in relation to specific components of the EIA process:
— engaging the public
— cumulative environmental effects
— addressing sustainability

9.151   Provisions for public involvement in EIA are increasingly being interpreted as one of the pillars of the EIA process in the UK. Whilst much of UK practice is still in defensive mode in terms of only fulfilling the requirements of the regulations, there is increasing interest in the advantages to be gained from going beyond the minimum requirements and being more proactive in engaging the public in the process. The context, benefits and methods of public involvement are discussed in this section.

9.152   Cumulative effects have traditionally been something of a footnote to the EIA Directive, but are now receiving greater prominence, as their role in undermining sustainability is increasingly being appreciated. Whilst most practitioners can agree on the importance of cumulative effects, their treatment within an EIA for a specific proposal is more problematic. If they are to be addressed effectively they will need to be considered throughout the EIA process rather than simply when the impacts of a proposal are being assessed.

9.153   An increasing number of ESs are addressing the issues of sustainability with varying degrees of success. This move is not in response to any regulatory change, but as a result of the increasing emphasis being placed on sustainability at the local level, and in particular in the planning context. This section discusses some of the approaches that can be used to address the issue of sustainability.

Engaging the public in EIA

9.154 Public participation has been established as an essential part of the EIA process since its inception in the USA. Virtually without exception, where EIA has been adopted around the world the public participation requirement has been incorporated. Whilst some systems pay lip service to involving the public, there is a greater pressure in democratic societies to deliver on the participation requirements. Set in the context of increased requirements for environmental information provision and availability to the public in regulations and improved information technology, together with enhanced public involvement and participation in a number of different contexts (risk management, local environmental improvement work, urban regeneration and Local Agenda 21), public participation within EIA is both a component and a reflection of a wider general development of public involvement in decision-making.[1]

1   J. Petts, *Public Participation and Environmental Impact Assessment*, in J Petts (1999), Handbook of Environmental Impact Assessment, Volume 1, Blackwell Science, Oxford.

9.155 The EIA Directive has moved from requiring consultation prior to project initiation to requiring it 'before development consent is granted'. Additional requirements for information provision have also enhanced the role of public involvement in the process. However, the Directive remains focused upon consultation and the provision of information, rather than participation. Nevertheless, the provision in the Directive for public involvement is being supported and strengthened by court decisions that have interpreted the exposure of the EIA process to the public as being one of the important features of the regime.[1]

1   S Tromans (2002), *"The Chicken Run Case" and Screening*, in The Environmentalist, Issue Number 14, December 2002, Institute of Environmental Management & Assessment, Lincoln.

9.156 The UNECE Convention on Access to Information, Public Participation in Decision Making and Access to Justice in Environmental Matters[1] (Aarhus, 1998) is the principal international treaty and most comprehensive legal instrument relating to public involvement. This treaty describes how public participation should work in cases of decision-making, and states that public participation should be effective, adequate, formal, and provide for information, notification, dialogue, consideration and response. Its provisions and implications are still being incorporated into EIA regulations and practice, and it is likely to set important new precedents for standards of public involvement. Specifically, requirements for early and effective participation are likely to be interpreted as a requirement to involve the public in the EIA process much earlier than current regulations demand and current practice allows.

1   UNECE (1998) Convention on Access to Information Public Participation in Decision – Making and Access to Justice in Environmental Matters. Fourth Ministerial Conference, Aarhus, Denmark, 23-25 June 1998. See further, para XXX above.

Benefits of engaging the public

9.157   Effective public participation within the EIA process offers a number of advantages to the proponent, the authorities and the public (see Table 1). Public participation can contribute to successful design, implementation, operation and management of proposals; provide a valuable source of information on key impacts, potential mitigation measures, aid identification and selection of alternatives; also it can provide a mechanism that ensures the EIA process is open, transparent, robust and characterised by defensible analysis.[1] Table 1 sets out some of the key benefits for different stakeholders of involving the public in the process.

1   B Sadler & K Fuller et al (2002), *United Nations Environment Programme Environmental Impact Assessment Training Resource Manual* 2nd Edition, UNEP, Geneva.

The Proponent	The Decision Maker	Third Parties
Raises the proponent's awareness of their potential impacts on the environment and receiving community.	Achieves more informed and accountable decision-making.	Provides an opportunity to raise concerns and influence the decision-making process.
Legitimises proposals and ensures greater acceptance and support.	Provides increased assurance that all issues of legitimate concern have been addressed.	Provides an opportunity to gain a better understanding and knowledge about the environmental impacts and risks that may arise.
Improves public trust.	Decision-making is seen to be open and transparent avoiding accusations of decisions being made 'behind closed doors'.	Increases awareness of how decision-making processes work, who makes decisions and on what basis.
Assists by obtaining local information and data.	Promotes good relations with the proponent and third parties.	Empowers people, providing the knowledge that they can influence decision-making and creating a greater sense of social responsibility.
Avoids potentially costly delays later in the process by resolving conflict early.	Avoids potentially costly delays later in the process by resolving conflict early.	Ensures all relevant issues and concerns are dealt with prior to decision.

Table 1: Advantages of public participation
Source: IEMA, 2002

Purpose and objectives

9.158 The purpose of public participation is to inform stakeholders about the proposal and its likely effects; canvass their inputs, views and concerns; and take account of the information and views of the public in the EIA and decision-making. The objectives of a public participation programme will differ from one project to another and according to the intentions of the developer, but they can include the following:[1]

— to obtain local knowledge that may be useful for decision making;
— to facilitate consideration of alternatives, mitigation measures and trade-offs;
— to ensure that important impacts are not overlooked and benefits are maximised;
— to reduce conflict through the early identification of contentious issues;
— to provide an opportunity for the public to influence project design in a positive manner (so helping create a sense of ownership of the proposal);
— to improve transparency and accountability of decision making; and
— to increase public confidence in the EIA process.

1 B Sadler & K Fuller et al (2002), *United Nations Environment Programme Environmental Impact Assessment Training Resource Manual* 2nd Edition, UNEP, Geneva.

Defining the public

9.159 Defining who 'the public' are can be a problem. Usually it is considered to be those communities that are likely to be significantly affected by the project. This becomes more problematical where there are people that have an intermittent interest in the area. For example, if a project is proposed for a National Park, should tourists that visit the National Park be considered part of the affected public? Usually the affected public would be defined by reference to those that have an economic interest in the area, or who would be affected in terms of quality of life.

9.160 Having identified the public, and other stakeholders, that may have an interest in the project, it may be necessary to identify a smaller number that actively participate in the public involvement programme. These may be randomly selected, chosen by the developer or by a third party. Whoever is responsible for the selection it will be important to ensure that particular social groups are not excluded from the process. For example, it may be tempting to think that a process will be easier to operate if dealing with the well educated section of a community, but this could have a result that changes are made to a project that more adversely affect the poorer and less well educated sections of a community. Similar concerns are associated with the use of an existing group as a proxy for the views of the local community. For example, a parish council may not be representative of the views of the wider community.

Levels of involvement

9.161 There are various levels of public involvement, that differ according to the level of participation. The level adopted at any one particular time will depend on the stage of the EIA process and the objectives of the public involvement programme. The different levels include:[1]

— **information provision** – a one way flow of information to the public
— **consultation** – a two way flow of information in which the public are provided with an opportunity to submit opinions about the development and / or the EIA
— **participation** – an interactive exchange between the developer and the public in which they share the setting of agendas, seek to understand each other's point of view and develop agreed positions on the project and / or the EIA. Participation offers greater influence and participation in the decision making processes than consultation that only provides an input into the process.
— **negotiation** – an interactive exchange designed to build consensus and reach a mutually acceptable resolution

1   Based on Sadler B & K Fuller et al (2002), *United Nations Environment Programme Environmental Impact Assessment Training Resource Manual* 2nd Edition, UNEP, Geneva.

9.162   There are 5 main stages of EIA at which public involvement can occur:
— **Screening**   Provision of information regarding the nature and significance of likely impacts that can assist in determining the need for an EIA (and at what level).
— **Scoping**   Critical to ensure that all significant issues are identified, local information collected, and alternatives considered.
— **Impact analysis and mitigation**   Can help to avoid biases and inaccuracies in analysis, identify local values and preferences, assist in the consideration of mitigation measures, and select a best practicable alternative.
— **EIA review**   To opinions on the outcomes of the EIA process, in terms of the nature of the development and the environmental effects
— **Implementation and follow up**   Helping to respond to problems, and promote good relations with affected local communities, verifying implementation of mitigation measures, notifying of significant or unanticipated environmental effects.

9.163   In practice public involvement in the UK tends to centre on the review stage. More extended forms of public involvement occur when:
— proponents are seeking to apply 'best practice';
— proponents are depending upon gaining the consent or support of local stakeholders; or
— the project could have significant social impacts.

Principles for engaging the public

9.164   There are seven basic principles for improving public participation in environmental decision-making:[1]
1.   Participation should be inclusive of a wide range of participants who are representative of affected and interested individuals and parties.

2. There should be openness and transparency with clearly defined roles and communication.
3. Participation should be interactive allowing for the effective contribution of all stakeholders.
4. Consideration should be given to the timing of participation. It should begin as early as possible, continue throughout the EIA process and into implementation and follow up.
5. The participation programme should be relevant in order to maintain focus and minimise in time and costs.
6. The process should be credible and constructive, with participants that respect all opinions.
7. Finally, participation should generate a response, informing and influencing the decision making process.

1   Institute of Environmental Management & Assessment (IEMA) (2002), *Perspectives – Guidelines on participation in environmental decision making*, IEMA, Lincoln.

Planning a public participation programme

9.165   The public participation programme will make a significant contribution to defining the nature of the relationship between the developer and the affected communities. A programme that is poorly planned and executed can undermine the credibility of the developer and the EIA and reduce the chances of gaining consent for the project. It is therefore important that the public participation elements of an EIA are as well planned as any other part of the EIA. This should be undertaken as early as possible in the process to allow for public involvement in the early stages of the EIA.

Planning a public involvement programme involves the following:[1]
— Consider the purpose of the participation exercise and issues that may arise.
— Consider the aims, objectives and expectations of participation of both your own and those of potential participants.
— Consider the decision-making process in which participation is proposed and determine the time-scale for participation.
— Identify potential participants.
— Identify the type and scope of public involvement appropriate to the issues and objectives of the EIA.
— Determine the techniques to be used.
— Identify the need for staff training or external expertise.
— Identify when and where the opportunities for public involvement should be provided.
— Consider how the results of participation will be analysed and used.
— Determine how the participation programme will be evaluated.
— Identify the resources required to deliver the public participation programme.

The consideration of the aims, objectives and expectations associated with the programme will be important in determining the other factors. For example, the expectations of the developer and the public may be very different, with the public anticipating a much greater influence on project decisions than the developer is willing to provide. Recognition of these differences in expectations will influence the nature of the programme, the techniques used and the type of feedback that is given to the participants in the programme.

1   Based on Institute of Environmental Management & Assessment (IEMA) (2002), *Perspectives – Guidelines on participation in environmental decision making*, IEMA, Lincoln and on Sadler B & K Fuller et al (2002), *United Nations Environment Programme Environmental Impact Assessment Training Resource Manual* 2nd Edition, UNEP, Geneva.

Public engagement techniques

9.166   Where public participation programmes extend beyond the minimum requirements in the UK, two approaches are generally used: first the public meeting at which the developer and his advisers present information on the project and the EIA and members of the audience are invited to raise questions or comments; and secondly the public exhibition at which information on the project and the EIA are presented on boards and the public are invited to comment or raise questions. The first technique is widely regarded as an approach that can often be unpredictable and, in some cases, can make a difficult situation worse. The second, whilst less adversarial, is often focused on information provision rather than an interactive exchange of views resulting in change to the project. More creative techniques are increasingly being used, but have been part of EIA practice in many other countries for some years. These are focused on avoiding an adversarial approach and promoting consensus building.

9.167   Factors that influence the selection of techniques are:
— The purpose and objectives of the participation exercise.
— The degree of interaction required between participants, and the extent to which participants are able to influence decisions.
— The timing of use, i.e. the stage in the decision-making process and the time available for participation.
— Resource availability – time and costs in particular.
— The number of participants involved (more interactive techniques can be used with smaller numbers of people, but could impractical with large groups).
— The complexity, controversy and level of interest in issues under consideration.

9.168   Table 2 illustrates the range of techniques that are available for engaging the public. Each has their advantages and disadvantages and there is no 'correct' technique to use in any particular situation. Nevertheless, the Table does indicate the range of possibilities enabling a public participation exercise to be planned to meet the objectives and avoid the unpredictable consequences of the techniques that are used more frequently in the UK. Box 9 provides an example of a more creative approach to public involvement developed to address the often controversial issue of waste management. The programme was integrated into the development of a waste management strategy, but directly impacted on easing the decision making process for three waste to energy plants that were proposed as a result of the strategy. Achieving a level of public 'buy in' to the strategy that they had helped to develop meant that there was an understanding of the need for the proposal.

Table 2: Methods of public participation[1]

Technique	Description and uses	Advantages	Disadvantages
Level 1: Education and Information Provision			
Leaflets/brochures	Written material used to convey information. The boundaries of distribution should be carefully considered.	• Potential to reach a wide audience. • Can be targeted at particular groups.	• Can be problems with interpretation and understanding. • May be treated as junk mail.
Newsletters	Written material used to convey information that may involve a series of publications.	• Information can be updated through ongoing contact. • Flexible approach that can be adapted to address the needs of the audience. • Potential for feedback.	• As for leaflets/ brochures.
Unstaffed exhibits/ displays	Information conveyed via exhibits or displays within public areas e.g. shopping centres.	• Convenient viewing for the public. • Use of graphical representations can help people visualise proposals.	• Can be problems with interpretation and understanding. • No staff present to respond to queries or comments.
Advertising	Advertising can be used to announce proposals, arrangements for meetings and other activities.	• Potential to reach a wide audience, dependant upon the circulation of the publication.	• Only reach those who read the publications chosen. • Only limited information can be conveyed.
Local newspapers	Article published in a local newspaper to convey information regarding proposals.	• Potentially cheap. • Reach a local audience	• Circulation may be limited. • May be problems with limited editorial control and misrepresentation of information.
National newspapers	Article published in a national newspaper to convey information regarding proposals.	• Potential to reach a very large audience.	• May only be of limited interest to the national press and a national audience if the proposals have gained a national profile.
Television and radio	Use of TV or radio to convey information regarding proposals.	• Potential to reach a very large audience. • People may watch a broadcast rather than read a leaflet or brochure.	• Broadcasts may need to be supported with further media containing greater information. • Relatively expensive.

Technique	Description and uses	Advantages	Disadvantages
Level 1: Education and Information Provision—contd			
Internet	Set up a web site dedicated to the proposal to provide information and enable copies of the ES to be downloaded.	• Information available when the public are available • Information more accessible • Reduced production costs for the ES	• Relies on the public being computer literate and owning equipment • Needs to be supported by other techniques to make people aware of the web site.
Video	Use of video can convey information regarding proposals. This may incorporate computer graphics and other images to enhance the viewers understanding.	• Editorially controlled by the producer. • Can be watched at the viewer's convenience.	• Can be perceived as biased propaganda. • Relatively expensive to produce a professional and credible end product.
Site visits	Organised case studies through site orientated meetings to provide first hand experience of a particular activity and the issues involved.	• Issues are brought to life through real examples.	• Difficulties in identifying a site which replicates all the issues under consideration. • Unsuitable for large groups.
Level 2: Information Feedback			
Staffed exhibits/ displays	Information conveyed via exhibits or displays within public areas e.g. shopping centres. These are staffed by specialists who can provide information, answer questions and receive comments.	• Convenient viewing for the public. • Use of graphical representations can help people visualise proposals. • One to one contact can be achieved. • Particular groups can be targeted.	• Requires major commitment of staff time. • May attract a small proportion of third parties.
Staffed telephone lines	The provision of a staffed telephone number for people to call and obtain information, ask questions or make comments.	• Convenient. • Not intimidating. • Accessible.	• Not as good as face to face communication. • Operating staff may not have technical knowledge to respond to questions.
Internet	The use of a website on the internet to provide information or invite feedback. The use of on-line forums and discussion groups can encourage more interactive forms of participation.	• Potentially global audience. • Reduction of costs due to less printing and postage. • Convenient for those with internet access.	• Access to internet is limited, and will not reach all interested parties. Therefore, alternative means of communication will also be required.

Technique	Description and uses	Advantages	Disadvantages
Level 2: Information Feedback—contd			
Public meetings	Formal gathering of interested and affected parties to present and exchange information and views on a proposal.	• Useful way of getting stakeholders together. • Demonstrates that the proponent is willing to meet other interested parties.	• Despite appearing simple, can be complex and unpredictable. • Can be intimidating and may be hijacked by interest groups and vocal individuals. • May result in no consultation and only information provision.
Surveys, interviews and questionnaires	Encompasses a wide range of techniques for obtaining information and opinions. These may be self administered, conducted face-to-face, by post or via telephone.	• Can reach people who would not attend a public meeting, or become involved in other activities. • Confidential surveys can elicit more candid responses. • Can identify existing knowledge and concerns.	• Can have a poor response rate. • Responses may not be representative. • Designing and implementing a good survey or questionnaire can be costly and time consuming.
Level 3: Involvement and Consultation			
Workshops	Meetings which involve a limited number of participants where background information is provided, issues can be discussed in detail and problems solved.	• A more open exchange of ideas that can facilitate mutual understanding. • Useful for dealing with complex, technical issues and allowing more in-depth consideration. • Can be targeted at particular stakeholder groups.	• In order to maximise effectiveness only a small number of individuals can participate. As a consequence the full range of interests may not be represented.
Focus Groups/For a	Invited participants attend a meeting designed to gauge the response to proposals, and gain a detailed understanding of people's perspectives, values and concerns.	• Quick method of gauging what the likely public reaction to proposals.	• May exclude certain sectors of the community. • Groups require facilitation. • Time consuming.
Open-House highlight the decision making process and the complexi	Interested parties are encouraged to visit a designated location on an informal basis to find out about a proposal and provide feedback.	• Convenient method where the public can visit at leisure and view materials and ask questions.	• Cost in time and money.

Technique	Description and uses	Advantages	Disadvantages
Level 4: Extended Involvement			
Community advisory/liaison groups	Meetings, consisting of small groups of people representing particular interests or areas of expertise, to discuss issues of concern and provide informed output.	• Allows for considera-tion of issues in detail and can ties involved. • Promotes a feeling of trust.	• A longer term process that requires more resources. • May not represent all interests. • Commitment is required from the participants.
Citizens' juries	Community representa-tives are brought together to consider a particular issue. Evidence from expert witnesses can be delivered and ques-tioned. A report is produced at the end of the process that sets out the views of the jury, including differences in opinion.	• Considers issues in detail in a relatively short period of time.	• May not represent all interests. • The limited time scale may restrict time available for adequate considera-tion of information received.
Consensus conference	A citizens' panel, selected from the public, questions experts on a particular topic, assesses re-sponses, discusses the issues raised and reports its conclusions.	• Can deal effectively with controversial issues of public concern. • Can provide an insight into public perceptions.	• May not represent all interests. • Limited time scale.
Visioning	Technique for developing a shared vision of a desirable future for a local community.	• Develops a common view of future needs. • Promotes trust and a sense of purpose.	• Lack of control over outcome. • Needs to be used early in the decision making process.

1   Source: Institute of Environmental Management & Assessment (IEMA) (2002), *Perspectives – Guidelines on participation in environmental decision making*, IEMA, Lincoln, based on J Petts, *Evaluating method for public participation: Literature review*. R&D Technical Report E135, Environment Agency, Bristol.

Box 9: *Identifying Issues, Concerns and Strategy Options for the*
Hampshire Waste Management Strategy

CONTEXT

In the late 1980s the county of Hampshire was faced with a problem of an ageing incinerator stock, which would not meet new emissions standards. There was increasing difficulty in finding new and environmentally acceptable landfill sites and there was pressure arising from increasing waste generation. The 1989 County Waste Management Plan endorsed the need for an integrated approach to waste management, supporting the need for waste minimisation and recycling and stressing the need for reduced reliance upon landfill. In 1991 a single large Energy-from-Waste (EfW) plant was proposed to provide a capacity of 400,000 tonnes per annum. The site was selected by the County Council. The proposal met with strong and well organised opposition from members of the local community and Portsmouth City Council. The basis of the opposition represented a mixture of policy, need and environmental impact issues. Whilst the Waste Management Plan had supported the need for EfW and had been subject to public consultation it was felt that this had been too passive a process and that the concerns and priorities of the community had not been recognised by the Council.

A voluntary, proactive public involvement programme was instigated by Hampshire County Council Waste Disposal Authority in 1993 to examine the options for dealing with household waste and to seek a broad base of public support for a strategy which could be translated into new facilities.

MECHANISM FOR PARTICIPATION

Hampshire employed independent public consultation consultants to devise and run the programme. The County did not have the necessary skills and the independence of the party running the programme was considered important. The key component of the community involvement programme was the formation of a Community Advisory Forum (CAF) in each of the areas of the three regional groupings for waste management within the County. Six CAF meetings were held, each lasting three hours during an evening once a month over the period November 1993 to April 1994. Over the same period the County conducted a more traditional public consultation programme including: exhibitions; a monthly newsletter; press releases; open days at waste facilities in the County; public meetings; and production of a resource pack and videos for loan to schools.

Potential participants were approached following a community analysis and appraisal exercise involving the identification of over 500 community groups and organisations and a telephone survey to ascertain people's awareness of waste and their expectations of public consultation.

Each CAF (maximum size 18) included a mix of people:
— people with different interests – community, environmental, business, health, conservation, parish;
— males and females;
— young and old;
— ethnic representatives;
— people with little knowledge of waste problems;
— those who were actively involved in recycling programmes;
— individuals who had led the opposition to the Portsmouth proposal.

Each forum was chaired by an independent member of the local community.

Objectives of the fora:
— to provide a sounding-board for the development of an integrated waste management strategy;
— to identify issues and areas of concern about different waste management options and the most appropriate options for Hampshire;
— to provide feedback to the County and districts;
— to comment on the proposed range of options for communicating information to the general public.

Key elements of the process:
— Members of the fora were provided with any information which they requested, whether 'for' or 'against' different waste management options.
— While each forum meeting was open to the public and press only the forum members had the right to participate.
— Visits to facilities and a one-day seminar were arranged. The seminar included papers presented by UK and overseas experts.

OUTCOME

The Hampshire community involvement programme:
— provided for consensus amongst some interested stakeholders that an integrated strategy is needed;
— opened up decision-making systems and decision criteria for public involvement;
— raised the profile of waste management;
— improved the credibility of officers responsible for waste disposal;
— improved officers' and key elected Members' understanding of public concerns;
— helped some key stakeholders to hear and be aware of (if not entirely sympathise with) the views of others;
— forced the County to slow down the normal local authority 'decision-making treadmill' to allow opinions to be expressed and to revisit the requirements for effective implementation of the strategy;
— allowed the County to say that it had consulted.

Source: IEMA (2002) based on Petts, J. (1995) Waste Management Strategy Development: *A Case Study of Community Involvement and Consensus-Building in Hampshire*. Journal of Environmental Planning and Management, Vol. 38, No. 4, pp519-536.

Cumulative effects assessment

9.169 Until recently cumulative effects have received little attention EIA practice in the UK. However, significant environmental effects still occur, despite the requirements of the EIA Directive, and despite most EIAs claiming to have mitigated the significant environmental effects to acceptable levels. This has resulted in more attention being given to the impact of multiple developments. Widespread adoption of strategic environmental assessment (SEA) in the planning system and the requirements of the Habitats Directive have also focused attention on the cumulative effects of development.

9.170 Cumulative effects have been described as the "stuff of sustainability",[1] meaning that the most significant environmental threats result from the accumulation of the smaller effects from multiple sources. If EIA is to fulfil the objective of protecting the environment and make a significant contribution to moving development to a sustainable level, then it is clear that EIA needs to give greater attention to the cumulative effects of development. The UK is several steps behind other mature EIA systems in this. For example, the assessment of cumulative effects is an explicit requirement of the Federal EIA system in Canada, as well as the provinces of Alberta and British Columbia. Despite this, the EIA Directive does require the assessment of effects to consider cumulative effects, but it has been common practice to date for EIAs to only consider direct effects. For this reason the European Commission has developed guidance on the assessment of cumulative and indirect effects.[2]

1   B Sadler (1999), personal communication.
2   Hyder (1999), *Guidelines for the Assessment of Cumulative and Indirect Impacts as well as Impact Interactions*, European Commission.

9.171 The ideal opportunity to assess cumulative effects is at the strategic level, when plans are being formulated that set the framework for proposed projects. The introduction of the SEA Directive should improve the practice of assessing cumulative effects. However, development plans cannot anticipate all development, neither can they anticipate all of the impacts for projects that are just concepts and for which no detail exists. Therefore, there will always be a need for cumulative effects to be considered at the project level as well.

Defining cumulative effects

9.172 There are a range of definitions of cumulative effects, but perhaps the simplest is:

'Cumulative effects are changes to the environment that are caused by an action in combination with other past, present and future human actions.'[1]

An understanding of such effects is better gained by considering practical examples of when and how they might occur:[2]

Physical-chemical transport: A physical or chemical emission is transported away from a proposed project where it then interacts with another pollutant (for example, air emissions, waste water effluent, sediment).   Several, entirely separate developments can therefore have a cumulative impact at a location some distance away from the project location.

Nibbling loss: Occurring as a result of the gradual disturbance and loss of land and habitat (for example, clearing of land for new housing and roads.)

Spatial and temporal crowding: Cumulative effects can occur when too much is happening within too small an area and in too brief a period of time. Spatial crowding results in an overlap of effects (for example, noise from a road adjacent to an industrial site, confluence of stack emission plumes. Temporal crowding may occur if effects from different actions overlap or occur before the receptor has had time to recover.

Growth-inducing potential: A project can induce further projects to occur (for example, a bypass for a town creating new development opportunities)

Combined effects: Occurring when different types of effects all affect the same receptor.   Assessed individually they may be considered to be insignificant, but when combined result in a significant effect on the receptor (for example, perceived change in the quality of life of a household or community).

1   The Cumulative Effects Assessment Working Group and Axys Environmental Consulting (1999), *Cumulative Effects Assessment Practitioners Guide*, Canadian Environmental Assessment Agency.

2   Based on Cumulative Effects Assessment Working Group (1999) and Hyder (1999), *Guidelines for the Assessment of Cumulative and Indirect Impacts as well as Impact Interactions*, European Commission.

9.173   The EIA Regulations indicate that the cumulative effects should be assessed alongside the more routine assessment of impacts undertaken as part of an EIA.   In practice, this is the case, but unless they are given specific treatment, it is unlikely that the assessment of cumulative effects will be successful.   Whilst the assessment of cumulative effects will be undertaken in accordance with the same process and using many of the same tools, the assessment of cumulative effects does have a different focus that does not normally appear in the assessment of more direct environmental effects.   Guidance issued by the President's Council on Environmental Quality in the USA sets out eight principles of cumulative effects that are designed to indicate how they differ from the other effects that are routinely addressed by EIA.   These are adapted and reproduced in box *.*.[1]   The principles emphasise that cumulative effects assessment is focused on the receptor (for example, air quality, habitat, species, landscape character) rather than on the effect of the proposal.   It examines the effect of the project, but in the context of the other factors which have affected it in the past, which will be concurrent with the proposed project, and are foreseeable in the future.   Of particular interest will be whether any environmental factors are close to a critical threshold that will generate an adverse change in its condition. The trends relating to a particular environmental factor will also be important. For example, if the population of a particular bird species has been in rapid decline, then a project that contributes to exacerbating the decline may be viewed with more concern than if the impact of the project is looked at in isolation.

1   Based on: Council on Environmental Quality (1997), *Considering Cumulative Effects Under the National Environmental Policy Act*, CEQ, Washington.

9.174   The process for assessing cumulative impacts is the same as for other environmental effects. The impacts are identified as part of the scoping process, they are assessed and any mitigation or management measures are designed to try and address the problem. However, some of the approaches differ to some degree.

SCOPING

9.175   Scoping of cumulative effects should be undertaken alongside the scoping of other impacts. Consideration should be given to all impacts, including those that may not be regarded as significant in terms of the direct effects. Questions such as whether there are any developments in the area that are having a similar effect, or whether there are any environmental resources that have been subjected to cumulative effects in the recent past, will need to be asked to determine whether cumulative effects are likely to be important. There are likely to be a range of cumulative effects, but as with the more direct effects, the purpose of scoping is to ensure that only those that are considered to be significant are assessed in any detail.

9.176   Given that cumulative effects assessment is about taking into consideration the environmental effects of other projects and actions, both in the past, present and future, it is important to set the boundaries for the assessment to ensure that the the study is sound, in terms of its consideration of the receptor, and reasonable, in terms of the resources that can be devoted to the assessment. The geographical boundaries and the time horizons are both likely to be expanded beyond those that would be considered for a more routine assessment. For example, for the impact on a particular habitat type, the study may be expanded to consider the frequency of occurrence of the habitat with the region, the importance of the habitat and any trends associated with its status. Setting the geographical boundaries may involve identifying natural resource boundaries rather than simply administrative ones. For example, the catchment area for a river is likely to have greater importance for CEA than a local authority boundary. There is likely to be some difficulty in identifying a reasonable time horizon. However, it would be usual to take into account projects that are being constructed, those that have received consent and those that are included in any development plans that affect the area. The consideration of any other future projects would normally be considered to be too speculative. The setting of a past time horizon may often be established by limitations of data. Otherwise, it may be relevant to go back several decades to monitor trends in changes to some environmental resources.

Assessing cumulative effects

9.177   Describing the baseline conditions for cumulative effects assessment is not markedly different from the description for other types of impacts. However, there is a greater focus on the other stresses and influences on the condition of the environment and on the capacity of the receiving environment to assimilate further change. The use of indicators may be helpful to indicate how the environment has changed over time.

9.178   Predicting the magnitude and significance of cumulative effects requires a clear understanding of the range of effects that may influence the resource that is of interest. It is likely that more attention would need to be given to indirect effects than might otherwise occur with a more routine EIA. The significance of the effect will be judged against regulations and standards, but also the understanding of any thresholds or capacity, which if exceeded might cause the resource to be irreversibly changed. The key difference between routine EIA and CEA is that the effects of other past, present and future actions are taken into account to determine the significance of effects.

Mitigation and management

9.179   The identification of any significant environmental effects should lead to the development of mitigation and management measures in order to avoid, reduce or offset the effects. These may relate to the particular proposal (for example, avoidance of particular areas of habitat so as not to contribute to the cumulative effect) or may involve the modification of past projects, or additional mitigation for other present or future projects. Imposing modifications on project that already have consent is likely to be difficult from a regulatory standpoint, although there may be opportunities associated with the renewal or variation of pollution control licenses. There is more scope for regulating other concurrent or future projects (for example, coordinating construction timing so as not to cause a significant cumulative noise effect on a local community).

9.180   The assessment of cumulative effects inevitably involves dealing with uncertainty and the techniques described in the chapter dealing with the EIA process can be adopted to address this. Specifically, monitoring and management is likely to form part of any mitigation package designed to address cumulative effects.

Sustainability and EIA for projects

9.181   The increasing emphasis being place on sustainability as a guiding principle for future economic development is now resulting in this issue being addressed by EIAs for many different types of project. The treatment of the issue is variable, ranging from a restatement of the mitigation measures to an analysis against the UK sustainability indicators. The variety of approaches reflects the lack of a current consensus on how sustainability should be treated at the project level. Nevertheless, it is clear that some of the approaches used are not supportable when subjected to testing against the principles of sustainable development.

9.182 Sustainability places the environment at the centre of future development and views it as an essential component of future economic and social development, rather than an alternative to it. Most projects that are subjected to an EIA are undertaken for financial gain, occasionally with an associated social purpose, for example urban regeneration projects. Any assessment of the sustainability of a project therefore focuses on environmental (and occasionally social) sustainability. The links between sustainability and EIA are further reinforced by the reference to EIA in the 1992 Rio Declaration (Principle 17).

9.183 Given that sustainability centres on the maintenance of resources for current and future generations it is implicit that any project that claims to be sustainable is claiming a certain level of environmental performance. For example, it implies that the impacts of the proposal are within the assimilative capacity of the environment. Understanding the basis for any sustainability claims is important.

9.184 ESs that attempt to address sustainability tend to focus on the extent to which the proposal includes measures that move the impacts of the development toward, rather than away from, sustainability. This assertion is usually made within the context of the proposal, rather than the existing environmental conditions. So, for example, the ES for a housing development that includes a transport plan designed to reduce the level of car use from that which would otherwise occur may claim the proposal is sustainable, with regard to its transport policy. However, a clearer understanding of the sustainability implications can be gained by considering the cumulative effects of the proposal with other actions, and the capacity of the receiving environment to accommodate any further stresses.

9.185 To try and steer development proposals to a more sustainable pattern the World Bank has developed sustainability tests, based on project inputs and outputs. These are given in box 10. Whilst this provides some indication of how the environmental sustainability of a project could be measured, in reality such a detailed measurement is likely to be impracticable, with the possible exception of assessing the energy demand of the project.

Box 10 World Bank Guidelines on Environmental Sustainability

OUTPUT GUIDE:

Waste emissions from a project should be within the assimilative capacity of the local environment to absorb without unacceptable degradation of its future waste absorptive capacity or other important services.

INPUT GUIDE:

Harvest rates of renewable resource inputs should be within regenerative capacity of the natural system that generates them; depletion rates of non-renewable resource inputs should be equal to the rate at which renewable substitutes are developed by human invention and investment.

Source: World Bank (1991), *Environmental Assessment Sourcebook*. Vol.1. Washington, D.C.: World, Bank Technical Paper No. 139.

9.186   Sadler has suggested that a modification of the World Bank guidelines could be used to develop EIA into a tool used for sustainability assurance.[1] Government guidelines and standards could be used as the basis for setting critical thresholds, but stricter interpretations of the precautionary principle would be required where there is a threat of significant or irreversible damage. Most EIAs set out to achieve the design of a project that does not exceed any regulatory thresholds. For issues such as biodiversity, strict definitions of thresholds and capacities are more difficult and the strict interpretation of the precautionary principle will be more frequently required.

1   B Sadler (1996), *International Study of the Effectiveness of Environmental Assessment Final Report: Environmental Assessment In A Changing World: Evaluating Practice to Improve Performance*, International Association for Impact Assessment & Canadian Environmental Assessment Agency.

9.187   In combination with the above approach, Sadler also suggests that where significant effects are likely to occur, affecting high value resources, the acceptability of the proposal should be assessed with particular attention given to the resources and functions that will be affected. The purpose would be for the project proponent to demonstrate that the benefits of the project far outweigh the cost of any impact. Failure to achieve this would result in a strict precautionary principle being applied, i.e. the project would not receive consent, and the effects on critical ecological resources and processes would be avoided.

9.188   The final element in this approach to sustainability is to implement 'in-kind' compensation for all residual impacts. This may be on the basis of strict replacement for those resources that are considered to be of high value. For those resources that are abundant it could be considered permissible to trade off against other resources or processes that are considered to be of higher value.

9.189   The approach outlined above is imprecise and open to varying interpretation. This reflects the present lack of sufficient tools to address sustainability within the framework of EIA. Nevertheless, the approach does indicate that the impact of a project should be tested, and suggests a proportionate response that may result in the project being refused or in the setting of significant mitigation hurdles that must be overcome in order for the project to proceed. The inclusion of the 'in-kind' compensation for all residual impacts could assist in arresting the adverse contribution that many projects make to the significant cumulative effects, despite having been subject to EIA.

Town and Country Planning (Environmental Impact Assessment) (England and Wales) Regulations 1999 (SI 1999/293)

Town and Country Planning (Environmental Impact Assessment)
(England and Wales) Regulations 1999*

1999 No 293

Made   10th February 1999

Laid before Parliament   19th February 1999

Coming into force   14th March 1999

The Secretary of State for the Environment, Transport and the Regions, as respects England, and the Secretary of State for Wales, as respects Wales, being designated Ministers for the purposes of section 2(2) of the European Communities Act 1972 in relation to measures relating to the requirement for an assessment of the impact on the environment of projects likely to have significant effects on the environment, in exercise of the powers conferred by that section and section 71A of the Town and Country Planning Act 1990 and of all other powers enabling them in that behalf, and having taken into account the selection criteria in Annex III to Council Directive 85/337/EEC as amended by Council Directive 97/11/EC hereby make the following Regulations:—

PART 1
GENERAL

1   Citation, commencement and application

(1)   These Regulations may be cited as the Town and Country Planning (Environmental Impact Assessment) (England and Wales) Regulations 1999 and shall come into force on 14 March 1999.

(2)   Subject to paragraph (3), these Regulations shall apply throughout England and Wales.

* NOTE: These Regulations apply to planning applications made after 14 March 1999.

(3)   Paragraphs (2) and (5)(a) of regulation 14 shall not apply to the Isles of Scilly and, in relation to the Isles of Scilly, the reference in paragraph (6) of that regulation to paragraph (5) of that regulation shall be construed as a reference to paragraph (5)(b).

2   Interpretation

(1)   In these Regulations—

'the Act' means the Town and Country Planning Act 1990 and references to sections are references to sections of that Act;

['the 1991 Act' means the Planning and Compensation Act 1991;]

['the 1995 Act' means the Environment Act 1995;]

'the consultation bodies' means—
  (a)   any body which the relevant planning authority is required to consult, or would, if an application for planning permission for the development in question were before them, be required to consult by virtue of article 10 (consultations before the grant of permission) of the Order or of any direction under that article; and
  (b)   the following bodies if not referred to in sub-paragraph (a)—
        (i)   any principal council for the area where the land is situated, if not the relevant planning authority;
        (ii)   where the land is situated in England, the Countryside Commission and [English Nature];
        (iii) where the land is situated in Wales, the Countryside Council for Wales; and
        (iv)   the Environment Agency;

'the Directive' means Council Directive 85/337/EEC;

['EEA State' means a State party to the Agreement on the European Economic Area;]

'EIA application' means an application for planning permission for EIA development;

'EIA development' means development which is either—
  (a)   Schedule 1 development; or
  (b)   Schedule 2 development likely to have significant effects on the environment by virtue of factors such as its nature, size or location;

'environmental information' means the environmental statement, including any further information, any representations made by any body required by these Regulations to be invited to make representations, and any representations duly made by any other person about the environmental effects of the development;

'environmental statement' means a statement—
  (a)   that includes such of the information referred to in Part I of Schedule 4 as is reasonably required to assess the environmental effects of the development and which the applicant can, having regard in particular to

current knowledge and methods of assessment, reasonably be required to compile, but
(b) that includes at least the information referred to in Part II of Schedule 4;

'exempt development' means development which comprises or forms part of a project serving national defence purposes or in respect of which the Secretary of State has made a direction under regulation 4(4);

'further information' has the meaning given in regulation 19(1);

'General Regulations' means the Town and Country Planning General Regulations 1992;

'inspector' means a person appointed by the Secretary of State pursuant to Schedule 6 to the Act to determine an appeal;

'the land' means the land on which the development would be carried out or, in relation to development already carried out, has been carried out;

'the Order' means the Town and Country Planning (General Development Procedure) Order 1995;

'principal council' has the meaning given by sub-section (1) of section 270 (general provisions as to interpretation) of the Local Government Act 1972;

'register' means a register kept pursuant to section 69 (registers of applications etc) and 'appropriate register' means the register on which particulars of an application for planning permission for the relevant development have been placed or would fall to be placed if such an application were made;

['relevant mineral planning authority' means the body to whom it falls, fell, or would, but for a direction under paragraph—
(a) 7 of Schedule 2 to the 1991 Act;
(b) 13 of Schedule 13 to the 1995 Act; or
(c) 8 of Schedule 14 to the 1995 Act,
    fall to determine the ROMP application in question;]

'relevant planning authority' means the body to whom it falls, fell, or would, but for a direction under section 77 (reference of applications to Secretary of State), fall to determine an application for planning permission for the development in question;

['ROMP application' means an application to a relevant mineral planning authority to determine the conditions to which a planning permission is to be subject under paragraph—
(a) 2(2) of Schedule 2 to the 1991 Act (registration of old mining permissions);
(b) 9(1) of Schedule 13 to the 1995 Act (review of old mineral planning permissions); or
(c) 6(1) of Schedule 14 to the 1995 Act (periodic review of mineral planning permissions);]

['ROMP development' means development which has yet to be carried out and which is authorised by a planning permission in respect of which a ROMP application has been or is to be made;]

'Schedule 1 application' and 'Schedule 2 application' mean an application for planning permission for Schedule 1 development and Schedule 2 development respectively;

'Schedule 1 development' means development, other than exempt development, of a description mentioned in Schedule 1;

'Schedule 2 development' means development, other than exempt development, of a description mentioned in Column 1 of the table in Schedule 2 where—
    (a) any part of that development is to be carried out in a sensitive area; or
    (b) any applicable threshold or criterion in the corresponding part of Column 2 of that table is respectively exceeded or met in relation to that development;

'scoping direction' and 'scoping opinion' have the meanings given in regulation 10;

'screening direction' means a direction made by the Secretary of State as to whether development is EIA development;

'screening opinion' means a written statement of the opinion of the relevant planning authority as to whether development is EIA development;

'sensitive area' means any of the following—
    (a) land notified under sub-section (1) of section 28 (areas of special scientific interest) of the Wildlife and Countryside Act 1981;
    (b) land to which sub-section (3) of section 29 (nature conservation orders) of the Wildlife and Countryside Act 1981 applies;
    (c) an area to which paragraph (u)(ii) in the table in article 10 of the Order applies;
    (d) a National Park within the meaning of the National Parks and Access to the Countryside Act 1949;
    (e) the Broads;
    (f) a property appearing on the World Heritage List kept under article 11(2) of the 1972 UNESCO Convention for the Protection of the World Cultural and Natural Heritage;
    (g) a scheduled monument within the meaning of the Ancient Monuments and Archaeological Areas Act 1979;
    (h) an area of outstanding natural beauty designated as such by an order made by the Countryside Commission, as respects England, or the Countryside Council for Wales, as respects Wales, under section 87 (designation of areas of outstanding natural beauty) of the National Parks and Access to the Countryside Act 1949 as confirmed by the Secretary of State;
        (i) a European site within the meaning of regulation 10 of the Conservation (Natural Habitats etc) Regulations 1994.

(2)   Subject to paragraph (3), expressions used both in these Regulations and in the Act have the same meaning for the purposes of these Regulations as they have for the purposes of the Act.

(3)   Expressions used both in these Regulations and in the Directive (whether or not also used in the Act) have the same meaning for the purposes of these Regulations as they have for the purposes of the Directive.

(4)   In these Regulations any reference to a Council Directive is a reference to that Directive as amended at the date these Regulations were made.

(5)   In these Regulations references to the Secretary of State shall not be construed as references to an inspector.

[(6)   In its application to Wales, these Regulations shall have effect, with any necessary amendments, as if each reference to 'the Secretary of State' were a reference to 'the National Assembly for Wales'.]

NOTES

Para (1): definition 'the 1991 Act' inserted by SI 2000/2867, reg 2(1), (2)(a). Date in force: 15 November 2000: see SI 2000/2867, reg 1(1).

Para (1): definition 'the 1995 Act' inserted by SI 2000/2867, reg 2(1), (2)(a). Date in force: 15 November 2000: see SI 2000/2867, reg 1(1).

Para (1): in definition 'the consultation bodies' in para (b)(ii) words 'English Nature' in square brackets substituted by virtue of the Countryside and Rights of Way Act 2000, s 73(2). Date in force: 30 January 2001: see the Countryside and Rights of Way Act 2000, s 103(2).

Para (1): definition 'EEA State' inserted by SI 2000/2867, reg 2(1), (2)(b). Date in force: 15 November 2000: see SI 2000/2867, reg 1(1).

Para (1): definition 'relevant mineral planning authority' inserted by SI 2000/2867, reg 2(1), (2)(c). Date in force: 15 November 2000: see SI 2000/2867, reg 1(1).

Para (1): definition 'ROMP application' inserted by SI 2000/2867, reg 2(1), (2)(d). Date in force: 15 November 2000: see SI 2000/2867, reg 1(1).

Para (1): definition 'ROMP development' inserted by SI 2000/2867, reg 2(1), (2)(d). Date in force: 15 November 2000: see SI 2000/2867, reg 1(1).

Para (6): inserted by SI 2000/2867, reg 2(1), (2)(e). Date in force: 15 November 2000: see SI 2000/ 2867, reg 1(1).

3   Prohibition on granting planning permission without consideration of environmental information

(1)   This regulation applies—
    (a)   to every EIA application received by the authority with whom it is lodged on or after the commencement of these Regulations; and
    (b)   to every EIA application lodged by an authority pursuant to regulation 3 or 4 (applications for planning permission) of the General Regulations on or after that date;

and for the purposes of this paragraph, the date of receipt of an application by an authority shall be determined in accordance with paragraph (3) of article 20 (time periods for decision) of the Order.

(2)   The relevant planning authority or the Secretary of State or an inspector shall not grant planning permission pursuant to an application to which this regulation applies unless they have first taken the environmental information into consideration, and they shall state in their decision that they have done so.

PART II
SCREENING

4 General provisions relating to screening

(1)   Subject to paragraphs (3) and (4), the occurrence of an event mentioned in paragraph (2) shall determine for the purpose of these Regulations that development is EIA development.

(2)   The events referred to in paragraph (1) are—
 (a) the submission by the applicant or appellant in relation to that development of a statement referred to by the applicant or appellant as an environmental statement for the purposes of these Regulations; or
 (b) the adoption by the relevant planning authority of a screening opinion to the effect that the development is EIA development.

(3)   A direction of the Secretary of State shall determine for the purpose of these Regulations whether development is or is not EIA development.

(4)   The Secretary of State may direct that particular proposed development is exempted from the application of these Regulations in accordance with Article 2(3) of the Directive (but without prejudice to Article 7 of the Directive) and shall send a copy of any such direction to the relevant planning authority.

(5)   Where a local planning authority or the Secretary of State has to decide under these Regulations whether Schedule 2 development is EIA development the authority or Secretary of State shall take into account in making that decision such of the selection criteria set out in Schedule 3 as are relevant to the development.

(6)   Where—
 (a) a local planning authority adopt a screening opinion; or
 (b) the Secretary of State makes a screening direction under these Regulations;
     to the effect that development is EIA development—
      (i) that opinion or direction shall be accompanied by a written statement giving clearly and precisely the full reasons for that conclusion; and
      (ii) the authority or the Secretary of State, as the case may be, shall send a copy of the opinion or direction and a copy of the written statement required by sub-paragraph (i) to the person who proposes to carry out, or who has carried out, the development in question.

(7)   The Secretary of State may make a screening direction irrespective of whether he has received a request to do so.

(8)   The Secretary of State may direct that particular development of a description mentioned in Column 1 of the table in Schedule 2 is EIA development in spite of the fact that none of the conditions contained in sub-paragraphs (a) and (b) of the definition of 'Schedule 2 development' is satisfied in relation to that development.

(9)   The Secretary of State shall send a copy of any screening direction to the relevant planning authority.

5 Requests for screening opinions of the local planning authority

(1)   A person who is minded to carry out development may request the relevant planning authority to adopt a screening opinion.

(2)   A request for a screening opinion shall be accompanied by—
   (a) a plan sufficient to identify the land;
   (b) a brief description of the nature and purpose of the development and of its possible effects on the environment; and
   (c) such other information or representations as the person making the request may wish to provide or make.

(3)   An authority receiving a request for a screening opinion shall, if they consider that they have not been provided with sufficient information to adopt an opinion, notify in writing the person making the request of the points on which they require additional information.

(4)   An authority shall adopt a screening opinion within three weeks beginning with the date of receipt of a request made pursuant to paragraph (1) or such longer period as may be agreed in writing with the person making the request.

(5)   An authority which adopts a screening opinion pursuant to paragraph (4) shall forthwith send a copy to the person who made the request.

(6)   Where an authority—
   (a) fail to adopt a screening opinion within the relevant period mentioned in paragraph (4); or
   (b) adopt an opinion to the effect that the development is EIA development;
   the person who requested the opinion may request the Secretary of State to make a screening direction.

(7)   The person may make a request pursuant to paragraph (6) even if the authority has not received additional information which is sought under paragraph (3).

6 Requests for screening directions of the Secretary of State

(1)   A person who pursuant to regulation 5(6) requests the Secretary of State to make a screening direction shall submit with his request—
   (a) a copy of his request to the relevant planning authority under regulation 5(1) and the documents which accompanied it;
   (b) a copy of any notification under regulation 5(3) which he has received and of any response;
   (c) a copy of any screening opinion he has received from the authority and of any accompanying statement of reasons; and
   (d) any representations that he wishes to make.

(2)   When a person makes a request pursuant to regulation 5(6) he shall send to the relevant planning authority a copy of that request and of any representations he makes to the Secretary of State.

(3)   The Secretary of State shall, if he considers that he has not been provided with sufficient information to make a screening direction, notify in writing the person making the request pursuant to regulation 5(6) of the points on which he requires additional information, and may request the relevant planning authority to provide such information as they can on any of those points.

(4)   The Secretary of State shall make a screening direction within three weeks beginning with the date of receipt of a request pursuant to regulation 5(6) or such longer period as he may reasonably require.

(5)   The Secretary of State shall send a copy of any screening direction made pursuant to paragraph (4) forthwith to the person who made the request.

PART III
PROCEDURES CONCERNING APPLICATIONS FOR PLANNING PERMISSION

7   Application made to a local planning authority without an environmental statement

(1)   Where it appears to the relevant planning authority that—
  (a) an application for planning permission which is before them for determination is a Schedule 1 application or Schedule 2 application; and
  (b) the development in question has not been the subject of a screening opinion or screening direction; and
  (c) the application is not accompanied by a statement referred to by the applicant as an environmental statement for the purposes of these Regulations,
paragraphs (3) and (4) of regulation 5 shall apply as if the receipt or lodging of the application were a request made under regulation 5(1).

(2)   Where an EIA application which is before a local planning authority for determination is not accompanied by a statement referred to by the applicant as an environmental statement for the purposes of these Regulations, the authority shall notify the applicant in writing that the submission of an environmental statement is required.

(3)   An authority shall notify the applicant in accordance with paragraph (2) within three weeks beginning with the date of receipt of the application or such longer period as may be agreed in writing with the applicant; but where the Secretary of State, after the expiry of that period of three weeks or of any longer period so agreed, makes a screening direction to the effect that the development is EIA development, the authority shall so notify the applicant within seven days beginning with the date the authority received a copy of that screening direction.

(4)   An applicant receiving a notification pursuant to paragraph (2) may, within three weeks beginning with the date of the notification, write to the authority stating—
  (a) that he accepts their view and is providing an environmental statement; or

(b) unless the Secretary of State has made a screening direction in respect of the development, that he is writing to the Secretary of State to request a screening direction.

(5)   If the applicant does not write to the authority in accordance with paragraph (4), the permission sought shall, unless the Secretary of State has made a screening direction to the effect that the development is not EIA development, be deemed to be refused at the end of the relevant three week period, and the deemed refusal—

(a) shall be treated as a decision of the authority for the purposes of paragraph (4)(c) of article 25 (register of applications) of the Order; but

(b) shall not give rise to an appeal to the Secretary of State by virtue of section 78 (right to appeal against planning decisions and failure to take such decisions).

(6)   An authority which has given a notification in accordance with paragraph (2) shall, unless the Secretary of State makes a screening direction to the effect that the development is not EIA development, determine the relevant application only by refusing planning permission if the applicant does not submit an environmental statement and comply with regulation 14(5).

(7)   A person who requests a screening direction pursuant to sub-paragraph (4)(b) shall send to the Secretary of State with his request copies of—

(a) his application for planning permission;

(b) all documents sent to the authority as part of the application; and

(c) all correspondence between the applicant and the authority relating to the proposed development,

and paragraphs (2) to (5) of regulation 6 shall apply to a request under this regulation as they apply to a request made pursuant to regulation 5(6).

8   Application referred to the Secretary of State without an environmental statement

(1)   Where it appears to the Secretary of State that an application for planning permission which has been referred to him for determination—

(a) is a Schedule 1 application or Schedule 2 application; and

(b) the development in question has not been the subject of a screening opinion or screening direction; and

(c) the application is not accompanied by a statement referred to by the applicant as an environmental statement for the purposes of these Regulations,

paragraphs (3) and (4) of regulation 6 shall apply as if the referral of the application were a request made by the applicant pursuant to regulation 5(6).

(2)   Where it appears to the Secretary of State that an application which has been referred to him for determination is an EIA application and is not accompanied by a statement referred to by the applicant as an environmental statement for the purposes of these Regulations, he shall notify the applicant in writing that the submission of an environmental statement is required and shall send a copy of that notification to the relevant planning authority.

(3)   The Secretary of State shall notify the applicant in accordance with paragraph (2) within three weeks beginning with the date he received the application or such longer period as he may reasonably require.

(4)   An applicant who receives a notification under paragraph (2) may within three weeks beginning with the date of the notification write to the Secretary of State stating that he proposes to provide an environmental statement.

(5)   If the applicant does not write in accordance with paragraph (4), the Secretary of State shall be under no duty to deal with the application; and at the end of the three week period he shall inform the applicant in writing that no further action is being taken on the application.

(6)   Where the Secretary of State has given a notification under paragraph (2), he shall determine the relevant application only by refusing planning permission if the applicant does not submit an environmental statement and comply with regulation 14(5).

9   Appeal to the Secretary of State without an environmental statement

(1)   Where on consideration of an appeal under section 78 (right to appeal against planning decisions and failure to take such decisions) it appears to the Secretary of State that—

    (a)   the relevant application is a Schedule 1 application or Schedule 2 application; and

    (b)   the development in question has not been the subject of a screening opinion or screening direction; and

    (c)   the relevant application is not accompanied by a statement referred to by the appellant as an environmental statement for the purposes of these Regulations,

paragraphs (3) and (4) of regulation 6 shall apply as if the appeal were a request made by the appellant pursuant to regulation 5(6).

(2)   Where an inspector is dealing with an appeal and a question arises as to whether the relevant application is an EIA application and it appears to the inspector that it may be such an application, the inspector shall refer that question to the Secretary of State and shall not determine the appeal, except by refusing planning permission, before he receives a screening direction.

(3)   Paragraphs (3) and (4) of regulation 6 shall apply to a question referred under paragraph (2) as if the referral of that question were a request made by the appellant pursuant to regulation 5(6).

(4)   Where it appears to the Secretary of State that the relevant application is an EIA application and is not accompanied by a statement referred to by the appellant as an environmental statement for the purposes of these Regulations, he shall notify the appellant in writing that the submission of an environmental statement is required and shall send a copy of that notification to the relevant planning authority.

(5)   An appellant who receives a notification under paragraph (4) may within three weeks beginning with the date of the notification write to the Secretary of State stating that he proposes to provide an environmental statement.

(6)   If the appellant does not write in accordance with paragraph (5), the Secretary of State or, where relevant, the inspector shall be under no duty to deal with the appeal; and at the end of the three week period he shall inform the appellant that no further action is being taken on the appeal.

(7)   Where the Secretary of State has given a notification under paragraph (4), the Secretary of State or, where relevant, the inspector shall determine the appeal only by refusing planning permission if the appellant does not submit an environmental statement and comply with regulation 14(5).

PART IV
PREPARATION OF ENVIRONMENTAL STATEMENTS

10 Scoping opinions of the local planning authority

(1)   A person who is minded to make an EIA application may ask the relevant planning authority to state in writing their opinion as to the information to be provided in the environmental statement (a 'scoping opinion').

(2)   A request under paragraph (1) shall include—
  (a) a plan sufficient to identify the land;
  (b) a brief description of the nature and purpose of the development and of its possible effects on the environment; and
  (c) such other information or representations as the person making the request may wish to provide or make.

(3)   An authority receiving a request under paragraph (1) shall, if they consider that they have not been provided with sufficient information to adopt a scoping opinion, notify the person making the request of the points on which they require additional information.

(4)   An authority shall not adopt a scoping opinion in response to a request under paragraph (1) until they have consulted the person who made the request and the consultation bodies, but shall, subject to paragraph (5), within five weeks beginning with the date of receipt of that request or such longer period as may be agreed in writing with the person making the request, adopt a scoping opinion and send a copy to the person who made the request.

(5)   Where a person has, at the same time as making a request for a screening opinion under regulation 5(1), asked the authority for an opinion under paragraph (1) above, and the authority have adopted a screening opinion to the effect that the development is EIA development, the authority shall, within five weeks beginning with the date on which that screening opinion was adopted or such longer period as may be agreed in writing with the person making the request, adopt a scoping opinion and send a copy to the person who made the request.

(6)   Before adopting a scoping opinion the authority shall take into account—
(a) the specific characteristics of the particular development;
(b) the specific characteristics of development of the type concerned; and
(c) the environmental features likely to be affected by the development.

(7)   Where an authority fail to adopt a scoping opinion within the relevant period mentioned in paragraph (4) or (5), the person who requested the opinion may under regulation 11(1) ask the Secretary of State to make a direction as to the information to be provided in the environmental statement (a 'scoping direction').

(8)   Paragraph (7) applies notwithstanding that the authority may not have received additional information which they have sought under paragraph (3).

(9)   An authority which has adopted a scoping opinion in response to a request under paragraph (1) shall not be precluded from requiring of the person who made the request additional information in connection with any statement that may be submitted by that person as an environmental statement in connection with an application for planning permission for the same development as was referred to in the request.

11 Scoping directions of the Secretary of State

(1)   A request made under this paragraph pursuant to regulation 10(7) shall include—
(a) a copy of the relevant request to the relevant planning authority under regulation 10(1);
(b) a copy of any relevant notification under regulation 10(3) and of any response;
(c) a copy of any relevant screening opinion received by the person making the request and of any accompanying statement of reasons; and
(d) any representations that the person making the request wishes to make.

(2)   When a person makes a request under paragraph (1) he shall send to the relevant planning authority a copy of that request, but that copy need not include the matters mentioned in sub-paragraphs (a) to (c) of that paragraph.

(3)   The Secretary of State shall notify in writing the person making the request of any points on which he considers the information provided pursuant to paragraph (1) is insufficient to enable him to make a scoping direction; and may request the relevant planning authority to provide such information as they can on any of those points.

(4)   The Secretary of State shall not make a scoping direction in response to a request under paragraph (1) until he has consulted the person making the request and the consultation bodies, but shall, within five weeks beginning with the date of receipt of that request or such longer period as he may reasonably require, make a direction and send a copy to the person who made the request and to the relevant planning authority.

(5)   Before making a scoping direction the Secretary of State shall take into account the matters specified in regulation 10(6).

(6)   Where the Secretary of State has made a scoping direction in response to a request under paragraph (1) neither he nor the relevant planning authority shall be

precluded from requiring of the person who made the request additional information in connection with any statement that may be submitted by that person as an environmental statement in connection with an application for planning permission for the same development as was referred to in the request.

12 Procedure to facilitate preparation of environmental statements

(1)   Any person who intends to submit an environmental statement to the relevant planning authority or the Secretary of State under these Regulations may give notice in writing to that authority or the Secretary of State under this paragraph.

(2)   A notice under paragraph (1) shall include the information necessary to identify the land and the nature and purpose of the development, and shall indicate the main environmental consequences to which the person giving the notice proposes to refer in his environmental statement.

(3)   The recipient of—
    (a)   such notice as is mentioned in paragraph (1); or
    (b)   a written statement made pursuant to regulation 7(4)(a), or 8(4) or 9(5)
    shall—
       (i)   notify the consultation bodies in writing of the name and address of the person who intends to submit an environmental statement and of the duty imposed on the consultation bodies by paragraph (4) to make information available to that person; and
      (ii)   inform in writing the person who intends to submit an environmental statement of the names and addresses of the bodies so notified.

(4)   Subject to paragraph (5), the relevant planning authority and any body notified in accordance with paragraph (3) shall, if requested by the person who intends to submit an environmental statement enter into consultation with that person to determine whether the [authority or] body has in its possession any information which he or they consider relevant to the preparation of the environmental statement and, if they have, the [authority or] body shall make that information available to that person.

(5)   Paragraph (4) shall not require the disclosure of information which is capable of being treated as confidential, or must be so treated, under regulation 4 of the Environmental Information Regulations 1992.

(6)   A reasonable charge reflecting the cost of making the relevant information available may be made by [an authority or body], which makes information available in accordance with paragraph (4).

NOTES

Para (4): words 'authority or' in square brackets in both places they occur inserted by SI 2000/2867, reg 2(1), (3)(a). Date in force: 15 November 2000: see SI 2000/2867, reg 1(1).
Para (6): words 'an authority or body' in square brackets substituted by SI 2000/2867, reg 2(1), (3)(b). Date in force: 15 November 2000: see SI 2000/2867, reg 1(1).

PART V
PUBLICITY AND PROCEDURES ON SUBMISSION OF ENVIRONMENTAL
STATEMENTS

13 Procedure where an environmental statement is submitted to a local planning authority

(1)   When an applicant making an EIA application submits to the relevant planning authority a statement which he refers to as an environmental statement for the purposes of these Regulations he shall provide the authority with three additional copies of the statement for transmission to the Secretary of State and, if at the same time he serves a copy of the statement on any other body, he shall—
   (a)   serve with it a copy of the application and any plan submitted with the application (unless he has already served these documents on the body in question);
   (b)   inform the body that representations may be made to the relevant planning authority; and
   (c)   inform the authority of the name of every body whom he has so served and of the date of service.

(2)   When a relevant planning authority receive in connection with an EIA application such a statement as is first mentioned in paragraph (1) the authority shall—
   (a)   send to the Secretary of State, within 14 days of receipt of the statement, three copies of the statement and a copy of the relevant application and of any documents submitted with the application;
   (b)   inform the applicant of the number of copies required to enable the authority to comply with sub-paragraph (c) below; and
   (c)   forward to any consultation body which has not received a copy direct from the applicant a copy of the statement and inform any such consultation body that they may make representations.

(3)   The applicant shall send the copies required for the purposes of paragraph (2)(c) to the relevant planning authority.

(4)   The relevant planning authority shall not determine the application until the expiry of 14 days from the last date on which a copy of the statement was served in accordance with this regulation.

14 Publicity where an environmental statement is submitted after the planning application

(1)   Where an application for planning permission has been made without a statement which the applicant refers to as an environmental statement for the purposes of these Regulations and the applicant proposes to submit such a statement, he shall, before submitting it, comply with paragraphs (2) to (4).

(2)   The applicant shall publish in a local newspaper circulating in the locality in which the land is situated a notice stating—

    (a) his name and that he is the applicant for planning permission and the name and address of the relevant planning authority;

    (b) the date on which the application was made and, if it be the case, that it has been referred to the Secretary of State for determination or is the subject of an appeal to him;

    (c) the address or location and the nature of the proposed development;

    (d) that a copy of the application and of any plan and other documents submitted with it together with a copy of the environmental statement may be inspected by members of the public at all reasonable hours;

    (e) an address in the locality in which the land is situated at which those documents may be inspected, and the latest date on which they will be available for inspection (being a date not less than 21 days later than the date on which the notice is published);

    (f) an address (whether or not the same as that given under sub-paragraph (e)) in the locality in which the land is situated at which copies of the statement may be obtained;

    (g) that copies may be obtained there so long as stocks last;

    (h) if a charge is to be made for a copy, the amount of the charge;

    (i) that any person wishing to make representations about the application should make them in writing, before the date named in accordance with sub-paragraph (e), to the relevant planning authority or (in the case of an application referred to the Secretary of State or an appeal) to the Secretary of State; and

    (j) in the case of an application referred to the Secretary of State or an appeal, the address to which representations should be sent.

(3)   The applicant shall, unless he has not, and was not reasonably able to acquire, such rights as would enable him to do so, post on the land a notice containing the information specified in paragraph (2), except that the date named as the latest date on which the documents will be available for inspection shall be not less than 21 days later than the date on which the notice is first posted.

(4)   The notice mentioned in paragraph (3) must—

    (a) be left in position for not less than seven days in the 28 days immediately preceding the date of the submission of the statement; and

    (b) be affixed firmly to some object on the land and sited and displayed in such a way as to be easily visible to, and readable by, members of the public without going on to the land.

(5)   The statement, when submitted, shall be accompanied by—

    (a) a copy of the notice mentioned in paragraph (2) certified by or on behalf of the applicant as having been published in a named newspaper on a date specified in the certificate; and

    (b) a certificate by or on behalf of the applicant which states either—

        (i) that he has posted a notice on the land in compliance with this regulation and when he did so, and that the notice was left in position for not less than seven days in the 28 days immediately preceding the date of the submission of the statement, or that, without any fault or intention on his part, it was removed, obscured or defaced before seven days had elapsed and he took reasonable steps for its protection or replacement, specifying the steps taken; or

   (ii) that the applicant was unable to comply with paragraphs (3) and (4) above because he did not have the necessary rights to do so; that he has taken such reasonable steps as are open to him to acquire those rights; and has been unable to do so, specifying the steps taken.

(6)   Where an applicant indicates that he proposes to provide such a statement and in such circumstances as are mentioned in paragraph (1), the relevant planning authority, the Secretary of State or the inspector, as the case may be, shall (unless disposed to refuse the permission sought) suspend consideration of the application or appeal until receipt of the statement and the other documents mentioned in paragraph (5); and shall not determine it during the period of 21 days beginning with the date of receipt of the statement and the other documents so mentioned.

(7)   If any person issues a certificate which purports to comply with the requirements of paragraph (5)(b) and which contains a statement which he knows to be false or misleading in a material particular, or recklessly issues a certificate which purports to comply with those requirements and which contains a statement which is false or misleading in a material particular, he shall be guilty of an offence and liable on summary conviction to a fine not exceeding level 3 on the standard scale.

(8)   Where it is proposed to submit an environmental statement in connection with an appeal, this regulation applies with the substitution, except in paragraph (2)(a), of references to the appellant for references to the applicant.

15 Provision of copies of environmental statements and further information for the Secretary of State on referral or appeal

Where an applicant for planning permission has submitted to the relevant planning authority in connection with his application a statement which he refers to as an environmental statement for the purposes of these Regulations, or further information, and—

(a) the application is referred to the Secretary of State under section 77 (reference of applications to Secretary of State); or

(b) the applicant appeals under section 78 (right to appeal against planning decisions and failure to take such decisions),

the applicant shall supply the Secretary of State with three copies of the statement and, where relevant, the further information unless, in the case of a referred application, the relevant planning authority have done so when referring the application to him.

16 Procedure where an environmental statement is submitted to the Secretary of State

(1)   This regulation applies where an applicant submits to the Secretary of State, in relation to an EIA application which is before the Secretary of State or an inspector for determination or is the subject of an appeal to the Secretary of State, a statement which the applicant or appellant refers to as an environmental statement for the purposes of these Regulations.

(2)   The applicant or appellant shall submit four copies of the statement to the Secretary of State who shall send one copy to the relevant planning authority.

(3)   If at the same time as he submits a statement to the Secretary of State the applicant or appellant serves a copy of it on any other body, he shall comply with regulations 13(1)(a) and 13(1)(b) as if the reference in regulation 13(1)(b) to the relevant planning authority were a reference to the Secretary of State, and inform the Secretary of State of the matters mentioned in regulation 13(1)(c).

(4)   The Secretary of State shall comply with regulation 13(2) (except sub-paragraph (a) of that regulation) and the applicant or appellant with regulation 13(3) as if—
  (a)   references in those provisions to the relevant planning authority were references to the Secretary of State; and,
  (b)   in the case of an appeal, references to the applicant were references to the appellant;
and the Secretary of State or the inspector shall comply with regulation 13(4) as if it referred to him instead of to the relevant planning authority.

17 Availability of copies of environmental statements

An applicant for planning permission or an appellant who submits in connection with his application or appeal a statement which he refers to as an environmental statement for the purposes of these Regulations shall ensure that a reasonable number of copies of the statement are available at the address named in the notices published or posted pursuant to article 8 of the Order or regulation 14 as the address at which such copies may be obtained.

18 Charges for copies of environmental statements

A reasonable charge reflecting printing and distribution costs may be made to a member of the public for a copy of a statement made available in accordance with regulation 17.

19 Further information and evidence respecting environmental statements

(1)   Where the relevant planning authority, the Secretary of State or an inspector is dealing with an application or appeal in relation to which the applicant or appellant has submitted a statement which he refers to as an environmental statement for the purposes of these Regulations, and is of the opinion that the statement should contain additional information in order to be an environmental statement, they or he shall notify the applicant or appellant in writing accordingly, and the applicant or appellant shall provide that additional information; and such information provided by the applicant or appellant is referred to in these Regulations as 'further information'.

(2)   Paragraphs (3) to (9) shall apply in relation to further information, except in so far as the further information is provided for the purposes of an inquiry held under the Act and the request for that information made pursuant to paragraph (1) stated that it was to be provided for such purposes.

(3)   The recipient of further information pursuant to paragraph (1) shall publish in a local newspaper circulating in the locality in which the land is situated a notice stating—
   (a) the name of the applicant for planning permission or the appellant (as the case may be) and the name and address of the relevant planning authority;
   (b) the date on which the application was made and, if it be the case, that it has been referred to the Secretary of State for determination or is the subject of an appeal to him;
   (c) the address or location and the nature of the proposed development;
   (d) that further information is available in relation to an environmental statement which has already been provided;
   (e) that a copy of the further information may be inspected by members of the public at all reasonable hours;
   (f) an address in the locality in which the land is situated at which the further information may be inspected and the latest date on which it will be available for inspection (being a date not less than 21 days later than the date on which the notice is published);
   (g) an address (whether or not the same as that given pursuant to sub-paragraph (f)) in the locality in which the land is situated at which copies of the further information may be obtained;
   (h) that copies may be obtained there so long as stocks last;
   (i) if a charge is to be made for a copy, the amount of the charge;
   (j) that any person wishing to make representations about the further information should make them in writing, before the date specified in accordance with sub-paragraph (f), to the relevant planning authority, the Secretary of State or the inspector (as the case may be); and
   (k) the address to which representations should be sent.

(4)   The recipient of the further information shall send a copy of it to each person to whom, in accordance with these Regulations, the statement to which it relates was sent.

(5)   Where the recipient of the further information is the relevant planning authority they shall send to the Secretary of State three copies of the further information.

(6)   The recipient of the further information may by notice in writing require the applicant or appellant to provide such number of copies of the further information as is specified in the notice (being the number required for the purposes of paragraph (4) or (5)).

(7)   Where information is requested under paragraph (1), the relevant planning authority, the Secretary of State or the inspector, as the case may be, shall suspend determination of the application or appeal, and shall not determine it before the expiry of 14 days after the date on which the further information was sent to all persons to whom the statement to which it relates was sent or the expiry of 21 days after the date that notice of it was published in a local newspaper, whichever is the later.

(8)   The applicant or appellant who provides further information in accordance with paragraph (1) shall ensure that a reasonable number of copies of the information is available at the address named in the notice published pursuant to paragraph (3) as the address at which such copies may be obtained.

(9)   A reasonable charge reflecting printing and distribution costs may be made to a member of the public for a copy of the further information made available in accordance with paragraph (8).

(10)   The relevant planning authority or the Secretary of State or an inspector may in writing require an applicant or appellant to produce such evidence as they may reasonably call for to verify any information in his environmental statement.

PART VI
AVAILABILITY OF DIRECTIONS ETC AND NOTIFICATION OF DECISIONS

20 Availability of opinions, directions etc for inspection

(1)   Where particulars of a planning application are placed on Part I of the register, the relevant planning authority shall take steps to secure that there is also placed on that Part a copy of any relevant—
   (a) screening opinion;
   (b) screening direction;
   (c) scoping opinion;
   (d) scoping direction;
   (e) notification given under regulation 7(2), 8(2) or 9(4);
   (f) direction under regulation 4(4);
   (g) environmental statement, including any further information;
   (h) statement of reasons accompanying any of the above.

(2)   Where the relevant planning authority adopt a screening opinion or scoping opinion, or receive a request under regulation 10(1) or 11(2), a copy of a screening direction, scoping direction, or direction under regulation 4(4) before an application is made for planning permission for the development in question, the authority shall take

steps to secure that a copy of the opinion, request, or direction and any accompanying statement of reasons is made available for public inspection at all reasonable hours at the place where the appropriate register (or relevant section of that register) is kept. Copies of those documents shall remain so available for a period of two years.

21 Duties to inform the public and the Secretary of State of final decisions

(1)   Where an EIA application is determined by a local planning authority, the authority shall—
- (a) in writing, inform the Secretary of State of the decision;
- (b) inform the public of the decision, by publishing a notice in a newspaper circulating in the locality in which the land is situated, or by such other means as are reasonable in the circumstances; and
- (c) make available for public inspection at the place where the appropriate register (or relevant section of that register) is kept a statement containing—
    - (i)   the content of the decision and any conditions attached thereto;
    - (ii) the main reasons and considerations on which the decision is based; and
    - (iii) a description, where necessary, of the main measures to avoid, reduce and, if possible, offset the major adverse effects of the development.

(2)   Where an EIA application is determined by the Secretary of State or an inspector, the Secretary of State shall—
- (a) notify the relevant planning authority of the decision; and
- (b) provide the authority with such a statement as is mentioned in sub-paragraph (1)(c).

(3)   The relevant planning authority shall, as soon as reasonably practicable after receipt of a notification under sub-paragraph (2)(a), comply with sub-paragraphs (b) and (c) of paragraph (1) in relation to the decision so notified as if it were a decision of the authority.

PART VII
SPECIAL CASES

22 Development by a local planning authority

(1)   Where the relevant planning authority is also (or would be) the applicant (whether alone or jointly with any other person), these Regulations shall apply to a Schedule 1 application or Schedule 2 application (or proposed application) subject to the following modifications—
- (a) subject to sub-paragraph (b) of this paragraph and to paragraphs (2) and (3) below, regulations 5 and 6 shall not apply;

(b) paragraphs (2) to (7) of regulation 7 shall not apply, and paragraph 7(1) shall apply as if the reference to paragraph (3) of regulation 5 were omitted;

(c) regulations 10 and 11 shall not apply;

(d) paragraphs (1) to (3) of regulation 12 shall not apply, and regulation 12(4) shall apply to any consultation body from whom the relevant planning authority requests assistance as it applies to a body notified in accordance with regulation 12(3);

(e) save for the purposes of regulations 16(3) and (4), regulation 13 shall apply as if—

    (i) for paragraph (1), there were substituted;

        '(1) When a relevant planning authority making an EIA application lodge a statement which they refer to as an environmental statement for the purposes of these Regulations, they shall—

        (a) serve a copy of that statement, the relevant application and any plan submitted with it on each consultation body;

        (b) inform each consultation body that representations may be made to the relevant planning authority; and

        (c) send to the Secretary of State within 14 days of lodging the statement three copies of the statement and a copy of the relevant application and of any documents submitted with the application.'

    (ii) paragraphs (2) and (3) were omitted;

(f) regulation 16 shall apply as if paragraph (2) were omitted.

(2)   An authority which is minded to make a planning application in relation to which it would be the relevant planning authority may adopt a screening opinion or request the Secretary of State in writing to make a screening direction, and paragraphs (3) and (4) of regulation 6 shall apply to such a request as they apply to a request made pursuant to regulation 5(6).

(3)   A relevant planning authority which proposes to carry out development which they consider may be—

(a) development of a description specified in Schedule 2 to the Town and Country Planning (General Permitted Development) Order 1995 other than development of a description specified in article 3(12) of that Order; or

(b) development for which permission would be granted but for regulation 23(1),

may adopt a screening opinion or request the Secretary of State to make a screening direction, and paragraphs (3) and (4) of regulation 6 shall apply to such a request as they apply to a request made pursuant to regulation 5(6).

(4)   A request under paragraph (2) or (3) shall be accompanied by—

(a) a plan sufficient to identify the land;

(b) a brief description of the nature and purpose of the development and of its possible effects on the environment; and

(c) such other information or representations as the authority may wish to provide or make.

(5)   An authority making a request under paragraph (2) or (3) shall send to the Secretary of State any additional information he may request in writing to enable him to make a direction.

23 Restriction of grant of permission by old simplified planning zone schemes or enterprise zone orders

(1)   Any:
   (a) adoption or approval of a simplified planning zone scheme;
   (b) order designating an enterprise zone; or
   (c) approval of a modified scheme in relation to an enterprise zone,
        which has effect immediately before the commencement of these Regulations to grant planning permission shall, on and after that date, cease to have effect to grant planning permission for Schedule 1 development, and cease to have effect to grant planning permission for Schedule 2 development unless either:
        (i)   the relevant planning authority has adopted a screening opinion; or
        (ii) the Secretary of State has made a screening direction,
              to the effect that the particular proposed development is not EIA development.

(2)   Paragraph (1) shall not affect the completion of any development begun before the commencement of these Regulations.

24 Restriction of grant of permission by new simplified planning zone schemes or enterprise zone orders

No:
   (a) adoption or approval of a simplified planning zone scheme;
   (b) order designating an enterprise zone made; or
   (c) modified scheme in relation to an enterprise zone approved,
        after the commencement of these Regulations shall:
        (i)   grant planning permission for EIA development; or
        (ii) grant planning permission for Schedule 2 development unless that grant is made subject to the prior adoption of a screening opinion or prior making of a screening direction that the particular proposed development is not EIA development.

25 Unauthorised development

Prohibition on the grant of planning permission for unauthorised EIA development

(1)   The Secretary of State shall not grant planning permission under sub-section (1) of section 177 (grant or modification of planning permission on appeals against enforcement notices) in respect of EIA development which is the subject of an enforcement notice under section 172 (issue of enforcement notice) ('unauthorised EIA development') unless he has first taken the environmental information into consideration, and he shall state in his decision that he has done so.

Screening opinions of the local planning authority

(2)   Where it appears to the local planning authority by whom or on whose behalf an enforcement notice is to be issued that the matters constituting the breach of planning control comprise or include Schedule 1 development or Schedule 2 development they shall, before the enforcement notice is issued, adopt a screening opinion.

(3)   Where it appears to the local planning authority by whom or on whose behalf an enforcement notice is to be issued that the matters constituting the breach of planning control comprise or include EIA development they shall serve with a copy of the enforcement notice a notice ('regulation 25 notice') which shall—
  (a) include the screening opinion required by paragraph (2) and the written statement required by regulation 4(6); and
  (b) require a person who gives notice of an appeal under section 174 to submit to the Secretary of State with the notice four copies of an environmental statement relating to that EIA development.

(4)   The authority by whom a regulation 25 notice has been served shall send a copy of it to—
  (a) the Secretary of State; and
  (I) the consultation bodies.

(5)   Where an authority provide the Secretary of State with a copy of a regulation 25 notice they shall also provide him with a list of the other persons to whom a copy of the notice has been or is to be sent.

Screening directions of the Secretary of State

(6)   Any person on whom a regulation 25 notice is served may apply to the Secretary of State for a screening direction and the following shall apply—
  (a) an application under this paragraph shall be accompanied by—
      (i)   a copy of the regulation 25 notice;
      (ii) a copy of the enforcement notice which accompanied it; and
      (iii) such other information or representations as the applicant may wish to provide or make;
  (b) the applicant shall send to the authority by whom the regulation 25 notice was served, at such time as he applies to the Secretary of State, a copy of the application under this paragraph and of any information or representations provided or made in accordance with sub-paragraph (a)(iii);
  (c) if the Secretary of State considers that the information provided in accordance with sub-paragraph (a) is insufficient to enable him to make a direction, he shall notify the applicant and the authority of the matters in respect of which he requires additional information; and the information so requested shall be provided by the applicant within such reasonable period as may be specified in the notice;
  (d) the Secretary of State shall send a copy of his direction to the applicant;

(e) without prejudice to sub-paragraph (d), where the Secretary of State directs that the matters which are alleged to constitute the breach of planning control do not comprise or include EIA development, he shall send a copy of the direction to every person to whom a copy of the regulation 25 notice was sent.

Provision of information

(7)   The relevant planning authority and any person, other than the Secretary of State, to whom a copy of the regulation 25 notice has been sent ('the consultee') shall, if requested by the person on whom the regulation 25 notice was served, enter into consultation with that person to determine whether the consultee has in his possession any information which that person or the consultee consider relevant to the preparation of an environmental statement and, if they have, the consultee shall make any such information available to that person.

(8)   The provisions of regulations 12(5) and 12(6) shall apply to information under paragraph (7) as they apply to any information falling within regulation 12(4).

Appeal to the Secretary of State without a screening opinion or screening direction

(9)   Where on consideration of an appeal under section 174 it appears to the Secretary of State that the matters which are alleged to constitute the breach of planning control comprise or include Schedule 1 development or Schedule 2 development and, in either case, no screening opinion has been adopted and no screening direction has been made in respect of that development, the Secretary of State shall, before any notice is served pursuant to paragraph (12), make such a screening direction.

(10)   If the Secretary of State considers that he has not been provided with sufficient information to make a screening direction he shall notify the applicant and the authority by whom the regulation 25 notice was served of the matters in respect of which he requires additional information; and the information so requested shall be provided by the applicant within such reasonable period as may be specified in the notice.

(11)   If an appellant to whom notice has been given under paragraph (10) fails to comply with the requirements of that notice:
   (a) the application which is deemed to have been made by virtue of the appeal made under section 174 ('the deemed application'); and
   (b) the appeal in so far as it is brought under the ground mentioned in section 174(2)(a) ('the ground (a) appeal'),
shall lapse at the end of the period specified in the notice.

Appeal to the Secretary of State without an environmental statement

(12)   Where the Secretary of State is considering an appeal under section 174 and the matters which are alleged to constitute the breach of planning control comprise or

include unauthorised EIA development, and the documents submitted to him for the purposes of the appeal do not include a statement referred to by the appellant as an environmental statement for the purposes of these Regulations, the following procedure shall apply—

    (a) the Secretary of State shall, subject to sub-paragraph (b), within the period of three weeks beginning with the day on which he receives the appeal, or such longer period as he may reasonably require, notify the appellant in writing of the requirements of sub-paragraph (c) below;

    (b) notice need not be given under sub-paragraph (a) where the appellant has submitted a statement which he refers to as an environmental statement for the purposes of these Regulations to the Secretary of State for the purposes of an appeal under section 78 (right to appeal against planning decisions and failure to take such decisions) which—

        (i) relates to the development to which the appeal under section 174 relates; and

        (ii) is to be determined at the same time as that appeal under section 174;

    and that statement, any further information, and the representations (if any) made in relation to it shall be treated as the environmental statement and representations for the purpose of paragraph (1) of this regulation;

    (c) the requirements of this sub-paragraph are that the appellant shall, within the period specified in the notice or such longer period as the Secretary of State may allow, submit to the Secretary of State four copies of an environmental statement relating to the unauthorised EIA development in question;

    (d) the Secretary of State shall send to the relevant planning authority a copy of any notice sent to the appellant under sub-paragraph (a);

    (e) if an appellant to whom notice has been given under sub-paragraph (a) fails to comply with the requirements of sub-paragraph (c), the deemed application and the ground (a) appeal (if any) shall lapse at the end of the period specified or allowed (as the case may be);

    (f) as soon as reasonably practicable after the occurrence of the event mentioned in sub-paragraph (e), the Secretary of State shall notify the appellant and the local planning authority in writing that the deemed application and the ground (a) appeal (if any) have lapsed.

Procedure where an environmental statement is submitted to the Secretary of State

(13)   Where the Secretary of State receives (otherwise than as mentioned in paragraph (12)(b)) in connection with an enforcement appeal a statement which the appellant refers to as an environmental statement for the purposes of these Regulations he shall—

    (a) send a copy of that statement to the relevant planning authority, advise the authority that the statement will be taken into consideration in determining the deemed application and the ground (a) appeal (if any), and inform them that they may make representations; and

    (b) notify the persons to whom a copy of the relevant regulation 25 notice was sent that the statement will be taken into consideration in determining the deemed application and the ground (a) appeal (if any), and inform them that they may make representations and that, if they wish to receive a copy of the statement or any part of it, they must notify the Secretary of State of their requirements within seven days of the receipt of the Secretary of State's notice; and

(c) respond to requirements notified in accordance with sub-paragraph (b) by providing a copy of the statement or of the part requested (as the case may be).

Further information and evidence respecting environmental statements

(14)   Regulations 19(1) and 19(10) shall apply to statements provided in accordance with this regulation with the following modifications—

(a) where the Secretary of State notifies the appellant under regulation 19(1), the appellant shall provide the further information within such period as the Secretary of State may specify in the notice or such longer period as the Secretary of State may allow;

(b) if an appellant to whom a notice has been given under sub-paragraph (a) fails to provide the further information within the period specified or allowed (as the case may be), the deemed application and the ground (a) appeal (if any) shall lapse at the end of that period.

(15)   Paragraph (13) shall apply in relation to further information received by the Secretary of State in accordance with paragraph (14) as it applies to such a statement as is referred to in that paragraph.

Publicity for environmental statements or further information

(16)   Where an authority receive a copy of a statement or further information by virtue of paragraph (13)(a) they shall publish in a local newspaper circulating in the locality in which the land is situated a notice stating—

(a) the name of the appellant and that he has appealed to the Secretary of State against the enforcement notice;

(b) the address or location of the land to which the notice relates and the nature of the development;

(c) that a copy of the statement or further information may be inspected by members of the public at all reasonable hours;

(d) an address in the locality in which the land is situated at which the statement or further information may be inspected, and the latest date on which it will be available for inspection (being a date not less than 21 days later than the date on which the notice is published);

(e) that any person wishing to make representations about any matter dealt with in the statement or further information should make them in writing, no later than 14 days after the date named in accordance with sub-paragraph (d), to the Secretary of State; and

(f) the address to which any such representations should be sent.

(17)   The authority shall as soon as practicable after publication of a notice in accordance with paragraph (16) send to the Secretary of State a copy of the notice certified by or on behalf of the authority as having been published in a named newspaper on a date specified in the certificate.

(18)   Where the Secretary of State receives a certificate under paragraph (17) he shall not determine the deemed application or the ground (a) appeal in respect of the development to which the certificate relates until the expiry of 14 days from the date stated in the published notice as the last date on which the statement or further information was available for inspection.

Public inspection of documents

(19)   The relevant planning authority shall make available for public inspection at all reasonable hours at the place where the appropriate register (or relevant part of that register) is kept a copy of—
   (a)   every regulation 25 notice given by the authority;
   (b)   every notice received by the authority under paragraph (12)(d); and
   (c)   every statement and all further information received by the authority under paragraph (13)(a);
and copies of those documents shall remain so available for a period of two years or until they are entered in Part II of the register in accordance with paragraph (20), whichever is the sooner.

(20)   Where particulars of any planning permission granted by the Secretary of State under section 177 are entered in Part II of the register the relevant planning authority shall take steps to secure that that Part also contains a copy of any of the documents referred to in paragraph (19) as are relevant to the development for which planning permission has been granted.

(21)   The provisions of regulations 21(2) and 21(3) apply to a deemed application and a grant of planning permission under section 177 as they apply to an application for and grant of planning permission under Part III of the Act.

26   Unauthorised development with significant transboundary effects

(1)   Regulation 27 shall apply to unauthorised EIA development as if—
   (a)   for regulation 27(1)(a) there were substituted—
      '(a) on consideration of an appeal under section 174 the Secretary of State is of the opinion that the matters which are alleged to constitute the breach of planning control comprise or include EIA development and that the development has or is likely to have significant effects on the environment in another [EEA State]; or'
   (b)   in regulation 27(3)(a) the words 'a copy of the application concerned' were replaced by the words 'a description of the development concerned';

    (c) in regulation 27(3)(b) the words 'to which that application relates' were omitted; and

    (d) in regulation 27(6) the word 'application' was replaced by the word 'appeal'.

NOTES

Para (1): in substituted sub-para (a) words 'EEA State' in square brackets substituted by SI 2000/2867, reg 2(1), (4). Date in force: 15 November 2000: see SI 2000/2867, reg 1(1).

[26A ROMP Applications]

General application of the Regulations to ROMP applications

(1)   These Regulations shall apply to—
    (a) a ROMP application as they apply to an application for planning permission;
    (b) ROMP development as they apply to development in respect of which an application for planning permission is, has been or is to be made;
    (c) a relevant mineral planning authority as they apply to a relevant planning authority;
    (d) a person making a ROMP application as they apply to an applicant for planning permission; and
    (e) the determination of a ROMP application as they apply to the granting of a planning permission,
subject to the modifications and additions set out below.

Modification of provisions on prohibition of granting planning permission

(2)   In regulation 3(1) (prohibition on granting planning permission without consideration of environmental information)—
    (a) in paragraph (a) for the words 'these Regulations' substitute 'the Town and Country Planning (Environmental Impact Assessment) (England and Wales) (Amendment) Regulations 2000';
    (b) in paragraph (b) for the words '3 or 4 (applications for planning permission)' substitute '11 (other consents)';
    (c) for the words 'determined in accordance with paragraph (3) of article 20 (time periods for decision) of the Order' substitute 'the date on which a ROMP application has been made which complies with the provisions of paragraphs 2(3) to (5) and 4 (1) of Schedule 2 to the 1991 Act, 9(2) of Schedule 13 to the 1995 Act, or 6(2) of Schedule 14 to the 1995 Act'.

Modification of provisions on application to local planning authority without an
environmental statement

(3)   In regulation 7(4) (application made to a local planning authority without an
environmental statement)—
- (a) for the word 'three' substitute 'six'; and
- (b) after 'the notification' insert ', or within such other period as may be agreed
       with the authority in writing,'.

Disapplication of Regulations and modification of provisions on application referred to or
appealed to the Secretary of State without an environmental statement

(4)   Regulations 7(5) and (6), 8(5) and (6), 9(6) and (7), 22, and 32 shall not apply.

(5)   In regulation 8(4) (application referred to the Secretary of State without an
environmental statement) and 9(5) (appeal to the Secretary of State without an
environmental statement)—
- (a) for the word 'three' substitute 'six';
- (b) after 'the notification' insert ', or within such other period as may be agreed
       with the Secretary of State in writing,'.

Substitution of references to section 78 right of appeal and modification of provisions on
appeal to the Secretary of State without an environmental statement

(6)   In regulations 9(1) and 15(b), for the references to 'section 78 (right to appeal
against planning decisions and failure to take such decisions)' substitute—
'paragraph 5(2) of Schedule 2 to the 1991 Act, paragraph 11(1) of Schedule 13 to the
1995 Act or paragraph 9(1) of Schedule 14 to the 1995 Act (right of appeal)'.

(7)   In regulation 9(2) (appeal to the Secretary of State without an environmental
statement) omit the words ', except by refusing planning permission,'.

Modification of provisions on preparation, publicity and procedures on submission of
environmental statements

(8)   In regulations 10(9) and 11(6) for the words 'an application for planning
permission for' substitute 'a ROMP application which relates to another planning
permission which authorises'.

(9)   In regulation 13 (procedure where an environmental statement is submitted to
a local planning authority) after paragraph (3) insert—
'(3A) Where an applicant submits an environmental statement to the authority in
     accordance with paragraph (1), the provisions of article 8 of and Schedule 3 to the
     Order (publicity for applications for planning permission) shall apply to a ROMP
     application under paragraph—

(a) 2(2) of Schedule 2 to the 1991 Act; and

(b) 6(1) of Schedule 14 to the 1995 Act,

as they apply to a planning application falling within paragraph 8(2) of the Order except that for the references in the notice in Schedule 3 to the Order to "planning permission" there shall be substituted "determination of the conditions to which a planning permission is to be subject" and that notice shall refer to the relevant provisions of the 1991 or 1995 Act pursuant to which the application is made.'

(10)   In regulation 14 (publicity where an environmental statement is submitted after the planning application)—

> (a) in paragraph (2)(a) for the words 'and that he is the applicant for planning permission' substitute—
>
> > ', that he has applied for determination of the conditions to which a planning permission is to be subject, the relevant provisions of the 1991 or 1995 Act pursuant to which the application is made';
>
> (b) in paragraph (6) for the words—
>
> > (i) '(unless disposed to refuse the permission sought) suspend consideration of the application or appeal until receipt of the statement and the other documents mentioned in paragraph (5)' substitute—
> >
> > > 'suspend consideration of the application or appeal until the date specified by the authority or the Secretary of State for submission of the environmental statement and compliance with paragraph (5)';
> >
> > (ii) 'so mentioned' substitute 'mentioned in paragraph (5)'.

(11)   In regulation 15 (provision of copies of environmental statements and further information for the Secretary of State on referral or appeal), in paragraph (a) for 'section 77' substitute 'paragraph 7(1) of Schedule 2 to the 1991 Act, paragraph 13(1) of Schedule 13 to the 1995 Act or paragraph 8(1) of Schedule 14 to the 1995 Act'.

(12)   In regulation 17 (availability of copies of environmental statements) after the words 'the Order' insert '(as applied by regulation 13(3A) or by paragraph 9(5) of Schedule 13 to the 1995 Act),'.

(13)   In regulation 19 (further information and evidence respecting environmental statements)—

> (a) in paragraph (3) for the words 'applicant for planning permission or the appellant (as the case may be)' substitute—
>
> > 'person who has applied for or who has appealed in relation to the determination of the conditions to which the planning permission is to be subject, the relevant provisions of the 1991 or 1995 Act pursuant to which the application is made';
>
> (b) in paragraph (7) after the words 'application or appeal' insert 'until the date specified by them or him for submission of the further information'.

Modification of provisions on application to the High Court and giving of directions

(14)   For regulation 30 (application to the High Court) substitute—
'Application to the High Court

30

For the purposes of Part XII of the Act (validity of certain decisions), the reference in section 288, as applied by paragraph 9(3) of Schedule 2 to the 1991 Act, paragraph 16(4) of Schedule 13 to the 1995 Act or paragraph 9(4) of Schedule 14 to the 1995 Act, to action of the Secretary of State which is not within the powers of the Act shall be taken to extend to the determination of a ROMP application by the Secretary of State in contravention of regulation 3.'.

(15)   The direction making power substituted by regulation 35(8) shall apply to ROMP development as it applies to development in respect of which a planning application is made.

Suspension of minerals development

(16)   Where the authority, the Secretary of State or an inspector notifies the applicant or appellant, as the case may be, that—
  (a)   the submission of an environmental statement is required under regulation 7(2), 8(2) or 9(4) then such notification shall specify the period within which the environmental statement and compliance with regulation 14(5) is required; or
  (b)   a statement should contain additional information under regulation 19(1) then such notification shall specify the period within which that information is to be provided.

(17)   Subject to paragraph (18), the planning permission to which the ROMP application relates shall not authorise any minerals development (unless the Secretary of State has made a screening direction to the effect that the ROMP development is not EIA development) if the applicant or the appellant does not—
  (a)   write to the authority or Secretary of State within the six week or other period agreed pursuant to regulations 7(4), 8(4) or 9(5);
  (b)   submit an environmental statement and comply with regulation 14(5) within the period specified by the authority or the Secretary of State in accordance with paragraph (16) or within such extended period as is agreed in writing; or
  (c)   provide additional information within the period specified by the authority, the Secretary of State or an inspector in accordance with paragraph (16) or within such extended period as is agreed in writing.

(18)   Where paragraph (17) applies, the planning permission shall not authorise any minerals development from the end of—
  (a)   the relevant six week or other period agreed in writing as referred to in paragraph (17)(a);

(b)   the period specified or agreed in writing as referred to in paragraphs (17)(b) and (c),

('suspension of minerals development') until the applicant has complied with all of the provisions referred to in paragraph (17) which are relevant to the application or appeal in question.

(19)   Particulars of the suspension of minerals development and the date when that suspension ends must be entered in the appropriate part of the register as soon as reasonably practicable.

(20)   Paragraph (17) shall not affect any minerals development carried out under the planning permission before the date of suspension of minerals development.

(21)   For the purposes of paragraphs (17) to (20) 'minerals development' means development consisting of the winning and working of minerals, or involving the depositing of mineral waste.

Determination of conditions and right of appeal on non-determination

(22)   Where it falls to—
   (a)   a mineral planning authority to determine a Schedule 1 or a Schedule 2 application, paragraph 2(6)(b) of Schedule 2 to the 1991 Act, paragraph 9(9) of Schedule 13 to the 1995 Act or paragraph 6(8) of Schedule 14 to the 1995 Act shall not have effect to treat the authority as having determined the conditions to which any relevant planning permission is to be subject unless either the mineral planning authority has adopted a screening opinion or the Secretary of State has made a screening direction to the effect that the ROMP development in question is not EIA development;
   (b)   a mineral planning authority or the Secretary of State to determine a Schedule 1 or a Schedule 2 application—
      (i)   section 69 (register of applications, etc), and any provisions of the Order made by virtue of that section, shall have effect with any necessary amendments as if references to applications for planning permission included ROMP applications under paragraph 9(1) of Schedule 13 to the 1995 Act and paragraph 6(1) of Schedule 14 to the 1995 Act; and
      (ii)   where the relevant mineral planning authority is not the authority required to keep the register, the relevant mineral planning authority must provide the authority required to keep it with such information and documents as that authority requires to comply with section 69 as applied by sub-paragraph (i), with regulation 20 as applied by paragraph (1), and with paragraph (19).

(23)   Where it falls to the mineral planning authority or the Secretary of State to determine an EIA application which is made under paragraph 2(2) of Schedule 2 to the 1991 Act, paragraph 4(4) of that Schedule shall not apply.

(24)   Where it falls to the mineral planning authority to determine an EIA application, the authority shall give written notice of their determination of the ROMP application

within 16 weeks beginning with the date of receipt by the authority of the ROMP application or such extended period as may be agreed in writing between the applicant and the authority.

(25)   For the purposes of paragraph (24) a ROMP application is not received by the authority until—
  (a) a document referred to by the applicant as an environmental statement for the purposes of these Regulations;
  (b) any documents required to accompany that statement; and
  (c) any additional information which the authority has notified the applicant that the environmental statement should contain,
has been received by the authority.

(26)   Where paragraph (22)(a) applies—
  (a) paragraph 5(2) of Schedule 2 to the 1991 Act, paragraph 11(1) of Schedule 13 to the 1995 Act and paragraph 9(1) of Schedule 14 to the 1995 Act (right of appeal) shall have effect as if there were also a right of appeal to the Secretary of State where the mineral planning authority have not given written notice of their determination of the ROMP application in accordance with paragraph (24); and
  (b) paragraph 5(5) of Schedule 2 to the 1991 Act, paragraph 11(2) of Schedule 13 to the 1995 Act and paragraph 9(2) of Schedule 14 to the 1995 Act (right of appeal) shall have effect as if they also provided for notice of appeal to be made within six months from the expiry of the 16 week or other period agreed pursuant to paragraph (24).

(27)   In determining for the purposes of paragraphs—
  (a) 2(6)(b) of Schedule 2 to the 1991 Act, 9(9) of Schedule 13 to the 1995 Act and 6(8) of Schedule 14 to the 1995 Act (determination of conditions); or
  (b) paragraph 5(5) of Schedule 2 to the 1991 Act, paragraph 11(2) of Schedule 13 to the 1995 Act and paragraph 9(2) of Schedule 14 to the 1995 Act (right of appeal) as applied by paragraph (26)(b),
the time which has elapsed without the mineral planning authority giving the applicant written notice of their determination in a case where the authority have notified an applicant in accordance with regulation 7(2) that the submission of an environmental statement is required and the Secretary of State has given a screening direction in relation to the ROMP development in question no account shall be taken of any period before the issue of the direction.

ROMP application by a mineral planning authority

(28)   Where a mineral planning authority proposes to make or makes a ROMP application to the Secretary of State under regulation 11 (other consents) of the General Regulations which is a Schedule 1 or a Schedule 2 application (or proposed application), these Regulations shall apply to that application or proposed application as they apply to a ROMP application referred to the Secretary of State under paragraph 7(1) of Schedule 2 to the 1991 Act, paragraph 13(1) of Schedule 13 to the 1995 Act or paragraph

8(1) of Schedule 14 to the 1995 Act (reference of applications to the Secretary of State) subject to the following modifications—

    (a) subject to paragraph (29) below, regulations 5, 6, 7, 9, 10, 11, 13 (save for the purposes of regulations 16(3) and (4)) 15 and 21(1) shall not apply;

    (b) in regulation 4 (general provisions relating to screening)—

        (i) in paragraph (4), omit the words 'and shall send a copy of such direction to the relevant planning authority';

        (ii) paragraph (9) shall be omitted;

    (c) in regulation 8(2) (application referred to the Secretary of State without an environmental statement), omit the words 'and shall send a copy of that notification to the relevant planning authority';

    (d) in regulation 12 (procedure to facilitate preparation of environmental statements)—

        (i) in sub-paragraph (3)(b) for the words '7(4)(a), or 8(4) or 9(5)' substitute '8(4)';

        (ii) in paragraph (4) omit the words 'the relevant planning authority and';

    (e) in regulation 14(2) (publicity where an environmental statement is submitted after the planning application)—

        (i) in sub-paragraph (a) omit the words 'and the name and address of the relevant planning authority';

        (ii) for sub-paragraph (b) substitute—

            '(b) the date on which the application was made and that it has been made to the Secretary of State under regulation 11 of the General Regulations;';

    (f) in regulation 16 (procedure where an environmental statement is submitted to the Secretary of State), in paragraph (2) omit the words 'who shall send one copy to the relevant planning authority';

    (g) in regulation 19(3) (further information and evidence respecting environmental statements)—

        (i) in sub-paragraph (a) omit the words 'and the name and address of the relevant planning authority';

        (ii) for sub-paragraph (b) substitute—

            '(b) the date on which the application was made and that it has been made to the Secretary of State under regulation 11 of the General Regulations;';

    (h) regulations 20 (availability of opinions, directions etc for inspection) and 21(2) (duties to inform the public and the Secretary of State of final decisions) shall apply as if the references to a 'relevant planning authority' were references to a mineral planning authority.

(29)   A mineral planning authority which is minded to make a ROMP application to the Secretary of State under regulation 11 of the General Regulations may request the Secretary of State in writing to make a screening direction, and paragraphs (3) and (4) of regulation 6 shall apply to such a request as they apply to a request made pursuant to regulation 5(6) except that in paragraph (3) the words ', and may request the relevant planning authority to provide such information as they can on any of those points' shall be omitted.

(30)   A request under paragraph (29) shall be accompanied by—
   (a)   a plan sufficient to identify the land;
   (b)   a brief description of the nature and purpose of the ROMP development and of its possible effects on the environment; and
   (c)   such other information as the authority may wish to provide or make.

(31)   An authority making a request under paragraph (29) shall send to the Secretary of State any additional information he may request in writing to enable him to make a direction.]

NOTES

Inserted by SI 2000/2867, reg 2(1), (5). Date in force: 15 November 2000: see SI 2000/2867, reg 1(1).

PART VIII
DEVELOPMENT WITH SIGNIFICANT TRANSBOUNDARY EFFECTS

27 Development in England and Wales likely to have significant effects in another [EEA State]

(1)   Where—
   (a)   it comes to the attention of the Secretary of State that development proposed to be carried out in England or Wales is the subject of an EIA application and is likely to have significant effects on the environment in another [EEA State]; or
   (b)   another [EEA State] likely to be significantly affected by such development so requests,
      the Secretary of State shall—
      (i)   send to the [EEA State] as soon as possible and no later than their date of publication in The London Gazette referred to in sub-paragraph (ii) below, the particulars mentioned in paragraph (2) and, if he thinks fit, the information referred to in paragraph (3); and
      (ii)   publish the information in sub-paragraph (i) above in a notice placed in The London Gazette indicating the address where additional information is available; and
      (iii) give the [EEA State] a reasonable time in which to indicate whether it wishes to participate in the procedure for which these Regulations provide.

(2)   The particulars referred to in paragraph (1)(i) are—
   (a)   a description of the development, together with any available information on its possible significant effect on the environment in another Member State; and
   (b)   information on the nature of the decision which may be taken.

(3)   Where a [EEA State] indicates, in accordance with paragraph (1)(iii), that it wishes to participate in the procedure for which these Regulations provide, the Secretary of State shall as soon as possible send to that [EEA State] the following information—
   (a)   a copy of the application concerned;
   (b)   a copy of the environmental statement in respect of the development to which that application relates; and
   (c)   relevant information regarding the procedure under these Regulations,
but only to the extent that such information has not been provided to the [EEA State] earlier in accordance with paragraph (1)(i).

(4)   The Secretary of State, insofar as he is concerned, shall also—
   (a)   arrange for the particulars and information referred to in paragraphs (2) and (3) to be made available, within a reasonable time, to the authorities referred to in Article 6(1) of the Directive and the public concerned in the territory of the [EEA State] likely to be significantly affected; and
   (b)   ensure that those authorities and the public concerned are given an opportunity, before planning permission for the development is granted, to forward to the Secretary of State, within a reasonable time, their opinion on the information supplied.

(5)   The Secretary of State shall in accordance with Article 7(4) of the Directive—
   (a)   enter into consultations with the [EEA State] concerned regarding, inter alia, the potential significant effects of the development on the environment of that [EEA State] and the measures envisaged to reduce or eliminate such effects; and
   (b)   determine in agreement with the other [EEA State] a reasonable period of time for the duration of the consultation period.

(6)   Where a [EEA State] has been consulted in accordance with paragraph (5), on the determination of the application concerned the Secretary of State shall inform the [EEA State] of the decision and shall forward to it a statement of—
   (a)   the content of the decision and any conditions attached thereto;
   (b)   the main reasons and considerations on which the decision is based; and
   (c)   a description, where necessary, of the main measures to avoid, reduce and, if possible, offset the major adverse effects of the development.

NOTES

Section heading: words 'EEA State' in square brackets substituted by SI 2000/2867, reg 2(1), (4). Date in force: 15 November 2000: see SI 2000/2867, reg 1(1).
Para (1): in sub-para (a) words 'EEA State' in square brackets substituted by SI 2000/2867, reg 2(1), (4). Date in force: 15 November 2000: see SI 2000/2867, reg 1(1).
Para (1): in sub-para (b) words 'EEA State' in square brackets in each place they occur substituted by SI 2000/2867, reg 2(1), (4). Date in force: 15 November 2000: see SI 2000/2867, reg 1(1).
Para (3): words 'EEA State' in square brackets in each place they occur substituted by SI 2000/2867, reg 2(1), (4). Date in force: 15 November 2000: see SI 2000/2867, reg 1(1).
Para (4): in sub-para (a) words 'EEA State' in square brackets substituted by SI 2000/2867, reg 2(1), (4). Date in force: 15 November 2000: see SI 2000/2867, reg 1(1).
Para (5): in sub-para (a) words 'EAA State' in square brackets in both places they occur substituted by SI 2000/2867, reg 2(1), (4). Date in force: 15 November 2000: see SI 2000/2867, reg 1(1).
Para (5): in sub-para (b) words 'EEA State' in square brackets substituted by SI 2000/2867, reg 2(1), (4). Date in force: 15 November 2000: see SI 2000/2867, reg 1(1).

Para (6): words 'Member State' in square brackets in both places they occur substituted by SI 2000/
2867, reg 2(1), (4). Date in force: 15 November 2000: see SI 2000/2867, reg 1(1).

28 Projects in another [EEA State] likely to have significant transboundary effects

(1)   Where the Secretary of State receives from another [EEA State] pursuant to Article 7(2) of the Directive information which that [EEA State] has gathered from the developer of a proposed project in that [EEA State] which is likely to have significant effects on the environment in England and Wales, the Secretary of State shall, in accordance with Article 7(4) of the Directive:

  (a) enter into consultations with that [EEA State] regarding, inter alia, the potential significant effects of the proposed project on the environment in England and Wales and the measures envisaged to reduce or eliminate such effects; and

  (b) determine in agreement with that [EEA State] a reasonable period, before development consent for the project is granted, during which members of the public in England and Wales may submit to the competent authority in that [EEA State] representations pursuant to Article 7(3)(b) of the Directive.

(2)   The Secretary of State, insofar as he is concerned, shall also—

  (a) arrange for the information referred to in paragraph (1) to be made available, within a reasonable time, both to the authorities in England and Wales which he considers are likely to be concerned by the project by reason of their specific environmental responsibilities, and to the public concerned in England and Wales; and

  (b) ensure that those authorities and the public concerned in England and Wales are given an opportunity, before development consent for the project is granted, to forward to the competent authority in the relevant [EEA State], within a reasonable time, their opinion on the information supplied.

NOTES

Section heading: words 'EEA State' in square brackets substituted by SI 2000/2867, reg 2(1), (4).
    Date in force: 15 November 2000: see SI 2000/2867, reg 1(1).
Para (1): words 'EEA State' in square brackets in each place they occur substituted by SI 2000/2867,
    reg 2(1), (4). Date in force: 15 November 2000: see SI 2000/2867, reg 1(1).
Para (1): in sub-para (a) words 'EEA State' in square brackets substituted by SI 2000/2867, reg 2(1),
    (4). Date in force: 15 November 2000: see SI 2000/2867, reg 1(1).
Para (1): in sub-para (b) words 'EEA State' in square brackets in both places they occur substituted
    by SI 2000/2867, reg 2(1), (4). Date in force: 15 November 2000: see SI 2000/2867, reg 1(1).
Para (2): in sub-para (b) words 'EEA State' in square brackets substituted by SI 2000/2867, reg 2(1),
    (4). Date in force: 15 November 2000: see SI 2000/2867, reg 1(1).

PART IX
MISCELLANEOUS

29 Service of notices etc

Any notice or other document to be sent, served or given under these Regulations may be served or given in a manner specified in section 329 (service of notices).

30 Application to the High Court

For the purposes of Part XII of the Act (validity of certain decisions), the reference in section 288 to action of the Secretary of State which is not within the powers of the Act shall be taken to extend to a grant of planning permission by the Secretary of State in contravention of regulations 3 or 25(1).

31 Hazardous waste and material change of use

A change in the use of land or buildings to a use for a purpose mentioned in paragraph 9 of Schedule 1 involves a material change in the use of that land or those buildings for the purposes of paragraph (1) of section 55 (meaning of 'development' and 'new development').

32 Extension of the period for an authority's decision on a planning application

(1)   In determining for the purposes of section 78 (right to appeal against planning decisions and failure to take such decisions) the time which has elapsed without the relevant planning authority giving notice to the applicant of their decision in a case where—
  (a) the authority have notified an applicant in accordance with regulation 7(2) that the submission of an environmental statement is required; and
  (b) the Secretary of State has given a screening direction in relation to the development in question,
no account shall be taken of any period before the issue of the direction.

(2)   Where it falls to an authority to determine an EIA application, article 20 (time periods for decision) of the Order shall have effect as if—
  (a) for the reference in paragraph (2)(a) of that article to a period of 8 weeks there were substituted a reference to a period of 16 weeks;
  (b) after paragraph (3)(b) of that article there were inserted—
    '(ba) the environmental statement required to be submitted in respect of the application has been submitted, together with the documents required to accompany that statement; and'.

33 Extension of the power to provide in a development order for the giving of directions as respects the manner in which planning applications are dealt with

The provisions enabling the Secretary of State to give directions which may be included in a development order by virtue of section 60 (permission granted by development order) shall include provisions enabling him to direct that development which is both of a description mentioned in Column 1 of the table in Schedule 2, and of a class described in the direction is EIA development for the purposes of these Regulations.

34 Revocation of Statutory Instruments and transitional provisions

(1)   The instruments in Schedule 5 are hereby revoked to the extent shown in that Schedule.

(2)   Nothing in paragraph (1) shall affect the continued application of the Instruments revoked by that paragraph to any application lodged or received by an authority before the commencement of these Regulations, to any appeal in relation to such an application, or to any matter in relation to which a local planning authority has before that date issued an enforcement notice under section 172; and these Regulations shall not apply to any such application, appeal, or matter.

35 Miscellaneous and consequential amendments

(1)   In section 55(2)(b) of the Act after the words 'improvement of the road' there are inserted the words 'but, in the case of any such works which are not exclusively for the maintenance of the road, not including any works which may have significant adverse effects on the environment'.

(2)   In Article 3(6) (Use Classes) of the Town and Country Planning (Use Classes) Order 1987, after sub-paragraph (i) there are inserted the words:
   '(j) as a waste disposal installation for the incineration, chemical treatment (as defined in Annex IIA to Directive 75/442/EEC under heading D9), or landfill of waste to which Directive 91/689/EEC applies.'

(3)   For paragraphs (10) and (11) of article 3 (permitted development) of the Town and Country Planning (General Permitted Development) Order 1995 there is substituted—
   '(10)   Subject to paragraph (12), Schedule 1 development or Schedule 2 development within the meaning of the Town and Country Planning (Environmental Impact Assessment) (England and Wales) Regulations 1999 ("the EIA Regulations") is not permitted by this Order unless:
      (a) the local planning authority has adopted a screening opinion under regulation 5 of those Regulations that the development is not EIA development;

     (b) the Secretary of State has made a screening direction under regulation 4(7) or 6(4) of those Regulations that the development is not EIA development; or

     (c) the Secretary of State has given a direction under regulation 4(4) of those Regulations that the development is exempted from the application of those Regulations.

(11)   Where:

     (a) the local planning authority has adopted a screening opinion pursuant to regulation 5 of the EIA Regulations that development is EIA development and the Secretary of State has in relation to that development neither made a screening direction to the contrary under regulation 4(7) or 6(4) of those Regulations nor directed under regulation 4(4) of those Regulations that the development is exempted from the application of those Regulations; or

     (b) the Secretary of State has directed that development is EIA development,

that development shall be treated, for the purposes of paragraph (10), as development which is not permitted by this Order.'

(4)   For the words '3rd June 1995' in articles 3(12)(e) and 3(12)(f) of the Town and Country Planning (General Permitted Development) Order 1995 there are substituted the words '14th March 1999'.

(5)   For Class A of Part 13 in Schedule 2 of the Town and Country Planning (General Permitted Development) Order 1995 there is substituted—

'A

The carrying out by a local highway authority—

     (a) on land within the boundaries of a road, of any works required for the maintenance or improvement of the road, where such works involve development by virtue of section 55(2)(b) of the Act; or

     (b) on land outside but adjoining the boundary of an existing highway of works required for or incidental to the maintenance or improvement of the highway.'

(6)   In sub-paragraph (a) of article 8(2) of the Order for the words 'the subject of an E.A. Schedule 1 or E.A. Schedule 2 application' there are substituted the words 'an EIA application'.

(7)   In article 8(7) of the Order for the definitions of 'E.A. Schedule 1 application' and 'E.A. Schedule 2 application' there is substituted—
'"EIA application" has the meaning given in regulation 2 of the Town and Country Planning (Environmental Impact Assessment) (England and Wales) Regulations 1999, and "environmental statement" means a statement which the applicant refers to as an environmental statement for the purposes of those Regulations'.

(8)   For article 14(2) of the Order there is substituted—

     '(2) The Secretary of State may give directions that development which is both of a description set out in Column 1 of the table in Schedule 2 to the Town and Country Planning (Environmental Impact Assessment) (England and Wales) Regulations 1999, and of a class described in the direction is EIA development for the purposes of those Regulations.'

Signed by authority of the Secretary of State for the Environment, Transport and the Regions

Richard G Caborn
Minister of State
Department of the Environment, Transport and the Regions

10th February 1999

Alun Michael
Secretary of State for Wales

10th February 1999

SCHEDULE I
DESCRIPTIONS OF DEVELOPMENT FOR THE PURPOSES OF THE DEFINITION OF 'SCHEDULE I DEVELOPMENT'

Regulation 2(1)

Interpretation

In this Schedule—

'airport' means an airport which complies with the definition in the 1944 Chicago Convention setting up the International Civil Aviation Organisation (Annex 14);

'express road' means a road which complies with the definition in the European Agreement on Main International Traffic Arteries of 15 November 1975;

'nuclear power station' and 'other nuclear reactor' do not include an installation from the site of which all nuclear fuel and other radioactive contaminated materials have been permanently removed; and development for the purpose of dismantling or decommissioning a nuclear power station or other nuclear reactor shall not be treated as development of the description mentioned in paragraph 2(b) of this Schedule.

Descriptions of development

The carrying out of development to provide any of the following—

I   Crude-oil refineries (excluding undertakings manufacturing only lubricants from crude oil) and installations for the gasification and liquefaction of 500 tonnes or more of coal or bituminous shale per day.

2

(a) Thermal power stations and other combustion installations with a heat output of 300 megawatts or more; and

(b) Nuclear power stations and other nuclear reactors (except research installations for the production and conversion of fissionable and fertile materials, whose maximum power does not exceed 1 kilowatt continuous thermal load).

3
(a) Installations for the reprocessing of irradiated nuclear fuel.
(b) Installations designed—
   (i)   for the production or enrichment of nuclear fuel,
   (ii) for the processing of irradiated nuclear fuel or high-level radioactive waste,
   (iii) for the final disposal of irradiated nuclear fuel,
   (iv) solely for the final disposal of radioactive waste,
   (v)   solely for the storage (planned for more than 10 years) of irradiated nuclear fuels or radioactive waste in a different site than the production site.

4
(a) Integrated works for the initial smelting of cast-iron and steel;
(b) Installations for the production of non-ferrous crude metals from ore, concentrates or secondary raw materials by metallurgical, chemical or electrolytic processes.

5   Installations for the extraction of asbestos and for the processing and transformation of asbestos and products containing asbestos—
(a) for asbestos-cement products, with an annual production of more than 20,000 tonnes of finished products;
(b) for friction material, with an annual production of more than 50 tonnes of finished products; and
(c) for other uses of asbestos, utilisation of more than 200 tonnes per year.

6   Integrated chemical installations, that is to say, installations for the manufacture on an industrial scale of substances using chemical conversion processes, in which several units are juxtaposed and are functionally linked to one another and which are—
(a) for the production of basic organic chemicals;
(b) for the production of basic inorganic chemicals;
(c) for the production of phosphorous-, nitrogen- or potassium-based fertilisers (simple or compound fertilisers);
(d) for the production of basic plant health products and of biocides;
(e) for the production of basic pharmaceutical products using a chemical or biological process;
(f) for the production of explosives.

7
(a) Construction of lines for long-distance railway traffic and of airports with a basic runway length of 2,100 metres or more;
(b) Construction of motorways and express roads;
(c) Construction of a new road of four or more lanes, or realignment and/or widening of an existing road of two lanes or less so as to provide four or more lanes, where such new road, or realigned and/or widened section of road would be 10 kilometres or more in a continuous length.

8
(a) Inland waterways and ports for inland-waterway traffic which permit the passage of vessels of over 1,350 tonnes;
(b) Trading ports, piers for loading and unloading connected to land and outside ports (excluding ferry piers) which can take vessels of over 1,350 tonnes.

9   Waste disposal installations for the incineration, chemical treatment (as defined in Annex IIA to Council Directive 75/442/EEC under heading D9), or landfill of hazardous waste (that is to say, waste to which Council Directive 91/689/EEC applies).

10   Waste disposal installations for the incineration or chemical treatment (as defined in Annex IIA to Council Directive 75/442/EEC under heading D9) of non-hazardous waste with a capacity exceeding 100 tonnes per day.

11   Groundwater abstraction or artificial groundwater recharge schemes where the annual volume of water abstracted or recharged is equivalent to or exceeds 10 million cubic metres.

12
(a) Works for the transfer of water resources, other than piped drinking water, between river basins where the transfer aims at preventing possible shortages of water and where the amount of water transferred exceeds 100 million cubic metres per year;
(b) In all other cases, works for the transfer of water resources, other than piped drinking water, between river basins where the multi-annual average flow of the basin of abstraction exceeds 2,000 million cubic metres per year and where the amount of water transferred exceeds 5% of this flow.

13   Waste water treatment plants with a capacity exceeding 150,000 population equivalent as defined in Article 2 point (6) of Council Directive 91/271/EEC.

14   Extraction of petroleum and natural gas for commercial purposes where the amount extracted exceeds 500 tonnes per day in the case of petroleum and 500,000 cubic metres per day in the case **of gas.**

15   Dams and other installations designed for the holding back or permanent storage of water, where a new or additional amount of water held back or stored exceeds 10 million cubic metres.

16   Pipelines for the transport of gas, oil or chemicals with a diameter of more than 800 millimetres and a length of more than 40 kilometres.

17   Installations for the intensive rearing of poultry or pigs with more than—
(a) 85,000 places for broilers or 60,000 places for hens;
(b) 3,000 places for production pigs (over 30 kg); or
(c) 900 places for sows.

18   Industrial plants for—
(a) the production of pulp from timber or similar fibrous materials;
(b) the production of paper and board with a production capacity exceeding 200 tonnes per day.

19   Quarries and open-cast mining where the surface of the site exceeds 25 hectares, or peat extraction where the surface of the site exceeds 150 hectares.

20   Installations for storage of petroleum, petrochemical or chemical products with a capacity of 200,000 tonnes or more.

SCHEDULE 2
DESCRIPTIONS OF DEVELOPMENT AND APPLICABLE THRESHOLDS AND CRITERIA FOR THE PURPOSES OF THE DEFINITION OF 'SCHEDULE 2 DEVELOPMENT'

Regulation 2(1)

1   In the table below—

'area of the works' includes any area occupied by apparatus, equipment, machinery, materials, plant, spoil heaps or other facilities or stores required for construction or installation;

'controlled waters' has the same meaning as in the Water Resources Act 1991;

'floorspace' means the floorspace in a building or buildings.

2   The table below sets out the descriptions of development and applicable thresholds and criteria for the purpose of classifying development as Schedule 2 development.

Description of development	Applicable thresholds and criteria
The carrying out of development to provide any of the following—	
1 *Agriculture and aquaculture*	
(a) Projects for the use of uncultivated land or semi-natural areas for intensive agricultural purposes;	The area of the development exceeds 0.5 hectare.
(b) Water management projects for agriculture, including irrigation and land drainage projects;	The area of the works exceeds 1 hectare.
(c) Intensive livestock installations (unless included in Schedule 1);	The area of new floorspace exceeds 500 square metres.
(d) Intensive fish farming;	The installation resulting from the development is designed to produce more than 10 tonnes of dead weight fish per year.
(e) Reclamation of land from the sea.	All development.
2 *Extractive industry*	
(a) Quarries, open cast mining and peat extraction (unless included in Schedule 1);	All development except the construction of buildings or other ancillary structures where the new floorspace does not exceed 1,000 square metres.
(b) Underground mining;	
(c) Extraction of minerals by fluvial dredging;	All development.
(d) Deep drillings, in particular—	i) In relation to any type of drilling, the area of the works exceeds 1 hectare; or

Description of development	Applicable thresholds and criteria
(i) geothermal drilling;	ii) in relation to geothermal drilling and drilling for the storage of nuclear waste material, the drilling is within 100 metres of any controlled waters.
(ii) drilling for the storage of nuclear waste material;	
(iii) drilling for water supplies;	
with the exception of drillings for investigating the stability of the soil.	
(e) Surface industrial installations for the extraction of coal, petroleum, natural gas and ores, as well as bituminous shale.	The area of the development exceeds 0.5 hectare.
3 *Energy industry*	
(a) Industrial installations for the production of electricity, steam and hot water (unless included in Schedule 1);	The area of the development exceeds 0.5 hectare.
(b) Industrial installations for carrying gas, steam and hot water;	The area of the works exceeds 1 hectare.
(c) Surface storage of natural gas;	(i) The area of any new building, deposit or structure exceeds 500 square metres; or (ii) a new building, deposit or structure is to be sited within 100 metres of any controlled waters.
(d) Underground storage of combustible gases;	(i) The area of any new building, deposit or structure exceeds 500 square metres; or (ii) a new building, deposit or structure is to be sited within 100 metres of any controlled waters.
(e) Surface storage of fossil fuels;	(i) The area of any new building, deposit or structure exceeds 500 square metres; or (ii) a new building, deposit or structure is to be sited within 100 metres of any controlled waters.
(f) Industrial briquetting of coal and lignite;	The area of new floorspace exceeds 1,000 square metres.
(g) Installations for the processing and storage of radioactive waste (unless included in Schedule 1);	(i) The area of new floorspace exceeds 1,000 square metres; or (ii) the installation resulting from the development will require an authorisation or the variation of an authorisation under the Radioactive Substances Act 1993.
(h) Installations for hydroelectric energy production;	The installation is designed to produce more than 0.5 megawatts.
(i) Installations for the harnessing of wind power for energy production (wind farms).	(i) The development involves the installation of more than 2 turbines; or (ii) the hub height of any turbine or height of any other structure exceeds 15 metres.

Description of development	Applicable thresholds and criteria
4 *Production and processing of metals*	
(a) Installations for the production of pig iron or steel (primary or secondary fusion) including continuous casting;	The area of new floorspace exceeds 1,000 square metres.
(b) Installations for the processing of ferrous metals— (i) hot-rolling mills; (ii) smitheries with hammers; (iii) application of protective fused metal coats.	The area of new floorspace exceeds 1,000 square metres.
(c) Ferrous metal foundries;	The area of new floorspace exceeds 1,000 square metres.
(d) Installations for the smelting, including the alloyage, of non-ferrous metals, excluding precious metals, including recovered products (refining, foundry casting, etc);	The area of new floorspace exceeds 1,000 square metres.
(e) Installations for surface treatment of metals and plastic materials using an electrolytic or chemical process;	The area of new floorspace exceeds 1,000 square metres.
(f) Manufacture and assembly of motor vehicles and manufacture of motor-vehicle engines;	The area of new floorspace exceeds 1,000 square metres.
(g) Shipyards;	The area of new floorspace exceeds 1,000 square metres.
(h) Installations for the construction and repair of aircraft;	The area of new floorspace exceeds 1,000 square metres.
(i) Manufacture of railway equipment;	The area of new floorspace exceeds 1,000 square metres.
(j) Swaging by explosives;	The area of new floorspace exceeds 1,000 square metres.
(k) Installations for the roasting and sintering of metallic ores.	The area of new floorspace exceeds 1,000 square metres.
5 *Mineral industry*	
(a) Coke ovens (dry coal distillation);	The area of new floorspace exceeds 1,000 square metres.
(b) Installations for the manufacture of cement;	The area of new floorspace exceeds 1,000 square metres.
(c) Installations for the production of asbestos and the manufacture of asbestos-based products (unless included in Schedule 1);	The area of new floorspace exceeds 1,000 square metres.
(d) Installations for the manufacture of glass including glass fibre;	The area of new floorspace exceeds 1,000 square metres.
(e) Installations for smelting mineral substances including the production of mineral fibres;	The area of new floorspace exceeds 1,000 square metres.
(f) Manufacture of ceramic products by burning, in particular roofing tiles, bricks, refractory bricks, tiles, stonewear or porcelain.	The area of new floorspace exceeds 1,000 square metres.

Description of development	Applicable thresholds and criteria
6 *Chemical industry (unless included in Schedule 1)*	
(a) Treatment of intermediate products and production of chemicals;	The area of new floorspace exceeds 1,000 square metres.
(b) Production of pesticides and pharmaceutical products, paint and varnishes, elastomers and peroxides;	The area of new floorspace exceeds 1,000 square metres.
(c) Storage facilities for petroleum, petrochemical and chemical products.	(i) The area of any new building or structure exceeds 0.05 hectare; or (ii) more than 200 tonnes of petroleum, petrochemical or chemical products is to be stored at any one time.
7 *Food industry*	
(a) Manufacture of vegetable and animal oils and fats;	The area of new floorspace exceeds 1,000 square metres.
(b) Packing and canning of animal and vegetable products;	The area of new floorspace exceeds 1,000 square metres.
(c) Manufacture of dairy products;	The area of new floorspace exceeds 1,000 square metres.
(d) Brewing and malting;	The area of new floorspace exceeds 1,000 square metres.
(e) Confectionery and syrup manufacture;	The area of new floorspace exceeds 1,000 square metres.
(f) Installations for the slaughter of animals;	The area of new floorspace exceeds 1,000 square metres.
(g) Industrial starch manufacturing installations;	The area of new floorspace exceeds 1,000 square metres.
(h) Fish-meal and fish-oil factories;	The area of new floorspace exceeds 1,000 square metres.
(i) Sugar factories.	The area of new floorspace exceeds 1,000 square metres.
8 *Textile, leather, wood and paper industries*	
(a) Industrial plants for the production of paper and board (unless included in Schedule 1);	The area of new floorspace exceeds 1,000 square metres.
(b) Plants for the pre-treatment (operations such as washing, bleaching, mercerisation) or dyeing of fibres or textiles;	The area of new floorspace exceeds 1,000 square metres.
(c) Plants for the tanning of hides and skins;	The area of new floorspace exceeds 1,000 square metres.
(d) Cellulose-processing and production installations.	The area of new floorspace exceeds 1,000 square metres.
9 *Rubber industry*	
Manufacture and treatment of elastomer-based products.	The area of new floorspace exceeds 1,000 square metres.

Description of development	Applicable thresholds and criteria
10 *Infrastructure projects*	
(a) Industrial estate development projects;	The area of the development exceeds 0.5 hectare.
(b) Urban development projects, including the construction of shopping centres and car parks, sports stadiums, leisure centres and multiplex cinemas;	The area of the development exceeds 0.5 hectare.
(c) Construction of intermodal transshipment facilities and of intermodal terminals (unless included in Schedule 1);	The area of the development exceeds 0.5 hectare.
(d) Construction of railways (unless included in Schedule 1);	The area of the works exceeds 1 hectare.
(e) Construction of airfields (unless included in Schedule 1);	(i) The development involves an extension to a runway; or (ii) the area of the works exceeds 1 hectare.
(f) Construction of roads (unless included in Schedule 1);	The area of the works exceeds 1 hectare.
(g) Construction of harbours and port installations including fishing harbours (unless included in Schedule 1);	The area of the works exceeds 1 hectare.
(h) Inland-waterway construction not included in Schedule 1, canalisation and flood-relief works;	The area of the works exceeds 1 hectare
(i) Dams and other installations designed to hold water or store it on a long-term basis (unless included in Schedule 1);	The area of the works exceeds 1 hectare.
(j) Tramways, elevated and underground railways, suspended lines or similar lines of a particular type, used exclusively or mainly for passenger transport;	The area of the works exceeds 1 hectare
(k) Oil and gas pipeline installations (unless included in Schedule 1);	(i) The area of the works exceeds 1 hectare; or, (ii) in the case of a gas pipeline, the installation has a design operating pressure exceeding 7 bar gauge.
(l) Installations of long-distance aqueducts;	(i) The area of the works exceeds 1 hectare; or, (ii) in the case of a gas pipeline, the installation has a design operating pressure exceeding 7 bar gauge.
(m) Coastal work to combat erosion and maritime works capable of altering the coast through the construction, for example, of dykes, moles, jetties and other sea defence works, excluding the maintenance and reconstruction of such works;	All development.
(n) Groundwater abstraction and artificial groundwater recharge schemes not included in Schedule 1;	The area of the works exceeds 1 hectare.

Description of development	Applicable thresholds and criteria
(o) Works for the transfer of water resources between river basins not included in Schedule 1;	The area of the works exceeds 1 hectare.
(p) Motorway service areas.	The area of the development exceeds 0.5 hectare.
11 *Other projects*	
(a) Permanent racing and test tracks for motorised vehicles;	The area of the development exceeds 1 hectare.
(b) Installations for the disposal of waste (unless included in Schedule 1);	(i) The disposal is by incineration; or (ii) the area of the development exceeds 0.5 hectare; or (iii) the installation is to be sited within 100 metres of any controlled waters.
(c) Waste-water treatment plants (unless included in Schedule 1);	The area of the development exceeds . 1,000 square metres.
(d) Sludge-deposition sites;	(i) The area of deposit or storage exceeds 0.5 hectare; or (ii) a deposit is to be made or scrap stored within 100 metres of any controlled waters.
(e) Storage of scrap iron, including scrap vehicles;	(i) The area of deposit or storage exceeds 0.5 hectare; or (ii) a deposit is to be made or scrap stored within 100 metres of any controlled waters.
(f) Test benches for engines, turbines or reactors;	The area of new floorspace exceeds 1,000 square metres.
(g) Installations for the manufacture of artificial mineral fibres;	The area of new floorspace exceeds 1,000 square metres.
(h) Installations for the recovery or destruction of explosive substances;	The area of new floorspace exceeds 1,000 square metres.
(i) Knackers' yards.	The area of new floorspace exceeds 1,000 square metres.
12 *Tourism and leisure*	
(a) Ski-runs, ski-lifts and cable-cars and associated developments;	(i) The area of the works exceeds 1 hectare; or (ii) the height of any building or other structure exceeds 15 metres.
(b) Marinas;	The area of the enclosed water surface exceeds 1,000 square metres.
(c) Holiday villages and hotel complexes outside urban areas and associated developments;	The area of the development exceeds 0.5 hectare.
(d) Theme parks;	The area of the development exceeds 0.5 hectare.
(e) Permanent camp sites and caravan sites;	The area of the development exceeds 1 hectare.
(f) Golf courses and associated developments.	The area of the development exceeds 1 hectare.

Description of development	Applicable thresholds and criteria

13

(a) Any change to or extension of development of a description listed in Schedule 1 or in paragraphs 1 to 12 of Column 1 of this table, where that development is already authorised, executed or in the process of being executed, and the change or extension may have significant adverse effects on the environment;

(i) In relation to development of a description mentioned in Column 1 of this table, the thresholds and criteria in the corresponding part of Column 2 of this table applied to the change or extension (and not to the development as changed or extended).

(ii) In relation to development of a description mentioned in a paragraph in Schedule 1 indicated below, the thresholds and criteria in Column 2 of the paragraph of this table indicated below applied to the change or extension (and not to the development as changed or extended):

Paragraph in Schedule 1	*Paragraph of this table*
1	6(a)
2(a)	3(a)
2(b)	3(g)
3	3(g)
4	4
5	5
6	6(a)
7(a)	10(d) (in relation to railways) or 10(e) (in relation to airports)
7(b) and (c)	10(f)
8(a)	10(h)
8(b)	10(g)
9	11(b)
10	11(b)
11	10(n)
12	10(o)
13	11(c)
14	2(e)
15	10(i)
16	10(k)
17	1(c)
18	8(a)
19	2(a)
20	6(c).

(b) Development of a description mentioned in Schedule 1 undertaken exclusively or mainly for the development and testing of new methods or products and not used for more than two years.

All development.

SCHEDULE 3
SELECTION CRITERIA FOR SCREENING SCHEDULE 2 DEVELOPMENT

Regulation 4(5)

I Characteristics of development

The characteristics of development must be considered having regard, in particular, to—

(a) the size of the development;
(b) the cumulation with other development;
(c) the use of natural resources;
(d) the production of waste;
(e) pollution and nuisances;
(f) the risk of accidents, having regard in particular to substances or technologies used.

2 Location of development

The environmental sensitivity of geographical areas likely to be affected by development must be considered, having regard, in particular, to—

(a) the existing land use;
(b) the relative abundance, quality and regenerative capacity of natural resources in the area;
(c) the absorption capacity of the natural environment, paying particular attention to the following areas—
    (i) wetlands;
    (ii) coastal zones;
    (iii) mountain and forest areas;
    (iv) nature reserves and parks;
    (v) areas classified or protected under Member States' legislation; areas designated by Member States pursuant to Council Directive 79/409/EEC on the conservation of wild birds and Council Directive 92/43/EEC on the conservation of natural habitats and of wild fauna and flora;
    (vi) areas in which the environmental quality standards laid down in Community legislation have already been exceeded;
    (vii) densely populated areas;
    (viii) landscapes of historical, cultural or archaeological significance.

3 Characteristics of the potential impact

The potential significant effects of development must be considered in relation to criteria set out under paragraphs 1 and 2 above, and having regard in particular to—

(a) the extent of the impact (geographical area and size of the affected population);
(b) the transfrontier nature of the impact;
(c) the magnitude and complexity of the impact;
(d) the probability of the impact;
(e) the duration, frequency and reversibility of the impact.

SCHEDULE 4
INFORMATION FOR INCLUSION IN ENVIRONMENTAL STATEMENTS

Regulation 2(1)

Part I

1   Description of the development, including in particular—
(a)   a description of the physical characteristics of the whole development and the land-use requirements during the construction and operational phases;
(b)   a description of the main characteristics of the production processes, for instance, nature and quantity of the materials used;
(c)   an estimate, by type and quantity, of expected residues and emissions (water, air and soil pollution, noise, vibration, light, heat, radiation, etc) resulting from the operation of the proposed development.

2   An outline of the main alternatives studied by the applicant or appellant and an indication of the main reasons for his choice, taking into account the environmental effects.

3   A description of the aspects of the environment likely to be significantly affected by the development, including, in particular, population, fauna, flora, soil, water, air, climatic factors, material assets, including the architectural and archaeological heritage, landscape and the inter-relationship between the above factors.

4   A description of the likely significant effects of the development on the environment, which should cover the direct effects and any indirect, secondary, cumulative, short, medium and long-term, permanent and temporary, positive and negative effects of the development, resulting from:
(a)   the existence of the development;
(b)   the use of natural resources;
(c)   the emission of pollutants, the creation of nuisances and the elimination of waste, and the description by the applicant of the forecasting methods used to assess the effects on the environment.

5   A description of the measures envisaged to prevent, reduce and where possible offset any significant adverse effects on the environment.

6   A non-technical summary of the information provided under paragraphs 1 to 5 of this Part.

7   An indication of any difficulties (technical deficiencies or lack of know-how) encountered by the applicant in compiling the required informa**tion.**

Part II

1   A description of the development comprising information on the site, design and size of the development.

2   A description of the measures envisaged in order to avoid, reduce and, if possible, remedy significant adverse effects.

3   The data required to identify and assess the main effects which the development is likely to have on the environment.

4   An outline of the main alternatives studied by the applicant or appellant and an indication of the main reasons for his choice, taking into account the environmental effects.

5   A non-technical summary of the information provided under paragraphs 1 to 4 of this Part.

SCHEDULE 5
STATUTORY INSTRUMENTS REVOKED

Regulation 34(1)

Title of Instrument	Reference	Extent of revocation
The Town and Country Planning (Assessment of Environmental Effects) Regulations 1988	SI 1988/1199	The whole of the Regulations
The Town and Country Planning (Assessment of Environmental Effects) (Amendment) Regulations 1990	SI 1990/367	The whole of the Regulations
The Town and Country Planning (Assessment of Environmental Effects) (Amendment) Regulations 1992	SI 1992/1494	The whole of the Regulations
The Town and Country Planning (Simplified Planning Zones) Regulations 1992	SI 1992/2414	Regulation 22
The Town and Country Planning (Assessment of Environmental Effects) (Amendment) Regulations 1994	SI 1994/677	The whole of the Regulations
The Town and Country Planning (Environmental Assessment and Permitted Development) Regulations 1995	SI 1995/417	The whole of the Regulations
The Town and Country Planning (General Permitted Development) Order 1995	SI 1995/418	Sub-paragraphs (a) and (c) of article 3(12)
The Town and Country Planning (Environmental Assessment and Unauthorised Development) Regulations 1995	SI 1995/2258	The whole of the Regulations

A Regulatory Impact Appraisal has been prepared in relation to these Regulations. It has been placed in the Library of each House of Parliament and copies may be obtained from PD5A Division, Department of the Environment, Transport and the Regions, Eland House, Bressenden Place, London SW1E 5DU (Telephone 0171-890 3893) or Planning Division, Welsh Office, Cathays Park, Cardiff CF1 3NQ (Telephone 01222-823882).

Directive 85/337/EEC of the European Council

Directive 85/337/EEC of the
European Council
of 27 June 1985

on the assessment of the effects of certain public and private projects
on the environment

(OJ L175 5.7.1985 p 40)
Amended by:
Council Directive 97/11/EC of 3 March 1997 L73 4.3.1997 p 5

This document is meant purely as a documentation tool and the institutions do not assume any liability for its contents

THE COUNCIL OF THE EUROPEAN COMMUNITIES,

Having regard to the Treaty establishing the European Economic Community, and in particular Articles 100 and 235 thereof,

Having regard to the proposal from the Commission,[1]

Having regard to the opinion of the European Parliament,[2]

Having regard to the opinion of the Economic and Social Committee,[3]

Whereas the 1973[4] and 1977[5] action programmes of the European Communities on the environment, as well as the 1983[6] action programme, the main outlines of which have been approved by the Council of the European Communities and the representatives of the Governments of the Member States, stress that the best environmental policy consists in preventing the creation of pollution or nuisances at source, rather than subsequently trying to counteract their effects; whereas they affirm the need to take effects on the environment into account at the earliest possible stage in all the technical planning and decision-making processes; whereas to that end, they provide for the implementation of procedures to evaluate such effects;

Whereas the disparities between the laws in force in the various Member States with regard to the assessment of the environmental effects of public and private projects may create unfavourable competitive conditions and thereby directly affect the functioning of the common market; whereas, therefore, it is necessary to approximate national laws in this field pursuant to Article 100 of the Treaty;

Whereas, in addition, it is necessary to achieve one of the Community's objectives in the sphere of the protection of the environment and the quality of life;

Whereas, since the Treaty has not provided the powers required for this end, recourse should be had to Article 235 of the Treaty;

Whereas general principles for the assessment of environmental effects should be introduced with a view to supplementing and coordinating development consent procedures governing public and private projects likely to have a major effect on the environment;

Whereas development consent for public and private projects which are likely to have significant effects on the environment should be granted only after prior assessment of the likely significant environmental effects of these projects has been carried out; whereas this assessment must be conducted on the basis of the appropriate information supplied by the developer, which may be supplemented by the authorities and by the people who may be concerned by the project in question;

Whereas the principles of the assessment of environmental effects should be harmonised, in particular with reference to the projects which should be subject to assessment, the main obligations of the developers and the content of the assessment;

Whereas projects belonging to certain types have significant effects on the environment and these projects must as a rule be subject to systematic assessment;

Whereas projects of other types may not have significant effects on the environment in every case and whereas these projects should be assessed where the Member States consider that their characteristics so require;

Whereas, for projects which are subject to assessment, a certain minimal amount of information must be supplied, concerning the project and its effects;

Whereas the effects of a project on the environment must be assessed in order to take account of concerns to protect human health, to contribute by means of a better environment to the quality of life, to ensure maintenance of the diversity of species and to maintain the reproductive capacity of the ecosystem as a basic resource for life;

Whereas, however, this Directive should not be applied to projects the details of which are adopted by a specific act of national legislation, since the objectives of this Directive, including that of supplying information, are achieved through the legislative process;

Whereas, furthermore, it may be appropriate in exceptional cases to exempt a specific project from the assessment procedures laid down by this Directive, subject to appropriate information being supplied to the Commission,

HAS ADOPTED THIS DIRECTIVE:

Article 1

1   This Directive shall apply to the assessment of the environmental effects of those public and private projects which are likely to have significant effects on the environment.

2   For the purposes of this Directive:
'project' means:
— the execution of construction works or of other installations or schemes,
— other interventions in the natural surroundings and landscape including those involving the extraction of mineral resources;

'developer' means:
the applicant for authorisation for a private project or the public authority which initiates a project;

'development consent' means:
the decision of the competent authority or authorities which entitles the developer to proceed with the project.

3   The competent authority or authorities shall be that or those which the Member States designate as responsible for performing the duties arising from this Directive.

4   Projects serving national defence purposes are not covered by this Directive.

5   This Directive shall not apply to projects the details of which are adopted by a specific act of national legislation, since the objectives of this Directive, including that of supplying information, are achieved through the legislative process.

Article 2

1   Member States shall adopt all measures necessary to ensure that, before consent is given, projects likely to have significant effects on the environment by virtue, inter alia, of their nature, size or location are made subject to a requirement for development consent and an assessment with regard to their effects. These projects are defined in Article 4.

2   The environmental impact assessment may be integrated into the existing procedures for consent to projects in the Member States, or, failing this, into other procedures or into procedures to be established to comply with the aims of this Directive.

2a   Member States may provide for a single procedure in order to fulfil the requirements of this Directive and the requirements of Council Directive 96/61/EC of 24 September 1996 on integrated pollution prevention and control.[7]

3   Without prejudice to Article 7, Member States may, in exceptional cases, exempt a specific project in whole or in part from the provisions laid down in this Directive.

In this event, the Member States shall:

(a) consider whether another form of assessment would be appropriate and whether the information thus collected should be made available to the public;
(b) make available to the public concerned the information relating to the exemption and the reasons for granting it;
(c) inform the Commission, prior to granting consent, of the reasons justifying the exemption granted, and provide it with the information made available, where applicable, to their own nationals.

The Commission shall immediately forward the documents received to the other Member States.

The Commission shall report annually to the Council on the application of this paragraph.

Article 3

The environmental impact assessment shall identify, describe and assess in an appropriate manner, in the light of each individual case and in accordance with Articles 4 to 11, the direct and indirect effects of a project on the following factors:
— human beings, fauna and flora;
— soil, water, air, climate and the landscape;
— material assets and the cultural heritage;
— the interaction between the factors mentioned in the first, second and third indents.

Article 4

1   Subject to Article 2(3), projects listed in Annex I shall be made subject to an assessment in accordance with Articles 5 to 10.

2   Subject to Article 2(3), for projects listed in Annex II, the Member States shall determine through:
(a) a case-by-case examination,
     or
(b) thresholds or criteria set by the Member State whether the project shall be made subject to an assessment in accordance with Articles 5 to 10.

Member States may decide to apply both procedures referred to in (a) and (b).

3   When a case-by-case examination is carried out or thresholds or criteria are set for the purpose of paragraph 2, the relevant selection criteria set out in Annex III shall be taken into account.

4   Member States shall ensure that the determination made by the competent authorities under paragraph 2 is made available to the public.

Article 5

1   In the case of projects which, pursuant to Article 4, must be subjected to an environmental impact assessment in accordance with Articles 5 to 10, Member States shall adopt the necessary measures to ensure that the developer supplies in an appropriate form the information specified in Annex IV inasmuch as:
(a)   the Member States consider that the information is relevant to a given stage of the consent procedure and to the specific characteristics of a particular project or type of project and of the environmental features likely to be affected;
(b)   the Member States consider that a developer may reasonably be required to compile this information having regard inter alia to current knowledge and methods of assessment.

2   Member States shall take the necessary measures to ensure that, if the developer so requests before submitting an application for development consent, the competent authority shall give an opinion on the information to be supplied by the developer in accordance with paragraph 1. The competent authority shall consult the developer and authorities referred to in Article 6(1) before it gives its opinion. The fact that the authority has given an opinion under this paragraph shall not preclude it from subsequently requiring the developer to submit further information.

Member States may require the competent authorities to give such an opinion, irrespective of whether the developer so requests.

3   The information to be provided by the developer in accordance with paragraph 1 shall include at least:
—   a description of the project comprising information on the site, design and size of the project,
—   a description of the measures envisaged in order to avoid, reduce and, if possible, remedy significant adverse effects,
—   the data required to identify and assess the main effects which the project is likely to have on the environment,
—   an outline of the main alternatives studied by the developer and an indication of the main reasons for his choice, taking into account the environmental effects,
—   a non-technical summary of the information mentioned in the previous indents.

4   Member States shall, if necessary, ensure that any authorities holding relevant information, with particular reference to Article 3, shall make this information available to the developer.

Article 6

1   Member States shall take the measures necessary to ensure that the authorities likely to be concerned by the project by reason of their specific environmental responsibilities are given an opportunity to express their opinion on the information supplied by the developer and on the request for development consent. To this end, Member States shall designate the authorities to be consulted, either in general terms

or on a case-by-case basis. The information gathered pursuant to Article 5 shall be forwarded to those authorities. Detailed arrangements for consultation shall be laid down by the Member States.

2   Member States shall ensure that any request for development consent and any information gathered pursuant to Article 5 are made available to the public within a reasonable time in order to give the public concerned the opportunity to express an opinion before the development consent is granted.

3   The detailed arrangements for such information and consultation shall be determined by the Member States, which may in particular, depending on the particular characteristics of the projects or sites concerned:
— determine the public concerned,
— specify the places where the information can be consulted,
— specify the way in which the public may be informed, for example by bill-posting within a certain radius, publication in local newspapers, organisation of exhibitions with plans, drawings, tables, graphs, models,
— determine the manner in which the public is to be consulted, for example, by written submissions, by public enquiry,
— fix appropriate time limits for the various stages of the procedure in order to ensure that a decision is taken within a reasonable period.

Article 7

1   Where a Member State is aware that a project is likely to have significant effects on the environment in another Member State or where a Member State likely to be significantly affected so requests, the Member State in whose territory the project is intended to be carried out shall send to the affected Member State as soon as possible and no later than when informing its own public, inter alia:
(a) a description of the project, together with any available information on its possible transboundary impact;
(b) information on the nature of the decision which may be taken, and shall give the other Member State a reasonable time in which to indicate whether it wishes to participate in the Environmental Impact Assessment procedure, and may include the information referred to in paragraph 2.

2   If a Member State which receives information pursuant to paragraph 1 indicates that it intends to participate in the Environmental Impact Assessment procedure, the Member State in whose territory the project is intended to be carried out shall, if it has not already done so, send to the affected Member State the information gathered pursuant to Article 5 and relevant information regarding the said procedure, including the request for development consent.

3   The Member States concerned, each insofar as it is concerned, shall also:
(a) arrange for the information referred to in paragraphs 1 and 2 to be made available, within a reasonable time, to the authorities referred to in Article 6(1) and the public concerned in the territory of the Member State likely to be significantly affected; and

(b) ensure that those authorities and the public concerned are given an opportunity, before development consent for the project is granted, to forward their opinion within a reasonable time on the information supplied to the competent authority in the Member State in whose territory the project is intended to be carried out.

4   The Member States concerned shall enter into consultations regarding, inter alia, the potential transboundary effects of the project and the measures envisaged to reduce or eliminate such effects and shall agree on a reasonable time frame for the duration of the consultation period.

5   The detailed arrangements for implementing the provisions of this Article may be determined by the Member States concerned.

Article 8

The results of consultations and the information gathered pursuant to Articles 5, 6 and 7 must be taken into consideration in the development consent procedure.

Article 9

1   When a decision to grant or refuse development consent has been taken, the competent authority or authorities shall inform the public thereof in accordance with the appropriate procedures and shall make available to the public the following information:
— the content of the decision and any conditions attached thereto,
— the main reasons and considerations on which the decision is based,
— a description, where necessary, of the main measures to avoid, reduce and, if possible, offset the major adverse effects.

2   The competent authority or authorities shall inform any Member State which has been consulted pursuant to Article 7, forwarding to it the information referred to in paragraph 1.

Article 10

The provisions of this Directive shall not affect the obligation on the competent authorities to respect the limitations imposed by national regulations and administrative provisions and accepted legal practices with regard to commercial and industrial confidentiality, including intellectual property, and the safeguarding of the public interest.

Where Article 7 applies, the transmission of information to another Member State and the receipt of information by another Member State shall be subject to the limitations in force in the Member State in which the project is proposed.

Article 11

1   The Member States and the Commission shall exchange information on the experience gained in applying this Directive.

2   In particular, Member States shall inform the Commission of any criteria and/or thresholds adopted for the selection of the projects in question, in accordance with Article 4(2).

3   Five years after notification of this Directive, the Commission shall send the European Parliament and the Council a report on its application and effectiveness. The report shall be based on the aforementioned exchange of information.

4   On the basis of this exchange of information, the Commission shall submit to the Council additional proposals, should this be necessary, with a view to this Directive's being applied in a sufficiently coordinated manner.

Article 12

1   Member States shall take the measures necessary to comply with this Directive within three years of its notification.[8]

2   Member States shall communicate to the Commission the texts of the provisions of national law which they adopt in the field covered by this Directive.

Article 14

This Directive is addressed to the Member States.

ANNEX I
PROJECTS SUBJECT TO ARTICLE 4(1)

1   Crude-oil refineries (excluding undertakings manufacturing only lubricants from crude oil) and installations for the gasification and liquefaction of 500 tonnes or more of coalor bituminous shale per day.

2
— Thermal power stations and other combustion installations with a heat output of 300 megawatts or more, and
— nuclear power stations and other nuclear reactors including the dismantling or decommissioning of such power stations or reactors[9] (except research installations for the production and conversion of fissionable and fertile materials, whose maximum power does not exceed 1 kilowatt continuous thermal load).

3

(a) Installations for the reprocessing of irradiated nuclear fuel.

(b) Installations designed:
- for the production or enrichment of nuclear fuel,
- for the processing of irradiated nuclear fuel or high-level radioactive waste,
- for the final disposal of irradiated nuclear fuel,
- solely for the final disposal of radioactive waste,
- solely for the storage (planned for more than 10 years) of irradiated nuclear fuels or radioactive waste in a different site than the production site.

4

- Integrated works for the initial smelting of cast-iron and steel;
- Installations for the production of non-ferrous crude metals from ore, concentrates or secondary raw materials by metallurgical, chemical or electrolytic processes.

5   Installations for the extraction of asbestos and for the processing and transformation of asbestos and products containing asbestos: for asbestos-cement products, with an annual production of more than 20 000 tonnes of finished products, for friction material, with an annual production of more than 50 tonnes of finished products, and for other uses of asbestos, utilisation of more than 200 tonnes per year.

6   Integrated chemical installations, ie those installations for the manufacture on an industrial scale of substances using chemical conversion processes, in which several units are juxtaposed and are functionally linked to one another and which are:

(i)   for the production of basic organic chemicals;

(ii)   for the production of basic inorganic chemicals;

(iii) for the production of phosphorous-, nitrogen- or potassium-based fertilizers (simple or compound fertilizers);

(iv)   for the production of basic plant health products and of biocides;

(v)   for the production of basic pharmaceutical products using a chemical or biological process;

(vi)   for the production of explosives.

7

(a) Construction of lines for long-distance railway traffic and of airports[10] with a basic runway length of 2 100 m or more;

(b) Construction of motorways and express roads;[11]

(c) Construction of a new road of four or more lanes, or realignment and/or widening of an existing road of two lanes or less so as to provide four or more lanes, where such new road, or realigned and/or widened section of road would be 10 km or more in a continuous length.

8

(a) Inland waterways and ports for inland-waterway traffic which permit the passage of vessels of over 1 350 tonnes;

(b) Trading ports, piers for loading and unloading connected to land and outside ports (excluding ferry piers) which can take vessels of over 1 350 tonnes.

9   Waste disposal installations for the incineration, chemical treatment as defined in Annex IIA to Directive 75/442/EEC[12] under heading D9, or landfill of hazardous waste (ie waste to which Directive 91/689/EEC[13] applies).

10   Waste disposal installations for the incineration or chemical treatment as defined in Annex IIA to Directive 75/442/EEC under heading D9 of non-hazardous waste with a capacity exceeding 100 tonnes per day.

11   Groundwater abstraction or artificial groundwater recharge schemes where the annual volume of water abstracted or recharged is equivalent to or exceeds 10 million cubic metres.

12
(a) Works for the transfer of water resources between river basins where this transfer aims at preventing possible shortages of water and where the amount of water transferred exceeds 100 million cubic metres/year;
(b) In all other cases, works for the transfer of water resources between river basins where the multi-annual average flow of the basin of abstraction exceeds 2 000 million cubic metres/year and where the amount of water transferred exceeds 5 % of this flow.

In both cases transfers of piped drinking water are excluded.

13   Waste water treatment plants with a capacity exceeding 150 000 population equivalent as defined in Article 2 point (6) of Directive 91/271/EEC.[14]

14   Extraction of petroleum and natural gas for commercial purposes where the amount extracted exceeds 500 tonnes/day in the case of petroleum and 500 000 m3/day in the case of gas.

15   Dams and other installations designed for the holding back or permanent storage of water, where a new or additional amount of water held back or stored exceeds 10 million cubic metres.

16   Pipelines for the transport of gas, oil or chemicals with a diameter of more than 800 mm and a length of more than 40 km.

17   Installations for the intensive rearing of poultry or pigs with more than:
(a) 85 000 places for broilers, 60 000 places for hens;
(b) 3 000 places for production pigs (over 30 kg); or
(c) 900 places for sows.

18   Industrial plants for the
(a) production of pulp from timber or similar fibrous materials;
(b) production of paper and board with a production capacity exceeding 200 tonnes per day.

19   Quarries and open-cast mining where the surface of the site exceeds 25 hectares, or peat extraction, where the surface of the site exceeds 150 hectares.

20   Construction of overhead electrical power lines with a voltage of 220 kV or more and a length of more than 15 km.

21   Installations for storage of petroleum, petrochemical, or chemical products with a capacity of 200 000 tonnes or more.

ANNEX II
PROJECTS SUBJECT TO ARTICLE 4(2)

1   Agriculture, silviculture and aquaculture

(a) Projects for the restructuring of rural land holdings;
(b) Projects for the use of uncultivated land or semi-natural areas for intensive agricultural purposes;
(c) Water management projects for agriculture, including irrigation and land drainage projects;
(d) Initial afforestation and deforestation for the purposes of conversion to another type of land use;
(e) Intensive livestock installations (projects not included in Annex I);
(f) Intensive fish farming;
(g) Reclamation of land from the sea.

2   Extractive industry

(a) Quarries, open-cast mining and peat extraction (projects not included in Annex I);
(b) Underground mining;
(c) Extraction of minerals by marine or fluvial dredging;
(d) Deep drillings, in particular:
    — geothermal drilling,
    — drilling for the storage of nuclear waste material,
    — drilling for water supplies,
      with the exception of drillings for investigating the stability of the soil;
(e) Surface industrial installations for the extraction of coal, petroleum, natural gas and ores, as well as bituminous shale.

3   Energy industry

(a) Industrial installations for the production of electricity, steam and hot water (projects not included in Annex I);
(b) Industrial installations for carrying gas, steam and hot water; transmission of electrical energy by overhead cables (projects not included in Annex I);
(c) Surface storage of natural gas;
(d) Underground storage of combustible gases;
(e) Surface storage of fossil fuels;
(f) Industrial briquetting of coal and lignite;
(g) Installations for the processing and storage of radioactive waste (unless included in Annex I);

(h) Installations for hydroelectric energy production;
(i)   Installations for the harnessing of wind power for energy production (wind farms).

4   *Production and processing of metals*

(a) Installations for the production of pig iron or steel (primary or secondary fusion) including continuous casting;
(b) Installations for the processing of ferrous metals:
    (i)   hot-rolling mills;
    (ii)   smitheries with hammers;
    (iii) application of protective fused metal coats;
(c) Ferrous metal foundries;
(d) Installations for the smelting, including the alloyage, of non-ferrous metals, excluding precious metals, including recovered products (refining, foundry casting, etc);
(e) Installations for surface treatment of metals and plastic materials using an electrolytic or chemical process;
(f) Manufacture and assembly of motor vehicles and manufacture of motor vehicle engines;
(g) Shipyards;
(h) Installations for the construction and repair of aircraft;
(i)   Manufacture of railway equipment;
(j)   Swaging by explosives;
(k) Installations for the roasting and sintering of metallic ores.

5   *Mineral industry*

(a) Coke ovens (dry coal distillation);
(b) Installations for the manufacture of cement;
(c) Installations for the production of asbestos and the manufacture of asbestos-products (projects not included in Annex I);
(d) Installations for the manufacture of glass including glass fibre;
(e) Installations for smelting mineral substances including the production of mineral fibres;
(f) Manufacture of ceramic products by burning, in particular roofing tiles, bricks, refractory bricks, tiles, stoneware or porcelain.

6   *Chemical industry (Projects not included in Annex I)*

(a) Treatment of intermediate products and production of chemicals;
(b) Production of pesticides and pharmaceutical products, paint and varnishes, elastomers and peroxides;
(c) Storage facilities for petroleum, petrochemical and chemical products.

7 Food industry

(a) Manufacture of vegetable and animal oils and fats;
(b) Packing and canning of animal and vegetable products;
(c) Manufacture of dairy products;
(d) Brewing and malting;
(e) Confectionery and syrup manufacture;
(f) Installations for the slaughter of animals;
(g) Industrial starch manufacturing installations;
(h) Fish-meal and fish-oil factories;
(i) Sugar factories.

8 Textile, leather, wood and paper industries

(a) Industrial plants for the production of paper and board (projects not included in Annex I);
(b) Plants for the pretreatment (operations such as washing, bleaching, mercerisation) or dyeing of fibres or textiles;
(c) Plants for the tanning of hides and skins;
(d) Cellulose-processing and production installations.

9 Rubber industry

Manufacture and treatment of elastomer-based products.

10 Infrastructure projects

(a) Industrial estate development projects;
(b) Urban development projects, including the construction of shopping centres and car parks;
(c) Construction of railways and intermodal transshipment facilities, and of intermodal terminals (projects not included in Annex I);
(d) Construction of airfields (projects not included in Annex I);
(e) Construction of roads, harbours and port installations, including fishing harbours (projects not included in Annex I);
(f) Inland-waterway construction not included in Annex I, canalisation and flood-relief works;
(g) Dams and other installations designed to hold water or store it on a long-term basis (projects not included in Annex I);
(h) Tramways, elevated and underground railways, suspended lines or similar lines of a particular type, used exclusively or mainly for passenger transport;
(i) Oil and gas pipeline installations (projects not included in Annex I);
(j) Installations of long-distance aqueducts;

(k) Coastal work to combat erosion and maritime works capable of altering the coast through the construction, for example, of dykes, moles, jetties and other sea defence works, excluding the maintenance and reconstruction of such works;
(l) Groundwater abstraction and artificial groundwater recharge schemes not included in Annex I;
(m) Works for the transfer of water resources between river basins not included in Annex I.

11   Other projects

(a) Permanent racing and test tracks for motorised vehicles;
(b) Installations for the disposal of waste (projects not included in Annex I);
(c) Waste-water treatment plants (projects not included in Annex I);
(d) Sludge-deposition sites;
(e) Storage of scrap iron, including scrap vehicles;
(f) Test benches for engines, turbines or reactors;
(g) Installations for the manufacture of artificial mineral fibres;
(h) Installations for the recovery or destruction of explosive substances;
(i) Knackers' yards.

12   Tourism and leisure

(a) Ski-runs, ski-lifts and cable-cars and associated developments;
(b) Marinas;
(c) Holiday villages and hotel complexes outside urban areas and associated developments;
(d) Permanent camp sites and caravan sites;
(e) Theme parks.

13— Any change or extension of projects listed in Annex I or Annex II, already authorised, executed or in the process of being executed, which may have significant adverse effects on the environment;
— Projects in Annex I, undertaken exclusively or mainly for the development and testing of new methods or products and not used for more than two years.

ANNEX III
SELECTION CRITERIA REFERRED TO IN ARTICLE 4(3)

1   Characteristics of projects

The characteristics of projects must be considered having regard, in particular, to:
— the size of the project,
— the cumulation with other projects,
— the use of natural resources,

— the production of waste,
— pollution and nuisances,
— the risk of accidents, having regard in particular to substances or technologies used.

2 Location of projects

The environmental sensitivity of geographical areas likely to be affected by projects must be considered, having regard, in particular, to:
— the existing land use,
— the relative abundance, quality and regenerative capacity of natural resources in the area,
— the absorption capacity of the natural environment, paying particular attention to the following areas:
  (a) wetlands;
  (b) coastal zones;
  (c) mountain and forest areas;
  (d) nature reserves and parks;
  (e) areas classified or protected under Member States' legislation; special protection areas designated by Member States pursuant to Directive 79/409/EEC and 92/43/EEC;
  (f) areas in which the environmental quality standards laid down in Community legislation have already been exceeded;
  (g) densely populated areas;
  (h) landscapes of historical, cultural or archaeological significance.

3 Characteristics of the potential impact

The potential significant effects of projects must be considered in relation to criteria set out under 1 and 2 above, and having regard in particular to:
— the extent of the impact (geographical area and size of the affected population),
— the transfrontier nature of the impact,
— the magnitude and complexity of the impact,
— the probability of the impact,
— the duration, frequency and reversibility of the impact.

ANNEX IV
INFORMATION REFERRED TO IN ARTICLE 5(1)

1 Description of the project, including in particular:
— a description of the physical characteristics of the whole project and the land-use requirements during the construction and operational phases,

— a description of the main characteristics of the production processes, for instance, nature and quantity of the materials used,

— an estimate, by type and quantity, of expected residues and emissions (water, air and soil pollution, noise, vibration, light, heat, radiation, etc) resulting from the operation of the proposed project.

2   An outline of the main alternatives studied by the developer and an indication of the main reasons for this choice, taking into account the environmental effects.

3   A description of the aspects of the environment likely to be significantly affected by the proposed project, including, in particular, population, fauna, flora, soil, water, air, climatic factors, material assets, including the architectural and archaeological heritage, landscape and the inter-relationship between the above factors.

4   A description[15] of the likely significant effects of the proposed project on the environment resulting from:
— the existence of the project,
— the use of natural resources,
— the emission of pollutants, the creation of nuisances and the elimination of waste, and the description by the developer of the forecasting methods used to assess the effects on the environment.

5   A description of the measures envisaged to prevent, reduce and where possible offset any significant adverse effects on the environment.

6   A non-technical summary of the information provided under the above headings.

7   An indication of any difficulties (technical deficiencies or lack of know-how) encountered by the developer in compiling the required information.

(1)   OJ C169 9.7.1980 p 14.
(2)   OJ C66 15.3.1982 p 89.
(3)   OJ C185 27.7.1981 p 8.
(4)   OJ C112 20.12.1973 p 1.
(5)   OJ C139 13.6.1977 p1.
(6)   OJ C46 17.2.1983 p 1.
(7)   OJ L257 10.10.1996 p 26.
(8)   This Directive was notified to the Member States on 3 July 1985.
(9)   Nuclear power stations and other nuclear reactors cease to be such an installation when all nuclear fuel and other radioactively contaminated elements have been removed permanently from the installation site.
(10) For the purposes of this Directive, 'airport' means airports which comply with the definition in the 1944 Chicago Convention setting up the International Civil Aviation Organisation (Annex 14).
(11) For the purposes of the Directive, 'express road' means a road which complies with the definition in the European Agreement on Main International Traffic Arteries of 15 November 1975.
(12)   OJ L194 25.7.1975 p 39. Directive as last amended by Commission Decision 94/3/EC (OJ L5 7.1.1994 p 15).
(13) OJ L377 31.12.1991 p 20. Directive as last amended by Directive 94/31/EC (OJ L168 2.7.1994 p 28).
(14)   OJ L135 30.5.1991 p 40. Directive as last amended by the 1994 Act of Accession.
(15) This description should cover the direct effects and any indirect, secondary, cumulative, short, medium and long-term, permanent and temporary, positive and negative effects of the project.

Town and Country Planning (Assessment of Environmental Effects) Regulations 1988 (SI 1988/1199)

Town and Country Planning
(Assessment of Environmental Effects) Regulations 1988*

1988 No 1199

Made   12th July 1988

NOTES

Revoked with savings by SI 1999/293, reg 34(1), Sch 5; for savings see reg 34(2) thereof. Date in force: 14 March 1999: see SI 1999/293, reg 1(1).

The Secretary of State for the Environment as respects England and the Secretary of State for Wales as respects Wales, being designated Ministers for the purposes of section 2(2) of the European Communities Act 1972 in relation to measures relating to the requirement for an assessment of the impact on the environment of projects likely to have significant effects on the environment, in exercise of the powers conferred upon them by the said section 2 hereby make the following Regulations, a draft of which has been laid before and approved by a resolution of each House of Parliament.

1   Citation, commencement and application

(1)   These Regulations may be cited as the Town and Country Planning (Assessment of Environmental Effects) Regulations 1988.

(2)   These Regulations shall come into force on the third day after the day on which they are made.

[(3)   Subject to paragraph (4), these Regulations apply throughout England and Wales.

(4)   Paragraphs (2) and (5)(a) of regulation 13 shall not apply to the Isles of Scilly and, in relation to the Isles of Scilly, the reference in paragraph (6) of that regulation to paragraph (5) of that regulation shall be construed as a reference to paragraph (5)(b).

(5)   These regulations apply to local authority applications mentioned in paragraph (1) of regulation 25A in accordance with the modifications set out in that paragraph.]

*Note: These Regulations apply to planning applications made on or after 15 July 1988 and before 14 March 1999.

NOTES

Paras (3)–(5): substituted, for para (3) as originally enacted, by SI 1992/1494, reg 3, Schedule, para 1.
Revoked with savings by SI 1999/293, reg 34(1), Sch 5; for savings see reg 34(2) thereof. Date in force: 14 March 1999: see SI 1999/293, reg 1(1).

2 Interpretation

(1)   In these Regulations, unless the contrary intention appears—

'the Act' means the Town and Country Planning Act 1971, references to sections are references to sections of that Act and expressions used in that Act and these Regulations have the meaning they have in the Act save that, in relation to an appeal, references to the Secretary of State shall not be construed as references to an inspector;

'aerodrome' means a defined area on land or water (including any buildings and other installations) intended to be used either wholly or in part for the arrival, departure and surface movement of aircraft;

'controlled waste' has the meaning assigned to it by section 30(1) of the Control of Pollution Act 1974;

'documents' include photographs, drawings, maps and plans;

'environmental information' means the environmental statement prepared by the applicant or appellant . . . , any representations made by any body required by these Regulations to be invited to make representations or to be consulted and any representations duly made by any other person about the likely environmental effects of the proposed development;

'environmental statement' means such a statement as is described in Schedule 3;

'exempt development' means particular proposed development which is the subject of a direction by the Secretary of State that these Regulations do not apply in relation to it;

'the General Development Order' means the Town and Country Planning General Development Order 1977;

. . .

'inspector' means a person appointed by the Secretary of State pursuant to Schedule 9 to the Act to determine an appeal;

'the land' means the land on which proposed development would be carried out;

'local planning authority' means the body to whom it falls or would but for a direction under section 35 fall, to determine an application for planning permission, or to whom it would fall (but for any such direction) to determine a proposed application;

'principal council' has the meaning assigned to that term by section 270(1) of the Local Government Act 1972;

'register' means a register kept pursuant to section 34 and 'appropriate register' means the register on which particulars of an application for planning permission for the relevant development would fall to be placed when such an application is made;

'Schedule' means a Schedule to these Regulations;

'Schedule 1 application' means an application for planning permission (other than an application made pursuant to section 31A or section 32) for the carrying out of development of any description mentioned in Schedule 1, which is not exempt development;

'Schedule 2 application' means, subject to paragraph (2), an application for planning permission (other than an application made pursuant to section 31A or section 32) for the carrying out of development of any description mentioned in Schedule 2, which is not exempt development and which would be likely to have significant effects on the environment by virtue of factors such as its nature, size or location;

'special road' means [any road which for the purposes of Part I of the New Roads and Street Works Act 1991 is a road subject to a concession and any other road] authorised by a scheme made by a local highway authority under section 16 of the Highways Act 1980 for the use of traffic within Classes I and II of Schedule 4 to that Act; and

['special waste' means waste which is special waste for the purposes of the Special Waste Regulations 1996.]

(2)   Where the Secretary of State gives a direction which includes a statement that in his opinion proposed development would be likely, or would not be likely, to have significant effects on the environment by virtue of factors such as its nature, size or location, or includes such a statement in a notification under regulation 10(1), that statement shall determine whether an application for planning permission for that development is, or is not, a Schedule 2 application by reason of the effects the development would be likely to have; and references in these Regulations to a Schedule 2 application shall be interpreted accordingly.

NOTES

Para (1): in definition 'environmental information' words omitted revoked, and definition omitted revoked, by SI 1992/1494, reg 3, Schedule, para 2; in definition 'special road' words in square brackets substituted by SI 1994/677, reg 2, Schedule, para 1; definition 'special waste' substituted by SI 1996/972, reg 21(1).

Revoked with savings by SI 1999/293, reg 34(1), Sch 5; for savings see reg 34(2) thereof. Date in force: 14 March 1999: see SI 1999/293, reg 1(1).

3   Extension of the power to provide in a development order for the giving of directions as respects the manner in which planning applications are dealt with

The provisions enabling the Secretary of State to give directions which may be included in a development order by virtue of section 31 shall include provisions enabling him to direct—

(a) that particular proposed development of a description set out in Schedule 1 or 2 is exempt development to which these Regulations do not apply [in accordance with Article 2(3) of Council Directive 85/337/EEC];

(b) that particular proposed development is not development in respect of which the consideration of environmental information is required before planning permission can be granted;

(c) that particular proposed development or development of any class is development in respect of which such consideration is required.

NOTES

Words in square brackets inserted by SI 1994/677, reg 2, Schedule, para 2.
Revoked with savings by SI 1999/293, reg 34(1), Sch 5; for savings see reg 34(2) thereof. Date in force: 14 March 1999: see SI 1999/293, reg 1(1).

4   Prohibition on the grant of planning permission without consideration of environmental information

(1)   This regulation applies to any Schedule 1 or Schedule 2 application received by the authority with whom it is lodged on or after 15th July 1988 . . . .

For the purposes of this paragraph, the date of receipt of an application by an authority shall be determined in accordance with article 7(6A) of the General Development Order.

(2)   The local planning authority or the Secretary of State or an inspector shall not grant planning permission pursuant to an application to which this regulation applies unless they have first taken the environmental information into consideration [and state in their decision that they have done so].

(3)   Subject to any direction of the Secretary of State, the occurrence of an event mentioned in paragraph (4) shall determine in the case of an application for planning permission for development, other than exempt development, that, for the purposes of this regulation, the application is a Schedule 1 or 2 application.

(4)   The events referred to in paragraph (3) are—

(i) the submission by the applicant of an environmental statement expressed to be for the purposes of these Regulations;

(ii) a failure by the applicant to apply to the Secretary of State for a direction where the local planning authority have given such an opinion as is mentioned in regulation 5(6)(a); and

(iii) the making to that authority by the applicant of a written statement agreeing or conceding that the submission of an environmental statement is required.

NOTES

Para (1): words omitted revoked by SI 1992/1494, reg 3, Schedule, para 3.
Para (2): words in square brackets inserted by SI 1994/677, reg 2, Schedule, para 3.
Revoked with savings by SI 1999/293, reg 34(1), Sch 5; for savings see reg 34(2) thereof. Date in force: 14 March 1999: see SI 1999/293, reg 1(1).

5 Opinion as to whether an application will be a Schedule 1 or 2 application

(1) A person who is minded to apply for planning permission may ask the local planning authority to state in writing whether in their opinion the proposed development would be within a description mentioned in Schedule 1 or 2 and, if so,—

(a) within which such description; and

(b) if it falls within a description in Schedule 2, whether its likely effects would be such that regulation 4 would apply.

(2) A request made pursuant to paragraph (1) shall be accompanied by—

(a) a plan sufficient to identify the land;

(b) a brief description of the nature and purpose of the proposed development and of its possible effects on the environment;

(c) such other information or representations as the person making the request may wish to provide or make.

(3) An authority receiving a request under paragraph (1) shall, if they consider that they have not been provided with sufficient information to give an opinion on the questions raised, notify the person making the request of the particular points on which they require further information.

(4) An authority shall respond to a request under paragraph (1) within 3 weeks beginning with the date [of receipt of the request] or such longer period as may be agreed in writing with the person making the request; and if they express an opinion to the effect that the consideration of environmental information would be required before planning permission could be granted for the proposed development, they shall provide with the opinion a written statement giving clearly and precisely their full reasons for their conclusion.

(5) An authority shall make a copy of any opinion given pursuant to a request under paragraph (1), and any accompanying statement of reasons and a copy of the relevant request and the accompanying documents available for public inspection at any reasonable hour at the place where the appropriate register (or relevant section of that register) is kept until such time, if any, as a copy of that opinion is required by regulation 7 to be placed on Part I of that register.

(6) Where an authority—

(a) give an opinion to the effect mentioned in paragraph (4); or

(b) fail to give an opinion within the relevant period mentioned in paragraph (4),

the person who requested the opinion may apply in accordance with regulation 6 to the Secretary of State for a direction on the matter.

(7) Paragraph (6)(b) applies notwithstanding that the authority may not have received further information which they have sought under paragraph (3).

NOTES

Para (4): words in square brackets substituted by SI 1994/677, reg 2, Schedule, para 4.

Revoked with savings by SI 1999/293, reg 34(1), Sch 5; for savings see reg 34(2) thereof. Date in force: 14 March 1999: see SI 1999/293, reg 1(1).

6   Pre-application directions

(1)   A person applying to the Secretary of State for a direction pursuant to regulation 5(6) shall submit with his application—
(a)   a copy of his request under regulation 5(1) to the local planning authority and the documents which accompanied it;
(b)   a copy of any notification under regulation 5(3) which he has received and of any response;
(c)   a copy of any opinion given by the authority and of the accompanying statement of reasons; and
(d)   any representations he wishes to make.

(2)   A person applying as aforesaid shall, when he makes the application, send the local planning authority a copy of the application and of any representations he makes to the Secretary of State.

(3)   The Secretary of State shall notify an applicant in writing of any points on which he considers the information provided pursuant to paragraph (1) is insufficient to enable him to give a direction; and may request the local planning authority to provide such information as they can on any of those points.

(4)   The Secretary of State shall issue a direction within 3 weeks beginning with the date of [receipt of the application] or such longer period as he may reasonably require.

(5)   The Secretary of State shall upon giving a direction send a copy to the applicant and the local planning authority; and where he gives a direction that the proposed application would be a Schedule 1 or Schedule 2 application, he shall at the same time send them a written statement giving his full reasons for his conclusion clearly and precisely.

NOTES

Para (4): words in square brackets substituted by SI 1994/677, reg 2, Schedule, para 5.
Revoked with savings by SI 1999/293, reg 34(1), Sch 5; for savings see reg 34(2) thereof. Date in force: 14 March 1999: see SI 1999/293, reg 1(1).

7   Availability of directions etc for inspection

(1)   Where particulars of a planning application are placed on Part I of the register, the local planning authority shall take steps to secure that there is also placed on that Part a copy of any direction which the Secretary of State has given as to whether the application is, or is not, a Schedule 1 or 2 application; and of any relevant opinion given pursuant to regulation 5.

(2)   Where the Secretary of State gives any such direction as is mentioned in paragraph (1) after particulars of the relevant application have been placed on Part I of the register or sends the applicant a notification under regulation 10, the local planning authority shall take steps to secure that a copy of that direction or notification is also placed on that Part of the register.

(3)   Where the local planning authority notify an applicant under regulation 9 that they consider his application cannot be granted unless he submits an environmental statement, they shall take steps to secure that a copy of that notification is placed on Part I of the register.

(4)   Where the Secretary of State gives, otherwise than pursuant to regulation 6, a direction as to whether the consideration of environmental information is required before planning permission can be granted for a particular proposed development he shall forthwith send a copy of the direction to the local planning authority and to such other persons as he considers it desirable to send a copy together, where necessary, with documents sufficient to identify the land and the development.

(5)   Where a copy of a direction is received by the local planning authority before application is made for planning permission for the development in question, the authority shall take steps to secure that a copy of the direction and any documents sent with it are available for public inspection at all reasonable hours at the place where the appropriate register (or section of that register) is kept.

NOTES

Revoked with savings by SI 1999/293, reg 34(1), Sch 5; for savings see reg 34(2) thereof. Date in force: 14 March 1999: see SI 1999/293, reg 1(1).

8   Procedure to facilitate preparation for environmental statements

(1)   A prospective applicant may give the local planning authority notice in writing that he intends to make a Schedule 1 or Schedule 2 application and to submit an environmental statement with his application.

(2)   A notice under paragraph (1) shall include the information necessary to identify, or be accompanied by documents identifying, the land and the nature and purpose of the proposed development, and shall indicate the main environmental consequences to which the prospective applicant proposes to refer in his environmental statement.

(3)   Paragraph (4) applies where—
(a)   the local planning authority receive in relation to a proposed planning application—
    (i)   such a notice as is mentioned in paragraph (1); or
    (ii)   such a statement as is mentioned in regulation 4(4)(iii); or
    (iii) a copy of a direction by the Secretary of State under regulation 6 that a proposed application would be a Schedule 1 or Schedule 2 application; . . .
(b)   . . .
    but only paragraph (4)(a) shall apply by virtue of sub-paragraph (b).

(4)   Where this paragraph applies, the authority in question shall—
(a)   notify the bodies mentioned in paragraph (5) in writing of the name and address of the prospective applicant and of the duty imposed upon them by regulation 22 to make information available to the prospective applicant;

(b) inform the prospective applicant in writing of the names and addresses of the bodies so notified.

(5)   The bodies referred to in paragraph (4) are—
(a) any body which the local planning authority would be required by article 15 of the General Development Order or any direction under that article to consult if the application were before them;
(b) the following bodies if not referred to in sub-paragraph (a),—
    (i)   any principal council for the area where the land is situated, if not the local planning authority;
    (ii) the Countryside Commission;
    (iii) the Nature Conservancy Council;
(c) where the proposed development is a development of a description referred to in paragraph (6), [the chief inspector for England and Wales appointed under Part I of the Environmental Protection Act 1990].

(6)   The development referred to in paragraph (5)(c) is any development which in the opinion of the local planning authority will—
(a) involve mining operations, or manufacturing industry or the disposal of waste; and
(b) is likely either—
    (i)   to give rise to waste, the disposal of which requires an authorisation under the Radioactive Substances Act 1960, or to discharges (other than of domestic sewage) which are controlled waste or special waste or are likely to require the licence or consent of [the [Environment Agency]]; or
    (ii) to involve works specified in Schedule 1 to the Health and Safety (Emissions to the Atmosphere) Regulations 1983.

(7)   Paragraph (4) shall apply (but subject to the modifications mentioned in paragraph (8)) where a Schedule 1 or Schedule 2 application has been made without an environmental statement and—
    (i)   the Secretary of State has given a direction to the effect that the consideration of environmental information is required before planning permission can be granted; or
    (ii) the applicant has informed the local planning authority or, where the application has been referred to the Secretary of State or is the subject of an appeal, the Secretary of State, that he proposes to submit an environmental statement.

(8)   In its application by virtue of paragraph (7), paragraph (4) shall have effect—
(a) as if references to the prospective applicant were references to the applicant or appellant, as appropriate; and
(b) where the application has been referred to the Secretary of State or is the subject of an appeal, as if references to the local planning authority in paragraphs (4) and (6) were references to the Secretary of State and regulation (5)(a) referred to such bodies as the Secretary of State considers would be required to be consulted by or under article 15 of the General Development Order if the case were before the local planning authority.

NOTES

Para (3): words omitted revoked by SI 1992/1494, reg 3, Schedule, para 4.
Para (5): words in square brackets substituted by SI 1994/677, reg 2, Schedule, para 6.
Para (6): first words in square brackets substituted by SI 1989/1968, reg 3, Sch 2, words in square
    brackets therein substituted by the Environment Act 1995, s 120, Sch 22, para 233(1).
Revoked with savings by SI 1999/293, reg 34(1), Sch 5; for savings see reg 34(2) thereof. Date in
    force: 14 March 1999: see SI 1999/293, reg 1(1).

9 Application made to a planning authority without an environmental statement

(1)   Where it appears to the local planning authority that an application for planning permission is a Schedule 1 or a Schedule 2 application, and it is not accompanied by an environmental statement, they shall (unless the application is the subject of a direction under section 35) within 3 weeks beginning with the date of receipt of the application, or such longer period as they may agree with the applicant in writing, notify the applicant in writing that they consider the submission of such a statement is required, giving their full reasons for their view clearly and precisely.

(2)   An applicant receiving a notification pursuant to paragraph (1) may within 3 weeks beginning with the date of the notification write to the authority to inform them that he—
    (i)   accepts their view and is providing an environmental statement; or
    (ii) is applying in writing to the Secretary of State for his direction on the matter.

(3)   If the applicant does not write in accordance with paragraph (2), the permission sought shall be deemed to be refused at the end of the 3 week period; but no appeal shall lie to the Secretary of State by virtue of section 36 or 37.

The deemed refusal shall be treated as a decision of the authority for the purposes of article 21(2)(c) of the General Development Order.

(4)   Except where the Secretary of State gives a direction to the effect that regulation 4 does not apply, an authority which has given a notification in accordance with paragraph (1) shall determine the relevant application only by refusing planning permission if the applicant does not submit an environmental statement and comply with regulation 13(5).

(5)   A person applying to the Secretary of State for a direction pursuant to paragraph (2) shall send with his application copies of—
(a) his application for planning permission;
(b) all documents sent to the authority as part of the application; and
(c) all correspondence with the authority relating to the development proposed,
and paragraphs [(2)] to (5) of regulation 6 shall apply in relation to the application.

NOTES

Para (5): reference to '(2)' in square brackets substituted by SI 1994/677, reg 2, Schedule, para 7.
Revoked with savings by SI 1999/293, reg 34(1), Sch 5; for savings see reg 34(2) thereof. Date in
    force: 14 March 1999: see SI 1999/293, reg 1(1).

10 Application referred to the Secretary of State without an environmental statement

(1)   Where it appears to the Secretary of State that an application for planning permission which has been referred to him for determination is a Schedule 1 or a Schedule 2 application, and it is not accompanied by an environmental statement, he shall within 3 weeks beginning with the date he received the application, or such longer period as he may reasonably require, notify the applicant in writing that the submission of an environmental statement is required, giving his full reasons for his view clearly and precisely.

(2)   An applicant receiving a notification pursuant to paragraph (1) may within 3 weeks beginning with the date of the notification write to the Secretary of State to inform him that he proposes to provide an environmental statement.

(3)   If the applicant does not write in accordance with paragraph (2), the Secretary of State shall be under no duty to deal with the application: and at the end of the 3 week period he shall inform the applicant in writing that no further action is being taken on the application.

(4)   Where the Secretary of State has given a notification in accordance with paragraph (1), he shall determine the relevant application only by refusing planning permission if the applicant does not submit an environmental statement and comply with regulation 13(5).

(5)   The Secretary of State shall send a copy of any notification under paragraph (1) to the local planning authority.

NOTES

Revoked with savings by SI 1999/293, reg 34(1), Sch 5; for savings see reg 34(2) thereof. Date in force: 14 March 1999: see SI 1999/293, reg 1(1).

11 Appeal to the Secretary of State without an environmental statement

(1)   Where the Secretary of State on consideration of an appeal under section 36 forms the view that the relevant application is a Schedule 1 or a Schedule 2 application, and the documents sent to him for the purposes of the appeal do not include a copy of an environmental statement, regulation 10 shall apply subject to any necessary modifications.

(2)   Where an inspector is dealing with an appeal and any question arises as to whether the relevant application is a Schedule 1 or a Schedule 2 application and it appears to the inspector that it may be such an application and no environmental statement has been submitted, the inspector shall refer the matter to the Secretary of State.

(3)   Where a question is referred pursuant to paragraph (2), the Secretary of State shall direct whether or not the application is a Schedule 1 or Schedule 2 application; and the inspector shall not determine the appeal, except by refusing planning permission, before he receives a direction.

(4)   Where the Secretary of State directs as aforesaid, he shall forthwith send copies of the direction to the appellant, the local planning authority and the inspector, and to any other person he considers desirable, and where he directs that the application is a Schedule 1 or Schedule 2 application he shall at the same time send those persons a written statement giving his full reasons for his conclusions clearly and precisely.

(5)   Where the Secretary of State directs that the application is a Schedule 1 or Schedule 2 application, the appellant may within 3 weeks beginning with the date of the direction write to the Secretary of State to inform him that he proposes to provide an environmental statement.

(6)   If the appellant does not write in accordance with paragraph (5), the inspector shall be under no duty to deal with the appeal; and at the end of the 3 week period he shall inform the appellant that no further action is being taken on the appeal.

(7)   Where the Secretary of State has directed that the relevant application is a Schedule 1 or Schedule 2 application, the inspector shall determine the appeal only by refusing planning permission if the appellant does not submit an environmental statement and comply with regulation 13(5).

NOTES

Revoked with savings by SI 1999/293, reg 34(1), Sch 5; for savings see reg 34(2) thereof. Date in force: 14 March 1999: see SI 1999/293, reg 1(1).

13 Publicity where an environmental statement is submitted in course of planning procedures

(1)   Where a Schedule 1 or a Schedule 2 application has been made without an environmental statement and the applicant proposes to submit one, he shall before submitting it, comply with paragraphs (2) to (5).

(2)   The applicant shall publish in a local newspaper circulating in the locality in which the land is situated (hereinafter referred to as 'the locality') a notice stating—
(a) his name and that he is the applicant for planning permission and the name and address of the local planning authority;
(b) the date on which the application was made and, if it be the case, that it has been referred to the Secretary of State for determination or is the subject of an appeal to him;
(c) the address or location and the nature of the proposed development;
(d) that a copy of the application and of the plans and other documents submitted with it together with a copy of the environmental statement may be inspected by members of the public at all reasonable hours;

(e) an address in the locality at which those documents may be inspected, and the latest date on which they will be available for inspection (being a date not less than 20 days later than the date on which the notice is published);

(f) an address in the locality (whether or not the same as that give pursuant to sub-paragraph (e)) at which copies of the environmental statement may be obtained;

(g) that copies may be obtained there so long as stocks last;

(h) if a charge is to be made for a copy, the amount of the charge; and

(i) that any person wishing to make representations about the application should make them in writing, before the date named in accordance with sub-paragraph (e), to the local planning authority or (in the case of an application referred to the Secretary of State or an appeal) to the Secretary of State.

(3)   The applicant shall, unless he has not, and was not reasonably able to acquire, such rights as would enable him to do so, post on the land a notice containing the information specified in paragraph (2), except that the date named as the latest date on which the documents will be available for inspection shall be not less than 20 days later than the date on which the notice is first posted.

(4)   The notice mentioned in paragraph (3) must—

(a) be left in position for not less than 7 days in the month immediately preceding the date of the submission of the environmental *statement; and*

(b) be affixed firmly to some object on the land and sited and displayed in such a way as to be easily visible to, and readable by, members of the public without going on to the land.

(5)   The environmental statement, when submitted, shall be accompanied by—

(a) a copy of the notice mentioned in paragraph (2) certified by or on behalf of the applicant as having been published in a named newspaper on a date specified in the certificate; and

(b) a certificate by or on behalf of the applicant which states either—

   (i)   that he has posted a notice on the land in compliance with this regulation and when he did so, and that the notice was left in position for not less than 7 days in the month immediately preceding the date of the submission of the statement, or that, without any fault or intention on his part, it was removed, obscured or defaced before 7 days had elapsed and he took reasonable steps for its protection or replacement, specifying the steps taken; or

   (ii) that the applicant was unable to comply with paragraph (3) and (4) above because he did not have the necessary rights to do so; that he has taken such reasonable steps as are open to him to acquire those rights; and has been unable to do so, specifying the steps taken.

(6) Where an applicant proposes to provide an environmental statement in the circumstances mentioned in paragraph (1), the local planning authority, the Secretary of State or the inspector, as the case may be, shall (unless disposed to refuse the permission sought) suspend consideration of the application or appeal until receipt of the statement and the other documents mentioned in paragraph (5); and shall not determine it during the period of 21 days beginning with the date of receipt of the statement and the other documents so mentioned.

(7) If any person issues a certificate which purports to comply with the requirements of paragraph (5)(b) and which contains a statement which he knows to be false or

misleading in a material particular, or recklessly issues a certificate which purports to comply with those requirements and which contains a statement which is false or misleading in a material particular, he shall be guilty of an offence and liable on summary conviction to a fine not exceeding level 3 on the standard scale.

(8) The reference in paragraph (7) to a fine not exceeding level 3 on the standard scale shall be construed in accordance with section 37 (standard scale of fines for summary offences) of the Criminal Justice Act 1982.

(9) Where it is proposed to submit an environmental statement in connection with an appeal, this regulation applies with the substitution, except in paragraph 2(a), of references to the appellant for references to the applicant.

NOTES

Revoked with savings by SI 1999/293, reg 34(1), Sch 5; for savings see reg 34(2) thereof. Date in force: 14 March 1999: see SI 1999/293, reg 1(1).

14 Procedure where the planning authority receive an environmental statement

(1)   When an applicant making a Schedule 1 or Schedule 2 application submits an environmental statement to the local planning authority he shall provide the authority with [three additional copies] of the statement for transmission to the Secretary of State and, if at the same time he serves a copy of the statement or of a part of it on any other body, he shall—

(a) serve with it a copy of the application and any plan submitted with it (unless he has already served these documents on the body in question);

(b) inform the body that representations may be made to the local planning authority;

(c) inform the authority of the name of every body whom he has so served, of the date of service and, where he has not served a copy of the whole of the statement, of the part of which a copy was served.

(2)   When a local planning authority receive an environmental statement in connection with a Schedule 1 or Schedule 2 application the authority shall—

(a) take steps to secure that a copy of the statement is placed on Part I of the register with the application;

(b) send to the Secretary of State [three copies of the statement, and a copy] of the relevant application and of any documents submitted with the application;

(c) advise any body mentioned in regulation 8(5) on whom the applicant has not served a copy of the statement or a part of it, that a statement will be taken into consideration in determining the application, elicit whether they wish to receive a copy of the statement or any part of it and inform them that they may make representations;

(d) inform the applicant of the copies required by those bodies and of the names and addresses of the bodies concerned and enquire of him whether he proposes to serve the required copy on each of those bodies or send the required copies to the authority for service;

(e) serve on the relevant body any copy sent to them by the applicant for service.

(3)   The applicant shall inform the authority which of the courses mentioned in paragraph 2(d) he proposes to follow and shall serve copies of the environmental statement or a part of it on each body on whom he has said he will serve a copy or send the necessary copies to the authority, as the case may be. Where the applicant elects to send copies to the bodies directly he shall inform the authority as mentioned in paragraph (1)(c).

(4)   The local planning authority shall not determine the application until the expiry of 14 days from the last date on which a copy of the environmental statement or a part of it was served in accordance with this regulation.

NOTES

Paras (1), (2): words in square brackets substituted by SI 1994/677, reg 2, Schedule, paras 8, 9.
Revoked with savings by SI 1999/293, reg 34(1), Sch 5; for savings see reg 34(2) thereof. Date in
    force: 14 March 1999: see SI 1999/293, reg 1(1).

15 Procedure where the Secretary of State receives an environmental statement

(1)   This regulation applies where an applicant submits to the Secretary of State an environmental statement relating to a Schedule 1 or Schedule 2 application which is before the Secretary of State for determination or is the subject of an appeal to him.

(2)   The applicant shall submit [four] copies of the statement to the Secretary of State who shall transmit one copy to the local planning authority.

(3)   The local planning authority shall take steps to secure that the copy so transmitted is placed on the register.

(4)   If at the same time as he submits a statement to the Secretary of State the applicant serves a copy of it or a part of it on any other body, the applicant shall comply with regulation 14(1)(a) and (b) and inform the Secretary of State of the matters mentioned in regulation 14(1)(c).

(5)   The Secretary of State shall comply with regulation 14(2)(c) to (e) and the applicant with regulation 14(3) as if—
(a) references in any of those provisions and regulation 8(6) to the local planning authority were references to the Secretary of State; and
(b) regulation 8(5)(a) referred to such bodies as the Secretary of State considers would be required to be consulted by or under article 15 of the General Development Order if the matter were before the local planning authority;
and the Secretary of State or the inspector shall comply with regulation 14(4) as if it referred to him instead of to the local planning authority.

(6)   . . .

(7)   In this regulation, references to the applicant include references to an appellant.

NOTES

Para (2): word in square brackets substituted by SI 1994/677, reg 2, Schedule, para 10.
Para (6): revoked by SI 1992/1494, reg 3, Schedule, para 6.
Revoked with savings by SI 1999/293, reg 34(1), Sch 5; for savings see reg 34(2) thereof. Date in
    force: 14 March 1999: see SI 1999/293, reg 1(1).

16 Extension of the period for an authority's decision on a planning application

(1)   In determining for the purposes of section 37 (appeal in default of planning decision) the time which has elapsed without the local planning authority giving notice to the applicant of their decision in a case where—
(a) the authority have notified an applicant in accordance with regulation 9(1) that the submission of an environmental statement is required; and
(b) the Secretary of State has given a direction in the matter,
no account shall be taken of any period before the issue of the direction.

[(2)   Where it falls to an authority determining an application for planning permission to take environmental information into consideration, article 23 of the Town and Country Planning General Development Order 1988 shall have effect as if—
(a) for the reference in paragraph (2)(a) of that article to a period of 8 weeks there was substituted a reference to a period of 16 weeks;
(b) after paragraph (3)(b) of that article there was inserted—
    '(ba)   the environmental statement required to be submitted in respect of the application has been submitted, together with the documents required to accompany that statement; and']

NOTES

Para (2): substituted by SI 1992/1494, reg 3, Schedule, para 7.
Revoked with savings by SI 1999/293, reg 34(1), Sch 5; for savings see reg 34(2) thereof. Date in
    force: 14 March 1999: see SI 1999/293, reg 1(1).

18 Availability of copies of an environmental statement

An applicant for planning permission or an appellant who submits an environmental statement in connection with his application or appeal shall ensure that a reasonable number of copies of the statement are available at the address named in the notices published or posted pursuant to [article 12B of the Town and Country Planning General Development Order 1988 or regulation 13] as the address at which such copies may be obtained.

NOTES

Words in square brackets substituted by SI 1992/1494, reg 3, Schedule, para 9.
Revoked with savings by SI 1999/293, reg 34(1), Sch 5; for savings see reg 34(2) thereof. Date in
    force: 14 March 1999: see SI 1999/293, reg 1(1).

19 Provision of a copy of an environmental statement for the Secretary of State

Where an applicant for planning permission has submitted an environmental statement in connection with his application and the application—
(a)   is directed to be referred to the Secretary of State under section 35; or
(b)   occasions an appeal under section 36,
the applicant shall supply the Secretary of State with [three copies] of the statement unless, in the case of a referred application, the local planning authority have done so when referring the application to him.

NOTES

Words in square brackets substituted by SI 1994/677, reg 2, Schedule, para 11.
Revoked with savings by SI 1999/293, reg 34(1), Sch 5; for savings see reg 34(2) thereof. Date in
    force: 14 March 1999: see SI 1999/293, reg 1(1).

20 Charges

(1)   A reasonable charge reflecting printing and distribution costs may be made to a member of the public for a copy of an environmental statement made available in accordance with regulation . . . 18 and for any copy, in excess of one, of the whole or part of a statement supplied to a body pursuant to regulation 14, [or 15].

(2)   A reasonable charge reflecting the cost of making the relevant information available may be made by a body supplying in accordance with regulation 22(1) information sought by an applicant or appellant.

NOTES

Para (1): words omitted revoked and words in square brackets substituted, by SI 1992/1494, reg 3,
    Schedule, para 10.
Revoked with savings by SI 1999/293, reg 34(1), Sch 5; for savings see reg 34(2) thereof. Date in
    force: 14 March 1999: see SI 1999/293, reg 1(1).

21 Further information and evidence respecting environmental statements

(1)   The local planning authority or the Secretary of State or an inspector, when dealing with an application or appeal in relation to which an environmental statement has been provided, may in writing require the applicant or appellant to provide such further information as may be specified concerning any matter which is required to be, or may be, dealt with in the statement; and where in the opinion of the authority or the Secretary of State or the inspector—

(a) the applicant or appellant could (having regard in particular to current knowledge and methods of assessment) provide further information about any matter mentioned in paragraph 3 of Schedule 3; and

(b) that further information is reasonably required to give proper consideration to the likely environmental effects of the proposed development,

they or he shall notify the applicant or appellant in writing accordingly, and the applicant or appellant shall provide that further information.

[(2) Paragraphs (3) to (9) shall apply in relation to further information required of an applicant or appellant after those paragraphs come into force except in so far as such further information is required to be provided for the purposes of a local inquiry held under the Act and the request for such further information states that it is to be provided for such purposes.

(3) The recipient of the further information shall publish in a local newspaper circulating in the locality in which the land is situated (hereinafter referred to as 'the locality') a notice stating—

(a) the name of the applicant for planning permission or the appellant (as the case may be) and the name and address of the local planning authority;

(b) the date on which the application was made and, if it be the case, that it has been referred to the Secretary of State for determination or is the subject of an appeal to him;

(c) the address or location and the nature of the proposed development;

(d) that further information is available in relation to an environmental statement which has already been provided;

(e) that a copy of the further information may be inspected by members of the public at all reasonable hours;

(f) an address in the locality at which the further information may be inspected and the latest date on which it will be available for inspection (being a date not less than 20 days later than the date on which the notice is published);

(g) an address in the locality (whether or not the same as that given pursuant to sub-paragraph (f)) at which copies of the further information may be obtained;

(h) that copies may be obtained there so long as stocks last;

(i) if a charge is to be made for a copy, the amount of the charge; and

(j) that any person wishing to make representations about the further information should make them in writing, before the date specified in accordance with sub-paragraph (f), to the local planning authority, the Secretary of State or the inspector (as the case may be).

(4) The recipient of the further information shall send a copy of it to each person to whom the environmental statement to which it relates was sent.

(5) Where the recipient of the further information is a local planning authority they shall—

(a) take steps to secure that a copy of the further information is placed on Part I of the register with the application and the environmental statement; and

(b) send to the Secretary of State three copies of the further information.

(6) The recipient of the further information may by notice in writing require the applicant or appellant to provide such number of copies of the further information as

is specified in the notice (being the number required for the purposes of paragraph (4) or (5)).

(7)   Where further information is required to be provided, the local planning authority, the Secretary of State or the inspector, as the case may be, shall suspend determination of the application or appeal; and shall not determine it before the expiry of 14 days after the date on which the further information was sent to all persons to whom the environmental statement was sent or the expiry of 21 days after the date that notice of it was published in a local newspaper, whichever is the later.

(8)   The applicant or appellant who provides further information in accordance with paragraph (1) shall ensure that a reasonable number of copies of the information is available at the address named in the notice published pursuant to paragraph (3) as the address at which such copies may be obtained.

(9)   A reasonable charge reflecting printing and distribution costs may be made to a member of the public for a copy of the further information made available in accordance with paragraph (8) and for any copy, in excess of one, of the whole or part of the further information supplied to a person pursuant to paragraph (4).]

[(10)]   The local planning authority or the Secretary of State or an inspector may in writing require an applicant or appellant to produce such evidence as they may reasonably call for to verify any information in his environmental statement.

NOTES

Para (2): original para (2) renumbered as para (10) and new para (2) inserted by SI 1994/677, reg 2, Schedule, para 12.
Paras (3)–(9): inserted by SI 1994/677, reg 2, Schedule, para 12.
Para (10): originally para (2), renumbered as such by SI 1994/677, reg 2, Schedule, para 12.
Revoked with savings by SI 1999/293, reg 34(1), Sch 5; for savings see reg 34(2) thereof. Date in force: 14 March 1999: see SI 1999/293, reg 1(1).

22 Provision of information

(1)   Subject to paragraph (2), the local planning authority and any body notified in accordance with these Regulations that a person has made or is proposing to make a Schedule 1 or Schedule 2 application, shall, if requested by the applicant (or prospective applicant) or may without such a request, enter into consultation with him to determine whether the body has in its possession any information which he or they consider relevant to the preparation of an environmental statement and, if they have, the body shall make any such information available to him.

(2)   Paragraph (1) shall not require the disclosure by a body of confidential information.

NOTES

Revoked with savings by SI 1999/293, reg 34(1), Sch 5; for savings see reg 34(2) thereof. Date in force: 14 March 1999: see SI 1999/293, reg 1(1).

[23 Duty to inform the Secretary of State]

[Where, after environmental information has been taken into consideration, a local planning authority determine an application for planning permission, they shall inform the Secretary of State of the decision taken and provide details of any conditions subject to which any planning permission was granted.]

NOTES

Substituted by SI 1992/1494, reg 3, Schedule, para 11.
Revoked with savings by SI 1999/293, reg 34(1), Sch 5; for savings see reg 34(2) thereof. Date in force: 14 March 1999: see SI 1999/293, reg 1(1).

24   Service of Notices etc

Any notice or other document to be sent, served or given under these Regulations may be served or given in a manner specified in section 283(1).

NOTES

Revoked with savings by SI 1999/293, reg 34(1), Sch 5; for savings see reg 34(2) thereof. Date in force: 14 March 1999: see SI 1999/293, reg 1(1).

25   Application to the High Court

For the purposes of Part XII of the Act (validity of certain decisions), the reference in section 245 to action of the Secretary of State which is not within the powers of the Act shall be taken to extend to a grant of planning permission in contravention of regulation 4 of these Regulations.

NOTES

Revoked with savings by SI 1999/293, reg 34(1), Sch 5; for savings see reg 34(2) thereof. Date in force: 14 March 1999: see SI 1999/293, reg 1(1).

[25A   Local authority applications]

[(1)   In the application of these Regulations to a Schedule 1 or Schedule 2 application (or proposed application) where the local planning authority is also (or would also be) the applicant (whether alone or jointly with any other person), the following modifications shall apply—
(a)   regulations 5 and 6 shall not apply;
(b)   regulation 8(1) to (3) shall not apply but regulation 8(4)(a) shall apply where an authority proposes to make a Schedule 1 or Schedule 2 application and to submit an environmental statement with that application;

(c)   regulation 9 shall not apply;
(d)   regulation 10(5) shall not apply;
(e)   save for the purposes of regulation 15(4) and (5), regulation 14 shall apply as if—
    (i)   in paragraph (1), for 'When an applicant' to 'other body, he shall' was substituted 'When an applicant making a Schedule 1 or Schedule 2 application submits an environmental statement and at the same time serves a copy of the statement or of a part of it on any other body, he shall' and subparagraph (c) was omitted;
    (ii) in paragraph (2), for subparagraphs (d) and (e) was substituted—
'(d)   serve on any such body that has expressed a wish to receive a copy of the statement or any part of it such a copy.';
    (iii) paragraph (3) was omitted;
(f)   regulation 15 shall apply as if—
    (i)   paragraph (2) was omitted;
    (ii) for paragraph (3) was substituted—

'(3)   The local planning authority shall take steps to secure that a copy of the environmental statement is placed on the register.'

(2)   An authority which is minded to make a planning application in relation to which it would be the local planning authority may request the Secretary of State in writing for a direction as to whether the proposed application would be a Schedule 1 or a Schedule 2 application.

(3)   A request made pursuant to paragraph (2) shall be accompanied by—
(a)   a plan sufficient to identify the land;
(b)   a brief description of the nature and purpose of the proposed development and of its possible effects on the environment;
(c)   such other information or representations as the authority may wish to provide or make.

(4)   An authority making a request under paragraph (2) shall send to the Secretary of State any further information he may request in writing to enable him to give a direction.]

NOTES

Inserted by SI 1992/1494, reg 2.
Revoked with savings by SI 1999/293, reg 34(1), Sch 5; for savings see reg 34(2) thereof. Date in force: 14 March 1999: see SI 1999/293, reg 1(1).

SCHEDULE I
DESCRIPTIONS OF DEVELOPMENT

Regulation 2(1)

NOTES

Revoked with savings by SI 1999/293, reg 34(1), Sch 5; for savings see reg 34(2) thereof. Date in force: 14 March 1999: see SI 1999/293, reg 1(1).

(1)　The carrying out of building or other operations, or the change of use of buildings or other land (where a material change) to provide any of the following—
1　A crude-oil refinery (excluding an undertaking manufacturing only lubricants from crude oil) or an installation for the gasification and liquefaction of 500 tonnes or more of coal or bituminous shale per day.
[2
　(a)　A thermal power station or other combustion installation with a heat output of 300 megawatts or more (not being an installation falling within paragraph (b)); and
　(b)　A nuclear power station or other nuclear reactor (excluding a research installation for the production and conversion of fissionable and fertile materials, the maximum power of which does not exceed 1 kilowatt continuous thermal load).]
3　An installation designed solely for the permanent storage or final disposal of radioactive waste.
4　An integrated works for the initial melting of cast-iron and steel.
5　An installation for the extraction of asbestos or for the processing and transformation of asbestos or products containing asbestos—
　(a)　where the installation produces asbestos-cement products, with an annual production of more than 20,000 tonnes of finished products; or
　(b)　where the installation produces friction material, with an annual production of more than 50 tonnes of finished products; or
　(c)　in other cases, where the installation will utilise more than 200 tonnes of asbestos per year.
6　An integrated chemical installation, that is to say, an industrial installation or group of installations where two or more linked chemical or physical processes are employed for the manufacture of olefins from petroleum products, or of sulphuric acid, nitric acid, hydrofluoric acid, chlorine or fluorine.
7　A special road; a line for long-distance railway traffic; or an aerodrome with a basic runway length of 2,100m or more.
8　A trading port, an inland waterway which permits the passage of vessels of over 1,350 tonnes or a port for inland waterway traffic capable of handling such vessels.
9　A waste-disposal installation for the incineration or chemical treatment of special waste.

(2)　The carrying out of operations whereby land is filled with special waste, or the change of use of land (where a material change) to use for the deposit of such waste.

NOTES

Para (1): sub-para 2 substituted by SI 1990/367, reg 2.
Revoked with savings by SI 1999/293, reg 34(1), Sch 5; for savings see reg 34(2) thereof. Date in
    force: 14 March 1999: see SI 1999/293, reg 1(1).

SCHEDULE 2
DESCRIPTIONS OF DEVELOPMENT

Regulation 2(1)

NOTES

Revoked with savings by SI 1999/293, reg 34(1), Sch 5; for savings see reg 34(2) thereof. Date in
    force: 14 March 1999: see SI 1999/293, reg 1(1).

Development for any of the following purposes—

1   Agriculture
(a) water-management for agriculture
(b) poultry-rearing
(c) pig-rearing
(d) a salmon hatchery
(e) an installation for the rearing of salmon
(f) the reclamation of land from the sea

2   Extractive industry
(a) extracting peat
(b) deep drilling, including in particular—
     (i)   geothermal drilling
     (ii) drilling for the storage of nuclear waste material
     (iii) drilling for water supplies
     but excluding drilling to investigate the stability of the soil
(c) extracting minerals (other than metalliferous and energy-producing minerals) such
     as marble, sand, gravel, shale, salt, phosphates and potash
(d) extracting coal or lignite by underground or open-cast mining
(e) extracting petroleum
(f) extracting natural gas
(g) extracting ores
(h) extracting bituminous shale
(i) extracting minerals (other than metalliferous and energy-producing minerals) by
     open-cast mining
(j) a surface industrial installation for the extraction of coal, petroleum, natural gas or
     ores or bituminous shale
(k) a coke oven (dry distillation of coal)
(l) an installation for the manufacture of cement

3   Energy industry
(a) a non-nuclear thermal power station, not being an installation falling within Schedule 1, or an installation for the production of electricity, steam and hot water
(b) an industrial installation for carrying gas, steam or hot water; or the transmission of electrical energy by overhead cables
(c) the surface storage of natural gas
(d) the underground storage of combustible gases
(e) the surface storage of fossil fuels
(f) the industrial briquetting of coal or lignite
(g) an installation for the production or enrichment of nuclear fuels
(h) an installation for the reprocessing of irradiated nuclear fuels
(i) an installation for the collection or processing of radioactive waste, not being an installation falling within Schedule 1
(j) an installation for hydroelectric energy production
[(k) a wind generator]

4   Processing of metals
(a) an ironworks or steelworks including a foundry, forge, drawing plant or rolling mill (not being a works falling within Schedule 1)
(b) an installation for the production (including smelting, refining, drawing and rolling) of non-ferrous metals, other than precious metals
(c) the pressing, drawing or stamping of large castings
(d) the surface treatment and coating of metals
(e) boilermaking or manufacturing reservoirs, tanks and other sheet-metal containers
(f) manufacturing or assembling motor vehicles or manufacturing motor-vehicle engines
(g) a shipyard
(h) an installation for the construction or repair of aircraft
(i) the manufacture of railway equipment
(j) swaging by explosives
(k) an installation for the roasting or sintering of metallic ores

5   Glass making
the manufacture of glass

6   Chemical industry
(a) the treatment of intermediate products and production of chemicals, other than development falling within Schedule 1
(b) the production of pesticides or pharmaceutical products, paints or varnishes, elastomers or peroxides
(c) the storage of petroleum or petrochemical or chemical products

7   Food industry
(a) the manufacture of vegetable or animal oils or fats
(b) the packing or canning of animal or vegetable products
(c) the manufacture of dairy products
(d) brewing or malting
(e) confectionery or syrup manufacture
(f) an installation for the slaughter of animals

(g) an industrial starch manufacturing installation
(h) a fish-meal or fish-oil factory
(i) a sugar factory

8   Textile, leather, wood and paper industries
(a) a wool scouring, degreasing and bleaching factory
(b) the manufacture of fibre board, particle board or plywood
(c) the manufacture of pulp, paper or board
(d) a fibre-dyeing factory
(e) a cellulose-processing and production installation
(f) a tannery or a leather dressing factor

9   Rubber industry
the manufacture and treatment of elastomer-based products

10   Infrastructure projects
(a) an industrial estate development project
(b) an urban development project
(c) a ski-lift or cable-car
(d) the construction of a road, or a harbour, including a fishing harbour, or an aerodrome, not being development falling within Schedule 1
(e) canalisation or flood-relief works
(f) a dam or other installation designed to hold water or store it on a long-term basis
(g) a tramway, elevated or underground railway, suspended line or similar line, exclusively or mainly for passenger transport
(h) an oil or gas pipeline installation
(i) a long-distance aqueduct
(j) a yacht marina
[(k) a motorway service area
(l) coast protection works]

11   Other projects
(a) a holiday village or hotel complex
(b) a permanent racing or test track for cars or motor cycles
(c) an installation for the disposal of controlled waste or waste from mines and quarries, not being an installation falling within Schedule 1
(d) a waste water treatment plant
(e) a site for depositing sludge
(f) the storage of scrap iron
(g) a test bench for engines, turbines or reactors
(h) the manufacture of artificial mineral fibres
(i) the manufacture, packing, loading or placing in cartridges of gunpowder or other explosives
(j) a knackers' yard

12   The modification of a development which has been carried out, where that development is within a description mentioned in Schedule 1.

13   Development within a description mentioned in Schedule 1, where it is exclusively or mainly for the development and testing of new methods or products and will not be permitted for longer than one year.

NOTES

Para 3: sub-para (k) inserted by SI 1994/677, reg 2, Schedule, para 13.
Para 10: sub-paras (k), (l) inserted by SI 1994/677, reg 2, Schedule, para 14.
Revoked with savings by SI 1999/293, reg 34(1), Sch 5; for savings see reg 34(2) thereof. Date in force: 14 March 1999: see SI 1999/293, reg 1(1).

SCHEDULE 3

Regulation 2(1)

NOTES

Revoked with savings by SI 1999/293, reg 34(1), Sch 5; for savings see reg 34(2) thereof. Date in force: 14 March 1999: see SI 1999/293, reg 1(1).

1   An environmental statement comprises a document or series of documents providing for the purpose of assessing the likely impact upon the environment of the development proposed to be carried out, the information specified in paragraph 2 (referred to in this Schedule as 'the specified information').

2   The specified information is—
(a)   a description of the development proposed, comprising information about the site and the design and size or scale of the development;
(b)   the data necessary to identify and assess the main effects which that development is likely to have on the environment;
(c)   a description of the likely significant effects, direct and indirect, on the environment of the development, explained by reference to its possible impact on—
      human beings;
      flora;
      fauna;
      soil;
      water;
      air;
      climate;
      the landscape;
      the inter-action between any of the foregoing;
      material assets;
      the cultural heritage;
(d)   where significant adverse effects are identified with respect to any of the foregoing, a description of the measures envisaged in order to avoid, reduce or remedy those effects; and
(e)   a summary in non-technical language of the information specified above.

3   An environmental statement may include, by way of explanation or amplification of any specified information, further information on any of the following matters—

(a) the physical characteristics of the proposed development, and the land-use requirements during the construction and operational phases;

(b) the main characteristics of the production processes proposed, including the nature and quality of the materials to be used;

(c) the estimated type and quantity of expected residues and emissions (including pollutants of water, air or soil, noise, vibration, light, heat and radiation) resulting from the proposed development when in operation;

(d) (in outline) the main alternatives (if any) studied by the applicant, appellant or authority and an indication of the main reasons for choosing the development proposed, taking into account the environmental effects;

(e) the likely significant direct and indirect effects on the environment of the development proposed which may result from—

  (i)   the use of natural resources;

  (ii) the emission of pollutants, the creation of nuisances, and the elimination of waste;

(f) the forecasting methods used to assess any effects on the environment about which information is given under subparagraph (e); and

(g) any difficulties, such as technical deficiencies or lack of know-how, encountered in compiling any specified information.

In paragraph (e), 'effects' includes secondary, cumulative, short, medium and long term, permanent, temporary, positive and negative effects.

4   Where further information is included in an environmental statement pursuant to paragraph 3, a non-technical summary of that information shall also be provided.

NOTES

Revoked with savings by SI 1999/293, reg 34(1), Sch 5; for savings see reg 34(2) thereof. Date in force: 14 March 1999: see SI 1999/293, reg 1(1).

Directive 85/337/EEC of the European Council

Directive 85/337/EEC of the
European Council
of 27 June 1985

on the assessment of the effects of certain public and private projects
on the environment

THE COUNCIL OF THE EUROPEAN COMMUNITIES,

Having regard to the Treaty establishing the European Economic Community, and in particular Articles 100 and 235 thereof,

Having regard to the proposal from the Commission,[1]

Having regard to the opinion of the European Parliament,[2]

Having regard to the opinion of the Economic and Social Committee,[3]

Whereas the 1973[4] and 1977[5] action programmes of the European Communities on the environment, as well as the 1983[6] action programme, the main outlines of which have been approved by the Council of the European Communities and the representatives of the Governments of the Member States, stress that the best environmental policy consists in preventing the creation of pollution or nuisances at source, rather than subsequently trying to counteract their effects; whereas they affirm the need to take effects on the environment into account at the earliest possible stage in all the technical planning and decision-making processes; whereas to that end, they provide for the implementation of procedures to evaluate such effects;

Whereas the disparities between the laws in force in the various Member States with regard to the assessment of the environmental effects of public and private projects may create unfavourable competitive conditions and thereby directly affect the functioning of the common market; whereas, therefore, it is necessary to approximate national laws in this field pursuant to Article 100 of the Treaty;

Whereas, in addition, it is necessary to achieve one of the Community's objectives in the sphere of the protection of the environment and the quality of life;

Whereas, since the Treaty has not provided the powers required for this end, recourse should be had to Article 235 of the Treaty;

Whereas general principles for the assessment of environmental effects should be introduced with a view to supplementing and coordinating development consent procedures governing public and private projects likely to have a major effect on the environment;

Whereas development consent for public and private projects which are likely to have significant effects on the environment should be granted only after prior assessment of the likely significant environmental effects of these projects has been carried out; whereas this assessment must be conducted on the basis of the appropriate information supplied by the developer, which may be supplemented by the authorities and by the people who may be concerned by the project in question;

Whereas the principles of the assessment of environmental effects should be harmonised, in particular with reference to the projects which should be subject to assessment, the main obligations of the developers and the content of the assessment;

Whereas projects belonging to certain types have significant effects on the environment and these projects must as a rule be subject to systematic assessment;

Whereas projects of other types may not have significant effects on the environment in every case and whereas these projects should be assessed where the Member States consider that their characteristics so require;

Whereas, for projects which are subject to assessment, a certain minimal amount of information must be supplied, concerning the project and its effects;

Whereas the effects of a project on the environment must be assessed in order to take account of concerns to protect human health, to contribute by means of a better environment to the quality of life, to ensure maintenance of the diversity of species and to maintain the reproductive capacity of the ecosystem as a basic resource for life;

Whereas, however, this Directive should not be applied to projects the details of which are adopted by a specific act of national legislation, since the objectives of this Directive, including that of supplying information, are achieved through the legislative process;

Whereas, furthermore, it may be appropriate in exceptional cases to exempt a specific project from the assessment procedures laid down by this Directive, subject to appropriate information being supplied to the Commission,

HAS ADOPTED THIS DIRECTIVE:

Article I

1. This Directive shall apply to the assessment of the environmental effects of those public and private projects which are likely to have significant effects on the environment.

2. For the purposes of this Directive:

'project' means:

    the execution of construction works or of other installations or schemes,

— other interventions in the natural surroundings and landscape including those involving the extraction of mineral resources;

'developer' means:
the applicant for authorisation for a private project or the public authority which initiates a project;

'development consent' means:
the decision of the competent authority or authorities which entitles the developer to proceed with the project.

3. The competent authority or authorities shall be that or those which the Member States designate as responsible for performing the duties arising from this Directive.

4. Projects serving national defence purposes are not covered by this Directive.

5. This Directive shall not apply to projects the details of which are adopted by a specific act of national legislation, since the objectives of this Directive, including that of supplying information, are achieved through the legislative process.

Article 2

1. Member States shall adopt all measures necessary to ensure that, before consent is given, projects likely to have significant effects on the environment by virtue inter alia, of their nature, size or location are made subject to an assessment with regard to their effects.

These projects are defined in Article 4.

2. The environmental impact assessment may be integrated into the existing procedures for consent to projects in the Member States, or, failing this, into other procedures or into procedures to be established to comply with the aims of this Directive.

3. Member States may, in exceptional cases, exempt a specific project in whole or in part from the provisions laid down in this Directive.

In this event, the Member States shall:
(a) consider whether another form of assessment would be appropriate and whether the information thus collected should be made available to the public;
(b) make available to the public concerned the information relating to the exemption and the reasons for granting it;
(c) inform the Commission, prior to granting consent, of the reasons justifying the exemption granted, and provide it with the information made available, where appropriate, to their own nationals.

The Commission shall immediately forward the documents received to the other Member States.

The Commission shall report annually to the Council on the application of this paragraph.

Article 3

The environmental impact assessment will identify, describe and assess in an appropriate manner, in the light of each individual case and in accordance with the Articles 4 to 11, the direct and indirect effects of a project on the following factors:
— human beings, fauna and flora,
— soil, water, air, climate and the landscape,
— the inter-action between the factors mentioned in the first and second indents,
— material assets and the cultural heritage.

Article 4

1. Subject to Article 2 (3), projects of the classes listed in Annex I shall be made subject to an assessment in accordance with Articles 5 to 10.

2. Projects of the classes listed in Annex II shall be made subject to an assessment, in accordance with Articles 5 to 10, where Member States consider that their characteristics so require. To this end Member States may inter alia specify certain types of projects as being subject to an assessment or may establish the criteria and/or thresholds necessary to determine which of the projects of the classes listed in Annex II are to be subject to an assessment in accordance with Articles 5 to 10.

Article 5

1. In the case of projects which, pursuant to Article 4, must be subjected to an environmental impact assessment in accordance with Articles 5 to 10, Member States shall adopt the necessary measures to ensure that the developer supplies in an appropriate form the information specified in Annex III inasmuch as:
(a)   the Member States consider that the information is relevant to a given stage of the consent procedure and to the specific characteristics of a particular project or type of project and of the environmental features likely to be affected;
(b)   the Member States consider that a developer may reasonably be required to compile this information having regard inter alia to current knowledge and methods of assessment.

2. The information to be provided by the developer in accordance with paragraph 1 shall include at least:
— a description of the project comprising information on the site, design and size of the project,
— a description of the measures envisaged in order to avoid, reduce and, if possible, remedy significant adverse effects,
— the data required to identify and assess the main effects which the project is likely to have on the environment,
— a non-technical summary of the information mentioned in indents 1 to 3.

3. Where they consider it necessary, Member States shall ensure that any authorities with relevant information in their possession make this information available to the developer.

Article 6

1. Member States shall take the measures necessary to ensure that the authorities likely to be concerned by the project by reason of their specific environmental responsibilities are given an opportunity to express their opinion on the request for development consent. Member States shall designate the authorities to be consulted for this purpose in general terms or in each case when the request for consent is made. The information gathered pursuant to Article 5 shall be forwarded to these authorities. Detailed arrangements for consultation shall be laid down by the Member States.

2. Member States shall ensure that:
— any request for development consent and any information gathered pursuant to Article 5 are made available to the public,
— the public concerned is given the opportunity to express an opinion before the project is initiated.

3. The detailed arrangements for such information and consultation shall be determined by the Member States, which may in particular, depending on the particular characteristics of the projects or sites concerned:
— determine the public concerned,
— specify the places where the information can be consulted,
— specify the way in which the public may be informed, for example by bill-posting within a certain radius, publication in local newspapers, organisation of exhibitions with plans, drawings, tables, graphs, models,
— determine the manner in which the public is to be consulted, for example, by written submissions, by public enquiry,
— fix appropriate time limits for the various stages of the procedure in order to ensure that a decision is taken within a reasonable period.

Article 7

Where a Member State is aware that a project is likely to have significant effects on the environment in another Member State or where a Member State likely to be significantly affected so requests, the Member State in whose territory the project is intended to be carried out shall forward the information gathered pursuant to Article 5 to the other Member State at the same time as it makes it available to its own nationals. Such information shall serve as a basis for any consultations necessary in the framework of the bilateral relations between two Member States on a reciprocal and equivalent basis.

Article 8

Information gathered pursuant to Articles 5, 6 and 7 must be taken into consideration in the development consent procedure.

Article 9

When a decision has been taken, the competent authority or authorities shall inform the public concerned of:
— the content of the decision and any conditions attached thereto,
— the reasons and considerations on which the decision is based where the Member States' legislation so provides. The detailed arrangements for such information shall be determined by the Member States.

If another Member State has been informed pursuant to Article 7, it will also be informed of the decision in question.

Article 10

The provisions of this Directive shall not affect the obligation on the competent authorities to respect the limitations imposed by national regulations and administrative provisions and accepted legal practices with regard to industrial and commercial secrecy and the safeguarding of the public interest.

Where Article 7 applies, the transmission of information to another Member State and the reception of information by another Member State shall be subject to the limitations in force in the Member State in which the project is proposed.

Article 11

1. The Member States and the Commission shall exchange information on the experience gained in applying this Directive.

2. In particular, Member States shall inform the Commission of any criteria and/or thresholds adopted for the selection of the projects in question, in accordance with Article 4 (2), or of the types of projects concerned which, pursuant to Article 4 (2), are subject to assessment in accordance with Articles 5 to 10.

3. Five years after notification of this Directive, the Commission shall send the European Parliament and the Council a report on its application and effectiveness. The report shall be based on the aforementioned exchange of information.

4. On the basis of this exchange of information, the Commission shall submit to the Council additional proposals, should this be necessary, with a view to this Directive's being applied in a sufficiently coordinated manner.

Article 12

1. Member States shall take the measures necessary to comply with this Directive within three years of its notification (1).

2. Member States shall communicate to the Commission the texts of the provisions of national law which they adopt in the field covered by this Directive.

Article 13

The provisions of this Directive shall not affect the right of Member States to lay down stricter rules regarding scope and procedure when assessing environmental effects.

Article 14

This Directive is addressed to the Member States.

Done at Luxembourg, 27 June 1985.

For the Council

The President

A. BIONDI

ANNEX I
PROJECTS SUBJECT TO ARTICLE 4(1)

1. Crude-oil refineries (excluding undertakings manufacturing only lubricants from crude oil) and installations for the gasification and liquefaction of 500 tonnes or more of coal or bituminous shale per day.

2. Thermal power stations and other combustion installations with a heat output of 300 megawatts or more and nuclear power stations and other nuclear reactors (except research installations for the production and conversion of fissionable and fertile materials, whose maximum power does not exceed 1 kilowatt continuous thermal load).

3. Installations solely designed for the permanent storage or final disposal of radioactive waste.

4. Integrated works for the initial melting of cast-iron and steel.

5. Installations for the extraction of asbestos and for the processing and transformation of asbestos and products containing asbestos: for asbestos-cement products, with an annual production of more than 20 000 tonnes of finished products, for friction material, with an annual production of more than 50 tonnes of finished products, and for other uses of asbestos, utilisation of more than 200 tonnes per year.

6. Integrated chemical installations.

7. Construction of motorways, express roads(1) and lines for long-distance railway traffic and of airports(2) with a basic runway length of 2 100 m or more.

8. Trading ports and also inland waterways and ports for inland-waterway traffic which permit the passage of vessels of over 1 350 tonnes.

9. Waste-disposal installations for the incineration, chemical treatment or land fill of toxic and dangerous wastes.

NOTES

(1) For the purposes of the Directive, 'express road' means a road which complies with the definition in the European Agreement on main international traffic arteries of 15 November 1975.
(2) For the purposes of this Directive, 'airport' means airports which comply with the definition in the 1944 Chicago Convention setting up the International Civil Aviation Organisation (Annex 14).

ANNEX II
PROJECTS SUBJECT TO ARTICLE 4(2)

1. Agriculture
(a) Projects for the restructuring of rural land holdings.
(b) Projects for the use of uncultivated land or semi-natural areas for intensive agricultural purposes.
(c) Water-management projects for agriculture.
(d) Initial afforestation where this may lead to adverse ecological changes and land reclamation for the purposes of conversion to another type of land use.
(e) Poultry-rearing installations.
(f) Pig-rearing installations.
(g) Salmon breeding.
(h) Reclamation of land from the sea.

2. Extractive industry
(a) Extraction of peat.
(b) Deep drillings with the exception of drillings for investigating the stability of the soil and in particular:
  — geothermal drilling,
  — drilling for the storage of nuclear waste material,
  — drilling for water supplies.
(c) Extraction of minerals other than metalliferous and energy-producing minerals, such as marble, sand, gravel, shale, salt, phosphates and potash.
(d) Extraction of coal and lignite by underground mining.
(e) Extraction of coal and lignite by open-cast mining.
(f) Extraction of petroleum.
(g) Extraction of natural gas.
(h) Extraction of ores.

(i) Extraction of bituminous shale.
(j) Extraction of minerals other than metalliferous and energy-producing minerals by open-cast mining.
(k) Surface industrial installations for the extraction of coal, petroleum, natural gas and ores, as well as bituminous shale.
(l) Coke ovens (dry coal distillation).
(m) Installations for the manufacture of cement.

3. Energy industry
(a) Industrial installations for the production of electricity, steam and hot water (unless included in Annex I).
(b) Industrial installations for carrying gas, steam and hot water; transmission of electrical energy by overhead cables.
(c) Surface storage of natural gas.
(d) Underground storage of combustible gases.
(e) Surface storage of fossil fuels.
(f) Industrial briquetting of coal and lignite.
(g) Installations for the production or enrichment of nuclear fuels.
(h) Installations for the reprocessing of irradiated nuclear fuels.
(i) Installations for the collection and processing of radioactive waste (unless included in Annex I).
(j) Installations for hydroelectric energy production.

4. Processing of metals
(a) Iron and steelworks, including foundries, forges, drawing plants and rolling mills (unless included in Annex I).
(b) Installations for the production, including smelting, refining, drawing and rolling, of nonferrous metals, excluding precious metals.
(c) Pressing, drawing and stamping of large castings.
(d) Surface treatment and coating of metals.
(e) Boilermaking, manufacture of reservoirs, tanks and other sheet-metal containers.
(f) Manufacture and assembly of motor vehicles and manufacture of motor-vehicle engines.
(g) Shipyards.
(h) Installations for the construction and repair of aircraft.
(i) Manufacture of railway equipment.
(j) Swaging by explosives.
(k) Installations for the roasting and sintering of metallic ores.

5. Manufacture of glass

6. Chemical industry
(a) Treatment of intermediate products and production of chemicals (unless included in Annex I).
(b) Production of pesticides and pharmaceutical products, paint and varnishes, elastomers and peroxides.
(c) Storage facilities for petroleum, petrochemical and chemical products.

7. Food industry
(a) Manufacture of vegetable and animal oils and fats.

(b) Packing and canning of animal and vegetable products.
(c) Manufacture of dairy products.
(d) Brewing and malting.
(e) Confectionery and syrup manufacture.
(f) Installations for the slaughter of animals.
(g) Industrial starch manufacturing installations.
(h) Fish-meal and fish-oil factories.
(i) Sugar factories.

8. Textile, leather, wood and paper industries
(a) Wool scouring, degreasing and bleaching factories.
(b) Manufacture of fibre board, particle board and plywood.
(c) Manufacture of pulp, paper and board.
(d) Fibre-dyeing factories.
(e) Cellulose-processing and production installations.
(f) Tannery and leather-dressing factories.

9. Rubber industry

Manufacture and treatment of elastomer-based products.

10. Infrastructure projects
(a) Industrial-estate development projects.
(b) Urban-development projects.
(c) Ski-lifts and cable-cars.
(d) Construction of roads, harbours, including fishing harbours, and airfields (projects not listed in Annex I).
(e) Canalisation and flood-relief works.
(f) Dams and other installations designed to hold water or store it on a long-term basis.
(g) Tramways, elevated and underground railways, suspended lines or similar lines of a particular type, used exclusively or mainly for passenger transport.
(h) Oil and gas pipeline installations.
(i) Installation of long-distance aqueducts.
(j) Yacht marinas.

11. Other projects
(a) Holiday villages, hotel complexes.
(b) Permanent racing and test tracks for cars and motor cycles.
(c) Installations for the disposal of industrial and domestic waste (unless included in Annex I).
(d) Waste water treatment plants.
(e) Sludge-deposition sites.
(f) Storage of scrap iron.
(g) Test benches for engines, turbines or reactors.
(h) Manufacture of artificial mineral fibres.
(i) Manufacture, packing, loading or placing in cartridges of gunpowder and explosives.
(j) Knackers' yards.

12. Modifications to development projects included in Annex I and projects in Annex I undertaken exclusively or mainly for the development and testing of new methods or products and not used for more than one year.

ANNEX III
INFORMATION REFERRED TO IN ARTICLE 5(1)

1. Description of the project, including in particular:
— a description of the physical characteristics of the whole project and the land-use requirements during the construction and operational phases,
— a description of the main characteristics of the production processes, for instance, nature and quantity of the materials used,
— an estimate, by type and quantity, of expected residues and emissions (water, air and soil pollution, noise, vibration, light, heat, radiation, etc) resulting from the operation of the proposed project.

2. Where appropriate, an outline of the main alternatives studied by the developer and an indication of the main reasons for his choice, taking into account the environmental effects.

3. A description of the aspects of the environment likely to be significantly affected by the proposed project, including, in particular, population, fauna, flora, soil, water, air, climatic factors, material assets, including the architectural and archaeological heritage, landscape and the inter-relationship between the above factors.

4. A description[7] of the likely significant effects of the proposed project on the environment resulting from:
— the existence of the project,
— the use of natural resources,
— the emission of pollutants, the creation of nuisances and the elimination of waste; and the description by the developer of the forecasting methods used to assess the effects on the environment.

5. A description of the measures envisaged to prevent, reduce and where possible offset any significant adverse effects on the environment.

6. A non-technical summary of the information provided under the above headings.

7. An indication of any difficulties (technical deficiencies or lack of know-how) encountered by the developer in compiling the required information.

NOTE

(1) This description should cover the direct effects and any indirect, secondary, cumulative, short, medium and long-term, permanent and temporary, positive and negative effects of the project.

(1) OJ C169 9.7.1980 p 14.
(2) OJ C66 15.3.1982 p 89.
(3) OJ C185 27.7.1981 p 8.
(4) OJ C112 20.12.1973 p 1.
(5) OJ C139 13.6.1977 p 1.

(6) OJ C46 17.2.1983 p 1.

(7) This Directive was notified to the Member States on 3 July 1985.

Circular 02/99
Environmental Impact Assessment

Circular 02/99
Environmental Impact Assessment

Office of the Deputy Prime Minister

Published 22 August 2002

CONTENTS

This Circular contains the following main sections:

INTRODUCTION

1   This Circular gives guidance on the Town and Country Planning (Environmental Impact Assessment) (England and Wales) Regulations 1999, SI 1999 No 293, (referred to in this Circular as 'the Regulations'). The Regulations implement Council Directive No 85/337/EEC on the assessment of the effects of certain public and private projects on the environment (the EIA Directive), as amended by Council Directive No 97/111/EC, in so far as it applies to development under the Town and Country Planning Act 1990. In this Circular, references to 'the Directive' mean the Directive as amended.

2   The Regulations apply to development in England and Wales:
a   for which an application for planning permission, is received by a local planning authority on or after 14 March 1999;
b   which is carried out under permitted development rights and which were not already begun on 14 March 1999;
c   which is the subject of a planning enforcement notice issued under section 172 of the 1990 Act (as substituted by section 5 of the Planning and Compensation Act 1991) on or after 14 March 1999; and
d   which is carried out under permission granted by a simplified planning zone scheme or enterprise zone order and which is not already begun on 14 March 1999.

3   Applications for planning permission received by a local planning authority before 14 March 1999 remain subject to the requirements of the Town and Country Planning (Assessment of Environmental Effects) Regulations 1988, as amended (see endnote 1). The Town and Country Planning (Environmental Assessment and Unauthorised Development) Regulations 1995 (see endnote 2) continue to apply to enforcement notices served before that date.

4   The Regulations consolidate all the existing Regulations which implement the requirements of Council Directive 85/337/EEC for projects which are 'development' (see endnote 3).

5   Similar provision for development subject to planning control is being made in Scotland and Northern Ireland. Procedures for projects which are granted consent under other legislation are the subject of separate legislation and guidance issued by the relevant Government departments or agencies.

6   Although the Regulations relate to England and Wales, this Circular relates only to development in England. Similar guidance will be issued by the Welsh Office in respect of development in Wales. The Circular is intended as a guide. It should be read in conjunction with the Regulations themselves. An authoritative statement of the law can only be made by the Courts.

7   This Circular replaces: C15/88; paragraphs 7 and 8 of Annex A to PPG 5 (Simplified Planning Zones); C7/94; C3/95; C13/95; paragraphs 15 and 16 of C15/92; paragraphs 36–40 of C19/92; paragraphs 2.78 and 2.79 of Annex 2 to Circular 10/97; and paragraph 22 of C9/95 in relation to applications for planning permission received by a local planning authority on or after 14 March 1999.

ENDNOTES

1   SI 1988/1199, as amended by SI 1990/367, SI 1992/1494 and SI 1994/677.
2   SI 1995/2258.
3   SI 1988/1199, SI 1990/367, SI 1992/1494, SI 1992/2414, SI 1994/677, SI 1995/417 and SI 1995/2258.

THE EIA DIRECTIVE

8   Council Directive 85/337/EEC came into force in 1988. Directive 97/11/EC, which amends Directive 85/337/EEC, comes into force on 14 March 1999. It extends the range of development to which the Directive applies and makes a number of small but important changes to EIA procedures.

9   The Directive's main aim is to ensure that the authority giving the primary consent (the 'competent authority') for a particular project makes its decision in the knowledge of any likely significant effects on the environment. The Directive, therefore, sets out a procedure that must be followed for certain types of project before they can be given 'development consent'. This procedure, known as Environmental Impact Assessment (EIA), is a means of drawing together, in a systematic way, an assessment of a project's likely significant environmental effects. This helps to ensure that the importance of the predicted effects, and the scope for reducing them, are properly understood by the public and the relevant competent authority before it makes its decision.

10   Projects of the types listed in Annex I to the Directive must always be subject to EIA. Projects of the types listed in Annex II must be subject to EIA whenever they are likely to have significant effects on the environment. A determination of whether or not EIA is required must be made for all projects of a type listed in Annex II.

11   Where EIA is required there are three broad stages to the procedure.
a   The developer must compile detailed information about the likely main environmental effects. To help the developer, public authorities must make available any relevant environmental information in their possession. The developer can also ask the 'competent authority' for their opinion on what information needs to be included. The information finally compiled by the developer is known as an 'Environmental Statement' (ES).
b   The ES (and the application to which it relates) must be publicised. Public authorities with relevant environmental responsibilities and the public must be given an opportunity to give their views about the project and ES.
c   The ES, together with any other information, comments and representations made on it, must be taken into account by the competent authority in deciding whether or not to give consent for the development. The public must be informed of the decision and the main reasons for it.

THE REGULATIONS

12   The Regulations must be interpreted in the context of the Directive itself. Neither the Directive nor the Regulations determine whether consent can or should be granted. Local planning authorities already have a well established general responsibility to consider the environmental implications of developments which are subject to planning control. The Regulations integrate the EIA procedures into this existing framework of local authority control. These procedures provide a more systematic method of assessing the environmental implications of developments that are likely to have significant effects. While only a very small proportion of development will require EIA, it is stressed that EIA is not discretionary. If significant effects on the environment are likely, EIA is required.

13   Where the EIA procedure reveals that a project will have an adverse impact on the environment, it does not follow that planning permission must be refused. It remains the task of the local planning authority to judge each planning application on its merits within the context of the Development Plan, taking account of all material considerations, including the environmental impacts.

14   For developers, EIA can help to identify the likely effects of a particular project at an early stage. This can produce improvements in the planning and design of the development; in decision-making by both parties; and in consultation and responses thereto, particularly if combined with early consultations with the local planning authority and other interested bodies during the preparatory stages. In addition, developers may find EIA a useful tool for considering alternative approaches to a development. This can result in a final proposal that is more environmentally acceptable, and can form the basis for a more robust application for planning permission. The presentation of environmental information in a more systematic way may also simplify the local planning authority's task of appraising the application and drawing up appropriate planning conditions, enabling swifter decisions to be reached.

The legal framework

15   In this Circular, Environmental Impact Assessment (EIA) refers to the whole process by which environmental information is collected, publicised and taken into account in reaching a decision on a relevant planning application. This process was formerly referred to in the UK as Environmental Assessment or EA.

16   Applications for planning permission for which EIA is required are referred to in the Regulations and the Circular as 'EIA applications'. Subject to any direction by the Secretary of State, an application is, or would be, an EIA application if:

a   the relevant planning authority has notified the developer in writing that EIA is required; or

b   the applicant submits a statement which he refers to as an Environmental Statement for the purposes of the Regulations.

17   Development that falls within a relevant description in Schedule 1 to the Regulations always requires EIA. Such development is referred to in this Circular and the Regulations as 'Schedule 1 development'.

18   Development of a type listed in Schedule 2 to the Regulations which:
a   meets one of the relevant criteria or exceeds one of the relevant thresholds listed in the second column of the table in Schedule 2; or
b   is located in a 'sensitive area', as defined in regulation 2(1);
is referred to in this Circular as 'Schedule 2 development'.

19   Regulation 3 prohibits the granting of planning permission for:
•   Schedule 1 development; or
•   Schedule 2 development which is likely to have significant environmental effects because of factors such as its nature, size or location; unless the EIA procedures have been followed. The prohibition applies to any development for which a planning application is received by the local planning authority on or after 14 March 1999.

20   For all Schedule 2 development (including that which would otherwise benefit from permitted development rights), the local planning authority must make its own formal determination of whether or not EIA is required (referred to in the Regulations and this Circular as a 'screening opinion'). This may be done before any planning application has been submitted (regulation 5) or after (regulation 7). In making this determination the local planning authority must take into account the relevant 'selection criteria' in Schedule 3 to the Regulations (Annex B to this Circular). Developers may appeal to the Secretary of State for a 'screening direction' where a local authority adopts a screening opinion that EIA is required (regulations 6 and 8). The local planning authority must make all screening opinions and directions available for public inspection (regulation 20).

21   Where EIA is required, information must be provided by the developer in an Environmental Statement (ES). This document (or series of documents) must contain the information specified by regulation 2(1) and in Schedule 4 to the Regulations. Regulation 10 allows developers to obtain a formal opinion from the relevant planning authority on what should be included in the Environmental Statement ('a scoping opinion'). Under regulation 12, certain public bodies (defined in regulation 2(1) as 'the consultation bodies') must, if requested, make information in their possession available to the developer for the purposes of preparing an ES.

22   Regulation 13 sets out the procedures which must be followed by applicants in submitting a planning application with an ES, and by local planning authorities in publicising it. Similar procedures apply where an ES is submitted to the Secretary of State (regulation 16). Where the statement is not submitted until after the planning application to which it relates, the applicant is responsible for publicising it (regulation 14). In all cases, applicants must also make a reasonable number of copies of the ES available to the public (regulation 17), and may make a reasonable charge for them (regulation 18).

23   For EIA applications, the period after which an appeal against non-determination may be made is extended to 16 weeks (regulation 32).

24   Where a statement has been submitted which does not contain all the required information, the local planning authority, Secretary of State or Inspector must ask the applicant to supply further information (regulation 19). This information must be publicised in the same way as the statement itself.

25   When determining an EIA application, the local planning authority or Secretary of State must inform the public of their decision (regulation 21).

26   The Regulations also implement the EIA Directive in relation to:
- development carried out by local planning authorities (regulation 22);
- development permitted by simplified planning zone schemes and enterprise zone orders (regulations 23 and 24);
- development subject to a planning enforcement notice (regulation 25);
- development likely to have significant environmental effects in other Member States (regulations 27 and 28); and
- permitted development (regulation 35(3)).

27   Regulation 35 makes consequential and miscellaneous amendments to the provisions of:
- section 55 of the Town and Country Planning Act 1990;
- the Town and Country Planning (Use Classes) Order 1987 (see endnote 4);
- the Town and Country Planning (General Development Procedure) Order 1995 ('GDPO') (see endnote 5); and
- the Town and Country Planning (General Permitted Development) Order 1995 ('GPDO') (see endnote 6).

ENDNOTES

4   SI 1987/764. relevant amending instruments are SI 1991/1567, SI 1992/61 and SI 1994/724.
5   SI 1995/419.
6   S1 1995/418.

ESTABLISHING WHETHER EIA IS REQUIRED

28   Generally, it will fall to local planning authorities in the first instance to consider whether a proposed development requires EIA. For this purpose they will first need to consider whether the development is described in Schedule 1 or Schedule 2 to the Regulations (see figure 1).

Schedule 1 development

Development of a type listed in Schedule 1 always requires EIA.

Schedule 2 development

Development listed in Schedule 2 requires EIA if it is likely to have significant effects on the environment by virtue of factors such as its size, nature or location.

Changes or extensions to Schedule 1 or Schedule 2 development

Changes or extensions to Schedule 1 or Schedule 2 development which may have significant adverse effects on the environment also fall within the scope of the Regulations. Where the change or extension itself would fall within one of the descriptions in Schedule 1, it constitutes a Schedule 1 development and EIA is always required (see endnote 7). Otherwise, and if the change or extension may have significant adverse effects on the environment, it is considered to be a Schedule 2 development. A screening opinion or direction is then required on whether the development is likely to have significant effects on the environment.

Identifying Schedule 2 development

29   Schedule 2 development is development of a type listed in Schedule 2 which:
a   is located wholly or in part in a 'sensitive area' as defined in regulation 2(1) (paragraph 36); or
b   meets one of the relevant criteria or exceeds one of the relevant thresholds listed in the second column of the table in Schedule 2

30   It is stressed that development in a sensitive area should only be considered to be Schedule 2 development if it falls within a description in Schedule 2. Most of the types of development listed in Schedule 2 have an inherent scale as emphasised by the headings (eg 'energy industry') contained in the Annexes to the Directive and included in Schedule 2. It follows that the majority of development proposals such as householder or small business developments will not fall within any of the descriptions. The criteria and thresholds in the second column of the table apply equally to changes or extensions to relevant development as they do to new development. Paragraph 13(a) of Schedule 2 provides that, in such cases, the thresholds and criteria are to be applied to the change or extension itself, not to the development as changed or extended.

31   Development falling below the thresholds or meeting none of the criteria in the second column of the table in Schedule 2 does not require EIA. However, there may be circumstances in which such small developments might give rise to significant environmental effects. In those exceptional cases the Secretary of State can use his powers under regulation 4(8) (paragraph 77) to direct that EIA is required.

Esablishing whether a development requires EIA

Is it listed in Schedule 1?
(paragraph 28)

Yes

No

Is it listed   in Schedule   2?
(paragraph 30)

Yes

No

Is it in a 'sensitive area'?
(paragraph 28)

Yes

No

Does it meet any of the relevant thresholds and criteria in Schedule 2?

Yes

No

Is this 'Schedule 2 development' likely to have significant effects on the environment?
(paragraph 32-47)

Yes

No

The need for EIA for Schedule 2 development

General considerations

32   The local planning authority must screen every application for Schedule 2 development in order to determine whether or not EIA is required. This determination is referred to as a 'screening opinion'. In each case, the basic question to be asked is 'Would this particular development be likely to have significant effects on the environment?'. The following paragraphs indicate the considerations which should be taken into account in making that determination.

33   As a starting point, authorities should study Schedule 3 to the Regulations (reproduced at Annex B to this Circular) which sets out the 'selection criteria' which must be taken into account in determining whether a development is likely to have significant effects on the environment. Not all of the criteria will be relevant in every case. It identifies three broad criteria which should be considered: the characteristics of the development (eg its size, use of natural resources, quantities of pollution and waste generated); the environmental sensitivity of the location; and the characteristics of the potential impact (eg its magnitude and duration). In the light of these, the Secretary of State's view is that, in general, EIA will be needed for Schedule 2 developments in three main types of case:
a   for major developments which are of more than local importance (paragraph 35);
b   for developments which are proposed for particularly environmentally sensitive or vulnerable locations (paragraphs 36–40); and
c   for developments with unusually complex and potentially hazardous environmental effects (paragraphs 41–42).

34   The number of cases of such development will be a very small proportion of the total number of Schedule 2 developments. It is emphasised that the basic test of the need for EIA in a particular case is the likelihood of significant effects on the environment. It should not be assumed, for example, that conformity with a development plan rules out the need for EIA. Nor is the amount of opposition or controversy to which a development gives rise relevant to this determination, unless the substance of opponents' arguments reveals that there are likely to be significant effects on the environment.

Major development of more than local importance

35   In some cases, the scale of a development can be sufficient for it to have wide-ranging environmental effects that would justify EIA. There will be some overlap between the circumstances in which EIA is required because of the scale of the development proposed and those in which the Secretary of State may wish to exercise his power to 'call in' an application for his own determination (see endnote 8). However, there is no presumption that all called-in applications require EIA, nor that all EIA applications will be called in.

Development in environmentally sensitive locations

36   The relationship between a proposed development and its location is a crucial consideration. For any given development proposal, the more environmentally sensitive the location, the more likely it is that the effects will be significant and will require EIA. Certain designated sites are defined in regulation 2(1) as 'sensitive areas' and the thresholds/criteria in the second column of Schedule 2 do not apply there. All developments must be screened for the need for EIA. These are:

a   Sites of Special Scientific Interest, any consultation areas around them (where these have been notified to the local planning authority under article l0(u)(ii) of the GDPO), land to which Nature Conservation Orders apply and international conservation sites; and

b   National Parks, the Broads (see endnote 9), Areas of Outstanding Natural Beauty, World Heritage Sites and scheduled monuments.

37   Special considerations apply to Sites of Special Scientific Interest (SSSIs), especially those which are also international conservation sites. In practice, the likely environmental effects of Schedule 2 development will often be such as to require EIA if it is to be located in or close to such sites, including classified and potential Special Protection Areas (SPAs) under the Wild Birds Directive (79/404/EEC); designated and candidate Special Areas of Conservation (SACs) under the Habitats Directive (92/43/EEC); and Ramsar sites (wetlands of international importance). Whenever local planning authorities are uncertain about the significance of a development's likely effects on an SSSI, they should consult English Nature. Other non-statutory bodies may have relevant information and can also be consulted. Where development is proposed within two kilometres of an SSSI, the developer should consult the local planning authority to discover whether the site of the proposed development falls within a consultation area as a result of a notification to the authority by a nature conservation body under article l0(u)(ii) of the GDPO.

38   For any Schedule 2 development, EIA is more likely to be required if it would be likely to have significant effects on the special character of any of the other types of 'sensitive area' or the New Forest Heritage Area (see endnote 10). However, it does not follow that every Schedule 2 development in (or affecting) these areas will automatically require EIA. In each case, it will be necessary to judge whether the likely effects on the environment of that particular development will be significant in that particular location. Any views expressed by the consultation bodies (paragraph 98) should be taken into account, and authorities should consult them in the cases where there is a doubt about the significance of a development's likely effects on a sensitive area.

39   In certain cases other statutory and non-statutory designations which are not included in the definition of 'sensitive areas', but which are nonetheless environmentally sensitive, may also be relevant in determining whether EIA is required. Where relevant, Local Biodiversity Action Plans will be of assistance in determining the sensitivity of a location. Urban locations may also be considered sensitive as a result of their heavier concentrations of population.

40   In considering the sensitivity of a particular location, regard should also be had to whether any national or internationally agreed environmental standards are already being approached or exceeded. An example is where a proposed development might affect air quality in a designated Air Quality Management Area (see endnote 11). Where there are local standards (for bathing water for example) consideration should be given to whether the proposed development would affect the standards or levels in those plans.

Development with particularly complex and potentially hazardous effects

41   A small number of developments may be likely to have significant effects on the environment because of the particular nature of their impact. Consideration should be given to development which could have complex, long-term or irreversible impacts, and where expert and detailed analysis of those impacts would be desirable and would be relevant to the issue of whether or not the development should be allowed. Industrial development involving emissions which are potentially hazardous to humans and nature may fall into this category. So, occasionally, may other types of development which are proposed for severely contaminated land and where the development might lead to more hazardous contaminants escaping from the site than would otherwise be the case if the development did not take place.

42   The Regulations do not alter the relationship between authorities' planning responsibilities and the separate statutory responsibilities exercised by local authorities and other pollution control bodies under pollution control legislation. However, they do strengthen the need for appropriate consultations with the relevant bodies at the planning application stage. Detailed guidance on the relevance of pollution controls to the exercise of planning functions in England is set out in PPG 23 (Planning and Pollution Control).

Indicative criteria and thresholds

43   Given the range of Schedule 2 development, and the importance of location in determining whether significant effects on the environment are likely, it is not possible to formulate criteria or thresholds which will provide a universal test of whether or not EIA is required. The question must be considered on a case-by-case basis. However, it is possible to offer a broad indication of the type or scale of development which is likely to be a candidate for EIA and, conversely, an indication of the sort of development for which EIA is unlikely to be necessary.

44   For each category of Schedule 2 development, Annex A to this Circular lists criteria and/or thresholds which indicate the types of case in which, in the Secretary of State's view, EIA is more likely to be required. Annex A also gives an indication of the types of impact that are most likely to be significant for particular types of development. It should not be presumed that developments falling below these thresholds could never give rise to significant effects, especially where the development is in an

environmentally sensitive location. Equally, developments which exceed the thresholds will not in every case require assessment. The fundamental test to be applied in each case is whether that particular type of development and its specific impacts are likely, in that particular location, to result in significant effects on the environment. **It follows that the thresholds should only be used in conjunction with the general guidance, and particularly that relating to environmentally sensitive locations (paragraphs 36–40).**

Applying the guidance to individual development

45   In general, each application (or request for an opinion) should be considered for EIA on its own merits. The development should be judged on the basis of what is proposed by the developer.

46   However, in judging whether the effects of a development are likely to be significant, local planning authorities should always have regard to the possible cumulative effects with any existing or approved development. There are occasions where the existence of other development may be particularly relevant in determining whether significant effects are likely, or even where more than one application for development should be considered together to determine whether or not EIA is required.

Multiple applications

For the purposes of determining whether EIA is required, a particular planning application should not be considered in isolation if, in reality, it is properly to be regarded as an integral part of an inevitably more substantial development (see endnote 12). In such cases, the need for EIA (including the applicability of any indicative thresholds) must be considered in respect of the total development. This is not to say that all applications which form part of some wider scheme must be considered together. In this context, it will be important to establish whether each of the proposed developments could proceed independently and whether the aims of the Regulations and Directive are being frustrated by the submission of multiple planning applications.

Changes or extensions to existing or approved development

Development which comprises a change or extension requires EIA only if the change or extension is likely to have significant environmental effects. This should be considered in the 'light of the general guidance in this Circular and the indicative thresholds in Annex A. However, the significance of any effects must be considered in the context of the existing development. For example. even a small extension to an airport runway might have the effect of allowing larger aircraft to land. thus significantly increasing the level of noise and emissions. In some cases, repeated small extensions may be made to development. Quantified thresholds cannot easily deal with this kind of 'incremental' development. In such instances, it should be borne in mind that the thresholds in Annex A are indicative only. An expansion of the same size as a previous expansion will not automatically lead to the same determination on the need for EIA because the environment may have altered since the question was last addressed

47   It should be noted that a developer can be asked to provide an Environmental Statement only in respect of the specific development he has proposed, though the statement will need to address not only direct, but also indirect effects of the development. Any wider implications would be for the local planning authority to consider, although it is open to developers to assist the local planning authority by supplying any additional information relevant to this consideration. Further guidance on the content of Environmental Statements is given in paragraphs 81–85.

Outline planning applications

48   Where EIA is required for a planning application made in outline, the requirements of the Regulations must be fully met at the outline stage since reserved matters cannot be subject to EIA. When any planning application is made in outline, the local planning authority will need to satisfy themselves that they have sufficient information available on the environmental effects of the proposal to enable them to determine whether or not planning permission should be granted in principle. In cases where the Regulations require more information on the environmental effects for the Environmental Statement than has been provided in an outline application, for instance, on visual effects of a development in a National Park, authorities should request further information under regulation 19. This may also constitute a request under article 3(2) of the GDPO.

Procedures for establishing whether or not EIA is required ('screening')

49   The determination of whether or not EIA is required for a particular development proposal can take place at a number of different stages.
a   The developer may decide that EIA will be required and submit a statement which he refers to as an Environmental Statement for the purpose of the Regulations with the planning application (paragraphs 52–54).
b   The developer may, before submitting any planning application, request a screening opinion from the local planning authority (paragraphs 55–58). If the developer disputes the need for EIA (or a screening opinion is not adopted within the required period), the developer may apply to the Secretary of State for a screening direction (paragraphs 59–60). Similar procedures apply to permitted development (paragraphs 61–65).
c   The local planning authority may determine that EIA is required following receipt of a planning application (paragraphs 67–70). Again, if the developer disputes the need for EIA, the applicant may apply to the Secretary of State for a screening direction (paragraph 71).

d   The Secretary of State may determine that EIA is required for an application that has been called in for his determination or is before him on appeal (paragraphs 72–76).

e   The Secretary of State may direct that EIA is required at any stage prior to the granting of consent for particular development (paragraph 77).

50   Applicants should bear in mind that if the need for EIA only arises after the planning application has been submitted, consideration of the application will be suspended pending submission of an Environmental Statement (regulation 32(2)(b)).

Procedures prior to submission of a planning application

51   Developers are advised to consult planning authorities at as early a stage as possible in cases where there is any question of EIA being required, particularly where the proposed development would otherwise benefit from permitted development rights. It will generally be helpful for developers to be aware of the concerns of local planning authorities and pollution control bodies well before a planning application is submitted. To provide some certainty for developers, they can obtain a screening opinion from the local planning authority before making a planning application (regulation 5). A valid planning application may be made without prior recourse to this procedure, but developers should bear in mind that any informal view from an authority has no legally-binding effect.

Environmental Statement submitted 'voluntarily' by a developer

52   Developers may decide for themselves (in the light of the Regulations, the guidance in this Circular and any discussions with the planning authority) that EIA will be required for their proposed development. A developer may, therefore, submit a statement with a planning application without having obtained a screening opinion to the effect that one is required.

53   If an applicant expressly states that they are submitting a statement which they refer to as an Environmental Statement (ES) for the purposes of the Regulations, the application is an EIA application and must be treated as such by the local planning authority (regulation 4(2)(a)). Exceptionally, where an authority is of the view that the application to which the statement relates is clearly not one which they would have determined to be an EIA application, they may request the Secretary of State for a direction on the matter.

54   Occasionally, the applicant may not have made it clear that the information submitted is intended to constitute an ES for the purposes of the Regulations. In such cases, the local planning authority should adopt a screening opinion (if they have not already done so), in accordance with the procedures in regulation 7 (paragraphs 67–70). If the local planning authority determine that it is an EIA application, it is open to the applicant to ask for the information already submitted to be treated as the ES for the purposes of the Regulations, or to submit the specified information in a new statement.

If the authority's opinion is that EIA is not required, the information provided by the applicant should still be taken into account in determining the application if it is material to the decision.

Obtaining a screening opinion from the local planning authority (regulation 5)

55   Before submitting an application for planning permission, developers who are in doubt whether EIA would be required, may request a screening opinion from the local planning authority (regulation 5(1)). The request should include a plan indicating the proposed location of the development, a brief description of the nature and purpose of the proposal and its possible environmental effects, giving a broad indication of their likely scale.

56   On receipt of a request, the authority should consider whether the proposed development is either Schedule 1 development or Schedule 2 development that is likely to have significant effects on the environment by virtue of factors such as its nature, size or location, taking into account the selection criteria in Schedule 3 (Annex B) (regulation 4(5)). The developer should normally be able to supply sufficient information about the development to enable the local planning authority to form a judgment and give a ruling on the need for EIA. However, where the authority considers that it needs further information, the developer should be asked to provide it (regulation 5(3)). Authorities should bear in mind that what is in question at this stage is the broad significance of the likely environmental effects of the proposal. This should not require as much information as would be expected to support a planning application. Very exceptionally, authorities may also wish to seek advice from one or more of the consultation bodies or non-statutory bodies.

57   The local planning authority must adopt its screening opinion within three weeks of receiving a request. This period may be extended if the authority and developer so agree in writing. When adopting an opinion that EIA is required, the authority must state the full reasons for their conclusion clearly and precisely (regulation 4(6)). A copy must be sent to the developer (regulations 5(5) and 4(6)). This will help him to prepare the ES by indicating those aspects of the proposed development's environmental effects which the authority considers to be likely to be significant (see also paragraphs 86–92).

58   Where a local planning authority adopts a screening opinion, a copy of the relevant documents must be made available for public inspection for two years at the place where the planning register is kept. If a planning application is subsequently made for the development, the opinion and related documents should be transferred to Part I of the register with the application (regulation 20).

Applying to the Secretary of State for a screening direction (regulation 6)

59   Where the local planning authority's opinion is that EIA is required and the developer disagrees, or where an authority fails to adopt any opinion within three

weeks (or any agreed extension), the developer may request the Secretary of State to make a screening direction (see endnote 13) (regulation 5(6)). The request must be accompanied by all the previous documents relating to the request for a screening opinion, together with any additional representations that the developer wishes to make. The developer should also send a copy of the request and any representations to the local planning authority, which is free to make its own further representations.

60   The Secretary of State should make a screening direction within three weeks from the date of receipt of the request, or such longer period as he may reasonably require. Where he directs that EIA is required, the direction must be accompanied by a clear and precise statement of his full reasons (regulation 4(6)). He must send copies of the direction to the developer and to the local planning authority (regulations 6(5) and 4(9)), which must ensure that a copy of the direction is made available for inspection with the other documents referred to in paragraph 59 (regulation 20).

Permitted development

61   The Town and Country Planning (General Permitted Development) Order 1995 ('GPDO') (see endnote 14) grants general permission (usually referred to as permitted development rights PDRs) for various specified types of development. The purpose and function of the Order is explained in Circular 9/95, although paragraph 22 of that Circular is superseded by the provisions set out below in paragraphs 62–65.

62   Permitted development rights largely concern development of a minor, non-contentious nature. The majority of permitted developments, such as development within the curtilage of a dwelling house, minor operations, temporary buildings and uses, and small business development are very unlikely to fall within any of the descriptions in Schedules 1 or 2.

63   The provisions of the GPDO (insofar as they relate to Schedule 1 or Schedule 2 development) are amended (regulation 35(3)) as follows:
a   Schedule 1 development is not permitted development. Such developments always require the submission of a planning application and an Environmental Statement.
b   Schedule 2 development does not constitute permitted development unless the local planning authority has adopted a screening opinion to the effect that EIA is not required. Where the authority's opinion is that EIA is required, permitted development rights are withdrawn and a planning application must be submitted and accompanied by an Environmental Statement.

These requirements do not apply to certain types of permitted development, described in paragraphs 151–156.

64   A request for a screening opinion in relation to permitted development should be made in accordance with the provisions which apply to requests for a pre-application screening opinion set out in regulation 5 (paragraphs 55–58). There are similar rights to request the Secretary of State to make a screening direction if a developer disagrees with an opinion that EIA is required, or where the local planning authority fails to adopt any opinion within three weeks (or such longer period as is agreed in writing).

Such requests should be made in accordance with the procedures in regulation 6 (paragraphs 59–60). Requests can be made at the same time as any prior notification required by a condition in the GPDO (but in many cases a screening opinion will be required by the Regulations even though no prior notification is required by the GPDO). The existing non-statutory consultation arrangements for statutory undertakers in relation to Article 4 Directions set out in Circular 9195 are not affected by these arrangements.

65   Local planning authorities are reminded that in exercising their functions under the Regulations they are to determine the significance or otherwise of the likely environmental effects of the proposed development, rather than to judge its planning merits. They should, therefore, make every effort to minimise disruption and delay, particularly where urgent development is required, for example for safety or security purposes or for essential improvements to public water and sewage treatment systems, or in any other case where improvements to public utilities are proposed.

Effect of screening opinions and screening directions

66   A screening opinion that development is EIA development determines, for the purposes of the Regulations, that it is EIA development, unless it is overridden by a direction from the Secretary of State. It is possible for the Secretary of State to cancel or vary an earlier direction if he has grounds for doing so. The local planning authority must observe any such direction, although they may in exceptional circumstances ask the Secretary of State to cancel or vary it if they consider that there is good reason to do so. However, a screening opinion can only be adopted on the basis of the information provided at the time it was given. There may, exceptionally, be cases where an opinion has been given that EIA is not required for a proposed development, but it subsequently becomes evident (for example, from further information submitted in support of a planning application) that it is nevertheless an EIA application. In such cases, the procedures described in paragraphs 67–70 below will apply as they apply in cases where no prior screening opinion has been adopted.

Planning application not accompanied by an Environmental Statement

Initial consideration by local planning authority (regulation 7)

67   When a local planning authority receives a planning application without an accompanying Environmental Statement, if there appears any possibility that it is for Schedule 1 or Schedule 2 development, they should check their records for any screening direction, or any pre-application screening opinion they may have adopted. Where no screening opinion or direction exists, the local planning authority must adopt such an opinion. If the authority needs further information to be able to adopt an opinion, the applicant should be asked to provide it.

68   Where the local planning authority's opinion is that EIA is not required, a screening opinion to that effect should be adopted and placed on Part I of the planning register with the planning application within three weeks of the receipt of the application (regulations 7 (1) and 20(1)). The application should then be determined in the normal way.

69   However, where the authority's opinion is that EIA is required, they must notify the applicant within three weeks of the date of receipt of the application, giving full reasons for their view clearly and precisely (regulations 7(2) and (3) and 4(6)). The three-week period may be extended if the applicant and the authority so agree in writing. A copy of the notification should be placed on Part I of the planning register with the application (regulation 20(1)(e)). For monitoring purposes, authorities are also asked to send a copy to the Secretary of State (see endnote 15).

70   An applicant who still wishes to continue with the application must reply within three weeks of the date of such a notification. The reply should indicate the applicant's intention either to provide an Environmental Statement or to ask the Secretary of State for a screening direction. If the applicant does not reply within the three weeks, the application will be deemed to have been refused. No appeal to the Secretary of State is possible against such a deemed refusal. If the applicant does reply to the notification, the authority should suspend consideration of the planning application (unless they are already minded to refuse planning permission because of other material considerations, in which case they should proceed to do so as quickly as possible). The 16 week period after which the applicant may appeal against non-determination of the planning application does not begin until an Environmental Statement and the documents required by regulation 14(5) have been submitted. If the Secretary of State directs that no such Statement is required the normal 8 week period applies, but the period begins to run at the date of the direction.

Application to Secretary of State for a screening direction (regulations 7(4) and 7(7))

71   An applicant requesting the Secretary of State for a screening direction (paragraph 70), must include a copy of the planning application together with all supporting documents and correspondence with the local planning authority concerning the proposed development. The same procedures apply to such requests as apply to requests for a screening direction prior to the submission of a planning application (paragraphs 59–60).

Called-in application not accompanied by an Environmental Statement (regulation 8)

72   When an application for planning permission is called in for determination by the Secretary of State (under section 77 of the Town and Country Planning Act 1990) and it is not accompanied by an Environmental Statement, the Secretary of State will consider whether it is for permission for Schedule 1 development or for Schedule 2

development for which EIA is required. Where necessary he will make a screening direction.

73   If the Secretary of State directs that EIA is required, the applicant and the local planning authority will be notified accordingly. There is no appeal against such a notification. An applicant who wishes to continue with the application must reply within three weeks of such a notification, stating that an Environmental Statement will be provided. Otherwise, at the end of the three-week period, the Secretary of State will inform the applicant that no further action will be taken on the application. Where the applicant indicates that an Environmental Statement will be provided, the Secretary of State will notify the consultation bodies (paragraph 98) accordingly.

74   If the Secretary of State concludes that EIA is not required, and there has been no previous screening opinion to that effect, he shall make a screening direction to that effect and send a copy to the local planning authority. They must ensure that the direction is placed on the planning register (regulation 20(1) (b)).

Appeal not accompanied by an Environmental Statement (regulation 9)

75   On receipt of an appeal made under section 78 of the 1990 Act which is not accompanied by an Environmental Statement, the Secretary of State will consider whether the proposed development is a Schedule 1 development or a Schedule 2 development for which EIA is required. Where necessary, he will make a screening direction. Where a Planning Inspector is dealing with an appeal, if the Inspector considers that EIA might be required, that question must be referred to the Secretary of State. The Inspector is then precluded from determining the appeal (except by refusing planning permission) until he receives a screening direction from the Secretary of State. If the Secretary of State directs that EIA is required, the Inspector may not determine the appeal (except by refusing permission) until the appellant submits an Environmental Statement. The Secretary of State may direct that EIA is required at any time before an appeal is determined.

76   The procedures set out in paragraphs 73–74 above apply to appeals as they apply to called-in applications.

Secretary of State's general power to make directions

77   The Secretary of State is empowered to make directions in relation to the need for EIA (regulations 4(7), 4(8) and article 14(2) of the GDPO). Such directions will normally be made in response to an application from a developer who is in dispute with the local planning authority about whether EIA is required (paragraphs 59–60). However, the Secretary of State also has a number of wider powers.

a   The Secretary of State may make a screening direction for any particular development of a type listed in Schedule 1 or Schedule 2 to the Regulations at any time prior to consent being granted, even where no application for a direction has been made to him. He may also make a screening direction in relation to development permitted under the GPDO (regulation 4(7)). There may be cases where information submitted to the Secretary of State by other bodies or persons suggests the need for EIA. In such cases it will be open to the Secretary of State to issue a direction.

b Local planning authorities may, exceptionally, draw the Secretary of State's attention to a particular development which, although listed in Schedule 2 does not constitute a Schedule 2 development for the purposes of the Regulations. The Secretary of State has powers to direct that such development is EIA development (regulation 4(8)).

c The Secretary of State may direct that EIA is always required for particular classes of development (article 14(2) of the GDPO). Any such general directions will be notified to all local planning authorities.

d The Secretary of State may direct that particular proposed Schedule 1 or Schedule 2 development is exempt from the application of the Regulations, even though it is likely to have significant effects on the environment (regulation 4(4)). While the Directive specifically provides such a power, the Secretary of State does not foresee any circumstances in which it would be used, although such circumstances may arise.

78 Before making a direction, the Secretary of State will normally give the local planning authority and applicant the opportunity to make representations. Any direction will be copied to the applicant (where known) and the local planning authority, which must make a copy of any direction available for public inspection. Where the Secretary of State has used any of these powers to direct that EIA is required for an application which is before a local planning authority, the authority must write to the applicant within seven days of receiving the copy of the screening direction to tell him that an Environmental Statement is required (regulation 7(3)). The procedures of regulation 7(4)–(6) then apply (paragraphs 67–70).

EIA and other types of environmental assessment

79 There are a number of other European Community Directives which require the assessment of effects on the environment. For example:

1 developments which will affect a Special Protection Area designated under the Wild Birds Directive (see endnote 16) or Special Area of Conservation designated under the Habitats Directive (see endnote 17) must be subject to an assessment of those effects in accordance with the Conservation (Natural Habitats &c.) Regulations 1994 (SI 1994/2716);

2 from October 1999, certain industrial developments will require a permit under the IPPC Directive (see endnote 18) (similar arrangements apply at present under the IPC regime (Environmental Protection Act 1990)); and

3 from April 1999, certain establishments which have the potential to cause a major accident hazard will require a consent under the Control of Major Accident Hazards Directive (see endnote 19).

80 These requirements and EIA are all independent of each other in that the requirement for one does not mean another automatically applies. The individual tests

set out in each system still apply. However, there are clearly some links between them and developers will benefit from identifying the different assessments required at an early stage and co-ordinating them to minimise undesirable duplication where more than one regime applies. Advice on the links between the EIA system and the requirements of the Habitats Regulations is offered in PPG 9 (Nature Conservation) and on the links between the Town and Country Planning system and the current IPC authorisation system in PPG 23 (Planning and Pollution Control).

ENDNOTES

7 Under section 77 of the 1990 Act, as amended by paragraph 18 of Schedule 7 to the Planning and Compensation Act 1991.

8 Under the Norfolk and Suffolk Broads Act 1988, the Broads have a status equal to that of a National Park.

9 The Government announced in July 1994 that the same planning principles apply to the New Forest Heritage Area as to a National Park (Commons Written Answers, 14 July 1994, column 768).

10 *Commission v Germany* [1995] ECR I-2189 in particular paragraph 36.

11 Air Quality and Land Use Planning. DETR/WO, December 1997.

12 Judgment in the case of *R v Swale BC, ex p RSPB* (1991) 1PLR 6.

13 Such requests should be sent to the relevant Government Office.

14 SI 1995/418.

15 The copy should be sent to the relevant Government Office.

16 Directive 79/409/EEC.

17 Directive 92/43/EEC.

18 Directive 96/61/EC.

19 Directive 96/82/EC.

PROCEDURES WHEN EIA IS REQUIRED

Preparation and content of an Environmental Statement

General requirements

81   It is the applicant's responsibility to prepare the Environmental Statement (ES). There is no statutory provision as to the form of an ES (which may consist of one or more documents). However, it must contain the information specified in Part II, and such of the relevant information in Part I of Schedule 4 to the Regulations (reproduced in Annex C to this Circular) as is reasonably required to assess the effects of the project and which the developer can reasonably be required to compile (see the definition of 'environmental statement' in regulation 2(1)).

82   Whilst every ES should provide a full factual description of the development, the emphasis of Schedule 4 is on the 'main' or 'significant' environmental effects to which a development is likely to give rise. In many cases, only a few of the effects will be significant and will need to be discussed in the ES in any great depth. Other impacts may be of little or no significance for the particular development in question and will need only very brief treatment to indicate that their possible relevance has been considered. While each ES must comply with the requirements of the Regulations, it is

important that they should be prepared on a realistic basis and without unnecessary elaboration.

83   Where alternative approaches to development have been considered, paragraph 2 of Part II of Schedule 4 now requires the developer to include in the ES an outline of the main ones, and the main reasons for his choice. Although the Directive and the Regulations do not expressly require the developer to study alternatives, the nature of certain developments and their location may make the consideration of alternative sites a material consideration (see, for example, paragraph 3.15 of PPG 23). In such cases, the ES must record this consideration of alternative sites. More generally, consideration of alternatives (including alternative sites, choice of process, and the phasing of construction) is widely regarded as good practice, and resulting in a more robust application for planning permission. Ideally, EIA should start at the stage of site and process selection, so that the environmental merits of practicable alternatives can be properly considered. Where this is undertaken, the main alternatives considered must be outlined in the ES.

84   The list of aspects of the environment which might be significantly affected by a project is set out in paragraph 3 of Part I of Schedule 4, and includes human beings; flora; fauna; soil; water; air; climate; landscape; material assets, including architectural and archaeological heritage; and the interaction between any of the foregoing. Paragraph 4 of Part I of Schedule 4 indicates, among other things, that consideration should also be given to the likely significant effects resulting from use of natural resources, the emission of pollutants, the creation of nuisances and the elimination of waste. In addition to the direct effects of a development, the ES should also cover indirect, secondary, cumulative, short, medium and long-term, permanent and temporary, positive and negative effects. These are comprehensive lists, and a particular project may of course give rise to significant effects, and require full and detailed assessment, in only one or two respects.

85   The information in the ES must be summarised in a non-technical summary (paragraph 5 of Part II of Schedule 4). The non-technical summary is particularly important for ensuring that the public can comment fully on the ES. The ES may, of necessity, contain complex scientific data and analysis in a form which is not readily understandable by the lay person. The non-technical summary should set out the main findings of the ES in accessible plain English.

Compiling an Environmental Statement

86   It is the developer's responsibility to prepare the ES. As a starting point, developers may like to study the Department's good practice guide (see endnote 20).

87   There is no obligation on the developer to consult anyone about the information to be included in a particular ES. However, there are good practical reasons to do so. Local planning authorities will often possess useful local and specialised information and may be able to give preliminary advice on those aspects of the proposal that are likely to be of particular concern to the authority. The timing of such informal consultations is at the developer's discretion. It will generally be advantageous for

them to take place as soon as the developer is in a position to provide enough information to form a basis for discussion. The developer can ask that any information provided at this preliminary stage be treated in confidence by the planning authority and any other consultees.

88   It will normally also be helpful to a developer preparing an ES to obtain information from the consultation bodies. Where a developer has formally notified the planning authority that an ES is being prepared (paragraphs 97–99) the local planning authority will inform each of the consultation bodies of the details of the proposed development and that they may be requested to provide relevant, non-confidential, information. Non-statutory bodies also have a wide range of information and may be consulted by the developer.

Provision to seek a formal opinion from the local planning authority on the scope of an ES ('scoping')(regulation 10)

89   Before making a planning application, a developer may ask the local planning authority for their formal opinion on the information to' be supplied in the ES (a 'scoping opinion'). This provision allows the developer to be clear about what the local planning authority considers the main effects of the development are likely to be and, therefore, the topics on which the ES should focus.

90   The developer must include the same information as would be required to accompany a request for a screening opinion (paragraph 55), and both requests may be made at the same time (regulations 10(2) and 10(5)). A developer may also wish to submit a draft outline of the ES, giving an indication of what he considers to be the main issues, to provide a focus for the local planning authority's considerations. If the authority considers that it needs further information to be able to adopt a scoping opinion, the developer should be asked to provide it. The authority must consult the consultation bodies and the developer before adopting its scoping opinion.

91   The local planning authority must adopt a scoping opinion within five weeks of receiving a request (or, where relevant, of adopting a screening opinion-regulation 10(5)). This period may be extended if the authority and developer so agree in writing. As a starting point, authorities should study the definition of environmental statement in regulation 2(1) and Schedule 4 to the Regulations (Annex C) and the guidance elsewhere in this Circular (paragraphs 81–85 and Annex A). In addition, authorities may find it useful to consult other published guidance, such as the European Commission's 'Guidance on Scoping', which was sent to all local planning authorities in late 1996 (see endnote 21).

92   The scoping opinion must be kept available for public inspection for two years (with the request including documents submitted by the developer as part of that request) at the place where the planning register is kept. If a planning application is subsequently made for development to which the scoping opinion relates, the opinion and related documents should be transferred to Part I of the register with the application (regulation 20).

Request to the Secretary of State for a scoping direction (regulation 11)

93   There is no provision for any disagreement between the developer and the local planning authority over the content of an ES to be referred to the Secretary of State. However, on call in or appeal the Secretary of State will need to form his own opinion on the matter. Where a local planning authority fails to adopt a scoping opinion within five weeks (or any agreed extension), the developer may apply to the Secretary of State for a scoping direction (regulation 10(7)). This application must be accompanied by all the previous documents relating to the request for a scoping opinion, together with any additional representations that the developer wishes to make. The developer should also send a copy of the request and any representations to the local planning authority, who are free to make their own additional representations.

94   The Secretary of State must make a scoping direction within five weeks from the date of receipt of a request, or such longer period as he may reasonably require. He must consult the consultation bodies and the developer beforehand. Copies of the scoping direction will be sent to the developer and to the local planning authority, which must ensure that a copy is made available for inspection with the other documents referred to in paragraph 93 above.

Effect of a scoping opinion or direction

95   An ES is not necessarily invalid if it does not fully comply with the scoping opinion or direction. However, as these documents represent the considered view of the local planning authority or the Secretary of State, a statement which does not cover all the matters specified in the scoping opinion or direction will probably be subject to calls for further information under regulation 19 (paragraphs 109–112).

96   The fact that a local planning authority or the Secretary of State has given a scoping opinion or scoping direction does not prevent them from requesting further information at a later stage under regulation 19. Where the Secretary of State has made a scoping direction in default of the local planning authority, the authority must still take into account all the information they consider relevant. In practice, there should rarely be any difference between the relevant information and that specified by the Secretary of State.

Provision of information by the consultation bodies (regulation 12)

97   Under the Environmental Information Regulations 1992 (see endnote 22), public bodies must make environmental information available to any person who requests it. The Regulations supplement these provisions in cases where a developer is preparing an ES. Once a developer has given the local planning authority notice in writing that he intends to submit an ES, the authority must inform the consultation bodies, and remind them of their obligation to make available, if requested, any relevant information in their possession (regulation 12). The local planning authority must also notify the

developer of the names and addresses of the bodies to whom they have sent such a notice. The notification to the local planning authority must include similar information to that which would be submitted if the developer were seeking a screening opinion under regulation 5 (paragraph 55).

98   The consultation bodies are—

a   the bodies who would be statutory consultees under article 10 of the GDPO for any planning application for the proposed development; and (if not already included)

b   any principal council for the area in which the land is situated (other than the local planning authority);

c   English Nature;

d   the Countryside Commission; and

e   the Environment Agency.

99   The consultation bodies are only required to provide information already in their possession. There is no obligation on public bodies to undertake research or otherwise to take steps to obtain information which they do not already have. Nor is there any obligation to make available information which is capable of being treated as confidential under the Environmental Information Regulations 1992. Public bodies may make a reasonable charge reflecting the cost of making available information requested by a developer. Further information on the application of the Environmental Information Regulations is contained in a guidance note prepared by the Department (see endnote 23).

Submission of EIA applications and initial publicity procedures

Environmental Statement submitted with planning application (regulation 13)

100   When submitting with a planning application a statement which he refers to as an Environmental Statement, the applicant should send to the local planning authority all the documents which must normally accompany a planning application, together with the requisite fee (which is not affected by the fact that an Environmental Statement is required). In addition, the applicant must submit:

a   four copies of the statement (three will be for onward transmission to the Secretary of State);

b   a note of the name of every body to whom the applicant has already sent or intends to send a copy of the statement under the procedures described in paragraph 102; and

c   such further copies of the statement as are needed to allow the local planning authority to send one to the other consultation bodies (paragraph 103).

101   Applicants must also make a reasonable number of copies of the ES available to the public, either free of charge or at a reasonable cost reflecting printing and distribution costs (regulations 17 and 18). Local planning authorities and applicants may wish to consider whether these copies should be held at the authority's offices, and whether

the authority's staff should collect any charges for those copies on behalf of the applicant.

102   On receipt, the local planning authority is required to treat a planning application submitted with a statement referred to by the applicant as an ES in the same way as any other planning application, with the following additional requirements:

a   The application and the statement must be publicised in accordance with the procedures set out in article 8 of the GDPO. Schedule 3 to the GDPO contains the appropriate form for the notices to be published in the local press and posted on site, which must:

    i   state that a copy of the statement is included in the documents which will be open to inspection by the public and give the address where the documents can be inspected free of charge;

    ii   give an address in the locality where copies of the statement may be obtained;

    iii state that a copy may be obtained there while stocks last and the amount of any charge to be made for supplying a copy; and

    iv   state the date (which must be at least 21 days after the date on which the notice was published) by which any written representations about the application should be made to the local planning authority.

b   Copies of the statement and application must be sent to those of the consultation bodies that have not received one direct from the developer.

c   Three copies of the statement and a copy of the application must be sent to the Secretary of State within 14 days of receipt (see endnote 24).

d   The statement must be placed on Part I of the planning register. Any related screening or scoping direction or opinion given under the pre-application procedures should also be placed on the register.

Copies of Environmental Statement for the consultation bodies

103   The local planning authority must consult the consultation bodies (paragraph 98). The applicant must provide one copy of the statement for each of the consultation bodies without charge. The applicant may either send a copy of the statement, together with a copy of the related planning application. and any relevant plan. direct to the bodies concerned, or may send copies of the statement to the local planning authority for onward transmission (paragraph 102b)). In practice, it will be sensible for the applicant and local planning authority to agree prior to submission of the application how the copies of the statement will be distributed.

104   A charge may be made for any extra copies of the statement requested by any of these bodies.

Additional publicity

105   Applicants, are encouraged to publish the non-technical summary (which must be included in every ES) as a separate document, and to make copies available free of

charge so as to facilitate wider public consultation. Applicants and local planning authorities may also wish to make further arrangements to make details of the development available to the public.

Environmental Statement submitted after a planning application (regulation 14)

106   Where an applicant is submitting an ES which relates to a planning application that has already been submitted, the procedures are the same as described in paragraphs 100–103 above. except that the applicant is responsible for publicising the statement. The applicant must publish notices in the local press and post them on site before the statement is submitted (regulation 14). When the copies of the statement are submitted to the local planning authority, they must be accompanied by a certificate stating that the publicity arrangements have been met (regulation 14(5)). Submission of false certificates is a criminal offence.

Consideration of EIA applications

107   The local planning authority should determine the application within 16 weeks from the date of receipt of the statement, instead of the normal 8 weeks from the receipt of the planning application (regulation 32). The period may be extended by written agreement between the authority and the applicant. Where the local planning authority has not determined the application after 16 weeks or any agreed extension, the applicant may appeal to the Secretary of State against non-determination.

108   The planning application may not be determined until at least 14 days after the last date on which a consultation body was served with a copy of the statement (regulation 13(4)). Where an EIA application is not submitted with a statement and the applicant indicates he proposes to provide one, consideration of the application is suspended until the statement is received. The application shall not be determined until at least 21 days after the receipt of the statement (regulation 14(6)).

Adequacy of the Environmental Statement

109   Local planning authorities should satisfy themselves in every case that submitted statements contain the information specified in Part II of Schedule 4 to the Regulations and the relevant information set out in Part I of that Schedule that the developer can reasonably be required to compile. To avoid delays in determining EIA applications, consideration of the need for further information and any necessary request for such information should take place as early as possible in the scrutiny of the planning application.

Provision of further information (regulation 19)

110   Where the required information has not been provided, the authority must use its powers under regulation 19 to require the applicant to provide further information concerning the relevant matters set out in Schedule 4. Any information provided in response to such a written request must be publicised, and consulted on, in a similar way to the document submitted as an ES (regulation 19(3)–(9)).

111   Authorities should only use their powers under regulation 19 when they consider that further information is necessary to complete the ES and thus enable them to give proper consideration to the likely environmental effects of the proposed development. The additional delay and costs imposed on applicants by the requirement to provide further information about environmental effects should be kept to the minimum consistent with compliance with the Regulations. Authorities should not use regulation 19 simply to obtain clarification or non-substantial information. However, where an applicant voluntarily submits additional information of a substantive nature, local planning authorities should consider advertising that information and sending it to the consultation bodies as if it had been provided in response to a formal request under regulation 19(1).

112   The period of 16 weeks referred to in paragraph 107 continues to run while any correspondence about the adequacy of the information in a statement is taking place. The applicant's right of appeal against non-determination at the end of that period (or any agreed extension) is not affected. A planning application is not invalid purely because an inadequate ES has been supplied nor because the applicant has failed to provided further information when required to do so under regulation 19. However, if a developer fails to provide enough information to complete the ES, the application can be determined only by refusal (regulation 3)).

Further information provided for a public inquiry

113   The Secretary of State may use regulation 19 to request further information for the purposes of a local inquiry under the 1990 Act (see endnote 25). By virtue of regulation 19(2), if the request specifically states that the information is to be provided for such purposes, the publicity procedures set out in regulation 19(3)–(9) do not apply. Rather, such information will be regulated by the Rules relating to the submission of evidence to local planning inquiries (see endnote 26). These Rules already require material provided by the applicant to be publicised appropriately. Further details of procedures relating to public inquiries are contained in Circular 15/96.

114   The Secretary of State or an Inspector may, in writing, require an applicant or appellant to produce such evidence as they may reasonably call for to verify any information in the ES.

Secretary of State's consideration of effects on other countries (regulations 27 and 28)

115   Local planning authorities are required to send copies of Environmental Statements and related planning applications to the Secretary of State within two weeks of receipt. This will enable him to consider whether the proposed development is likely to have significant effects on the environment of any other EC Member State or any other country that has ratified the UNECE Convention on Environmental Impact Assessment in a Transboundary Context (the Espoo Convention) (see endnote 27). This will also enable the Secretary of State to respond promptly if a country asks for information about a particular development.

116   Developments that are likely to have significant effects on the environment of another country will be rare in England. However, should they occur, the Secretary of State must send information about the development to the government of the affected country, and invite them to participate in the consultation procedures. At the same time, the Secretary of State will publish a notice in the London Gazette giving details of the development and any available information on its possible transboundary impact. In any such case, the Secretary of State will direct (under article 14(1) of the GDPO) that planning permission may not be granted until the end of such time as may be necessary for consultations with that government.

117   In the Department's view, a decision by the Secretary of State to call in an application involving a development proposal that is likely to have significant effects on the environment of another Member State would be consistent with published policy guidelines for exercising this power. These are set out in a statement by the then Secretary of State, John Gummer, on 26 January 1995 (Hansard cols 314–315).

118   Where the environment in England is likely to be significantly affected by a project in another country, the Secretary of State will agree with that country how the UK and its public are to be consulted so that they may participate fully in that country's EIA procedure.

Determining the planning application

119   Before determining any EIA application, the local planning authority, the Secretary of State or an Inspector as the case may be, must take into consideration the information contained in the Environmental Statement (ES) (including any further information), any comments made by the consultation bodies, and any representations from members of the public about environmental issues.

Securing mitigation measures

120   Mitigation measures proposed in an ES are designed to limit the environmental effects of the development. Planning authorities will need to consider carefully how

such measures are secured, particularly in relation to the main mitigation measures specified in the decision (paragraph 125).

121   Conditions attached to a planning permission may include mitigation measures. However, a condition requiring the development to be 'in accordance with the Environmental Statement' is unlikely to be valid unless the ES was exceptional in the precision with which it specified the mitigation measures to be undertaken. Even then, the condition would need to refer to the specific part of the ES rather than the whole document.

122   A planning condition may require a scheme of mitigation for more minor measures to be submitted to the local planning authority and approved in writing before any development is undertaken. However, planning conditions should not duplicate other legislative controls. In particular, planning authorities should not seek to substitute their own judgment on pollution control issues for that of the bodies with the relevant expertise and the statutory responsibility for that control (paragraph 1.34 of PPG 23). Advice on planning conditions is contained in Circular 11/95.

123   Another possible method of securing mitigation measures is through planning obligations (see endnote 28), which are enforceable by the local planning authority. Planning obligations may be entered into unilaterally by a developer or by agreement between a developer and the local planning authority. Detailed guidance on the use of such agreements is contained in Circular 1/97.

124   In addition, developers may adopt environmental management systems such as the Eco-Management and Audit Scheme (EMAS) to demonstrate implementation of mitigation measures and to monitor their effectiveness.

Publicising determinations of EIA applications (regulation 21)

125   When the local authority has determined an EIA application, they must, in addition to the normal requirement to notify the applicant, notify the Secretary of State. The authority must also publish a notice in the local press, giving the content of the determination and stating that the documents relating to the determination will be open to inspection by the public. They must give the address where the documents can be inspected free of charge (paragraph 126). Where either the Secretary of State or an Inspector has determined an EIA application he will send a copy of his determination to the local authority for them to publicise.

126   A copy of the decision, including any conditions imposed, should be kept in the same place as the register with such other documents as contain:
a   the main reasons and considerations on which the decision is based; and
b   a description, where permission has been granted, of the main measures to avoid, reduce and, if possible, offset the major adverse effects of the development.

127   The requirement to make available the main reasons and considerations on which the decision is based now applies equally to cases where planning permission is granted and where it is refused. In practice, authorities may find that this requirement is met by the relevant planning officer's report to the Planning Committee.

ENDNOTES

20 Preparation of Environmental Statements for Planning Projects that Require Environmental Assessment — A Good Practice Guide, 1995 Available from the Stationery Office.
21 Environmental Impact Assessment — Guidance on Scoping, May 1996 Available from Mrs M-C Beeckmans, European Commission. DG XI B2 Fax No, 00 322 2969561.
22 SI 1992/3240, as amended by SI 1998/1447.
23 Freedom of Access to Information on the Environment 1992.
24 Copies should be sent to the relevant Government Office.
25 Including local inquiries held into planning appeals arising under section 78 of that Act and into planning applications referred to the Secretary of State under section 77 of the Act.
26 Rule 6 (service of statements of case etc) and rule 13 (proofs of evidence) of the Town and Country Planning (Inquiries Procedure) Rules 1992 SI 1992/2038. Similar provisions are also included in the Town and Country Planning Appeals Determination by Inspectors) (Inquiries Procedure) Rules 1992 SI 1992/2039.
27 Cm 1645.
28 Made under section 106 of the Town and Country Planning Act 1990.

SPECIAL CASES

Local authorities' own development (regulation 22)

128   Where a local authority lodges an application for planning permission, the procedures for EIA set out in the Regulations apply to the applicant authority (subject to necessary modifications set out in regulation 22) as they apply to any other applicant.

129   The authority is required to adopt a screening opinion for any Schedule 2 development in accordance with the relevant procedures in regulation 7(1). Where the development requires EIA, the authority is required to prepare an Environmental Statement (ES); place the ES on the planning register; and publish and consult on the ES in the same way as any other EIA application. The ES, any comments made by the consultation bodies, and any representations from members of the public must be taken into consideration before planning permission can be granted.

130   The procedures and considerations to be taken into account in deciding whether Schedule 2 development requires EIA, apply to proposals for development by local authorities whether on their own land or other land. The Secretary of State's power to make a screening direction applies to local authority development as it does to any other development.

131   The procedures for permitted development apply to local planning authorities' own development as they do to any other developer's use of such rights (paragraphs 61–65).

Simplified Planning Zones (SPZs) and Enterprise Zones (EZs) (regulations 23 and 24)

132   No EIA development can be granted planning permission by the adoption or approval of an SPZ or through the designation or modification of an EZ. This applies equally to permission granted under existing and new schemes.

133   Schedule 2 development may be included in SPZs and EZ. It can be granted permission by them providing the particular development has been the subject of a screening opinion or direction that it is not EIA development.

Development which is the subject of a planning enforcement notice (regulations 25 and 26)

134   The Regulations provide for EIA of development which is the subject of a planning enforcement notice (see endnote 29) (regulation 25). Where such development requires EIA, it is referred to in this Circular and the Regulations as 'unauthorised EIA development'.

135   An appeal against a planning enforcement notice (see endnote 30) ('an enforcement appeal') could, if successful, result in the grant of planning permission (see endnote 31). All enforcement appeals which involve unauthorised EIA development will be determined by the Secretary of State (see endnote 32). The Secretary of State is prohibited from granting planning permission for unauthorised EIA development unless EIA has first been carried out (regulation 25(1)).

136   Neither the need to provide an ES nor the facility to seek a direction from the Secretary of State (paragraph 139) should be allowed to delay the enforcement appeal process. If the recipient of an enforcement notice wishes to appeal against it, any appeal must be received by the Secretary of State before the effective date specified in the notice.

Determining whether EIA is needed

Determinations by the local planning authority

137   When deciding to take enforcement action, the local planning authority must consider whether the particular development is either Schedule 1 development or Schedule 2 development and, if so, adopt a screening opinion.

138   Where the local planning authority determines that EIA is required, they must serve a 'regulation 25 notice' with the enforcement notice. The regulation 25 notice must include the authority's full reasons for their screening opinion. A model regulation 25 notice is attached to this Circular at Annex D. The local planning authority are required to send a copy of the regulation 25 notice to the Secretary of State (see endnote 33) and to the consultation bodies.

Directions by the Secretary of State

139   A recipient of a regulation 25 notice may apply to the Secretary of State for a screening direction. The application must be accompanied by a copy of the notice, a copy of the enforcement notice and any additional representations the applicant wishes to make. A copy of the application and the additional representations (if any) should be sent to the local planning authority. If the Secretary of State considers that further information is needed before a screening direction can be made, the applicant must provide it within a specified time period (regulation 25(6)(c)). No screening direction will be made until the information is provided. However, any delay in providing additional information will not affect the period for compliance with the enforcement notice or extend the period for submitting an enforcement notice appeal.

140   The Secretary of State will notify the applicant and the local planning authority of the screening direction (regulations 25(6)(d) and 4(9)). If he directs that EIA is required, the screening direction must be accompanied by a clear and precise statement of his full reasons (regulation 4(6)). If he directs that EIA is not required, he will also send a copy of his direction to every recipient of the regulation 25 notice.

Enforcement appeal not accompanied by an Environmental Statement

141   On receipt of an enforcement appeal without a statement referred to by the appellant as an Environmental Statement, the Secretary of State will consider whether the appeal relates to unauthorised EIA development. If he determines that it does, he will send a copy of his screening direction to the appellant and local planning authority within 21 days of receiving the appeal (or such longer period as he may reasonably require), giving the full reasons for his conclusion. The appellant will be required to submit four copies of an ES within a period specified by the Secretary of State. If the appellant fails to do so by the due date, both the application deemed to be made by section 174 of the 1990 Act and any appeal under ground (a) in section 174(2) of the Act will lapse. The Secretary of State will then notify the appellant and local planning authority in writing accordingly.

142   If the appellant has already submitted an ES for the purpose of an appeal under section 78 of the 1990 Act which relates to the same development as the enforcement appeal, and the two appeals are to be determined at the same time, the ES already provided will be regarded as supporting both appeals.

Provision of information

143   The local planning authority and the consultation bodies are required, if requested, to provide to the person who has been served with a regulation 25 notice any information (other than 'confidential' information under the Environmental Information Regulations 1992) which is relevant to the preparation of an ES (paragraphs 97–99).

Procedure where the Secretary of State receives an Environmental Statement

144   On receipt of a statement, the Secretary of State will send a copy to the local planning authority, and advise them that the statement will be taken into consideration in determining the deemed planning application and ground (a) appeal, if any. Any persons who received a copy of the regulation 25 notice will also be similarly notified and may obtain a copy of the statement if they notify the Secretary of State within 7 days of receipt of notification. They may also put forward their views.

PUBLICITY FOR ENVIRONMENTAL STATEMENTS

145   When the local planning authority receive a copy of a statement from the Secretary of State, they are required by regulation 25(16) to publish a notice in a local newspaper. This must state the name of the appellant and the address or location of the land; and advise members of the public where and when the ES may be inspected, and the closing date for inspection. The authority must also send a certified copy of the newspaper notice to the Secretary of State as soon as practicable after publication (regulation 25(17)).

146   Anyone wishing to comment should do so in writing to the Secretary of State within 14 days of the closing date for public inspection of the statement. The deemed application or ground (a) appeal will not be determined by the Secretary of State until the period has elapsed.

147   The local planning authority are required to make every regulation 25 notice; any screening direction received from the Secretary of State; every notice received by the authority from the Secretary of State under regulation 25(12)(d); and every ES received by the authority under regulation 25(13)(a) available for public inspection for two years or until particulars of the notice or direction are entered into Part II of the appropriate register.

FURTHER INFORMATION AND EVIDENCE RESPECTING ENVIRONMENTAL STATEMENTS

148   The Secretary of State may require an appellant who has submitted a statement which he refers to as an ES to provide more information, within a specified period. The information provided will be copied to the local planning authority and to those persons who received a copy of the regulation 25 notice. If the appellant fails to provide the information required within the time specified, the deemed application and ground (a) appeal, if any, shall lapse. The Secretary of State will then notify the appellant and the local planning authority in writing.

149   The arrangements for publicity for additional information are the same as those for the statements by virtue of regulations 25(13) and (15) (paragraphs 145–147).

150   The procedures for development which is likely to have significant effects on the environment of another Member State (paragraphs 115–118) apply, with necessary modifications, to unauthorised EIA development (regulation 26).

Permitted development (regulation 35(3))

151   The provisions described in paragraphs 61–65 do not apply to development within the following classes in Schedule 2 to the General Permitted Development Order ('GPOO'):

a   Part 7 (forestry buildings and operations);

b   Class D of Part 8 (development comprising deposit of waste material resulting from an industrial process);

c   Part 11 (development under local or private acts or orders);

d   Class B of Part 12 (development comprising deposit of waste material by a local authority);

e   Class F(a) of Part 17 (development by public gas suppliers);

f   Class A of Part 20 (development by licensees of the Coal Authority);

g   Class B of Part 20 (development by licensees of the British Coal Corporation); and

h   Class B of Part 21 (deposit of mining waste).

Development is also excluded if it consists of the carrying out by a drainage body (see endnote 34) of improvement works within the meaning of the Land Drainage Improvement Works (Assessment or Environmental Effects) Regulations 1988.

152   Development permitted (see endnote 35) under Class A(a) and (b) of Part 11 is excluded by virtue of Article 1.5 of the Directive, which states that the Directive shall not apply to projects the details of which are adopted by a specific act of national legislation. As an exemption this is, under Community law, to be construed narrowly. Accordingly, development of a nature or in a location that was not specifically designated in the relevant Act or order (see Part 11, Class A) are subject to the procedures in paragraphs 61, 65. New Private Acts of Parliament which would benefit from Part 11 permitted development rights are subject to EIA procedures by Parliamentary Standing Order 27 A.

153   Development permitted under Part 7, Class A(c) of Part 11, Part 14 and Class F(a) of Part 17 is the subject of alternative consent procedures to which separate Regulations apply. Development permitted under Class D of Part 8, Class B of Part 12, Classes A and B of Part 20 and Class B of Part 21 is excluded as it concerns projects begun on or before 1 July 1948, before the date on which the Directive came into operation.

154   Projects begun before 14 March 1999 are also excluded, if they comprise development:

a   under Class C or Class D of Part 20 on the same authorised site as development begun under the same Class before that date;

b   under Class A of Part 21 on the same premises or the same ancillary mining land as the premises or land on which development under the same Class was begun before that date; and

c   under Class B of Part 22 on the same land or on land adjoining land on which development under the same Class was begun before that date.

155   Development which comprises or forms part of a project serving national defence purposes is excluded by virtue of Article 1.4 of the Directive (see the definition of 'exempt development' in regulation 2(1)).

156   For all other Parts not covered by specific exclusions the provisions of paragraph (10) of article 3 of the GPDO will not apply to the completion of development begun before 14 March 1999. Development carried out under permitted development rights and consisting of building operations or engineering operations will be excluded from the new provisions where such operations are already underway under permitted development rights at the time of these Regulations coming into force.

Crown development

157   Like the Town and Country Planning Act, the Regulations do not bind the Crown. Developments by Crown bodies which would require planning permission if they were proposed by any other person and which require EIA under the terms of the Regulations are likely to be uncommon in England. When any such development is proposed, the Crown body concerned will submit an Environmental Statement to the local planning authority when consulting them under the arrangements set out in Part IV of the Memorandum to Circular 18/84. In addition, the Ministry of Defence will, in appropriate circumstances and subject to considerations affecting national security, provide Environmental Statements in respect of major defence projects. Proposals have been published for the removal of Crown exemption in planning matters. Pending the necessary legislation, the arrangements in Circular 18/84 continue to apply.

ENDNOTES

29   Issued under section 172 of the 1990 Act, as substituted by section 5 of the Planning and Compensation Act 1991.
30   Under section 174 of the 1990 Act.
31   Under section 177 (l) of the 1990 Act.
32   By virtue of the Town and Country Planning (Determination of Appeals by Appointed Persons) (Prescribed Classes) (Amendment) Regulations 1995.
33   Send the copy to The Planning Inspectorate, PO Box 326, Bristol BS99 7XF.
34   Section 72(1) of the Land Drainage Act 1991.
35   SI 1988/1217.

FINANCIAL AND MANPOWER IMPLICATIONS

158   Developers who are required to prepare Environmental Statements will incur some additional costs in doing so. However, in most cases much of the information in the Statement would be likely to be provided in support of the planning application, particularly if the proposal is one which under existing planning procedures would go to public inquiry. In deciding on the extent of the information required to be submitted, planning authorities' aim should be to keep the costs imposed on developers to the minimum consistent with compliance with the Regulations.

159   The implications for local planning authorities will vary from authority to authority according to the incidence of environmentally significant development projects. There will be a small amount of additional work involved in deciding on the need for EIA particularly in Schedule 2 cases. However, in general it is expected that this will form part of normal pre, application consultations between the developer and the authority. Where an Environmental Statement is submitted, the systematic analysis of the project's effects should result in administrative savings in considering the application, and the possibility of an earlier decision. There may be additional costs for planning authorities where consultants have to be engaged to advise on the appraisal of highly technical or specialist evidence. Such cases should be exceptional.

ANNEX A: INDICATIVE THRESHOLDS AND CRITERIA FOR IDENTIFICATION OF SCHEDULE 2 DEVELOPMENT REQUIRING EIA

The criteria and thresholds in this Annex (referred to in paragraphs 43–44) are only indicative. In determining whether significant effects are likely, the location of a development is of crucial importance. The more environmentally sensitive the location, the lower will be the threshold at which significant effects will be likely.

It follows, therefore, that the thresholds below should only be used in conjunction with the more general guidance in this Circular on 'Establishing whether EIA is required' and, in particular, the guidance on environmentally sensitive locations (paragraphs 36–40).

Agricultural development

A1   In general, agricultural operations fall outside the scope of the Town and Country Planning system and, where relevant, will be regulated under other consent procedures. The descriptions below apply only to projects that are considered to be 'development' for the purposes of the Town and Country Planning Act 1990.

Use of uncultivated or semi-natural land for intensive agricultural purposes

A2   Development (such as greenhouses, farm buildings etc) on previously uncultivated land is unlikely to require EIA unless it covers more than five hectares. In considering whether particular development is likely to have significant effects, consideration should be given to impacts on the surrounding ecology, hydrology and landscape.

Water management for agriculture, including irrigation and land drainage works

A3   EIA is more likely to be required if the development would result in permanent changes to the character of more than five hectares of land. In assessing the significance of any likely effects, particular regard should be had to whether the development would have damaging wider impacts on hydrology and surrounding ecosystems. It follows that EIA will not normally be required for routine water management projects undertaken by farmers.

Intensive livestock installations

A4   The significance or otherwise of the impacts of intensive livestock installations will often depend upon the level of odours, increased traffic and the arrangements for waste handling. EIA is more likely to be required for intensive livestock installations if they are designed to house more than 750 sows, 2,000 fattening pigs, 60,000 broilers or 50,000 layers, turkeys or other poultry.

Intensive fish farming

A5   Apart from the physical scale of any development, the likelihood of significant effects will generally depend on the extent of any likely wider impacts on the hydrology and ecology of the surrounding area. Developments designed to produce more than 100 tonnes (dead weight) of fish per year will be more likely to require EIA.

Reclamation of land from the sea

A6   In assessing the significance of any development, regard should be had to the likely wider impacts on natural coastal processes beyond the site itself, as well as to the scale of reclamation works themselves. EIA is more likely to be required where work is proposed on a site which exceeds one hectare.

Extractive industry

Surface and underground mineral working

A7   The likelihood of significant effects will tend to depend on the scale and duration of the works, and the likely consequent impact of noise, dust, discharges to water and visual intrusion. All new open cast mines and underground mines will generally require EIA. For clay, sand and gravel workings, quarries and peat extraction sites, EIA is more likely to be required if they would cover more than 15 hectares or involve the extraction of more than 30,000 tonnes of mineral per year.

Extraction of minerals by dredging in fluvial waters

A8   Particular consideration should be given to noise, and any wider impacts on the surrounding hydrology and ecology. EIA is more likely to be required where it is expected that more than 100,000 tonnes of mineral will be extracted per year.

Deep drilling

A9   EIA is more likely to be required where the scale of the drilling operations involves development of a surface site of more than five hectares. Regard should be had to the likely wider impacts on surrounding hydrology and ecology. On its own, exploratory deep drilling is unlikely to require EIA. It would not be appropriate to require EIA for exploratory activity simply because it might eventually lead to some form of permanent activity.

Surface industrial installations for the extraction of coal, petroleum, natural gas, ores, or bituminous shale

A10   The main considerations are likely to be the scale of development, emissions to air, discharges to water, the risk of accident and the arrangements for transporting the fuel. EIA is more likely to be required if the development is on a major scale (site of 10 hectares or more) or where production is expected to be substantial (eg more than 100,000 tonnes of petroleum per year).

Energy industry

Power stations

A11   EIA will normally be required for power stations which require approval from the Secretary of State at the Department of Trade and Industry (ie those with a thermal output of more than 50 MW). EIA is unlikely to be required for smaller new conventional power stations. Small stations using novel forms of generation should be considered carefully in line with the guidance in PPG 22 (Renewable Energy). The main considerations are likely to be the level of emissions to air, arrangements for the transport of fuel and any visual impact.

Surface storage of fossil fuel and natural gas, underground storage of combustible gases, storage facilities for petroleum, petrochemical and chemical products

A12   In addition to the scale of the development, significant effects are likely to depend on discharges to water, emissions to air and risk of accidents. EIA is more likely to be required where it is proposed to store more than 100,000 tonnes of fuel. Smaller installations are unlikely to require EIA unless hazardous chemicals are stored.

Installations for the processing and storage of radioactive waste

A13   EIA will normally be required for new installations whose primary purpose is to process and store radioactive waste, and which are located on sites not previously authorised for such use. In addition to the scale of any development, significant effects are likely to depend on the extent of routine discharges of radiation to the environment. In this context EIA is unlikely to be required for installations where the processing or storage of radioactive waste is incidental to the main purpose of the development (eg installations at hospitals or research facilities).

Installations for hydroelectric energy production

A14   In addition to the physical scale of the development, particular regard should be had to the potential wider impacts on hydrology and ecology. EIA is more likely to be required for new hydroelectric developments which have more than 5 MW of generating capacity.

Wind farms

A15   The likelihood of significant effects will generally depend upon the scale of the development, and its visual impact, as well as potential noise impacts. EIA is more likely to be required for commercial developments of five or more turbines, or more than 5 MW of new generating capacity.

Industrial and manufacturing development

A16   New manufacturing or industrial plants of the types listed in the Regulations, may well require EIA if the operational development covers a site of more than 10 hectares. Smaller developments are more likely to require EIA if they are expected to give rise to significant discharges of waste, emission of pollutants or operational noise. Among the factors to be taken into account in assessing the significance of such effects are:

·   whether the development involves a process designated as a 'scheduled process' for the purpose of air pollution control;
·   whether the process involves discharges to water which require the consent of the Environment Agency;
·   whether the installation would give rise to the presence of environmentally significant quantities of potentially hazardous or polluting substances;

·   whether the process would give rise to radioactive or other hazardous waste;
·   whether the development would fall under Council Directive 96182/EC on the control of major accident hazards involving dangerous substances (COMAH).

However, the need for a consent under other legislation is not itself a justification for EIA.

Infrastructure developments

Industrial estates

A17   EIA is more likely to be required if the site area of the new development is more than 20 hectares. In determining whether significant effects are likely, particular consideration should be given to the potential increase in traffic, emissions and noise.

Urban development projects (including the construction of shopping centres and car parks, sports stadiums, leisure centres and multiplex cinemas)

A18   In addition to the physical scale of such developments, particular consideration should be given to the potential increase in traffic, emissions and noise. EIA is unlikely to be required for the redevelopment of land unless the new development is on a significantly greater scale than the previous use, or the types of impact are of a markedly different nature or there is a high level of contamination (paragraph 41).

A19   Development proposed for sites which have not previously been intensively developed are more likely to require EIA if:
·   the site area of the scheme is more than 5 hectares; or
·   it would provide a total of more than 10,000 m^2 of new commercial floorspace; or
·   the development would have significant urbanising effects in a previously non, urbanised area (eg a new development of more than 1,000 dwellings).

Intermodal transshipment facilities and intermodal terminals

A20   In addition to the physical scale of the development, particular impacts for consideration are increased traffic, noise, emissions to air and water. Developments of more than five hectares are more likely to require EIA.

Motorway service areas

A21   Impacts likely to be significant are traffic, noise, air quality, ecology and visual impact. EIA is more likely to be required for new motorway service areas which are proposed for previously undeveloped sites and if the proposed development would cover an area of more than five hectares.

Construction of roads, railways (including elevated and underground) and tramways

A22   For linear transport schemes, the likelihood of significant effects will generally depend on the estimated emissions, traffic, noise and vibration and degree of visual intrusion and impact on the surrounding ecology. EIA is more likely to be required for new development over 2 km in length.

Construction of inland waterways and canalisation

A23   The likelihood of significant impacts is likely to depend primarily on the potential wider impacts on the surrounding hydrology and ecology. EIA is more likely to be required for development of over 2 km of canal.

Flood relief works

A24   The impact of flood relief works is especially dependent upon the nature of the location and the potential effects on the surrounding ecology and hydrology. Schemes for which the area of the works would exceed five hectares or which are more than 2 km in length would normally require EIA.

Construction of airfields

A25   The main impacts to be considered in judging significance are noise, traffic generation and emissions. New permanent airfields will normally require EIA, as will major works (such as new runways or terminals with a site area of more than 10 hectares) at existing airports. Smaller scale development at existing airports is unlikely to require EIA unless it would lead to significant increases in air or road traffic.

Construction of harbours and port installations, including fishing harbours

A26   Primary impacts for consideration are those on hydrology, ecology, noise and increased traffic. EIA is more likely to be required if the development is on a major scale (eg would cover a site of more than 10 hectares). Smaller developments may also have significant effects where they include a quay or pier which would extend beyond the high water mark or would affect wider coastal processes.

Dams and other installations designed to hold water or store it on a long-term basis

A27   In considering such developments, particular regard should be had to the potential wider impacts to the hydrology and ecology, as well as to the physical scale of the development EIA is likely to be required for any major new dam (eg where the construction site exceeds 20 hectares).

Installation of oil pipelines, gas pipelines and long-distance aqueducts (including water and sewerage pipelines)

A28   For underground pipelines, the major impact to be considered will generally be the disruption to the surrounding ecosystems during construction, while for overground pipelines visual impact will be a key consideration. EIA is more likely to be required for any pipeline over 5 km long. EIA is unlikely to be required for pipelines laid underneath a road, or for those installed entirely by means of tunnelling.

Coastal works to combat erosion and maritime works capable of altering the coast

A29   The impact of such works will depend largely on the nature of the particular site and the likely wider impacts on natural coastal processes outside of the site. EIA will be more likely where the area of the works would exceed one hectare.

Groundwater abstraction and artificial groundwater recharge schemes, works for the transfer of water resources between river basins

A30   Impacts likely to be significant are those on hydrology and ecology. Developments of this sort can have significant effects on environments some kilometres distant. This is particularly important for wetland and other sites where the habitat and species are particularly dependent on an aquatic environment. EIA is likely to be required for developments where the area of the works exceeds one hectare.

Tourism and leisure

Ski-runs, ski-lifts and cable-cars and associated developments

A31   EIA is more likely to be required if the development is over 500 metres in length or if it requires a site of more than five hectares. In addition to any visual or ecological impacts, particular regard should also be had to the potential traffic generation.

Marinas

A32   In assessing whether significant effects are likely, particular regard should be had to any wider impacts on natural coastal processes outside the site, as well as the potential noise and traffic generation. EIA is more likely to be required for large new marinas, for example where the proposal is for more than 300 berths (seawater site) or 100 berths (freshwater site). EIA is unlikely to be required where the development is located solely within an existing dock or basin.

Holiday villages and hotel complexes outside urban areas and associated developments, permanent camp sites and caravan sites, and theme parks

A33   In assessing the significance of tourism development, visual impacts, impacts on ecosystems and traffic generation will be key considerations. The effects of new theme parks are more likely to be significant if it is expected that they will generate more than 250,000 visitors per year. EIA is likely to be required for major new tourism and leisure developments which require a site of more than 10 hectares. In particular, EIA is more likely to be required for holiday villages or hotel complexes with more than 300 bed spaces, or for permanent camp sites or caravan sites with more than 200 pitches.

Golf courses

A34   New 18-hole golf courses are likely to require EIA. The main impacts are likely to be those on the surrounding hydrology, ecosystems and landscape, as well as those from traffic generation. Developments at existing golf courses are unlikely to require EIA.

Other projects

Permanent racing and test tracks for motorised vehicles

A35   Particular consideration should be given to the size, noise impacts, emissions and the potential traffic generation. EIA is more likely to be required for developments with a site area of 20 hectares or more.

Installations for the disposal of non-hazardous waste

A36   The likelihood of significant effects will generally depend on the scale of the development and the nature of the potential impact in terms of discharges, emissions or odour. For installations (including landfill sites) for the deposit, recovery and/or disposal of household, industrial and/or commercial wastes (as defined by the Controlled

Waste Regulations 1992) EIA is more likely to be required where new capacity is created to hold more than 50,000 tonnes per year, or to hold waste on a site of 10 hectares or more. Sites taking smaller quantities of these wastes, sites seeking only to accept inert wastes (demolition rubble etc) or Civic Amenity sites, are unlikely to require EIA.

Sludge-deposition sites (sewage sludge lagoons)

A37   Similar considerations will apply for sewage sludge lagoons as for waste disposal installations. EIA is more likely to be required where the site is intended to hold more than 5,000 m^3 of sewage sludge.

Storage of scrap Iron, including scrap vehicles

A38   Major impacts are likely to be discharges to soil, site noise and traffic generation. EIA is more likely to be required where it is proposed to store scrap on an area of 10 hectares or more.

Waste-water treatment plants

A39   Particular consideration should be given to the size, treatment process, pollution and nuisance potential, topography, proximity of dwellings and the potential impact of traffic movements. EIA is more likely to be required if the development would be on a substantial scale (eg site area of more than 10 hectares) or if it would lead to significant discharges (eg capacity exceeding 100,000 population equivalent). EIA should not be required simply because a plant is on a scale which requires compliance with the Urban Waste Water Treatment Directive (91/271/EEC).

ANNEX B: SELECTION CRITERIA FOR SCREENING SCHEDULE 2 DEVELOPMENT

This is a reproduction of Schedule 3 of the Regulations (paragraphs 20 and 33)

I   Characteristics of development

The characteristics of development must be considered having regard, in particular, to
a   the size of the development;
b   the cumulation with other development;
c   the use of natural resources;
d   the production of waste;

e   pollution and nuisances;
f   the risk of accidents, having regard in particular to substances or technologies
used.

2   Location of development

The environmental sensitivity of geographical areas likely to be affected by
development must be considered, having regard, in particular, to:
a   the existing land use;
b   the relative abundance, quality and regenerative capacity of natural resources in
the area;
c   the absorption capacity of the natural environment, paying particular attention to
the following areas—
   i   wetlands;
   ii   coastal zones;
   iii mountain and forest areas;
   iv   nature reserves and parks;
   v   areas classified or protected under Member States' legislation; areas
designated by Member States pursuant to Council Directive 79/409/EEC on
the conservation of wild birds (see endnote 36) and Council Directive 92/43/
EEC on the conservation of natural habitats and of wild fauna and flora (see
endnote 37);
   vi   areas in which the environmental quality standards laid down in Community
legislation have already been exceeded;
   vii densely populated areas;
   viii landscapes of historical, cultural or archaeological significance.

3   Characteristics of the potential impact

The potential significant effects of development must be considered in relation to
criteria set out under paragraphs 1 and 2 above, and having regard in particular to:
a   the extent of the impact (geographical area and size of the affected population);
b   the transfrontier nature of the impact;
c   the magnitude and complexity of the impact;
d   the probability of the impact;
e   the duration, frequency and reversibility of the impact.

ENDNOTES

36   OJ L103 25.4.1979 p 1.
37   OJ L206 22.7.1992 p 7.

ANNEX C: INFORMATION TO BE INCLUDED IN AN ENVIRONMENTAL

STATEMENT

This is a reproduction of Schedule 4 of the Regulations (paragraphs 81–85 and 91).

Part I

1   Description of the development, including in particular
a   a description of the physical characteristics of the whole development and the land use requirements during the construction and operational phases;
b   a description of the main characteristics of the production processes, for instance, nature and quantity of the materials used;
c   an estimate, by type and quantity, of expected residues and emissions (water, air and soil pollution, noise, vibration, light, heat, radiation, etc) resulting from the operation of the proposed development.

2   An outline of the main alternatives studied by the applicant or appellant and an indication of the main reasons for his choice, taking into account the environmental effects.

3   A description of the aspects of the environment likely to be significantly affected by the development, including, in particular, population, fauna, flora, soil, water, air, climatic factors, material assets, including the architectural and archaeological heritage, landscape and the interrelationship between the above factors.

4   A description of the likely significant effects of the development on the environment, which should cover the direct effects and any indirect, secondary, cumulative, short, medium and long-term, permanent and temporary, positive and negative effects of the development, resulting from:
a   the existence of the development;
b   the use of natural resources;
c   the emission of pollutants, the creation of nuisances and the elimination of waste, and the description by the applicant of the forecasting methods used to assess the effects on the environment.

5   A description of the measures envisaged to prevent, reduce and where possible offset any significant adverse effects on the environment.

6   A non-technical summary of the information provided under paragraphs 1 to 5 of this Part.

7   An indication of any difficulties (technical deficiencies or lack of know-how) encountered by the applicant in compiling the required information.

Part II

1   A description of the development comprising information on the site, design and size of the development.

2   A description of the measures envisaged in order to avoid, reduce and, if possible, remedy significant adverse effects.

3   The data required to identify and assess the main effects which the development is likely to have on the environment.

4   An outline of the main alternatives studied by the applicant or appellant and an indication of the main reasons for his choice, taking into account the environmental effects.

5   A non-technical summary of the information provided under paragraphs 1 to 4 of this Part.

ANNEX D: MODEL REGULATION 25 NOTICE

Important: This communication affects your property

Town and Country Planning (Environmental Impact Assessment) (England and Wales) Regulations 1999 (SI 1999 No 293)

Regulation 25 Notice

1   This notice is served by [*name of Council*] ('the Council') under regulation 25 of the Town and Country Planning (Environmental Impact Assessment) (England and Wales) Regulations 1999 (SI 1999 No 293) in connection with the Council's enforcement notice, dated [*date of enforcement notice*], issued in respect of—

.... [*insert description of alleged unauthorised development*]

at.. [*insert address*]

2   It is the Council's opinion that development to which the enforcement notice relates is

either:

'Schedule 1 development' within the meaning of the Town and Country Planning (Environmental Impact Assessment) (England and Wales) Regulations 1999 (SI 1999 No 293) (ie [*set out the description within Schedule 1 in which the unauthorised EIA development is deemed to fall*]).

or:

'Schedule 2 development' within the meaning of the Town and Country Planning (Environmental Impact Assessment) (England and Wales) Regulations 1999 (SI 1999 No 293) (ie [set out the description within Column 1 of the table in Schedule 2 in which the unauthorised EIA development is deemed to fall and the relevant threshold or criterion in Column 2 of the table in Schedule 2 which is exceeded or met]) which is considered likely to have significant effects on the environment for the following reasons:

(a)..

(b)..

(c) etc.

[complete as appropriate setting out clearly and precisely the full reasons why the development is considered likely to have significant effects on the environment]

3   Accordingly, subject to any direction of the Secretary of State to the contrary, any appeal under section 174 against the enforcement notice must be accompanied by four copies of an Environmental Statement. Please read the notes below for information about appeals, directions and Environmental Statements.

Dated: *[insert date of issue]*

Signed: *[signature of officer authorised to issue regulation 25 notices]*

Notes

Appeals

If you wish to appeal against the enforcement notice, you must follow the instructions provided with that notice. Please remember that the Secretary of State cannot consider your arguments against the enforcement notice if you fail to observe the time limit for appeal specified in that notice.

Directions

You may apply to the Secretary of State (see endnote 38) for a direction as to whether the development requires the submission of an Environmental Statement.

The Secretary of State will give his direction in writing and will send a copy of it to the Council.

Environmental Statements

An Environmental Statement is a document or series of documents prepared for the purpose of enabling the Secretary of State to assess the likely impact on the environment of the development to which this notice relates.

For guidance on Environmental Statements generally please see Department of the Environment, Transport and the Regions Circular 02/99. General guidance about preparing environmental statements can be found in the HMSO publication 'Preparation of Environmental Statements for Planning Projects that Require Environmental Assessment: A Good Practice Guide' (ISBN 0-11-753207-X) although it should be read in conjunction with the Town and Country Planning (Environmental Impact Assessment) (England and Wales) Regulations 1999 (SI 1999 No 293) themselves since the guidance predates these revised requirements.

Important: Please remember that an application for a direction in connection with this regulation 25 notice does *not* affect the time limit for appeal specified in the enforcement notice. Any appeal against that notice must be received by the Secretary of State before the date specified in the enforcement notice as the date on which it takes effect.

ENDNOTES

38   Apply to The Planning Inspectorate. PO Box 326, Bristol BS99 7XF.

Environmental Impact Assessment — A Guide to Procedures

Office of the Deputy Prime Minister

Published 7 February 2001, updated 8 July 2002

INTRODUCTION

Environmental impact assessment (EIA) is an important procedure for ensuring that the likely effects of new development on the environment are fully understood and taken into account before the development is allowed to go ahead. This booklet, which is intended primarily for developers and their advisers, explains how European Community (EC) requirements for the environmental impact assessment of major projects have been incorporated into consent procedures in the UK. It revises the booklet 'Environmental Assessment: A Guide to the Procedures', first published in 1989, to take account of the requirements of Directive 97/11/EC, which was adopted on 3 March 1997 and came into effect on 14 March 1999.

Directive 97/11/EC amends the original Directive 85/337/EEC on 'The assessment of the effects of certain public and private projects on the environment', which came into effect in July 1988. The text of the Directive as amended (with amendments shown in italics) is reproduced in Appendix 1 to this booklet. Throughout this booklet, references to 'the Directive' mean Directive 85/337/EEC as amended by Directive 97/11/EC. The effect of the Directive is to require environmental impact assessment to be carried out, before development consent is granted, for certain types of major project which are judged likely to have significant environmental effects.

Parts 1 and 2 of this booklet explain the procedures which apply to projects falling within the scope of the Directive and requiring planning permission in England and Wales. For such projects the Directive was given legal effect through the Town and Country Planning (Environmental Impact Assessment) (England and Wales) Regulations 1999 (SI No 293 http://www.legislation.hmso.gov.uk/si/si1995/uksi_19950418_en_1.htm) ('the EIA Regulations') which came into force on 14 March 1999 and apply to relevant planning applications lodged on or after that date. The full text of the Regulations is published separately by The Stationery Office. For ease of reference, those parts of the Regulations which list the types of project to which they apply, and specify what information an environmental statement must contain, are reproduced in Appendices 2 to 4 to this booklet. The booklet is not intended to be an authoritative interpretation of the law and does not remove the need to refer to the Regulations.

Formal guidance on procedures under the Regulations, directed principally at local planning authorities, was issued in DETR Circular 2/99 (Welsh Office Circular 11/99). Although the present booklet, like its predecessor, is meant to be reasonably self-contained, developers may need to refer to that Circular, particularly for fuller information on how planning authorities are expected to judge the significance of a project's likely effects for the purpose of deciding whether environmental impact assessment is required.

Parts 1 and 2 also give some general guidance, applicable to all types of project, on the nature of environmental impact assessment and on the practical aspects of preparing an environmental statement.

Part 3 gives a brief account of the procedures which apply to other projects within the scope of the Directive but which are not approved under planning procedures, for example, motorways, harbour works and long distance pipe-lines. It also deals very briefly with environmental impact assessment procedures in Scotland and Northern Ireland. For the detailed requirements, reference will need to be made to the relevant statutory instruments and associated guidance (see Appendix 8 to this booklet).

Throughout this booklet, the term 'environmental impact assessment' (EIA) is used to describe the whole process whereby information about the environmental effects of a project is collected, assessed and taken into account in reaching a decision on whether the project should go ahead or not. The process was formerly referred to in the UK as 'environmental assessment' (EA). An 'environmental statement' is a document setting out the developer's own assessment of a project's likely environmental effects, which is prepared and submitted by the developer in conjunction with the application for consent.

CHAPTER 1: ENVIRONMENTAL IMPACT ASSESSMENT AND PROJECTS WHICH REQUIRE PLANNING PERMISSION

What is environmental impact assessment?

1   The term 'environmental impact assessment' (EIA) describes a procedure that must be followed for certain types of project before they can be given 'development consent'. The procedure is a means of drawing together, in a systematic way, an assessment of a project's likely significant environmental effects. This helps to ensure that the importance of the predicted effects, and the scope for reducing them, are properly understood by the public and the relevant competent authority before it makes its decision.

2   Environmental impact assessment enables environmental factors to be given due weight, along with economic or social factors, when planning applications are being considered. It helps to promote a sustainable pattern of physical development and land and property use in cities, towns and the countryside. If properly carried out, it benefits all those involved in the planning process.

3   From the developer's point of view, the preparation of an environmental statement in parallel with project design provides a useful framework within which environmental considerations and design development can interact. Environmental analysis may indicate ways in which the project can be modified to avoid possible adverse effects, for example through considering more environmentally friendly alternatives. Taking these steps is likely to make the formal planning approval stages run more smoothly.

4   For the planning authority and other public bodies with environmental responsibilities, environmental impact assessment provides a basis for better decision making. More thorough analysis of the implications of a new project before a planning application is made, and the provision of more comprehensive information with the application, should enable authorities to make swifter decisions. While the responsibility for compiling the environmental statement rests with the developer, it is expected that the developer will consult those with relevant information, and the Regulations specifically require that public authorities which have information in their possession which is relevant to the preparation of the environmental statement should make it available to the developer.

5   The general public's interest in a major project is often expressed as concern about the possibility of unknown or unforeseen effects. By providing a full analysis of a project's effects, an environmental statement can help to allay fears created by lack of information. At the same time, early engagement with the public when plans are still fluid can enable developers to make adjustments which will help to secure a smoother passage for the proposed development and result in a better environmental outcome. The environmental statement can also help to inform the public on the substantive issues which the local planning authority will have to consider in reaching a decision. It is a requirement of the Regulations that the environmental statement must include a description of the project and its likely effects together with a summary in non-technical language. One of the aims of a good environmental statement should be to enable readers to understand for themselves how its conclusions have been reached, and to form their own judgments on the significance of the environmental issues raised by the project.

6   Environmental impact assessment can therefore be helpful to all those concerned with major projects. The following paragraphs describe the procedures for deciding whether EIA is necessary in a particular case and, where it is, for carrying out the assessment. The procedure is intended to make the most of the potential benefits of EIA, while keeping the process as simple and flexible as possible, and avoiding any duplication of existing planning procedures.

When is environmental impact assessment needed?

7   The Regulations apply to two separate lists of projects:
(i)   'Schedule 1 projects', for which EIA is required in every case;
(ii) 'Schedule 2 projects', for which EIA is required only if the particular project in question is judged likely to give rise to significant environmental effects.

Lists of Schedule 1 and Schedule 2 projects are given in, respectively, Appendices 2 and 3 to this booklet.

8   For Schedule 1 projects, whether or not a particular project falls within the scope of the Regulations will normally be clear: several of the definitions of Schedule 1 projects incorporate an indication of scale, in the form of a quantified threshold, which clearly identifies the projects requiring EIA. Where there is any doubt about a project's inclusion in Schedule 1, the procedures described in paragraphs 14–19 below can be used to obtain an opinion from the planning authority or a direction from the Secretary of State (or, in Wales, the National Assembly for Wales).

9   For the much longer list of Schedule 2 projects, the issue turns on the likelihood of 'significant environmental effects'. For the different types of project described in column 1 of Schedule 2, the 1999 Regulations introduced a system of thresholds and criteria, shown in column 2, as a method of discounting development which is not likely to have significant effects on the environment. For development where the applicable threshold or criterion is not exceeded or met, EIA is not normally required. However, even where the threshold or criterion is not met or exceeded, EIA may be required if the proposed development is in, or partly in, a 'sensitive area' (see paragraph 10). In exceptional circumstances the Secretary of State (or, in Wales, the National Assembly for Wales) may exercise his power under the Regulations to direct that a particular type of Schedule 2 development requires EIA even if it is not to be located in a sensitive area and does not exceed or meet the applicable threshold or criterion.

10   The more environmentally sensitive the location, the more likely it is that the effects of development will be significant and that EIA will be required. That is why the thresholds and criteria do not apply where development is proposed in, or partly in, a 'sensitive area' as defined in the Regulations. Such areas include Sites of Special Scientific Interest (SSSIs), National Parks, Areas of Outstanding Natural Beauty, the Broads, World Heritage Sites and scheduled monuments. There is no general presumption that every Schedule 2 development in a sensitive area will require EIA. Nevertheless, in the case of development to be located in or close to SSSIs, especially those which are also international conservation sites such as Ramsar sites or Special Protection Areas for birds, the likely environmental effects will often be such as to require EIA.

How 'significance' will be assessed

11   Developments which meet or exceed the applicable threshold are considered on a case-by-case basis. For the purpose of determining whether EIA is necessary, those of the selection criteria set out in Schedule 3 to the Regulations which are relevant to the proposed development, must be taken into account. The selection criteria fall into the three broad headings: characteristics of the development, location of the development, and characteristics of the potential impact.

12   For obvious reasons there can be no general definition of what constitutes significance. General guidance on how to assess 'significance' is contained in DETR Circular 2/99 (Welsh Office Circular 11/99); and rulings may be obtained from the local

planning authority or the Secretary of State (or, in Wales, the National Assembly for Wales) on whether EIA is required in particular cases. Essentially the Circular suggests that there are three main criteria of significance:

(i)   major developments which are of more than local importance;
(ii) developments which are proposed for particularly environmentally sensitive or vulnerable locations;
(iii) developments with unusually complex and potentially hazardous environmental effects.

13   These are very general guidelines and, to assist in their application to particular cases, the Circular also sets out indicative thresholds and criteria by reference to particular categories of development listed in Schedule 2 to the Regulations. These are reproduced in the last column of the Table in Appendix 3 to this booklet. It will be obvious that none of these guidelines can be applied as hard and fast rules; circumstances are bound to vary greatly from case to case. Some large-scale projects which exceed the indicative thresholds may not be significant enough to require EIA; some smaller projects, particularly in sensitive locations, may be candidates for EIA. Nevertheless, the guidance in the Circular should provide a starting point for consideration by the developer and the planning authority of the need for EIA. If the matter is referred to the Secretary of State (or, in Wales, the National Assembly for Wales), he will have regard to the published criteria.

Obtaining a ruling on the need for EIA

14   Where there is a possibility that a proposed development will require environmental impact assessment, developers are advised to consult the relevant planning authority well in advance of a planning application. Developers can decide for themselves that a given project falls within the scope of the Regulations so that an environmental statement will be needed. But the Regulations also provide a procedure which enables developers to apply to the planning authority for an opinion ('screening opinion') on whether EIA is needed in a particular case, as soon as a basic minimum of information can be provided about the proposal. This must include a plan on which the site of the proposed development is identified, and a brief description of its nature and purpose and of its possible effects on the environment. This can, of course, be supplemented with other information if the developer wishes.

15   Where such information can be provided, the developer may approach the planning authority at any time for an opinion on the need for EIA. This can be done well in advance of any formal planning application, although any approach to the planning authority before the planning application stage is entirely voluntary. Where such an approach is made, the planning authority must give its opinion within three weeks, unless the developer agrees to a longer period. The planning authority may request further information from the developer, but this in itself does not extend the three-week time limit, unless the developer agrees. The planning authority must make its determination available for public inspection at the place where the appropriate register (or relevant section of that register) is kept.

16   Where the planning authority express the opinion that a particular proposal requires EIA — whether in response to a request from a developer prior to a planning application, or following a planning application — it must provide a written statement giving clear and precise reasons for its opinion. Both that statement and the developer's application for an opinion are then made available for public inspection at the same place as the register.

17   A developer who is dissatisfied with the planning authority's opinion that EIA is required may refer the matter to the Secretary of State (or, in Wales, the National Assembly for Wales). The developer is simply required to copy the relevant papers to the Government Office in the region concerned (or the Assembly) and add any representations which are considered to be appropriate in the light of the planning authority's statement. The Secretary of State (or the Assembly) will then normally give a direction within three weeks of the developer's application; and, if the direction is to the effect that EIA is required, it will be accompanied by a statement of reasons. The developer may, when requesting a screening opinion from the planning authority, simultaneously request an opinion on what should be included in any environmental statement (see paragraph 25 below).

18   The broad intention of this procedure is to ensure that developers can obtain a clear ruling on the need for EIA well before they reach the stage of lodging a formal planning application. This should minimise the possibility of delay or uncertainty at that stage. Where the matter is not raised until a formal planning application is lodged, the developer risks serious delay if either the planning authority or the Secretary of State (or, in Wales, the National Assembly for Wales) rules that an environmental statement must be prepared. No action will be taken on the planning application until the developer has prepared an environmental statement and submitted it to the planning authority.

19   In most cases this procedure will give developers a firm decision on the need for EIA as soon as they can provide basic information about their project. There may occasionally be cases where the receipt of information directly leads the Secretary of State (or, in Wales, the National Assembly for Wales) to issue a direction when there has been no request for one from the developer; or to overrule a planning authority's opinion that EIA is not required; or even, very exceptionally, to reverse an earlier direction. This could, for instance, happen where a development proposal came to the Secretary of State's (or the Assembly's) notice on 'call-in'; or where third party representations drew attention to aspects of a proposed development which were not known to the Secretary of State (or the Assembly) when the initial direction was given. Exceptionally, also, a planning authority which has given a pre-application opinion that EIA is not required might consider it necessary to reverse that decision when the planning application is formally submitted. In that case the developer could, of course, apply to the Secretary of State (or the Assembly) for a direction.

'Permitted development rights' (PDRs)

20   Developments which do not require planning permission because of the provisions of the Town and Country Planning (General Permitted Development) Order 1995 (SI No 418) http://www.legislation.hmso.gov.uk/si/si1995/ Uksi_19950418_en_1.htm continue to enjoy PDRs provided that they do not fall into Schedule 1 or 2 of the EIA Regulations. For developments that do fall within Schedule 1 or 2, the general position is as follows. Schedule 1 projects are not permitted development, and always require the submission of a planning application and an environmental statement. PDRs for Schedule 2 projects which either exceed or meet the applicable threshold or criterion, or are wholly or partly in a sensitive area, are also withdrawn, unless the local planning authority has adopted a screening opinion (or the Secretary of State (or, in Wales, the National Assembly for Wales) has directed) to the effect that EIA is not required. There are exceptions to these provisions in the case of the following classes in Schedule 2 to the 1995 Order: Part 7, Class D of Part 8, Part 11, Class B of Part 12, Class F(a) of Part 17, Class A of Part 20, Class B of Part 20, and Class B of Part 21. These exceptions exist for a variety of reasons. For example, some relate to projects subject to alternative consent procedures, and others to projects begun before Directive 85/337/EEC came into operation.

Further information about the exceptions, and about permitted development and EIA generally, can be found in DETR Circular 2/99 (Welsh Office Circular 11/99) paragraphs 61–65 and 151–156.

Simplified planning zones and enterprise zones

21   Special considerations apply to projects proposed for simplified planning zones (SPZs) and enterprise zones (EZs).

Simplified planning zones

22   All Schedule 1 projects are excluded from the scope of SPZs and therefore require EIA as part of the application for planning permission. Where the terms of SPZ schemes would permit Schedule 2 projects to be undertaken without specific planning permission, developers must notify the planning authority that they intend to undertake such development. This notification will give the planning authority and, where appropriate, the Secretary of State (or, in Wales, the National Assembly for Wales) the opportunity to consider whether the project is likely to give rise to significant environmental effects. If so, planning permission will be required in the normal way and an environmental statement must be prepared. If not, the project will enjoy the benefit of the general permission granted by the SPZ scheme, and no separate application for planning permission will be necessary.

Enterprise zones

23   If the planning scheme allows for Schedule 1 projects, EIA must be carried out. As regards Schedule 2 projects, the same procedures apply as those for SPZs described above.

24   The arrangements in SPZs and EZs are explained in DETR Circular 2/99 (Welsh Office Circular 11/99).

2   PREPARING AN ENVIRONMENTAL STATEMENT:THE PLANNING PROCEDURES

25   The developer is responsible for preparing the environmental statement which must be submitted with the planning application. A developer may choose to engage consultants for some or all of the work. The preparation of the statement should be a collaborative exercise involving discussions with the local planning authority, statutory consultees and possibly other bodies as well. There is no prescribed form of statement, provided that the requirements of the Regulations are met. The Regulations enable a developer, before making a planning application, to ask the local planning authority for its formal opinion ('scoping opinion') on the information to be included in an environmental statement. The developer can therefore be clear as to what the authority considers are the aspects of the environment which would be affected. The request may be made at the same time as for the screening opinion, and must be accompanied by the same information as for the screening opinion (paragraph 14 above). A developer may also wish to submit a draft outline of the environmental statement, indicating what the developer thinks the main issues are, as a focus for the authority's consideration. The authority must consult certain bodies (see paragraph 36) and the developer before adopting a scoping opinion, and must adopt the scoping opinion within five weeks of receiving the request. This period may be extended provided that the developer agrees. The scoping opinion must be kept available for public inspection for two years, with the request (including documents submitted by the developer as part of that request), at the place where the planning register is kept.

26   There is no provision for an appeal to the Secretary of State (or, in Wales, the National Assembly for Wales) if the developer and local planning authority disagree about the content of an environmental statement. If an authority fails to adopt a scoping opinion within five weeks (or any agreed extension), the developer may apply to the Secretary of State (or the Assembly) for a scoping direction. The application must be accompanied by the previous documents relating to the request for a scoping opinion, plus any additional representations the developer wishes to make. The developer should also send a copy of the request and any representations to the authority. The Secretary of State (or the Assembly) must make a scoping direction within five weeks of receiving the request, or such longer period as he may reasonably require. He must consult the developer and certain bodies beforehand. A copy of the scoping direction will be sent to the developer and the authority.

27   The aim should be to provide as systematic and objective an account as is possible of the significant environmental effects to which the project is likely to give rise. Where the statement embodies or summarises the conclusions of more detailed work, sufficient information should be provided to enable those who wish to do so to verify the statement's conclusions and to identify the source of the information provided. The environmental statement must contain a non-technical summary which will enable non-experts to understand its findings.

Preliminary consultations

28   One of the main emphases of the process of environmental impact assessment is on the need for fuller and earlier consultation by the developer with bodies which have an interest in the likely environmental effects of the development proposal. If important issues are not considered at a very early stage, they may well emerge when a project's design is well advanced, and necessitate rethinking and delay. Ideally, EIA should start at the stage of site selection and (where relevant) process selection, so that the environmental merits of practicable alternatives can be properly considered.

29   While a developer is under no formal obligation to consult about the proposal before the submission of a formal planning application, there are good practical reasons for doing so. Authorities will often possess useful local and specialised information which is relevant to a project's design, and officers may be able to give preliminary advice about local problems and about those aspects of the proposal that are likely to be of particular concern to the authority.

30   The timing of such informal consultations is at the developer's discretion; but it will generally be advantageous for them to take place as soon as the developer is in a position to provide sufficient information about the proposal to form a basis for discussion. The developer can ask that any information provided at this preliminary stage should be treated in confidence by the planning authority and any other consultees. If the developer is seeking a formal opinion from the planning authority on the need for environmental impact assessment (see paragraph 14), the information about the project which accompanies that request will be made public by the authority.

Content of the environmental statement

31   Developers and authorities should discuss the scope of an environmental statement before its preparation is begun. The formal requirements as to the content of environmental statements are set out in Schedule 4 to the Regulations, which is reproduced in Appendix 4 to this booklet. The information is given under separate headings: Part I and Part II. The statement must include at least the information included in Part II, and such of the information in Part I as is reasonably required to assess the environmental effects of the development and which the applicant can reasonably be required to complete. As a practical guide to the range of issues which may need to be considered, developers may find it helpful to use the checklist at Appendix 5 to this

booklet as a basis for their discussions with the planning authority. The checklist is not meant to be regarded as a prescribed framework for all environmental statements. Its main purpose is to act as a guide or agenda for the preliminary discussions about the scope of the statement.

32   The comprehensive nature of the checklist at Appendix 5 should not be taken to imply that all environmental statements should cover every conceivable aspect of a project's potential environmental effects at the same level of detail. They should be tailored to the nature of the project and its likely effects. Whilst every environmental statement should provide a full factual description of the project, the emphasis of Schedule 4 is on the main or significant effects to which a project is likely to give rise. In some cases, only a few of the aspects set out in the checklist will be significant in this sense and will need to be discussed in the statement in any great depth. Other issues may be of little or no significance for the particular project in question, and will need only very brief treatment, to indicate that their possible relevance has been considered.

33   It should be noted that developers are now required to include in the environmental statement an outline of the main alternative approaches to the proposed development that they may have considered, and the main reasons for their choice. It is widely regarded as good practice to consider alternatives, as it results in a more robust application for planning permission. Also, the nature of certain developments and their location may make the consideration of alternatives a material consideration. Where alternatives are considered, the main ones must be outlined in the environmental statement.

34   Even where a local planning authority has adopted a scoping opinion, the developer is responsible for the content of the statement which is finally submitted. Developers should bear in mind that planning authorities have powers to call for additional information when considering environmental statements and planning applications, and that they are likely to use those powers if they consider that aspects of a submitted environmental statement are inadequate (see paragraph 48 below). There is no provision for any disagreement between the developer and the planning authority over the content of an environmental statement to be referred to the Secretary of State (or, in Wales, the National Assembly for Wales), except through normal planning appeal procedures (see paragraph 52 below).

35   Developers should consider at an early stage whether an assessment of environmental effects may also be required under another European Community Directive, such as the Habitats Directive (92/43/EEC), the Wild Birds Directive (79/409/ EEC), the Integrated Pollution Prevention and Control Directive (96/61/EC) or the Control of Major Accident Hazards Directive (96/82/EC). Although the requirements of these and of the EIA Directive are all independent of each other, there are clearly links between them. Where more than one regime applies, developers could save unnecessary time and effort if they identify and co-ordinate the different assessments required. Advice on the links between the EIA system and the requirements of the Habitats Regulations is offered in PPG 9 on Nature Conservation (or, in Wales, Planning Guidance (Wales) Planning Policy First Revision), and on the links between the Town and Country Planning system and the IPPC authorisation system in PPG 23 on Planning

and Pollution Control (or, in Wales, Planning Guidance (Wales) Planning Policy First Revision and Planning Guidance (Wales) Technical Advice Note (Wales) 5 'Nature Conservation and Planning').

Statutory and other consultees; the general public

36   The Regulations give a particular role in environmental impact assessment to those public bodies with statutory environmental responsibilities who must be consulted by the planning authority before a Schedule 1 or a Schedule 2 planning application is determined. A full list of these statutory consultation bodies is given in Appendix 6 to this booklet.

37   Where the planning authority or the Secretary of State (or, in Wales, the National Assembly for Wales) rules that EIA is required, those bodies which are statutory consultees for the particular project in question will be notified and the developer will be informed accordingly. The effect of this notification is to put those bodies under an obligation to provide the developer (on request) with any information in their possession which is likely to be relevant to the preparation of the environmental statement. An example might be information held by English Nature (or, in Wales, the Countryside Council for Wales) about the ecology of a particular area, which could be relevant to the assessment of a project's likely effects.

38   It is up to the developer to approach the statutory consultees and indicate what sort of information would be helpful in preparing the environmental statement. The obligation on statutory consultees relates only to information already in their possession; they are not required to undertake research on behalf of the developer. Nor, at this stage, would consultees be expected to express a view about the merits of the proposal; their views on merits are invited at a later stage (see paragraph 46 below). Consultees may make a reasonable charge to cover the cost of making information requested by a developer available.

39   Developers should also consider whether to consult the general public, and non-statutory bodies concerned with environmental issues, during the preparation of the environmental statement. Bodies of this kind may have particular knowledge and expertise to offer. Some are national organisations, for instance, the Royal Society for the Protection of Birds; in most areas there are also active local amenity societies and environmental groups. While developers are under no obligation to publicise their proposals before submitting a planning application, consultation with local amenity groups and with the general public can be useful in identifying key environmental issues, and may put the developer in a better position to modify the project in ways which would mitigate adverse effects and recognise local environmental concerns. It will also give the developer an early indication of the issues which are likely to be important at the formal application stage if, for instance, the proposal goes to public inquiry.

Techniques of assessment; sources of advice

40   Extensive literature is available on how to assess the effects on the environment of particular processes and activities. The assessment techniques used, and the degree of detail in which any particular subject is treated in an environmental statement, will depend on the character of the proposal, the environment which it is likely to affect, and the information available. While a careful study of the proposed location will generally be needed (including environmental survey information), original scientific research will not normally be necessary. The local planning authority and statutory consultees may be able to advise the developer on sources of specialist information, for example, about particular local conditions.

41   Environmental statements will often need to recognise that there is some uncertainty attached to the prediction of environmental effects. Where there is uncertainty, it needs to be explicitly recognised. Uncertainty is not in itself a reason for discounting the importance of particular potential environmental effects, simply because other effects can be more confidently predicted.

Submission of environmental statement with planning application

42   To enable a planning application to be processed as quickly as possible, it is in the developer's interest to submit an environmental statement at the same time as the application is made. It will be for the planning authority to judge how much information is required in the particular case, but the preparation of an environmental statement is bound to require the developer to work out proposals in some detail; otherwise any thorough appraisal of likely effects will be impossible. Where an application is in outline, the planning authority will still need to have sufficient information on a project's likely effects to enable it to judge whether the development should take place or not. The information given in the environmental statement will have an important bearing on whether matters may be reserved in an outline permission; it will be important to ensure that the development does not take place in a form which would lead to significantly different effects from those considered at the planning application stage.

43   When the developer submits an environmental statement at the same time as the planning application, three further copies must also be submitted for onward transmission by the planning authority to the Secretary of State (or, in Wales, the National Assembly for Wales). The developer is also required to provide the planning authority with sufficient copies of the environmental statement to enable one to be sent to each of the statutory consultees. Alternatively, the developer may send copies of the statement directly to the consultees. When submitting the application, the developer must inform the planning authority of the name of every body — whether or not it is a statutory consultee — to which a copy of the statement has been sent.

44   The developer should make a reasonable number of copies of the statement available for members of the public. A reasonable charge reflecting printing and distribution costs may be made.

Handling by the planning authority

45 Where the environmental statement is submitted with the planning application, the local planning authority will arrange for a notice to be published in a local newspaper and displayed at or near the site of the proposed development. If the environmental statement is submitted after the planning application, responsibility for publicising it falls to the developer.

46 The planning authority will place the planning application on Part I of the planning register, together with the environmental statement. The authority and the developer may wish to consider the need for further publicity at this stage, for example, publication of further details of the project in a local newspaper, or an exhibition. The planning authority will also need to notify statutory consultees of the application (unless the developer has already done so) and invite them to comment on the environmental statement. Consultees must be allowed at least 14 days from receipt of the statement in which to comment before a decision is taken. It will often be useful for the planning authority to discuss the project with consultees who have a particular interest in its environmental effects before reaching its conclusions on the planning applications.

47 The copies of the environmental statement that are forwarded by the planning authority to the Secretary of State (or, in Wales, the National Assembly for Wales), will assist in monitoring. In those exceptional circumstances where a proposed development is likely to have significant effects on the environment in another country, they will also enable certain international obligations for exchange of information with other countries to be met.

Requests for further information

48 Where the planning authority considers that the information provided in the developer's environmental statement, together with that available to the authority from other sources, is insufficient to permit a proper evaluation of the project's likely environmental effects, the authority can require further information, or evidence to verify the information that has already been provided. The use of these powers should not normally be necessary, especially if the parties have worked together during the preparation of the environmental statement. Nevertheless, further consultation between the planning authority and the developer may be necessary at this stage, in particular to consider comments made by consultees and, possibly, amendments to the proposal to meet objections that have been raised.

49 Where an authority considers that it does not have the necessary expertise to evaluate the information contained in an environmental statement, it may decide to seek advice from consultants or other suitably qualified persons or organisations.

Determination of application

50   The planning authority is required to determine a planning application which is the subject of environmental impact assessment within 16 weeks from the date of receipt of the environmental statement, unless the developer agrees to a longer period. In determining the application, the authority is, of course, required to have regard to the environmental statement, as well as to other material considerations. As with any other planning application, the planning authority may refuse permission or grant it with or without conditions.

51   The planning authority cannot take the view that a planning application is invalid because it considers that an inadequate environmental statement has been submitted or because the developer has failed to provide any further information required under the powers described in paragraph 48 above. However, if the developer fails to provide enough information to complete the environmental statement, the application can be determined only by refusal.

Appeals and call-ins

52   The right of appeal to the Secretary of State (or, in Wales, the National Assembly for Wales) against an adverse decision by a planning authority (or against an authority's failure to determine an application within the 16-week time limit) is the same for planning applications to which the EIA Regulations apply as for other applications. Similarly, the Secretary of State's (or the Assembly's) power to call in a planning application applies in these cases. Where an environmental statement has been prepared to accompany a planning application, the information which it contains will be among the material considerations which an Inspector will take into account in considering an appeal. The Secretary of State (or the Assembly) and Inspectors, like the planning authority, have power to request the developer to provide further information where they consider that the environmental statement is inadequate as it stands. Any additional information provided by the developer in response to such a request will be made available to all parties to an appeal.

Procedural stages

53   Appendix 7 to this booklet provides illustrative flow charts for the five main procedural stages: application to the planning authority for a screening opinion; application to the Secretary of State (or, in Wales, the National Assembly for Wales) for a screening direction; application to the planning authority for a scoping opinion; application to the Secretary of State (or the Assembly) for a scoping direction; and submission of an environmental statement to the planning authority in conjunction with a planning application.

3   ARRANGEMENTS FOR OTHER PROJECTS

54   The advice given in Parts 1 and 2 of this booklet is generally applicable to all projects. However, those Parts specifically describe the arrangements for EIA of projects in England and Wales which are approved through the planning system. Part 3 gives brief guidance on the legislative provisions on EIA for projects insofar as they are outside the scope of the planning system.

55   For all the following projects the Regulations described, which implement the Directive, include provisions for seeking a scoping opinion from the competent authority, for consulting statutory and other bodies, for the submission of an environmental statement in the prescribed form, and for publicising the statement. Where applicable, the Regulations disapply any thresholds for Annex II projects which are at least partly in a 'sensitive area', this term being defined in the same or almost the same way as in the planning EIA Regulations (see paragraph 10 above).

Projects not subject to planning control

The trunk road network

56   EIA is mandatory for projects to construct new motorways and certain other roads, including those with four or more lanes, and for certain road improvements (see Directive Annex I.7(b) and (c)). Projects to construct roads other than those in Annex I automatically fall within Annex II.10(e).

57   Roads in England and Wales for which the Secretary of State for Transport or the National Assembly for Wales is the highway authority, are approved under procedures set out in the Highways Act 1980. These roads — the trunk road network — currently include nearly all motorways. The Department concerned will normally consult the public widely about alternative routes before selecting a preferred route for a new road. Once the preferred route has been announced, detailed design work is carried out leading to the publication of statutory orders. In most cases these orders are the subject of a public inquiry held by an independent inspector.

58   For these roads, the Directive has been implemented in England and Wales by the Highways (Assessment of Environmental Effects) Regulations 1999 (SI No 369) http://www.legislation.hmso.gov.uk/si/si1999/19990369.htm. These Regulations replace the Highways (Assessment of Environmental Effects) Regulations 1988 (SI No 1241), except for projects begun before the new Regulations came into force on 13 March 1999.

59   The Regulations incorporate an exclusive threshold for the purpose of screening Annex II projects: only those in which the area of the completed works and the area occupied during the road construction or improvement period exceeds one hectare, or are wholly or partly in a sensitive area, need to be screened for EIA.

60   Roads developed by local planning authorities, and roads developed by private developers, require planning permission and the provisions described in Parts I and 2 of this booklet apply to such roads.

Oil and gas pipe-lines

61   Oil and gas pipe-lines with a diameter of more than 800 millimetres and a length of more than 40 kilometres fall within Annex I of the Directive. Pipe-line installations which are below either of these thresholds fall within Annex II. Oil and gas pipe-lines 10 miles long or less are approved under planning legislation.

ONSHORE PIPE-LINE WORKS

62   Proposed onshore pipes (but not those of public gas transporters — see below) which are more than 10 miles long require a pipe-line construction authorisation (PCA) from the Secretary of State for Trade and Industry under the Pipe-lines Act 1962. The Pipe-line Works (Environmental Impact Assessment) Regulations 2000 (SI No 1928) http://www.legislation.hmso.gov.uk/si/si2000/20001928.htm, which replace the provisions relating to pipe-lines in the Electricity and Pipe-line Works (Assessment of Environmental Effects) Regulations 1990, implement the Directive in England, Wales and Scotland in respect of pipe-lines which require a PCA. They require 'relevant pipe-line works' to be subject to EIA unless the Secretary of State makes a determination that EIA is not necessary.

PUBLIC GAS TRANSPORTER PIPE-LINE WORKS

63   Under the licensing regime introduced by the Gas Act 1995, companies wishing to convey gas may be licensed as public gas transporters. As such, they are exempt from the need to obtain authorisation for their pipes under the Pipe-lines Act 1962.

64   The Public Gas Transporter Pipe-line Works (Environmental Impact Assessment) Regulations 1999 (SI No 1672) http://www.legislation.hmso.gov.uk/si/si1999/19991672.htm came into force on 15 July 1999 and implement the Directive in England, Wales and Scotland. They require a public gas transporter proposing to undertake pipe-line works which fall in Annex I of the Directive to submit an environmental statement and apply to the Secretary of State for Trade and Industry for consent to carry them out. Pipe-line works in Annex II of the Directive may be subject to EIA if they have a design operating pressure exceeding 7 bar gauge or either wholly or in part cross a sensitive area. In these circumstances, the public gas transporter must, before commencing construction, either obtain a determination from the Secretary of State that an environmental statement is not required, or give notice that it intends in any event to produce an environmental statement. The Regulations also provide for the Secretary of State to require an environmental statement where proposed works do not

meet these criteria but nevertheless it is considered that there are likely to be significant environmental effects.

Offshore oil and gas projects

65   Annex 1.14 of the Directive covers the extraction of petroleum and natural gas for commercial purposes where the amount extracted exceeds 500 tonnes per day in the case of petroleum and 500 000 cubic metres per day in the case of gas.

66   For such projects, the Offshore Petroleum Production and Pipe-lines (Assessment of Environmental Effects) Regulations 1999 (SI No 360) http:// www.legislation.hmso.gov.uk/si/si1999/19990360.htm implement the Directive. They apply to the whole of the UK. They replace the Offshore Petroleum and Pipe-lines (Assessment of Environmental Effects) Regulations 1998 (SI No 968), which are revoked except for saving provisions for applications for consent received before 14 March 1999.

67   The Regulations are linked to licences granted by the Secretary of State for Trade and Industry under the Petroleum Act 1998. Such licences require the Secretary of State's consent to be obtained to the drilling of a well, the getting of petroleum (where the amount exceeds 500 tonnes per day in the case of oil and 500 000 cubic metres per day in the case of gas) and the erection of any structure in connection with a development. They require, subject to an exception for floating installations whose use commenced before 30 April 1998 (when the 1998 Regulations came into force), the Secretary of State's consent for the use of a floating installation in prescribed circumstances. The Regulations also require the Secretary of State's consent to the use of a mobile installation for the purposes of the extraction of petroleum where the main purpose of such extraction is the testing of a well.

68   For projects which fall outside Annex I of the Directive, the Secretary of State decides whether the project is likely to have significant effects and therefore whether EIA is required.

Nuclear power stations

69   Annex 1.2 of the Directive covers nuclear power stations and other nuclear reactors, and now includes their dismantling or decommissioning, so EIA is mandatory for these projects. It does not cover research installations for the production and conversion of fissionable and fertile material, whose maximum power does not exceed 1 kilowatt continuous thermal load.

70   For new nuclear power stations over 50 megawatts, the Secretary of State for Trade and Industry is the competent authority, and the Directive has been implemented in England and Wales by the Electricity Works (Assessment of Environmental Effects) Regulations 2000 (SI No 1927) http://www.legislation.hmso.gov.uk/si/si2000/ 20001927.htm, which also applies to thermal power stations and overhead power lines

(see below). Power stations of less than 50 megawatts, and other buildings to house small nuclear reactors, are given consent through the normal planning system and are subject to the provisions described in Parts 1 and 2 of this booklet.

71   The Directive's provisions on the dismantling and decommissioning of nuclear power stations and reactors have been implemented by the Nuclear Reactors (Environmental Impact Assessment for Decommissioning) Regulations 1999 (SI No 2892) http://www.legislation.hmso.gov.uk/si/si1999/19992892.htm, which apply to England, Wales and Scotland. They prohibit dismantling or decommissioning from being carried out without the consent of the Health and Safety Executive. A licensee who applies for consent is required to provide the Executive with an environmental statement. The Regulations also apply to changes to existing dismantling or decommissioning projects which may have significant effects on the environment (Annex II.13 of the Directive).

Other power stations and overhead power lines

72   Annex I of the Directive includes thermal power stations with a heat output of 300 megawatts or more, and the construction of overhead power lines with a voltage of 220 kilovolts or more and a length of more than 15 kilometres. Overhead cables which are not in Annex I fall within Annex II.

73   The construction or extension of power stations exceeding 50 megawatts, and the installation of overhead power lines, require consent from the Secretary of State for Trade and Industry under sections 36 and 37 of the Electricity Act 1989, and the requirement for EIA has been implemented as part of the procedure for applications under those provisions. The Electricity Works (Environmental Impact Assessment) Regulations 2000 (SI No 1927) http://www.legislation.hmso.gov.uk/ si/si2000/ 20001927.htm require EIA for all projects which fall within Annex I of the Directive. They also require proposed power stations not covered by Annex I, and all overhead power lines of 132 kilovolts or more, to be screened for EIA. Overhead power lines below 132 kilovolts are not normally expected to have significant environmental effects and do not need to be considered for EIA unless local circumstances demand it. The Regulations also make provisions relating to nuclear power stations (see paragraph 70 above).

74   The Regulations apply to England and Wales and replace that part of the Electricity and Pipe-line Works (Assessment of Environmental Effects) Regulations 1990 dealing with power stations and overhead cables. The 1990 Regulations, however, remain in force in respect of applications lodged before the new Regulations came into force.

75   Power stations of 50 megawatts or less are approved under planning legislation and are subject to the provisions described in Parts 1 and 2 of this booklet.

Forestry projects

76   Projects in Annex II of the Directive include 'Initial afforestation and deforestation for the purposes of conversion to another type of land use'. The Environmental Impact Assessment (Forestry) (England and Wales) Regulations 1999 (SI No 2228) http://www.legislation.hmso.gov.uk/si/si1999/19992228.htm require anyone who proposes to carry out a forestry project that is likely to have significant effects on the environment to apply for a consent from the Forestry Commission before starting work. Those who apply for consent will be required to prepare an environmental statement.

77   There are four categories of forestry project that fall within the Regulations: afforestation (creating new woodlands), deforestation (conversion of woodland to another use), constructing forest roads, and quarrying material to construct forest roads. The Regulations incorporate thresholds below which the project is taken to be unlikely to have significant effects on the environment. The thresholds are 5 hectares for afforestation and 1 hectare for other categories, although projects in sensitive areas have lower and in some cases no thresholds. In considering whether EIA is necessary for projects which meet the appropriate threshold, the Forestry Commission takes account of the nature and scale of the project and the sensitivity of the site. Given the variability of forestry developments and the importance of location in determining whether significant effects on the environment are likely, it is not possible to formulate criteria which will provide a universal test of whether or not EIA is required. The question must be considered on a case-by-case basis. Anyone contemplating a forestry project is advised to contact the appropriate Forestry Commission Conservancy Office for advice on whether or not EIA will be required.

78   An applicant who disagrees with the Commission's opinion that consent is required for a project may ask the appropriate Minister (in England, the Secretary of State for the Environment, Food and Rural Affairs) for a direction.

79   If the Forestry Commission discovers that work is being carried out that would have required its consent or has breached the conditions of consent, it may serve an Enforcement Notice. This can require the person carrying out the work, or someone else with sufficient interest in the land, to do one or more of the following: stop the work, apply for consent, restore the land to its condition before the work was started, carry out work to secure compliance with the conditions of consent, remove or alleviate any injury to the environment which has been caused by the work.

Land drainage improvements

80   Land drainage projects fall within Annex II.1(c) of the Directive. New land drainage works, including flood defence works and defences against the sea, require planning permission and the provisions described in Parts 1 and 2 of this booklet apply to such works. Land drainage improvement works undertaken by drainage bodies are permitted development under the Town and Country Planning (General Permitted Development) Order 1995 (see paragraph 20) and are therefore exempt from planning

permission. As such works might have significant effects on the environment, the principles of EIA need to be applied to them. This is done through the Environmental Impact Assessment (Land Drainage Improvement Works) Regulations 1999 (SI No 1783) http://www.legislation.hmso.gov.uk/si/si1999/19991783.htm, which apply to England and Wales and revoke and replace earlier Regulations which came into force in 1988 and were amended in 1995.

81   The 1999 Regulations require a drainage body to consider whether proposed improvement works are likely to have significant effects on the environment. Where the drainage body considers that there are unlikely to be such effects, it must publicise its intention to carry out the works. If the drainage body receives representations that there are likely to be significant effects but it still thinks otherwise, it must apply for a determination to the appropriate authority (Secretary of State for the Environment, Food and Rural Affairs or, in Wales, the National Assembly for Wales). Where the drainage body concludes that the works are likely to have significant environmental effects, it must publicise its intention to prepare an environmental statement and notify specified consultation bodies (English Nature, the Countryside Agency and any other authority or organisation which might have an interest).

82   The environmental effects of the improvement works must be assessed in the light, in particular, of the environmental statement and any representations received. If there are no objections, the drainage body may determine that it will proceed with the works. If there are objections, the proposal must be referred to the appropriate authority for a determination giving or refusing consent to the works. The determination must be publicised.

Ports and harbours

83   Annex 1.8 of the Directive includes trading ports, piers for loading and unloading connected to land and outside ports (excluding ferry piers) which can take vessels of over 1350 tonnes. Annex II.10(e) includes construction of harbours and port installations, including fishing harbours, which do not fall within Annex I.

84   Proposed development at ports and harbours down to the low water mark is subject to Town and Country Planning EIA Regulations. For other works, the requirements of the Directive have been implemented in England, Wales and Scotland by the Harbour Works (Environmental Impact Assessment) Regulations 1999 (SI No. 3445) http://www.legislation.hmso.gov.uk/si/si1999/19993445.htm. These Regulations incorporate a revised Schedule 3 to the Harbour Works Act 1964, which gives the procedures for harbour revision orders and harbour empowerment orders, and replace the Harbour Works (Assessment of Environmental Effects) (No 2) Regulations 1989 governing harbour works not needing to be authorised by harbour order.

85   Whether or not proposed works are subject to a harbour order, the appropriate Minister (generally the Secretary of State for Transport) is responsible for deciding whether EIA is required and, if so, whether the works should proceed in the light of the assessment and the comments of environmental bodies.

86   In general, works under harbour empowerment orders are likely to fall within Annex I of the Directive and require EIA in every case, whereas works under harbour revision orders are likely to fall within Annex II and the need for EIA will depend on whether there are likely to be significant environmental effects. Proposed works which are subject to harbour orders are not subject to EIA if the area of works comprised in the project does not exceed 1 hectare, unless any part falls within a 'sensitive area' or the Secretary of State decides that EIA is needed in a particular case.

Marine fish farming

87   Intensive fish farming is an Annex II project. Developments of onshore fish farming facilities may require planning permission and the provisions described in Parts 1 and 2 of this booklet apply to proposals for such facilities.

88   Off-shore facilities do not require planning permission but require a lease from the Crown Estate Commissioners (or, where appropriate, from the Shetlands Islands Council or Orkney Islands Council). The Environmental Impact Assessment (Fish Farming in Marine Waters) Regulations 1999 (SI No 367) http://www.legislation.hmso.gov.uk/si/si1999/19990367.htm, which apply to England, Wales and Scotland, set indicative criteria which, when triggered, require the Commissioners to screen applications to determine whether EIA is needed. They apply where the development is designed to hold a biomass of 100 tonnes or more, or where it will extend to 0.1 hectare or more of the surface area of the marine waters (including any proposed structures or excavations), or where any part of the development is to be carried out in a sensitive area. The Regulations prohibit a lease from being granted before the environmental statement provided by the developer, and comments on it from consultees and the general public, have been considered.

89   The Crown Estate Commissioners have, in consultation with the Scottish Executive Rural Affairs Department, issued an Environmental Assessment Guidance Manual for Marine Salmon Farmers which provides guidance to developers on how to conduct EIA and prepare an environmental statement. Guidance on the practical implications of the 1999 Regulations has also been issued by the Scottish Executive Rural Affairs Department (see Appendix 8).

Marine dredging for minerals

90   Extraction of minerals by marine dredging falls within Annex II.2(c) of the Directive. The Environmental Impact Assessment and Habitats (Extraction of Minerals by Marine Dredging) Regulations, which are likely to come into force early in 2001, will implement the Directive in waters around the UK (but excluding waters around Scotland). They will also implement the Habitats Directive (92/43/EEC).

91   Unless the regulator (Secretary of State in respect of English Waters or National Assembly in respect of Welsh waters) has provided, in response to a request, a written determination that proposed dredging is not likely to have significant effects, application

for permission must be obtained and the application must be accompanied by an environmental statement. The only exceptions to this are where the Secretary of State has determined that the dredging would form part of a project serving national defence purposes, or where the regulator has determined that it is exempted under Article 2.3 of the Directive.

Transport and Works Act 1992

92   The Transport and Works Act 1992 (TWA) enables orders to be made authorising the construction or operation of railways, tramways, other guided transport systems and inland waterways; and works interfering with rights of navigation. Orders may also authorise ancillary matters such as compulsory purchase and creating or extinguishing rights over land. Applicants for TWA orders may apply at the same time for a direction that planning permission is deemed to be granted.

93   The procedures for making applications for orders under Part 1 of the Act are contained in the Transport and Works (Applications and Objections Procedure) (England and Wales) Rules 2000 (SI No 2190) http://www.legislation.hmso.gov.uk/ si/ si2000/20002190.htm, which also implement the Directive. These Rules apply in England and Wales and replace the earlier 1992 Rules (SI No 2902) except for applications made and not determined before the new Rules come into force on 16 October 2000. In England, most applications for orders are determined by the First Secretary of State. Applications for orders relating wholly to Wales fall to be determined by the National Assembly for Wales.

94   The procedures include provision for opposed orders to be considered by way of a public inquiry, hearing or exchanges of written representations. Schemes that are identified by the Secretary of State or the Assembly as being of national significance are also subject to Parliamentary approval prior to a public inquiry being held.

Projects arising in Scotland and Northern Ireland

95   The arrangements for environmental impact assessment in Scotland and Northern Ireland are broadly similar to those applying in England and Wales, but are mainly subject to separate legislative provisions. The Environmental Impact Assessment (Scotland) Regulations 1999 (SSI 1999/1) http://www.scotland-legislation.hmso.gov.uk/ legislation/ scotland/ssi1999/19990001.htm implement the Directive in Scotland for projects which are subject to planning permission and for certain trunk road projects and land drainage works. Scottish Executive Development Department Circular 15/ 1999 explains the Regulations, and Planning Advice Note (PAN 58) http:// www.scotland.gov.uk/library/pan/pan58-02.htm on Environmental Impact Assessment also provides background information and guidance on best practice. The preceding section, in paragraphs 56 to 94, of this booklet indicates which of those Regulations relating to projects outside the planning system in England and Wales, also apply in Scotland.

96   The Planning (Environmental Impact Assessment) Regulations (Northern Ireland) 1999 (SR 1999/73) http://www.northernireland-legislation.hmso.gov.uk/ sr/ sr1999/19990073.htm implement the Directive in Northern Ireland for projects subject to planning permission. Development Control Advice Note 10 (Revised 1999) issued by the Planning Service, an agency of the Department of the Environment for Northern Ireland, explains the Regulations.

97   Appendix 8 includes a list of all implementing legislation currently in force in England and Wales, Scotland and Northern Ireland, and a list of available guidance.

* * *

APPENDIX 5:
CHECKLIST OF MATTERS TO BE CONSIDERED FOR INCLUSION IN AN ENVIRONMENTAL STATEMENT

This checklist is intended as a guide to the subjects that need to be considered in the course of preparing an environmental statement. It is unlikely that all the items will be relevant to any one project. (See paragraphs 31 and 32 of the main text.)

The environmental effects of a development during its construction and commissioning phases should be considered separately from the effects arising whilst it is operational. Where the operational life of a development is expected to be limited, the effects of decommissioning or reinstating the land should also be considered separately.

Section I

Information describing the project

1.1   Purpose and physical characteristics of the project, including details of proposed access and transport arrangements, and of numbers to be employed and where they will come from.

1.2   Land use requirements and other physical features of the project:
(a) during construction;
(b) when operational;
(c) after use has ceased (where appropriate).

1.3   Production processes and operational features of the project:
(a) type and quantities of raw materials, energy and other resources consumed;
(b) residues and emissions by type, quantity, composition and strength including:
     (i)   discharges to water;
     (ii)   emissions to air;
     (iii) noise;
     (iv)   vibration;
     (v)   light;

(vi) heat;

(vii) radiation;

(viii)   deposits/residues to land and soil;

(ix) others.

1.4   Main alternative sites and processes considered, where appropriate, and reasons for final choice.

Section 2

Information describing the site and its environment

PHYSICAL FEATURES

2.1   Population — proximity and numbers.

2.2   Flora and fauna (including both habitats and species) — in particular, protected species and their habitats.

2.3   Soil: agricultural quality, geology and geomorphology.

2.4   Water: aquifers, water courses, shoreline, including the type, quantity, composition and strength of any existing discharges.

2.5   Air: climatic factors, air quality, etc.

2.6   Architectural and historic heritage, archaeological sites and features, and other material assets.

2.7   Landscape and topography.

2.8   Recreational uses.

2.9   Any other relevant environmental features.

THE POLICY FRAMEWORK

2.10   Where applicable, the information considered under this section should include all relevant statutory designations such as national nature reserves, sites of special scientific interest, national parks, areas of outstanding natural beauty, heritage coasts, regional parks, country parks and designated green belt, local nature reserves, areas affected by tree preservation orders, water protection zones, conservation areas, listed buildings, scheduled ancient monuments, and designated areas of archaeological importance. It should also include references to relevant national policies (including Planning Policy Guidance notes) and to regional and local plans and policies (including approved or emerging development plans).

2.11   Reference should also be made to international designations, eg those under the EC 'Wild Birds' or 'Habitats' Directives, the Biodiversity Convention and the Ramsar Convention.

Section 3

Assessment of effects

Including direct and indirect, secondary, cumulative, short, medium and long-term, permanent and temporary, positive and negative effects of the project.

EFFECTS ON HUMAN BEINGS, BUILDINGS AND MAN-MADE FEATURES

3.1   Change in population arising from the development, and consequential environment effects.

3.2   Visual effects of the development on the surrounding area and landscape.

3.3   Levels and effects of emissions from the development during normal operation.

3.4   Levels and effects of noise from the development.

3.5   Effects of the development on local roads and transport.

3.6   Effects of the development on buildings, the architectural and historic heritage, archaeological features, and other human artefacts, eg through pollutants, visual intrusion, vibration.

EFFECTS ON FLORA, FAUNA AND GEOLOGY

3.7   Loss of, and damage to, habitats and plant and animal species.

3.8   Loss of, and damage to, geological, palaeontological and physiographic features.

3.9   Other ecological consequences.

EFFECTS ON LAND

3.10   Physical effects of the development, eg change in local topography, effect of earth-moving on stability, soil erosion, etc.

3.11   Effects of chemical emissions and deposits on soil of site and surrounding land.

3.12   Land use/resource effects:
  (a)   quality and quantity of agricultural land to be taken;
  (b)   sterilisation of mineral resources;
  (c)   other alternative uses of the site, including the 'do nothing' option;
  (d)   effect on surrounding land uses including agriculture;
  (e)   waste disposal.

EFFECTS ON WATER

3.13   Effects of development on drainage pattern in the area.

3.14   Changes to other hydrographic characteristics, eg groundwater level, water courses, flow of underground water.

3.15   Effects on coastal or estuarine hydrology.

3.16   Effects of pollutants, waste, etc on water quality.

EFFECTS ON AIR AND CLIMATE

3.17   Level and concentration of chemical emissions and their environmental effects.

3.18   Particulate matter.

3.19   Offensive odours.

3.20   Any other climatic effects.

OTHER INDIRECT AND SECONDARY EFFECTS ASSOCIATED WITH THE PROJECT

3.21   Effects from traffic (road, rail, air, water) related to the development.

3.22   Effects arising from the extraction and consumption of materials, water, energy or other resources by the development.

3.23   Effects of other development associated with the project, eg new roads, sewers, housing, power lines, pipe-lines, telecommunications, etc.

3.24   Effects of association of the development with other existing or proposed development.

3.25   Secondary effects resulting from the interaction of separate direct effects listed above.

Section 4

Mitigating measures

4.1   Where significant adverse effects are identified, a description of the measures to be taken to avoid, reduce or remedy those effects, eg:
(a)   site planning;
(b)   technical measures, eg:
       (i)   process selection;
       (ii)   recycling;
       (iii)   pollution control and treatment;

       (iv) containment (eg, bunding of storage vessels).

(c) aesthetic and ecological measures, eg:

       (i)   mounding;

       (ii) design, colour, etc;

       (iii) landscaping;

       (iv) tree plantings;

       (v) measures to preserve particular habitats or create alternative habitats;

       (vi) recording of archaeological sites;

       (vii) measures to safeguard historic buildings or sites.

4.2   Assessment of the likely effectiveness of mitigating measures.

Section 5

Risk of accidents and hazardous development

5.1   Risk of accidents as such is not covered in the EIA Directive or, consequently, in the implementing Regulations. However, when the proposed development involves materials that could be harmful to the environment (including people) in the event of an accident, the environmental statement should include an indication of the preventive measures that will be adopted so that such an occurrence is not likely to have a significant effect. This could, where appropriate, include reference to compliance with Health and Safety legislation.

5.2   There are separate arrangements in force relating to the keeping or use of hazardous substances and the Health and Safety Executive provides local planning authorities with expert advice about risk assessment on any planning application involving a hazardous installation.

5.3   Nevertheless, it is desirable that, wherever possible, the risk of accidents and the general environmental effects of developments should be considered together, and developers and planning authorities should bear this in mind.

Note on Environmental Impact Assessment Directive For Local Planning Authorities (1999 EIA Regulations)

Office of the Deputy Prime Minister

Published 1 July 2002

ENVIRONMENTAL IMPACT ASSESSMENT

Background

In the UK, environmental issues have long been taken into account during the planning process. But practice varied throughout the European Community. Member States agreed in 1985 that procedures should be harmonised so that environmental issues were addressed in a more rigorous, scientific and transparent manner. In 1988 the European Directive on the effects of certain public and private projects on the environment came into effect. The Directive, referred to as the EIA Directive, was amended in 1997. The consolidated text of the Directive is reproduced at Appendix 1 of our publication 'Environmental Impact Assessment; a guide to procedures'. An electronic copy is available at www.planning.odpm.gov.uk/eia/guide/index.htm. You can also order copies from: www.thomastelford.com/books/.

For projects that are subject to approval through the planning system the requirements of the Directive have been transposed into domestic legislation by the Town and Country Planning (Environmental Impact Assessment) (England and Wales) Regulations 1999 (SI 1999 No 293). A copy of these Regulations is available at www.legislation.hmso.gov.uk/si/si1999/19990293.htm

Although the Directive has now been in force for many years some planning authorities will have had limited experience of it. This note, in the form of answers to frequently asked questions, offers a brief guide to the Directive, the Regulations and planning authority responsibilities. The guide does not offer definitive guidance and is *not* a substitute for the Regulations or for guidance provided in the official Departmental Circular (DETR Circular 02/99, Environmental Impact Assessment). You *need* to be familiar with these documents and refer to them when dealing with applications where EIA is involved. But it may provide a useful aide-memoire to remind you of some the potential pitfalls in cases involving EIA and offer some advice on how you can avoid them. And it refers to some important judgments involving EIA that you should be aware of and take note of.

What do the Regulations require?

For qualifying projects they require a planning authority to consider, first, whether a proposed project is likely to have a significant effect on the environment. If so, the authority *must* ensure that the applicant carries out an assessment and prepares and submits to the planning authority a report that identifies, describes and assesses the effects that the project is likely to have on the environment. The process is referred to as Environmental Impact Assessment (EIA), the report as the Environmental Statement (ES).

The ES has to address the direct and indirect effects of the development on a number of factors including the population, fauna, flora, soil, air, water, climatic factors, landscape and archaeology. Full details of the information that has to be included is listed in Schedule 4 of the Regulations. The ES must also contain a non-technical summary so that lay persons can understand what is being proposed and its likely effects.

Members of the public, and statutory consultees, must be given the opportunity to comment on the ES. Before any decision to approve the application may be taken, the planning authority must take into account the ES and any representations made about the environmental effects by the public or consultees. And they must state in their decision that they have done so.

Is there a standard format for an ES?

There is no prescribed format. But in the case of *Berkeley v SSETR* (2000), the House of Lords commented that an ES must not be a paper chase. Lord Hoffman said, 'the point about the environmental statement contemplated by the Directive is that it constitutes a single and accessible compilation, produced by the applicant at the very start of the application process, of the relevant environmental information and the summary in non-technical language'.'

Do the Regulations apply to all applications for planning permission?

There are two classes of project. Schedule 1 of the EIA Regulations lists those for which EIA is *mandatory*. Schedule 2 lists those where the planning authority *is required to consider* whether the project is likely to have a significant effect on the environment. Where this is the case, EIA *must* also be carried out. There is no discretion not to require EIA simply because other information about the project is available.

What action does the planning authority have to take?

The authority's roles involve 'screening' to determine whether a project requires EIA; 'scoping' to advise the applicant of the likely, significant effects on the environment that it wants to see addressed in the ES; consultation with statutory consultees, members of the public and others who may have views on the proposal and the ES; and evaluation of the environmental information presented in the ES and any representations made on it prior to making its decision.

Screening

An applicant for planning permission may ask the planning authority for a 'screening opinion' before submitting the application. If it receives such a request, the authority has to issue an opinion within 3 weeks of the date of receipt. A copy of the opinion has to be made available for public inspection where the planning register is kept.

Where a planning application is submitted without an ES, and a screening opinion has not previously been issued, the authority must determine whether the application falls within a class of development listed in either Schedule 1 or 2 of the Regulations and, for any that fall within Schedule 2, whether the project will have a significant effect on the environment. The authority will then issue a 'screening opinion' to the applicant and place a copy on the planning register. Again a period of 3 weeks is allowed from the date the application is received.

Who has to carry out the screening opinion?

It is the responsibility of the *local planning authority* to ensure that planning applications are 'screened' to establish whether an EIA is required. Normally this will be carried out by the officer dealing with the planning application. But the decision is taken on behalf of the planning authority. If the decision is to be made by officers, it is important to ensure that they have delegated authority to do so.

In *R v St Edmundsbury Borough Council, ex parte Walton* (1999) a decision of the planning authority to grant planning permission was overturned because a decision not to require EIA was taken by an officer who had no formal delegation.

What factors are taken into consideration when reaching a screening opinion?

Given their scale and nature, Schedule 1 projects should be easily identified and it is expected the applicant would not submit such a proposal without an EIA. But if not, it should be a fairly straightforward matter to decide that EIA is required.

For projects within a category of development listed in Schedule 2 a screening opinion *has to be made* if the project meets or exceeds the thresholds and criteria listed in column 2 of the Table at Schedule 2.

Schedule 3 of the Regulations gives some guidance on how to decide whether these projects are likely to have significant environmental effects. Further indicative guidance is provided in Annex A of DETR Circular 2/99 on Environmental Impact Assessment (reproduced in column 3 of the Table at Appendix 3 of the guide to procedures). Decisions need to be taken on a case-by-case basis. Thresholds shown within the indicative guidance are ***not determinative***. Individual projects that fall below the indicative thresholds and criteria may require EIA. The important thing is to consider whether the proposed development is likely to have significant environmental effects and to be clear of the reasons for the decision.

Projects that fall below the thresholds and criteria in Column 2 of the Table at Schedule 2 do not generally require EIA and the authority need not adopt a screening opinion. In effect, the Regulations have already provided a negative screening opinion. The exceptions to this are where the proposed project falls in or partly within a sensitive area as defined in Regulation 2(1), or where the Secretary of State has exercised powers under Regulation 4(8) to direct that EIA is required even though it does not meet these thresholds ands criteria. Such a direction will usually be in response to a request by the planning authority.

Does the screening opinion have to give reasons for the decision?

Where an EIA is required, the authority ***must*** provide a written statement giving full reasons for its decision. There is no similar requirement where the authority decides that EIA is not required. However, it would be prudent for the authority to make and retain for its own use a clear record of the issues considered and the reason for its decision. This would be very useful in the event of any challenge to the planning decision based on EIA grounds.

Can screening opinion still be issued outside of the 3-week timescale?

To avoid unnecessary delays it's important that every attempt should be made to issue screening opinions within the statutory 3-week period. The regulations do, however, allow for the authority and the applicant to agree a longer period. Unless there is such agreement, the authority has no legal authority to request an EIA beyond the 3-week period.

But if it had not issued a screening opinion and it considered that EIA was required the authority could seek to persuade the applicant voluntarily to carry out an assessment and provide an ES which would be submitted in accordance with the Regulations. It can also request the Secretary of State to issue a screening direction to determine whether EIA is required.

Can the authority change its screening opinion?

Yes. But this should done within the statutory period unless there is prior agreement of the applicant to extend the period.

It's possible that additional information about the effects of the project not known to the authority when its screening opinion was given will come to light before a decision is taken on the application. If that information indicates that EIA is required the authority *must not* ignore it simply because it has already issued an opinion that EIA is not required. If the authority itself is unable to change its opinion, it should request a screening direction from the Secretary of State before any decision is taken on the application.

This case of *Fernback and Others v Harrow LBC* **(2000)** addressed this issue. In this case the Court held that a 'negative' screening opinion issued by an LPA did not determine whether an application for planning permission was 'EIA Development' and a 'positive' one by the LPA was determinative only in the absence of one by the Secretary of State. On the other hand, an opinion by the Secretary of State, either way, is determinative.

Scoping

Applicants for planning permission may request the planning authority to provide a 'scoping opinion' on the impacts and issues that the EIA should address — ie those impacts that are likely to be significant. The statutory process requires discussion between the authority, applicant and statutory bodies and a scoping opinion to be issued within 5 weeks of the request or such longer period as may be agreed.

The Regulations require the authority to issue a scoping opinion only in cases where the application has not yet been submitted. But authorities are encouraged to respond favourably to any request from the applicant for a scoping opinion. They may also wish to consider whether they should extend consultations to involve the public and other interested bodies.

Once a scoping opinion is issued can I request further information?

A scoping opinion agreed by all interested parties at the outset should ensure that the relevant issues and potential impacts are identified and reported in the ES. Provided the EIA is properly carried out this should minimise the need to request further information. However, if it believes that further information is necessary it is able to request it under Regulation 19.

It is important to stress that the authority *must* obtain all the information it needs to assess and evaluate the likely significant environmental effects of the proposal *before* it reaches its decision. It cannot adopt a 'wait and see' approach or impose a condition requesting further work to identify the likely environmental effects after permission has been granted. It must be sure that all of these have been identified and taken into account before granting planning permission.

R v Cornwall County Council ex parte Jill Hardy (2001) refers to a case in which the applicant carried out an EIA and provided an ES. Although it was known that the conditions at the site were those favoured by a protected species, bats, the applicant did not investigate for their presence. The planning authority, advised by English Nature, imposed a condition requiring the applicant to carry out a survey to establish whether bats were present prior to commencing the development. The Court held that this information should have been included in the ES, otherwise the authority could not comply with the EIA Regulations (Regulation 3(2)). The planning permission was quashed.

Consultation

Who has to be consulted, and when?

The Regulations require a planning authority to consult with specified statutory consultees prior to issuing any scoping opinion. It must also give statutory consultees and members of the public an opportunity to comment on any ES and its associated planning application and it must take any relevant views expressed by them into account in reaching its decisions.

There is no requirement to consult either statutory consultees or the public about screening opinions.

Do special provisions apply in advertising development subject to EIA?

Where the ES is submitted with the planning application the authority has to advertise the fact and specify where the application and ES may be inspected at a place on or near the site to which the application relates for a minimum period of 21 days before it may determine the application *and* must also publicise it in a local newspaper. There is also a specific form of Notice for EIA applications. See Article 8 and Schedule 3 of the General Development Procedure Order 1995. www.legislation.hmso.gov.uk/si/si1995/Uksi_19950419_en_1.htm

Where the ES is submitted after the planning application the applicant is responsible for publicity.

Does further information requested under Regulation 19 also have to be advertised?

Yes. The authority will have to advertise in the manner set out in Regulation 19.

What if the applicant changes the ES rather than simply provides further information?

There is no specific provision dealing with amendments or additions to an ES that has already been submitted. Such information would not be regarded as 'further information' as this is very specifically defined in the EIA Regulations.

The safest approach is to treat any addition or amendment as an ES submitted during the course of a planning application and to advise the applicant to advertise the whole of the ES, with the amendment/addition, in compliance with regulation 14. This will ensure compliance with the general intent of the EIA Directive to notify and inform people of the possible environmental effects of a proposed development.

Evaluating the Environmental Statement

The planning authority is responsible for evaluating the ES to ensure it addresses all of the relevant environmental issues and that the information is presented accurately, clearly and systematically. It should be prepared to challenge the findings of the ES if it believes they are not adequately supported by scientific evidence. If it believes that key issues are not fully addressed, or not addressed at all, it *must* request further information. The authority has to ensure that it has in its possession *all* relevant environmental information about the likely significant environmental effects of the project *before* it makes its decision whether to grant planning permission. It is too late to address the issues after planning permission has been granted.

Does this also apply to applications for outline planning permission where some matters may be reserved for later determination?

Yes. Where it applies, the Directive requires EIA to be carried out prior to the grant of 'development consent'. Development consent is defined as 'the decision of the competent authority or authorities which entitled the developer to proceed with the development'. Under the UK planning system, it is the planning permission that enables the applicant to proceed with the development. Therefore, in the case of outline applications, an EIA application *must* be properly assessed for possible environmental effects *prior* to the grant of outline permission. It will not be possible to carry out an EIA at the reserved matters stage. The planning permission and the conditions attached to it must be designed to prevent the development from taking a form — and having effects — different from what was considered during the EIA.

This was confirmed in the case of *R v SSTLR ex parte Diane Barker* (2001).

For outline planning applications, how should an EIA be carried out so as to comply with the Directive and Regulations?

The cases of *R v Rochdale MBC ex parte Tew* (1999) and *R v Rochdale MBC ex parte Milne* **(2000)** set out the approach that planning authorities need to take when considering EIA in the context of an application for outline planning permission if they are to comply with the Directive and the Regulations.

Both cases dealt with a legal challenge to a decision of the authority to grant outline planning permission for a business park. In both cases an ES was provided. In *ex parte Tew* the Court upheld a challenge to the decision and quashed the planning permission. In *ex parte Milne*, the Court rejected the challenge and upheld the authority's decision to grant planning permission.

In *ex parte Tew*, the authority authorised a scheme based on an illustrative masterplan showing how the development might be developed, but with all details left to reserved matters. The ES assessed the likely environmental effects of the scheme by reference to the illustrative masterplan. However, there was no requirement for the scheme to be developed in accordance with the masterplan and in fact a very different scheme could have been built, the environmental effects of which would not have been properly assessed. The Court held that description of the scheme was not sufficient to enable the main effects of the scheme to be properly assessed, in breach of Schedule 4 of the EIA Regulations.

In **ex parte Milne**, *the ES was more detailed; a Schedule of Development set out the details of the buildings and likely environmental effects, and the masterplan was no longer merely illustrative. Conditions were attached to the permission 'to tie the outline permission for the business park to the documents which comprise the application'. The outline permission was restricted so that the development that could take place would have to be within the parameters of the matters assessed in the ES. Reserved matters would be restricted to matters that had previously been assessed in the ES. Any application for approval of reserved matters that went beyond the parameters of the ES would be unlawful, as the possible environmental effects would not have been assessed prior to approval.*

The Judge emphasised that the Directive and Regulations required the permission to be granted in the full knowledge of the likely significant effects on the environment. This did not mean that developers would have no flexibility in developing a scheme. But such flexibility would have to be properly assessed and taken into account prior to granting outline planning permission.

He also commented that the ES need not contain information about every single environmental effect. The Directive refers only to those that are likely and significant. To ensure it complied with the Directive the authority would have to ensure that these were identified and assessed before it could grant planning permission. The Court of Appeal in *ex parte Diane Barker* **(2001)** confirmed this approach.

What are the lessons of these cases?

You will want to read these judgments carefully, but there are some general points about applications for outline planning permission:

i) An application for a 'bare' outline permission with all matters reserved for later approval is extremely unlikely to comply with the requirement of the EIA Regulations;

ii)   When granting outline consent, the permission must be 'tied' to the environmental information provided in the ES, and considered and assessed by the authority prior to approval. This can be usually done by conditions although it would also be possible to achieve this by a section 106 agreement. An example of a condition was referred to in *ex parte Milne* (2000). 'The development on this site shall be carried out in substantial accordance with the layout included within the Development Framework document submitted as part of the application and shown on (a) drawing entitled "Master Plan with Building Layouts".' The reason for this condition was given as 'The layout of the proposed Business Park is the subject of an Environmental Impact Assessment and any material alteration to the layout may have an impact which has not been assessed by that process.' (see paras 28 and 131 of the judgment);

iii)   Developers are not precluded from having a degree of flexibility in how a scheme may be developed. But each option will need to have been properly assessed and be within the remit of the outline permission;

iv)   Development carried out pursuant to a reserved matters consent granted for a matter that does not fall within the remit of the outline consent will be unlawful.

What if I fail to comply with the Regulations?

It's possible that proceedings will be initiated by an aggrieved party either through the domestic Courts or by reference to the European Commission.

Domestic challenges

It should be evident from the Court cases referred to that failing to comply with the Regulations may make a decision to grant planning permission unlawful and lead to it being quashed by the Court. Although the Court has the power not to quash planning decisions where there has been procedural impropriety, this discretion is very limited in cases involving EIA because of the duty to comply with EC legislation. It can only be exercised where there had been 'substantial compliance' with the Directive.

If the project is one to which the Regulations apply it is essential to comply fully with them. It is not sufficient to argue that EIA was not necessary because all of the information that could have been in the ES was available elsewhere and was taken into account before the decision was taken; or that had an ES been available the decision would have been the same.

In *Berkeley v SSETR* **(2000)**, the House of Lords unanimously emphasised the need to comply with the Regulations. It took the view that when considering compliance with the Regulations it was necessary to consider the EIA Directive. The Lords stressed that the importance of the EIA process extended beyond the decision on the application. Its purpose is to provide individual citizens with sufficient information about the possible effects and give them the opportunity to make representations. The Court was not entitled to decide after the decision had been made that the requirement of an

EIA could be dispensed with on the ground that the outcome would have been the same even if these procedures had been followed. In his leading judgment, Lord Hoffman noted that the Directive did not allow Member States to treat 'a disparate collection of documents produced by parties other than the developer and traceable only by a person with a good deal of energy and persistence as satisfying the requirement to make available to the public the information which should have been provided by the developer'.

Complaints to the European Commission

Individuals may, and frequently do, complain to the European Commission that planning applications should have been subject to EIA, or that where an EIA was undertaken the procedures were not followed correctly or the information in the Environmental Statement was inadequate. This can lead to formal legal proceedings between the Commission and the United Kingdom. This can be lengthy and prolonged and can increase uncertainty for developers and planning authorities.

How can I avoid legal challenge?

Nothing can guarantee there will be no legal challenge. But you can minimise the risk of such challenge being successful by ensuring compliance with all of the Regulations. In particular you should ensure that:

Planning applications are properly screened and copies of screening opinions placed on the planning register:
— Environmental Statements contain all of the information required by Schedule 4 of the Regulations;
— All of the likely significant effects that the project will have on the environment have been identified and taken into account prior to a decision to allow the project to go ahead;
— The permission that is granted relates only to the project whose environmental effects have been described, assessed and mitigated in the ES. If the ES describes and assesses the effects of burning a single specific type of fuel in a manufacturing process, the consent for the project should be limited to its operation only with the fuel that has been assessed;
— Keep a record of your decisions and why you have reached them.

Town and Country Planning (General Development Procedure) Order 1995 (SI 1995/419)

Town and Country Planning (General Development Procedure) Order 1995

1995 No 419

Made   22nd February 1995

The Secretary of State for the Environment, as respects England, and the Secretary of State for Wales, as respects Wales, in exercise of the powers conferred on them by sections 59, 61(1), 65, 69, 71, 73(3), 74, 77(4), 78, 79(4), 188, 193, 196(4), and 333(7) of, and paragraphs 5, 6, 7(6) and 8(6) of Schedule 1 to, the Town and Country Planning Act 1990 and of all other powers enabling them in that behalf, hereby make the following Order—

1   Citation, commencement and interpretation

(1)   This Order may be cited as the Town and Country Planning (General Development Procedure) Order 1995 and shall come into force on 3 June 1995.

(2)   In this Order, unless the context otherwise requires—

'the Act' means the Town and Country Planning Act 1990;

'building' includes any structure or erection, and any part of a building, as defined in this article, but does not include plant or machinery or any structure in the nature of plant or machinery;

'dwellinghouse' does not include a building containing one or more flats, or a flat contained within such a building;

'environmental information' and 'environmental statement' have the same meanings respectively as in regulation 2 of the Town and Country Planning (Assessment of Environmental Effects) Regulations 1988 (interpretation);

'erection', in relation to buildings as defined in this article, includes extension, alteration, or re-erection;

'flat' means a separate and self-contained set of premises constructed or adapted for use for the purpose of a dwelling and forming part of a building from some other part of which it is divided horizontally;

'floor space' means the total floor space in a building or buildings;

'landscaping' means the treatment of land (other than buildings) being the site or part of the site in respect of which an outline planning permission is granted, for the purpose of enhancing or protecting the amenities of the site and the area in which it is situated and includes screening by fences, walls or other means, the planting of trees, hedges, shrubs or grass, the formation of banks, terraces or other earthworks, the laying out of gardens or courts, and the provision of other amenity features;

'by local advertisement' means by publication of the notice in a newspaper circulating in the locality in which the land to which the application relates is situated;

'mining operations' means the winning and working of minerals in, on or under land, whether by surface or underground working;

'outline planning permission' means a planning permission for the erection of a building, which is granted subject to a condition requiring the subsequent approval of the local planning authority with respect to one or more reserved matters;

['planning obligation' means an obligation entered into by agreement or otherwise by any person interested in land pursuant to section 106 of the Act;]

'proposed highway' has the same meaning as in section 329 of the Highways Act 1980 (further provision as to interpretation);

'1988 Regulations' means the Town and Country Planning (Applications) Regulations 1988;

'reserved matters' in relation to an outline planning permission, or an application for such permission, means any of the following matters in respect of which details have not been given in the application, namely—
(a) siting,
(b) design,
(c) external appearance,
(d) means of access,
(e) the landscaping of the site;

['section 278 agreement' means an agreement entered into pursuant to section 278 of the Highways Act 1980;]

'by site display' means by the posting of the notice by firm affixture to some object, sited and displayed in such a way as to be easily visible and legible by members of the public;

'special road' means a highway or proposed highway which is a special road in accordance with section 16 of the Highways Act 1980 (general provisions as to special roads);

'trunk road' means a highway or proposed highway which is a trunk road by virtue of sections 10(1) or 19 of the Highways Act 1980 (general provisions as to trunk roads, and certain special roads and other highways to become trunk roads) or any other enactment or any instrument made under any enactment.

NOTES

Para (2): definition 'planning obligation' inserted, in relation to England, by SI 2002/828, art 3(a). Date in force: 1 July 2002: see SI 2002/828, art 1(1).
Para (2): definition 'section 278 agreement' inserted, in relation to England, by SI 2002/828, art 3(b). Date in force: 1 July 2002: see SI 2002/828, art 1(1).

8   Publicity for applications for planning permission

(1)   An application for planning permission shall be publicised by the local planning authority to which the application is made in the manner prescribed by this article.

(2)   In the case of an application for planning permission for development which—
(a)   is [an EIA application] accompanied by an environmental statement;
(b)   does not accord with the provisions of the development plan in force in the area in which the land to which the application relates is situated; or
(c)   would affect a right of way to which Part III of the Wildlife and Countryside Act 1981 (public rights of way) applies,
the application shall be publicised in the manner specified in paragraph (3).

(3)   An application falling within paragraph (2) ('a paragraph (2) application') shall be publicised by giving requisite notice—
(a)   by site display in at least one place on or near the land to which the application relates for not less than 21 days, and
(b)   by local advertisement.

(4)   In the case of an application for planning permission which is not a paragraph (2) application, if the development proposed is major development the application shall be publicised by giving requisite notice—
(a)
    (i)   by site display in at least one place on or near the land to which the application relates for not less than 21 days, or
    (ii)   by serving the notice on any adjoining owner or occupier,
    and
(b)   by local advertisement.

(5)   In a case to which neither paragraph (2) nor paragraph (4) applies, the application shall be publicised by giving requisite notice—
(a)   by site display in at least one place on or near the land to which the application relates for not less than 21 days, or
(b)   by serving the notice on any adjoining owner or occupier.

(6)   Where the notice is, without any fault or intention of the local planning authority, removed, obscured or defaced before the period of 21 days referred to in paragraph (3)(a), (4)(a)(i) or (5)(a) has elapsed, the authority shall be treated as having complied with the requirements of the relevant paragraph if they have taken reasonable steps for protection of the notice and, if need be, its replacement.

(7)   In this article—

'adjoining owner or occupier' means any owner or occupier of any land adjoining the land to which the application relates;

['EIA application' has the meaning given in regulation 2 of the Town and Country Planning (Environmental Impact Assessment) (England and Wales) Regulations 1999, and 'environmental statement' means a statement which the applicant refers to as an environmental statement for the purposes of those Regulations];

'major development' means development involving any one or more of the following—
(a) the winning and working of minerals or the use of land for mineral-working deposits;
(b) waste development;
(c) the provision of dwellinghouses where—
    (i) the number of dwellinghouses to be provided is 10 or more; or
    (ii) the development is to be carried out on a site having an area of 0.5 hectare or more and it is not known whether the development falls within paragraph (c)(i);
(d) the provision of a building or buildings where the floor space to be created by the development is 1,000 square metres or more; or
(e) development carried out on a site having an area of 1 hectare or more;

'requisite notice' means notice in the appropriate form set out in Schedule 3 to this Order or in a form substantially to the like effect;

'waste development' means any operational development designed to be used wholly or mainly for the purpose of, or a material change of use to, treating, storing, processing or disposing of refuse or waste materials.

NOTES

Para (2): in sub-para (a) words 'an EIA application' in square brackets substituted by SI 1999/293, reg 35(6). Date in force: 14 March 1999: see SI 1999/293, reg 1(1).
Para (7): definition 'EIA application' substituted by SI 1999/293, reg 35(7). Date in force: 14 March 1999: see SI 1999/293, reg 1(1).

10 Consultations before the grant of permission

(1)   Before granting planning permission for development which, in their opinion, falls within a category set out in the table below, a local planning authority shall consult the authority or person mentioned in relation to that category, except where—
(i) the local planning authority are the authority so mentioned;
(ii) the local planning authority are required to consult the authority so mentioned under articles 11 or 12; or
(iii) the authority or person so mentioned has advised the local planning authority that they do not wish to be consulted.

[(1A)   The exception in article 10(1)(iii) shall not apply where, in the opinion of the local planning authority, development falls within paragraph (zb) of the table below.]

TABLE

Para	Description of Development	Consultee
(a)	Development likely to affect land in Greater London or in a metropolitan county [or, in relation to Wales, land in the area of another local planning authority]	The local planning authority concerned
(b)	Development likely to affect land in a non-metropolitan county [in England], other than land in a National Park	The district planning authority concerned*
(c)	Development likely to affect land in a National Park [in England]	The county planning authority concerned
(d)	Development within an area which has been notified to the local planning authority by the Health and Safety Executive for the purpose of this provision because of the presence within the vicinity of toxic, highly reactive, explosive or inflammable substances and which involves the provision of— (i) residential accommodation; (ii) more than 250 square metres of retail floor space; (iii) more than 500 square metres of office floor space; or (iv) more than 750 square metres of floor space to be used for an industrial process, or which is otherwise likely to result in a material increase in the number of persons working within or visiting the notified area	The Health and Safety Executive
(e)	Development likely to result in a material increase in the volume or a material change in the character of traffic— (i) entering or leaving a trunk road; or	In England, the Secretary of State for Transport and, in Wales, the Secretary of State for Wales
	(ii) using a level crossing over a railway	The operator of the network which includes or consists of the railway in question, and in England, the Secretary of State for Transport and, in Wales, the Secretary of State for Wales
(f)	Development likely to result in a material increase in the volume or a material change in the character of traffic entering or leaving a classified road or proposed highway	The local highway authority concerned
(g)	Development likely to prejudice the improvement or construction of a classified road or proposed highway	The local highway authority concerned
(h)	Development involving— (i) the formation, laying out or alteration of any means of access to a highway (other than a trunk road); or	The local highway authority concerned

Para	Description of Development	Consultee
	(ii) the construction of a highway or private means of access to premises affording access to a road in relation to which a toll order is in force	The local highway authority concerned, and in the case of a road subject to a concession, the concessionaire
(i)	Development which consists of or includes the laying out or construction of a new street	The local highway authority
(j)	Development which involves the provision of a building or pipe-line in an area of coal working notified by the Coal Authority to the local planning authority	The Coal Authority
(k)	Development involving or including mining operations	The [Environment Agency]
(l)	Development within three kilometres of Windsor Castle, Windsor Great Park, or Windsor Home Park, or within 800 metres of any other royal palace or park, which might affect the amenities (including security) of that palace or park	The Secretary of State for National Heritage
(m)	Development of land in Greater London involving the demolition, in whole or part, or the material alteration of a listed building	The Historic Buildings and Monuments Commission for England
(n)	Development likely to affect the site of a scheduled monument	In England, the Historic Buildings and Monuments Commission for England, and, in Wales, the Secretary of State for Wales
(o)	Development likely to affect any garden or park of special historic interest which is registered in accordance with section 8C of the Historic Buildings and Ancient Monuments Act 1953 (register of gardens) and which is classified as Grade I or Grade II.	The Historic Buildings and Monuments Commission for England
(p)	Development involving the carrying out of works or operations in the bed of or on the banks of a river or stream	The [Environment Agency]
(q)	Development for the purpose of refining or storing mineral oils and their derivatives	The [Environment Agency]
(r)	Development involving the use of land for the deposit of refuse or waste	The [Environment Agency]
(s)	Development relating to the retention, treatment or disposal of sewage, trade-waste, slurry or sludge (other than the laying of sewers, the construction of pumphouses in a line of sewers, the construction of septic tanks and cesspools serving single dwellinghouses or single caravans or single buildings in which not more than ten people will normally reside, work or congregate, and works ancillary thereto)	The [Environment Agency]
(t)	Development relating to the use of land as a cemetery	The [Environment Agency]

Para	Description of Development	Consultee
(u)	Development— (i) in or likely to affect a site of special scientific interest of which notification has been given, or has effect as if given, to the local planning authority by [English Nature] or the Countryside Council for Wales, in accordance with section 28 of the Wildlife and Countryside Act 1981 (areas of special scientific interest); or (ii) within an area which has been notified to the local planning authority by [English Nature] or the Countryside Council for Wales, and which is within two kilometres of a site of special scientific interest of which notification has been given or has effect as if given as aforesaid	The Council which gave, or is to be regarded as having given, the notice
(v)	Development involving any land on which there is a theatre	The Theatres Trust
(w)	Development which is not for agricultural purposes and is not in accordance with the provisions of a development plan and involves— (i) the loss of not less than 20 hectares of grades 1, 2 or 3a agricultural land which is for the time being used (or was last used) for agricultural purposes; or (ii) the loss of less than 20 hectares of grades 1, 2 or 3a agricultural land which is for the time being used (or was last used) for agricultural purposes, in circumstances in which the development is likely to lead to a further loss of agricultural land amounting cumulatively to 20 hectares or more	In England, the Minister of Agriculture, Fisheries and Food and, in Wales, the Secretary of State for Wales
(x)	Development within 250 metres of land which— (i) is or has, at any time in the 30 years before the relevant application, been used for the deposit of refuse or waste; and (ii) has been notified to the local planning authority by the waste regulation authority for the purposes of this provision	The waste regulation authority concerned
(y)	Development for the purposes of fish farming	The [Environment Agency]
[(z)	Development which: (i) is likely to prejudice the use, or lead to the loss of use, of land being used as a playing field; or (ii) is on land which has been: (aa) used as a playing field at any time in the 5 years before the making of the relevant application and which remains undeveloped; or (bb) allocated for use as a playing field in a development plan or in proposals for such a plan or its alteration or replacement; or	In England, the Sports Council for England; in Wales, the Sports Council for Wales]

Para	Description of Development	Consultee
	(iii) involves the replacement of the grass surface of a playing pitch on a playing field with an artificial, man-made or composite surface	
[(za)	Development likely to affect (i) any inland waterway (whether natural or artificial) or reservoir owned or managed by the British Waterways Board; or (ii) any canal feeder channel, watercourse, let off or culvert, which is within an area which has been notified for the purposes of this provision to the local planning authority by the British Waterways Board	The British Waterways Board]
[(zb)	Development (i) involving the siting of new establishments; or (ii) consisting of modifications to existing establishments which could have significant repercussions on major-accident hazards; or (iii) including transport links, locations frequented by the public and residential areas in the vicinity of existing establishments, where the siting or development is such as to increase the risk or consequences of a major accident.	The Health and Safety Executive and the Environment Agency, and, where it appears to the local planning authority that an area of particular natural sensitivity or interest may be affected, in England, [English Nature], or in Wales, the Countryside Council for Wales.]

* For cases where functions have been transferred from the county council to the district council or vice versa see regulation 5 of the Local Government Changes for England Regulations 1994 (SI 1994/867) and section 1 of the Act.

(2)   In the above table—

(a)   in paragraph (d)(iv), 'industrial process' means a process for or incidental to any of the following purposes—

    (i)   the making of any article or part of any article (including a ship or vessel, or a film, video or sound recording);

    (ii)   the altering, repairing, maintaining, ornamenting, finishing, cleaning, washing, packing, canning, adapting for sale, breaking up or demolition of any article; or

    (iii) the getting, dressing or treatment of minerals in the course of any trade or business other than agriculture, and other than a process carried out on land used as a mine or adjacent to and occupied together with a mine (and in this sub-paragraph, 'mine' means any site on which mining operations are carried out);

(b)   in paragraph (e)(ii), 'network' and 'operator' have the same meaning as in Part I of the Railways Act 1993 (the provision of railway services);

(c)   in paragraphs (f) and (g), 'classified road' means a highway or proposed highway which—

    (i)   is a classified road or a principal road by virtue of section 12(1) of the Highways Act 1980 (general provision as to principal and classified roads); or

    (ii)   is classified for the purposes of any enactment by the Secretary of State by virtue of section 12(3) of that Act;

(d)   in paragraph (h), 'concessionaire', 'road subject to a concession' and 'toll order' have the same meaning as in Part I of the New Roads and Street Works Act 1991 (new roads in England and Wales);

(e)   in paragraph (i), 'street' has the same meaning as in section 48(1) of the New Roads and Street Works Act 1991 (streets, street works and undertakers), and 'new street' includes a continuation of an existing street;

(f)   in paragraph (m), 'listed building' has the same meaning as in section 1 of the Planning (Listed Buildings and Conservation Areas) Act 1990 (listing of buildings of special architectural or historic interest);

(g)   in paragraph (n), 'scheduled monument' has the same meaning as in section 1(11) of the Ancient Monuments and Archaeological Areas Act 1979 (schedule of monuments);

(h)   in paragraph (s), 'slurry' means animal faeces and urine (whether or not water has been added for handling), and 'caravan' has the same meaning as for the purposes of Part I of the Caravan Sites and Control of Development Act 1960 (caravan sites);

(i)   in paragraph (u), 'site of special scientific interest' means land to which section 28(1) of the Wildlife and Countryside Act 1981 (areas of special scientific interest) applies;

(j)   in paragraph (v), 'theatre' has the same meaning as in section 5 of the Theatres Trust Act 1976 (interpretation); . . .

(k)   in paragraph (x), 'waste regulation authority' has the same meaning as in section 30(1) of the Environmental Protection Act 1990 (authorities for purposes of Part II)[; . . .

(l)   in paragraph (z)—

(i) 'playing field' means the whole of a site which encompasses at least one playing pitch;

(ii) 'playing pitch' means a delineated area which, together with any run-off area, is of 0.4 hectares or more, and which is used for association football, American football, rugby, cricket, hockey, lacrosse, rounders, baseball, softball, Australian football, Gaelic football, shinty, hurling, polo or cycle polo][; and

(m) the expressions used in paragraph (zb), have the same meaning as in Council Directive 96/82/EC on the control of major-accident hazards involving dangerous substances.]

(3)   The Secretary of State may give directions to a local planning authority requiring that authority to consult any person or body named in the directions, in any case or class of case specified in the directions.

(4)   Where, by or under this article, a local planning authority are required to consult any person or body ('the consultee') before granting planning permission—

(a) they shall, unless an applicant has served a copy of an application for planning permission on the consultee, give notice of the application to the consultee; and

(b) they shall not determine the application until at least 14 days after the date on which notice is given under paragraph (a) or, if earlier, 14 days after the date of service of a copy of the application on the consultee by the applicant.

(5)   The local planning authority shall, in determining the application, take into account any representations received from a consultee.

NOTES

Para (1A): inserted by SI 1999/981, reg 6(1), (2)(a). Date in force: 20 April 1999: see SI 1999/981, reg 1(1).

Table: in para (u) words 'English Nature' in square brackets in both places they occur substituted by virtue of the Countryside and Rights of Way Act 2000, s 73(2). Date in force: 30 January 2001: see the Countryside and Rights of Way Act 2000, s 103(2).

Table: in para (zb) words 'English Nature' in square brackets substituted by virtue of the Countryside and Rights of Way Act 2000, s 73(2). Date in force: 30 January 2001: see the Countryside and Rights of Way Act 2000, s 103(2).

Table: words in square brackets in paras (a), (b), (c) inserted by SI 1996/525, art 3, Schedule, para 20(2).

Table: words in square brackets in paras (k), (p), (q), (r), (s), (t), (y) substituted by the Environment Act 1995, s 120, Sch 22, para 233(1).

Table: para (z) inserted by SI 1996/1817, art 2.

Table: para (za) inserted by SI 1997/858, art 2.

Table: para (zb) inserted by SI 1999/981, reg 6(1), (2)(b). Date in force: 20 April 1999: see SI 1999/981, reg 1(1).

Para (2): word 'and' at the end of para (j) revoked, para (l) and the word 'and' immediately preceding it inserted, by SI 1996/1817, art 3.

Para (2): word 'and' at the end of para (k) revoked by SI 1999/981, reg 6(1), (3)(a). Date in force: 20 April 1999: see SI 1999/981, reg 1(1).

Para (2): para (m) and the word 'and' immediately preceding it inserted by SI 1999/981, reg 6(1), (3)(b). Date in force: 20 April 1999: see SI 1999/981, reg 1(1).

SCHEDULE 3
NOTICE UNDER ARTICLE 8 OF APPLICATION FOR PLANNING PERMISSION

Article 8

Town and Country Planning (General Development Procedure) Order 1995

NOTICE UNDER ARTICLE 8

(*to be published in a newspaper, displayed on or near the site, or served on owners and/or occupiers of adjoining land*)

Proposed development at (a)...

I give notice that (b)...

is applying to the (c)..Council

for planning permission to (d)...

The proposed development does not accord with the provisions of the development plan in force in the area in which the land to which the application relates is situated*

Members of the public may inspect copies of:
— the application
— the plans
— and other documents submitted with it

at (e)...during

all reasonable hours until (I)...

Anyone who wishes to make representations about this application should write to the   Council   at   (g)
....

.... by (f) ....

Signed...

. . . .
(Council's authorised officer)

On behalf of...............................Council

Date..

*delete where inappropriate

Insert:
(a)   address or location of the proposed development
(b)   applicant's name

(c)   name of Council
(d)   description of the proposed development
(e)   address at which the application may be inspected
(f)   date giving a period of 21 days, beginning with the date when the notice is first displayed on or near the site or served on an owner and/or occupier of adjoining land, or a period of 14 days, beginning with the date when the notice is published in a newspaper (as the case may be)
(g)   address of Council

Town and Country Planning (General Development Procedure) Order 1995

NOTICE UNDER ARTICLE 8 OF APPLICATION FOR PLANNING PERMISSION ACCOMPANIED BY AN ENVIRONMENTAL STATEMENT

(to be published in a newspaper and displayed on or near the site)

Proposed development at (a)..

I give notice that (b)..

is applying to the (c)..Council

for planning permission to (d)..

and that the application is accompanied by an environmental statement

The proposed development does not accord with the provisions of the development plan in force in the area in which the land to which the application relates is situated*

Members of the public may inspect copies of:
— the application
— the plans
— the environmental statement

—   and other documents submitted with the application

at (e)..during

all reasonable hours until (f)..

Members of the public may obtain copies of the environmental statement from (g)
....

so long as stocks last, at a charge of (h)..

Anyone who wishes to make representations about this application should write to the   Council   at   (i)
....

by (f) ....

Signed..

. . . .

(Council's authorised officer)

On behalf of...................................Council

Date..

*delete where inappropriate

Insert:
(a)   address or location of the proposed development
(b)   applicant's name
(c)   name of Council
(d)   description of the proposed development
(e)   address at which the application may be inspected
(f)   date giving a period of 21 days, beginning with the date when the notice is first displayed on or near the site, or a period of 14 days, beginning with the date when the notice is published in a newspaper (as the case may be)
(g)   address from where copies of the environmental statement may be obtained (whether or not the same as (e))
(h)   amount of charge, if any
(i)   address of Council

Town and Country Planning (Environmental Impact Assessment) (England and Wales) (Amendment) Regulations 2000 (SI 2000/2867)

Town and Country Planning (Environmental Impact Assessment) (England and Wales) (Amendment) Regulations 2000

2000 No 2867

Made   18th October 2000

Laid before Parliament   25th October 2000

Coming into force   15th November 2000

The Secretary of State for the Environment, Transport and the Regions, as respects England and Wales, being a designated Minister for the purposes of section 2(2) of the European Communities Act 1972, in relation to measures relating to the requirement for an assessment of the impact on the environment of projects likely to have significant effects on the environment, in exercise of the powers conferred upon him by that section and of all other powers enabling him in that behalf, hereby makes the following Regulations:—

I   Citation, commencement, interpretation and extent

(1)   These Regulations may be cited as the Town and Country Planning (Environmental Impact Assessment) (England and Wales) (Amendment) Regulations 2000 and shall come into force on 15th November 2000.

(2)   In these Regulations, 'the Regulations' means the Town and Country Planning (Environmental Impact Assessment) (England and Wales) Regulations 1999.

(3)   These Regulations extend to England and Wales only.

2   Amendment of the Regulations

(1)   The Regulations shall be amended as follows.

(2)   In regulation 2 (interpretation)—
    (a) after the definition of 'the Act' insert—
       '"the 1991 Act" means the Planning and Compensation Act 1991;
       "the 1995 Act" means the Environment Act 1995;';
    (b) after the definition of 'the Directive' insert—
       '"EEA State" means a State party to the Agreement on the European Economic Area;';
    (c) after the definition of 'appropriate register' (included in the definition of 'register') insert—
       '"relevant mineral planning authority" means the body to whom it falls, fell, or would, but for a direction under paragraph—
       (a) 7 of Schedule 2 to the 1991 Act;
       (b) 13 of Schedule 13 to the 1995 Act; or
       (c) 8 of Schedule 14 to the 1995 Act,
          fall to determine the ROMP application in question;';
    (d) after the definition of 'relevant planning authority' insert—
       '"ROMP application" means an application to a relevant mineral planning authority to determine the conditions to which a planning permission is to be subject under paragraph—
       (a) 2(2) of Schedule 2 to the 1991 Act (registration of old mining permissions);
       (b) 9(1) of Schedule 13 to the 1995 Act (review of old mineral planning permissions); or
       (c) 6(1) of Schedule 14 to the 1995 Act (periodic review of mineral planning permissions);
       "ROMP development" means development which has yet to be carried out and which is authorised by a planning permission in respect of which a ROMP application has been or is to be made;';
    (e) after paragraph (5) add—
       '(6) In its application to Wales, these Regulations shall have effect, with any necessary amendments, as if each reference to "the Secretary of State" were a reference to "the National Assembly for Wales".'

(3)   In regulation 12 (procedure to facilitate preparation of environmental statements)—
    (a) in paragraph (4), before the words 'body has' and 'body shall' insert 'authority or';
    (b) in paragraph (6) for the words 'a body, including the relevant planning authority' substitute 'an authority or body'.

(4)   In regulations 26 to 28, for each reference to 'Member State' substitute 'EEA State'.

(5)   After regulation 26 (unauthorised development with significant transboundary effects) add—
    'ROMP Applications

26A

General application of the Regulations to ROMP applications

(1)   These Regulations shall apply to—
    (a) a ROMP application as they apply to an application for planning permission;
    (b) ROMP development as they apply to development in respect of which an application for planning permission is, has been or is to be made;
    (c) a relevant mineral planning authority as they apply to a relevant planning authority;
    (d) a person making a ROMP application as they apply to an applicant for planning permission; and
    (e) the determination of a ROMP application as they apply to the granting of a planning permission,
subject to the modifications and additions set out below.

Modification of provisions on prohibition of granting planning permission

(2)   In regulation 3(1) (prohibition on granting planning permission without consideration of environmental information)—
    (a) in paragraph (a) for the words "these Regulations" substitute "the Town and Country Planning (Environmental Impact Assessment) (England and Wales) (Amendment) Regulations 2000";
    (b) in paragraph (b) for the words "3 or 4 (applications for planning permission)" substitute "11 (other consents)";
    (c) for the words "determined in accordance with paragraph (3) of article 20 (time periods for decision) of the Order" substitute "the date on which a ROMP application has been made which complies with the provisions of paragraphs 2(3) to (5) and 4 (1) of Schedule 2 to the 1991 Act, 9(2) of Schedule 13 to the 1995 Act, or 6(2) of Schedule 14 to the 1995 Act".

Modification of provisions on application to local planning authority without an environmental statement

(3)   In regulation 7(4) (application made to a local planning authority without an environmental statement)—
    (a) for the word "three" substitute "six"; and
    (b) after "the notification" insert ", or within such other period as may be agreed with the authority in writing,".

Disapplication of Regulations and modification of provisions on application referred to or appealed to the Secretary of State without an environmental statement

(4)   Regulations 7(5) and (6), 8(5) and (6), 9(6) and (7), 22, and 32 shall not apply.

(5)   In regulation 8(4) (application referred to the Secretary of State without an environmental statement) and 9(5) (appeal to the Secretary of State without an environmental statement)—
  (a) for the word "three" substitute "six";
  (b) after "the notification" insert ", or within such other period as may be agreed with the Secretary of State in writing,".

Substitution of references to section 78 right of appeal and modification of provisions on appeal to the Secretary of State without an environmental statement

(6)   In regulations 9(1) and 15(b), for the references to "section 78 (right to appeal against planning decisions and failure to take such decisions)" substitute— "paragraph 5(2) of Schedule 2 to the 1991 Act, paragraph 11(1) of Schedule 13 to the 1995 Act or paragraph 9(1) of Schedule 14 to the 1995 Act (right of appeal)".

(7)   In regulation 9(2) (appeal to the Secretary of State without an environmental statement) omit the words ", except by refusing planning permission,".

Modification of provisions on preparation, publicity and procedures on submission of environmental statements

(8)   In regulations 10(9) and 11(6) for the words "an application for planning permission for" substitute "a ROMP application which relates to another planning permission which authorises".

(9)   In regulation 13 (procedure where an environmental statement is submitted to a local planning authority) after paragraph (3) insert—

"(3A) Where an applicant submits an environmental statement to the authority in accordance with paragraph (1), the provisions of article 8 of and Schedule 3 to the Order (publicity for applications for planning permission) shall apply to a ROMP application under paragraph—
  (a) 2(2) of Schedule 2 to the 1991 Act; and
  (b) 6(1) of Schedule 14 to the 1995 Act,
as they apply to a planning application falling within paragraph 8(2) of the Order except that for the references in the notice in Schedule 3 to the Order to 'planning permission' there shall be substituted 'determination of the conditions to which a planning permission is to be subject' and that notice shall refer to the relevant provisions of the 1991 or 1995 Act pursuant to which the application is made."

(10)   In regulation 14 (publicity where an environmental statement is submitted after the planning application)—

(a) in paragraph (2)(a) for the words 'and that he is the applicant for planning permission' substitute—
", that he has applied for determination of the conditions to which a planning permission is to be subject, the relevant provisions of the 1991 or 1995 Act pursuant to which the application is made";

(b) in paragraph (6) for the words—
(i) "(unless disposed to refuse the permission sought) suspend consideration of the application or appeal until receipt of the statement and the other documents mentioned in paragraph (5)" substitute—
"suspend consideration of the application or appeal until the date specified by the authority or the Secretary of State for submission of the environmental statement and compliance with paragraph (5)";
(ii) "so mentioned" substitute "mentioned in paragraph (5)".

(11) In regulation 15 (provision of copies of environmental statements and further information for the Secretary of State on referral or appeal), in paragraph (a) for "section 77" substitute "paragraph 7(1) of Schedule 2 to the 1991 Act, paragraph 13(1) of Schedule 13 to the 1995 Act or paragraph 8(1) of Schedule 14 to the 1995 Act".

(12) In regulation 17 (availability of copies of environmental statements) after the words "the Order" insert "(as applied by regulation 13(3A) or by paragraph 9(5) of Schedule 13 to the 1995 Act),".

(13) In regulation 19 (further information and evidence respecting environmental statements)—
(a) in paragraph (3) for the words "applicant for planning permission or the appellant (as the case may be)" substitute—
"person who has applied for or who has appealed in relation to the determination of the conditions to which the planning permission is to be subject, the relevant provisions of the 1991 or 1995 Act pursuant to which the application is made";
(b) in paragraph (7) after the words "application or appeal" insert "until the date specified by them or him for submission of the further information".

Modification of provisions on application to the High Court and giving of directions

(14) For regulation 30 (application to the High Court) substitute—

"Application to the High Court

30

For the purposes of Part XII of the Act (validity of certain decisions), the reference in section 288, as applied by paragraph 9(3) of Schedule 2 to the 1991 Act, paragraph 16(4) of Schedule 13 to the 1995 Act or paragraph 9(4) of Schedule 14 to the 1995 Act, to action of the Secretary of State which is not within the powers of the Act shall be taken to extend to the determination of a ROMP application by the Secretary of State in contravention of regulation 3.".

(15)   The direction making power substituted by regulation 35(8) shall apply to ROMP development as it applies to development in respect of which a planning application is made.

Suspension of minerals development

(16)   Where the authority, the Secretary of State or an inspector notifies the applicant or appellant, as the case may be, that—
   (a) the submission of an environmental statement is required under regulation 7(2), 8(2) or 9(4) then such notification shall specify the period within which the environmental statement and compliance with regulation 14(5) is required; or
   (b) a statement should contain additional information under regulation 19(1) then such notification shall specify the period within which that information is to be provided.

(17)   Subject to paragraph (18), the planning permission to which the ROMP application relates shall not authorise any minerals development (unless the Secretary of State has made a screening direction to the effect that the ROMP development is not EIA development) if the applicant or the appellant does not—
   (a) write to the authority or Secretary of State within the six week or other period agreed pursuant to regulations 7(4), 8(4) or 9(5);
   (b) submit an environmental statement and comply with regulation 14(5) within the period specified by the authority or the Secretary of State in accordance with paragraph (16) or within such extended period as is agreed in writing; or
   (c) provide additional information within the period specified by the authority, the Secretary of State or an inspector in accordance with paragraph (16) or within such extended period as is agreed in writing.

(18)   Where paragraph (17) applies, the planning permission shall not authorise any minerals development from the end of—
   (a) the relevant six week or other period agreed in writing as referred to in paragraph (17)(a);
   (b) the period specified or agreed in writing as referred to in paragraphs (17)(b) and (c),

("suspension of minerals development") until the applicant has complied with all of the provisions referred to in paragraph (17) which are relevant to the application or appeal in question.

(19)   Particulars of the suspension of minerals development and the date when that suspension ends must be entered in the appropriate part of the register as soon as reasonably practicable.

(20)   Paragraph (17) shall not affect any minerals development carried out under the planning permission before the date of suspension of minerals development.

(21)   For the purposes of paragraphs (17) to (20) "minerals development" means development consisting of the winning and working of minerals, or involving the depositing of mineral waste.

Determination of conditions and right of appeal on non-determination

(22)   Where it falls to—
   (a)   a mineral planning authority to determine a Schedule 1 or a Schedule 2 application, paragraph 2(6)(b) of Schedule 2 to the 1991 Act, paragraph 9(9) of Schedule 13 to the 1995 Act or paragraph 6(8) of Schedule 14 to the 1995 Act shall not have effect to treat the authority as having determined the conditions to which any relevant planning permission is to be subject unless either the mineral planning authority has adopted a screening opinion or the Secretary of State has made a screening direction to the effect that the ROMP development in question is not EIA development;
   (b)   a mineral planning authority or the Secretary of State to determine a Schedule 1 or a Schedule 2 application—
      (i)   section 69 (register of applications, etc), and any provisions of the Order made by virtue of that section, shall have effect with any necessary amendments as if references to applications for planning permission included ROMP applications under paragraph 9(1) of Schedule 13 to the 1995 Act and paragraph 6(1) of Schedule 14 to the 1995 Act; and
      (ii)   where the relevant mineral planning authority is not the authority required to keep the register, the relevant mineral planning authority must provide the authority required to keep it with such information and documents as that authority requires to comply with section 69 as applied by sub-paragraph (i), with regulation 20 as applied by paragraph (1), and with paragraph (19).

(23)   Where it falls to the mineral planning authority or the Secretary of State to determine an EIA application which is made under paragraph 2(2) of Schedule 2 to the 1991 Act, paragraph 4(4) of that Schedule shall not apply.

(24)   Where it falls to the mineral planning authority to determine an EIA application, the authority shall give written notice of their determination of the ROMP application within 16 weeks beginning with the date of receipt by the authority of the ROMP application or such extended period as may be agreed in writing between the applicant and the authority.

(25)   For the purposes of paragraph (24) a ROMP application is not received by the authority until—
   (a)   a document referred to by the applicant as an environmental statement for the purposes of these Regulations;
   (b)   any documents required to accompany that statement; and
   (c)   any additional information which the authority has notified the applicant that the environmental statement should contain,
has been received by the authority.

(26)   Where paragraph (22)(a) applies—
    (a) paragraph 5(2) of Schedule 2 to the 1991 Act, paragraph 11(1) of Schedule 13 to the 1995 Act and paragraph 9(1) of Schedule 14 to the 1995 Act (right of appeal) shall have effect as if there were also a right of appeal to the Secretary of State where the mineral planning authority have not given written notice of their determination of the ROMP application in accordance with paragraph (24); and
    (b) paragraph 5(5) of Schedule 2 to the 1991 Act, paragraph 11(2) of Schedule 13 to the 1995 Act and paragraph 9(2) of Schedule 14 to the 1995 Act (right of appeal) shall have effect as if they also provided for notice of appeal to be made within six months from the expiry of the 16 week or other period agreed pursuant to paragraph (24).

(27)   In determining for the purposes of paragraphs—
    (a) 2(6)(b) of Schedule 2 to the 1991 Act, 9(9) of Schedule 13 to the 1995 Act and 6(8) of Schedule 14 to the 1995 Act (determination of conditions); or
    (b) paragraph 5(5) of Schedule 2 to the 1991 Act, paragraph 11(2) of Schedule 13 to the 1995 Act and paragraph 9(2) of Schedule 14 to the 1995 Act (right of appeal) as applied by paragraph (26)(b),

the time which has elapsed without the mineral planning authority giving the applicant written notice of their determination in a case where the authority have notified an applicant in accordance with regulation 7(2) that the submission of an environmental statement is required and the Secretary of State has given a screening direction in relation to the ROMP development in question no account shall be taken of any period before the issue of the direction.

ROMP application by a mineral planning authority

(28)   Where a mineral planning authority proposes to make or makes a ROMP application to the Secretary of State under regulation 11 (other consents) of the General Regulations which is a Schedule 1 or a Schedule 2 application (or proposed application), these Regulations shall apply to that application or proposed application as they apply to a ROMP application referred to the Secretary of State under paragraph 7(1) of Schedule 2 to the 1991 Act, paragraph 13(1) of Schedule 13 to the 1995 Act or paragraph 8(1) of Schedule 14 to the 1995 Act (reference of applications to the Secretary of State) subject to the following modifications—
    (a) subject to paragraph (29) below, regulations 5, 6, 7, 9, 10, 11, 13 (save for the purposes of regulations 16(3) and (4)) 15 and 21(1) shall not apply;
    (b) in regulation 4 (general provisions relating to screening)—
        (i)   in paragraph (4), omit the words "and shall send a copy of such direction to the relevant planning authority";
        (ii) paragraph (9) shall be omitted;
    (c) in regulation 8(2) (application referred to the Secretary of State without an environmental statement), omit the words "and shall send a copy of that notification to the relevant planning authority";

(d) in regulation 12 (procedure to facilitate preparation of environmental statements)—

    (i) in sub-paragraph (3)(b) for the words "7(4)(a), or 8(4) or 9(5)" substitute "8(4)";

    (ii) in paragraph (4) omit the words "the relevant planning authority and";

(e) in regulation 14(2) (publicity where an environmental statement is submitted after the planning application)—

    (i) in sub-paragraph (a) omit the words "and the name and address of the relevant planning authority";

    (ii) for sub-paragraph (b) substitute—

        "(b) the date on which the application was made and that it has been made to the Secretary of State under regulation 11 of the General Regulations;";

(f) in regulation 16 (procedure where an environmental statement is submitted to the Secretary of State), in paragraph (2) omit the words "who shall send one copy to the relevant planning authority";

(g) in regulation 19(3) (further information and evidence respecting environmental statements)—

    (i) in sub-paragraph (a) omit the words "and the name and address of the relevant planning authority";

    (ii) for sub-paragraph (b) substitute—

        "(b) the date on which the application was made and that it has been made to the Secretary of State under regulation 11 of the General Regulations;";

(h) regulations 20 (availability of opinions, directions etc for inspection) and 21(2) (duties to inform the public and the Secretary of State of final decisions) shall apply as if the references to a "relevant planning authority" were references to a mineral planning authority.

(29) A mineral planning authority which is minded to make a ROMP application to the Secretary of State under regulation 11 of the General Regulations may request the Secretary of State in writing to make a screening direction, and paragraphs (3) and (4) of regulation 6 shall apply to such a request as they apply to a request made pursuant to regulation 5(6) except that in paragraph (3) the words ", and may request the relevant planning authority to provide such information as they can on any of those points" shall be omitted.

(30) A request under paragraph (29) shall be accompanied by—

(a) a plan sufficient to identify the land;

(b) a brief description of the nature and purpose of the ROMP development and of its possible effects on the environment; and

(c) such other information as the authority may wish to provide or make.

(31) An authority making a request under paragraph (29) shall send to the Secretary of State any additional information he may request in writing to enable him to make a direction.'

Signed by authority of the Secretary of State for the Environment, Transport and the Regions

Nick Raynsford
Minister of State,
Department of the Environment, Transport and the Regions

18th October 2000

Directive 2001/42/EC of the European Parliament and of the Council of 27 June 2001

on the assessment of the effects of certain plans and programmes on the environment

(OJ L 197, 21.7.2001, p 30)

Directive 2001/42/EC of the European Parliament and of the Council of 27 June 2001 on the assessment of the effects of certain plans and programmes on the environment

THE EUROPEAN PARLIAMENT AND THE COUNCIL OF THE EUROPEAN UNION,

Having regard to the Treaty establishing the European Community, and in particular Article 175(1) thereof,

Having regard to the proposal from the Commission,[1]

Having regard to the opinion of the Economic and Social Committee,[2]

Having regard to the opinion of the Committee of the Regions,[3]

Acting in accordance with the procedure laid down in Article 251 of the Treaty,[4] in the light of the joint text approved by the Conciliation Committee on 21 March 2001,

Whereas:

(1)   Article 174 of the Treaty provides that Community policy on the environment is to contribute to, inter alia, the preservation, protection and improvement of the quality of the environment, the protection of human health and the prudent and rational utilisation of natural resources and that it is to be based on the precautionary principle. Article 6 of the Treaty provides that environmental protection requirements are to be integrated into the definition of Community policies and activities, in particular with a view to promoting sustainable development.

(2)   The Fifth Environment Action Programme: Towards sustainability – A European Community programme of policy and action in relation to the environment and

sustainable development,[5] supplemented by Council Decision No 2179/98/EC[6] on its review, affirms the importance of assessing the likely environmental effects of plans and programmes.

(3)   The Convention on Biological Diversity requires Parties to integrate as far as possible and as appropriate the conservation and sustainable use of biological diversity into relevant sectoral or cross-sectoral plans and programmes.

(4)   Environmental assessment is an important tool for integrating environmental considerations into the preparation and adoption of certain plans and programmes which are likely to have significant effects on the environment in the Member States, because it ensures that such effects of implementing plans and programmes are taken into account during their preparation and before their adoption.

(5)   The adoption of environmental assessment procedures at the planning and programming level should benefit undertakings by providing a more consistent framework in which to operate by the inclusion of the relevant environmental information into decision making. The inclusion of a wider set of factors in decision making should contribute to more sustainable and effective solutions.

(6)   The different environmental assessment systems operating within Member States should contain a set of common procedural requirements necessary to contribute to a high level of protection of the environment.

(7)   The United Nations/Economic Commission for Europe Convention on Environmental Impact Assessment in a Transboundary Context of 25 February 1991, which applies to both Member States and other States, encourages the parties to the Convention to apply its principles to plans and programmes as well; at the second meeting of the Parties to the Convention in Sofia on 26 and 27 February 2001, it was decided to prepare a legally binding protocol on strategic environmental assessment which would supplement the existing provisions on environmental impact assessment in a transboundary context, with a view to its possible adoption on the occasion of the 5th Ministerial Conference "Environment for Europe" at an extraordinary meeting of the Parties to the Convention, scheduled for May 2003 in Kiev, Ukraine. The systems operating within the Community for environmental assessment of plans and programmes should ensure that there are adequate transboundary consultations where the implementation of a plan or programme being prepared in one Member State is likely to have significant effects on the environment of another Member State. The information on plans and programmes having significant effects on the environment of other States should be forwarded on a reciprocal and equivalent basis within an appropriate legal framework between Member States and these other States.

(8)   Action is therefore required at Community level to lay down a minimum environmental assessment framework, which would set out the broad principles of the environmental assessment system and leave the details to the Member States, having regard to the principle of subsidiarity. Action by the Community should not go beyond what is necessary to achieve the objectives set out in the Treaty.

(9)   This Directive is of a procedural nature, and its requirements should either be integrated into existing procedures in Member States or incorporated in specifically established procedures. With a view to avoiding duplication of the assessment, Member

States should take account, where appropriate, of the fact that assessments will be carried out at different levels of a hierarchy of plans and programmes.

(10)   All plans and programmes which are prepared for a number of sectors and which set a framework for future development consent of projects listed in Annexes I and II to Council Directive 85/337/EEC of 27 June 1985 on the assessment of the effects of certain public and private projects on the environment,[7] and all plans and programmes which have been determined to require assessment pursuant to Council Directive 92/43/EEC of 21 May 1992 on the conservation of natural habitats and of wild flora and fauna,[8] are likely to have significant effects on the environment, and should as a rule be made subject to systematic environmental assessment. When they determine the use of small areas at local level or are minor modifications to the above plans or programmes, they should be assessed only where Member States determine that they are likely to have significant effects on the environment.

(11)   Other plans and programmes which set the framework for future development consent of projects may not have significant effects on the environment in all cases and should be assessed only where Member States determine that they are likely to have such effects.

(12)   When Member States make such determinations, they should take into account the relevant criteria set out in this Directive.

(13)   Some plans or programmes are not subject to this Directive because of their particular characteristics.

(14)   Where an assessment is required by this Directive, an environmental report should be prepared containing relevant information as set out in this Directive, identifying, describing and evaluating the likely significant environmental effects of implementing the plan or programme, and reasonable alternatives taking into account the objectives and the geographical scope of the plan or programme; Member States should communicate to the Commission any measures they take concerning the quality of environmental reports.

(15)   In order to contribute to more transparent decision making and with the aim of ensuring that the information supplied for the assessment is comprehensive and reliable, it is necessary to provide that authorities with relevant environmental responsibilities and the public are to be consulted during the assessment of plans and programmes, and that appropriate time frames are set, allowing sufficient time for consultations, including the expression of opinion.

(16)   Where the implementation of a plan or programme prepared in one Member State is likely to have a significant effect on the environment of other Member States, provision should be made for the Member States concerned to enter into consultations and for the relevant authorities and the public to be informed and enabled to express their opinion.

(17)   The environmental report and the opinions expressed by the relevant authorities and the public, as well as the results of any transboundary consultation, should be taken into account during the preparation of the plan or programme and before its adoption or submission to the legislative procedure.

(18)   Member States should ensure that, when a plan or programme is adopted, the relevant authorities and the public are informed and relevant information is made available to them.

(19)   Where the obligation to carry out assessments of the effects on the environment arises simultaneously from this Directive and other Community legislation, such as Council Directive 79/409/EEC of 2 April 1979 on the conservation of wild birds,[9] Directive 92/43/EEC, or Directive 2000/60/EC of the European Parliament and the Council of 23 October 2000 establishing a framework for Community action in the field of water policy,[10] in order to avoid duplication of the assessment, Member States may provide for coordinated or joint procedures fulfilling the requirements of the relevant Community legislation.

(20)   A first report on the application and effectiveness of this Directive should be carried out by the Commission five years after its entry into force, and at seven-year intervals thereafter. With a view to further integrating environmental protection requirements, and taking into account the experience acquired, the first report should, if appropriate, be accompanied by proposals for amendment of this Directive, in particular as regards the possibility of extending its scope to other areas/sectors and other types of plans and programmes,

HAVE ADOPTED THIS DIRECTIVE:

Article 1

Objectives

The objective of this Directive is to provide for a high level of protection of the environment and to contribute to the integration of environmental considerations into the preparation and adoption of plans and programmes with a view to promoting sustainable development, by ensuring that, in accordance with this Directive, an environmental assessment is carried out of certain plans and programmes which are likely to have significant effects on the environment.

Article 2

Definitions

For the purposes of this Directive:
  (a) "plans and programmes" shall mean plans and programmes, including those co-financed by the European Community, as well as any modifications to them:
      — which are subject to preparation and/or adoption by an authority at national, regional or local level or which are prepared by an authority for

adoption, through a legislative procedure by Parliament or Government, and

— which are required by legislative, regulatory or administrative provisions;

(b) "environmental assessment" shall mean the preparation of an environmental report, the carrying out of consultations, the taking into account of the environmental report and the results of the consultations in decision-making and the provision of information on the decision in accordance with Articles 4 to 9;

(c) "environmental report" shall mean the part of the plan or programme documentation containing the information required in Article 5 and Annex I;

(d) "The public" shall mean one or more natural or legal persons and, in accordance with national legislation or practice, their associations, organisations or groups.

Article 3

Scope

1   An environmental assessment, in accordance with Articles 4 to 9, shall be carried out for plans and programmes referred to in paragraphs 2 to 4 which are likely to have significant environmental effects.

2   Subject to paragraph 3, an environmental assessment shall be carried out for all plans and programmes,

(a) which are prepared for agriculture, forestry, fisheries, energy, industry, transport, waste management, water management, telecommunications, tourism, town and country planning or land use and which set the framework for future development consent of projects listed in Annexes I and II to Directive 85/337/EEC, or

(b) which, in view of the likely effect on sites, have been determined to require an assessment pursuant to Article 6 or 7 of Directive 92/43/EEC.

3   Plans and programmes referred to in paragraph 2 which determine the use of small areas at local level and minor modifications to plans and programmes referred to in paragraph 2 shall require an environmental assessment only where the Member States determine that they are likely to have significant environmental effects.

4   Member States shall determine whether plans and programmes, other than those referred to in paragraph 2, which set the framework for future development consent of projects, are likely to have significant environmental effects.

5   Member States shall determine whether plans or programmes referred to in paragraphs 3 and 4 are likely to have significant environmental effects either through case-by-case examination or by specifying types of plans and programmes or by combining both approaches. For this purpose Member States shall in all cases take into account relevant criteria set out in Annex II, in order to ensure that plans and programmes with likely significant effects on the environment are covered by this Directive.

6   In the case-by-case examination and in specifying types of plans and programmes in accordance with paragraph 5, the authorities referred to in Article 6(3) shall be consulted.

7   Member States shall ensure that their conclusions pursuant to paragraph 5, including the reasons for not requiring an environmental assessment pursuant to Articles 4 to 9, are made available to the public.

8   The following plans and programmes are not subject to this Directive:
  — plans and programmes the sole purpose of which is to serve national defence or civil emergency,
  — financial or budget plans and programmes.

9   This Directive does not apply to plans and programmes co-financed under the current respective programming periods[11] for Council Regulations (EC) No 1260/1999[12] and (EC) No 1257/1999.[13]

Article 4

General obligations

1   The environmental assessment referred to in Article 3 shall be carried out during the preparation of a plan or programme and before its adoption or submission to the legislative procedure.

2   The requirements of this Directive shall either be integrated into existing procedures in Member States for the adoption of plans and programmes or incorporated in procedures established to comply with this Directive.

3   Where plans and programmes form part of a hierarchy, Member States shall, with a view to avoiding duplication of the assessment, take into account the fact that the assessment will be carried out, in accordance with this Directive, at different levels of the hierarchy. For the purpose of, inter alia, avoiding duplication of assessment, Member States shall apply Article 5(2) and (3).

Article 5

Environmental report

1   Where an environmental assessment is required under Article 3(1), an environmental report shall be prepared in which the likely significant effects on the environment of implementing the plan or programme, and reasonable alternatives taking into account the objectives and the geographical scope of the plan or programme, are identified, described and evaluated. The information to be given for this purpose is referred to in Annex I.

2   The environmental report prepared pursuant to paragraph 1 shall include the information that may reasonably be required taking into account current knowledge and methods of assessment, the contents and level of detail in the plan or programme, its stage in the decision-making process and the extent to which certain matters are more appropriately assessed at different levels in that process in order to avoid duplication of the assessment.

3   Relevant information available on environmental effects of the plans and programmes and obtained at other levels of decision-making or through other Community legislation may be used for providing the information referred to in Annex I.

4   The authorities referred to in Article 6(3) shall be consulted when deciding on the scope and level of detail of the information which must be included in the environmental report.

Article 6

Consultations

1   The draft plan or programme and the environmental report prepared in accordance with Article 5 shall be made available to the authorities referred to in paragraph 3 of this Article and the public.

2   The authorities referred to in paragraph 3 and the public referred to in paragraph 4 shall be given an early and effective opportunity within appropriate time frames to express their opinion on the draft plan or programme and the accompanying environmental report before the adoption of the plan or programme or its submission to the legislative procedure.

3   Member States shall designate the authorities to be consulted which, by reason of their specific environmental responsibilities, are likely to be concerned by the environmental effects of implementing plans and programmes.

4   Member States shall identify the public for the purposes of paragraph 2, including the public affected or likely to be affected by, or having an interest in, the decision-making subject to this Directive, including relevant non-governmental organisations, such as those promoting environmental protection and other organisations concerned.

5   The detailed arrangements for the information and consultation of the authorities and the public shall be determined by the Member States.

Article 7

Transboundary consultations

1   Where a Member State considers that the implementation of a plan or programme being prepared in relation to its territory is likely to have significant effects on the environment in another Member State, or where a Member State likely to be significantly affected so requests, the Member State in whose territory the plan or programme is being prepared shall, before its adoption or submission to the legislative procedure, forward a copy of the draft plan or programme and the relevant environmental report to the other Member State.

2   Where a Member State is sent a copy of a draft plan or programme and an environmental report under paragraph 1, it shall indicate to the other Member State whether it wishes to enter into consultations before the adoption of the plan or programme or its submission to the legislative procedure and, if it so indicates, the Member States concerned shall enter into consultations concerning the likely transboundary environmental effects of implementing the plan or programme and the measures envisaged to reduce or eliminate such effects.

Where such consultations take place, the Member States concerned shall agree on detailed arrangements to ensure that the authorities referred to in Article 6(3) and the public referred to in Article 6(4) in the Member State likely to be significantly affected are informed and given an opportunity to forward their opinion within a reasonable time-frame.

3   Where Member States are required under this Article to enter into consultations, they shall agree, at the beginning of such consultations, on a reasonable timeframe for the duration of the consultations.

Article 8

Decision making

The environmental report prepared pursuant to Article 5, the opinions expressed pursuant to Article 6 and the results of any transboundary consultations entered into pursuant to Article 7 shall be taken into account during the preparation of the plan or programme and before its adoption or submission to the legislative procedure.

Article 9

Information on the decision

1   Member States shall ensure that, when a plan or programme is adopted, the authorities referred to in Article 6(3), the public and any Member State consulted

under Article 7 are informed and the following items are made available to those so informed:

(a) the plan or programme as adopted;

(b) a statement summarising how environmental considerations have been integrated into the plan or programme and how the environmental report prepared pursuant to Article 5, the opinions expressed pursuant to Article 6 and the results of consultations entered into pursuant to Article 7 have been taken into account in accordance with Article 8 and the reasons for choosing the plan or programme as adopted, in the light of the other reasonable alternatives dealt with, and

(c) the measures decided concerning monitoring in accordance with Article 10.

2 The detailed arrangements concerning the information referred to in paragraph 1 shall be determined by the Member States.

Article 10

Monitoring

1 Member States shall monitor the significant environmental effects of the implementation of plans and programmes in order, inter alia, to identify at an early stage unforeseen adverse effects, and to be able to undertake appropriate remedial action.

2 In order to comply with paragraph 1, existing monitoring arrangements may be used if appropriate, with a view to avoiding duplication of monitoring.

Article 11

Relationship with other Community legislation

1 An environmental assessment carried out under this Directive shall be without prejudice to any requirements under Directive 85/337/EEC and to any other Community law requirements.

2 For plans and programmes for which the obligation to carry out assessments of the effects on the environment arises simultaneously from this Directive and other Community legislation, Member States may provide for coordinated or joint procedures fulfilling the requirements of the relevant Community legislation in order, inter alia, to avoid duplication of assessment.

3 For plans and programmes co-financed by the European Community, the environmental assessment in accordance with this Directive shall be carried out in conformity with the specific provisions in relevant Community legislation.

Article 12

Information, reporting and review

1   Member States and the Commission shall exchange information on the experience gained in applying this Directive.

2   Member States shall ensure that environmental reports are of a sufficient quality to meet the requirements of this Directive and shall communicate to the Commission any measures they take concerning the quality of these reports.

3   Before 21 July 2006 the Commission shall send a first report on the application and effectiveness of this Directive to the European Parliament and to the Council.

With a view further to integrating environmental protection requirements, in accordance with Article 6 of the Treaty, and taking into account the experience acquired in the application of this Directive in the Member States, such a report will be accompanied by proposals for amendment of this Directive, if appropriate. In particular, the Commission will consider the possibility of extending the scope of this Directive to other areas/sectors and other types of plans and programmes.

A new evaluation report shall follow at seven-year intervals.

4   The Commission shall report on the relationship between this Directive and Regulations (EC) No 1260/1999 and (EC) No 1257/1999 well ahead of the expiry of the programming periods provided for in those Regulations, with a view to ensuring a coherent approach with regard to this Directive and subsequent Community Regulations.

Article 13

Implementation of the Directive

1   Member States shall bring into force the laws, regulations and administrative provisions necessary to comply with this Directive before 21 July 2004. They shall forthwith inform the Commission thereof.

2   When Member States adopt the measures, they shall contain a reference to this Directive or shall be accompanied by such reference on the occasion of their official publication. The methods of making such reference shall be laid down by Member States.

3   The obligation referred to in Article 4(1) shall apply to the plans and programmes of which the first formal preparatory act is subsequent to the date referred to in paragraph 1. Plans and programmes of which the first formal preparatory act is before that date and which are adopted or submitted to the legislative procedure more than 24 months thereafter, shall be made subject to the obligation referred to in Article 4(1) unless Member States decide on a case by case basis that this is not feasible and inform the public of their decision.

4   Before 21 July 2004, Member States shall communicate to the Commission, in addition to the measures referred to in paragraph 1, separate information on the types of plans and programmes which, in accordance with Article 3, would be subject to an environmental assessment pursuant to this Directive. The Commission shall make this information available to the Member States. The information will be updated on a regular basis.

Article 14

Entry into force

This Directive shall enter into force on the day of its publication in the Official Journal of the European Communities.

Article 15

Addressees

This Directive is addressed to the Member States.

Done at Luxembourg, 27 June 2001.

For the European Parliament
The President
N. Fontaine

For the Council
The President
B. Rosengren

(1) OJ C 129, 25.4.1997, p. 14 and OJ C 83, 25.3.1999, p. 13.
(2) OJ C 287, 22.9.1997, p. 101.
(3) OJ C 64, 27.2.1998, p. 63 and OJ C 374, 23.12.1999, p. 9.
(4) Opinion of the European Parliament of 20 October 1998 (OJ C 341, 9.11.1998, p. 18), confirmed on 16 September 1999 (OJ C 54, 25.2.2000, p. 76), Council Common Position of 30 March 2000 (OJ C 137, 16.5.2000, p. 11) and Decision of the European Parliament of 6 September 2000 (OJ C 135, 7.5.2001, p. 155). Decision of the European Parliament of 31 May 2001 and Decision of the Council of 5 June 2001.
(5) OJ C 138, 17.5.1993, p. 5.
(6) OJ L 275, 10.10.1998, p. 1.
(7) OJ L 175, 5.7.1985, p. 40. Directive as amended by Directive 97/11/EC (OJ L 73, 14.3.1997, p. 5).
(8) OJ L 206, 22.7.1992, p. 7. Directive as last amended by Directive 97/62/EC (OJ L 305, 8.11.1997, p. 42).
(9) OJ L 103, 25.4.1979, p. 1. Directive as last amended by Directive 97/49/EC (OJ L 223, 13.8.1997, p. 9).
(10) OJ L 327, 22.12.2000, p. 1.

(11) The 2000–2006 programming period for Council Regulation (EC) No 1260/1999 and the 2000–2006 and 2000–2007 programming periods for Council Regulation (EC) No 1257/1999.

(12) Council Regulation (EC) No 1260/1999 of 21 June 1999 laying down general provisions on the Structural Funds (OJ L 161, 26.6.1999, p. 1).

(13) Council Regulation (EC) No 1257/1999 of 17 May 1999 on support for rural development from the European Agricultural Guidance and Guarantee Fund (EAGGF) and amending and repealing certain regulations (OJ L 160, 26.6.1999, p. 80).

ANNEX I

Information referred to in Article 5(1)

The information to be provided under Article 5(1), subject to Article 5(2) and (3), is the following:

(a)   an outline of the contents, main objectives of the plan or programme and relationship with other relevant plans and programmes;

(b)   the relevant aspects of the current state of the environment and the likely evolution thereof without implementation of the plan or programme;

(c)   the environmental characteristics of areas likely to be significantly affected;

(d)   any existing environmental problems which are relevant to the plan or programme including, in particular, those relating to any areas of a particular environmental importance, such as areas designated pursuant to Directives 79/409/EEC and 92/43/EEC;

(e)   the environmental protection objectives, established at international, Community or Member State level, which are relevant to the plan or programme and the way those objectives and any environmental considerations have been taken into account during its preparation;

(f)   the likely significant effects[1] on the environment, including on issues such as biodiversity, population, human health, fauna, flora, soil, water, air, climatic factors, material assets, cultural heritage including architectural and archaeological heritage, landscape and the interrelationship between the above factors;

(g)   the measures envisaged to prevent, reduce and as fully as possible offset any significant adverse effects on the environment of implementing the plan or programme;

(h)   an outline of the reasons for selecting the alternatives dealt with, and a description of how the assessment was undertaken including any difficulties (such as technical deficiencies or lack of know-how) encountered in compiling the required information;

(i)   a description of the measures envisaged concerning monitoring in accordance with Article 10;

(j)   a non-technical summary of the information provided under the above headings.

(1)   These effects should include secondary, cumulative, synergistic, short, medium and long-term permanent and temporary, positive and negative effects.

ANNEX II

Criteria for determining the likely significance of effects referred to in Article 3(5)

1   The characteristics of plans and programmes, having regard, in particular, to
— the degree to which the plan or programme sets a framework for projects and other activities, either with regard to the location, nature, size and operating conditions or by allocating resources,
— the degree to which the plan or programme influences other plans and programmes including those in a hierarchy,
— the relevance of the plan or programme for the integration of environmental considerations in particular with a view to promoting sustainable development,
— environmental problems relevant to the plan or programme,
— the relevance of the plan or programme for the implementation of Community legislation on the environment (e.g. plans and programmes linked to waste-management or water protection).

2   Characteristics of the effects and of the area likely to be affected, having regard, in particular, to
— the probability, duration, frequency and reversibility of the effects,
— the cumulative nature of the effects,
— the transboundary nature of the effects,
— the risks to human health or the environment (e.g. due to accidents),
— the magnitude and spatial extent of the effects (geographical area and size of the population likely to be affected),
— the value and vulnerability of the area likely to be affected due to:
— special natural characteristics or cultural heritage,
— exceeded environmental quality standards or limit values,
— intensive land-use,
— the effects on areas or landscapes which have a recognised national, Community or international protection status.

Directive 2003/35/EC of the European Parliament and of the Council of 26 May 2003

providing for public participation in respect of the drawing up of certain plans and programmes relating to the environment and amending with regard to public participation and access to justice Council Directives 85/337/EEC and 96/61/EC

Directive 2003/35/EC of the European Parliament and of the Council of 26 May 2003 providing for public participation in respect of the drawing up of certain plans and programmes relating to the environment and amending with regard to public participation and access to justice Council Directives 85/337/EEC and 96/61/EC*

THE EUROPEAN PARLIAMENT AND THE COUNCIL OF THE EUROPEAN UNION,

Having regard to the Treaty establishing the European Community, and in particular Article 175 thereof,

Having regard to the proposal from the Commission,[1]

Having regard to the opinion of the European Economic and Social Committee,[2]

Having regard to the opinion of the Committee of the Regions,[3]

Acting in accordance with the procedure laid down in Article 251 of the Treaty,[4] in the light of the joint text approved by the Conciliation Committee on 15 January 2003,

Whereas:

* NOTE: This Directive (Article 3) amends the EIA Directive to reflect the requirements of the UN/ECE Convention on Public Participation and Access to Justice.

(1)   Community legislation in the field of the environment aims to contribute to preserving, protecting and improving the quality of the environment and protecting human health.

(2)   Community environmental legislation includes provisions for public authorities and other bodies to take decisions which may have a significant effect on the environment as well as on personal health and well-being.

(3)   Effective public participation in the taking of decisions enables the public to express, and the decision-maker to take account of, opinions and concerns which may be relevant to those decisions, thereby increasing the accountability and transparency of the decision-making process and contributing to public awareness of environmental issues and support for the decisions taken.

(4) Participation, including participation by associations, organisations and groups, in particular non-governmental organisations promoting environmental protection, should accordingly be fostered, including inter alia by promoting environmental education of the public.

(5)   On 25 June 1998 the Community signed the UN/ECE Convention on Access to Information, Public Participation in Decision-Making and Access to Justice in Environmental Matters (the Århus Convention). Community law should be properly aligned with that Convention with a view to its ratification by the Community.

(6)   Among the objectives of the Århus Convention is the desire to guarantee rights of public participation in decision-making in environmental matters in order to contribute to the protection of the right to live in an environment which is adequate for personal health and well-being.

(7)   Article 6 of the Århus Convention provides for public participation in decisions on the specific activities listed in Annex I thereto and on activities not so listed which may have a significant effect on the environment.

(8)   Article 7 of the Århus Convention provides for public participation concerning plans and programmes relating to the environment.

(9)   Article 9(2) and (4) of the Århus Convention provides for access to judicial or other procedures for challenging the substantive or procedural legality of decisions, acts or omissions subject to the public participation provisions of Article 6 of the Convention.

(10)   Provision should be made in respect of certain Directives in the environmental area which require Member States to produce plans and programmes relating to the environment but which do not contain sufficient provisions on public participation, so as to ensure public participation consistent with the provisions of the Århus Convention, in particular Article 7 thereof. Other relevant Community legislation already provides for public participation in the preparation of plans and programmes and, for

the future, public participation requirements in line with the Århus Convention will be incorporated into the relevant legislation from the outset.

(11)   Council Directive 85/337/EEC of 27 June 1985 on the assessment of the effects of certain public and private projects on the environment,[5] and Council Directive 96/61/EC of 24 September 1996 concerning integrated pollution prevention and control[6] should be amended to ensure that they are fully compatible with the provisions of the Århus Convention, in particular Article 6 and Article 9(2) and (4) thereof.

(12)   Since the objective of the proposed action, namely to contribute to the implementation of the obligations arising under the Århus Convention, cannot be sufficiently achieved by the Member States and can therefore, by reason of the scale and effects of the action, be better achieved at Community level, the Community may adopt measures in accordance with the principle of subsidiarity as set out in Article 5 of the Treaty. In accordance with the principle of proportionality, as set out in that Article, this Directive does not go beyond what is necessary in order to achieve that objective,

HAVE ADOPTED THIS DIRECTIVE:

Article 1

Objective

The objective of this Directive is to contribute to the implementation of the obligations arising under the Århus Convention, in particular by:
(a) providing for public participation in respect of the drawing up of certain plans and programmes relating to the environment;
(b) improving the public participation and providing for provisions on access to justice within Council Directives 85/337/EEC and 96/61/EC.

Article 2

Public participation concerning plans and programmes

1   For the purposes of this Article, "the public" shall mean one or more natural or legal persons and, in accordance with national legislation or practice, their associations, organisations or groups.

2   Member States shall ensure that the public is given early and effective opportunities to participate in the preparation and modification or review of the plans or programmes required to be drawn up under the provisions listed in Annex I.

To that end, Member States shall ensure that:

(a) the public is informed, whether by public notices or other appropriate means such as electronic media where available, about any proposals for such plans or programmes or for their modification or review and that relevant information about such proposals is made available to the public including inter alia information about the right to participate in decision-making and about the competent authority to which comments or questions may be submitted;

(b) the public is entitled to express comments and opinions when all options are open before decisions on the plans and programmes are made;

(c) in making those decisions, due account shall be taken of the results of the public participation;

(d) having examined the comments and opinions expressed by the public, the competent authority makes reasonable efforts to inform the public about the decisions taken and the reasons and considerations upon which those decisions are based, including information about the public participation process.

3   Member States shall identify the public entitled to participate for the purposes of paragraph 2, including relevant non-governmental organisations meeting any requirements imposed under national law, such as those promoting environmental protection.

The detailed arrangements for public participation under this Article shall be determined by the Member States so as to enable the public to prepare and participate effectively.

Reasonable time-frames shall be provided allowing sufficient time for each of the different stages of public participation required by this Article.

4   This Article shall not apply to plans and programmes designed for the sole purpose of serving national defence or taken in case of civil emergencies.

5   This Article shall not apply to plans and programmes set out in Annex I for which a public participation procedure is carried out under Directive 2001/42/EC of the European Parliament and of the Council of 27 June 2001 on the assessment of the effects of certain plans and programmes on the environment[7] or under Directive 2000/60/EC of the European Parliament and of the Council of 23 October 2000 establishing a framework for Community action in the field of water policy.[8]

Article 3

Amendment of Directive 85/337/EEC

Directive 85/337/EEC is hereby amended as follows:

1   in Article 1(2), the following definitions shall be added:

"'the public' means: one or more natural or legal persons and, in accordance with national legislation or practice, their associations, organisations or groups;

'the public concerned' means: the public affected or likely to be affected by, or having an interest in, the environmental decision-making procedures referred to in Article 2(2); for the purposes of this definition, non-governmental organisations promoting environmental protection and meeting any requirements under national law shall be deemed to have an interest; "

2   in Article 1, paragraph 4 shall be replaced by the following:
"4   Member States may decide, on a case-by-case basis if so provided under national law, not to apply this Directive to projects serving national defence purposes, if they deem that such application would have an adverse effect on these purposes.";

3   in Article 2(3), points (a) and (b) shall be replaced by the following:
"(a) consider whether another form of assessment would be appropriate;
 (b) make available to the public concerned the information obtained under other forms of assessment referred to in point (a), the information relating to the exemption decision and the reasons for granting it.";

4   in Article 6, paragraphs 2 and 3 shall be replaced by the following paragraphs:
"2   The public shall be informed, whether by public notices or other appropriate means such as electronic media where available, of the following matters early in the environmental decision-making procedures referred to in Article 2(2) and, at the latest, as soon as information can reasonably be provided:
(a) the request for development consent;
(b) the fact that the project is subject to an environmental impact assessment procedure and, where relevant, the fact that Article 7 applies;
(c) details of the competent authorities responsible for taking the decision, those from which relevant information can be obtained, those to which comments or questions can be submitted, and details of the time schedule for transmitting comments or questions;
(d) the nature of possible decisions or, where there is one, the draft decision;
(e) an indication of the availability of the information gathered pursuant to Article 5;
(f) an indication of the times and places where and means by which the relevant information will be made available;
(g) details of the arrangements for public participation made pursuant to paragraph 5 of this Article.

3   Member States shall ensure that, within reasonable time-frames, the following is made available to the public concerned:
(a) any information gathered pursuant to Article 5;
(b) in accordance with national legislation, the main reports and advice issued to the competent authority or authorities at the time when the public concerned is informed in accordance with paragraph 2 of this Article;
(c) in accordance with the provisions of Directive 2003/4/EC of the European Parliament and of the Council of 28 January 2003 on public access to environmental information(9), information other than that referred to in paragraph 2 of this Article which is relevant for the decision in accordance with Article 8 and which only

becomes available after the time the public concerned was informed in accordance with paragraph 2 of this Article.

4   The public concerned shall be given early and effective opportunities to participate in the environmental decision-making procedures referred to in Article 2(2) and shall, for that purpose, be entitled to express comments and opinions when all options are open to the competent authority or authorities before the decision on the request for development consent is taken.

5   The detailed arrangements for informing the public (for example by bill posting within a certain radius or publication in local newspapers) and for consulting the public concerned (for example by written submissions or by way of a public inquiry) shall be determined by the Member States.

6   Reasonable time-frames for the different phases shall be provided, allowing sufficient time for informing the public and for the public concerned to prepare and participate effectively in environmental decision-making subject to the provisions of this Article."

5   Article 7 shall be amended as follows:
(a) paragraphs 1 and 2 shall be replaced by the following:
   "1   Where a Member State is aware that a project is likely to have significant effects on the environment in another Member State or where a Member State likely to be significantly affected so requests, the Member State in whose territory the project is intended to be carried out shall send to the affected Member State as soon as possible and no later than when informing its own public, inter alia:
   (a) a description of the project, together with any available information on its possible transboundary impact;
   (b) information on the nature of the decision which may be taken,
   and shall give the other Member State a reasonable time in which to indicate whether it wishes to participate in the environmental decision-making procedures referred to in Article 2(2), and may include the information referred to in paragraph 2 of this Article.
   2   If a Member State which receives information pursuant to paragraph 1 indicates that it intends to participate in the environmental decision-making procedures referred to in Article 2(2), the Member State in whose territory the project is intended to be carried out shall, if it has not already done so, send to the affected Member State the information required to be given pursuant to Article 6(2) and made available pursuant to Article 6(3)(a) and (b)."
(b) paragraph 5 shall be replaced by the following:
   "5   The detailed arrangements for implementing this Article may be determined by the Member States concerned and shall be such as to enable the public concerned in the territory of the affected Member State to participate effectively in the environmental decision-making procedures referred to in Article 2(2) for the project."

6   Article 9 shall be amended as follows:
(a)   Paragraph 1 shall be replaced by the following:
        "1   When a decision to grant or refuse development consent has been taken, the
              competent authority or authorities shall inform the public thereof in
              accordance with the appropriate procedures and shall make available to the
              public the following information:
              — the content of the decision and any conditions attached thereto,
              — having examined the concerns and opinions expressed by the public
                 concerned, the main reasons and considerations on which the decision
                 is based, including information about the public participation process,
              — a description, where necessary, of the main measures to avoid, reduce
                 and, if possible, offset the major adverse effects."
      (b)   Paragraph 2 shall be replaced by the following:
              "2   The competent authority or authorities shall inform any Member State
                    which has been consulted pursuant to Article 7, forwarding to it the
                    information referred to in paragraph 1 of this Article.
                    The consulted Member States shall ensure that that information is made
                    available in an appropriate manner to the public concerned in their own
                    territory.";

7   the following Article shall be inserted:
"Article 10a

Member States shall ensure that, in accordance with the relevant national legal system,
members of the public concerned:
(a) having a sufficient interest, or alternatively,
(b) maintaining the impairment of a right, where administrative procedural law of a
     Member State requires this as a precondition,
have access to a review procedure before a court of law or another independent and
impartial body established by law to challenge the substantive or procedural legality
of decisions, acts or omissions subject to the public participation provisions of this
Directive.

Member States shall determine at what stage the decisions, acts or omissions may be
challenged.

What constitutes a sufficient interest and impairment of a right shall be determined by
the Member States, consistently with the objective of giving the public concerned
wide access to justice. To this end, the interest of any non-governmental organisation
meeting the requirements referred to in Article 1(2), shall be deemed sufficient for the
purpose of subparagraph (a) of this Article. Such organisations shall also be deemed
to have rights capable of being impaired for the purpose of subparagraph (b) of this
Article.

The provisions of this Article shall not exclude the possibility of a preliminary review
procedure before an administrative authority and shall not affect the requirement of

exhaustion of administrative review procedures prior to recourse to judicial review procedures, where such a requirement exists under national law.

Any such procedure shall be fair, equitable, timely and not prohibitively expensive.

In order to further the effectiveness of the provisions of this article, Member States shall ensure that practical information is made available to the public on access to administrative and judicial review procedures.";

8   in Annex I, the following point shall be added:
"22 Any change to or extension of projects listed in this Annex where such a change or extension in itself meets the thresholds, if any, set out in this Annex.";
9   in Annex II, No 13, first indent, the following shall be added at the end:
"(change or extension not included in Annex I)".

Article 4

Amendment of Directive 96/61/EC

Directive 96/61/EC is hereby amended as follows:

1   Article 2 shall be amended as follows:
(a) the following sentence shall be added to point 10(b):
"For the purposes of this definition, any change to or extension of an operation shall be deemed to be substantial if the change or extension in itself meets the thresholds, if any, set out in Annex I.";
(b) the following points shall be added:
"13   'the public' shall mean one or more natural or legal persons and, in accordance with national legislation or practice, their associations, organisations or groups;
14 'the public concerned' shall mean the public affected or likely to be affected by, or having an interest in, the taking of a decision on the issuing or the updating of a permit or of permit conditions; for the purposes of this definition, non-governmental organisations promoting environmental protection and meeting any requirements under national law shall be deemed to have an interest; "
2   in Article 6(1), first subparagraph, the following indent shall be added:
"— the main alternatives, if any, studied by the applicant in outline."

3   Article 15 shall be amended as follows:
(a) paragraph 1 shall be replaced by the following:
"1   Member States shall ensure that the public concerned are given early and effective opportunities to participate in the procedure for:
— issuing a permit for new installations,
— issuing a permit for any substantial change in the operation of an installation,
— updating of a permit or permit conditions for an installation in accordance with Article 13, paragraph 2, first indent.

The procedure set out in Annex V shall apply for the purposes of such participation.";
(b)   the following paragraph shall be added:
"5 When a decision has been taken, the competent authority shall inform the public in accordance with the appropriate procedures and shall make available to the public the following information:
(a)   the content of the decision, including a copy of the permit and of any conditions and any subsequent updates; and
(b)   having examined the concerns and opinions expressed by the public concerned, the reasons and considerations on which the decision is based, including information on the public participation process.";

4   the following Article shall be inserted:

"Article 15a

Access to justice

Member States shall ensure that, in accordance with the relevant national legal system, members of the public concerned:
(a)   having a sufficient interest, or alternatively,
(b)   maintaining the impairment of a right, where administrative procedural law of a Member State requires this as a precondition;
have access to a review procedure before a court of law or another independent and impartial body established by law to challenge the substantive or procedural legality of decisions, acts or omissions subject to the public participation provisions of this Directive.

Member States shall determine at what stage the decisions, acts or omissions may be challenged.

What constitutes a sufficient interest and impairment of a right shall be determined by the Member States, consistently with the objective of giving the public concerned wide access to justice. To this end, the interest of any non-governmental organisation meeting the requirements referred to in Article 2(14) shall be deemed sufficient for the purpose of subparagraph (a) of this Article. Such organisations shall also be deemed to have rights capable of being impaired for the purpose of subparagraph (b) of this Article.

The provisions of this Article shall not exclude the possibility of a preliminary review procedure before an administrative authority and shall not affect the requirement of exhaustion of administrative review procedures prior to recourse to judicial review procedures, where such a requirement exists under national law.

Any such procedure shall be fair, equitable, timely and not prohibitively expensive.

In order to further the effectiveness of the provisions of this Article, Member States shall ensure that practical information is made available to the public on access to administrative and judicial review procedures.";

5   Article 17 shall be amended as follows:
(a) paragraph 1 shall be replaced by the following:
"1   Where a Member State is aware that the operation of an installation is likely to have significant negative effects on the environment of another Member State, or where a Member State likely to be significantly affected so requests, the Member State in whose territory the application for a permit pursuant to Article 4 or Article 12(2) was submitted shall forward to the other Member State any information required to be given or made available pursuant to Annex V at the same time as it makes it available to its own nationals. Such information shall serve as a basis for any consultations necessary in the framework of the bilateral relations between the two Member States on a reciprocal and equivalent basis.";
(b) the following paragraphs shall be added:
"3   The results of any consultations pursuant to paragraphs 1 and 2 must be taken into consideration when the competent authority reaches a decision on the application.
4   The competent authority shall inform any Member State, which has been consulted pursuant to paragraph 1, of the decision reached on the application and shall forward to it the information referred to in Article 15(5). That Member State shall take the measures necessary to ensure that that information is made available in an appropriate manner to the public concerned in its own territory.";

6   an Annex V shall be added, as set out in Annex II to this Directive.

Article 5

Reporting and review

By 25 June 2009, the Commission shall send a report on the application and effectiveness of this Directive to the European Parliament and to the Council. With a view to further integrating environmental protection requirements, in accordance with Article 6 of the Treaty, and taking into account the experience acquired in the application of this Directive in the Member States, such a report will be accompanied by proposals for amendment of this Directive, if appropriate. In particular, the Commission will consider the possibility of extending the scope of this Directive to other plans and programmes relating to the environment.

Article 6

Implementation

Member States shall bring into force the laws, regulations and administrative provisions necessary to comply with this Directive by 25 June 2005 at the latest. They shall forthwith inform the Commission thereof.

When Member States adopt these measures, they shall contain a reference to this Directive or shall be accompanied by such a reference on the occasion of their official publication. The methods of making such reference shall be laid down by Member States.

Article 7

Entry into force

This Directive shall enter into force on the day of its publication in the Official Journal of the European Union.

Article 8

Addressees

This Directive is addressed to the Member States.

Done at Brussels, 26 May 2003.

For the European Parliament
The President
P. Cox

For the Council
The President
G. Drys

(1)   OJ C 154 E, 29.5.2001, p. 123.
(2)   OJ C 221, 7.8.2001, p. 65.
(3)   OJ C 357, 14.12.2001, p. 58.
(4)   Opinion of the European Parliament of 23 October 2001 (OJ C 112, 9.5.2002, p. 125 (E)), Council Common Position of 25 April 2002 (OJ C 170 E, 16.7.2002, p. 22) and Decision of the European Parliament of 5 September 2002 (not yet published in the Official Journal). Decision of the European Parliament of 30 January 2003 and Decision of the Council of 4 March 2003.
(5)   OJ L 175, 5.7.1985, p. 40. Directive as amended by Directive 97/11/EC (OJ L 73, 14.3.1997, p. 5).

(6) OJ L 257, 10.10.1996, p. 26.
(7) OJ L 197, 21.7.2001, p. 30.
(8) OJ L 327, 22.12.2000, p. 1. Directive as amended by Decision No 2455/2001/EC (OJ L 331, 15.12.2001, p. 1).
(9) OJ L 41, 14.2.2003, p. 26.

ANNEX I

Provisions for plans and programmes referred to in Article 2

(a) Article 7(1) of Council Directive 75/442/EEC of 15 July 1975 on waste.[1]

(b) Article 6 of Council Directive 91/157/EEC of 18 March 1991 on batteries and accumulators containing certain dangerous substances.[2]

(c) Article 5(1) of Council Directive 91/676/EEC of 12 December 1991 concerning the protection of waters against pollution caused by nitrates from agricultural sources.[3]

(d) Article 6(1) of Council Directive 91/689/EEC of 12 December 1991 on hazardous waste.[4]

(e) Article 14 of Directive 94/62/EC of the European Parliament and of the Council of 20 December 1994 on packaging and packaging waste.[5]

(f) Article 8(3) of Council Directive 96/62/EC of 27 September 1996 on ambient air quality assessment and management.[6]

(1) OJ L 194, 25.7.1975, p. 39. Directive as last amended by Commission Decision 96/350/EC (OJ L 135, 6.6.1996, p. 32).
(2) OJ L 78, 26.3.1991, p. 38. Directive as last amended by Commission Directive 98/101/EC (OJ L 1, 5.1.1999, p. 1).
(3) OJ L 375, 31.12.1991, p. 1.
(4) OJ L 377, 31.12.1991, p. 20. Directive as last amended by Directive 94/31/EC (OJ L 168, 2.7.1994, p. 28).
(5) OJ L 365, 31.12.1994, p. 10.
(6) OJ L 296, 21.11.1996, p. 55.

ANNEX II

In Directive 96/61/EC, the following Annex shall be added:

"ANNEX V

Public participation in decision-making

1   The public shall be informed (by public notices or other appropriate means such as electronic media where available) of the following matters early in

the procedure for the taking of a decision or, at the latest, as soon as the information can reasonably be provided:

(a)   the application for a permit or, as the case may be, the proposal for the updating of a permit or of permit conditions in accordance with Article 15(1), including the description of the elements listed in Article 6(1);

(b)   where applicable, the fact that a decision is subject to a national or transboundary environmental impact assessment or to consultations between Member States in accordance with Article 17;

(c)   details of the competent authorities responsible for taking the decision, those from which relevant information can be obtained, those to which comments or questions can be submitted, and details of the time schedule for transmitting comments or questions;

(d)   the nature of possible decisions or, where there is one, the draft decision;

(e)   where applicable, the details relating to a proposal for the updating of a permit or of permit conditions;

(f)   an indication of the times and places where, or means by which, the relevant information will be made available;

(g)   details of the arrangements for public participation and consultation made pursuant to point 5.

2   Member States shall ensure that, within appropriate time-frames, the following is made available to the public concerned:

(a)   in accordance with national legislation, the main reports and advice issued to the competent authority or authorities at the time when the public concerned were informed in accordance with point 1;

(b)   in accordance with the provisions of Directive 2003/4/EC of the European Parliament and of the Council of 28 January 2003 on public access to environmental information,[1] information other than that referred to in point 1 which is relevant for the decision in accordance with Article 8 and which only becomes available after the time the public concerned was informed in accordance with point 1.

3   The public concerned shall be entitled to express comments and opinions to the competent authority before a decision is taken.

4   The results of the consultations held pursuant to this Annex must be taken into due account in the taking of a decision.

5   The detailed arrangements for informing the public (for example by bill posting within a certain radius or publication in local newspapers) and consulting the public concerned (for example by written submissions or by way of a public inquiry) shall be determined by the Member States. Reasonable time-frames for the different phases shall be provided, allowing sufficient time for informing the public and for the public concerned to prepare and participate effectively in environmental decision-making subject to the provisions of this Annex.

(1)   OJ L 41, 14.2.2003, p. 26."

Index